# INTERNATIONAL POLITICAL ECONOMY

*The Struggle for Power and Wealth*

# INTERNATIONAL POLITICAL ECONOMY

*The Struggle for Power and Wealth*

Second Edition

**Thomas D. Lairson**

*Rollins College*

**David Skidmore**

*Drake University*

**Harcourt Brace College Publishers**

Fort Worth    Philadelphia    San Diego    New York    Orlando    Austin    San Antonio
Toronto    Montreal    London    Sydney    Tokyo

| | |
|---|---|
| Publisher | Christopher P. Klein |
| Senior Acquisitions Editor | David Tatom |
| Developmental Editor | Christopher Nelson |
| Senior Project Editor | Laura J. Hanna |
| Senior Production Manager | Annette Wiggins |
| Art Director | Candice Clifford |

Cover image: © Cyberimage/Tony Stone Images

Harcourt Brace may provide complimentary instructional aids and supplements or supplement packages to those adopters qualified under our adoption policy. Please contact your sales representative for more information. If as an adopter or potential user you receive supplements you do not need, please return them to your sales representative or send them to: Attn: Returns Department, Troy Warehouse, 465 South Lincoln Drive, Troy, MO 63379.

Requests for permission to make copies of any part of the work should be mailed to: Permissions Department, Harcourt Brace & Company, 6277 Sea Harbor Drive, Orlando, Florida 32887-6777.

Address for Editorial Correspondence: Harcourt Brace College Publishers, 301 Commerce Street, Suite 3700, Fort Worth, TX 76102.

Address for Orders: Harcourt Brace & Company, 6277 Sea Harbor Drive, Orlando, FL 32887-6777, 1-800-782-4479, or 1-800-433-0001 (in Florida).

Printed in the United States of America

ISBN: 0-15-503026-4

Library of Congress Catalog Card Number: 96-76310

6 7 8 9 0 1 2 3 4 5   016   9 8 7 6 5 4 3 2 1

# PREFACE

This edition of *International Political Economy: The Struggle for Power and Wealth* carries over many of the objectives and themes central to the first edition, while also addressing a number of new topics and issues. Once again, our goal has been to produce a clear and readable text without sacrificing sophistication or rigor. We recognize the difficulties that students face in mastering a subject that lies at the intersection of two complex fields—political science and economics. We therefore take great care to explain basic economic concepts and to offer a balanced blend of theory, history, and policy. We believe that the resulting volume is accessible enough to be used as a supplement in an introductory course on international relations, but challenging enough to be assigned as a main textbook for upper-level courses.

As before, we depict the international political economy as a realm of both struggle and cooperation. We show how these contrary imperatives coexist and how the mix between the two varies over time, across countries, and among issues. In pursuing this theme, we weave together theory, concepts, and arguments throughout and tie these ideas closely to the topics under discussion.

Like the first edition, this one includes a number of pedagogical aids, including illustrations and tables, anecdotes, an annotated bibliography at the end of each chapter, and a glossary of essential terms.

Alongside these continuities, the second edition offers numerous innovations. Throughout the book, we have updated our analysis of recent events and incorporated new data. More significantly, we have broadened the book's scope, addressing a number of new topics and themes. Some of these new features include:

- A new chapter on the globalization of production and finance.
- A new chapter on hunger, population and sustainable development.
- A comparison of different methods for measuring development.
- Country studies of economic liberalization in China, India, and Brazil.
- More material on regional economic blocs in North America, Latin America, Europe, and Asia.
- A discussion of recent efforts to reform foreign aid.
- Expanded discussion of the winners and losers from free trade.
- A new discussion of the Uruguay Round and the World Trade Organization.
- An analysis of portfolio investment in the Third World.

- An examination of the Mexican financial crisis of 1994–1995.
- A comparison of post-communist systems in Russia, China, and Vietnam.
- A list of acronyms at the end of the book.

We thank the editors at Harcourt Brace and Company, including David Tatom, Senior Acquisitions Editor, who has actively supported this project from its genesis; Fritz Schanz and Chris Nelson, Developmental Editors, who provided valuable assistance at different stages in the preparation of the manuscript and Laura Hanna, Senior Project Editor, who guided the book through production. We also appreciate the advice offered by Steve Chan, University of Colorado—Boulder; Roxanne Lynn Doty, Arizona State University; Yale H. Ferguson, Rutgers University; Christopher L. Holomon, SUNY—Buffalo; Mark Peceny, University of New Mexico; Michael Shafer, Rutgers University; Scott E. Tarry, Southern Illinois University; and Kenneth P. Thomas, University of Missouri—St. Louis. Finally, we each thank our spouses, Sally Lairson and Charlene Skidmore, for their patience and support.

Thomas Lairson and David Skidmore

# CONTENTS

*Chapter 4*
## THE POLITICAL ECONOMY OF
## AMERICAN HEGEMONY: 1938–1973    63

*Chapter 5*
## GLOBALIZATION AND THE WORLD ECONOMY    95

## Chapter 6
## COOPERATION AMONG ADVANCED INDUSTRIAL STATES    126

## Chapter 7
## COMPETITION AND CONFLICT AMONG ADVANCED INDUSTRIAL STATES    165

# INTERNATIONAL POLITICAL ECONOMY
## The Struggle for Power and Wealth

# Chapter 1

# Introduction:
# The Politics of International
# Political Economy

Understanding international affairs is exceedingly difficult and perhaps impossible without a clear sense of how politics and economics are related. This assertion, very controversial even fifteen years ago, may still provoke dissent and perhaps confusion from students today. After all, political science is taught in one department and economics in another. One looks at power and the other at money and products. But consider the following set of anecdotes drawn from recent events and notice how power, money, and profits are entangled.

> With some frequency after 1975, the United States and Japan have experienced significant political conflict over their trade relations. First over textiles, then automobiles, next semiconductors, then with automobiles again, these two countries have struggled to manage the level of their trade. Conflict over trade is neither new nor unusual; nations have often turned to political negotiations to try to resolve economic disagreements. The U.S.–Japanese conflict is noteworthy because these are the two largest economic powers in the world and because they are bound together in a very close security alliance. Each episode of conflict involved significant public rancor, with threats, deadlines, and recrimination frequently heard. At one point, a U.S. congressman resorted to demolishing Japanese goods with a sledge hammer. Many others in Congress wanted to retaliate against Japan by blocking the sale of Japanese goods in the United States. In 1995, it was revealed that the U.S. Central Intelligence Agency provided the U.S. trade negotiator with a daily briefing about secret communications among members of the Japanese negotiating delegation. Behind the disputes is a complex mix of somewhat conflicting economic interests. The U.S. and Japanese economies are linked by large and increasing amounts of trade, investment, technological, and security interdependence. At the same time, the results of this interdependence have often been unbalanced toward Japan. The consequences of the trade conflicts have been significant. Leaders in both countries have

engaged in a debate over the merits of free trade and protectionism and over the nature of the U.S. and Japanese economies. Negotiations focused on politically arranged trade outcomes and alterations in the basic structure of each nation's economic system. "Voluntary" restrictions on Japanese auto sales in the United States, a quota for sales of U.S. semiconductors and autos in Japan, reduction of the U.S. budget deficit, and changes in Japanese public spending were among the deals. One important byproduct of the trade conflicts was worry over whether these disputes would lead to bigger problems.[1]

In 1986, the communist leaders of Vietnam faced a severe crisis. Having won the thirty-year war to gain independence and reunite the country in 1975, they found the economic and political program that followed was in tatters. Close association with the Soviet Union produced aid and some tourists. But the effort to collectivize the agricultural breadbasket in the south had failed, generating serious food shortages. The shelves of state-run stores were starkly bare, and economic growth had failed to keep pace with population increases. A huge Vietnamese army was bogged down in Cambodia, and the nation faced diplomatic isolation. Radical change seemed afoot in the Soviet Union, while Vietnam's neighbors in China, Malaysia, Thailand, and Indonesia were moving toward even more rapid economic growth. Many members of the ruling politburo of the Communist Party saw their nation falling very far behind these other states' economic capabilities. Vietnamese leaders, their entire lives devoted to achieving national independence and scarred by many years of terrible war, were nonetheless moved by desperate circumstances to engage in a somewhat open debate about the failings of their system. In the end, they chose to join the world capitalist economy. Over the next ten years, markets were freed of much state control; many thousands of small enterprises selling plentiful goods emerged; rice production soared to make Vietnam a big exporter; foreign direct investment poured in; Vietnam withdrew from Cambodia and received diplomatic recognition from the United States; and economic growth jumped to more than 8 percent annually.[2]

Often, the economic policies within one nation have major consequences for other nations. And political decisions can have a big effect on the economy. Such is the case with the reunification of West and East Germany. The size of the West German economy and the role of the government bank—the Bundesbank—in managing the monetary affairs of Europe had made this country the dominant economic power in Europe. Other countries in Europe were required to follow the leadership of the Bundesbank in order to make their

---

[1] See Timothy O'Shea, *The U.S.-Japanese Semiconductor Problem*, Washington, D.C.: Pew Case Studies, 1994; Stephen D. Cohen, "United States–Japanese Trade Relations," *Current History*, 90, April 1991, 152–155; Simon Reich, *The Reagan Administration, the Auto Producers, and the 1981 Agreement with Japan*; and Simon Reich, *Restraining Trade to Invoke Investment: MITI and the Japanese Auto Producers*, both Washington, D.C.: Pew Case Studies, 1992. The most recent auto dispute is covered in David Sanger "Trade Fight with Japan Is Widening," *New York Times*, May 19, 1995; and David Sanger, "U.S. Settles Trade Dispute," *New York Times*, June 29, 1995.

[2] Michael Williams, *Vietnam at the Crossroads*, New York: CFR Press, 1992; Borje Ljunggren (ed.), *The Challenge of Reform in Indochina*, Cambridge: Harvard University Press, 1993.

system of fixed exchange rates work effectively. Stability of exchange rates required coordination of monetary policy and interest rates by European countries, and they did this by following the Bundesbank. This became much more difficult after the reunification of the two Germanys. The dislocation and even trauma associated with integrating East and West and especially converting the East from a communist to a capitalist economy were the source of the problem. For East Germans, prices rose dramatically, and many enterprises closed in bankruptcy. Perhaps as many as 40 percent of those previously employed lost their jobs. Large sums were spent by the German government to stabilize and rebuild the East. The resources came from government borrowing and amounted in 1991 to almost 5 percent of total output. To stem the feared inflation, the Bundesbank used its economic powers to raise interest rates to more than double the level before reunification. This confronted other countries in Europe with a choice between raising interest rates and dropping the fixed exchange rate system. Because many of these countries were in a serious recession, they resisted interest rate hikes. Eventually some, like the British, left the fixed exchange rate system. The pound fell by nearly 25 percent in less than a week, producing shock waves throughout Europe and the world. Some foreign exchange rate speculators made hundreds of millions of dollars by correctly predicting the outcome of the crisis.[3]

Those who believe that private enterprise freed of governmental interference is the only source of dynamism in the world economy will find the close cooperation between business and government in Japan, Taiwan, South Korea, Singapore, and Malaysia somewhat perplexing. The U.S. version of these arrangements—though much less well developed—is an obscure unit of the Defense Department known as the Advanced Research Projects Agency (ARPA). Its bureaucratic location is a consequence of the willingness of Americans to tolerate close government–business ties in defense production and illustrates the strong connection between technology and national security. ARPA has played a key role in the development of several industries, especially computers and software. The Internet, now used by millions daily, was originally created in the 1960s as ARPAnet. Today, ARPA has a budget of over $1 billion to support the development of dual-use technologies. These are technologies with both defense and commercial applications. But ARPA also provokes strong criticism from those who fear any governmental role in defining industrial development and from others who support the principle underlying the agency but who object to the role of the military. Perhaps the key question raised by ARPA is whether success in the world economy today demands a major role for government in subsidizing and even selecting where research and development funds for expensive and risky high technology should be spent.[4]

The politics of business and government relations is also a crucial element of the world aircraft industry. Recent gains in global market share by the

---

[3] Alexander Dyck, *Germany in the 1990s: Managing Reunification,* Cambridge, Harvard Business School Case Study, 1994.

[4] James Kitfield, "The New Partnership," *National Journal,* August 6, 1994, 1840–1844.

European consortium Airbus have hurt U.S. companies that have historically dominated this market. And the fact that Airbus is partially state-owned has led to complaints of unfair subsidies and threats of a trade war. Between 1988 and 1990, Airbus increased its world market share of commercial jet aircraft from 15 percent to 34 percent, cutting Boeing's from 59 percent to 34 percent and McDonnell Douglas's from 22 percent to 15 percent. Government subsidies for development costs may have permitted Airbus, which is owned by private companies from Germany and Great Britain and state-owned companies in France and Spain, to undercut the prices of the American firms. The Airbus case has helped prompt calls for similar actions by the U.S. government in order to preserve America's market share. Meanwhile, Boeing and McDonnell Douglas are independently scrambling to devise a plan to counter this new competitive environment. One option even calls for a merger between the two companies.[5]

Our last vignette helps to point out the consequences of international economic interdependence and the role of government power and money in supporting that system. During the winter of 1994–1995, the collapse of the Mexican peso threatened the stability of the international financial system. The United States and several important international economic organizations responded by providing Mexico with large loans. They did this not out of beneficence, but rather because an unchecked crisis in Mexico could have brought on a global financial crisis with great potential harm to many countries. What caused the crisis? Primarily, it was serious economic problems in Mexico that became clear in late 1994. Beginning in the mid-1980s, the Mexican government chose economic opening and liberalization and moved toward freer trade with the United States and Canada in the North American Free Trade Agreement (NAFTA). The Mexican economy expanded, trade grew, and foreign investors moved into Mexico. But Mexico experienced a large deficit in its international accounts, inflation was high, savings were low, and the exchange rate of the peso (managed by the government) was too high. This all became clear when the government attempted to reduce the peso's value. The result was that domestic and then international investors began to flee Mexico, driving the peso's value much lower. With Mexico standing at the precipice of a default on its international debt, President Clinton moved to support Mexico. Along with the International Monetary Fund and the Bank for International Settlements, the United States organized a $50 billion line of credit for Mexico with $20 billion from the United States. The falling peso had by now spread to other emerging market countries in Latin America and Asia. Had Mexico been unable to meet the payments due on its debt, this would have led to a collapse of the peso and Mexican securities and to a major decline in other countries, including the United States. For its part, Mexico moved to reduce government spending, lower money supply growth, and increase the privatization of its state enterprises. This was not the first time that something like this had happened. During a serious recession in

---

[5] Artemis March, "The Future of the U.S. Aircraft Industry," *Technology Review*, January 1990, 26–36; Eric Vayle, *Collision Course in Commercial Aircraft: Boeing–McDonnell Douglas*, Cambridge: Harvard Business School Case Study, 1993.

1982, the U.S. government took steps to prevent a loan default by Mexico to U.S. and other foreign banks. The U.S. government provided additional loans to Mexico, supported loans by the International Monetary Fund, and lowered interest rates, thereby reducing the annual payments of Mexico and other debtor states. These actions also served to protect the interests of those U.S. banks who had lent Mexico and other Third World states nearly $100 billion. U.S. Secretary of the Treasury Donald Regan—a former Wall Street tycoon—defended this policy before Congress. He pointed out that a loan default would invariably lead to a contraction in U.S. bank lending at home and would probably force interest rates higher.

> . . . we are not talking here just about the big money-center banks and the multinational corporations. Well over 1,500 U.S. banks, or more than 10 percent of the total number of U.S. banks, have loaned money to Latin America alone. . . . Those loans, among other things, financed exports, exports that resulted in jobs, housing and investment being maintained or created throughout the United States.[6]

> For Mr. Regan, an immensely practical man with a strong commitment to private enterprise and American interests, it was essential that the U.S. government spend considerable sums on protecting and preserving the international financial system.[7]

This set of vignettes should make clear that the connections between politics and economics in international affairs are many and complex. We have seen how international political negotiations can lead to significant changes in the ways people live and work; how all nations are caught up in an immense world economy of production, technology, and competition that can affect the very foundations of their society; how systems of economic interdependence can have unexpected consequences for prices and profits as a result of political changes thousands of miles away; and how deeply involved governments are in helping private businesses succeed in the world economy.

These examples could be multiplied many times, but political scientists prefer to establish categories of relationships that can help us economize and organize our thinking. By way of introduction, we will focus on two broad categories: the political economy of relationships within a nation and among nations.

## DOMESTIC POLITICAL ECONOMY

The nature and scope of a country's participation in the world economy are greatly affected by political decisions made within its borders. The politics of

---

[6] As quoted in John C. Pool and Steve Stamos, *The ABC's of International Finance*, Lexington: Lexington Books, 1987, 80.

[7] The debt crisis of 1982 is detailed in Chapter 13 of this book. The 1994–1995 crisis can be followed in *The Economist* issues for December 1994 and January–February 1995. Also see International Monetary Fund, *World Economic Outlook*, May 1995, Washington D.C.: IMF, 90–97.

this decision making is often influenced by the fact that different groups are affected in different ways by involvement in the world economy: Some groups win, while others can be disadvantaged, which sets up a political struggle over what to do. Taxes, interest rates, decisions about tariffs, and economic negotiations with other nations are but a few of the choices involved in this process. The outcome is typically a result of both the power relationships and resources of the groups involved and the degree to which governmental leaders can act independently of those interests.

A more general version of this process is the long-standing question of how governments and private business interests are to be related in making economic decisions. Within Western capitalist states, the experience of depression and war from the 1930s to the 1950s worked to politicize economic choices and to focus them on the national government. Political leaders became much more deeply involved in regulating the economy, and national prosperity became their responsibility. Presidents and prime ministers now regularly win and lose elections based on whether the economy is expanding or contracting. Further, the intensification of international economic competition has prompted many governments (like the Europeans supporting Airbus) to play a much more important role in supporting particular industries.

The increasing role of the state in economic affairs is a defining element in our study of international political economy. Even in the United States, with its long-standing and now mostly mythological notions of a sharp separation of government and business, political leaders are deeply involved in business decisions. Regulating banks and bailing out bank failures, subsidizing basic research, giving tax breaks to investors, spending on defense, maintaining incomes for the poor, imposing regulations on polluters, and attempting to manage the economy through fiscal and monetary policy are but a few of the many areas of government direction of the economy. At the same time, many other nations—especially those first moving toward industrialization in the twentieth century—have gone beyond the Western model toward an intimate business–government partnership in promoting economic growth. These governments mobilize national resources and energies, build up certain industrial sectors, and restrict access to their markets in the name of a national economic strategy. The result is the establishment of a competitive environment in which the capabilities of entire nations are being harnessed to succeed in the world economy.

## INTERNATIONAL POLITICAL ECONOMY

The frequent and extensive economic interactions among nations define our second category. Perhaps the most general and least obvious point here is the relationship of the world economy to the power politics among nations. The organization of markets is made possible by the political agreements that nations reach. It is international power that defines legal relationships, creates and destroys economic opportunities, and raises and lowers profits. This comes about in many ways. The French conquest of Indochina in the nineteenth century opened that area to French entrepreneurs, many of whom made vast fortunes. The creation of the International Monetary Fund in the 1940s, made possible by the preponderance of U.S. power, eventually helped create legal rules that today permit the movement of money around the world. And raising or lowering tariffs, which affect whether and how much of a good is imported, is closely linked to simultaneous negotiations among more than one hundred nations.

Similarly broad in its relevance to world affairs is the fact that the international military and political power of a nation rests largely on the dynamism of its economy. The ability to support a large military system depends on a nation's wealth, and its success in war depends on how this wealth and productive capability compares to other nations. Both the technological prowess of a nation and its ability to turn its new developments into profitable products and implements of war are central to gaining the nation's objectives in the international arena. The extraordinary advantages enjoyed by the United States in the 1990–1991 war against Iraq and the temporary American monopoly of atomic weapons are but two of many examples of this fact. Over the past 150 years, international competition has been defined by an ever tightening relationship among military, economic, technological, and political processes.

When we probe these links between power and economics, matters become more complex. Things are usually not quite as simple as "the strong always win, and the weak lose," though this sometimes happens. One of the most important ways of thinking about the origins of a world economy examines the role of the most powerful state in establishing an open international economy, where goods and money move about with few hindrances. But this gets complicated very quickly. An especially powerful nation—what political scientists call a *hegemon*—wants other, weaker nations to participate in the system voluntarily. This may require bribing them or winning the support of their political and economic leadership. At the same time, the hegemon must be careful not to let its economic advantages wipe out the economies of those nations whose cooperation it needs. Much less clear is whether this process of spending money to support the system actually weakens the hegemon in the long run. Also uncertain are the consequences of hegemonic decline. Does that mean the international economic system will also decline?

Power relationships are also crucial when we shift attention to the interactions of nations of sharply different capabilities. Much of the Third World is at a considerable disadvantage in the world economy. Many of these nations were subjected to Western imperialism in the nineteenth and twentieth centuries and have poorly developed mechanisms for international competition. Their corporations are small and undercapitalized, their educational and technological systems are underfunded, and their political systems are fragmented and conflictual. It is unclear whether this state of affairs is primarily the result of the capitalist world economy and the power disadvantages of these countries or if it is the result of weaknesses in their societies. Equally uncertain is whether the few Third World states who have been able to accomplish strong economic growth are exceptions or are models that others need to emulate.

Also of interest is how nations more equal in power interact. The growth of the world economy in trade and money connects nations in webs of interdependence, and this forces them to work together in order to manage the consequences. Interdependence sets up a tension between the domestic politics of making decisions and the international politics of reaching agreements. When we remember that national decisions are related to domestic interests, we can see that making compromises and sacrifices to smooth out international problems may be difficult. Equally important, nations may try to manipulate the fact that they are less dependent than others on the world economy in order to gain advantages in negotiations; winning their support for an agreement may require that more-dependent nations make special concessions.

Thus cooperation among nations, even when there are important gains from such arrangements, may not be easy. This is also true because nations who are partners in cooperation are also engaged in competition. The examples of Airbus, U.S.-Japan trade, and ARPA show some of the ways in which governments can become involved in the process of economic competition. The politics of cooperation and competition in the world economy are never far apart. For example, many of the nations in Europe have recently accelerated their cooperation in creating a free market for goods, services, and people. Much of the reason for this action comes from the need for these nations to improve their ability to compete against the Japanese and the United States. Sometimes these efforts to promote competitiveness can have unexpected and even unwanted consequences. In the 1950s and 1960s, the United States promoted the efforts of its multinational corporations to set up operations in Europe and elsewhere. But over time, the logic of the global marketplace has turned many of these corporations into truly transnational firms that produce and sell based upon attention to costs and markets around the world. In many ways, their identity as American firms may have declined, and their profit-based decisions may not further U.S. interests in competition with other countries. How does nation-based politics, intent on promoting national economic interests and supplemented by limited arenas of international cooperation, cope with the development of transnational firms that carry out a large proportion of world trade and innovation?

The shifting tides of world affairs have helped reveal the enormous importance of international political economy for understanding global politics. The processes of struggle, competition, and cooperation—always the main elements of international relations—have become increasingly focused on national capacities for generating wealth and technological innovation and for supporting institutions capable of adjusting rapidly to a changing environment. New and powerful interests in preserving and extending a global economy have been created. Nations and their leaders are involved as never before in each other's "domestic affairs." More and more, issues must be decided in international forums because behaviors and consequences spill across borders. And the global economy itself has advanced to the point that markets and exchange can sometimes constrain nations and corporations.

## APPROACHES TO INTERNATIONAL POLITICAL ECONOMY

What is the best way to learn about international political economy? Before answering that question, you should realize that economic and political interests are deeply engaged by how people think about this subject. Different forms of analysis contain different implications for how political-economic relations are arranged and thus for who wins and who loses. Consequently, several strongly held ideologies have grown up around international political economy. Historically, three broad perspectives (sometimes theories) compete for our loyalties: Liberalism, Mercantilism, and Radicalism. Each makes an important contribution, but each also has important limitations; each has its best day in answering certain questions and in pointing us in the right direction.

Liberalism can trace its lineage back more than two hundred years to Adam Smith and David Ricardo. Today, liberals are found among economists, much of the business community in the West, writers for the *Wall Street Journal*, *The Economist*, and the *Far Eastern Economic Review*, and officials at the International Monetary Fund and the World Bank. Liberalism, also known as *neoclassical thinking*, extols the virtues of free markets and trade. Its ideas are complex and often provide a convincing case for the power and efficacy of markets. Perhaps the most important contribution of liberals is the idea that all participants in a system of free trade are beneficiaries. But the arguments of liberals sometimes extend beyond respecting to worshiping markets; their views often have the effect of rationalizing the interests of powerful groups; and liberals almost never understand the role of politics and power in creating and conditioning markets. More recently, a new version of liberalism (neoliberalism) has built on older versions of political economy. Neoliberals make broad claims about the impact of markets, international interdependence, and the possibilities for cooperation among nations.[8]

Mercantilists can lay claim to the longest intellectual tradition because this perspective emphasizes the importance of nations and power in thinking about economic issues. The mercantile perspective is an aspect of nationalism, and mercantilists often call on governments to manipulate markets so as to capture special benefits for their nation. The criterion for judging policies and actions is the need to preserve and enhance the power and prosperity of the nation. Mercantilists contrast most sharply with liberals in asserting that the gains of one nation usually come at the expense of others. The

---

[8] Discussion of neoliberalism is found in David Baldwin (ed.), *Neorealism and Neoliberalism: The Contemporary Debate*, New York: Columbia University Press, 1993. You can find examples of liberalism on the editorial pages of any issue of *The Economist* and the *Wall Street Journal*.

international economy is closely linked to the competitive system of states. Consequently, mercantilism sees a close relationship between economic strength, technological prowess, economic competitiveness, military strength, and national influence. Mercantilists can be found among the military and economic planners of most nations. Frequently, groups disadvantaged by international trade will cast self-serving arguments in terms of protecting national economic and military strength. Military and economic planners in countries like the United States, Japan, South Korea, and China pay close attention to the relative capabilities of other nations. The contribution of mercantilists is to recognize that international economic relations operate within a world of competitive and conflictual nations. Economic capabilities do make a major contribution to military and political influence. Power and politics are always a part of economics. But, like liberalism, mercantilism is frequently tied closely to the interests of certain groups or at most to a nation-centered view. This leads to proposals that privilege these groups over others or that undermine cooperation among nations.[9]

A third perspective—Radicalism—by contrast believes that the system of national and international capitalism biases economic outcomes to the benefit of certain social classes within the most powerful capitalist nations. Drawing their ideas from a Marxist perspective on political economy, radicals focus our attention on the area of greatest weakness for liberalism and mercantilism: the way that economic power and political power create interests and shape outcomes. The merit of radical arguments is that they tend to see power relationships that others miss (or want obscured). The central purpose of radical analysis is to uncover the role of power in seemingly "voluntary" market relations. One variant of radical theory is dependent development, which argues that market relations between rich and poor states are based on and reinforce inequality. This helps us see how power can affect the distribution of economic benefits, but radicals may not adequately appreciate how nations organized effectively for economic competition can turn the weak into the strong in a market system.[10]

Beyond the three broad categories are dozens of permutations and combinations of these and other forms of thinking, most with great confidence in one point of view. There sometimes seem to be nearly as many theories as facts. This buzzing confusion of theories and facts is a sign of the complexity, of the political and economic significance of the subject, and of the newness of the study of international political economy. For scholars, complexity and

---

[9] A small sample of writing that expounds or explains mercantilism includes: Theodore Moran, *American Economic Policy and National Security*, New York: CFR Press, 1993; James Fallows, *Looking at the Sun*, New York: Pantheon, 1994; and Wayne Sandholtz et al., *The Highest Stakes*, New York: Oxford University Press, 1992.

[10] For discussion and exposition of radical views, see Stephan Haggard, *Pathways from the Periphery*, Ithaca, N.Y.: Cornell University Press, 1990; Stephen Gill, *American Hegemony and the Trilateral Commission*, Cambridge: Cambridge University Press, 1990; and Immanuel Wallerstein, *The Capitalist World Economy*, Cambridge: Cambridge University Press, 1979.

even confusion make this an exciting field; for the uninitiated student, this is surely frightening and even intimidating.

We are of the view that simply learning the intricacies of theories won't "stick" without a rich sense of context, and likewise, that mere presentation of the facts devoid of analysis is equally doomed. Understanding theories is much easier when they can be related to concrete events and situations. And the real significance of events can be comprehended only through theories. The key to learning about international political economy is to strike the right balance between theory and information. Hopefully, we have found such a balance.

We will follow the lead of contemporary research in international political economy and focus on a set of overlapping and specific theoretical questions. The questions we address include:

- How do governments and domestic interests affect foreign economic policy?
- How do we understand the different ways that political leaders and institutions are entangled in managing and conditioning market outcomes?
- What are the roles of political power and international institutions in shaping the terms of trade flows and capital transfers?
- How does the globalization of finance and production alter the options and behaviors of nations and multinational corporations?
- How does a nation's economic growth and technological prowess affect its international influence?
- What are the sources of the development gap between the North and South?
- How do domestic and international factors affect the choice of development strategies?
- What are the sources of and barriers to international cooperation?
- How has the character of international economic competition changed?
- Why do different development strategies succeed or fail?
- How do the political interests of rich states and poor states affect the success of foreign aid?
- How do we understand the relative bargaining power of North and South over the terms of foreign investment and borrowing?

These analytical themes are always wrapped in a context of background, events, stories, and anecdotes.

The purpose of this approach is to give students information they can use both to appreciate and to evaluate theoretical arguments. Much attention is devoted to the history of the world economy before 1945. This period is rich in events that offer perspective on the main points of analysis: the political origins of free trade; industrialization by poor states; the shifting tides of competitive advantage; the effects of war on economic relationships; and examples of cooperation, conflict, and competition. These and many other topics are considered in the post-1945 era in terms of the rise and decline of U.S. power, the explosion of interdependence and globalization, and tenuous efforts at development in the Third World.

The plan of this book progresses the student toward a deepening understanding of the issues involved in international political economy. Chapters 2 and 3 are designed to serve as a further orientation to the subject. Chapter 2 does this by offering a basic literacy in economics, developing those concepts that are indispensable to understanding international political economy, and Chapter 3 gives some historical depth to the concept of a world economy, offering a sense of how we got to the present and some perspective on the outcome of past efforts at cooperation and struggles for international economic and political power. Chapter 4 moves on to consider the special role of the United States in creating the political and economic basis for the new shape for the world economy and international interdependence after 1945. Chapter 5 examines the complex matter of the globalization of finance and production after 1973. Chapters 6 and 7 address two central concepts in international political economy as applied to relations among advanced industrial states. Chapter 6 considers international cooperation in managing the global economy and in the formation of economic blocs. Chapter 7 focuses on the problems of conflict and competition. We look at Japan and the implications for international competition along with the rise of a new protectionism as a response to an uncertain world economy.

Chapter 8 begins a new section focusing on developing nations in the Third World. It gives students a clear understanding of the different ways of thinking about the problems of development and the relationship of North and South. Several strategies of economic development have been followed by nations in the Third World. Chapter 9 evaluates these strategies in terms of case studies of success and failure. Chapter 10 evaluates the role of foreign aid in promoting or inhibiting development. The topic of Chapter 11 is the bargaining power and distribution of benefits between multinational corporations and nations in the Third World. The political issues involved in the Third World debt crisis and the problems associated with suggested solutions are the focus of Chapter 12. The critical questions associated with food, population, and sustainable development are the focus of Chapter 13. Chapter 14 provides a consideration of the integration of postcommunist states into the world economy. And Chapter 15 offers some general conclusions focusing on possible future directions for the world economy, in particular the balance between struggle and cooperation and the competitive positions of several nations.

International political economy is certainly not an easy subject. It takes two areas of intellectual inquiry and mixes them together in new and complicated ways, but we expect that the following presentation will help you sort through these difficulties and emerge with a much clearer understanding of an immensely important area. With patience and some dedication on your part, this will be the case.

# Chapter 2

# THE ECONOMICS OF INTERNATIONAL POLITICAL ECONOMY

Studying the intersection of politics and economics at the international level cannot proceed very far without a firm grasp of basic economic relationships. Reading this or any book on international political economy requires that you understand a somewhat diverse set of economic concepts. This chapter is designed to introduce these ideas in a straightforward and nontechnical manner. At each stage of the book we will mix economic and political matters, with the balance sometimes shifting in one direction or another. This is just such an occasion, and its purpose is to provide a basic literacy in economics.

The most important task is to see how international and domestic economies are related, especially the ways in which the international environment constrains and directs national decisions. Governments strive to maintain control over their economies and at the same time to reap the benefits of international trade. Increasing global interdependence makes this effort much more difficult and uncertain. Understanding how these spheres of economic activity affect each other requires a common language of concepts that summarizes the most elemental features of each.

Acquiring a command of the language will involve a mastery of five basic tasks. First, it is necessary to have a clear sense of why trade takes place among nations in the first place. The prevailing understanding of this is the theory of free trade, and the basic elements of this theory and some alternative approaches will be considered. Second, we need to learn how to measure the movement of goods, services, and money across national boundaries—the balance of payments—and how to interpret this somewhat complex and daunting array of statistics. Third, we need to understand the tools of economic management by the central government that define the basic features of domestic political economy. The most important of these tools are fiscal and monetary policy, in which the government, by its spending, taxing, and banking policies, has a major impact on the economy. Fourth, the fact that international transactions require the exchange of one national currency for another creates a special set of problems that must be explored. Fluctuation in exchange rates not only influences the level of imports and exports but also creates an opportunity and need for political intervention. Finally, these concepts are brought together through an examination of the dynamics of monetary and fiscal policy, interest rates, exchange rates, financial markets, and the balance of payments.

These are complex matters, but they must be understood in order to deal with the rest of the material in this book. Consider reading this chapter at least twice and playing with the ideas and relationships so that you are quickly able to see causal linkages. After these are clearly in mind, the rest is much easier.

## FREE TRADE

Free trade is a variant on the notion of free markets and is probably the most important contribution that liberals make to the study of international political economy. The central assertion is that if trade is unrestricted, production will take place where it is most efficiently done and all nations will benefit. Standing behind this view is a concept of allocating resources to the production of goods in the most efficient way; that is, a division of labor operates among nations so that each concentrates on the set of goods to which it is best suited as compared with other nations and with all the kinds of goods it could produce. Economists focus their assessment of the benefits and costs of free trade on efficiency and the lowest prices for goods and focus less on the politically relevant costs of the economic adjustments that people must make to satisfy the demands of free trade.

Why not just produce and consume for yourself? Why trade at all? One undesirable consequence of such a strategy is that it cuts the country off from goods that might be especially desirable, and that cannot be produced at home. Thus, one somewhat eccentric but popular view of trade sees it as an involuntary act: buying those goods that you cannot produce for yourself and selling goods abroad in order to make these purchases. Another, more mercantilist view sees trade as a sort of weapon used to enrich the country. By selling more than you buy, the nation will be better off. Somehow, you need to restrict imports and make sure that others do not respond by blocking your goods. The notions of trade as compulsion and enrichment have frequently dominated thinking. By contrast, liberals argue that trade should be seen as mutually beneficial—where all nations are better off trading than restricting trade.

How does the argument for free trade work? It rests on the fact that countries differ in their ability to produce goods. Often any given nation will possess an absolute advantage in the cost of production of a particular good. That is, one country can produce a good at a lower cost than can another. This concept can be illustrated very easily with some simplifying assumptions: two countries, Great Britain and the United States; and two products, wheat and iron. Workers in each country are better at producing one good than the other; this can be seen from the per-worker production of each.

|  | WHEAT | IRON |
|---|---|---|
|  | *bushels* | *tons* |
| Britain | 100 | 250 |
| United States | 200 | 150 |

Clearly, Britain has an absolute advantage in iron, whereas the United States enjoys an absolute advantage in wheat.

Suppose that each country has 200 workers. If both devote half their work force to each good and avoid trade, they obtain the following output:

|  | WHEAT | IRON |
|---|---|---|
|  | *bushels* | *tons* |
| Britain | 10,000 | 25,000 |
| United States | 20,000 | 15,000 |
| Total Output | 30,000 | 40,000 |

The benefits of specialization and trade should be apparent by inspecting the figures. The United States can produce 200 bushels of wheat per worker, and Britain can produce 250 tons of iron per worker. If each shifts all its workers into the production of the good at which it is best, the total output of both will increase. Britain will produce 50,000 tons of iron by itself, and the United States will produce 40,000 bushels of wheat. Then trade can take place at the rate of 4 bushels of wheat for every 5 tons of iron, and both countries will benefit.

The amount of trade depends on how much of each good is needed. But notice that Britain can trade 5 tons of iron for 4 bushels of wheat. If Britain produces wheat itself, Britain will need to give up 10 tons of iron for every 4 bushels of wheat.[1] For simplicity's sake, assume that Britain and the United States are happy trading 16,000 bushels of wheat for 20,000 tons of iron. The following is the amount of wheat and iron that each can consume as a result of this specialization and trade:

|  | WHEAT | IRON |
|---|---|---|
|  | *bushels* | *tons* |
| Britain | 16,000 | 30,000 |
| United States | 24,000 | 20,000 |
| Total Output | 40,000 | 50,000 |

---

[1] Remember that British workers can produce 2.5 times as much iron in tons as wheat in bushels. So to get four bushels of wheat from their own workers, they will need to give up 4 times 2.5, or ten tons of iron.

Both the United States and Great Britain end up with more wheat and iron in this scenario than if they try to produce each commodity by themselves.

The benefits of trade in instances of absolute advantage are intuitively plausible and can be measured by the increase in total output and in the additional consumption in both countries. But economists argue convincingly that trade can benefit both nations even if one is inferior in the production of both goods. As long as the inferior nation has a comparative advantage in one good over the other, trade can be beneficial. This can be illustrated by assuming that the British–U.S. production ratios are now:

|  | WHEAT | IRON |
|---|---|---|
|  | *bushels* | *tons* |
| Britain | 300 | 1200 |
| United States | 100 | 200 |

This depicts a situation in which a British worker has an absolute advantage in the production of both wheat and iron. But because the United States is not equally inferior in both goods, the basis for trade is available. Notice that the trade-off in transferring resources from the production of iron to wheat is 4:1 for Britain, whereas it is only 2:1 for the United States. It is this comparative advantage that can be used to make trade profitable.

The easiest way to show this relationship is to examine the difference between the cost of producing the goods at home and the cost of buying them from the other country. If it costs less to buy the good abroad, specialization and trade is the best path. If we assume that cost is measured in terms of the ratios of production capabilities, comparative advantage is somewhat obvious. Thus, for Britain the cost of producing the good in which it has a comparative *disadvantage*—wheat—is 4 units of iron. But the U.S. cost is only two units of iron, and Britain should be able to buy the wheat at that price. For the United States, the domestic cost of each unit of iron is one-half unit of wheat, but Britain should be willing to trade iron at its cost, which is one unit of iron per one-quarter unit of wheat. The United States is clearly better off paying the British price for iron, and Britain is better off paying the U.S. price for wheat. Thus, comparative advantage makes trade beneficial for both countries. Although the benefits of trade are less pronounced under a situation of comparative advantage, this is the most difficult and unlikely case. Most nations will possess an absolute advantage in the production of some goods. But, demonstrating the benefits of trade under comparative advantage makes a very strong case for free trade.

David Ricardo first explained the merits of free trade nearly two centuries ago, just at the start of the industrial transformation of Great Britain. He made some assumptions to simplify the scope of his arguments—assumptions that were appropriate then but are less so today. Ricardo's argument assumed a world of simple national firms, a fixed distribution of the factors of production, where large firms don't have cost advantages over small ones and where trade is mostly exchanging manufactured goods for agricultural goods. Does this still work in a world of complex and rapidly changing technology, large transnational firms, government involvement with firms and markets, and where international trade is much more the exchange of manufactured goods? One necessary change is that instead of seeing comparative advantage as coming from fixed natural endowments, we need to entertain the possibility that advantages now come more from the ability to create capabilities through new technology, skills, and innovation. And this may derive from malleable features of the national and international environment in which firms operate. These differences may indicate that free trade and free markets are only part of the story.

Those more sensitive to the political consequences of trade—radicals and mercantilists—have raised other arguments against an unrestrained enthusiasm for free trade. Specialization may not produce the type and degree of economic development desired. If a country concentrates on food and raw materials, whose price relative to manufactured goods is falling over time, it will inevitably fall behind these industrial states in national income. Further, the great gains in income and social development to be had from advanced technological production will be denied to the state concentrating on low-value-added and low-technology production. The population of such a state will be condemned to a permanently inferior position in the international hierarchy.

In addition, certain goods are often thought to be essential to national security—for example, those used to produce armaments. An infrastructure of technological capability may be critical for maintaining military parity with other states. Specialization can expose nations to dependence on external supplies of such goods and thereby compromise security and other international goals. For example, many defense analysts in the United States have worried that purchasing high-technology goods from Japan compromises defense capabilities because this exposes the United States to a cutoff during a crisis.  Lastly, movement toward free trade and specialization would require shifting resources away from some goods and toward others. This entails political consequences because those affected are likely to resist the personal costs and disruption associated with change. Adopting free trade or protection is an intensely political process involving differences in who will receive the benefits and who will bear the costs. When we consider the added dimensions of changed circumstances, development, security, and redistribution, the choice of free trade becomes somewhat less clear; it should not be surprising to learn that free trade is the exception and not the rule over the past 175 years.

Why this is so can be understood through a consideration of the political economy of free trade. We have seen that free trade leads a nation to shift resources from the production of goods where it has a comparative disadvantage (CD) to the production of goods where it has a comparative advantage (CA). Exactly what does "shift" mean? Businesses unable to compete because their products are at a comparative disadvantage in global markets will go broke and workers here will lose their jobs. Only if businesses move to production of goods where the nation has a comparative advantage can these resources be profitably employed. How are we to understand this process politically? After all, this "shift" is likely to be difficult; some workers and businesses will not be able to make the transition. By the same token, those already producing CA goods will benefit from free trade.

If we think of national politics in terms of different groups based on their economic positions, several important conclusions about how trade affects politics are possible. A nation will have a comparative advantage in goods where the main factor of production (land, labor, capital) is plentiful relative to that factor's availability throughout the world. By contrast, that nation will be at a comparative disadvantage in producing a good using a factor that is scarce relative to the rest of the world. From this, we can see that increased or freer trade will produce significant benefits to those groups in a country whose economic position is based on an abundant factor and that it will harm those whose economic position is based upon scarce factors. The key point is that free trade does not help all producer groups (although it will help the interests of consumers).

Free trade will benefit those in a nation who control relatively abundant resources that give them a comparative advantage in global markets; it will damage those who produce goods using a relatively scarce factor. This sets up a political conflict between such groups as they struggle over whether the nation will have free trade or trade barriers. For example, suppose that labor in a nation is scarce relative to labor's much greater abundance in the rest of the world. Closing off this nation to trade will permit labor there to receive higher wages than if free trade were adopted. An open economy would force workers to compete against the much more plentiful workers in the rest of the world, and their wages would fall. If capital (banking and finance) is abundant there relative to other nations, this group will prefer openness because it can increase its returns through trade. The choice made by the country will probably depend on the political strength of labor versus capital.[2]

## THE BALANCE OF PAYMENTS

One of the most basic and essential concepts for understanding the international economy is the balance of payments, which focuses on a particular nation and its transactions with the rest of the world. This accounting technique records the movement of goods, services, and capital across national boundaries for some period of time (month, quarter, year). The notion of "balance" here is somewhat misleading, for although this statistic always balances

[2] Ronald Rogowski, *Commerce and Coalitions: How Trade Affects Domestic-Political Alignments*, Princeton: Princeton University Press, 1989.

(because of the requirements of double-entry bookkeeping), we are really interested in the imbalances that inevitably appear in its various components.

Given that the parts are more important than the whole, what are the main items in the balance of payments? First, note that we want to measure all transactions of resources and claims on resources that the citizens of one nation have with the rest of the world.[3] For the purposes of this book, we will focus on eight major categories:

1. **Merchandise Exports and Imports**

   This refers to tangible goods produced at home and sold abroad (exports) and tangible goods produced abroad and sold in the home country (imports). This is the most familiar item in the balance of payments and includes all goods from clothing to computers to auto parts.

2. **Exports and Imports of Services**

   This refers to more intangible items, such as the transportation costs for goods and people, insurance, information, satellite transmissions, and banking.

3. **Investment Income and Payments**

   When someone invests resources in another country, he/she expects a return in the form of interest or dividends. This item measures payments of investment income by foreigners to citizens of the home country and by the home country to foreigners.

4. **Government Exports/Imports and Foreign Aid**

   The government may be engaged in selling or buying goods internationally, such as weapons. Additionally, the government may give or receive foreign aid.

5. **Balance on Current Account**

   The Balance on Current Account is a summary measure of items 1–4, that is, Merchandise, Services, Investment Income, and Government. Along with the Merchandise Account taken alone, the Current Account balance is the most frequently used measure of a nation's international transactions.

6. **Capital Account**

   This measures the actual investment of resources abroad or in the home country by foreigners. Typically, a distinction is made between short-term investments, which have a maturity of less than one year, and long-term investments, which have a maturity beyond one year. For example, when a Japanese bank purchases a U.S. government security, such as a Treasury note, that matures in 180 days, this is recorded in the short-term Capital Account. (When the government pays interest to the Japanese bank, this is recorded in the Investment Account, which is described in number three above.)

---

[3] There are many complications about who counts as a citizen. One important example is a company with units overseas; the branches or facilities abroad are treated as foreigners.

**TABLE 2.1**

| | CREDIT | DEBIT | BALANCE |
|---|---|---|---|
| | | (IN BILLIONS OF DOLLARS) | |
| 1. Merchandise | | | |
| Exports | 164.3 | | |
| Imports | | 129.6 | |
| 2. Services | | | |
| Exports | 21.1 | | |
| Imports | | 19.3 | |
| Trade Balance | 185.4 | 148.9 | +36.5 |
| 3. Investment Income and Payments | | | |
| Income | 14.6 | | |
| Payments | | 21.4 | |
| 4. Government | | | |
| Exports | 13.5 | | |
| Imports | | 2.6 | |
| Aid (net) | | .7 | |
| 5. Balance on Current Account | 213.5 | 173.6 | +39.9 |
| 6. Capital Account | | | |
| Exports (long- and short-term) | | 58.4 | |
| Imports (long- and short-term) | 31.7 | | |
| Balance on Capital Account | | | -26.7 |
| 7. Official Reserves | | 7.0 | -7.0 |
| 8. Statistical Discrepancy | | 6.2 | -6.2 |

**7. Official Reserves**

The central bank of a country holds reserves of foreign exchange and gold that it uses when it conducts transactions with the central banks of other nations and when it intervenes in foreign exchange markets to buy or sell currency. The effect of these actions is to balance the net differences of other items in this list.

**8. Statistical Discrepancy**

The measurement of the balance of payments is an inexact process, owing to its complexity and to the fact that some transactions are concealed (for example, trade in illegal drugs). This item is a statistical device used to express the imprecision of measurement and to bring the overall credits and debits into balance.

A handy way to think of the balance of payments is to consider whether a transaction results in a payment to the country (credit) or a payment to a foreigner (debit). Or, as a famous student of politics once said, "Follow the money." Table 2.1 offers a hypothetical example.

**TABLE 2.2**

| | YEAR | | | |
|---|---|---|---|---|
| | 1 | 2 | 3 | 4 |
| Goods/Services | | | | |
|     Exports | 102.2 | 156.7 | 185.4 | 191.4 |
|     Imports | 119.9 | 140.1 | 148.9 | 227.5 |
| Investments | | | | |
|     Income | 3.2 | 3.7 | 14.6 | 20.2 |
|     Payments | 8.4 | 11.9 | 21.4 | 23.1 |
| Government | 1.5 | 11.8 | 10.2 | 8.1 |
| Current Account Balance | -21.4 | 20.2 | 39.9 | -30.9 |
| Capital Account | | | | |
|     Exports | 12.2 | 32.6 | 58.4 | 27.7 |
|     Imports | 26.8 | 29.1 | 31.7 | 50.3 |
| Capital Account Balance | 14.6 | -3.5 | -26.7 | 22.6 |
| Reserve Account | 3.2 | -11.0 | -7.0 | 4.1 |
| Statistical Discrepancy | 3.6 | -5.7 | -6.2 | 4.2 |

The balancing in the balance of payments is due not only to the accounting technique but also to the fact that everyone must get paid in one form or another. For example, imbalances in the merchandise, services, and investment accounts tend to be offset by the capital account. A current account surplus permits investment abroad, or, to put it another way, it allows the accumulation of foreign assets. The nation gets paid for its current account surplus with the assets of foreign countries. In Table 2.1, the $39.9 billion surplus on current account is partly offset by the outflow of funds recorded in the capital account. A trade deficit, on the other hand, encourages foreigners to invest in your country. This would mean that a deficit in the current account would be offset by an inflow of funds in the capital account.

To see how this process works and also gain some practice in understanding the balance of payments, look at Table 2.2. This is a comparison of our hypothetical nation's balance of payments over a four-year period. Note that the figures for Table 2.1 are in year three.

What can we learn about the dynamics of the balance of payments from Table 2.2? Perhaps the simplest matter is comparison of each item across the four years. The hypothetical country experiences a growth in exports, but imports grow even more rapidly. These different growth rates produce a shift from a current account deficit to surplus and then back to deficit. You can see this as the current account swings from a deficit of $21.4 billion to two years of surplus and then back to a deficit of $30.9 billion. The capital account tends to mirror these changes, with a net inflow of funds followed by two years of outflow and then a return to an inflow. In this hypothetical case, the country is able to invest more abroad and reap the benefits in income in the two intermediate years as a result of surpluses. The swing back to a deficit, however, sharply curtails this investment and, instead, pulls in foreign investment. This process can be followed in the sharp drop in capital exports and the rise in capital imports in year four.[4]

This may seem to be good since other countries are willing to make investments in our hypothetical country. Nevertheless, this situation has important and potentially costly consequences for the future. The increase in capital imports means you must pay income to foreign investors in the future, while future payments from abroad will diminish due to the decline in capital investments overseas. If the combination of a trade deficit and an increase in capital imports persists for a long period, it will set up some unpleasant choices for the future. One option is to reverse the current account deficit in order to pay income on investments to foreign investors, perhaps by curtailing imports. Alternatively, continuing the current account deficit will force the country to borrow more from abroad to pay income on past investments. But, the ability to use foreign debt to pay for a deficit depends on the willingness of those abroad to invest; they are not compelled to do so.[5] Thus, the need for everyone to get paid means that the nation must make adjustments for a current account deficit. The adjustments may come in market responses and/or in political action.

A related measurement is the nation's international standing as a creditor or debtor. This denominates the accumulated investment abroad by your citizens and by foreigners in your country, including governments and private actors. The position of our hypothetical state in year four might look something like Table 2.3.

The table reveals that our hypothetical country is a debtor in the sense that foreigners own more of its assets than its citizens own of foreign assets. This is the result of the fact that deficits in the current account have, on a net basis over several years, been financed by investment from abroad. Worthy of note is the fact that a debtor state will likely pay out more in interest and dividends to foreigners than it receives (notice, in year four, the payments of $23.1 billion and $20.2 billion in receipts as shown in Table 2.2), which is a further negative item in the balance of payments. This will continue until the

---

[4] The relation between the current and capital accounts is not a necessary one. A surplus in the current account means that the country in question is accumulating foreign exchange. This permits, but does not require, it to use those resources to make investments abroad. By contrast, a current account deficit results in foreigners accumulating the country's currency (or claims on its currency), and this allows them to purchase its assets (investments). What happens if these investments don't occur? The balancing factor then becomes the official reserve account, which entails transfers of liquid international assets among central banks. So a current account deficit not offset by investments from abroad will produce the transfer of official reserve assets to foreign countries.

[5] When this investment fails to happen, several things may occur. The country's exchange rate may fall, interest rates may rise to attract the investment, and the reserve account may be drawn upon to pay the bills for imports.

**TABLE 2.3**

| Assets Abroad | |
|---|---|
| Official (government-held) | $ 41.4 |
| Private (direct investment and securities) | 219.6 |
| Foreign Holdings of Country Assets | |
| Official (government-held) | 49.0 |
| Private (direct investment and securities) | 238.0 |
| Net Position (debtor) | $-26.0 |

current account can be brought into surplus for several years.[6] Had the situation been the opposite, and had the nation had more assets abroad than were held by foreigners, then it would be described as a creditor state. It then would likely receive a net income from abroad, a positive addition to its balance of payments.

To repeat, the balance of payments is most important for what it reveals about imbalances, especially persistent ones in the current account. But how do deficits and surpluses affect a nation's prosperity and financial position? What options does a government have for correcting or ameliorating these problems? To answer these questions, we must clearly see the relationships between national and international economies, and this requires a discussion of some of the basics of macroeconomic management: interest rates, money supply, and monetary and fiscal policy.

## MONETARY AND FISCAL POLICY

For much of the twentieth century, governments have expanded their role in influencing the overall level of national prosperity. The two most basic and well-established areas are fiscal and monetary policy. *Fiscal policy* refers to decisions about spending, taxes, and borrowing by the central government, whereas *monetary policy* involves efforts by the central bank to manage the money supply and interest rates. Of the two, monetary policy has the longest tradition, is the best institutionalized, and generally is the most effective. Fiscal policy, by contrast, tends to be much more politicized, because interest groups are easily able to identify its costs and benefits and act to influence decisions. The result is that efforts to use fiscal policy as a tool of macroeconomic management have a checkered legacy.

---

[6] In this case, the size of its debtor position is small and not terribly worrisome. However, the trends in its balance of payments toward a current account deficit create the possibility of continuing additions to its international debt. Should this debt become large, especially the proportion of interest payments in relation to exports, the potential for trouble would grow. Only when debt reaches these levels, such as with the United States and some Third World nations in recent years, does debtor or creditor status take on important consequences.

The decision to establish a central bank in the United States came early in 1913. The combination of financial panics and the management capabilities of other central banks pushed even conservative leaders to create the Federal Reserve.[7] The United States was much later in creating a central bank than were other large and prosperous countries. Great Britain did so in the 1840s, Germany in the 1870s, and upstart Japan in the 1880s.[8] One important distinction among central banks is the degree to which they act independently or are subject to political control. On that score, the German central bank—the Bundesbank—is certainly the most independent, with the Bank of England and the Banque de France generally following the direction of the government. The Federal Reserve falls somewhere between the two extremes, able to act on its own but often responding to political pressure to expand the money supply or lower interest rates.[9]

## Monetary Policy

Today, the Fed, as it is commonly called, has two major tools for managing the economy: open market operations and the discount rate. The purpose of both is to affect the availability of credit—that is, the willingness of banks to make loans and of individuals and corporations to borrow.

Most of what we treat as money is intangible, found in checking accounts and not in bills and coins. Usually, we pay for goods and services by ordering a bank to transfer a computer entry from ourselves to someone else (writing a check). Moreover, increases and decreases in the money supply for a nation typically come much more from banks making loans than from the government printing money. The Fed manages the money supply by affecting this process. When banks lend money to their customers, whether to buy a boat, computer, or office building, this expands economic activity. The production of goods and services to meet this demand boosts employment, and these additional workers spend their incomes and perhaps borrow money for purchases. The process also works in reverse: When banks decrease the rate of lending, purchases of goods and services shrink, unemployment increases, and further decreases in spending result.

How do actions of the Federal Reserve affect this process? First, we need to know that the Fed is connected to member banks in several ways: It determines the proportion of bank assets that must be held as reserves; it has the

---

[7] One of the recurring features of capitalism and free markets is a boom and bust cycle, often characterized in financial arenas by a panic. For an interesting history of financial crises, see Charles P. Kindleberger, *Manias, Panics, and Crashes*, New York: Basic Books, 1989.

[8] For detail on this process, see Charles Goodhart, *The Evolution of Central Banks*, Cambridge: MIT Press, 1988, 105–160. For establishment of the Federal Reserve, see Richard H. Timberlake, *The Origins of Central Banking in the United States*, Cambridge: Harvard University Press, 1978.

[9] For detail on the politics of Fed decision making, see John T. Woolley, *Monetary Politics: The Federal Reserve and the Politics of Monetary Policy*, Cambridge: Cambridge University Press, 1984. On the Bundesbank, see Ellen Kennedy, *The Bundesbank*, London: Pinter Publishers, 1991.

right to inspect, without notice, bank records and force changes in lending policies; and it lends money to member banks. The most commonly used technique for management of the money supply is open market operations. Here the Fed is either pumping funds into or draining funds from the banking system by buying or selling U.S. government securities. When several billion dollars of securities are purchased, the selling institutions (usually banks and insurance companies) will receive a check from the Fed that will expand the money available for lending. In adding funds to the banking system, and thereby increasing the potential lending power of banks, the Fed is pursuing an expansionary monetary policy. By contrast, a policy designed to contract or tighten the money supply would involve selling government securities. In this case, the Fed receives payment and effectively drains resources from the banking system.[10]

The discount rate is also a powerful instrument for managing the money supply. This is the interest rate charged by the Fed to member banks when they borrow money from it. The discount rate also functions as an anchor interest rate, and changes in it tend to spark changes in other interest rates. If the discount rate is 7.5 percent, the prime rate (the rate that banks charge their most credit-worthy customers) might be 9.5 percent, first mortgage loans at 10.5 percent, and credit cards at 18 percent. When the discount rate increases, other interest rates also rise, though not always in lockstep. The reverse is also true: A fall in the discount rate will probably produce a drop in other interest rates.[11] Once again, the object is to expand or contract the money supply and thereby the economy as a whole. Raising the discount rate increases the price of money, discourages borrowing, and should slow down economic expansion. Lowering the rate encourages borrowing and should accelerate economic activity.

The role of the Federal Reserve in the United States is to provide stability to financial markets during times of crisis and to promote economic growth consistent with low inflation. The Fed was created in the early twentieth century largely to moderate the financial panics that had become increasingly severe. A panic is a time when frightened investors attempt to sell securities all at once or when depositors lose confidence in the banking system and try to remove their money. The Fed also serves as a lender of last resort to provide liquidity (meaning a money supply sufficient for the transactions people want

---

[10] These actions also affect interest rates. Changes in the supply of money cause changes in the price of money, namely interest rates. Two key interest rates that often reflect open market operations are the Federal Funds and Treasury bill rates. When these rise, this may indicate that the Fed is following a tight money path by selling government securities. When they fall, the Fed may be pursuing an expansionary policy through open market purchases. The same goals of open market operations can be achieved through changes in the reserve requirement. Increasing the proportion of a bank's assets that it must hold in reserve decreases its lending capacity, whereas reductions in the reserve requirement increase the ability to make loans. Because changing the reserve requirement is such a public act, it is an infrequently used tool.

[11] Note that interest rates also rise and fall independent of Fed action, based on market-driven changes in the supply and demand for funds.

to make) to the economy when fear paralyzes the actions of other lenders. An equally important role of the Fed is to control inflation while encouraging economic growth. Inflation is especially harmful to persons who lend money or who have their assets in fixed-income instruments (such as government bonds). The fixed rates of future income are effectively reduced by inflation. Rising prices mean that interest received in the future has less purchasing power. In acting to control inflation, the Fed is protecting the interests of lenders and others who are hurt by rising prices.[12]

The decision makers at the Fed pay close attention to the capital and credit markets as well as to the indicators of economic expansion and contraction. If the evidence suggests that expansion is moving too fast and inflationary pressures are increasing, the Fed is likely to take action. The quiet and short-term method of attacking inflation would be open market sales of government securities, thereby reducing the money supply and pushing up interest rates. A more public declaration of policy would be an increase in the discount rate. Depending on the severity of the problem, some combination of these actions may continue for many months or even years. During much of the 1970s and 1980s, when inflationary pressures were strong, the Fed pursued a "tight money" policy, pushing interest rates to unprecedented levels. In early 1994, the Fed acted in anticipation of rising inflation to push up interest rates and slow the U.S. economy.

## Fiscal Policy

The other major instrument of economic management is fiscal policy—the use of taxing and spending by the national government to affect the economy. The basic ideas of fiscal policy can be traced to the thinking of John Maynard Keynes, an influential British economist. Keynes and others argued that fiscal policy need not, and should not, be tied to the rigid orthodoxy of a balanced budget, but instead could be used to manage the economy and smooth out the business cycle of expansion and recession (or depression).[13]

The notion of "pump priming" by the government to stimulate economic expansion involves deficit spending. Here, government spending exceeds tax revenue, with the difference made up by having the Treasury Department sell government bonds. Before about 1960, the theory supporting deficit spending was that selling bonds and spending the funds on government projects stimulated the economy by returning unused savings into the spending and income stream. With the Kennedy–Johnson tax cut of 1964, the rationale changed. Rather than rely on increased government spending, economists

---

[12] For a discussion of the contesting interests over inflation, see William Grieder, *Secrets of the Temple*, New York: Simon and Schuster, 1987, 11-47, 75-123.

[13] There was great resistance to Keynes among conservatives, especially from the 1930s to the 1960s. An interesting discussion of the political struggles over Keynesianism is in Robert Collins, *The Business Response to Keynes*, New York: Columbia University Press, 1981.

promoted cutting taxes and maintaining spending to produce a stimulative deficit. Here, recipients of lower taxes were expected to spend their increased income to accomplish the same result.[14]

The great weakness of fiscal policy as a means of macroeconomic management is that decisions about spending and taxes are rarely based on judgments about the "correct"-size deficit or surplus to fine-tune the economy. Not only do many groups—from the military to Social Security recipients—use political pressure to increase government spending, but politicians often use tax cuts to win votes, whether or not this is best for the economy. In 1966 and 1967, President Johnson chose not to increase taxes to pay for the Vietnam War because he felt that this would undermine an already weakened base of support for his policies. These extraneous factors may be rational as short-term political calculations, but they are harmful for economic management purposes. Often, the tendency to increase spending and to decrease taxes has overstimulated the economy, resulting in inflation. This was clearly the consequence of Johnson's decisions in the 1960s. In the 1980s, budget proposals of the president became blatantly political documents in a struggle with Congress. Budgets served more as a way to score points with constituents than to manage the economy.[15] In the mid-1990s, following years of gargantuan fiscal deficits, Congress and the president began to compete for votes by proposing several versions of a balanced budget and even a constitutional amendment to require such a balanced budget. In Chapter 5 we will see how the globalization of finance puts pressure on governments to control deficits.

## EXCHANGE RATES AND TRADE DEFICITS

The one remaining set of concepts essential to understanding international political economy concerns the relationship between exchange rates and international trade. For trade to occur, money must change hands. But in international trade, one country's currency must be exchanged for another country's currency, and the rate of this exchange has significant consequences for the terms of trade and for the network of relationships linking domestic and international politics. This section explains how foreign exchange trading works, how exchange rates can affect trade, explores the reasons for government intervention in foreign exchange markets, and examines the impact of interest rates on exchange rates.

The *exchange rate* for a currency refers simply to how much of another country's money can be purchased with a specified amount of your own

---

[14] Some economists, known as "supply siders," justified the Reagan tax cut of 1981 by predicting increased work and risk taking as an additional economic stimulus.

[15] Another complicating factor is that fiscal and monetary policies are made in different political settings. The president and Congress are the chief actors in fiscal policy, whereas the Fed makes decisions about monetary policy. There is no guarantee of policy consistency, and actions at cross-purposes are not uncommon.

country's money. At the end of 1995, one U.S. dollar would purchase 101.5 Japanese yen, .65 British pounds, and 1.45 German marks.[16] Or reciprocally, one Japanese yen would buy .0098 U.S. dollars (just less than one cent); one British pound would purchase 1.53 U.S. dollars; and one German mark could be exchanged for .691 U.S. dollars (69 cents). These values are the result of daily trading in foreign exchange markets. That is, one currency is used to purchase another currency, and this trading comes at different rates of exchange, or different prices for currencies. Most of this trading is done by private individuals, banks, financial institutions, corporations, and occasionally governments. Part of the reason for foreign exchange trading is that these individuals and corporations are engaged in international trade or finance and need to buy or sell currencies. But a very large part of trading is to speculate on changes in the price of currencies.

The exchange rate or price of a currency is determined by the demand for, and supply of, one currency in relation to another. Buying and selling currencies is partly the result of transactions recorded in the balance of payments between the two countries.[17] For example, trade between two countries generates a demand and a supply of both currencies as exporters return to their home currency. Exchange rates can be measured in terms of a single foreign currency or as an average of several currencies. The volume of foreign exchange trading is truly enormous, generally averaging in 1994–1995 $1.3 trillion per day around the world. By comparison, all equities trading in the United States for one day is about $50 billion. Global foreign exchange trading is *twenty-five* times bigger than stock trading in the United States.

The exchange rate is something about which governments are vitally interested. Governments use several ways to influence exchange rates. One way is to establish fixed rates, typically involving substantial governmental intervention in markets to keep the price of a currency from moving up or down. A fixed exchange rate system operated in much of the world from 1958 to 1973 and during the forty years before World War I. The opposite is a floating rate system, in which the value of a currency is determined entirely by market forces without government intervention. The current set of arrangements is a complex mixture. About fifty countries have some form of modified float, whereby the government intervenes periodically to affect markets. Fewer than twenty states have adopted arrangements that provide for somewhat fixed rates in relation to a group of other currencies. The vast majority of states, mostly small and poor, have fixed their currency's value to one or more stronger currencies. An important distinction to remember is between hard and soft currencies. Hard currencies are those few currencies that are especially stable and secure, that may be accepted in payment for

---

[16] Most newspapers carry reports of daily transactions on foreign exchange markets, usually in the business pages.

[17] In addition, speculators hoping to profit from fluctuations in the price of a currency will affect demand and supply. The transactions of speculators may or may not be recorded in the balance of payments.

**FIGURE 2.1**

**Real Effective Exchange Rate Indexes**
**United States, Germany, Japan**
**(Based on Relative Wholesale Prices)**

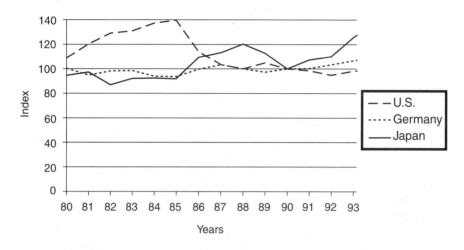

SOURCE: The data are taken from International Monetary Fund, *International Financial Statistics Yearbook*, 1995.

international transactions, and that international financiers can readily exchange for other currencies. Soft currencies lack these characteristics and are used only within the nation of issue.

Figure 2.1 demonstrates the erratic changes in the exchange rates of three major currencies—the dollar, deutsche mark, and yen—since 1980. The values are adjusted for inflation in wholesale goods prices and are based on a weighted average of each currency against twenty other currencies. Even when these adjustments are provided (they tend to reduce fluctuation to real changes in value), we can see significant volatility in the value of the three currencies. This is especially true for the dollar, which rose during the 1980–1985 period and then fell.

There are almost no examples of exchange rates determined entirely by market forces. As we have seen, the central bank (government-owned) of a country sometimes intervenes in foreign exchange markets, buying or selling in hopes of influencing the price of their currency. But why would a central bank want to influence the value of its money? What effect does a particular exchange rate have on a nation's economic prosperity? Economists and government officials have long recognized that the value of a nation's currency affects the prices of its goods involved in foreign trade and the prices of foreign goods sold in its home market. By changing the value of its nation's currency, these officials typically want to change the prices of imports and exports and thereby affect its overall balance of trade.

**FIGURE 2.2**

SOURCE: The data are taken from Department of Commerce, *National Trade Data Bank*, October 1991.

## How Exchange Rates Affect Trade

How is this supposed to work? First, remember that when people engage in foreign trade, they must price their goods in the currency of the selling market, whereas they want to end up with their own currency. This means that the money received from selling goods must be exchanged for the home currency. Thus, changes in the exchange rate directly influence the prices that can or must be charged.

To see this in action, consider the following situation. A U.S. exporter is selling computer disc drives in Great Britain. The exchange rate is £1 equals $2 (or $1 equals one half of a pound). The disc drives sell for $500 apiece in the United States, and the exporter is prepared to absorb the costs of transportation in order to establish a position in Britain. Thus, he/she prices the disc drives at £250 since this can be exchanged for the $500 he/she actually wants. Now, suppose the exchange rate changes to £1 equals $3. The pound has appreciated in value (it now brings $3 instead of only $2) while the dollar has depreciated (because you need $3 instead of only $2 to get £1). What effect does this have on our exporter? Remember that he/she wants to end up with $500. To do this, he/she now needs charge only £166.67 in order to convert to $500 (166.67 times 3). A depreciating dollar *permits* (but does not require) U.S. exporters to lower their prices abroad.

The opposite result occurs when the dollar appreciates in value. Suppose that the original exchange rate of £1 equals $2 becomes £1 equals $1. The pound has depreciated while the dollar has appreciated. Our exporter now has a big problem. In order to end up with $500, he/she must increase the price to £500. Thus, an appreciating dollar virtually forces exporters to raise prices or else see their profits fall. As an important aside, we should note that these effects also work, but in the opposite direction, for British exports to the United States.

This example gives us the basis for understanding how the government hopes to influence the nation's trade balance. We have a convenient example, namely the effort by the Reagan administration, beginning in 1985, to first "talk down" and later push down the value of the dollar. This came in the face of an unprecedented deficit in the balance of trade. Why try to force down the value of the dollar? The purposes can be summarized in Figure 2.2 as a causal chain.

**FIGURE 2.3**

**U.S. Merchandise Trade Balance Compared to Dollar Exchange Rate**

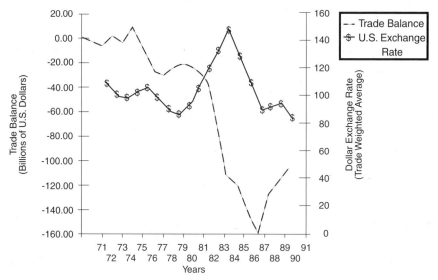

SOURCE: The data are taken from Department of Commerce, *National Trade Data Bank*, October 1991.

Verbally, this shows the expectation that a drop in the exchange rate of the dollar should lead to a drop in the prices of U.S. exports while the prices of imports rise. A decline in export prices should also lead to an increased demand for these goods, while rising import prices should lead U.S. citizens to purchase fewer imported goods. As a result, the amount of exports should rise while imports decline, and the trade deficit should improve.

But there are important limits on the ability of an exchange rate depreciation to eliminate a deeply entrenched deficit such as that of the United States. Look at Figure 2.3, which shows a trade-weighted average of the value of the dollar and the U.S. merchandise trade balance.[18] It should be clear that the U.S. trade deficit has been only marginally affected by previous declines in the dollar. Although the dollar generally fell from 1971 to 1980, the trade balance worsened. Since 1985 the dollar has fallen by as much as 50 percent, while the trade deficit continued rising until 1987. The figures for 1988–1990 recovered to only about 1984 levels.

There are several fairly simple reasons why the desired reduction in the trade deficit has been limited. Perhaps the most important unrealized expectation is that, instead of falling, imports have continued to rise in spite of a

---

[18] A trade-weighted average means that the value of the dollar is computed against an average value of several of its main trading partners. The average is weighted by the amount of trade conducted with the United States, with some countries' currencies counting more than others.

**FIGURE 2.4**

**U.S. Exports and Imports, 1981–1994**

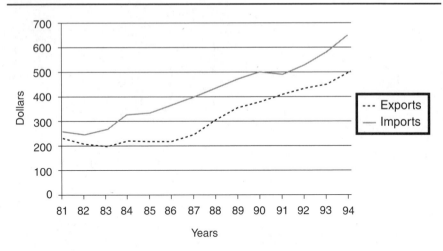

SOURCE: The data are taken from International Monetary Fund, *International Financial Statistics Yearbook*, 1995.

falling dollar. Look at Figure 2.4, which shows an increasing trend line for imports after 1983. Two factors contribute to this problem. First, U.S. consumers believe that many foreign-made products are superior to those made in the United States, so even when the prices of imports rise, demand may not fall very much.[19] A second reason is that businesspersons who are selling goods in the United States may choose not to raise prices but instead to absorb some of the effects of a declining dollar. They might take this step in order to remain competitive, retaining their market share in hopes of a rising dollar. Or they might decide to hold their money in dollars, investing in U.S. assets rather than reverting to a foreign currency. (Indeed, the growth of multinational firms, with permanent operations abroad and less need to convert to a "home" currency, increases the chances of this happening.) On the export

[19] This relationship between the amount of change in demand produced by a change in price is referred to by economists as the *elasticity of demand*. Frequently, economists and others refer to this relationship between the volume of trade and the prices of goods traded as the *J curve*. This term pays close attention to the effects of elasticity over time, in particular to the fact that the prices of imports and exports may rise or fall immediately following a change in exchange rates, while the intended changes in demand may require some time. The J curve indicates that the immediate result of a fall in a currency's value may be a *worsening* of the trade balance. If export prices fall and import prices rise, with little initial change in demand, then exports (measured as volume times price) will fall, and imports will rise. The deterioration in the trade balance, however, should be followed by improvement (thus the J curve) in the balance as elasticities in demand for exports and imports take over and swell the export volume beyond the fall in prices while lowering the volume of imports beyond the rise in prices.

side, those who sell abroad have options that would not necessarily help the trade deficit. Remember that a declining dollar permits, but does not require, the exporter to lower prices. But if exporters are already competitive in price, they may choose to keep prices about the same and reap the extra profits when the pounds (or whatever the currency of transaction) are exchanged for dollars. Once again, the presence of large, multinational firms, who are in a position to benefit from continuing exchange rate transactions, may nullify much of the anticipated impact of a declining dollar.[20]

## EXCHANGE RATES, TRADE, AND MACROECONOMIC POLICY

We can now begin to see how the complexities of national and international economies work. Frequently, actions in one economic arena complicate the situation elsewhere. International economic interdependence creates important difficulties for economic management. This section discusses some of the ways this can happen.

First, we need to extend our earlier discussion of exchange rates to see how a purely economic or market-based analysis of this process might work. In a system in which exchange rates are a result of only the forces of supply and demand for foreign exchange as generated by exports and imports, market processes can act to adjust trade balances automatically. For example, a trade deficit in country X adds to the supply of its currency in the hands of foreigners. (If you don't see why this is true, review the sections on exchange rates and the balance of payments.) When foreigners exchange country X's currency for their own, assuming that other factors don't change, the price of X's currency should fall. This decline activates the process, discussed earlier, of falling export prices and rising demand for exports, accompanied by rising import prices resulting in lower demand. This fall in prices should continue until the trade deficit has disappeared. A trade surplus brings the same arrangements into play, except in the opposite direction. But caution should be used in accepting this rather neat system. We have already considered how the connections among exchange rates, prices, and demand are subject to important qualifications. Another major problem with market-based solutions to trade imbalances is that foreign exchange trading has become disconnected from international trade. As we shall see in Chapter 5, the foreign exchange market is affected by trade in only a small way. Equally significant are other complications that emerge when we consider the political and other eco-

---

[20] A detailed discussion of the adjustment process is found in Paul R. Krugman, *Has the Adjustment Process Worked?*, Washington: Institute for International Economics, 1991. Krugman answers this question in the affirmative. See Chapter 6 of this book for more discussion of this issue in relation to the question of competitiveness.

nomic dimensions of the relationship between domestic and international economic systems.

Allowing exchange rates to cure a trade deficit, or attempting to manipulate these rates toward the same end, can have unpleasant consequences. A fall in the dollar, if it works right, should force up import prices, thereby increasing inflationary pressures and even permitting domestic producers to raise their prices. Equally, export prices may fall abroad, leading to increased demand that spurs the domestic economy. But, the combination of rising import prices and accelerating economic growth also creates the specter of inflation. This brings on the Federal Reserve (or the central bank of most countries), who, as we know, has a major commitment to fighting inflation.

As we have seen, one of the main weapons in the Fed's arsenal for combating inflation is interest rates. Specifically, the Fed may use the discount rate and open market operations to force interest rates to rise, in anticipation of the inflationary effects of a falling dollar, so as to reduce business investment and consumer spending. This, the Fed hopes, will reduce overall economic activity and hold down inflationary pressures. In other words, the Fed may try to induce a recession, or at least an economic slowdown, in order to counteract the inflationary consequences of a falling dollar. In addition to helping control inflation, a recession can result in a declining demand for imported goods as the economy contracts.[21]

But this effort to counter the effects of the falling dollar can have negative consequences for the stock market, which is very sensitive to changes in interest rates. The individuals and institutions who own stocks pay closer attention to the somewhat more certain returns from securities that pay a fixed return rather than in the more speculative form of dividends or price appreciation. When interest rates rise, especially if the expectation is for continuing increases, many investors may sell stocks and buy securities that offer the new (increased) interest rates. Rising interest rates frequently lead to a declining stock market. Often, the sequence works like this: The trade deficit for the month is announced, and it shows a larger than expected gap between imports and exports. People who own stock, anticipating actions by the Fed to cope with the expected inflation from a falling dollar, will sell stocks, sometimes creating frightening declines. This is part of what happened in October 1987, when the Dow Jones Industrial Average fell more than one thousand points, or more than one third of its total value, over the space of a few days.

Thus, the effort to improve the trade deficit through a declining dollar can lead to inflation, higher interest rates, and even a recession. But matters do not stop here. Interest rates themselves also affect exchange rates. Remember that the value of a currency is a result of the demand and supply in foreign exchange markets. Interest rates affect the capital account portion of the bal-

---

[21] This is similar to the adjustment often imposed by the International Monetary Fund on countries having persistent trade deficits. The "belt tightening" usually means cutting government spending, raising taxes, and increasing interest rates.

ance of payments by influencing the level of investment in a country. To see this, suppose you are a foreign banker with the choice of investing in the government bonds of five countries. The interest rates on these bonds are:

| U.S. | JAPAN | FRANCE | BRITAIN | GERMANY |
| --- | --- | --- | --- | --- |
| 8.7% | 3.6% | 6.1% | 9.2% | 4.8% |

If the Fed raises the discount rate and drives U.S. bond yields up to 10 percent, this will attract investors. In order to purchase U.S. bonds, the foreign banker must first buy dollars with his/her currency. If large numbers of investors do this, the increased demand for dollars will drive up the exchange rate.[22]

So what do we have? A declining dollar designed to improve the trade deficit ignites inflation. This prompts the Fed to raise interest rates, attracting foreign investors. And this pushes up the value of the dollar, which we know could make the trade deficit expand. Economic interdependence makes policy choices much more complicated because the international and domestic consequences of actions may negate each other.

This happens in other ways as well. If one country chooses to pursue an expansionary economic policy, it must consider the international consequences. An expanding economy, especially if accompanied by inflation, pulls in imports. If this occurs when other nations' economies are not expanding, the consequence is likely to be a weakening of the current account balance. Because other countries are experiencing an economic slowdown, they are not likely to be very good markets for exports. A declining current account surplus or widening deficit acts as a drag on overall gross national product (GNP) and may even negate the expansionary stimulus. This was the situation confronting the French government in the early 1980s as it sought to stimulate its economy at a time when other Western capitalist economies were in or entering a recession. The result was a serious worsening in the current account balance. As exports faltered and imports poured in, the value of the franc fell, and inflation rose.

Clearly, international economic interdependence means that domestic economic policies frequently must be coordinated with other states in order to be effective. Furthermore, it is too simple to say that market systems, left alone, can solve the problems created by a payments imbalance or that intervention by governments can always smooth out market imperfections. There are several markets at work, sometimes operating at cross-purposes, and

---

[22] An additional consideration for foreign investors is the stability of the exchange rate, because this affects the net yield. A falling exchange rate reduces the net return because you must have more foreign currency to get back to the home currency. Conversely, a rising exchange rate adds to the overall return; thus, the combination of high interest rates and a rising exchange rate tends to be self-reinforcing. But the key to the process is high interest rates relative to the rest of the world. Consequently, rates don't actually have to rise for the exchange rate to increase; they simply need to remain *relatively* high.

always functioning both with some autonomy and with powerful linkages to each other. Exchange rates, interest rates, and the markets for exports and imports certainly share this interesting combination of contradictory effects, independent operation, and interdependence.

Beyond the economics, there is the politics of the problem of managing domestic and international economic relations. Two situations are worth emphasizing here. Manipulating exchange rates, either by active intervention or passive acceptance of market forces, is a politically cheap way of trying to solve a trade deficit. Because most persons do not understand the mechanisms involved, the costs of such a policy can be disguised or hidden. A limited political impact is produced by assertions that a trade deficit results in transferring claims against a nation's resources to the rest of the world or that it means that a nation is consuming more than it is producing. Certainly, exchange rates are politically preferable to a strategy of economic restructuring or deflation and recession. But equally clear is the possibility that exchange rates may fail to solve the problem.

Also worthy of emphasis is the complex problem of international political cooperation to manage interdependent economic systems. Obviously, such cooperation is influenced by the status of political relationships in other matters. As we shall see in later chapters, success in cooperation is entangled in a web of conflicting and common interests and in the ability of leaders to maneuver and build a set of acceptable compromises among internal and external constituencies. This game of complex interdependence is at the heart of the problems of cooperation and conflict. But before we can talk intelligently about the present, we need to understand the paths of the past in the historical origins of a world economy.

## CONCLUSIONS

This chapter was designed to give you many of the concepts of economic analysis that are essential for understanding international political economy. At this point you should be comfortable with the following:

1. The concepts of free trade, absolute advantage, and comparative advantage are the keys to understanding why trade occurs and how the benefits of free trade are spread to all who participate. But remember that the benefits are not equal and that nations seeking security do not always gain what they need.

2. The components of the balance of payments, including some of the summary measures, such as the *current account* and related terms like *creditor* and *debtor nation*, should be familiar concepts. Additionally, you need to understand the relationship of the current account and capital account.

3. The differences between fiscal and monetary policy and the basic mechanisms of their operation must be almost second nature. Pay spe-

cial attention to the use of monetary policy and interest rates to manage the domestic economy.

4. The lines of influence between exchange rates and the prices and demand for exports and imports are an especially important set of relationships. You need to be able to work through this process quickly and to apply it to various policy options. Equally significant, however, is the plethora of factors that undermine and distort this process.

5. Finally, the most difficult but also most important matter is the interacting effects of the balance of payments, monetary and fiscal policy, and exchange rates. This is a major topic, in more complex form, in subsequent chapters.

There are other important economic concepts left for consideration in subsequent chapters, including the gold standard, fixed exchange rate systems, key currency, and protectionism. But with the ideas of this chapter in mind, you are now prepared to begin thinking seriously about international political economy.

## ANNOTATED BIBLIOGRAPHY

Richard Caves et al., *World Trade and Payments: An Introduction*, New York: Harper-Collins, 1993.
    Provides an excellent introduction to the entire field of international economics.
Robert Heilbroner and Lester Thurow, *Economics Explained*, New York: Touchstone, 1982.
    A very clear and basic introduction to economics.
Paul Krugman, *The Age of Diminished Expectations*, Cambridge: MIT Press, 1991.
    Offers a series of clearly written essays relating to many of the central topics of economics and economic policy.
Michael Melvin, *International Money and International Finance*, New York: Harper-Collins, 1992.
    Provides a very clear and understandable introduction to the complications of exchange rates.
John C. Pool and Steve Stamos, *The ABC's of International Finance*, Lexington: Lexington Books, 1987.
    A theoretically limited but very clear introduction to the basics of international economics.
Paul Samuelson, *Economics*, New York: McGraw-Hill, 1990.
    The standard textbook in the field of economics.

# Chapter 3

# THE ORIGINS OF A WORLD ECONOMY

In some respects a world economy is very much like other economic systems: Goods are produced and services provided; wealth is accumulated and destroyed; investments are made on the basis of maximizing returns; and prices fluctuate according to supply and demand. And yet, because these things are taking place across national borders, we know that something different is happening. We are accustomed to thinking of economies as coextensive with the nation. Historically, nations have guarded their borders jealously; after all, this is one of the things that makes them nations. Governments have always tried to place some controls on trade, immigration, and monetary transactions with the outside world. Consequently, the stupendous growth of a world economy over the past 150 to 175 years calls for understanding on its own terms.

The purpose of this chapter is to provide the student with the tools and information needed to begin thinking about the world economy as a special phenomenon. The approach is largely historical so that the student can appreciate the long-term background to contemporary events and gain some perspective on the many different outcomes of international economic cooperation and conflict. Especially important is understanding how the transformation of the world economy is inextricably enmeshed with international political and military developments. The discussion will follow two related lines. The first part deals with developments within nations, such as technology and production, special advantages in raw materials, labor skills, and entrepreneurial strategies and behaviors. The second part considers economic relations among nations, including the flow of goods, capital, information, and technology, and competitive advantages and their effects on political and military relations. The focus includes the beginnings of international trade in manufactured goods in the early nineteenth century, the formation of a world economy of expanding trade and interdependence from 1840 to 1875, and the breakdown and collapse of this system in World War I and the Great Depression.

# INDUSTRIALIZATION AND INTERNATIONAL TRADE

We begin our story with the late eighteenth and early nineteenth centuries. This is when the industrial system spread from England across Europe and, in conjunction with the explosion of British trade in manufactures, began to create a world economy somewhat like our own. Of course, international economic relations of substantial proportions did exist before this time. For example, during the sixteenth and seventeenth centuries a complex economic system grew up in Asia. It was organized by the British, Dutch, Spanish, and Portuguese around cloth, spice, and silver.[1] But what distinguishes our starting point from previous periods is the sense of potential economic gains for all from world trade, the growing importance of manufactured goods in foreign trade, and the enormous increase in the degree of interdependence among nations.[2] These factors combined to create new forms of production and thereby expanded dramatically the benefits from trade. The growth of world trade changed the willingness of nations to participate in this new system even as expanding profits encouraged overseas investments at unprecedented levels. This process extended from 1780 to 1850 and resulted in a world economy with features resembling that of our time.[3]

## British Industrialization

An enduring and exceedingly important characteristic of the world economy is its unevenness. Nations compete with each other on quite unequal terms based on distinct advantages in technology, economic organization, and resources. Such was the case with the industrial development of Britain in the late eighteenth century and with the changes in the world economy that followed. The British enjoyed the benefits of being the leaders in new

---

[1] Mark Borthwick, *Pacific Century*, Boulder: Westview, 1992, 77-89. Fernand Braudel believes that a world economy of significant proportions has existed for a very long time. Fernand Braudel, *Civilization and Capitalism, 15th-18th Centuries, Vol. 3: The Perspective of the World*, trans. by Sian Reynolds, New York: Harper & Row, 1984.

[2] The ideas associated with free trade contrast sharply with those of mercantilism. Operating from a zero-sum concept of a world economy, mercantilism asserts that the gains made from trade by one nation must come at the expense of all others. Nations, under this thesis, try to protect their own markets while seeking to take export markets from others. See Jacob Viner, "Power Versus Plenty as Objectives of Trade in the Seventeenth and Eighteenth Centuries," *World Politics*, 1.1, October 1946.

[3] In the period from 1500 to 1750, localism and barter were still predominant, with international trade largely confined to luxury goods, including foodstuffs, silk, hides, copper, spices, metals, and timber. The slow and uneven growth of world trade probably contributed to a zero-sum attitude. See Kristof Glamann, "European Trade, 1500-1750," in Carlo Cipolla (ed.), *The Fontana Economic History of Europe: The Sixteenth and Seventeenth Centuries*, Glasgow: Collins/Fontana Books, 1974, 427-526; and P. J. Cain, *Economic Foundations of British Overseas Expansion 1815-1914*, London: Macmillan, 1980.

manufacturing processes because of a particular configuration of factors favoring this development.

In 1750, Britain was already a highly commercialized society with the largest market in Europe. Rising agricultural productivity over much of the eighteenth century supported a rapidly increasing population. A monetary economy (in contrast to one based on barter) was widely accepted, and the country had a long and successful tradition of international trade.[4] In terms of labor, Britain had few restrictions on movement from agriculture to manufacturing and also possessed a significant number of persons competent in the somewhat low-level technical skills needed for the manufacturing processes of the period. Additionally, sufficient capital was available for the scale of investment in manufacturing processes.[5] The focus of these activities initially was in the production of wool cloth and, by the late eighteenth century, in manufacturing cotton cloth. Buoyed by the opportunities in domestic and foreign markets, British entrepreneurs quickly adopted new techniques of production. The result was a dramatic decline in costs and prices and a consequent explosion in sales.[6] British political and military power also mattered. Already a major power, Britain became the world's foremost state during the period of the industrial revolution. This meant Britain could defend itself and could capture and preserve the benefits of its new capabilities. Had the innovations in Britain taken place elsewhere—in India, for example—the Indian ability to retain these advantages would have been compromised, as it was dominated by foreign powers and interests. India could not have prevented control from slipping into others' hands.[7]

It was the sale of cotton goods abroad that fueled a general rise in British exports from 1784 to 1814. "Exports became, for the first time, a powerful 'engine of growth' of national income."[8] Sales abroad accounted for 18 percent of national income in 1801, and the cotton industry alone represented 7 percent of all national products in the same year.[9] Of equal significance was the fact that markets and sources of supply increasingly came from areas that were outside the Empire and, consequently, not under British political control. Trade

---

[4] Eric Hobsbawm, *Industry and Empire*, New York: Penguin, 1969, 53; E. L. Jones, "Agriculture, 1700–1800," in Roderick Floud and Donald McCloskey (eds.), *The Economic History of Britain Since 1700*, Cambridge: Cambridge University Press, 66–86; P. K. O'Brien, "Agriculture and the Industrial Revolution," *Economic History Review*, 30.1, 1977, 166–181; David Landes, *The Unbound Prometheus*, Cambridge: Cambridge University Press, 1969, 52–54, 46–49. Landes reports that Britain had the highest per-capita income in Europe, which meant that Britain had the highest wage rates and a significant domestic market for consumer goods.

[5] Hobsbawm, *Industry ...*, 39; Landes, *The Unbound . . .*, 61–66.

[6] D. N. McCloskey, "The Industrial Revolution 1780–1860: A Survey," in Floud and McCloskey (eds.), *Economic History . . .*, 110–111.

[7] Cain, *Economic Foundations . . .*, 24–25.

[8] P. J. Cain and A. G. Hopkins, "The Political Economy of British Expansion Overseas, 1750–1914," *The Economic History Review*, 33.4, November 1980, 472.

[9] McCloskey, "The Industrial Revolution . . .," 112.

relationships with other sovereign states were eventually to take on quite a different color than those with colonial areas. Unfortunately, these tendencies were interrupted somewhat by the international conflicts of 1792-1814 (the wars between revolutionary and Napoleonic France and much of Europe). The combination of the British blockade of continental ports and extreme protection by the French from British products retarded economic development in Europe and let Britain move into French overseas markets.

But we should not overestimate the impact of industrial production or international trade on Britain during this period. Industrialization, although rapid, did not transform Britain or the world economy all at once. For this to happen, British political and economic leaders had to develop an understanding of trading relationships based on something other than a mercantile effort at national aggrandizement. That is, we need to understand how developments in British political economy, the adoption of industrial systems and the growth of markets in Europe, and the unilateral British decision for freer trade produced a world economy with familiar features.

After 1815, many nations in Europe raised protectionist barriers to British goods, fearing competition and the political consequences of a flood of foreign goods.

> The cardinal fact for most French producers after 1815 was the existence of an overwhelmingly dominant and powerful industrial producer not only as their nearest neighbor but as a mighty force in all foreign markets and sometimes in their own heavily-protected domestic market.[10]

For several reasons, these same nations were unable to match British productivity quickly, often taking nearly fifty years to catch up in any meaningful sense. In some cases, it was technological backwardness (often rectified by industrial spies); in other cases, the growing scale of competitive enterprise had outpaced the capital capacities of family firms. Many European countries were disadvantaged by higher costs, by attitudes that undermined effective entrepreneurship, and most of all by their patchwork nature as countries and markets. The complex set of political and cultural divisions often carved markets up into areas too small to support the most efficiently sized production unit.[11] In some instances, patterns of industrialization can be linked to abundant coal reserves (Belgium), whereas others took advantage of human capital, awaited political efforts at national unity, depended on the agricultural sector, or simply failed in their efforts to make the transition.[12] In spite of the

---

[10] Alan Milward and S. B. Saul, *The Economic Development of Continental Europe 1780-1870* (2nd ed.), London: Allen and Unwin, 1979, 307-309.

[11] Landes, *The Unbound . . .*, 125, 127-132, 142, 145-150.

[12] Rondo Cameron, "A New View of European Industrialization," *Economic History Review*, 38.1, February 1985, 9-16. France, for example, was restrained by relatively high-cost coal. Behind a wall of protection it was able to develop a textile industry but could export only specialized and high-priced textiles. Milward and Saul, *Economic Development . . .*, 312-331.

myriad paths and fitful efforts at industrialization, many European states had made a significant beginning by midcentury, and this process accelerated considerably thereafter.[13]

# THE TURN TO FREER TRADE

## Repeal of the Corn Laws

Meanwhile, several developments in the British and world economies contributed to a British-led effort to create a more open international economy. In Britain, agriculture remained an important but declining sector. Indeed, between 1815 and 1845, Britain lost the capacity to feed itself as population growth outstripped agricultural output. At the same time, exports failed to expand at a rate sufficient to provide employment to a growing population. Stagnation in exports was due mainly to falling prices and to successful efforts in mainland Europe and the United States to protect their infant industries. The combination of greater dependence on imported food and slow economic growth fueled radical political challenges to the government and helped prompt a somewhat novel political and economic response.[14]

Traditionally, Britain had followed a policy, reflecting the political power of its landed interests, of protecting agriculture with tariffs and other restrictions—the Corn Laws. But these restraints on trade increasingly came to be seen by manufacturing and financial interests and by political leaders as a barrier to solving the problems of food and exports. Some hoped that a unilateral reduction in British tariffs would induce a freeing of trade elsewhere and that this would lead to an international division of labor resting on British manufacturing with agricultural and raw material production elsewhere. (Not inconsequentially, this arrangement would nip in the bud the growing industrial competition from Europe and the United States.) The 1840s produced repeal of the Corn Laws and of the Navigation Acts restricting transport to British ships and brought about the revival of British trade.[15]

---

[13] A helpful discussion of the various means for transmitting industrialization to Europe is in Sidney Pollard, *Peaceful Conquest: The Industrialization of Europe, 1760-1970*, Oxford: Oxford University Press, 1982, 142-190.

[14] Ralph Davis, *The Industrial Revolution and British Overseas Trade*, Leicester: Leicester University Press, 1979, 15.

[15] This paragraph is based on Cain and Hopkins, "The Political Economy . . . ," 474-481; and on P. J. Cain, *Economic Foundations of British Overseas Expansion, 1814-1914*, London: Macmillan, 1980, 17-21. Accompanying the move toward free trade was an end to efforts designed to prevent other nations from obtaining British technology and manpower skills. In the 1820s, laws barring the export of machinery and the immigration of skilled artisans were relaxed and, by 1843, repealed. See Pollard, *Peaceful Conquest* ..., 144. The Navigation Acts are discussed in R. P. Thomas and D. N. McCloskey, "Overseas Trade and Empire 1700-1860," in Floud and McCloskey, *Economic History* . . ., 94. For an interesting variant on the Corn Laws, see Scott James and David Lake, "The Second Face of Hegemony: Britain's Repeal of the Corn Laws and the American Walker Tariff of 1846," *International Organization*, 43.1, Winter 1989, 1-29. Later we shall raise questions about the appropriateness of the hegemonic thesis as applied to nineteenth-century Britain.

The repeal of the Corn Laws is important for two reasons. First, this helps us see the role of domestic political alignments in producing foreign economic policy. "Economic theories prevail . . . only when they have mobilized political authority, that is, only if those who believe the theories get the resources that enable them to take authoritative action."[16] For decades before 1846, economists had promoted the benefits of free trade. But only when the coalition of political forces favoring free trade was able to convince government leaders and to defeat protectionist agriculture could this become national policy.[17] Second, this unilateral move to free trade was of crucial importance in shaping the world economy. In 1860, Britain and France signed the Cobden–Chevalier Treaty, substantially reducing tariffs on trade between the two nations. This was followed by tariff reductions in eight other European countries and ushered in the first major period of relatively free trade.[18] Equally important, a system of multilateral trade and capital flows, centering largely on Britain, emerged to form a world economy of substantial proportions.

## The Expansion of the World Economy

The movement toward freer and increased trade was influenced by and helped to advance several related developments between 1850 and 1875. The political unification of Germany, pushed by the need for unified markets and the desire for greater international influence, changed the economic landscape in central Europe. Much of the process of economic change was centered on building railroads—an activity that required substantial amounts of capital and had the consequence of expanding dramatically the scope and scale of markets. Initially, much of the capital for railroads in Belgium and France came from Britain. Later, France became a capital exporter even as Germany was able to meet its own needs.

In the midst of these developments, industrial progress in Europe produced a widened scope of economic relationships. Expansion of textile production in France and Germany, along with continuing growth in Britain, resulted in sharp increases in wool and cotton imports from the United States, Australia, and New Zealand. The improvements in continental and oceanic

---

[16] Peter Gourevitch, *Politics in Hard Times: Comparative Responses to International Economic Crises*, Ithaca: Cornell University Press, 54.

[17] An alternative view emphasizing the ideological power of the idea of free trade is in Charles Kindleberger, "The Rise of Free Trade in Western Europe, 1820-1875," in his *Economic Response: Comparative Studies in Trade, Finance, and Growth*, Cambridge: Harvard University Press, 53. Two other approaches to understanding The adoption of free trade are found in Paul E. Rohrlich, "Economic Culture and Foreign Policy: the Cognitive Analysis of Economic Policy Making," *International Organization*, 41.1, Winter 1987, 61–92; and Cheryl Schonhardt-Bailey, "Specific Factors, Capital Markets, Portfolio Diversification, and Free Trade: Domestic Determinants of the Repeal of the Corn Laws," *World Politics*, 43.4, July 1991, 545–569.

[18] Kindleberger, "The Rise of . . .," 54–56. For a view of French behavior emphasizing domestic political and economic interests, see Michael S. Smith, *Tariff Reform in France 1860-1900: The Politics of Economic Interest*, Ithaca: Cornell University Press, 1980.

transportation, beginning especially in the 1860s and 1870s, led to dramatic increases in European imports of grain and meat. A multilateral division of labor based on the level of industrialization and geography developed within Europe. British goods, especially railroad equipment, machinery, coal, and textiles, were sold in advanced sections of Europe while German industry, for example, was successful in central and eastern European markets. Ironically, British trade in machinery and railroads helped the newly industrializing areas of Germany and France to utilize their own advantages (for example, German wages were lower than those in Britain) to close the gap with Britain and to adopt the role of leading other European states into the world economy.[19]

Equally telling, in addition to these general reservations about free trade, are the calculations made by countries who chose to participate in freer trade in the mid-nineteenth century. France used the 1860 treaty to deflect Britain from interfering in a conflict with Austria over Italy. The German free trade area—the Zollverein—recognized that its substantial sales of grain in Great Britain would be protected by lowering tariffs on British goods. In the United States, the new possibilities for trade with Britain created by lower tariffs helped solidify a political coalition supporting lower U.S. tariffs. These examples strongly reinforce the importance of understanding matters like free trade in terms of political economy—a perspective that acknowledges a relationship between economic and political influences.[20]

# THE PERILS OF INTERDEPENDENCE: 1873–1914

## Transformation of the World Economy

The period from 1873 to 1914 produced changes in the world economy equal in importance to those of the preceding hundred years. The pace of change accelerated, with an extraordinary shift in the distribution of relative international economic power resulting from the decline of Great Britain and the rise of the United States and Germany. Accompanying this were the first stirrings of industrialization in what we today call the Third World. This was true in India, China, and especially in Japan. The continuing expansion of international trade and finance led to a growing interdependence of national

---

[19] The discussion in this paragraph rests on Pollard, *Peaceful Conquest* . . ., 172–183; E. J. Hobsbawm, *The Age of Capital, 1848-1875*, New York: New American Library, 1975, 27–71; William Woodruff, "The Emergence of an International Economy 1700-1914," in Carlo M. Cipolla (ed.), *The Fontana Economic History of Europe*, London: Fontana Press, 1973, 658–672; Hobsbawm, *Industry* . . ., 97–140; Landes, *The Unbound* . . ., 158–219; and Alan Milward and S. B. Saul, *The Economic Development of Continental Europe 1780-1870* (2nd ed.), London: Allen and Unwin, 1979, 309–310, 352–353, 380–396, 404–414.

[20] See James Foreman-Peck, *A History of the World Economy: International Economic Relations Since 1850*, Totowa, N.J.: Barnes & Noble Books, 1983, 57-58; James and Lake, "The Second Face . . .," 13-14.

economies, as measured by price movements, common financial crises and economic fluctuations, increasing proportions of foreign trade and investment, and a more coherently organized international monetary system centered on gold.

At the same time, the free trade system created after 1846 was eventually dismantled and reversed by widespread protectionist sentiments. Higher tariffs were a reflection of an intensification of competition for markets and of the political and economic dislocations caused by dramatic increases in trade. And finally, the very character of industrial life began to change in fundamental ways. New industrial systems such as chemicals, oil, electricity, and steel emerged in the late nineteenth century not only as leading, but even as dominant sectors. In these and other industries a new type of enterprise developed—one of much greater size and designed to take advantage of significant economies of scale in production and national and international marketing and distribution networks.

The changes in the distribution of international economic and industrial power can be seen in Tables 3.1-3.5:

**TABLE 3.1**

**Distribution of World Industrial Production, 1870–1913**
*(in Percentages)*

| YEARS | UNITED STATES | GREAT BRITAIN | GERMANY | FRANCE | RUSSIA | JAPAN | INDIA | REST OF WORLD |
|---|---|---|---|---|---|---|---|---|
| 1870 | 23 | 32 | 13 | 10 | 4 | — | — | 17 |
| 1881–1885 | 29 | 27 | 14 | 9 | 3 | — | — | 19 |
| 1896–1900 | 30 | 20 | 17 | 7 | 5 | 1 | 1 | 19 |
| 1906–1910 | 35 | 15 | 16 | 6 | 5 | 1 | 1 | 20 |
| 1913 | 36 | 14 | 16 | 6 | 6 | 1 | 1 | 20 |

SOURCE: Walt Rostow, *The World Economy*, Austin: University of Texas Press, 1978, 52–53.

The precipitous decline of Great Britain and France and the equally rapid rise of the United States, and to a lesser extent Germany, are the most striking features of Table 3.1. That Britain, in the space of two generations, could fall relatively so far in spite of a growing economy over most of this period is testimony to the tenuous position of all in the modern world economy.[21] The United States and Germany, along with Russia, also experienced a rapid expansion in population, with growth from 1890 to 1913 of 55 percent, 36 percent,

---

[21] The effects of compound rates of growth can be seen in the statistics of economic expansion spread out over forty years. The average annual growth rate from 1870 to 1913 for Britain was 1.6 percent, for the United States 5 percent, and for Germany 4.7 percent. Seemingly small differences, extended over such a long period, produced the dramatic relative decline by Britain. See Aaron Friedberg, *The Weary Titan: Britain and the Experience of Relative Decline*, Princeton: Princeton University Press, 1988, 25.

**TABLE 3.2**

**Iron/Steel Production, 1890–1913**
*(Millions of Tons)*

|                | 1890 | 1900 | 1910 | 1913 |
|----------------|------|------|------|------|
| United States  | 9.3  | 10.3 | 26.5 | 31.8 |
| Great Britain  | 8.0  | 5.0  | 6.5  | 7.7  |
| Germany        | 4.1  | 6.3  | 13.6 | 17.6 |

SOURCE: This table is adapted from Kennedy, *The Rise* . . . , 200.

and 50 percent, respectively. By contrast, British population growth for the same period was only 22 percent, while in France it amounted to less than 4 percent.[22] In selected areas, the shift toward a U.S. and German advantage was even more dramatic.

**TABLE 3.3**

**Energy Consumption, 1890–1913**
*(in Millions of Metric Tons of Coal Equivalent)*

|                | 1890 | 1900 | 1910 | 1913 |
|----------------|------|------|------|------|
| United States  | 147  | 248  | 483  | 541  |
| Great Britain  | 145  | 171  | 185  | 195  |
| Germany        | 71   | 112  | 158  | 187  |

SOURCE: This table is adapted from Kennedy, *The Rise* . . . , 201.

Clearly, by 1913 British dominance of world industrial capabilities had been swept away.

How are we to understand this remarkable transformation? Perhaps the best explanation lies in the simple but powerful fact that certain special advantages in the United States and Germany were well suited to the industrial developments of the age. In Germany, an extensive and diversified system of scientific education produced large numbers of trained scientists and technical personnel who were able to take advantage of a cascade of theoretical innovations. This was especially true in the newly emerging chemical industry and in the production of complex machine tools. Further, Germany used its raw materials and industrial capabilities to press rapidly ahead in steel and coal production and in railroad construction (including in central and eastern Europe).[23]

Similarly, the United States used its substantial raw material resources and very large and affluent domestic market as the base for creating the biggest economy in the world.

---

[22] The data on population growth are computed from Paul Kennedy, *The Rise and Fall of the Great Powers*, New York: Random House, 1987, 199. Britain retained second position in per-capita industrialization. See Kennedy, page 200, Table 14.

[23] Alan Milward and S. B. Saul, *The Development of the Economies of Continental Europe, 1850-1914*, Cambridge: Harvard University Press, 1977, 19-20, 27, 30, 33-38.

**TABLE 3.4**

**Gross Domestic Product: United States, Great Britain, and Germany**
*(1970 U.S. Prices)*

| COUNTRY | 1870 | 1913 |
|---|---|---|
| United States | | |
| Gross Domestic Product (billions) | $3.050 | $17.628 |
| Gross Domestic Product (per capita) | $764 | $1,813 |
| Great Britain | | |
| Gross Domestic Product (billions) | $3.036 | $6.808 |
| Gross Domestic Product (per capita) | $972 | $1,491 |
| Germany | | |
| Gross Domestic Product (billions) | $2.099 | $7.184 |
| Gross Domestic Product (per capita) | $535 | $1,073 |

SOURCE: Albert Chandler, *Scale and Scope: The Dynamics of Industrial Capitalism,* Cambridge: Harvard University Press, 1990, 52.

The unification of markets produced by the introduction of the railroad and the telegraph had its greatest impact in the United States. It was here that the system of modern managerial capitalism was born and developed furthest in the pre–World War I era. Over a wide array of products, U.S. firms launched into mass production, distribution, and marketing for the giant domestic market, thereby taking advantage of substantial returns to scale.[24] The organization and direction of these firms rapidly shifted to professional, hierarchically arranged, salaried managers and away from owner-managers. It was this structural innovation that permitted the coordination and direction of these vast enterprises.[25]

The evolution of the world economy in the forty years before World War I generated substantial levels of financial and trade interdependence. In many ways, similar levels of interdependence have been reached again only in the 1990s. As reflected in Table 3.5, international financial transactions were large and growing. Purchase of international stocks and bonds was common throughout Europe, where few regulations or restrictions existed to limit these transactions. The gold standard (discussed later) operated to stabilize currency values and to establish an environment facilitating financial flows. As we have seen, trade grew dramatically after 1850 in spite of growing protectionism. The difficulty was that interdependence generated the need for greater international cooperation. Unfortunately, arrangements to manage the system of financial and trade flows were mostly ad hoc and private.[26]

---

[24] The concept of *economies of scale* refers to a decline in the per-unit cost of production as a result of increases in the volume of production. Typically, this is greatest for those firms with large fixed costs. Larger volume of production permits them to spread these costs over more units, thereby reducing the per-unit cost.

[25] Chandler, *Scale and Scope . . .,* 52–89.

[26] Giulio Gallarotti, *The Anatomy of an International Monetary Regime: The Classical Gold Standard, 1880–1914,* Oxford: Oxford University Press, 1995.

TABLE 3.5

**Overseas Investments of the Major Economic Powers, 1870–1914**
*(in Millions of Dollars)*

| | 1870 | 1900 | 1914 | % OF WORLD IN 1914 |
|---|---|---|---|---|
| Great Britain | 4,900 | 12,000 | 20,000 | 44.0 |
| France | 2,500 | 5,800 | 9,050 | 19.9 |
| Germany | — | 4,800 | 5,800 | 12.8 |
| United States | 100 | 500 | 3,500 | 7.8 |
| Others | 500 | 1,100 | 7,100 | 15.5 |

SOURCE: Sidney Pollard, "Capital Exports, 1870-1914: Harmful or Beneficial?" *The Economic History Review*, 38.4, November 1985, 492.

## British Hegemony?

What about Great Britain during this period? One important point to recognize is that Britain remained the dominant force in international trade and finance. Even in 1913, Britain accounted for 31 percent of world trade in manufactured goods, with Germany at 27.5 percent, and the United States at 13 percent.[27] In 1914, the British share of international investments was clearly in a commanding position and perhaps still growing. But this strong international investment position cannot disguise the serious relative decline in the British economy—a decline from which Britain never really recovered.

One important source of difficulty was Britain's incomplete adaptation to the emerging world of capital-intensive, large-scale, scientifically based, and professionally managed firms. British businesses and investors were content with retaining a much more personal system of management, often resting with the founder's family. This meant smaller enterprises with relatively limited managerial hierarchies. The reasons for these developments are complex but lie mainly in the fact that British advantages contributing to their leading role in the first industrial revolution did not transfer into advantages for the second industrial revolution. The British domestic market, once the largest in Europe, not only was small in comparison with the United States and Germany, but also grew much more slowly. Large domestic markets were crucial in supporting U.S. and German industries in their move into new industrial areas and provided the justification for creating large and sophisticated enterprises. The domestic British market simply did not support the widespread adoption of this kind of business organization. Moreover, the areas of early British advantage—textiles, iron, and ships—did not lend themselves to economies of scale, nor were they greatly affected by the new systems of communication and transportation. Thus, British export markets remained in the older industries even as the United States and Germany, resting on the

[27] Friedberg, *The Weary* . . ., 24.

large base of a domestic market, pushed their exports in the new industries such as "refined oil, processed foodstuffs, mass-produced light machinery, and electrical equipment." In the emerging age of large-scale production, marketing, and distribution, British industry lacked the advantages that would push its entrepreneurs to take the lead in developing these areas.[28]

Almost certainly, the most important British roles during this period were to extend international capital markets, contribute to a loosely organized international monetary system based on gold, and maintain open markets in a time of increasing protectionism. Britain's dominance resulted from the importance of the city of London in short-term financing of international trade, from the role of sterling as virtually equivalent to an international currency, and from the vast sums of capital that flowed abroad into long-term foreign investments. These bases of power enabled the London banking system to affect interest rates around the world, to provide international liquidity during times of crisis, and to finance, over many years, the balance of payments deficits of a variety of countries without harsh adjustments.[29]

Central to this process was an international monetary system based on the gold standard and sterling. This developed in the 1870s when several countries in addition to Britain adopted a gold backing for their currencies and permitted the free movement of gold exports and imports. The effect was to fix the exchange rates of these currencies based on the ratio of gold backing. That is, the exchange rate between any two currencies was simply the ratio of the amount of gold backing those currencies. The result was a rudimentary but evolving international monetary system, built around British management and protection of its own position along with an almost constant outflow of British capital to cushion the adjustment problems created by its perpetual current account surplus.[30]

The combination of economic growth (especially in the United States and Germany), increasing world trade, and expanding capital flows generated both greater interdependence among nations and a reaction designed to reduce the costs of this connectedness. The links among nations and the importance of these links can be seen in the increasing tendency for simultaneous expansion and contraction in national economies, including both production

---

[28] This paragraph is based on the analysis found in Chandler, *Scale and Scope* . . ., 235-294; with quote at page 250. Also helpful in filling out the picture of the competitive system of the 1873-1914 era are Derek H. Aldcroft, *The Development of British Industry and Foreign Competition: 1875-1914*, Toronto: University of Toronto Press, 1968, especially pages 11-36; and Foreman-Peck, *A History* . . ., 94-110.

[29] Robert J. A. Skidelsky, "Retreat from Leadership: The Evolution of British Economic Foreign Policy, 1870-1939," in Benjamin Rowland et al. (eds.), *Balance of Power or Hegemony: The Interwar Monetary System*, New York: New York University Press, 1976, 152-163; Foreman-Peck, *A History* . . ., 67-84; Milward and Saul, *The Development* . . ., 487-492.

[30] Barry Eichengreen, "Editor's Introduction," in Barry Eichengreen (ed.), *The Gold Standard in Theory and History*, New York: Methuen, 1985, 5-19; Barry Eichengreen, "Conducting the International Orchestra: Bank of England Leadership under the Classical Gold Standard," *Journal of International Money and Finance*, 6, March 1987.

and finance. By the late 1850s, the price of wheat in any given country was heavily influenced by world market conditions. In 1857, both an oversupply of wheat in the world and falling prices produced a financial panic in the United States that had serious effects in Great Britain and Germany. Throughout the 1860s, the American Civil War greatly affected financial conditions in Britain and land prices in India. By 1873, the French indemnity payment to Germany (following their 1870 war) produced such imbalances in the international financial system as to precipitate an international depression.[31]

This depression coincided with a growing supply of wheat, especially from the United States, made possible by improvements in land and sea transportation and in the technology of production. Price declines in many commodities were substantial, accelerating a trend common to much of the nineteenth century. This continued until an upturn began in the 1890s. The result was to rearrange the economic and political interests of several groups, especially with regard to tariff questions. Many agricultural and industrial producers were confronted with the possibility of being forced out of business, suffering major losses, or substantially changing their methods of production. Their demands for protection were not ignored, and several governments, led by Germany and France, began raising tariffs. By 1890, much of the system of freer trade had been reversed.[32]

The major exception to these trends was Britain, who resisted domestic pressure for protection and refused to retaliate against other nations. And yet any consideration of Britain's behavior during the late nineteenth century raises questions about the role and importance of the world's leading economic power in creating and sustaining a stable and orderly world economy. How important was British leadership for the nineteenth-century world economy? Did British leaders see themselves as responsible for maintaining a system of free trade and international economic prosperity? Or rather, did they simply look to extend their position and engage in leadership only when it could be linked to narrow national interests?

This question has usually been framed in terms of whether or not Britain acted as a hegemonic state, that is, whether the British were willing to apply overwhelming economic, military, and political strength to the formation and preservation of an international economic order. The evidence for this is mixed. Clearly, British market power in the 1840–1860 period helped move several nations toward freer trade, while British financial power was key to

---

[31] Foreman-Peck, *A History* . . ., 84–88. Foreman-Peck also reports on the "fairly close synchronization of price movements . . ." among gold standard economies. See pages 161–163.

[32] Gourevitch, *Politics in* . . ., 71–123. What was the consequence of increasing protectionism? In political terms it was to solidify conservative regimes. Economically, the consequence was to redistribute the costs and benefits of production and trade. Tariffs almost always raise the prices paid by consumers for goods associated with international trade, increase government revenues, and provide protected domestic producers with greater profits. Moreover, they remove or reduce the competitive incentives to innovate and lower costs for those domestic industries receiving protection.

the functioning of a world trading and monetary system for much of the century. Further, British policies, capital, and businessmen served to transmit technology and to bring many peripheral areas into the world economy. Perhaps most important was the willingness of private financiers to supply credit during periods of financial distress.[33] But, on the whole, Britain acted as a passive hegemon, reflecting the laissez-faire political economy of the day. It led largely by example and not by organizing multilateral efforts to manage the system. The instruments and practices of domestic economic management were limited, thereby restricting similar efforts at the international level. The failure to punish those nations who increased tariffs after 1873 suggests a much more aloof Britain, rather than one who saw its role as responsible for keeping an open system in place.

If we think beyond economic relationships, British military power was certainly important for forcibly opening China and Japan to the world, controlling India, and preserving free movement on the world's oceans. But, Britain was equally important in the process of expanding imperialism and thereby closing off areas from the world economy (except as trade went through Britain itself). Britain certainly made no effort to oppose the principle of international aggrandizement in the non-Western world (again, except as it encroached on British interests). We can safely say that the link between British security, international security, and the world economy was a tenuous one. The effect of this was to remove a key element providing incentives for a stronger involvement in managing world affairs. Thus, when nations began raising trade barriers in the 1870s, Britain stuck to its policy of splendid isolation from the continent, accepted this outcome, and shifted much of its trade to the Empire.[34]

The first great test of Britain's and other nations' ability to manage the vicissitudes of economic interdependence and international competition resulted in failure. Economic and political nationalism reinforced military competition, and nations increasingly found themselves unable to find a secure basis for pursuing prosperity within an open international system. The growing tide of protectionism and destructive competition did not eliminate the web of interdependence in the world economy. At the same time, the level and nature of political and economic cooperation were stunted and, consequently, did not provide mechanisms for collective gain. The spiral of struggle, alliances, armaments, and planning for war overwhelmed the logic of comparative advantage and mutual benefits from trade.

[33] Charles Kindleberger, "International Public Goods Without International Government," *American Economic Review*, 76.1, March 1986, 1–13; and Charles Kindleberger, *Manias, Panics, and Crashes*, New York: Basic Books, 1989, 201–231. British power was also very important in promoting "a politically stable environment for trade and investment." Charles Lipson, *Standing Guard: Protecting Foreign Capital in the Nineteenth and Twentieth Centuries*, Berkeley: University of California Press, 1985, 42. The strongest and clearest statement of Britain as hegemon is in Skidelsky, "Retreat from . . . ," 151–163.

[34] In some ways, this acquiescence to tariffs is similar to acceptance of German unification in the 1864–1871 period.

# JAPAN AND LATE ECONOMIC DEVELOPMENT

One of the most important and enduring questions of international political economy concerns the relationship between more-developed and less-developed states. Do advanced states, through trade and capital investments, serve to transmit the technology, money, and ideas for industrialization? Or, do these more-powerful states use their leverage to exploit weaker states and perpetuate underdevelopment? We will reserve a more thorough treatment of these questions for Chapter 8. For now, one very important part of the answer lies in determining whether any less-developed and non-Western states have been able to break through from backwardness to industrialization. Japan, over the last third of the nineteenth century, surely presents the most remarkable example of such a case.

It was Western determination to gain access to Japan that set this process into motion. Isolated for more than two hundred years and beset by a feudal system and a weak government, the Japanese were overwhelmed by Western military technology. In 1853–1854, and continuing over the next fifteen years, Japan was subjected to demands by the United States and Great Britain (among others) for special privileges and rights that compromised its sovereignty. The effort to cope with these demands without inviting war destroyed the legitimacy of the Japanese government. At the same time, the Western presence activated a virulent antiforeign reaction among the samurai (a military caste that had declined over the preceding two centuries of peace). Additionally, access to and the ability to utilize Western military technology effectively became the decisive factor in determining the outcome of the domestic political struggle that ensued. The result was a new Japanese government with the political strength and unflinching determination to make Japan into a modern nation capable of maintaining its independence.

Nonindustrialized states entering the world economy at such a late date are often said to face a special set of disadvantages in comparison with early industrializers. Late arrivers encounter established competitors who have more-complex systems of technology and education and a set of institutions that are experienced in adjusting to the demands of international competition. Those who hope to succeed must adopt some way of compensating for their weaknesses. Often, this has meant relying on the government to finance, or even establish, enterprises, especially when the capital requirements for large industries such as coal or steel are needed.[35] Equally important, the state has usually provided the means for creating the broad social infrastructure needed for a modern society.

The pattern of Japanese development conforms in several respects to these expectations, but in others it deviates in significant ways. In 1868, the year of the Meiji Restoration, Japan had already developed a substantial market

---

[35] This argument is traditionally acknowledged to come from Alexander Gerschenkron, *Economic Backwardness in Historical Perspective*, Cambridge: Harvard University Press, 1962.

economy based largely on rural enterprises.[36] Over the next thirty years, much of Japan's economic growth derived from agricultural improvements and from rural industrial enterprises. These small-scale industries were primarily silk-worm, silk reeling, and cotton textile operations, and most of the production was for export.[37] Unlike the tendency toward large-scale, capital-intensive heavy industries found in other late industrializers, the first wave of Japanese industrialization was concentrated in areas of comparative advantage.

This may have been the result of a convergence of two factors: Japan's forced exposure to the world economy and changes in the competitive position of several more-advanced states. One of the consequences of the unequal treaties of the 1850s and 1860s was that Japan forfeited control over its tariff policy. In addition, a decline in Britain's ability to dominate the cotton indus-try opened the door for Japan. The technology of production was readily available and inexpensive (compared to heavy industry) and much easier to adopt. The sensitivity to the world market, the presence of a disciplined, reli-able labor force, and entrepreneurial experience in the countryside gave Japan enough of an advantage to enter the world market successfully.

The greatest similarity between Japan and other late industrializers is the role of the state. The new Meiji government acted rapidly to reshape the country based on the needs of centralized power and economic develop-ment. It abolished the regional authorities (the domains), enacted a central-ized tax system, eliminated the special status of the samurai, started conscription, and created a national educational system all within seven years.[38] This extraordinary capacity for moving Japan so far so fast constitutes the distinctive quality of the Japanese state.[39] But, like most European states in the 1820–1870 period, the Japanese government mobilized capital, invested in infrastructure, started demonstration enterprises, offered subsidies, promoted market unification, and regulated industries needing help in establishing com-mon production standards.[40] And yet, the greatest part of the industrialization

---

[36] Thomas C. Smith, *Native Sources of Japanese Industrialization, 1750-1920*, Berkeley: Univer-sity of California Press, 1988, 71-102, 133-147, 199-235.

[37] Sidney Crawcour, "Industrialization and Technical Change," in Marius Jansen (ed.), *Cambridge History of Modern Japan*, Cambridge: Cambridge University Press, 1989, 388, 407-414; W. G. Beasley, *The Rise of Modern Japan*, New York: St. Martin's Press, 1990, 102-114; Osamu Saito, "Commercial Agriculture, By-Employment, and Wage Work," in Marius Jansen and Gilbert Rozman (eds.), *Japan in Transition: From Tokugawa to Meiji*, Princeton: Princeton University Press, 1986, 400-420.

[38] Richard Rubinger, "Education From One Room to One System," in Jansen and Rozman, *Japan in . . .*, 191-230; and W. G. Beasley, *The Meiji Restoration*, Stanford: Stanford University Press, 1973.

[39] I am grateful to Albert Craig for clarifying this point for me.

[40] Barry Supple, "The State and the Industrial Revolution, 1700-1914," in C. M. Cippola, *The Fontana Economic History of Europe: The Industrial Revolution*, Glasgow: Fontana/Collins, 1973, 301-357; William Lockwood, "The State and Economic Enterprise in Modern Japan, 1868-1938," in Simon Kutznets et al. (eds.), *Economic Growth in Brazil, India and Japan*, Durham: Duke University Press, 1955, 540-547, 563; Henry Rosovsky, *Capital Formation in Japan, 1868-1940*, New York: Free Press, 1961, 53-104; David Landes, "Japan and Europe: Con-trasts in Industrialization," in Lockwood (ed.), *The State and Economic Enterprise in Japan*, Princeton: Princeton University Press, 1965, 93-182.

process came from private action, even when supported by the state. This is true not only of Japan but also of France and Germany in the mid-nineteenth century. What may have been most unusual about Japan was the extraordinary cooperation of private and public actors.

## WORLD WAR I AND AFTERMATH

The world war that began in August 1914 was the culmination of the failure of nations to find security and prosperity within a context of tightening interdependence. Even more important was the extraordinary restructuring of the world economy caused by the war: It redistributed international economic power, disrupted the world economy, and destroyed trade and financial relations. The period from 1919 to 1939 is largely the story of limited, and somewhat unsuccessful, efforts to reorganize a functioning and prosperous world economic system.

There were three major impediments to international economic stability after World War I. First, most governments lacked the political strength and experience to design and carry out a managerial role in the domestic and international economies. As a result, the world economy lacked effective mechanisms for transferring capital from surplus to deficit countries, especially during times of economic distress. Second, the failure of the world's largest economic power, the United States, to accept a leadership role opened a major void. British weakness prevented a resumption of its nineteenth-century role, and the U.S. political system was too immature to support an assumption of this responsibility. Third, the ferocity of the downturn in the world economy after 1929 almost guaranteed a retreat into autarchy and protection as nations struggled to defend their domestic economies. But, in spite of these barriers, there were significant elements of reconstruction and cooperation. Private efforts frequently attempted to fill the vacuum created by government reticence. In the 1930s, the United States became less timid about organizing international cooperation. As it happened, though, these actions almost never proved sufficient.

### The Economic Consequences of World War I

The pattern of participation and fighting in the war helps explain many of its economic consequences. Britain and France, allied with Russia, fought Germany and Austria-Hungary for nearly three years before the United States joined the war. The United States acted as a neutral but emerged quickly as the chief supplier of war-related material to Britain and France. Before the United States entered the war in April 1917, the Allies paid for these goods by liquidating their overseas investments and by using credit provided by private U.S. banks. After U.S. involvement, credit was supplied by the U.S. government. By the war's end, Britain and France had accumulated more than $10 billion in debts, and the United States had become the largest creditor nation in the world.[41] Equally significant, European reliance on external suppliers and the disruption of export markets provided a major boost to production in several peripheral states, but especially in the United States and Japan.[42] The latter experienced dramatic improvements in its industrial and technological development from expanded markets in Europe and Asia. For other states, the breakdown of trade patterns provided incentives to develop domestic industries that could substitute for European imports. Thus, the European focus of the war helped shift industrial production to outlying nations and created an immense international debt burden.

Added to these hardships were problems created by worn-down and destroyed production facilities in Europe and by the financial disruption from measures used to finance the war. Four years of maximum production and difficulties in replacing old equipment reduced European competitiveness in the world economy. The war also forced abandonment of the gold standard at home and abroad—currency could no longer be exchanged for gold—along with a rapid expansion of the money supply to support deficit spending by the government. The result was unparalleled inflation, further deterioration in Europe's competitive position, and a continuation of a large trade deficit into the postwar period.[43] On top of the imbalances experienced by the victors in the war were the problems faced by Germany. The political importance of vengeance and the economic need to recoup losses combined to prompt Britain and France to demand reparations (payments for war losses) from Germany.[44] But reparations had to come from a German current account surplus or from capital supplied from abroad. The combination of trade imbalances and debt payments created a very unstable situation for the world economy.

## A Failure of Political Vision

Effective solutions to these difficulties were hampered by the fact that political thinking failed to keep up with the real changes produced by the war. Statesmen and publics in many countries were eager to return to the world of 1914 and acted as though they expected few problems in doing this. This was reflected in the almost blind faith in the need to reestablish the gold standard,

---

[41] Kathleen Burk, *Britain, America and the Sinews of War, 1914-1918*, Boston: Allen and Unwin, 1985; Ross Gregory, *The Origins of American Involvement in the First World War*, New York: Norton, 1971, 63. The inter-Allied financing system was more complex than simply sending funds from the United States to Britain and France. Several states operated as both borrower and lender, creating a tangled web of debts. See Derek Aldcroft, *From Versailles to Wall Street, 1919-1929*, Berkeley: University of California Press, 1977, 93.

[42] Aldcroft, *From Versailles ...*, 37-41.

[43] Aldcroft, *From Versailles ...*, 30-33, 63.

[44] The amount of reparations was never fixed in a permanent sense. But in 1921, the Reparations Commission determined the amount to be equal to $33 billion. See Aldcroft, *From Versailles . . .*, 81.

create monetary stability, and fix exchange rates. Wartime governmental controls were lifted quickly, and, at the same time, little thought was given at the peace conference to the importance of continuing intervention by governments in stabilizing the world economy.[45] Perhaps most shortsighted was the U.S. insistence on repayment of all war debts. This overlooked the payments deficit position of the Europeans and the negative impact that repayment would place on recovery. The U.S. commitment to war debts made France especially determined to force Germany to make large reparation payments. But, lest we see war-debt forgiveness as an easy matter, to do anything other than exacting payment would have required raising taxes to absorb the debts into the U.S. budget. Although such a plan was highly rational in terms of world reconstruction and stability, the U.S. government did not have the political strength required for such an act. Conservatives and nationalists rejected any U.S. responsibility for these problems and demanded the debts be repaid.[46]

In spite of domestic pressures to ignore any international responsibilities and to insist on war-debt repayment, the leadership of the U.S. government and financial community could not ignore the difficulties created by such a policy. They understood only too well the potential for great trouble resulting from imbalances in the world economy. The current account deficits of European states obviously hampered the payment of reparations and war debts. But in 1922, the already protective U.S. tariff rose (even if only by a small amount), thereby undermining the ability of Europeans to sell in the United States, achieve a current account surplus, and make debt payments. Exchange rates, due to financial dislocations caused by the war, could not be fixed. These fluctuations undercut the ability of businesspersons to make calculations for investments. From the standpoint of American leaders, European stability was judged to be an important but not vital interest. The domestic economy took priority over U.S. efforts to promote European recovery.[47]

A more active U.S. policy had to await French military action in 1923 to collect German reparations and the virtual financial and economic collapse of Germany over the next year. A coalition of U.S. government officials and private financial interests took steps to deal with the situation. The Dawes Plan, negotiated in conjunction with Britain and France, called for reductions in annual reparation payments and provided for private American loans to

---

[45] Aldcroft, *From Versailles . . .*, 3–6.

[46] Joan Hoff Wilson, *American Business and Foreign Policy, 1920–1933*, Boston: Beacon Press, 1971, 70–80, 105–112, 121–133.

[47] Melvyn Leffler, *The Elusive Quest: America's Pursuit of European Security and French Security, 1919–1933*, Chapel Hill: University of North Carolina Press, 1979, 79–81 and generally 40–81. Many U.S. officials believed that economic expansion abroad was beneficial but did not think that U.S. prosperity depended on it. At the same time, major figures in the New York financial community were committed to making New York the world's financial center, displacing London. See Leffler, *The Elusive . . .*, 147, 173; and Carl Parrini, *Heir to Empire: United States Economic Diplomacy, 1916–1923*, Pittsburgh: University of Pittsburgh Press, 1969, 101–137. For a good sense of U.S. domestic politics as reflected in presidential thinking, see Robert K. Murray, *The Politics of Normalcy*, New York: Norton, 1972.

Germany. Over the next five years, a large volume of foreign loans, mostly from the United States, provided Germany with the capital to make its reparations payments and to achieve an uneven economic recovery.[48] But this was a fragile and precarious arrangement, dependent as it was on an unending supply of foreign capital, which itself was contingent on calculations of profit by private bankers. Any interruption in foreign loans would prompt a return to the chaos of 1923-1924.

A second, and equally problematic, effort at producing stability came from Britain's decision to restore the gold standard and fix the value of the pound at the prewar rate. Wartime inflation had exacerbated the problem of British competitiveness, which was evident well before 1914. Rather than use a postwar recession to drive prices down and recoup some of its competitive position, Britain chose to let the pound float. Its price initially fell, but by 1925 had returned to near prewar exchange rates, at which point the pound was placed on the gold standard. The success of such a system depended on two crucial factors. London had to be able to meet the demand for gold, which was complicated by the emergence of New York and Paris as alternative international financial centers. The greater strength of the dollar and the franc put pressure on the weaker pound and produced a constant drain of gold from London. Equally important was the need to provide for capital flows from surplus to deficit countries (which was part of the Dawes Plan). But Britain's ability to fulfill this function was greatly damaged by the financial restructuring of the war, and the U.S. ability to take its place was hampered by the domestic priorities of the government and private bankers. When U.S. lending and imports both contracted from 1928 to 1930, the strains on the world economy were simply too great, and the system collapsed.[49]

## Collapse of the World Economy

Although the imbalances created by the First World War and the patchwork efforts to resolve these problems were not the precipitating cause of the Great Depression, they did serve to transform a downturn in the business cycle into a hurricane of deflation and unemployment. The Federal Reserve in the United States, worried about the boom and speculation in the American

---

[48] Aldcroft, *From Versailles* ..., 84-86; William C. McNeil, *American Money and the Weimar Republic*, New York: Columbia University Press, 1986, 24-34, 97-235. A view giving more weight to the stability of this postwar system is in Charles Maier, *Recasting Bourgeois Europe*, Princeton: Princeton University Press, 1974.

[49] Skidelsky, "Retreat from . . .," 168-173; Aldcroft, *From Versailles* . . ., 168-186. Because the American government could not appear to be intervening in European affairs, the task of managing the unavoidable U.S. involvement fell to the relatively invisible Federal Reserve Bank of New York and its governor, Benjamin Strong. Strong developed a close working relationship with Montagu Norman, governor of the Bank of England. These men understood that the international financial system could not function on its own and acted to supply the leadership needed to keep an unbalanced system in place, at least until the late 1920s. See Stephen V. O. Clarke, *Central Bank Cooperation, 1924-31*, New York: Federal Reserve Bank of New York, 1967.

economy, moved to restrict credit in 1928. The result was the aforementioned decline in U.S. foreign lending, a drop in U.S. production, and a bursting of the stock market bubble in October 1929. U.S. foreign lending was cut in half from 1928 to 1929 and halved again by 1930. This led to a decline in investment and production in Europe, which, combined with the slowdown in the United States, meant a sharp fall in commodity prices and contributed to the break in stock prices.[50]

The rush of world economic decline between 1930 and 1931 exposed the weaknesses in the system of trade, finance, and economic management. In the United States during 1930, manufacturing production declined by 20 percent and exports by 35 percent. During the same time, unemployment in Britain rose from 10 percent to 16 percent and in Germany from 13 percent to 22 percent.[51] Initial government reaction was largely to accept these events, based on the expectation that investment would revive when prices fell far enough. What finally prompted government action was the impending collapse in May and June of 1931 of the debt system built up around reparations, war debts, and U.S. loans. Fearing a "complete collapse of Germany's credit structure within a day or two . . ." and that collapse's effect on the American banking system, President Hoover granted a moratorium on reparation payments.[52]

When this proved insufficient to halt the German banking crisis, Hoover pulled back, preferring to shift any additional relief burden to private U.S. bankers. But this was impossible, and in mid-July the German government closed German banks and placed severe restrictions on foreign exchange transactions. The effect was to freeze all foreign assets in Germany. The crisis then shifted to London, and the threat to international financial stability moved Hoover to reverse the ten-year-old U.S. policy of refusing official (direct and open) participation in European affairs. He agreed to send Secretary of State Henry Stimson to a conference in London to address the crisis. Notwithstanding this break with the past, the U.S. government remained hamstrung by a deep reluctance to expand its budget deficit and by political forces insisting on domestic solutions to the depression. Consequently, the London Conference failed to solve the problem.[53]

The crisis continued throughout August and September as Britain was forced to exchange gold for pounds. When additional credits from private and central bankers were exhausted, the British left the gold standard in a dramatic decision on September 21, 1931. The next day, the United States suffered massive gold withdrawals and, by the end of October, the first of an

---

[50] Aldcroft, *From Versailles* . . ., 261-267, 280-284, 231-236.

[51] Leffler, *The Elusive* . . ., 231-232; Charles Kindleberger, *The World in Depression, 1929-1939,* Berkeley: University of California Press, 1973, 128-145.

[52] Leffler, *The Elusive* . . ., 238-239, 246. The crisis in Germany started in neighboring Austria, where a major bank, Credit-Anstalt, failed due to its own weaknesses and panicky withdrawals by foreign depositors. The effect was to frighten depositors into similar withdrawals in Germany and elsewhere in Europe. See Kindleberger, *The World* . . ., 146-153.

[53] Leffler, *The Elusive* ..., 248-256.

unceasing wave of bank failures. The spiral of declining world trade and domestic production; falling prices, investments, and profits; and rising loan defaults and bank failures continued throughout 1931 and 1932. By early 1933,
the banking system in the United States was perilously close to complete collapse. Only a decision to close the entire system and rebuild it from the
ground up averted this outcome.[54]

## Autarchy and Cooperation

The disintegration of the international monetary and trading systems ushered
in a period in which many countries tried to cope with the depression apart
from the world economy.[55] Earlier, in 1930, Congress passed, and President
Hoover signed, the Smoot–Hawley tariff legislation, which increased U.S. protection substantially. This triggered a round of tariff increases around the
world.[56] In 1931, Japan invaded Manchuria in China hoping to secure markets
and resources.[57] After Britain left the gold standard in 1931, the pound fell in
value by more than 30 percent, producing a substantial boost to the competitiveness of British exports. Britain also tried, with limited success, to organize
a trading bloc of nations tied closely to the use of sterling. Coupled with
cheap money and a housing boom, Britain began to crawl out of the hole in
1932.[58] France also organized a trading bloc of states remaining on the gold
standard, but with little effect on recovery.[59] Germany, under the Nazis, used a
vicious form of national economic planning, deficit spending, conscription,
and arms production to spark recovery.[60] And in 1933, President Roosevelt left
the gold standard to foster depreciation of the dollar, rejected international
cooperation, and concentrated on using government reorganization of the domestic economy to encourage recovery.[61]

Notwithstanding the retreat into autarchy and the recovery that this
sometimes produced, most nations could not ignore their relation to the
broader world economy. In June 1934, only one year after launching a
strongly nationalistic recovery program, the United States adopted the Reciprocal Trade Agreements Act (RTAA). This authorized the president to negotiate
substantial tariff reductions on a reciprocal and bilateral basis with other

---

[54] Susan Kennedy, *The Banking Crisis of 1933*, Lexington: University Press of Kentucky, 1973,
152-223; Kindleberger, *The World* . . ., 167-177, 186-198; Leffler, *The Elusive* . . ., 256-272.

[55] Kindleberger, *The World* . . ., 172, reports that world trade shrank from an average of $2.9 bil-
lion per month in 1929 to $1.1 billion per month in 1933.

[56] Leffler, *The Elusive* . . ., 195-202.

[57] Michael Barnhart, *Japan Prepares for Total War: The Search for Economic Security*, Ithaca: Cornell University Press, 1987, 22-58.

[58] Kindleberger, *The World* . . ., 162-167; 179-181; Skidelsky, "Retreat from . . .," 178-188.

[59] Kindleberger, *The World* . . ., 247-261.

[60] Gourevitch, *Politics in* . . ., 140-147.

[61] Albert Romasco, *The Politics of Recovery: Roosevelt's New Deal*, New York: Oxford University
Press, 1983.

nations. Although many agreements did result and tariffs fell on many items, the importance of the RTAA is mostly symbolic in indicating a shift by the United States away from a nationalist-protectionist tariff policy.[62] Also important for its symbolic value was the Tripartite Monetary Agreement of 1936 among the United States, Great Britain, and France. This agreement was designed to stabilize currencies and to end the process of competitive devaluation. The scope of the agreement was somewhat limited, and stabilization continued to be an elusive goal.[63] A more thoroughgoing and effective organization of the world economy awaited the restructuring of domestic and international politics produced by World War II.

## CONCLUSIONS

This chapter has focused on the development of a world economy over the century from the Corn Laws to the Great Depression. Several key themes emerge that will help us understand later events, in particular the processes of competition, economic transformation, and the growing importance of international cooperation for managing the world economy. This new system of economic relations originates with the growing industrial power of Britain and its special needs for imports and ability to sell abroad. By 1870, tariffs had fallen substantially, and a system of freer trade encompassing much of the globe had formed around Britain. The accumulated profits from British manufacturing began flowing into foreign investments, which helped to finance sales abroad as well as to transmit the technology of a modern economy. The availability of technology and improvements in infrastructure meant that many countries could begin competing with Britain on equal terms. But changes in technology, transportation, and communication—especially the ability to deliver goods and to manage large and dispersed organizations—altered the nature of business firms and markets. This worked to Britain's disadvantage and benefited the United States and Germany. By 1914, Britain had lost its position as the world's leading economy.

Understanding the world economy in these terms helps to underline its extraordinary dynamism. This dynamism can be seen in the tremendous growth in productive capacity, self-sustaining economic growth, and the rapid changes in technology. Competition among states meant that these economic changes produced substantial shifts in the balance of world power. The capacity for war and international influence was rearranged along with the world economy. Further, circumstances that provided advantages at one point in time did not last. Leading states, by selling, buying, and investing in other

---

[62] Robert Pastor, *Congress and the Politics of U.S. Foreign Economic Policy*, Berkeley: University of California Press, 1980, 84–93; Stephan Haggard, "The Institutional Foundations of Hegemony: Explaining the Reciprocal Trade Agreements Act of 1934," *International Organization*, 42.1, Winter 1988, 91–119; Wilson, *American Business . . .*, 98–100.

[63] Skidelsky, "Retreat from . . .," 186–188.

states, transferred their advantages. Moreover, the deep structural dynamism of the world economy transformed the very bases of advantage. What works to benefit a nation at one time is eroded, and new arrangements of competition emerge that privilege other nations at a later time.

The management of the world economy, a necessarily political process, became both more problematic and more important over this century. British interests and power worked to provide leadership and organization in the early stages, and Britain's financial predominance supported an international monetary system until 1914. But the move away from free trade and toward economic nationalism in the last quarter of the nineteenth century marked the limits of British power. The intensification of competition and conflict accompanying these trends suggests a general failure to cope with the new relationships of interdependence. The First World War itself generated massive changes in economic power, but these did not lead to corresponding procedures for effective international cooperation. This made the world economy especially vulnerable and contributed greatly to the catastrophic depression of the 1930s. Only the combination of war and depression would produce new forms of domestic and international political power committed to new arrangements of international management.

## ANNOTATED BIBLIOGRAPHY

W. G. Beasley, *The Rise of Modern Japan*, New York: St. Martin's Press, 1990.
    A detailed history of Japan from the 1850s to the present.
P. J. Cain, *Economic Foundations of British Overseas Expansion 1815–1914*, London: Macmillan, 1980.
    Provides a political economy approach to understanding nineteenth-century British foreign economic relations.
P. J. Cain and A. G. Hopkins, *British Imperialism, Innovation and Expansion: 1688–1914*, London: Longman, 1993.
    A remarkable overview, emphasizing the impact of financial interests.
Albert D. Chandler, Jr., *Scale and Scope: The Dynamics of Industrial Capitalism*, Cambridge: Harvard University Press, 1990.
    A masterful study of the competitive capacities of the largest firms in the United States, Germany, and Great Britain between 1890 and 1914.
James Foreman-Peck, *A History of the World Economy: International Economic Relations Since 1850*, Totowa, N.J.: Barnes & Noble Books, 1983.
    Perhaps the best general overview of the world economy for the nineteenth and twentieth centuries.
Aaron Friedberg, *The Weary Titan*, Princeton: Princeton University Press, 1988.
    A very important study of the domestic politics, economics, and foreign policy related to British economic decline in the late nineteenth and early twentieth centuries.
E. J. Hobsbawm, *The Age of Capital, 1848–1875*, New York: Mentor, 1975.
E. J. Hobsbawm, *Industry and Empire*, New York: Penguin, 1969.
    Two indispensable studies of the origins and development of nineteenth-century capitalism.

Paul Kennedy, *The Rise and Fall of the Great Powers*, New York: Random House, 1987.
    An important comparative study of the relationship between economic and military powers.

Charles Kindleberger, *The World in Depression*, Berkeley: University of California Press, 1973.
    The best single source for understanding the world economy during the Depression years of the 1930s.

David Landes, *The Unbound Prometheus*, Cambridge: Cambridge University Press, 1969.
    The classic study of technological and economic change over the past two centuries.

Charles Maier, *Recasting Bourgeois Europe*, Princeton: Princeton University Press, 1974.
    The most important examination of the interaction of European interest groups, domestic politics, and the world economy in the 1920s.

Alan Milward and S. B. Saul, *The Economic Development of Continental Europe 1780-1870*, London: Allen and Unwin, 1979.
    An important study of industrial change in Europe.

Joel Mokyr (ed.), *The British Industrial Revolution: An Economic Perspective*, Boulder: Westview, 1993.
    A thorough review of recent research.

Sidney Pollard, *Peaceful Conquest: The Industrialization of Europe, 1760-1970*, Oxford: Oxford University Press, 1982.
    An important study of industrial change in Europe.

Walt Rostow, *The World Economy*, Austin: University of Texas Press, 1978.
    A very rich source of data on the history of the world economy.

# Chapter 4

# THE POLITICAL ECONOMY OF AMERICAN HEGEMONY: 1938–1973

The years following World War II produced dramatic, even epoch-making, changes in the world economy. Unprecedented prosperity, the development of new international economic institutions, an explosion in world trade, and an extraordinary expansion in international cooperation were the key elements in this new international economic order. This chapter will describe these developments and the political structures that supported them and also provide a detailed examination of the reasons for these events. How and why did these changes in the world economy occur? A considerable portion of the answer to this question rests with the actions of the United States. We have seen that prior to 1940 the United States was unwilling to commit any substantial resources to stabilizing either the world economy or the international political system. The consequence was a catastrophic depression and, ultimately, war. But during and after the war, the United States moved assertively to reconstruct the world economy. Understanding the political sources of this change and the consequences of this activity occupies the greatest part of this chapter.

This thirty-five-year period offers a rich set of events for understanding international political economy. Several of the most important empirical issues and theoretical questions are linked to this era. The first part of this chapter provides a detailed discussion of the essential features of the postwar international economic order, in particular the patterns of economic growth and the basic institutions created to manage the system. These include the International Monetary Fund (IMF), the World Bank, and the General Agreement on Tariffs and Trade (GATT). The second part of the chapter examines the very important question of how political power affects economic outcomes. What were the nature and significance of U.S. leadership in producing the postwar international economic order? What were the motives for U.S. actions? Could the United States design the system alone? Who benefited from this system? The third part of the chapter considers several crucial developments that emerge from the era of U.S. hegemony: the growth of multinational corporations, the political economy of U.S. foreign policy, and economic integration in Europe. Finally, the last part of the chapter examines the two events that marked a change in the world economy: the collapse of fixed exchange rates and the end of cheap oil, both of which took place between 1971 and 1973.

## STRUCTURES AND TRENDS IN THE POSTWAR WORLD ECONOMY

### Growth of the World Economy

International trade and investment grew more quickly between 1938 and 1973 than in any other previous period after 1815.

**TABLE 4.1**

**World Exports, 1938–1974**
*(Current Value in Billions of U.S. Dollars)*

| YEAR | VALUE |
| --- | --- |
| 1938 | 21.1 |
| 1948 | 53.9 |
| 1958 | 96.0 |
| 1960 | 107.8 |
| 1965 | 156.5 |
| 1970 | 265.7 |
| 1972 | 355.3 |
| 1974 | 729.2 |

SOURCE: Robert A. Pastor, *Congress and the Politics of U.S. Foreign Economic Policy*, Berkeley: University of California Press, 1980, 99.

Comparison of the rates of GNP change for the pre- and postwar eras shows a substantial acceleration of growth after 1950. Most industrial countries experienced a near doubling of the rates of growth between 1950 and 1960 as compared with 1913-1950.[1] International trade was a key ingredient in this growth, with world trade in manufacturing expanding faster than world manufacturing output by a ratio of 1.4:1 between 1950 and 1970.[2]

The importance of the United States to this process is evident from Table 4.2.

[1] W. M. Scammell, *The International Economy Since 1945* (2nd ed.), New York: St. Martin's Press, 1983, 53.

[2] Scammell, *The International* ..., 127. Scammell notes that between 1876 and 1913 the ratio of manufacturing trade to manufacturing output was less than one. Walt Rostow, *The World Economy*, Austin: University of Texas Press, 1978, 67, provides a comparison of growth rates in world trade and in manufacturing from 1720 to 1971. David Landes, *The Unbound Prometheus*, Cambridge: Cambridge University Press, 1969, 512, provides data on growth rates in world trade from 1890 to 1960.

**TABLE 4.2**
**U.S. Trade and World Trade, 1949–1973**
*(Exports at Current Value in Billions of U.S. Dollars)*

| YEAR | U.S. | INDUSTRIAL NATIONS | WORLD EXPORTS | U.S. AS % OF INDUSTRIAL NATIONS | U.S. AS % OF WORLD |
|------|------|--------------------|--------------------|----------------------------|-------------------|
| 1949 | 12.1 | 33.8  | 55.2  | 35.8 | 21.9 |
| 1960 | 20.6 | 78.8  | 114.6 | 26.1 | 17.5 |
| 1970 | 43.2 | 208.3 | 283.7 | 20.7 | 15.2 |
| 1973 | 71.3 | 376.8 | 524.2 | 18.9 | 13.6 |

SOURCE: International Monetary Fund, *International Financial Statistics Yearbook, 1979,* 62–67.

The recovery of Western Europe and Japan was also a driving force in this economic growth. The surge in exports of industrial nations is a measure of this process. The expansion in world trade was in many ways generated by declining tariff levels, convertible currencies, and more openness. The near elimination of tariffs shown in Table 4.3 is also found in tariff levels for other advanced capitalist states who participated equally in the general reductions.

Also contributing to this process of economic growth was the availability of oil at stable prices. Inexpensive imported oil became the primary energy source supporting the dramatic increases in economic output. The shift from reliance on coal to imported oil occurred principally in Europe and Japan. Between 1950 and 1970, Western Europe increased its dependence on oil for total energy needs from 14.3 percent to 55.6 percent, while Japan increased from 5 percent to 68.8 percent. From 1962 to 1972, combined West European and Japanese imports of oil rose from 6.17 to 18.84 million barrels per day.[3]

## International Institutions

The growth of the world economy took place within a context created by several new international institutions conceived of and established near the end of World War II at an international conference in Bretton Woods, New Hampshire. These include the International Monetary Fund, the International Bank for Reconstruction and Development (commonly known as the World Bank), and the General Agreement on Tariffs and Trade (GATT). The IMF was designed to manage exchange rates and payments imbalances among nations, the World Bank to supplement private capital for international investment, and GATT to serve as a negotiating forum for the reduction of tariffs and other barriers to trade.

---

[3] Darmstadter and Landsberg, "The Crisis," 20–21.

**TABLE 4.3**
**Average Global Tariffs**

| YEAR | AVERAGE TARIFF |
|------|----------------|
| 1940 | 40% |
| 1950 | 25% |
| 1960 | 17% |
| 1970 | 13% |
| 1980 | 7% |
| 1990 | 5% |

SOURCE: Peter Dicken, *Global Shift*, New York: Guilford, 1992, 153. For additional comparative data on tariffs, see United Nations, *World Economic Survey*, New York, 1991, 52.

**TABLE 4.4**
**World Energy Consumption by Source, 1950–1972**
*(Percentage Shares)*

| SOURCE | 1950 | 1960 | 1965 | 1970 | 1972 |
|--------|------|------|------|------|------|
| Coal | 55.7 | 44.2 | 39.0 | 31.2 | 28.7 |
| Oil | 28.9 | 35.8 | 39.4 | 44.5 | 46.0 |
| Natural Gas | 8.9 | 13.5 | 15.5 | 17.8 | 18.4 |
| Electricity | 6.5 | 6.4 | 6.2 | 6.5 | 6.9 |

SOURCE: Joel Darmstadter and Hans H. Landsberg, "The Crisis," in Raymond Vernon (ed.), *The Oil Crisis*, New York: Norton, 1976, 19.

One of the most distinctive and important features of the post-1945 world economy was this set of formal and informal institutions for managing the economic relations among nations. During the 1920s, a significant array of mostly informal institutions had been created to deal with the new complexity of economic ties among nations.[4] Those designed and established between 1942 and 1948 were framed by certain principles of international economic relations. These principles included a preference for convertible currencies, a lowering of trade barriers, a system of fixed exchange rates, and generally the promotion of a multilateral system of trade and payments.

The desire for fixed exchange rates was the result of a deeply felt need for stability in international transactions—a sentiment reinforced by the negative experience of floating exchange rates in the 1930s and memories of the "golden age" of fixed rates under the nineteenth-century gold standard. The United States possessed the vast majority of the world's gold in 1945, and this

---

[4] See Michael Hogan, *Informal Entente: The Private Structure of Cooperation in Anglo-American Economic Diplomacy, 1918-1928*, Columbia: University of Missouri Press, 1977. The most formal institution and the predecessor to the IMF was the Bank for International Settlements, established in 1929. See Frank Costigliola, "The Other Side of Isolationism: The Establishment of the First World Bank, 1929-1930," *Journal of American History*, 59, December 1972, 602-620.

was used as the basis for establishing fixed rates.[5] The dollar was fixed in value to gold at $35 per ounce, while other governments fixed their currencies to the dollar and pledged to intervene in foreign exchange markets to keep values within a narrow band around the fixed rate. All this came within the basic rules of operation of the International Monetary Fund (IMF), which itself was established through payments of gold and national currencies from member states. The United States provided the lion's share of the IMF's resources, 31 percent, and consequently received the largest share of voting power.

The primary purpose of the IMF was to provide short-term loans to countries experiencing a current account deficit in their balance of payments. The loans would typically be used to support the fixed value of a country's currency and were usually contingent on adoption of a national policy designed to reverse the deficit. This often meant some combination of cutting government spending and restricting the money supply. This "belt tightening" would produce an economic downturn, higher unemployment, and lower inflation, which was expected to lead to higher exports and lower imports.[6] The IMF became the enforcer of the views of a conservative U.S. financial community, where trade deficits were seen as an indicator of domestic profligacy, and adjustments were expected to come in the domestic economy so as to make it more competitive internationally.[7]

If the current account deficit were serious enough—that is, if it were structural and not just temporary—the IMF would permit an alteration of the exchange rate (called a *devaluation* when the rate falls against other currencies). The British devaluation of the pound from $2.80 to $2.40 in 1967 is an example of this process. Burdened by an uncompetitive manufacturing sector, Britain faced an expanding current account deficit whenever the economy expanded. Because of the importance of the pound to the world economy, the United States and the IMF were ready to provide financial aid to

---

[5] Cohen reports the level at 75 percent, whereas Calleo sets it at 60 percent. Benjamin Cohen, *Organizing the World's Money*, New York: Basic Books, 1977, 95; David Calleo, *Beyond American Hegemony*, New York: Basic Books, 1987, 227.

[6] Remember that a recession should cause some decline (or at least a lower rate of increase) in the prices of domestically produced goods. This should make the country's goods more competitive abroad and also cause a fall in imports.

[7] This somewhat harsh policy applied more to Third World nations than to economically advanced nations. But the tension over the importance of domestic adjustment to international requirements presents a classic case of a conflict of interests between debtors and creditors. This was present in the negotiation of the Bretton Woods agreements, especially between the United States and Britain. See Alfred E. Eckes, *A Search for Solvency: Bretton Woods and the International Monetary System, 1941–1971*, Austin: University of Texas Press, 1975; and Fred Block, *The Origins of International Economic Disorder*, Berkeley: University of California Press, 1974. The discussion that follows, about the actual functioning of Bretton Woods, will emphasize the arrangements of "embedded liberalism," in which efforts were made to establish a working compromise between forcing domestic adjustment and permitting efforts to achieve high levels of economic growth. See John Gerard Ruggie, "International Regimes, Transactions, and Change: Embedded Liberalism in the Postwar Economic Order," *International Organization*, 36.2, Spring 1982, 379–415.

help support the currency. Eventually, the British government concluded that only a devaluation would produce a current account surplus and stay the need for additional borrowing. This decision was made in conjunction with the IMF.

The International Bank for Reconstruction and Development, or World Bank, was also established at Bretton Woods. Eventually, the Bank was allocated $10 billion in capital with the ability to borrow funds in capital markets. Over its first decade, the World Bank played only a marginal role in the actual postwar reconstruction process. But in the late 1950s and early 1960s, an increasing interest in the Third World prompted lending at the rate of well over $1 billion annually in new loans.[8] In Chapter 9 we will consider in more detail the role of the World Bank in providing aid to developing states.

The mechanisms for managing international trade had a somewhat more checkered history. Originally, the United States hoped to create an international organization for this purpose but found the goals of other states to be incompatible with its own. Concurrent negotiations in 1947 and 1948 produced first a General Agreement on Tariffs and Trade and an International Trade Organization. But the U.S. government was dissatisfied with the ITO because it placed restrictions on the United States while creating exceptions for other nations, and the president refused to submit the treaty to the Senate for ratification.[9] GATT was acceptable and has served for over forty years as the chief international organization for trade. It has provided a forum for negotiating reductions in tariffs and some other barriers to trade. In a series of meetings beginning in 1947 and continuing with various "rounds" through 1992, GATT has produced a substantial drop in world tariff levels.[10] In the period from 1890 to 1935, U.S. tariff levels fluctuated between 30 percent and 45 percent of dutiable imports. By 1955 these had been cut to 15 percent and by 1970 to 12 percent.[11] This helps illustrate a key fact about GATT and U.S. postwar trade objectives. American leaders were strongly in favor of lowering tariffs and other barriers to trade, that is, they were interested in freer trade; they were really not interested, in spite of much rhetoric to the contrary, in *free* trade. But GATT did embody a commitment by its members to establish a schedule of tariff rates and a set of trade principles designed to produce uniformity and predictability in international commercial relations. Although tariff barriers on manufactured goods fell substantially, trade in agriculture and services remained largely outside GATT (as did the communist bloc and many

---

[8] A detailed discussion of the origins and development of the World Bank is found in Edward S. Mason and Robert Asher, *The World Bank Since Bretton Woods*, Washington, D.C.: The Brookings Institution, 1973.

[9] Robert Pastor, *Congress and the Politics of Foreign Economic Policy*, Berkeley: University of California Press, 1980, 96–98.

[10] The GATT rounds include: 1947, Geneva; 1949, Annecy; 1950–1951, Torquay; 1955–1956, Geneva; 1959–1962, Geneva (Dillon Round); 1963–1967, Geneva (Kennedy Round); 1973–1979, Tokyo Round; 1986–1992, Uruguay Round.

[11] Pastor, *Congress* . . ., 78.

Third World nations). Beginning with the Tokyo Round, negotiations moved on to tackle nontariff barriers to trade, and the Uruguay Round took up these matters, along with the areas of agriculture and services.

The growth and dynamism of the world economy, along with the new set of international institutions, produced an epochal change in international economic relations. How this change came about, in particular the role of the United States in it, is the subject of the next section.

## U.S. HEGEMONY AND THE WORLD ECONOMY

A common characteristic of all the social sciences, especially one as new as international political economy, is disputation over the most basic of theoretical and empirical relationships. Perhaps the most important question for this emerging field—and the topic producing the greatest discussion—is the relationship of politics and power to the creation and management of the world economy. Scholars have sought to trace the emergence of a liberal international economic order to the presence of a single dominant power in the international system. The "hegemonic stability" theory holds that such a nation has the opportunity to construct an open and stable international economic system. Because this hegemonic state possesses a preponderance of military and economic power, it is in a position to convince other nations to enter into a system of relatively free trade and regular procedures for monetary relations. That is, the hegemon has the power and the reasons "to make and enforce the rules for the world political economy."[12]

Application of these ideas to understanding the period after World War II has produced a set of important insights but also several points of intellectual conflict. What follows is a consideration of these issues in terms of asking and answering five basic questions. First, what was the nature of U.S. leadership? Over what issues or problems was U.S. power the key element? Second, what were the aims of the United States? Was it primarily interested in acting for the benefit of all states in providing international peace and prosperity, or was it more concerned with designing a system to benefit itself even to the point of turning a profit? Third, what factors motivated the United States to assume the responsibilities of world leadership? What mixture of domestic interests and external political, military, and economic concerns provided the incentives for these actions? Fourth, how important was U.S. leadership to

---

[12] Robert Keohane, *After Hegemony*, Princeton: Princeton University Press, 1984, 37. Other works promoting the hegemonic stability theory are Stephen Krasner, "State Power and the Structure of International Trade," *World Politics*, 27, April 1975, 314-347; Charles Kindleberger, *The World in Depression*, Berkeley: University of California Press, 1973; Robert Gilpin, *U.S. Power and the Multinational Corporation*, New York: Basic Books, 1975; Robert Gilpin, *War and Change in World Politics*, Cambridge: Cambridge University Press, 1981; and Robert Keohane, "The Theory of Hegemonic Stability and Changes in International Regimes, 1967-1977," in Ole Holsti et al. (eds.), *Change in the International System*, Boulder: Westview Press, 1980.

international cooperation and political and economic stability? What were the extent and limits to U.S. power in engineering and/or coercing these outcomes? Fifth, what were the consequences of U.S. hegemony, particularly the distribution of benefits? These are broad and complex questions, and the answers are sometimes not yet clear. But they point out the basic elements of international political economy for the postwar world.

## Economic Consequences of World War II

Some historical background about the Second World War and its political and economic impact is helpful in providing a context for answering these questions. First and foremost was the importance of productivity in fighting and winning the war. World War II was essentially a contest of physical capabilities, with victory going to the side best able to amass the implements and manpower of war. Events from 1939 to 1945 both revealed and accentuated the productive advantages of the U.S. economy. Not only did the United States possess the greatest concentration of productive resources, but also its productivity—output per unit of input, usually labor—was far higher than that of any other nation. By 1944, the United States was producing 40 percent of the world's armaments, and its productivity was twice that of Germany and five times that of Japan.[13] The result was that the U.S. gross national product increased, in real terms, from $88.6 billion in 1939 to $135 billion in 1944.[14]

The war had equally profound effects on patterns of international trade and finance. The United States supplied vast quantities of Allied war material and financed this through Lend Lease. In spite of this largess, Britain liquidated its foreign reserves and large portions of its overseas investments to pay for imports from the United States. By the war's end, the pattern of British trade deficits financed by U.S. capital was firmly established. In addition, the rupture created by military operations made reestablishing prewar trade practices difficult. This was most evident in central and Eastern Europe, where Soviet control served to remove this area from its traditional role in European trade. Added to this was the physical destruction of the war, which represented approximately 13 percent of the prewar capital stock in Germany and 8 percent in France.[15] The result was a high demand for imports, significant barriers to exports, and a substantial payments imbalance between Europe and the United States.

---

[13] Alan Milward, *War, Economy and Society, 1939-1945*, Berkeley: University of California Press, 1977, 67. The sources of this advantage came from economies of scale, new capital investment, and incentives in winning the war. Much of the new investment was financed by the government. U.S. productivity was so great that it was able to increase war production on a vast scale without reducing civilian consumption below the levels of 1939. See Milward, *War . . .*, 63-68.

[14] Milward, *War . . .*, 63.

[15] Milward, *War . . .*, 333. He reports that the gross value of U.S. Lend Lease aid to the British was about $30 billion. See pages 351, 345-352, 359-360. Also useful is Scammell, *The International . . .*, 24-25.

The war and depression of the 1930s also had psychological and political consequences that influenced economic choices. The fear of recurrent depression helped reinforce affirmative government action in guaranteeing domestic prosperity. The depression left a legacy of significant barriers to trade and a memory of the dangers of economic warfare. More ominous were the German and Japanese experiences of military and economic organization designed to obtain secure access to the resources needed for autarchy. Finally, the military outcome not only disrupted traditional European trade but also brought a politically and economically alienated great power—the Soviet Union—into the heart of Europe.

## The United States and World Order

Now, what are the main issues in which U.S. power played the key role in defining the postwar international order? We will emphasize four: trade and finance, international security, vital resources, and international and domestic politics.[16] First, the United States was consistently the central actor in establishing and managing a framework of rules for international trade and finance, and also made the system work by providing financial support. We have seen how the Bretton Woods institutions and GATT were created largely through political initiatives from the United States. At the same time, these institutions confronted striking imbalances in the world economy measurable in terms of the sizable current account deficits between Europe and the United States.[17] Continuing the policy established under Lend Lease, in 1946 the United States provided additional funds to Britain and France to make up the payments gap. When this proved insufficient, the leadership in the United States moved to supply even more funds so that the recovery of Europe could continue. The Marshall Plan provided the financing needed to cover this imbalance. This can be seen in Table 4.5.

During the first four years after the war, the U.S. government and private sources supplied $28 billion to finance the payments imbalance with the rest of the world. This pattern continued with Marshall Plan aid in 1950–1951 and largely with military aid thereafter. The chief consequence of these actions was to ensure European recovery and to enshrine the dollar as the key international currency. That is, the dollar became the primary medium of international payment and the currency serving as the store of value for all others participating in the system.

Beyond these immediate economic issues lay a set of political and security matters that cried out for U.S. attention. Further, the U.S. ability to persuade the leadership of many nations to participate in the new liberal

---

[16] This list builds on and extends similar lists proposed by Robert Keohane, *After* . . ., 139, and Susan Strange, "The Persistent Myth of Lost Hegemony," *International Organization*, 41.4, Autumn 1987, 565.

[17] Remember that the main reason for the imbalance was the war itself. U.S. productivity, European destruction, disruption of traditional trading patterns, and the political importance of making a strong economic recovery all contributed to the difficulties in the 1945–1948 period.

**TABLE 4.5**
**World Payments Imbalances, 1946–1949**
*(Billions of U.S. Dollars)*

|  | 1946 | 1947 | 1948 | 1949 |
|---|---|---|---|---|
| U.S. Current Account Balance | +7.8 | +11.5 | +6.8 | +6.3 |
| Financed by: | | | | |
|     U.S. government | -4.9 | -5.8 | -5.1 | -5.9 |
|     Private loans and gifts | -1.1 | -1.5 | -1.6 | -1.1 |
|     IMF and World Bank | 0.0 | -0.8 | -0.4 | -0.1 |
|     Liquidating foreign assets | -1.9 | -4.5 | -0.8 | 0.0 |
|     Errors and omissions | +0.1 | +1.1 | +1.1 | +0.9 |
| Total | -7.8 | -11.5 | -6.8 | -6.3 |

SOURCE: W. M. Scammell, *The International . . .* , 21.

world order depended on their confidence in the United States and its willingness to ensure their security. The recent war had demonstrated the vulnerability of many parts of the world to a determined and aggressive state. Much of the leadership in Europe that was considering joining the U.S.-defined system was deeply worried about the political effects of Soviet military power in the heart of Europe. Thus, when events such as the Soviet-inspired coup in Czechoslovakia or the Soviet blockade of Berlin intensified these fears, the United States felt compelled to act. The result, by 1949, was the North Atlantic Treaty Organization (NATO), which represented a standing U.S. commitment to defend Western Europe. U.S. international leadership depended on the ability to use its superior power to reassure allies and to contain the Soviet Union. Especially critical was preventing Soviet actions from undermining confidence in and encouraging challenges to the United States. Many in the U.S. government concluded that the success of the postwar system rested on the image of U.S. power in Europe and on preventing the use or threat of force from affecting the shape of international politics.

A related set of political and security issues was defined by relations among states in the emerging Western system. The United States played a crucial role in encouraging cooperation, including convincing some—like the French—that their security would be ensured even as the German economy was being revived. A U.S.-imposed requirement for receiving Marshall Plan aid was European cooperation in coming together to define the scope of their economic problems and in administration of the funds. Much of the impetus for European unity came from constant encouragement by the United States. The occupation of Germany (a collective enterprise with the British and the French)[18] and the occupation of Japan (entirely by the United States) produced substantial efforts to change the domestic politics of these nations.

---

[18] The Soviet Union, of course, occupied the eastern third of Germany. But the failure of joint occupation in May 1947 moved the United States to reorganize its plans and to press forward with the Marshall Plan and unification of the three western zones.

A final and equally important element of U.S. hegemony was ensuring access to vital resources through the normal course of market relationships. Nations should not feel the need to use military force to gain a special position on these resources. Perhaps the most important of these resources was oil. The principal agents of control of this resource were the large American, British, and Dutch multinational oil corporations, but U.S. political and military power in the Middle East was an equally important ingredient.[19] This was especially evident in the U.S. effort to force the Soviets out of Iran in 1946, in the intervention in Iran in 1953, and in the close relationship with Saudi Arabia. The consequence was to ensure plentiful supplies at relatively cheap and stable prices.

## U.S. Purposes?

Although we can identify the main issues of international order in which U.S. hegemony played an essential role, scholars have disagreed about the basic aims of U.S. policy. Some have seen U.S. actions in trade, money, politics, security, and resources as an effort to provide many nations with the generalized benefits of peace and prosperity, sacrificing U.S. short-term interests for the good of the world community. In this case, the United States was involved in providing what are called *collective* or *public goods*. Thought of very precisely, *collective goods* refer to identifiable benefits that are available to all who participate in the system (even if they don't pay part of the cost), and consumption of the good by one does not diminish consumption by others. In one version of hegemonic stability theory, collective goods, such as security and prosperity, will emerge only if the most powerful nation accepts the costs of providing them and defers its benefits to the future. This country, in effect, must be willing to think in terms of benefits to a wide set of nations.[20]

A second perspective proposes that the collective benefits of international order will be supplied only if the dominant state can extract a disproportionate amount of the benefits. This view sees the United States as able to use its leverage to gain special privileges or to compel member states to make contributions to the costs of world order, so as to make providing international order a profitable venture.[21] A third perspective rejects the collective goods concept of international order and suggests instead that hegemonic power produced a substantial array of private benefits to the United States.[22]

---

[19] Lawrence Frank, "The First Oil Regime," *World Politics*, 37.4, July 1985, 586; Keohane, *After . . .*, 150–181; John Blair, *The Control of Oil*, New York: Pantheon Books, 1976.

[20] Kindleberger, *The World . . .*, is a good example of this viewpoint.

[21] Gilpin, *U.S. Power . . .*, and Krasner, "State Power . . .," promote this position.

[22] Bruce Russett, "The Mysterious Case of Vanishing Hegemony; or, Is Mark Twain Really Dead?" *International Organization*, 39.2, Spring 1985, 207–231, is the sole proponent of this position. Additional discussion of the importance of collective goods theory in understanding hegemony is found in Duncan Snidal, "The Limits of Hegemonic Stability Theory," *International Organization*, 39, Autumn 1985, 579–614; John Conybeare, "Public Goods, Prisoners' Dilemmas, and the International Political Economy," *International Studies Quarterly*, 28, March 1984, 5–22; and Fred Hirsch and Michael W. Doyle, *Alternatives to Monetary Disorder*, New York: McGraw-Hill, 1977, 11–64.

As is often the case, the actual situation contains a complex mixture of all three perspectives. In terms of bearing the costs of international order, the United States was clearly the only state capable of providing capital and guaranteeing the security of nations. The proportion of GNP spent on defense by the United States was much higher than that of other states in the "free world," and U.S. troops did a disproportionate share of the fighting and dying in wars for international stability. At the same time, free trade can provide great benefits to the most productive and low-cost nations because their exports are likely to expand relative to others. Further, the nation with the world's key currency receives special benefits by avoiding the need to adjust its domestic economy to payments deficits. Because the dollar functioned as a key currency and because other nations accepted it as payment for goods, the United States was able to force these nations to bear some of the costs of its international operations.[23] At the same time, peace and prosperity in the postwar period were general, at least for developed nations.[24]

But the real key to understanding U.S. motives in promoting international stability lies with the perceptions of U.S. leaders about the military and political costs that would come from dissolution of world order. The experience of depression and war convinced many key government officials that U.S. prosperity and security depended on prosperity abroad and on eliminating or blocking the acts of hostile and aggressive states. Should the United States not act to ensure these outcomes, international economic conflict would doom any chance for full employment and free enterprise in the United States, while control of the resources of Europe and Asia by a hostile power would certainly force a garrison state in the United States and cause another world war.[25] In an important sense, the benefits of a liberal world order derived from the unacceptable costs that could be forgone with its presence.

## Power and Outcomes

Should we conclude from this discussion that U.S. power was so dominant that the United States could get whatever it wanted? The answer is certainly "no," but for reasons that may not be obvious. Two critical examples help illustrate the point. Throughout the war, in negotiations leading to Lend Lease, in the discussions of the Bretton Woods institutions, and in the agreements for

---

[23] Allies of the U.S., like Germany and France, accepted dollars in payment for a U.S. current account deficit, resulting in expansion of their money supply and inflation rates. The matter of a key currency and its benefits and costs is the subject of more discussion later in this chapter.

[24] Because nations could be excluded from the GATT and IMF institutions and from the benefits of U.S. aid, the system of liberal world order does not qualify precisely as a collective good.

[25] These arguments, linking politics and economics in ways not always recognized by scholars in international political economy, can be found in Waldo Heinrichs, *Threshold of War: Franklin D. Roosevelt and American Entry into World War II*, New York: Oxford University Press, 1988; John Gaddis, *Strategies of Containment*, New York: Oxford University Press, 1982; and Gaddis, *The Long Peace*, New York: Oxford University Press, 1987.

the British loan in 1945–1946, the United States pressed the British very hard to dismantle the Imperial Preference System. This was the trade and monetary bloc created by Britain among past and present colonial areas to cope with the depression and the war. The U.S. position was consistent with a multilateral and open world order and would have eliminated the various mechanisms used to protect British trade.[26] The British grudgingly gave verbal assurances and, as a first step in 1947, moved to make the pound fully convertible. The result was to expose the weaknesses in the British economic position as the British were forced to use most of the $3.75 billion loan to support the pound. After a six-week trial, the idea of convertibility was shelved.

The U.S. objective of European political unity, a key element of Marshall Plan aid, suffered a similar fate. The idea was to create a stronger and more prosperous Europe through political and economic integration, and the expectation was for rapid movement toward this goal. One important consequence would be to establish an offsetting system of power in Europe and thereby reduce U.S. responsibilities. The other consequence would be to move more rapidly toward a multilateral trading system based on convertible currencies. This plan ran headlong into British resistance. They genuinely feared the economic and political effects of integration into Europe. British leaders worried about ties to Commonwealth nations, about the loss of political and economic independence, about the economic consequences of competition with the United States and the rapid swings in the U.S. business cycle, and about their status as a world power. Other countries also feared the consequences of a single integrated market in Europe.[27]

Despite its overwhelming power advantages and the apparent leverage created by the importance of Marshall Plan aid to Europe, the United States could not always obtain its objectives.[28] Three factors contributed to this result. First was the audacity of the proposal; bringing Europe—an area of intense political conflict for centuries—toward political and economic integration within a few years was probably unrealistic. Moving Britain and Europe toward a liberal system had to wait until their economies could compete with that of the United States. Second, and more interesting, was the effect of European and British weakness. The importance of bringing these nations into a Western political and economic bloc meant that overt intimidation and

---

[26] Similar actions were taken against the French bloc as part of a U.S. effort to break down the structure of colonialism built up in the nineteenth century.

[27] Stafford Cripps, the British chancellor of the Exchequer, asserted in November 1949 that "trade liberalization had gone far enough," and that the American proposal for European integration "amounted to a 'fifty-year programme.'" This quote and information on the U.S.–British dispute on European union are from Michael Hogan, *The Marshall Plan*, Cambridge: Cambridge University Press, 1987, 291. For evidence that Cripps had the timetable about right, see the discussion of Europe and 1992 in Chapter 6.

[28] A very useful discussion of these questions, along with a detailed historical analysis, is found in G. John Ikenberry, "Rethinking the Origins of American Hegemony," *Political Science Quarterly*, 104.3, 1989, 375–400.

coercion were likely to prove counterproductive. At the very least, adopting the U.S. vision of an unbridled multilateral world would have proved devastating to the economies of Europe. Pushing too hard would have produced either collapse of U.S.-oriented political elites or cooperation without actual consent. Finally, the very nature of U.S. hegemony placed sharp limits on the ability to achieve U.S. demands. From the U.S. standpoint, world stability required a collective and collaborative effort to contain the Soviet Union and to create a more liberal international system. Achieving a genuinely cooperative arrangement among Western nations forced the United States to make many compromises. U.S. hegemony was based mostly on leadership and not on coercion.[29]

## The Consequences of U.S. Hegemony

Understanding the overall effects of U.S. hegemony is a very difficult problem, and much of the rest of this book can be seen as an extended answer to such a question. One major consequence of this hegemony was an extraordinary level of peace and prosperity, certainly with disproportionate benefits accruing to developed states but also with some previously poor states gaining in economic strength. The rapid recovery of West Germany, most of Europe, and Japan owed much to U.S. aid, investment, and a favorable political and security climate. The Third World as a whole did not fare as well, losing in share of world trade and total output. Much of this came as a result of a relative decline in the importance of primary products and food and an increase in the importance of manufactured goods. After the mid-1960s, some Third World states were able to break into the world market for manufactures. (See Chapters 8 and 12 for more discussion of this process.) For the United States, many special benefits flowed from hegemony—the foreign policy benefits from having the key currency and the advantages to its corporations operating on a world scale are two examples—but it, too, experienced a relative decline in world product and trade. After 1971, U.S. policy took on a much more unilateral cast in trying to manipulate the world economy to its advantage. The Vietnam War experience from 1961 to 1973 also made the United States much more resentful of the military costs of hegemony and led to pressures on allies to share more of the burdens.

Unquestionably, U.S. economic, military, and political power shaped the post-1945 world economy. Examining in more detail the costs and benefits of that system for industrial states is the subject of the next section.

---

[29] The last point relating to the nature of hegemony is not the same as the second point, relating to weakness. U.S. leadership needed to be based primarily on persuasion even, and perhaps especially, had Europe and Japan been strong. The United States needed a commitment of political, economic, and military resources from its allies that was based on a belief in the justice of their cause. Under these circumstances, neither weak nor strong states could be coerced into this position.

# THE HEYDAY OF U.S. HEGEMONY: 1958–1970

Although the United States commanded great power resources after World War II, it was not until 1958–1959 that its vision of a multilateral and liberal world economy began to be realized. The ten years from 1948 to 1958 produced several new and significant features in the world economy, the most important being the development of new institutions for economic cooperation, dramatic economic growth in Europe, rising U.S. military spending, U.S. foreign aid in the Third World, and the emergence of U.S.-based multinational corporations. These factors helped to generate the stability and prosperity that gave nations the confidence to participate in this liberal system. But each factor also contributed to an outflow of dollars, and this ultimately brought down the Bretton Woods system. In this section we will briefly consider these developments and then turn to the problems they created.

## The European Economic Community

Perhaps the most important event during these ten years came in March 1957 with the signing of the Treaty of Rome. This treaty, signed by France, the Federal Republic of Germany (West Germany), Belgium, Luxembourg, Italy, and the Netherlands, called for the creation of the European Economic Community (EEC) beginning on January 1, 1958.[30] Several steps had preceded this decision. Marshall Plan aid had been made contingent on European cooperation, and the United States pressed hard for much greater levels of economic and political unity.[31] But in Europe, leadership for integration was supplied by the French, who were initially motivated by the need to bring German industrial power under international supervision and later by a recognition of the importance of creating a European system capable of dealing with the United States and the Soviet Union on equal terms. Under the U.S. concept of world leadership, this notion of independent power centers was actually encouraged, and the tariff discrimination and political independence that almost inevitably followed were tolerated. Further, the United States wanted German power accommodated to its other European partners and available to deal with the Soviets. First, in 1948 Belgium, Luxembourg, and the Netherlands had established a customs union,[32] and in 1950 the European Coal and Steel

---

[30] Continuing its reluctance to join in European economic integration, Britain was not a member of the EEC. Instead, the British helped organize the European Free Trade Area (EFTA) along with Norway, Switzerland, Austria, Sweden, Denmark, and Portugal in 1960. The main difference with the EEC was that the EFTA did not have a common external tariff.

[31] In response, the Organization for European Economic Cooperation (OEEC) was set up in 1948 to coordinate Marshall Plan aid and reconstruction efforts.

[32] Basically, a customs union acts to reduce tariffs and other trade barriers within the particular set of nations and also works to establish a common trade policy with outside states.

Community was created to manage and control German industrial power.[33] In 1955 negotiations began for a broader customs union, which reached fruition in the 1957 Rome treaty.

The basic purpose of the agreement was to establish a schedule for reducing tariffs and quantitative restrictions on trade. On the whole, the timetable was met or exceeded, with tariffs slashed dramatically and quotas eliminated entirely.[34] Shortly after the inauguration of the EEC—late 1958 and early 1959—fourteen European nations, including Great Britain, moved to accept full convertibility of their currencies.[35] The same economic growth in the 1950s that made the EEC possible also gave these and other nations the financial strength to close their payments gap and to accumulate the reserves needed to support a currency at a fixed price against the dollar. This also coincided with expansion of the resources at the IMF and a more liberal lending policy, both of which facilitated convertibility.[36]

## Military Keynesianism and Foreign Aid

The 1950s also witnessed important developments in U.S. political economy, in particular the increasing role of military spending, the rise of foreign aid, and a persistent balance of payments deficit. The combination of Soviet development of an atomic bomb in 1949 and the outbreak of the Korean War in 1950 produced a militarization of the Cold War and a consequent rise in U.S. military spending. Actual spending increased more than threefold by 1952 and stood at more than 10 percent of GNP by 1953. The legacy of Keynesianism of the 1930s, the postwar commitment to high levels of employment, and the need for high military spending merged to form a relatively coherent national policy. Keynes's idea was to use increases in government spending during periods of economic recession to stimulate the economy. From a political standpoint, the easiest way to raise spending was to pay for the military requirements of the Cold War. By the early 1960s, the new Kennedy administration had added the notion of reducing taxes while increasing spending so as to provide an extra boost to the economy.

A key element in U.S. postwar aims was dismantling the nineteenth-century colonial system established by the European powers. The late 1940s and 1950s produced a wave of new nations as this process came to fruition. However, the Soviet Union moved to take advantage of this development and

---

[33] The year 1950 also produced the European Payments Union, designed to manage payments imbalances within Europe.

[34] Scammell, *The International Economy* . . ., 137-138.

[35] Convertibility, in the 1958-1971 period, occurred when a currency could be freely traded for gold or for a foreign currency. The economic dislocations from the war led most countries to place substantial restrictions on convertibility until 1958. After 1971, gold was no longer an element of convertibility.

[36] Eckes, *A Search* ..., 231-233; Scammell, *The International Economy* . . ., 109-116.

increased its political and economic activities in what emerged as the Third World. The U.S. response was to utilize its military capabilities to engage in selective intervention and to increase its aid—economic and military—so as to reinforce its political and military position in the Third World. Castro's victory in Cuba and his swing toward the Soviet Union in 1959-1960 gave strong incentives to accelerate this trend. The Third World and its economic and military orientation in the Cold War became important enough to warrant much more attention and resources.

## Dollar Glut

The revival and integration of Western Europe and the growing demands of the Cold War came against the backdrop of troubling trends in the U.S. international economic situation. The 1950s, which began with a dollar shortage, ended with the United States wanting to reverse a persistent balance of payments deficit. In the early part of the decade, a payments deficit was created through military and economic aid; this was desirable because it helped close the dollar gap with the still economically weak Europeans. By the late 1950s Europe had recovered, and the deficit presented new problems. Although the United States enjoyed a substantial surplus in its goods and services and investment income accounts, this was more than offset by foreign aid, military expenditures abroad, and private overseas investment.[37] The sudden shrinkage in the surplus accounts in 1958-1959 produced a much wider payments deficit and instability in the dollar.

Remember that under the Bretton Woods system the dollar was fixed in terms of gold at $35 an ounce. This meant that the U.S. government was required to redeem dollars held by foreigners at that price—a commitment that served as the core of the fixed exchange rate system. The likelihood of exercising this option was based on the ratio of dollars held by foreigners to the gold held by the United States. If the amount of dollars abroad surpassed the amount of U.S. gold, all claimants could not be paid unless the United States changed the price of gold. Raising the price of gold in terms of dollars—in effect devaluing the dollar—automatically increased the dollar quantity of gold. Speculators in foreign exchange and others who feared this possibility would anticipate such an action and convert their dollars for gold—producing a "run" on the dollar and contributing to the very outcome they wanted to avoid or profit from. Because confidence in the dollar was a key element of the Bretton Woods system, and because this confidence meant persuading those holding dollars to continue doing so, the U.S. balance of payments became a prime indicator of the stability of the system. A larger payments deficit meant more dollars abroad and more potential claimants on U.S. gold.

---

[37] The late 1950s are discussed in Robert Pollard and Samuel F. Wells, Jr., "1945-1960: The Era of American Economic Hegemony," in William H. Becker and Samuel F. Wells, Jr. (eds.), *Economics and World Power*, New York: Columbia University Press, 1984, 379-381.

## Political Economy and Hegemony

It was this problem that dominated international monetary management in the 1960s and ultimately led to the demise of the Bretton Woods system. In a sense, the requirements of hegemony—as expressed in U.S. foreign and economic policies from 1961 to 1969—undermined a major pillar of that system. Kennedy and Johnson are the clearest examples of presidents who not only had policies guided by the political, military, and economic demands of hegemony but also who point out the costs and contradictions of such policies. President Kennedy was determined to marshal U.S. power in order to contain the Soviet Union and communism on a global scale. Expansion of military power and foreign aid was the chief means to this end. Kennedy was also concerned about the economic performance of the United States at home and abroad. He expected rapid domestic economic growth—the result of a fiscal policy based on military Keynesianism—to ameliorate the costs of the military buildup. Coupled with accelerating the liberalization of world trade, the improved productivity from growth was also expected to solve the balance of payments problem.

Links between domestic and international economies were more tightly drawn in the 1960s. Expectations about economic growth were driven by the requirements of competition with the Soviet Union. Moreover, the U.S. position in the world economy, as measured by the balance of payments, became a serious concern of the new president and his successor. One important advisor warned that "[we] will not be able to sustain in the 1960s a world position without solving the balance of payments problem."[38] But the harder the United States tried to meet its global responsibilities, the more it damaged the balance of payments and undermined its ability to act as hegemon. This behavior also began to prompt a backlash from allies who came to resent the privileges and consequences of the dollar as key currency. Their chief complaint was that the unrelenting U.S. payments deficit—a product of U.S. foreign operations—presented a major policy dilemma. They were forced either to hold dollars and expand their money supply and inflation or to exchange the dollars for gold and undermine the value of the dollars remaining in foreign hands. The French were especially critical, arguing that they and others were being required to pay part of the costs of a mistaken U.S. policy in Southeast Asia.

Over the decade, the U.S. response was to reject the option of devaluation and instead to devise a variety of mechanisms to cope with what was hoped to be a short-run balance of payments problem. These mechanisms included efforts to have Europeans use their gold and currencies to support the dollar, voluntary and mandatory measures to restrict the movement of U.S.

---

[38] The quote by Walt Rostow, special assistant to the president for national security, is from William S. Borden, "Defending Hegemony: American Foreign Economic Policy," in Thomas G. Paterson (ed.), *Kennedy's Quest for Victory: American Foreign Policy, 1961-1963*, New York: Oxford University Press, 1989, 63.

private capital abroad, and defending the value of the pound as the first line in defense of the dollar. The most lasting result of the efforts to salvage the dollar–gold connection was the establishment of a new form of international money. The Special Drawing Rights (SDR) established in the International Monetary Fund was a checking account that central banks could use to supplement their international reserves. Nations in deficit could use this overdraft privilege to settle international accounts with other central banks. The hope was that the liquidity role of the dollar could be eased by SDRs. But the small size of SDR allocations and reluctance to rely on "fiat" money limited the usefulness of SDRs.[39]

On a more fundamental level, the United States pushed for additional liberalization of world trade. Congress passed the Trade Expansion Act in 1962, giving the president broadened powers to negotiate lower tariffs. In large part, this act was a response to the challenges presented by the new European Economic Community. The EEC created a common external tariff on goods from outside the six members while reducing tariffs within the group. This threatened to hurt U.S. trade and to further weaken the balance of payments. The resulting Kennedy Round of GATT lasted from 1963 to 1967 and produced significant tariff reductions over a broad range of goods.[40] But, as we shall see, the U.S. trade balance, and with it the balance of payments, did not improve.

## The Emergence of Multinational Corporations

The efforts to cope with the EEC and payments difficulties also affected another very important development in the U.S. economy and the world economy: the rise of the multinational corporation and new international capital markets. The combination of the EEC and convertibility helped spur U.S. corporations to invest in Europe after 1958. The fear of tariff walls around the EEC provided the incentive, and the ability to convert profits back into dollars offered large U.S. corporations the opportunity to establish production facilities in Europe.[41] Multinational corporations (MNCs)—those with production and/or marketing facilities in at least two countries—have given rise to a new language for the analysis of international relations. Scholars now speak of the internationalization of production, the integration of national economies, global calculations of market relations, and the power of transnational actors in relation to nations themselves. These are matters that we will take up in subsequent chapters. For now, our concern is with understanding the political consequences of MNCs and the economic motivations behind their expansion abroad.

---

[39] Moffitt, *The World's* . . ., 33; Eckes, *A Search* . . ., 256–257.

[40] Pastor, *Congress and* . . ., 104–120; Borden, "Defending Hegemony . . .," 69–80.

[41] Gilpin, *The Political Economy* . . ., 233. An additional factor in the growth of MNCs was transportation and communication innovations in the form of regular jet travel and the telex.

**TABLE 4.6**

**U.S. Foreign Direct Investment: 1950–1970**
*(Book Value in Billions of U.S. Dollars)*

|  | TOTAL | MANUFACTURING | PETROLEUM & MINING | TRADE & PUBLIC UTILITIES |
|---|---|---|---|---|
| 1950 | 11.79 | 3.83 | 4.52 | 2.18 |
| 1960 | 31.82 | 11.05 | 13.76 | 4.95 |
| 1970 | 78.18 | 32.26 | 27.88 | 9.42 |

SOURCE: Adapted from Mira Wilkins, *The Maturing of Multinational Enterprise: American Business Abroad from 1914 to 1970*, Cambridge: Harvard University Press, 1974, 330.

A key feature of multinational corporations is direct investment abroad designed to establish and control a production and/or distribution unit.[42] The levels of foreign direct investment (FDI) and its geographic and business direction can be seen in Tables 4.6 and 4.7. Clearly, expansion abroad is substantial in all categories but especially in manufacturing. Table 4.7 shows the geographic distribution of foreign direct investment in manufacturing. Several areas of the world, but especially Canada, the EEC, and Asia, received U.S. direct investment.

The process of foreign direct investment was overwhelmingly an American phenomenon. By the early 1970s, the book value of U.S. investments was $86 billion, which represented 52 percent of all foreign direct investment for all market economies. Even more impressive is the fact that U.S. companies produced $172 billion worth of goods and services abroad. This is compared with $43.5 billion worth of goods produced within the United States for export. That is, production abroad by U.S. firms was almost four times as great as all U.S. exports.[43]

The growth of multinational corporations in the period from 1958 to 1970 was the consequence of a complex mixture of political and economic factors. In political terms, the interests of the United States and the Europeans were accommodated, and this created the climate within which U.S. MNCs in Europe could flourish. Specifically, this meant acceptance by the United States of the EEC and its discriminatory and competitive effects on American

---

[42] This process of direct foreign investment can be distinguished from portfolio investment, which seeks merely to provide a noncontrolling form of equity or debt to a foreign firm in the hopes of receiving returns in the future. Portfolio investment was characteristic of British foreign investment in the nineteenth century and is discussed in Chapter 3. See Robert Gilpin, *U.S. Power ...*, 9–11.

[43] Gilpin, *U.S. Power . . .*, 15. The propensity of U.S. firms to invest and produce abroad is indicated by the fact that only two other countries—Britain and Switzerland—produced more abroad than at home for export. And neither country did so to the same degree.

**TABLE 4.7**
**U.S. Foreign Direct Investment in Manufacturing, 1955–1970**
*(Book Value in Billions of U.S. Dollars)*

|  | EEC | U.K. | EUROPE OTHER | CANADA | LATIN AMERICA | OTHER | TOTAL |
|---|---|---|---|---|---|---|---|
| 1955 | 0.6 | 0.9 | 0.1 | 2.8 | 1.4 | 0.5 | 6.3 |
| 1960 | 1.4 | 2.2 | 0.3 | 4.8 | 1.5 | 0.9 | 11.1 |
| 1965 | 3.7 | 3.3 | 0.6 | 6.9 | 2.9 | 1.9 | 19.3 |
| 1970 | 7.2 | 5.0 | 1.5 | 10.1 | 4.6 | 3.9 | 32.3 |

SOURCE: This is adapted from Wilkins, *The Maturing* . . . , 331.

trade, and in return the Europeans (especially the Germans) agreed to finance the U.S. balance of payments deficit by holding dollars. This would permit operations such as stationing U.S. troops in Europe to continue and helped to make possible other major actions, such as in Vietnam. As part of this process, the United States persuaded the Europeans to give U.S. MNCs access to the EEC and to treat them as if they were a European company.[44]

Thought of only in economic terms, multinational corporations had a somewhat cloudy set of benefits for the United States. In 1971 U.S. MNCs engaged in $4.8 billion in foreign direct investment (remember that this is a negative item in the balance of payments) while generating $9 billion in investment income (a positive item).[45] More difficult to measure is the loss of jobs in the United States to overseas production, the transfer of technology abroad, and the exports back to the United States (our imports) of goods produced elsewhere by U.S. MNCs. But in terms of the immediate political needs of generating a positive return in the balance of payments, multinational corporations represented a support system for U.S. international responsibilities.[46]

From the standpoint of the multinationals themselves, the political climate created by U.S. hegemony and the economic climate of stability and opportunity intersected with a set of more specifically economic motivations. Several somewhat complementary explanations have been offered for the expansion of multinationals, each of which begins with the fact that these are typically firms that are operating in an oligopolistic environment and that are

---

[44] This argument is found in Gilpin, *U.S. Power* . . ., 107–108, 154–155. Gilpin (124–125) points out the importance of the dollar as key currency, especially as the balance of payments deficit persisted and made the dollar overvalued. U.S. firms could use an overvalued dollar to purchase European assets and establish European branches without having to earn this currency through a balance of payments surplus.

[45] United Nations, "Multinational Corporations in World Development," in George Modelski (ed.), *Transnational Corporations and World Order*, San Francisco: W. H. Freeman, 1979, 25.

[46] See Gilpin, *U.S. Power* . . ., 156–157.

seeking to maintain or extend their competitive advantages.[47] Because market share is an important asset for oligopolistic companies, these companies may expand operations abroad simply to make certain that they are positioned to participate in any new or expanding market. Or, a giant firm that enjoys some special competitive advantage may look to production in foreign markets to exploit this advantage. Finally, the firm may be at a particular point in the evolution of its products such that foreign production becomes an economic necessity. Initially, the combination of a large home market and technological advantages makes production for export a profitable strategy. But as the technology of the product and its production processes become more commonplace and available, the company may be forced to move abroad to take advantage of lower costs and/or to compete with a foreign producer. This "product cycle" theory may be especially relevant to U.S. firms in the 1950s and 1960s who faced rising European firms moving into markets that U.S. firms had pioneered in the preceding ten to fifteen years.[48]

Lagging somewhat behind multinational corporations were U.S. banks, who began in the mid-1960s to expand substantially their foreign operations. Once again, several factors were at work. The dollar as key currency, acceptable for most international transactions, and the U.S. payments imbalance must be judged as critical ingredients. The transition from a dollar shortage to a dollar surplus in 1957-1958 resulted in the accumulation of dollars in foreign banks. London bankers, an ingenious lot, decided to begin lending these dollars rather than returning them to the United States. Thus was born the Eurodollar or Eurocurrency (because some other currencies were also involved) market—essentially an unregulated international money supply. When the U.S. government acted in 1963 to stem the dollar outflow for loans through the interest equalization tax, many U.S. banks established operations abroad to continue their foreign lending and thereby took advantage of the Eurodollar process. The rise of the Eurodollar market, the expansion of U.S. international banking, and the growth of U.S. multinational firms were linked together throughout the 1960s.

Beyond this relationship, the Eurocurrency system became a phenomenon in its own right. Because no single state could regulate it effectively and because of the unceasing U.S. payments deficits, a Euromarket system developed consisting of the dollar and other currencies, a system of bank credit, and a Eurobond market (bonds denominated in dollars but floated outside the United States). A massive volume of funds emerged that, without much restriction, could move across borders in search of the highest yields

---

[47] An oligopoly means that the number of firms in the industry is very small, with each firm controlling a significant portion of the market. The size of the firm in relation to the market and to the economy permits it to influence the price of the good. That is, the firm is powerful enough to affect, in some significant way, the competitive environment in which it operates.

[48] This discussion relies on Gilpin, *U.S. Power* . . ., 115-125; and Gilpin, *The Political Economy* . . ., 232-238. Also see Charles Kindleberger, "The Monopolistic Theory of Direct Foreign Investment," in Modelski, *Transnational* . . ., 91-107; also see Raymond Vernon, "The Product Cycle Model," in Modelski, *Transnational* . . ., 108-117.

available on a global basis (discounting for risk). By 1970 this market approached $70 billion and would triple in size in the next three years.[49]

The 1958-1970 period produced an extraordinarily complex set of developments for the world economy. It was simultaneously a time of American dominance and American decline. Bearing the burdens of military competition and Vietnam, the United States was acutely aware of the continued importance of preserving global security and stability. The United States also encouraged the establishment of the EEC and the economic revitalization of Japan, both to marshal its assets against the Soviets and to facilitate the multilateral economic order sought since the 1940s. U.S. resources flowed abroad to preserve a liberal world order even as allies improved their competitive position in the world economy. But neither planned nor entirely desired was the acceleration of U.S. private investment abroad. As we shall see, this combination of events led to the breakdown of the Bretton Woods system so important to the United States and contributed to dramatic changes in the control of oil.

## MONEY AND OIL, 1971–1973

Between 1970 and 1973, two of the pillars of U.S. hegemony—fixed exchange rates and control of oil—came under pressure and eventually disintegrated, only to be replaced by new relationships. Several basic weaknesses of the Bretton Woods system were exposed by the continuing U.S. payments deficit and growing international financial interdependence, and between 1971 and 1973 the system largely collapsed. The ability of the United States to guarantee ample oil supplies at low prices ran aground on imbalances of supply and demand and growing nationalism in those Third World nations where the oil was located. Notwithstanding the collapse of these arrangements, U.S. power remained sufficient to organize new mechanisms for money and oil. But these new regimes required even greater coordination, cooperation, and compromise and cast doubt on the future of the world economy.

### The End of Bretton Woods

The economic growth of Western Europe and Japan, a weakening position in the U.S. balance of trade, and the growth of international capital markets spelled doom for the Bretton Woods system of fixed exchange rates based on a fixed dollar–gold exchange rate. As early as 1960, the liabilities created by foreign-held dollars exceeded the U.S. supply of gold. In that same year, the price of gold in private markets rose to $40 an ounce. During the next decade and more, the situation deteriorated.[50]

---

[49] See Jeffrey A. Frieden, *Banking on the World: The Politics of American International Finance*, New York: Harper & Row, 1987, 79-85; Benjamin J. Cohen, *In Whose Interest? International Banking and American Foreign Policy*, New Haven: Yale University Press, 1986, 19-33; Michael Moffitt, *The World's Money*, New York: Simon and Schuster, 1983, 43-55.

[50] John Odell, *U.S. International Monetary Policy*, Princeton: Princeton University Press, 1982, 85-87.

TABLE 4.8

**Proportion of World Exports**
*(Billions of U.S. Dollars with Percentage of World Totals)*

|  | 1960 | % | 1965 | % | 1970 | % | 1971 | % | 1972 | % |
|---|---|---|---|---|---|---|---|---|---|---|
| U.S. | 20.6 | 18.0 | 27.5 | 16.5 | 43.2 | 15.2 | 44.1 | 13.9 | 49.8 | 13.2 |
| Great Britain | 10.6 | 9.3 | 13.8 | 8.2 | 19.6 | 6.9 | 22.6 | 7.1 | 24.7 | 6.6 |
| W. Germany | 11.4 | 9.9 | 17.9 | 10.7 | 34.2 | 12.1 | 39.1 | 12.3 | 46.7 | 12.4 |
| France | 6.9 | 6.0 | 10.2 | 6.1 | 18.1 | 6.4 | 20.8 | 6.6 | 26.5 | 7.0 |
| Japan | 4.1 | 3.6 | 8.5 | 5.1 | 19.3 | 6.8 | 24.1 | 7.6 | 29.1 | 7.7 |
| World Exports | 114.6 | | 167.1 | | 283.7 | | 317.4 | | 376.8 | |

SOURCE: The figures are calculated from International Monetary Fund, *International Financial Statistics Yearbook*, 1979, 62–63.

This deterioration can be seen in several ways but especially in the growing importance of several countries in world trade and in the U.S. balance of payments. Table 4.8 shows a steady decline in the world proportion of home-based exports by the United States. (Remember the jump in U.S. MNC production abroad.) The same was true for Great Britain. At the same time, West Germany, France, and especially Japan made steady relative gains. U.S. exports rose throughout the period but not as fast as those of the world or of its industrial competitors. By 1972 West Germany had nearly equalled the United States in dollar volume of exports.

A close examination of the U.S. balance of payments for this period reveals some important refinements for our understanding of the U.S. problem.[51]

TABLE 4.9

**U.S. Balance of Payments, 1960–1972**
*(Billions of Dollars)*

| YEAR | EXPORTS | IMPORTS | NET | MILITARY | INVEST INC. | CURRENT ACCOUNT BALANCE | CAPITAL ACCOUNT BALANCE | ERROR | NET LIQUIDITY BALANCE |
|---|---|---|---|---|---|---|---|---|---|
| 1960 | 19.7 | -14.8 | 4.9 | -2.8 | 2.8 | 1.8 | -3.0 | -1.1 | -3.7 |
| 1965 | 26.5 | -21.5 | 5.0 | -2.1 | 5.3 | 4.3 | -6.1 | -0.5 | -2.5 |
| 1967 | 30.7 | -26.9 | 3.8 | -3.1 | 5.8 | 2.1 | -5.5 | -0.9 | -4.7 |
| 1968 | 33.6 | -33.0 | 0.6 | -3.1 | 6.2 | -0.4 | -3.4 | -0.4 | -1.6 |
| 1969 | 36.4 | -35.8 | 0.6 | -3.3 | 6.0 | -1.1 | -2.0 | -2.4 | -6.1 |
| 1970 | 42.0 | -39.8 | 2.2 | -3.4 | 6.4 | 0.4 | -3.4 | -1.2 | -3.9 |
| 1971 | 42.8 | -45.5 | -2.7 | -2.9 | 8.9 | -2.8 | -6.8 | -10.8 | -22.0 |
| 1972 | 48.8 | -55.7 | -6.9 | -3.6 | 9.8 | -8.4 | -1.5 | -3.1 | -13.9 |

*NOTE: Some items in the balance of payments have been omitted. The result is that only net exports/imports adds across.*

SOURCE: The table is reconstructed from data in Odell, *U.S. International . . .*, 203-205.

---

[51] The use of different sources for trade and balance of payments produces a slight variation in the export totals.

Several points stand out in the data shown in Table 4.9. Perhaps most important is the slow growth of exports relative to imports, especially after 1967, and the development of a trade deficit in 1971. Although investment income (remember MNC direct investments) grew steadily and the capital account and military spending abroad were mostly under control, the U.S. deficit persisted and grew much worse from the deteriorating trade balance.[52] Another perspective on this process is revealed from data on exports and imports of manufactured goods.

**TABLE 4.10**

**U.S. Trade in Manufactured Goods, 1960–1971**

|  | 1960 | 1965 | 1970 | 1971 |
|---|---|---|---|---|
| Low-technology goods |  |  |  |  |
| Exports | 3.573 | 4.409 | 6.778 | 6.262 |
| Imports | 4.494 | 7.350 | 12.928 | 14.550 |
| Balance | -.921 | -2.941 | -6.150 | -8.288 |
| High-technology goods |  |  |  |  |
| Exports | 9.010 | 13.030 | 22.565 | 24.187 |
| Imports | 2.369 | 3.895 | 12.978 | 15.898 |
| Balance | 6.641 | 9.135 | 9.587 | 8.289 |

SOURCE: These data are taken from Gilpin, *U.S. Power . . .* , 193.

Two points are notable from this evidence. First, imports of both low- and high-technology manufactures were growing more rapidly than were exports of these goods. Second, by 1971 the deficit in low-tech goods equalled the surplus in high-tech goods.

The difficulties in the U.S. trade and payments balances can be traced in substantial part to the interaction of domestic and foreign policy in the mid-1960s. The decision to escalate U.S. involvement in the Vietnam War in 1965 came in the context of substantial increases in domestic spending for new poverty and welfare programs and was followed by the decision not to raise taxes. In many ways this combination of choices was consistent with the Keynesian notions of fiscal policy except that it came at a time of near full employment and a booming economy. During the period from 1965 to 1973, the inflation rate rose (as measured by the Consumer Price Index), and the budget deficit widened.

In simple terms, the budget deficit contributed greatly to the rise in inflation, both by overstimulating the economy and by increases in the money supply encouraged by the Federal Reserve to help finance the deficit. The rising price of U.S. goods encouraged imports and discouraged exports. In 1968–1969, policy changed with a tax increase and tighter money. The

[52] The large "Error" item for 1971–72 in Table 4.9 reflects the substantial volume of speculation against the dollar discussed next.

result of this "belt tightening" was a budget surplus, an improvement in the balance of trade, and a stronger dollar. But the economy also went into recession even as inflation remained high. Later, in 1970, economic policy shifted back to stimulation.[53]

**TABLE 4.11**
**Budget Deficits and Inflation**

|                  | 1965 | 1966 | 1967 | 1968  | 1969  | 1970 | 1971  | 1972  | 1973 |
|------------------|------|------|------|-------|-------|------|-------|-------|------|
| CPI %            | 1.7  | 2.9  | 2.9  | 4.2   | 5.4   | 5.9  | 4.3   | 3.3   | 6.2  |
| Budget deficit $ | -1.6 | -3.8 | -8.7 | -25.2 | +3.2  | -2.8 | -23.0 | -23.4 | 14.8 |

SOURCE: The data on the Consumer Price Index are taken from David Calleo, *The Imperious Economy*, Cambridge: Harvard University Press, 1982, 201. The data on the budget deficit are taken from Calleo, *Beyond . . .*, 243.

The overall trade deficit in 1971 represented the culmination of several years of deterioration and, combined with the deficit in military and capital accounts, produced a major international monetary crisis. With pressure mounting against the dollar, on August 15, 1971, President Nixon announced a new policy. The United States suspended indefinitely the commitment to redeem gold for dollars, imposed domestic wage and price controls, demanded depreciation of the dollar, and placed a 10 percent tariff surcharge on U.S. imports. These actions amounted to a unilateral rejection of the basic rules of international monetary behavior and a demand for adjustment by U.S. military and economic allies.

What followed was more than eighteen months of coercion and pressure, resistance, seemingly solid agreements, and continued market instability. At issue was the future of the dollar-gold link, fixed exchange rates, the rate of exchange, and which countries would be forced to make the adjustments and trade concessions. The United States wanted substantial revaluations of major currencies, elimination of "unfair" restrictions on trade, and greater sharing of the costs of keeping U.S. forces abroad. The French and the Japanese resisted the most strongly, with the French refusing to alter the franc-gold price and the Japanese arguing that the United States should change its domestic economic system. Only after National Security Adviser Henry Kissinger became concerned about the damage this was doing to the alliance system did the United States accept the need for concessions. In December 1971, at the Smithsonian Institution in Washington, a compromise agreement was reached. The United States devalued the dollar in terms of gold (but made no commitment to redeem dollars for gold) and dropped the import surcharge. The

---

[53] Discussions of the links between domestic and foreign economic policy are found in Calleo, *The Imperious . . .*, 25-61; and Odell, *U.S. International . . .*, 110-111.

other major capitalist states revalued their currencies against the dollar by an average of 8 percent (Japan's was 16.9 percent against the dollar) and adjusted their currencies against each other. Trade issues were postponed. The result was a temporary return to fixed rates.[54]

This system held together through 1972 in spite of continuing U.S. trade deficits. But in February 1973, renewed selling of the dollar produced another currency crisis and a U.S. decision to devalue the dollar 10 percent (without consultation) accompanied by the threat to devalue another 10 percent unless the Japanese and the West Europeans agreed to float their currencies against the dollar. Acceptance of this arrangement led not to stability but rather to further selling of the dollar and the complete collapse of fixed exchange rates in March 1973.[55]

Two main reasons can be identified for the decline and fall of the Bretton Woods system. First, the system was inherently unstable because the mechanisms for adjustment of exchange rates were so inflexible. This was particularly true for the United States, where the value of the dollar also became the measure of the stability of the world economy, especially in the minds of U.S. leaders. The economic relations that developed after 1948 were structured by these fixed values even as the shift from U.S. surplus to deficit increasingly demanded adjustment of exchanges rates. The world of 1971 was significantly different from the world of 1945–1950, but the Bretton Woods system made few accommodations to that reality.

Second, and perhaps most reflective of those changes, was the massive growth of the market power of international capital and its impact on fixed rates. This is reflected in the emergence of transnational actors—multinational corporations and international banks—and in the vast Eurocurrency market over the years from 1958 to 1973. As late as 1966, the Eurocurrency market and U.S. international reserves were of approximately equal size. But by 1973 the Eurocurrency market was almost nine times bigger than U.S. reserves.[56] Such an immense collection of resources was capable of overwhelming even concerted government action. Between 1971 and 1973 these new transnational actors collectively lost confidence in the system of fixed exchange rates and the ability of governments to establish any viable system. Eventually, in March 1973, the governments of the capitalist world were forced to accept the immense market power of these actors and to adopt a new system of floating exchange rates.[57]

---

[54] The best-detailed discussion of these events is in Odell, *U.S. International* ..., 188–291.

[55] Odell, *U.S. International* . . ., 292–326.

[56] Calleo, *The Imperious* . . ., 208. Additional measures can be found in Robert Keohane and Joseph Nye, *Power and Interdependence* (2nd ed.), Glenview: Scott Foresman, 1989, 81–82; Eckes, *A Search* . . ., 240–241.

[57] Once again, Odell has the best discussion of this matter. See Odell, *U.S. International* . . ., 299–305. The arrangement adopted was a managed or "dirty" float in which governments periodically intervened to keep rate fluctuations within some acceptable bounds.

## Loss of Control Over Oil

Concurrent with these dramatic changes in the international monetary order was an equally significant structural transformation of the international oil market. Several basic forces converged in the early 1970s to lead to an over-turning of the control of oil. These forces included changes in the political and military relationship of the United States and Great Britain in the Middle East, shifts in supply and demand for oil, increasing political control over oil exercised by Third World countries, and the 1973 Yom Kippur War. U.S. domi-nation of the international oil market, operating through large multinational oil companies, came to an end as the price for oil skyrocketed and an em-bargo created shortages in the United States.

Between 1968 and 1971, Great Britain withdrew from its military commit-ments in the Middle East, leaving a political and military vacuum that it had filled for more than a century. During this time the United States was mired in the Vietnam War, which greatly hampered its ability to use military force any-where else in the world. These developments damaged the ability of the West to defend its interests in cheap and plentiful oil.[58]

The early 1970s also provided the culmination of the trends of the pre-ceding fifteen years, during which the world became increasingly dependent on oil from the Middle East. From 1957 to 1972, the proportion of world oil produced in the United States declined from 43.1 percent to 21.1 percent, while the Middle East raised its proportion from 19.4 percent to 41 percent. Over the same period, U.S. oil imports rose from 11 percent of consumption to 35.5 percent.[59] Rapid increases in world production were linked to even more rapid increases in demand for oil. However, by the early 1970s world supplies of oil failed to match increases in demand, primarily due to flat U.S. production growth. This combination created the potential for substantial price increases.[60]

Accompanying these trends was a growing boldness by the countries where the oil was located to challenge control over production and pricing decisions by the great oil multinationals. Beginning in Libya in 1970 and soon spreading to other states, governments used various forms of intimidation to increase their take, their level of participation in ownership of the oil, and even in the price charged. The tightening supply situation helped accelerate this process as countries began leapfrogging each other in terms of price and control. The devaluations of the dollar in 1971 and 1973 also prompted price increases because oil was denominated in dollars. When the United States was

---

[58] The story of the oil crisis of the early 1970s is ably told in Daniel Yergin, *The Prize: The Quest for Oil, Money and Power*, New York: Simon and Schuster, 1991, 563–652.

[59] Darmstadter and Landsberg, "The Economic . . . ," 31–33.

[60] Rostow, *The World . . .*, 257, reports that U.S. growth in oil consumption outstripped produc-tion throughout the postwar era. U.S. production peaked in 1970 and fell each year from 1971 to 1975.

forced to lift import quotas for oil in April 1973, the signal was given for a new round of negotiations.[61]

It was in this context of growing dependence on Middle East oil that Anwar Sadat, president of Egypt, launched an attack on Israel to begin the Yom Kippur War. U.S. support of Israel led several members of the Organization of Petroleum Exporting Countries (OPEC) to push prices up dramatically (from $3.01 to $5.12 per barrel) and to impose an embargo. This consisted of reductions in overall production and a ban on shipments to the United States (and the Netherlands). By January 1974, prices had risen to $11.65 a barrel, and the United States was confronted with a shift in power relations that, in the words of Henry Kissinger, "altered irrevocably the world as it had grown up in the postwar period."[62]

## CONCLUSIONS

In 1941, Henry Luce, publisher of *Life* magazine, wrote effusively of "The American Century." In many ways he was right; the United States was the key player in determining the outcome of World War II and the shape of the postwar world. American money and military might provided the base for projecting a vision of a liberal world order of peace and prosperity. Confrontation with the Soviet Union pushed the United States beyond its original plans and led to a major effort to organize the political and economic resources of the industrial world for containment. Out of this process came a new set of international institutions, new forms of cooperation, and an unprecedented expansion of international trade, capital transfer, and world economic growth. Seen against the record of the preceding century, the years after 1945 were truly epochal.

The economic relationships of the American Century did not last as long as the political and military relationships. The United States largely retained its ability to foster military security but in the process lost many of its economic advantages. The effort to rebuild Europe and Japan as economic powers capable of resisting Soviet pressure worked very well. In the meantime, military spending, foreign aid, and direct investment—the *sine qua non* of U.S. hegemony—kept the balance of payments in deficit and undermined the dollar-gold link that stabilized the international monetary system. When America's political and economic allies took advantage of the liberal system of international trade and greatly expanded their exports in the 1960s, the United States found itself unable to maintain a favorable trade balance. Further, when the growth of the world economy and demand for oil expanded in the 1960s and early 1970s, the United States was unable to prevent Western loss of control over oil production and pricing.

---

[61] For more detail, see Edith Penrose, "The Development of Crisis," in Vernon, *The Oil Crisis*, New York: Norton, 1976, 39-57; and Yergin, *The Prize* ..., 577-587.

[62] Quoted in Yergin, *The Prize* . . ., 588.

Nevertheless, the United States retained great strength; it was by far the largest economy in the world, the predominant source of capital, the biggest export market, and continued as the guarantor of Western security. But in important ways, the game of international political economy had changed. In the first decade or so after the war, the Europeans and Japanese gained their leverage in negotiating with the United States from weakness; and the United States accepted the necessity for sharply limiting any use of coercion to bring about actions it favored. Instead, providing aid and accepting and even promoting discriminatory arrangements such as the EEC were common fare. By the 1970s, increasing European and Japanese economic strength tilted the bargaining relationship. Now adjustments had to come from them, and the United States sometimes found it necessary to coerce these concessions. A much more complex system emerged in which the major capitalist states found that their economic interdependence created a new balance of opposing and conflicting interests. Even parts of the Third World, long simply an arena of military and economic struggle with the Soviets, gained the capacity for independent action. The trick to international order changed from one of U.S. dominance to one of bargaining over the terms for creating and re-creating a framework within which economic competition on a global scale could take place.

American hegemony was essential to creating a political context for restoring international stability and reconstructing a world economy. One very significant consequence was increasing levels of interdependence, especially among industrial states. Paradoxically, the events of the early 1970s led not to fragmentation in the world economy but rather to an explosion of international financial flows, rapidly growing trade, and an increasingly complex interdependence. This globalization process over the next quarter century is our next subject.

## ANNOTATED BIBLIOGRAPHY

William H. Becker and Samuel F. Wells (eds.), *Economics and World Power*, New York: Columbia University Press, 1984.
    Contains several insightful pieces on the history of U.S. foreign economic policy.
Fred Block, *The Origins of International Economic Disorder*, Berkeley: University of California Press, 1977.
    Offers a penetrating analysis of U.S. international monetary policy for the postwar era.
Benjamin Cohen, *Organizing the World's Money*, New York: Basic Books, 1977.
    Very helpful on the economics of international finance.
Jeffrey Frieden, *Banking on the World: The Politics of American International Finance*, New York: Harper & Row, 1987.
    A very useful study of the internationalization of U.S. financial institutions and the international financial system.

Robert Gilpin, *U.S. Power and the Multinational Corporation*, New York: Basic Books, 1975.
> Perhaps the best theoretically informed analysis of U.S. multinational corporations.

Robert Keohane and Joseph Nye, *Power and Interdependence*, Glenview: Scott Foresman, 1989.
> The most important study of the politics of bargaining within a framework of economic interdependence.

Charles Maier, "The Politics of Productivity: Foundations of American International Economic Policy After World War II," *International Organization*, Autumn 1977, 607-633.
> A very perceptive argument concerning the expression of domestic political economy in foreign policy.

John Odell, *U.S. International Monetary Policy*, Princeton: Princeton University Press, 1982.
> The best study of the breakdown and collapse of the Bretton Woods system.

Robert Pollard, *Economic Security and the Origins of the Cold War, 1945-1950*, New York: Columbia University Press, 1985.
> The best single source for understanding the relationship of U.S. political economy and national security from 1945 to 1950.

John G. Ruggie (ed.), *Multinationalism Matters*, New York: Columbia University Press, 1993.
> A collection of articles that help in understanding the multilateral dimension of U.S. hegemony.

W. M. Scammell, *The International Economy Since 1945*, New York: St. Martin's Press, 1983.
> An excellent overview.

Daniel Yergin, *The Prize: The Quest for Oil, Money and Power*, New York: Simon and Schuster, 1991.
> A comprehensive survey of the role of oil in twentieth-century international politics.

## Studies of U.S. Hegemony Include:

Simon Bromley, *American Hegemony and World Oil*, University Park: Pennsylvania State University Press, 1991.

David Calleo, *The Imperious Economy*, Cambridge: Harvard University Press, 1982.
> Defends the thesis that U.S. spending on foreign commitments undermined the domestic economy.

David Calleo, *Beyond American Hegemony*, New York: Basic Books, 1987.
> Relates the end of U.S. hegemony to Europe and NATO.

Stephen Gill, *American Hegemony and the Trilateral Commission*, Cambridge: Cambridge University Press, 1990.
> A brilliant investigation of elite interests in hegemony.

Robert Gilpin, *War and Change in World Politics*, Cambridge: Cambridge University Press, 1981.
> A theoretical investigation of the relationship of international systems, hegemony, and economic decline.

Robert Keohane, *After Hegemony*, Princeton: Princeton University Press, 1984.
    A very important study of international cooperation in the period after U.S. hegemony.
Stephen Krasner, "State Power and the Structure of International Trade," *World Politics*, April 1975, 314–347.
    A key statement of the hegemonic stability thesis.
Joseph Nye, *Bound to Lead*, New York: Basic Books, 1990.
    Counters the thesis that U.S. hegemony has waned.

# Chapter 5

---

# GLOBALIZATION AND
# THE WORLD ECONOMY

The combination of a collapse of the Bretton Woods system of fixed exchange rates and Western control of oil prices and production not only served to end the postwar international economic system. The events also unleashed powerful forces of change that have progressively transformed the world economy. Over the past twenty-five years, cascading waves of change have generated widespread commentary about rising unemployment levels, uncontrolled inflation, skyrocketing interest rates, debt crises, increasing economic integration, massive trade and fiscal deficits, rapid technological change, intensified economic competition, and enormous growth in the international economy. The concept of globalization is the most effective way to understand the nature and consequences of this change.

In the best of circumstances, understanding the present is a very difficult task; real perspective requires some distance in time. This is especially true when change is rapid and involves arrangements with few precedents. Observers often disagree about what is happening: Different people use the same terms to mean quite different things; there are strong debates about the nature and character of change; and it is very hard to sort out definitions, causes, and consequences. But just because it is confusing and hard is no excuse to give up. Our ability to think and act intelligently depends on how we understand the present world.

This chapter uses research on globalization to gain an understanding of the contemporary world economy. We will define *globalization* and discuss several ways of thinking about its causes and consequences. Rising levels of involvement in the world economy, increasing interdependence, the establishment of global markets, prices, and production, and the diffusion of technology and ideas all serve to define *globalization*. This has been brought on by an explosion of international transactions in money, including foreign direct investment by transnational corporations, declines in the cost of transportation and communication, and technological developments. The results of globalization include new constraints on states' ability to manage their economies, shifts in domestic political conflict, new forms of production relationships among transnational firms, and alterations of the terms and stakes associated with international cooperation and competition. Further, the complexity of globalization raises a number of problems for the way we think about international affairs, especially the basic architecture of the world economy and the relationship between firms and states.

The globalization of the world economy is a continuation and extension of trends present since the 1950s but at levels that require new concepts and understanding.[1] Specifically, *globalization* refers to a process of deepening and tightening of the interdependence among actors in the world economy such that the level and character of participation in international economic relations have increased in significant ways. International economic exchange has grown as a proportion of total economic activity, linkages among actors have been intensified and restructured, and new forms of economic relationships have emerged to define a distinctive stage in the development of the world economy. As we shall see, globalization is a process of ongoing change rather than an end state in which borders are meaningless. We do not have a fully globalized world economy, but instead we have experienced new levels and forms of interdependence.

What has happened to provoke observers of the world economy to develop new terminology for thinking about recent changes? We can identify five major developments that define globalization: (1) extremely rapid growth in international financial transactions, (2) rapid growth in trade, especially among transnational firms, (3) very rapid growth in foreign direct investment (FDI), especially by multinational corporations, (4) a decline in market segmentation, the emergence of global markets, and the convergence of many prices on a global scale, and (5) the global diffusion of technology and ideas via a global transportation and communication system. We will regroup these together into changes involving finance and production.[2]

## THE GLOBALIZATION OF FINANCE

Understanding the nature and sources of change can best be done by reviewing events after 1971, isolating the various elements of globalization and the reasons for these developments. As we have seen in Chapter 4, the combination of widespread currency convertibility, pumping dollars into foreign

---

[1] Indeed, a longer perspective shows that we have now returned to levels of interdependence found at the beginning of the twentieth century. For a detailed comparison of earlier and present-day interdependence, see David Henderson, "International Economic Integration: Progress, Prospects and Implications," *International Affairs*, 68.4, 1992, 633–653. See Chapter 3 for a discussion of the earlier era.

[2] This chapter will not attempt to examine all the many features of globalization. For a discussion of transnational social actors and globalization, see George Lopez, Jackie Smith, and Ron Pagnucco, "The Global Tide," *Bulletin of Atomic Scientists,* July/August 1995, 33–39.

hands via U.S. current account deficits, the expansion of U.S. multinational corporations abroad with the ability to transfer funds across national boundaries, and the emergence and growth of the Eurodollar market generated a large volume of internationalized resources. What's more, many of these resources were very liquid; that is, they could be converted to cash and moved quickly from country to country. The actual and potential conversion of dollars into gold, combined with speculative purchases of undervalued currencies such as yen and deutsche marks, helped precipitate the financial crises that ended the Bretton Woods system.

The collapse of fixed exchange rates in 1973 opened the door to much greater volatility in exchange rates and the growth of foreign exchange markets. But the most important immediate spur to internationalization came from the quadrupling of oil prices in 1973–1974 and the tripling of prices in 1979–1980. The massive transfer of funds from global consumers to oil producers had complex consequences for international finance. Many oil states preferred keeping balances of dollars and other convertible currencies in large Western banks. These banks needed to find investment outlets for their new-found deposits and turned to developing countries who were often eager to borrow. Over the rest of the 1970s, loans to such nations were readily available, and Third World debt grew rapidly. Between 1973 and 1979, the debt of Third World nations rose sixfold, from $100 billion to $600 billion.[3]

The growth of international deposits and debt—of a system of markets for international borrowers, investors, and speculators—exploded in size and complexity in the 1980s. Two events played a key role: the financial and trade imbalances of the United States after 1981 and a series of decisions by governments to end controls on the movement of capital across their borders.

The unprecedented increase in oil prices in 1973–1974 and 1979–1980 forced several important adjustments to the world economy. Paying for higher oil prices had a major impact on the economies of the developed and developing worlds. Because oil was essential for the functioning of all these economic systems, demand can be described as highly inelastic. That is, the short-term and near-term demands for oil remained about the same in spite of the price increases. The consequence was a combination of reduced purchases of other goods and a substantial rise in inflation as monetary authorities increased the quantity of money in circulation in order to offset oil price increases. Between 1974 and 1976 and between 1980 and 1982, many countries in the developed world experienced a serious case of stagflation— declining economic activity and rising prices. Historically, these rarely went together because recessions were thought to be a cure for inflation and vice versa. For the first time since the end of World War II, significant and persistent economic dislocation descended on the world economy.

---

[3] John C. Pool and Steve Stamos, *The ABC's of International Finance*, Lexington: Lexington Books, 1987, 86. See Chapter 12 for more detail on the debt crisis.

The United States also faced a declining dollar in addition to rising prices and a stagnant economy. But politically there was very strong support for addressing the problems of inflation and the dollar, even if that led to a weaker economy. The Federal Reserve, under Paul Volcker, adopted a very tight monetary policy that pushed interest rates to unprecedented levels and brought on a deep recession in 1981–1982. These actions also contributed to a serious world recession.

Largely in response to the economic difficulties of the 1970s and early 1980s, several strategies for economic revitalization emerged in the United States and elsewhere. Deregulation and large tax cuts were thought by many conservatives to be the mechanism for a return to strong economic growth and higher rates of savings and investment. Parallel to these ideas were worries about Soviet military power and risk taking, which reached a peak following the Soviet invasion of Afghanistan in late 1979. The solution was seen in much higher U.S. defense spending. The election of Ronald Reagan in 1980 brought together, once again, the political economy of the early 1960s: tax cuts and sharply higher defense spending. The result was a series of the largest peacetime budget deficits in U.S. history.

Imbalances in the U.S. economy spilled over into the world economy. Indeed, it was this link to the rest of the world that permitted some success for Reaganomics. The large budget deficits, combined with a looser monetary policy, produced a significant stimulus to demand and economic growth in the United States after 1982, including a significant rise in consumer and business spending. But as proportions of gross domestic product (GDP), both savings and investment fell while consumption rose. The greatest beneficiaries of the Reagan years were those at the highest income levels. Also accompanying the budget deficits were interest rates that were high relative to those in other countries. This served to attract funds into U.S. investments (these investments provided the funds that otherwise would need to be diverted from U.S. consumption to buy the government debt that closed the government spending gap), which produced large increases in the exchange rate of the dollar. The rising dollar tended to raise the prices of U.S. exports and to lower the prices of imports. This led to massive increases in the trade deficit, especially with the Japanese. The effort at revitalization worked in the sense that world economic growth occurred. But this came at a price—large trade deficits, even larger budget deficits, massive increases in the national debt and U.S. foreign debt, and very large swings in exchange rates.

The imbalances in the world economy are shown in Figure 5.1, which details the current account balances of the three major trading states. The current account balances of the United States, Germany, and Japan hovered around zero until 1981, when the expansion of the U.S. deficit was mirrored in the large German and Japanese surpluses. Remember from the earlier discussion of the balance of payments that a deficit (or surplus) in the current account is offset by a surplus (or deficit) in the capital account. The large and persistent U.S. current account deficit of the 1980s was sustained by a flow of

**FIGURE 5.1**

**Comparative Balance of Payments
Current Account Balance**

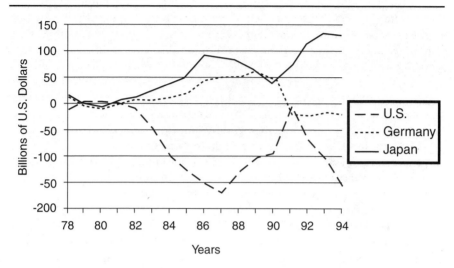

SOURCE: International Monetary Fund, *International Financial Statistics Yearbook*, 1995, 144.

capital into the United States from abroad, and this contributed much to the globalization of capital.

Also important to this process was a series of decisions—from the mid-1970s to the early 1990s—by many nations to eliminate long-standing restrictions on the ability of capital to cross their borders. Following the onset of the world depression in 1929, many states had turned to capital controls to insulate themselves from the impact of short-term capital flows on economic policy. The Bretton Woods system provided for extensive controls, and until the 1980s most states had used them to restrict (but not prevent) international flows of capital. The end of Bretton Woods led most wealthy states to end capital controls. These decisions both reflected the progression of globalization and contributed to this process.

During the period of 1971 to 1973, when the Bretton Woods order was in severe crisis, Europe and Japan preferred efforts by all states to cooperate in establishing new and much more restrictive controls on capital movement. In an effort to save the system, they wanted to reduce speculation against currencies that was undermining fixed exchange rates. These efforts were blocked by the United States, thereby ensuring the end of Bretton Woods. And in 1974 the United States moved unilaterally to end its own capital controls.[4]

---

[4]Eric Helleiner, *States and the Reemergence of Global Finance,* Ithaca: Cornell University Press, 1994, 102–112.

The U.S. decision did not lead immediately to similar actions by other states. Rather, for the next several years some powerful states needed to learn the growing ability of capital markets to influence their choices. In 1976, Great Britain was engaged in deficit spending (financed in part by foreign borrowing) to recover from the deep recession that began two years earlier. When creditors withdrew from providing additional lending, some British leaders looked to the option of extreme capital restrictions. This would prevent capital from exiting Britain, reduce pressure on the pound, and permit domestic borrowing to resume. The Labour government eventually rejected this option and instead accepted an internationally arranged deal that required Britain to cut government spending in return for additional loans.

Similarly, in 1978-1979 the United States was pursuing a stimulative policy, the effect of which was to require international support of the dollar. When this support faltered, the dollar began to plummet. Like the British, the United States rejected capital controls and moved toward restricting government spending and higher interest rates rather than return to capital controls.

And the French, suffering from economic recession in the wake of oil price increases, in 1981 elected a government committed to unilateral economic expansion. Financial markets quickly began selling francs, and the French government confronted the same choices that the British and Americans had. Over a two-year period, the Mitterrand government was forced to adopt an ever more restrictive economic policy in order to preserve France's international financial position. In each of these cases, the British, French, and Americans had the option of imposing capital controls as a way of avoiding unpleasant economic choices. This was rejected because to do so would require a withdrawal from the world economy at enormous political and economic costs.[5]

The U.S. capital liberalization of 1974, and the weakening of capital controls as an option in the three cases just discussed, came against a backdrop of rapidly growing international financial markets (see below for more detail). During the 1980s and 1990s, most nations in the advanced world removed all controls on capital movement—actions that acknowledged the power of these markets and contributed to their growth. In large part, these decisions were motivated by competition among states to attract international financial business or simply to avoid being left behind. In 1981, looking to shift some of the burgeoning Euromarket business to its shores, the United States legalized international banking facilities. In 1984, desperately needing international funds to finance its massive budget deficits, the United States reached a yen-dollar agreement with Japan that liberalized Japanese finance and made possible large Japanese investments in the United States. Propelled by competition from the United States, the British government of Margaret Thatcher abolished all capital controls and in 1986 opened the London Stock Exchange

---

[5] Helleiner, *States and ...,* 123-145.

to foreign securities dealers. The competitive dynamic between the United States and Great Britain resulted from the fact that international capital was attracted to those areas with the greatest freedom of action and the most liquid markets.

The lead taken by the Americans and British in capital liberalization was followed by most other industrial countries. Japan, since 1950 the most vigorous practitioner of capital restrictions, was moved toward relaxation by a combination of U.S. pressure, lobbying by foreign multinationals and segments of Japanese business, and the huge profit opportunities available to Japan in international finance. After 1981 the enormous current account surpluses with the United States and the rest of the world provided Japan with hundreds of billions of dollars for international investment. These realities helped shift the Japanese government to expand the limited liberalization adopted before 1981, primarily by permitting yen-based activity in Euromarkets, progressively lifting de facto capital controls, and allowing international banking facilities (offshore operations) in Japan.[6]

Led by Germany, Denmark, and the Netherlands, states in the European Economic Community also took steps to liberalize policies on capital movement in the early 1980s. Later in the decade, they were joined by France and Italy. In many ways these were defensive acts, made necessary by the U.S. and British liberalizations. In order to keep capital from migrating to New York and London, these states needed to lift existing restrictions. In the late 1980s, jumping onto the bandwagon, New Zealand, Australia, Norway, and Finland engaged in the deregulation and liberalization of finance.[7]

In one sense, removing restrictions on capital movement simply restored the openness of the late nineteenth and early twentieth centuries. Liberals would see this as the natural and most efficient state of affairs. But this view is too easy because these changes were really a continuation of the demise of Bretton Woods. Fixed exchange rates and capital controls went together, and the end of fixed rates made controls less viable. Why did these changes happen? The Bretton Woods order resulted, in part, from an effort by states to manage markets to their own ends—mainly expanding domestic economic growth. Events after 1971 suggest a sharp decline in the ability of states to control markets. This is not to say that states were not essential for creating a political context for market activity. Rather, what happened was a shift in the power relationship of states and markets.

---

[6] Helleiner, *States and . . .,* 152–156; Frances M. Rosenbluth, *Financial Politics in Contemporary Japan,* Ithaca: Cornell University Press, 1989, 50–89; Dennis Encarnation and Mark Mason, "Neither MITI nor America: The Political Economy of Capital Liberalization in Japan," *International Organization,* 44.1, Winter 1990, 25–54; John Goodman and Louis Pauly, "The Obsolescence of Capital Controls? Economic Management in an Age of Global Markets," *World Politics,* 46.1, October 1993, 64–70; Yoichi Shinkai, "The Internationalization of Finance in Japan," in Takashi Inoguchi and Daniel Okimoto (eds.), *The Political Economy of Japan: The Changing International Context,* Stanford: Stanford University Press, 1988, 249–271.

[7] Helleiner, *States and . . .,* 156–166; Goodman and Pauly, "The Obsolescence . . ."

## Indicators of Financial Globalization

The cumulative result of changes after 1973 was the exponential growth of the global trading of foreign exchange and the less spectacular but significant growth in international lending and equities trading. The basic point of trying to understand the globalization of finance is to see how much international financial flows have grown in proportion to other international activity and in proportion to national resources.

By the 1980s, global trading in foreign exchange had come to dwarf global trade in goods and services, and until the present it has grown much more rapidly than has trade. This can be seen Figure 5.2, which displays the level of daily foreign exchange trading in relation to the level of global trade. In 1986 foreign exchange trading was twenty-five times the level of world trade; by 1995, it had expanded to a level that was eighty-one times the level of trade.

**FIGURE 5.2**
**Ratio of Daily Foreign Exchange Trading to World Exports, 1986–1995**

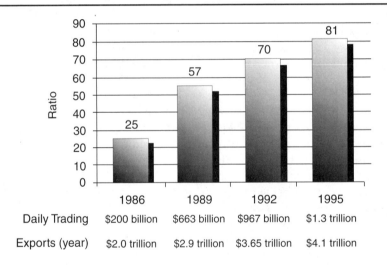

| | 1986 | 1989 | 1992 | 1995 |
|---|---|---|---|---|
| Daily Trading | $200 billion | $663 billion | $967 billion | $1.3 trillion |
| Exports (year) | $2.0 trillion | $2.9 trillion | $3.65 trillion | $4.1 trillion |

Historically, most buying and selling of foreign exchange was the result of international trade, as buyers and sellers of foreign goods and services needed another currency to settle their transactions. But clearly, the foreign exchange market is now largely disconnected from trade. The players in these markets are large banks and corporations attempting to make money and/or defend profits.

Other indicators of financial globalization include the growth of foreign exchange trading relative to the reserves of foreign exchange held by states, the dispersal of reserves away from the United States, growth in international lending and equities trading, and the increasing integration of global financial markets. Figure 5.3 provides data about the relationship between foreign exchange trading and the foreign exchange reserves of states. It is these reserves that nations use to intervene in markets to try to influence exchange rates.

**FIGURE 5.3**

**Foreign Exchange Trading/Reserves**
*(Billions of U.S. Dollars)*

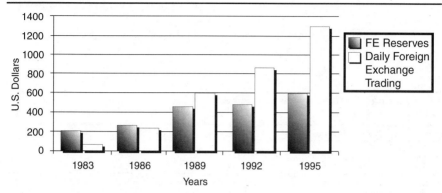

SOURCE: *The Economist,* October 7, 1995

We can see that even as late as 1983 the foreign exchange reserves of the largest industrial countries were more than double the level of daily foreign exchange trading. By 1995 trading was double the level of reserves. This probably overstates the ability of states to influence foreign exchange markets because reserves are now much less concentrated and much more globalized.

Table 5.1 presents data about the distribution of foreign exchange reserves among nations.

**TABLE 5.1**

**Globalization of Foreign Exchange Reserves, 1964–1995**
*(Billions of U.S. Dollars)*

| COUNTRY | 1964 | 1973 | 1986 | 1995 |
|---|---|---|---|---|
| Industrial: | | | | |
|     United States | 16.7 | 11.9 | 39.8 | 54.0 |
|     Germany | 7.9 | 27.5 | 45.6 | 74.9 |
|     France | 5.7 | 7.1 | 28.6 | — |
|     Japan | 2.0 | 10.2 | 35.4 | 170.0 |
|     Switzerland | 3.3 | 7.1 | 20.7 | — |
|     United Kingdom | 2.3 | 5.4 | 15.7 | 37.0 |
| Developing: | | | | |
|     Taiwan | 0.3 | 0.9 | 38.1 | 84.0 |
|     China | — | — | 9.8 | 71.0 |
|     Singapore | 0.4 | 1.9 | 10.6 | 63.0 |
|     Hong Kong | — | — | — | 53.0 |
|     Brazil | 0.2 | 5.3 | 4.8 | 44.0 |
|     Thailand | 0.7 | 1.1 | 2.4 | 31.0 |
| Industrial Total | 58.2 | 111.6 | 279.6 | 650.0 |
| Developing Total | 10.9 | 41.1 | 172.7 | 690.0 |
| World Total | 69.1 | 152.7 | 452.3 | 1,340.0 |

SOURCE: International Monetary Fund, *International Financial Statistics Yearbook,* 1994; *The Economist,* November 18, 1995, 82.

The data make clear the dramatic shift in foreign exchange holdings over the thirty years from 1964 to 1995. Resources have shifted away from the United States toward Japan and away from industrial countries generally and toward developing states.

The volume of international borrowing and trading in equities has also increased substantially. Table 5.2 shows the annual levels of international lending.

**TABLE 5.2**
**International Capital Markets Annual Borrowing**
*(Billions of U.S. Dollars)*

| 1990 | 1991 | 1992 | 1993 | 1994 |
| --- | --- | --- | --- | --- |
| $435 | $536 | $610 | $819 | $955 |

SOURCE: Organization for Economic Cooperation and Development, *International Financial Markets*, 1995.

The level of activity more than doubled from 1990 to 1994. By 1994 outstanding international bonds and international bank loans totaled $6 trillion. Regarding international equity markets, in 1991 there was approximately $1.1 trillion in transactions involving just the United States, Britain, and Japan.[8] Perhaps the strongest arguments for financial globalization and also for understanding the limits of globalization come from analysis of the degree of integration of financial markets. There are several ways to think about market integration. One way is accessibility—can trading take place in various markets at roughly the same cost for transactions? The immense volume in international financial markets indicate a high level of accessibility and rapidly declining barriers to trading. A second and more precise indicator of market integration is whether the same security asset trades at the same price in different markets. One measure shows that after capital controls were eliminated, the wide differences in French franc-denominated interest rates declined to practically zero.[9] This is not to say that international financial markets are completely integrated. Domestic savings is still much more important for investment, and investors still prefer domestic investment over foreign. But stock markets and interest rates move together, driven by the vast sums that do cross borders.

## Explaining the Globalization of Finance

Trying to understand the reasons for the globalization of finance is entangled with sorting out the consequences of these changes. Put another way, scholars

[8] The data on outstanding international lending are found in International Monetary Fund, *World Economic Outlook*, May 1995, 80; the information about equity trading is in Andrew C. Sobel, *Domestic Choices, International Markets*, Ann Arbor: University of Michigan Press, 1994, 52.

[9] "The World Economy," *The Economist*, October 7, 1995, 6; IMF, *World Economic Outlook*, May 1995, 80–81; and R. J. Barry Jones, *Globalisation and Interdependence in the International Political Economy*, London: Pinter, 1995, 104–118.

have not been able to agree about cause and effect. As with most important phenomena in the study of political economy, identifying causation is a complex matter. Disagreement often results from different broad theories about how political and economic life is constructed. And such theories sometimes turn on differences in whether causal priority is given to states or to markets. When governments acted to liberalize capital markets or to shift from fixed to floating exchange rates, were they being carried along by overwhelming market forces or were they acting to manage market forces to their advantage?

How you answer this question may depend on whether you believe that politics or markets has primal force in moving events.[10] Or you might adopt the view, as we do, that politics and markets are always codetermined but that over time the primacy of one over the other can change. Another way to see this process is to notice that actors whose main arena is markets—banks and corporations—sometimes gain strength relative to actors whose main arena is politics—presidents, prime ministers, and heads of central banks. A useful way to think about globalization is to ask why the evident power shift from state actors to market players has taken place.

We have seen how political and economic events such as the breakdown of Bretton Woods, the oil crisis, and the debt crisis contributed to globalization. But in significant ways, these events were made possible by the extraordinary changes in technology after 1970. The combination of developments in computers, telecommunications, and satellites has altered the cost and the scale of communications systems. Not only have costs fallen dramatically, but also it is now possible for even small economic units to maintain or participate in an instantaneous and continuous communication system on a global scale. Moreover, the creation of a global system with millions of members has made information and its interpretation an extremely important commodity. Events like those we have considered helped create the opportunities for profit and the need for sophisticated global communications, and advances in microcircuitry have made possible a larger and larger scale for communication systems. Responding to market opportunities made possible by technology, firms have developed a much greater variety of international financial instruments that have the effect of expanding markets further. And as markets grew larger—with more participants, markets became more regularized—understanding increased and more banks and corporations became participants.[11]

The rapid growth in international financial markets confronted states with difficult choices related to monetary policies and capital controls. Over

---

[10] For examples of very different approaches to the process of capital liberalization, see Richard McKenzie and Dwight Lee, *Quicksilver Capital*, New York: Free Press, 1991. McKenzie and Lee celebrate what they see as the irresistible force of markets on governments. By contrast, see Philip Cerny, "The Limits of Deregulation: Transnational Interpenetration and Policy Change," *European Journal of Political Research*, 19, 1991, 173-196. Cerny makes a compelling case that deregulation of one sort was replaced by reregulation of another, so as to make supposedly free markets work.

[11] A fascinating discussion of various techniques for using computers to make investment decisions is in "Frontiers of Finance," *The Economist*, October 9, 1993.

the 1970s and 1980s, an increasingly large volume of money controlled by many global actors could be moved across borders in search of profit and often in response to government policies. And these actors—usually banks, large institutional investors, and multinational corporations—developed strong interests in this freedom of international financial maneuvering. The size of markets and changes in technology made certain government policies—especially capital controls—more and more difficult. And markets would reward other policies, especially liberalization, by increasing resources and business in the most liberal locations. Governments essentially confronted the choice between absolute controls—which were very difficult to enforce and required virtual withdrawal from the world economy—and no controls at all. Over time, most countries chose to attract or retain their share of these resources by eliminating controls and liberalizing the opportunities for investment. At stake was the competitive position and future prosperity of the nation and its firms.[12]

## The Consequences of Financial Globalization

In the most elemental sense, globalization means that money moves quickly in large volume and with few restrictions across national boundaries. The decisions of money managers and speculators are very sensitive to expectations about financial, production, and political conditions, and their task is to act before events occur. They want to profit from change or at least to avoid losses.[13] What does this mean? As globalization proceeds, financial capital is increasingly able to leave a country, responding to conditions judged adverse to profits, and to shift to currencies where profit opportunities are relatively better. This ability to leave—capital holders essentially "vote" with their "feet"—enhances greatly the structural power of capital. That is, "international capital mobility systematically constrains state behavior by rewarding some actions and punishing others."[14]

Increased power to capital has significant political and economic consequences. Capital mobility and flexible exchange rates tend to negate the monetary policy adopted by a single nation. That is, a nation acting to establish its

---

[12] Goodman and Pauly, "The Obsolescence . . ."

[13] We should keep in mind that there is actually only a small number of currencies for holding short-term financial resources. Traders in foreign exchange have a small range of opportunities to place their funds. Most short-term trades are in five currencies: the dollar, yen, deutsche mark, pound, and Swiss franc. More than 70 percent of the pairs (remember that foreign exchange trading is one currency for another) in foreign exchange trading involve two of these five currencies. Further, 80 percent of all foreign exchange trading has the dollar as one of the pair of currencies. See David Eitenman, *Multinational Business Finance*, Reading: Addison-Wesley, 1995, 87, 90.

[14] David Andrews, "Capital Mobility and State Autonomy: Toward a Structural Theory of International Monetary Relations," *International Studies Quarterly,* 38, 1994, 197. Also see Vincent Cable, "The Diminished Nation-State: A Study in the Loss of Economic Power," *Daedalus,* Spring 1995, 23–53. For a review of this process as it affects specific countries, see Chapters 1 and 6.

monetary policy alone may have its purposes thwarted by globalized capital. Consider the following situation. Nation A wants to dampen inflation in its country by raising interest rates and slowing the growth of its money supply. But the effect of raising interest rates alone is to attract international capital, which results in increasing the money supply. The reverse situation is also common. Nation B wants to stimulate its economy by lowering interest rates and expanding government spending and deficits. Holders of liquid assets in B's currency are likely to flee because interest rates are falling relative to the rest of the world. Further, increasing budget deficits in B point to higher inflation. The decline in the money supply and in international investment could easily offset any expansion from monetary and fiscal policy.

The key point is that global capital flows penalize states whose economic policies are not in sync with the rest of the world. The only way to engage in an effective monetary policy is to cooperate, overtly or tacitly, with other states so as to raise and lower interest rates together.[15] In this way relative changes in interest rates are minimal, and international capital flows should be small. But, in practice, this often means that monetary and fiscal policies are sharply constricted because coordination among several states may be difficult to organize. Politically, this challenges the viability of basic arrangements worked out after World War II.

A fundamental element of the Bretton Woods system of fixed exchange rates was to shield each nation from having international trade and exchange rates influence its domestic economic policy. Remember that liberalization of the world economy under Bretton Woods was limited by the belief that governments could and should promote economic growth through independent actions. Memories of the 1930s Great Depression were strong, as was the need to diffuse radicalism among workers through sustained economic growth. Expanding the economic pie through managed economic growth was seen by many as the best strategy. A compromise between capitalists and workers could be arranged through government efforts to pump up the economy whenever growth waned. The Bretton Woods system of fixed exchange rates and limits on capital movement insulated domestic economies from international pressure to reverse growth policies.

This arrangement—known as Keynesianism or "embedded liberalism"—has been distinctly eroded by the globalization of capital markets.[16] Moreover, various groups in many countries have seen their economic and political positions helped and hurt by the same changes. Generally, holders of mobile capital have seen their rewards and bargaining power enhanced relative to groups

---

[15] This assumes that states want to influence monetary policy and are not willing to let the exchange rate of the currency rise and fall to any level. If a government is willing to forfeit any influence on exchange rates, then an independent monetary policy is possible.

[16] For the concept of "embedded liberalism," see John Gerard Ruggie, "International Regimes, Transactions, and Change: Embedded Liberalism in the Postwar Economic Order," *International Organization*, 36.2, 1982, 379–415.

whose resources are less mobile. This usually means that workers and manufacturers with large fixed investments that cannot easily be liquidated and moved. Once again, it is the option to shift resources to places with higher returns that enhances the structural power of capital. The rise of global capital opportunities means that mobile capital will invest in areas where, for example, the cost of labor relative to productivity is lowest. This puts downward pressure on wages and bargaining leverage by workers in high-cost countries. Some of the consequences of globalization are the lack of growth in real incomes in the United States for twenty years (in spite of growth in productivity) and very high unemployment rates in Europe.

The political leadership of many countries has been forced to shift their efforts away from growth via monetary and fiscal policy. Instead, most have concentrated on actions that enhance the competitiveness of their nation. That is, governments focus on making their territory as attractive to business as possible. This can include giving tax and other incentives, creating a favorable regulatory environment, and giving subsidies that shift costs of production to the entire society. The competitiveness strategy chosen may differ depending on whether the government in power is left or right. Left governments may be more likely to facilitate efforts by workers to adjust quickly to changes in the world markets. This usually means increasing the productivity of labor and subsidies to investment rather than forcing down wages. Conservative governments are more likely to reduce welfare programs so as to reduce wage levels and lower tax levels in order to increase returns to business.[17]

In brief, the consequences of the globalization of capital are substantial. The basic structure of political arrangements in postwar domestic politics has been undermined, and the autonomy of states has been reduced. Prior to about 1980, governments throughout the industrialized world regularly focused substantial attention on domestic economic management through fiscal and monetary policy. Today, the maneuverability on fiscal policy has been greatly restricted, and monetary policy is closely tied to the interests of global capital. Governments devote much more attention to coordinating monetary and fiscal policies. Their chief concern is to adopt policies that are consistent with the investment priorities of global capital. The previous concerns over raising wages and expanding employment have given way to fears of the effects of too much growth and employment on inflation. Governments cannot take steps that might lead holders of liquid capital to shift their funds to other sites. Global capital's preference for slow economic growth in production of goods and services—an environment conducive to low inflation and preserving the value of liquid capital—is in the ascendancy. Reports of "excessive" economic growth or falling unemployment rates spark rising interest rates

---

[17] Geoffrey Garrett and Peter Lange, "Political Responses to Interdependence: What's Left for the Left?" *International Organization*, 45.4, 1991, 539-564; and Geoffrey Garrett, "Capital Mobility, Trade, and the Domestic Politics of Economic Policy," *International Organization*, 49.4, Autumn 1995, 657-687.

and quick government efforts to reassure global capital thorough restrictive monetary policy. Labor unions have declined in political influence, and welfare states have eroded, while active market players have seen their interests, positions, and incomes enhanced.

# THE GLOBALIZATION OF PRODUCTION

Advances in the globalization of production and direct investment have not been as dramatic and fast paced as those in finance. Nevertheless, changes in the past twenty-five years have been very significant and are the result mainly of the growth and development of multinational corporations (MNCs) as major actors in world affairs. Indeed, the actions of multinational financial, production, and distribution enterprises are primarily responsible for globalization. In this section, we will examine both the reasons for the increasingly international activities of these organizations and the consequences of this activity. Especially important are the magnitude of MNCs, the expansion of foreign direct investment, changing patterns of the organization of international production and trade, the diffusion of technology, and new forms of relationships among firms.

## Trade Globalization

The globalization of trade since the 1970s has restored and even surpassed the levels of trade interdependence seen earlier in the twentieth century. World exports as a proportion of world production rose consistently after 1840, peaked in 1913, recovered after 1950, but surpassed 1913 levels only in the mid-1970s. That is, after 1970 more and more production has been destined for international trade.[18] During the decade from 1985 to 1994, trade grew twice as fast as global output. Periods of global economic expansion are especially prone to rapid increases in trade. For example, in 1994 world output grew by 5 percent while world trade increased by over 9 percent. The United States has experienced more change than have most advanced countries. Since 1978 exports plus imports of goods and services have increased from 17.3 percent to 22.3 percent of U.S. GDP.[19]

It is multinational corporations who dominate international production and trade, controlling "over one quarter of the world's economic activity

---

[18] For reasons that we will explain later, using international trade understates the level of international production. This measure misses production by multinational firms that takes place abroad for sale in the country of production. That is, international trade misses much of the production resulting from foreign direct investment (FDI).

[19] International Monetary Fund, *International Financial Statistics*, 1995, 150–152. Bank for International Settlements, *65th Annual Report*, Basel, June 12, 1995, 45; Janice Thompson and Stephen Krasner, "Global Transactions and the Consolidation of Sovereignty," in Robert Art and Robert Jervis (eds.), *International Politics*, New York: HarperCollins, 1996, 323.

*outside* their home countries; over half the world trade in manufactured goods and even more of the growing trade in services; 80 percent of the world's land cultivated for export crops, and the lion's share of the world's technological innovations."[20]

What is the geography of this trade? Figure 5.4 reveals a triad of global trade focused on Europe, East Asia, and North America and the exchange among these regions. More than one fifth of world trade occurs among European states and another 30 percent between these European states and North America, Asia, and the rest of the world.

**FIGURE 5.4**

**Distribution of World Trade**
*(Percent of Total World Trade)*

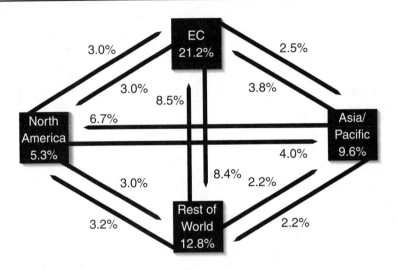

SOURCE: *The Economist,* September 22, 1990, special section on "World Trade," page 6.

In Chapter 6 we will consider whether this and other data demonstrate globalization or regionalization.

Which countries have the greatest impact on trade? Table 5.3 shows a "top ten" list of exporters and importers for 1993. How important are exports to the economic prosperity of nations? From Figure 5.5 we can see considerable variance in the impact of trade on national economies. But, except for Japan, each of these fifteen rich nations has seen exports increase as a proportion of GDP over the past thirty-five years.

---

[20] John Stopford and Susan Strange, *Rival States, Rival Firms: Competition for World Market Shares,* Cambridge: Cambridge University Press, 1991, 15.

**TABLE 5.3**

**Exports and Imports of Goods and Services**
*(Billions of Current Dollars; Figures Are for 1993–1994)*

| COUNTRY | EXPORTS GOODS | EXPORTS SERVICES | TOTAL G&S EXPORTS | IMPORTS GOODS | IMPORTS SERVICES | TOTAL G&S IMPORTS |
|---|---|---|---|---|---|---|
| United States | 503 | 195 | 698 | 669 | 133 | 802 |
| Germany | 427 | 61 | 488 | 376 | 100 | 476 |
| Japan | 384 | 61 | 445 | 238 | 110 | 348 |
| France | 223 | 92 | 315 | 214 | 73 | 287 |
| U.K. | 207 | 59 | 266 | 223 | 52 | 275 |
| Italy | 190 | 60 | 250 | 154 | 58 | 212 |
| Canada | 164 | 19 | 183 | 151 | 27 | 188 |
| Netherlands | 138 | 39 | 177 | 123 | 38 | 161 |
| Belgium | 107 | 37 | 144 | 100 | 31 | 131 |
| South Korea | 94 | 20 | 114 | 97 | 21 | 118 |

SOURCE: IMF, *International Financial Statistics Yearbook*, 1995.

**FIGURE 5.5**

**Exports of Goods and Services as a percent of GDP**

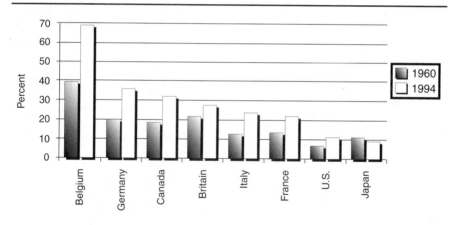

SOURCE: *The Economist,* April 1, 1995, 89.

The expansion of international trade is the product of firms, mostly multinational firms. The term *multinational corporation* refers to a corporation that has a significant commitment of its resources (including sales and production) to operations in several nations. For example, Toyota—the Japanese car company, which in 1975 operated mostly in Japan—has substantially globalized its operations. In 1995 Toyota had nine parts plants in seven countries other than Japan, twenty-nine assembly plants in twenty-five countries, and four research and development facilities in two countries. Toyota's international sales represent 42 percent of its total sales.[21] The United Nations estimated in the early 1990s that parent company MNCs totaled 35,000 worldwide with 147,000 foreign affiliates. More than 85 percent of the parent companies are from developed countries.[22] Many of these companies rival large nations in the resources they control. This can be seen in Table 5.4.

**TABLE 5.4**

**One Hundred Fifty of the Largest Countries and Industrial Corporations**
*(Ranked by Annual GDP and Sales in Millions of Dollars, 1992)*

| | | | | | |
|---|---|---|---|---|---|
| 1 | United States | 5,920,199 | 26 | Saudi Arabia | 111,343 |
| 2 | Japan | 3,670,979 | 27 | Thailand | 110,337 |
| 3 | Germany | 1,789,261 | 28 | Iran | 110,258 |
| 4 | France | 1,319,883 | 29 | South Africa | 103,651 |
| 5 | Italy | 1,222,962 | 30 | Exxon | 103,547 |
| 6 | United Kingdom | 903,126 | 31 | Ford Motor | 100,785.6 |
| 7 | Spain | 574,844 | 32 | Turkey | 99,696 |
| 8 | China | 506,075 | 33 | Royal Dutch/Shell Group | 98,935.3 |
| 9 | Canada | 493,602 | 34 | Ukraine | 94,831 |
| 10 | Russia | 387,476 | 35 | Finland | 93,869 |
| 11 | Brazil | 360,405 | 36 | Poland | 83,823 |
| 12 | Mexico | 329,011 | 37 | Portugal | 79,547 |
| 13 | Netherlands | 320,290 | 38 | Toyota Motor | 79,114.2 |
| 14 | Rep of Korea | 296,136 | 39 | Hong Kong | 77,828 |
| 15 | Australia | 294,760 | 40 | Israel | 69,762 |
| 16 | Switzerland | 241,406 | 41 | IRI | 67,547.4 |
| 17 | Argentina | 228,779 | 42 | Greece | 67,278 |
| 18 | Sweden | 220,834 | 43 | IBM | 65,096 |
| 19 | Belgium | 218,836 | 44 | Daimler-Benz | 63,339.5 |
| 20 | India | 214,598 | 45 | General Electric | 62,202 |
| 21 | Austria | 185,235 | 46 | Hitachi | 61,465.5 |
| 22 | General Motors | 132,744.9 | 47 | Venezuela | 61,137 |
| 23 | Indonesia | 126,364 | 48 | British Petroleum | 59,215.7 |
| 24 | Denmark | 123,546 | 49 | Malaysia | 57,568 |
| 25 | Norway | 112,906 | 50 | Matsushita Electric | 57,480.8 |

[21] Toyota, *Annual Report*, 1995, 14–15; "Multinationals," *The Economist*, March 27, 1993, 7. Ford Motor Company is much more globalized in its operations than is Toyota. Ford produces almost three fifths of its production outside the United States, mostly in Europe. See Peter Dicken, *Global Shift*, New York: Guilford Press, 1992, 290, 298.

[22] United Nations, *World Investment Report, 1992: Transnational Corporations as Engines of Growth,* New York: United Nations, 1992, 12.

**TABLE 5.4 (CONTINUED)**

## One Hundred Fifty of the Largest Countries and Industrial Corporations
*(Ranked by Annual GDP and Sales in Millions of Dollars, 1992)*

| | | | | | |
|---|---|---|---|---|---|
| 51 | Mobil | 57,389 | 90 | Hoescht | 29,570.6 |
| 52 | Volkswagen | 56,734.1 | 91 | Peugeot | 29,387.4 |
| 53 | Philppines | 52,462 | 92 | Kazakhstan | 28,580 |
| 54 | Siemens | 51,401.9 | 93 | BASF | 28,494.3 |
| 55 | Nissan Motor | 50,247.5 | 94 | Morocco | 28,401 |
| 56 | Philip Morris | 50,157 | 95 | NEC | 28,376.5 |
| 57 | Samsung | 49,559.6 | 96 | Daewoo | 28,333.9 |
| 58 | Colombia | 48,583 | 97 | Fujitsu | 27,910.7 |
| 59 | Fiat | 47,928.7 | 98 | Bayer | 26,625.3 |
| 60 | Singapore | 46,025 | 99 | Mitsubishi Electric | 26,502.3 |
| 61 | Unilever | 43,962.6 | 100 | Czech Republic | 26,187 |
| 62 | Ireland | 43,294 | 101 | Total | 26,141.5 |
| 63 | United Arab Emirates | 42,467 | 102 | Amoco | 25,543 |
| 64 | Pakistan | 41,904 | 103 | Mitsubishi Motors | 25,482.2 |
| 65 | New Zealand | 41,304 | 104 | Romania | 24,438 |
| 66 | Chile | 41,203 | 105 | Nippon Steel | 23,990.8 |
| 67 | ENI | 40,365.5 | 106 | Bangladesh | 23,783 |
| 68 | ELF Aquitane | 39,717.8 | 107 | Mitsubishi Heavy Industries | 23,011.3 |
| 69 | Nestle | 39,057.9 | 108 | Thyssen | 22,731.5 |
| 70 | Chevron | 38,523 | 109 | Peru | 22,100 |
| 71 | Myanmar | 37,749 | 110 | Pepsico | 22,083.7 |
| 72 | Toshiba | 37,471.6 | 111 | Robert Bosch | 22,036.5 |
| 73 | E.L. Du Pont de Nemours | 37,386 | 112 | United Technologies | 22,032 |
| 74 | Texaco | 37,130 | 113 | INI | 21,654.2 |
| 75 | Chrysler | 36,897 | 114 | Imperial Chemical Industries | 21,548.9 |
| 76 | Algeria | 35,674 | 115 | PDVSA | 21,375 |
| 77 | Hungary | 35,218 | 116 | PEMEX | 21,292.8 |
| 78 | Puerto Rico | 33,969 | 117 | Conagra | 21,219 |
| 79 | Renault | 33,884.9 | 118 | Mazda Motor | 20,867.4 |
| 80 | Egypt | 33,553 | 119 | BMW | 20,611.2 |
| 81 | Honda Motor | 33,369.6 | 120 | Eastman Kodak | 20,577 |
| 82 | Philips Electronics | 33,269.7 | 121 | Nippon Oil | 19,863.8 |
| 83 | Sony | 31,451.9 | 122 | Dow Chemical | 19,080 |
| 84 | ABB ASEA Brown Boveri | 30,536 | 123 | Repsol | 18,618.3 |
| 85 | Alcatel Alstbom | 30,529.1 | 124 | Mannesmann | 18,234.8 |
| 86 | Boeing | 30,414 | 125 | Xerox | 18,089 |
| 87 | Belarus | 30,125 | 126 | Atlantic Richfield | 18,061 |
| 88 | Procter & Gamble | 29,890 | 127 | British Aerospace | 17,838.9 |
| 89 | Nigeria | 29,667 | 128 | McDonnell Douglas | 17,513 |

**TABLE 5.4 (CONTINUED)**
## One Hundred Fifty of the Largest Countries and Industrial Corporations
*(Ranked by Annual GDP and Sales in Millions of Dollars, 1992)*

| | | | | | |
|---|---|---|---|---|---|
| 129 | Petrofina | 17,468.8 | 140 | BTR | 15,726.1 |
| 130 | Syria | 17,236 | 141 | Ruhrkohle | 15,712 |
| 131 | Hewlett-Packard | 16,427 | 142 | Preussag | 15,697.8 |
| 132 | Usinor-Sacilor | 16,418.6 | 143 | Idemitsu Kosan | 15,662.9 |
| 133 | Metallgesellschaft | 16,390.5 | 144 | Canon | 15,348.9 |
| 134 | USX | 16,186 | 145 | Volvo | 14,920.7 |
| 135 | Ferruzzi Finanziaria | 16,136.8 | 146 | Uzbekistan | 14,875 |
| 136 | Ciba-Geigy | 16,119.4 | 147 | Fried. Krupp | 14,820.5 |
| 137 | Rhone-Poulenc | 15,886.5 | 148 | Ssangyong | 14,609.7 |
| 138 | Viag | 15,784.7 | 149 | NKK | 14,605.5 |
| 139 | RJR Nabisco Holdings | 15,734 | 150 | Petrobras | 14,599.8 |

SOURCE: World Bank, *World Development Report*, 1994, 166-167; *Fortune*, July 26, 1993, 191-192. Prepared by Masao Doi.

## Foreign Direct Investment

An important measure of the global activity of multinational corporations is foreign direct investment (FDI).[23] We have seen how international trade has grown as a proportion of world production. But FDI has grown even more rapidly than trade: In the 1960s FDI grew twice as fast as GDP; in the 1980s FDI grew four times as fast as GDP.[24] This growth can be seen in Table 5.5: We can see the sharp rise in FDI flows from Europe and Japan after 1985 and from other Asian states in the 1990s; major recipients of FDI include the United States, Europe, China and Asia, and Latin America.

Foreign direct investment at these levels has created the need for a new measure of international production—one that captures not just goods and services crossing borders, but also goods and services produced abroad by foreign affiliates. This measure includes not only an automobile produced in Great Britain for sale in Germany, but also an American company's production of a car in Britain for sale in Britain. Analysts have concluded that trillions of dollars of international production are not counted by traditional balance of payments accounting because no good or service crosses a border. Instead, FDI crossed a border. When a U.S. firm establishes a production facility in Britain, FDI takes place, and international production follows. Unless the goods produced in Britain are exported, this global production is not counted. In 1989 estimates of international production give a measure almost

---

[23] Remember that FDI refers to investment in another country, the effect of which is managerial control of the enterprise.

[24] DeAnne Julius, *Global Companies and Public Policy,* London: Pinter, 1990, 6.

**TABLE 5.5**

**Foreign Direct Investment**
*(Billions of U.S. Dollars)*

*Global pattern of direct investment*

| | 1976–80 | 1981–85 | 1986–90 | 1991 | 1992 | 1993 | 1994[1] |
|---|---|---|---|---|---|---|---|
| *In billions of U.S. dollars, annual averages* | | | | | | | |
| Total outflows | 39.7 | 43.2 | 167.7 | 187.1 | 179.4 | 199.0 | 233.5 |
| Industrial countries | 39.0 | 41.4 | 158.6 | 177.7 | 161.4 | 168.4 | 197.8 |
| of which: | | | | | | | |
| United States | 16.9 | 7.6 | 25.3 | 31.3 | 41.0 | 57.9 | 58.4 |
| Japan | 2.3 | 5.1 | 32.1 | 30.7 | 17.2 | 13.7 | 17.9 |
| United Kingdom | 7.8 | 9.2 | 28.1 | 16.4 | 19.4 | 25.7 | 30.9 |
| Other Europe | 10.0 | 15.1 | 63.9 | 91.3 | 80.2 | 63.2 | 80.1 |
| Developing Countries[2] | 0.8 | 1.8 | 9.1 | 9.5 | 18.0 | 30.5 | 35.7 |
| of which: | | | | | | | |
| Asia | 0.1 | 1.1 | 7.8 | 7.2 | 15.3 | 26.4 | 30.2 |
| Latin America | 0.2 | 0.2 | 0.6 | 1.3 | 0.8 | 2.2 | 2.9 |
| Total inflows | 31.8 | 55.3 | 152.4 | 152.0 | 153.2 | 177.4 | 239.7 |
| Industrial Countries | 25.3 | 36.2 | 126.8 | 108.7 | 94.8 | 96.8 | 135.1 |
| of which: | | | | | | | |
| United States | 9.0 | 18.6 | 53.4 | 26.1 | 9.9 | 21.4 | 60.1 |
| Japan | 0.1 | 0.3 | 0.3 | 1.4 | 2.7 | 0.1 | 0.9 |
| United Kingdom | 5.6 | 4.3 | 21.7 | 16.1 | 16.5 | 14.6 | 10.9 |
| Other Europe | 8.7 | 9.9 | 38.8 | 57.5 | 55.7 | 52.4 | 51.5 |
| Developing countries[2] | 6.4 | 19.1 | 25.6 | 43.3 | 58.4 | 80.6 | 104.6 |
| of which: | | | | | | | |
| China | — | 1.0[3] | 3.1 | 4.4 | 11.2 | 25.8 | 33.8 |
| Other Asia | 2.1 | 4.6 | 12.1 | 20.5 | 26.2 | 25.5 | 33.3 |
| Latin America | 3.6 | 5.6 | 6.6 | 11.2 | 12.6 | 16.1 | 25.9 |

[1] *Preliminary*    [2] *Including Eastern Europe*    [3] *1982-85.*
SOURCE: Bank for International Settlements, *Annual Report*, 1995, 66

twice as large as international trade alone. Because the United States has a long history of FDI, the ratio of global production to international trade is even greater. In 1989 the global production of U.S. firms (outside the United States) was $1.266 trillion. For the same year, U.S. firms exported only $307 billion—a ratio of more than 4:1.[25]

Another indicator of the role of FDI in globalization is the increasing proportion that is geographically dispersed. FDI historically has mirrored the

---

[25] United Nations, *World Investment . . .*, 52–56. Also see Julius, *Global Companies . . .*, and *The Economist*, February 5, 1994, 71.

**TABLE 5.6**
**Changing Direction of FDI Flows**

| 1982–1986 | 80% Developed States | 20% Developing States |
|---|---|---|
| 1994 | 60% Developed States | 40% Developing States |
| 2010 (Estimated) | 50% Developed States | 50% Developing States |

*(Percentages are for amount of FDI directed toward this area.)*
SOURCE: *The Economist,* April, 22, 1995, 7.

trade triad of North America, Europe, and Japan.[26] This triad, of course, includes the major developed states. But FDI is increasingly directed toward developing states.

Table 5.5 shows that much of the growth of FDI inflows to developing states is toward China and Asia, which now receive more than the United States. The consequence of large and persistent FDI flows has been an increasing globalization of assets and production, not just trade. Approximately one third of the assets of the largest U.S. MNCs are foreign; for Great Britain, the figure is almost one half; and for Switzerland, Sweden, and Canada, almost all assets are foreign.[27] The fifty largest MNCs have approximately 40 percent of their assets located abroad.[28]

## Sources of the Globalization of Production

The enormous growth of FDI and international assets raises several important questions. Why has this globalization occurred? How do these levels of FDI affect the behavior of firms? Has this influenced the organization of firms and the way they interact? What are the consequences for nations?

We have seen in Chapter 4 that explanations for the expansion abroad of U.S. corporations have focused on the hegemonic position of the United States and on the cyclical process of product development. The decline of U.S. hegemony and the global complexity of FDI make these arguments more appropriate for the pre-1975 era.[29] The best explanation for the acceleration in FDI growth can be found in the organizational advantages of MNCs over domestic-based firms. The surge of FDI is a result of the widespread conclusion by the executives of multinational enterprises that profits could be

---

[26] See United Nations, *World Investment . . .,* 21.

[27] *The Economist,* June 24, 1995, special section, "Big Is Back," 15. An important reminder that we are studying the *process* of globalization and not an end result is the scale of FDI relative to GDP. If we add together one year's inflows and outflows of FDI for a nation, this represents only a small fraction of its GDP. The figures for 1994 are: Belgium, 7%; Sweden, 6.5%; Great Britain, 4%; United States, 2%; Germany, 1%; and Japan, 1%. See *The Economist,* July, 22, 1995, 99.

[28] Calculated from "Multinationals," *The Economist,* 6–7.

[29] Raymond Vernon, "The Product Cycle Hypothesis in a New International Environment," *Oxford Bulletin of Economics and Statistics,* 41.4, November 1979, 255–267.

expanded or protected through globalized productive assets. Recent innovations in FDI involve moving beyond the process of simply producing in the home market and selling abroad; FDI means acquiring productive assets in another country and selling there and/or elsewhere. For this to happen, and to expand, MNCs must be able to gain some competitive advantage from moving abroad. They must have, or believe they have, the ability to compete more effectively through globalization.

What are the advantages enjoyed by MNCs that let them generate large amounts of FDI?[30] The most important involve the ability to operate a global enterprise and derive benefits from that operation. The globalization of technology raises the cost of innovation and increases the risks associated with new product competition. The ability to sell in global markets permits MNCs to spread the risks and costs of innovation over a much larger number of sales units. This allows MNCs to accept risks and undertake innovation that otherwise would not happen and thereby to gain competitive advantages. The ability to engage in innovation can yield improvements in the product and in the process of production, in marketing techniques, and in management skills. Global operations also give MNCs a much greater scope of access to resources and capital. They can borrow funds and mobilize resources over a much wider set of opportunities.

In a context of globalizing technology, innovation, and information, MNCs increasingly gain advantages by operating an effective global scanning capacity: gathering, integrating and cross-fertilizing knowledge drawn from around the world. This process presents a major organizational challenge. Solving the difficulties this presents may require a special ability to use the organization of the MNC to control and reduce costs and to create advantages in the many sites where an MNC locates. An example might be the ability to coordinate the supply of materials, production, and distribution over several geographically distant locations through an information-processing system created by sophisticated global telecommunications. A successful MNC may use its global locations to obtain the latest technology,[31] integrate that technology into product or production innovation, and organize production and distribution on a global scale to take maximum advantage of the new knowledge. The advantages of an MNC increasingly come from the ability of its units to act effectively as "knowledge brokers" within and outside the organization.[32]

---

[30] We should note that firms in different industries often operate in different circumstances and that the following list of advantages is a summary that cumulates across industries.

[31] This includes not only the "hard" technology in machines but also "soft" technology, which could include knowledge about how machines and people can best be organized.

[32] The theoretical basis for the discussion of MNC advantages is found in John Dunning, "The Eclectic Paradigm of International Production: A Restatement and Some Possible Extensions," *Journal of International Business Studies*, 19.1, 1988, 1–31. Also very important is Lorraine Eden, "Bringing the Firm Back In: Multinationals in International Political Economy," *Millennium*, 20.2, 1991, 197–224. A summary is in Peter Cowhey and Jonathan Aronson, *Managing the World Economy,* New York: CFR Press, 1993, 43–55.

## Consequences of the Globalization of Production

Several developments of great significance are associated with the globalization of production. We will examine three: changes in the technology of production, the emergence of complex systems of global production, and the establishment of an increasing number and variety of intercorporate alliances.

The intensification of globalization after 1973 has magnified the impact of a new technology of production that found its highest development in Japan. There, largely as a result of intense competition and resource scarcity, many Japanese companies developed production forms that deviated dramatically from the mass production of standardized units typically known as "Fordism."[33] In its place, the Japanese organized a complex system of information-based, flexible manufacturing that emphasized lean production and very high quality standards. Using computer-directed production, Japanese companies began to produce small batches of significantly different products for different customers using the same production line. These production lines were designed to be reorganized quickly and cheaply to accommodate production of goods to customer specifications. Cost control was improved through "just in time" inventory control, in which the part reached the plant just as it was needed for production. Perhaps most stunning, Japanese producers were able to achieve much higher quality control than under "Fordism."[34]

One important consequence of globalization has been the rapid transmission of this new technological system to the United States, Europe, newly industrialized countries (NICs), and even to developing states. The system of information-based, flexible manufacturing defines the standard for efficiency, quality, and the ability to meet customer needs. The combination of increased international competition, global information and technology flows, and intercorporate alliances has led to rapid emulation of the Japanese system. Increased globalization produces a more rapid and geographically wider spread of innovation. Not only does information move faster and to more recipients, but globalization also expands the institutional and infrastructural bases that permit firms in many countries to adopt and use these innovations.[35]

---

[33] David Friedman, *The Misunderstood Miracle*, Ithaca: Cornell University Press, 1988; and Laura Tyson and John Zysman, "Developmental Strategy and Production Innovation in Japan," in Chalmers Johnson et al. (eds.), *Politics and Productivity,* New York: Harper & Row, 1989, 59–140.

[34] In addition to Friedman, *The Misunderstood . . .,* and Tyson and Zysman, "Developmental Strategy . . . ," see "Manufacturing Technology," *The Economist,* March 5, 1994; Michael Piore and Charles Sabel, *The Second Industrial Divide,* New York: Basic Books, 1984; and Mitchell Bernard, "Post-Fordism, Transnational Production, and the Changing Global Political Economy," in Richard Stubbs and Geoffrey Underhill (eds.), *Political Economy and the Changing Global Order*, New York: St. Martin's, 1994, 216–229.

[35] Although innovations are quickly spread globally, it is less clear whether the development of innovations has experienced globalization. In the most elementary sense, the proportion of global R&D activity has expanded from the United States to Japan. Between 1970 and 1987, U.S. R&D expenditures fell from 61.7 percent of world totals to 54 percent, while Japan's proportions increased from 12.3 percent to 20.9 percent But there have been few changes in the proportion of R&D activity outside the home country. See John Dunning, "Multinational Enterprises and the Globalization of Innovatory Capacity," *Research Policy*, 23, 1994, 69, 73. For contrasting views

A second institutional consequence of the globalization of production is the development of new and more complex forms for the organization of production. The organization of production is usually understood in terms of production or commodity chains, that is, the way the various elements of production—finance, technology R&D, design, materials procurement, assembly, sales, and distribution—are linked together.[36] Further, organization can be thought of geographically. As we move down the list, the increasing scope and complexity of the organization of production involve a network of relationships. Geography comes into play in terms of integrating local advantages into a global web.

**TABLE 5.7**
**Globalization of the Organization of Production**

Home-based firm (all functions): Exports finished products

Home-based: International distribution division

Home-based: Production of home-defined product abroad

Home-based: Production in several foreign sites—exports

Home-based headquarters: Production and distribution organized across several countries, with flexible production for local markets—exports are global, including to home market

Home-based headquarters: Global sourcing, financing, sales, production, and distribution; R&D organized globally

SOURCE: Based in part on Dicken, *Global Shift*, 211, 189-227.

The rapid decline in the costs of communication and information processing, the growth of flexible manufacturing, and the emergence of global networks of production, sourcing, finance, innovation, and communication have altered the nature of many MNCs. They have become global knowledge brokers: knowledge-based producers, acquirers, processors, and appliers of knowledge. In this environment, the global division of labor among nations is much more fluid than is the notion of trading raw materials for manufactured goods. What is increasingly emerging is a division that cuts across nations, with a division defined by technological sophistication: Some areas are knowledge generators, others may be capable of producing the high-technology components of the product, while others are responsible for the low-technology elements of a product.[37]

---

about the globalization of Japanese R&D, see D. Hicks et al., "Japanese Corporations, Scientific Research, and Globalization," *Research Policy*, 23, 1994, 375-384; and Richard Florida and Martin Kenny, "The Globalization of Japanese R&D," *Economic Geography*, 70.4, October 1994, 344-369.

[36] Dicken, *Global Shift*, 189-190. Also useful is Peter Dicken, "Global–Local Tensions: Firms and States in the Global Space-Economy," *Economic Geography*, 70, 1994, 101-128.

[37] Organization for Economic Cooperation and Development, *Globalization of Industrial Activities, Four Case Studies: Auto Parts, Chemicals, Construction and Semiconductors*, Paris: OECD, 1992.

The location of the various elements of the production chain has become sufficiently globalized that placement decisions are based on cost/productivity calculations and much less on geography.[38] An example of this process is the development of an advanced electronics industry in Malaysia since 1988. Driven by FDI, much of it from the United States and Taiwan, Malaysia has become a major site for the production of semiconductors. Bringing advanced technology with their manufacturing facilities, foreign firms have found Malaysia to be a very cost-effective location.[39]

In spite of the considerable strengths of MNCs, these organizations face increasingly daunting problems in coping with globalization. With the pace of technological change and global competition accelerating, the costs of innovation have increased dramatically, and the life cycle of products has declined significantly. This is especially true in the semiconductor industry, where every eighteen months microprocessor speeds double and the manufacturing process becomes equally demanding and costly. The Intel plant completed during 1995 in New Mexico cost $1.8 billion, and the next-generation facilities may cost over $3 billion.

Changes in semiconductors have dramatic consequences for computers and information processing. Processing power has made quantum leaps, and the cost per computation has fallen as rapidly. Every eighteen months the processing speed of computers doubles. In 1987 a $2,000 personal computer could process roughly four million commands per second, operated with 512 kilobytes of random access memory (RAM), and could store thirty million bits of information. In 1995 the same-price computer could process one hundred million commands per second, operated with sixteen million bytes of RAM, and could store 1.2 billion bits of information.[40] Firms producing semiconductors and computers must deal with rising costs to remain competitive and with shorter periods of time in which to recover these costs. The dynamism in global markets created by global competition simply adds to the risks and uncertainties that firms must manage. The response is to turn to strategic alliances, in which firms pool resources in order to share costs and spread risks.

A strategic alliance is an arrangement between two or more independent firms. It involves an ongoing and continuous relationship, which could include production, marketing, and/or research and development, in which the sharing and transfer of information, products, and even production occur.[41] A key element in the bargain is that each firm needs access to the capabilities generated by or available to the other. The most interesting strategic alliances have increasingly come from MNCs in different countries. Firms that are otherwise competitors and that have strong connections to different countries

---

[38] Martin Carnoy et al., *The New Global Economy in the Information Age*, University Park: Penn State University Press, 1993, 31.

[39] Alasdair Bowie, "The Dynamics of Business–Government Relations in Industrialising Malaysia," in Andrew MacIntyre (ed.), *Business and Government in Industrialising Asia*, Ithaca: Cornell University Press, 1994, 186–187.

[40] This is not unlike an eight-year change from a Model T at $2,000 to a Lexus LS 400 for $2,000.

[41] Cowhey and Aronson, *Managing ...*, 7.

develop a formal and continuing relationship. They may jointly produce a product, share the costs of development, organize a joint research facility, or simply exchange vital information.

One example of an international strategic alliance is an arrangement begun in the 1980s between General Motors and Toyota in which Toyota was responsible for producing in California an automobile sold by GM. Toyota wanted experience in producing cars in the United States, while GM needed to learn the technology associated with flexible, lean manufacturing. Similar alliances have occurred between Mazda and Ford and between GM and Isuzu. Rapid technological change in semiconductors and computers has led to a dense network of global strategic alliances. A complex system of strategic alliances in microelectronics during the late 1980s included Intel (United States), NEC (Japan), Siemens (Germany), Advanced Micro Devices (United States), Philips (Netherlands), Toshiba (Japan), Thomson (France), Motorola (United States), and Matsushita (Japan). An even wider web of arrangements linked more than thirty additional firms from an equally wide array of countries.[42]

The rising number and significance of strategic alliances are a response to globalizing processes in technology and markets; they also serve to deepen globalization in new and important ways. Firms find that they are unable to cope with rapid changes in markets and the rising costs of innovation. Strategic alliances are a response to some of the consequences of globalization. There are several very significant outcomes of strategic alliances. These relationships among firms from different countries alter the way we need to think about the nationality of firms in international competition. In some ways, strategic alliances, in conjunction with growing trade and FDI, undermine the connection between nation and firm. Some analysts believe that the emerging global networks of finance, trade, information, and innovation operate in contradiction to the territorial world of states. This can be seen most easily in the difficulties of traditional national trade policy. Efforts to promote or control the trade activities of "national" firms tend to ignore the geographic fluidity and flexibility generated by international strategic alliances, in conjunction with FDI and global production. The competitive advantages of firms seem to rest more with transnational relationships than simply with advantages given by one nation.[43] In addition, strategic alliances increase the pace of innovation and add to the dynamism of the world economy. Innovations spread globally more quickly by increasing the "mobility of capital, information, technology, and personnel."[44]

---

[42] For strategic alliances in information technology firms, see John Hagedoorn and Jos Schakenraad, "Leading Companies and Networks of Strategic Alliances in Information Technologies," *Research Policy*, 21, 1992, 178; and Cowhey and Aronson, *Managing ...,* 148-149. For automobiles, see Cowhey and Aronson, *Managing ...,* 91-124; and *The Economist*, "The Car Industry," October 17, 1992, special section. More comprehensive data can be found in "Multinationals," *The Economist*, March 27, 1993, 16.

[43] Mitchell Bernard and John Ravenhill, "Beyond Product Cycles and Flying Geese: Regionalization, Hierarchy, and the Industrialization of East Asia," *World Politics*, 47, January 1995, 171-172; Cowhey and Aronson, *Managing ...,* 83-85 and generally 80-88.

[44] Cowhey and Aronson, *Managing ...,* 34.

## CONCLUSIONS

Many of the most important features and trends in the world economy can be traced to the process of globalization. We have concentrated on the arrangements in finance and production. Flexible exchange rates, new and less expensive technologies in communication and computing, and a series of historical events have combined to produce a genuine sea change in global finance. A veritable explosion of foreign exchange trading and huge leaps in international lending and international equities trading have generated a major advance in the globalization of finance. Additionally, the expansion of the operations of multinational corporations through foreign direct investment has altered the world economy in the direction of greater globalization. The vast web of investment generates international production and a complex system of international corporate alliances. These arrangements both reflect and accelerate the processes of technological change, innovation, and global competition.

At the same time, most will acknowledge that globalization has not proceeded to the point that national economies are simply a subset of international transactions and relationships. National economies still account for the preponderance of economic activity: trade, investment, capital formation, and economic decision making. Globalization is taking place at an increasing pace, but the world economy does not overwhelm most national economies.

How much further globalization will take us is difficult to say. Somewhat clearer, though still debatable, are the consequences for states. Nations remain very important actors in the world economy. The economic strength of the home base of the MNC is a very important (some would say the most important) factor in determining the competitiveness of the MNC in the world economy.[45] Not only do nations retain the capacity for regulation, but also their efforts to control MNC behavior are essential features of a stable world economy. The liberalization of the past twenty years could be reversed by states; MNC are not stateless; and borders retain great significance.

But these qualifications must not divert us from understanding the profound consequences for nations, for the relations among nations, and for other actors in world affairs of the current level of globalization. The nature and significance of the nationality of MNCs are anything but clear. MNCs are not "stateless," but they are not "stated" or national in the same way as before 1970. The ability to operate a large business enterprise across many countries and to control investment, technology, and innovation makes MNCs very important actors in world affairs. Some scholars argue that the expansion of multinational corporations and globalization has proceeded to the point that the "game" of international politics has been altered. Because states must now compete for the opportunity to create wealth within their borders, they must

---

[45] Michael Porter, *The Competitive Advantage of Nations,* New York: Free Press, 1990; Yao-Su Hu, "Global or Stateless Corporations Are National Firms with International Operations," *California Management Review,* 34, Winter 1992, 107–126; Ethan Kapstein, "We Are US: The Myth of the Multinational," *The National Interest,* Winter 1991/92, 55–62.

bargain with MNCs.[46] These corporate entities are the main agents of wealth creation because they control the necessary resources—in particular the ability to move and organize capital on a global scale. The long-term consequences of these changes are difficult to discern. One scholar speculates that MNCs are not functional substitutes for states but that the scale of their operation alters the intellectual foundation of the state system. Drawing on an analogy to the medieval world, Ruggie suggests

> . . . the new wealth they produced, the new instruments of economic transactions they generated, the new ethos of commerce they spread, the new regulatory arrangements they required, and the expansion of cognitive horizons they effected all helped undermine . . . [the ideas upon which the existing system of government rested].[47]

In a less speculative vein, we have shown several significant consequences of globalization.

1. It is now much more difficult for states to initiate economic expansion via monetary and fiscal policy. Unless most states act together, international financial markets will impose penalties through interest rates and exchange rates. This substantially alters the economic basis for the embedded liberalism of the postwar world.

2. Financial market penalties have not eliminated deficit spending. States have actually expanded the gap between revenue and spending in recent years. Between 1974 and 1994, the public debt of OECD states has increased from 15 percent to 40 percent of GDP.[48] This may be the result of the fact that markets need a growing supply of high-quality investments and thus are willing to finance this debt. And the globalization of financial markets means that states can regularly borrow abroad.

3. The integration of financial markets can also impose penalties on countries whose fiscal and monetary policies have not changed. When interest rates rise in the United States (as in 1994, due to fears of increased inflation), this can drive up interest rates in other countries, such as Japan.

4. When nations cooperate, they still are able to affect prices in foreign exchange markets. Success usually requires acting in a manner consistent with underlying market forces. And long-term or strong trends cannot be controlled by governments. But if market timing is right, as

---

[46] Stopford and Strange, *Rival States* . . . .

[47] John Gerard Ruggie, "Territoriality and Beyond: Problemitizing Modernity in International Relations," *International Organization*, 47, Winter 1993, 155.  For a brief realist critique of this view, see Ethan Kapstein, "Territoriality and Who Is 'Us'?" *International Organization*, 47, Summer 1993, 501–503.

[48] "The World Economy," *The Economist*, October 7, 1995, 16; and International Monetary Fund, *International Capital Markets*, Washington: IMF, September 1994, 35.

with the 1995 effort by Japan and the United States to push up the dollar against the yen, governments can still influence prices.

5. There is now tremendous pressure on states to make their territory more attractive to MNCs for production and investment. Leaders of governments understand that for funds and production to move to or remain in their territory, the incentives and advantages must be clear to the holders of these resources. The role of the government of most countries has been focused on the competitive strength of their nation.[49]

Several very important questions remain to be resolved. Globalization simultaneously pushes states toward greater cooperation and greater competition. The incentives for cooperation can be seen in efforts to create and manage the political context needed for markets to function effectively. International cooperation has become more important in the process of managing exchange rates, coordinating economic policies, homogenizing regulations, negotiating rules for trade and investment, and coping with the difficulties in integrating postcommunist states into the world economy. Globalization can proceed only as states cooperate to maintain an effective framework for these transactions.

At the same time that cooperation increases in response to globalization, there are strong pressures for greater competition. The rising number of players in the world economy—both states and firms—intensifies the struggle for markets and growth. The very nature of this competition is in dispute. Economists argue that only firms compete while the trade and investment crossing national boundaries can only benefit all states. Others point out that rates of economic growth differ substantially in response to international exchange and that many people care about these differences. Globalization may increase the need for a state to enhance the ability of firms operating within its territory to compete in the world economy. Certainly the leadership and populace of most states see themselves in competition with each other for the means to wealth and power.

The following two chapters address the issues of cooperation and competition. In Chapter 6 we will explore the nature of international cooperation in relation to the process of globalization. We will consider the problems and prospects for cooperation, understand the conflicting incentives for cooperation, and apply these ideas to several cases of successful and attempted cooperation. Chapter 7 explores the nature and impact of competition and conflict among advanced states. We will examine the indicators of national competitive advantage and disadvantage, the challenge posed by Japan, the competitive strategies available, and the costs and benefits of these strategies.

---

[49] For a discussion of the liberalization of trade and capital policies in several developing states after 1985, see Stephan Haggard, *Developing Nations and the Politics of Global Integration*, Washington, D.C.: Brookings, 1995.

# ANNOTATED BIBLIOGRAPHY

Peter Cowhey and Jonathan Aronson, *Managing the World's Economy*, New York: CFR Press, 1993.
> The best discussion of global strategic alliances among multinational corporations.

Peter Dicken, *Global Shift*, New York: Guilford, 1992.
> The most comprehensive analysis of globalization with a special emphasis on multinational corporations.

Stephan Haggard, *Developing Nations and the Politics of Global Integration*, Washington, D.C.: Brookings, 1995.
> A very useful short discussion of the impact of globalization on developing states.

Eric Helleiner, *States and the Reemergence of Global Finance*, Ithaca, N.Y.: Cornell University Press, 1994.
> The best discussion of capital liberalization.

Richard Herring and Robert Litan, *Financial Regulation in the Global Economy*, Washington, D.C.: Brookings, 1995.
> A detailed examination of the problems of harmonization of financial regulations.

R. J. Barry Jones, *Globalisation and Interdependence in the International Political Economy*, London: Pinter, 1995.
> Offers insights into theoretical and empirical aspects of globalization.

Gregory Millman, *The Vandal's Crown*, New York: Free Press, 1995.
> A description of foreign exchange traders.

Henk Overbeek (ed.), *Restructuring Hegemony in the Global Political Economy: The Rise of Transnational Neo-Liberalism in the 1980s*, London: Routledge, 1993.
> Offers a very insightful radical perspective on liberal ideology.

Steven Solomon, *The Confidence Game: How Unelected Central Bankers Are Governing the Changed Global Economy*, New York: Simon and Schuster, 1995.
> A useful description of international financial crises.

John Stopford and Susan Strange, *Rival States and Rival Firms,* Cambridge: Cambridge University Press, 1991.
> The best discussion of the impact of globalization on the relationship of states and firms.

Andrew Walter, *World Power and World Money*, New York: St. Martin's Press, 1991.
> Provides a very good short discussion of political power and international finance.

# Chapter 6

## COOPERATION AMONG ADVANCED INDUSTRIAL STATES

Four major structural trends define much of the background for the contemporary world economy: (1) the decline, or at least change, in American hegemony, (2) the globalization of finance and production, (3) the development of a web of institutions of international cooperation, and (4) the intensification of competition among states and firms. We have seen how the economic weight of the United States has declined from the lofty levels immediately after World War II. And, consequently, the behavior of the United States has changed from broadly supporting the stability of the world economy to a leadership based on a narrower definition of national self-interest. Perhaps surprisingly, the decline of U.S. hegemony has been accompanied by increasing levels of global interdependence. Restrictions on the flow of money and goods have fallen dramatically. Rapid expansion of financial flows, the organization of production on a global scale, the rapid transmission of information and technology around the world, and new forms of relationships among firms and states are indications of these trends.

Often responding to the effects of U.S. decline and the globalization of finance and production, many institutions of global and regional cooperation have expanded the scale and scope of their activities. One of the sharpest differences in the nature of interdependence in the late nineteenth and late twentieth centuries is the presence today of many significant international institutions reflecting and contributing to cooperation. The scale and intensity of trade and financial flows have produced new efforts at cooperation and coordination, along with an accentuation of international competition. Nations and corporations frequently have found their interests bound together by the need to manage the burgeoning system of interdependence and thereby continue to reap the mutual benefits of free trade and capital movement. This process has given rise to new attempts at cooperation. Some of the most important are recurring efforts to manage newly floating exchange rates and to coordinate macroeconomic policies. Heads of state, finance ministers and their staffs, and central bankers have become deeply involved in these matters. Also interesting, for the mixture of cooperative and competitive features, is the growth of trading blocs in Europe, North America, and perhaps in Asia.

Even as we consider the role of cooperation, we must also keep in mind an appreciation of the impact of conflicting interests because a capitalist world economy generates powerful competitive incentives for nations and firms alike. Those that are able to define the rules for exchange or bring the best or least expensive product to the marketplace win a disproportionate set of the gains. Similarly, those that consistently fail to meet these demands fall further and further behind, whether it be in market share, technological innovation, the ability to attract investment, standard of living, or military competition. Thus the need for international cooperation is often tempered by a countervailing need for institutions and national strategies capable of adapting to and flourishing in an intensely competitive environment. In recent years the level of world trade, the swiftness of change, the declining dominance of the United States, and the astonishing success of the Japanese have combined to raise significant concerns about competitiveness across much of the world.

This chapter is the first of two that will focus on the complex mixture of cooperation and competition among advanced capitalist states. We begin with a detailed discussion of the concept of *cooperation*. This is an elusive term, and it requires some extended discussion in order for us to understand its several dimensions. Under what conditions can we expect cooperation to occur? What are the main obstacles to resolving problems through cooperation? Is cooperation likely to increase? In answering these questions, our goal is to provide an understanding of the contexts in which cooperation is possible. We follow a discussion of the factors supporting, and the barriers to, cooperation with a consideration of three very important cases: macroeconomic coordination through economic summits, management of exchange rates, and the creation of economic blocs, especially the European Union (EU), the North American Free Trade Agreement (Nafta), and a potential Asian bloc. These cases will offer some basis for reaching conclusions about the effectiveness of and prospects for cooperation among the largest and most prosperous states.

## THEORIES OF COOPERATION

Examination of the incidence and potential for cooperation engages some of the most basic questions about the nature of international politics. There is significant debate about whether we can expect any meaningful cooperation to take place in an international system based on sovereign states whose security depends on their own efforts. One approach sees anarchy among nations as the central obstacle to cooperation, driving states to compete for relative gains and thereby making any cooperation difficult and tenuous. Another perspective believes that in spite of these barriers, cooperation is both possible and even likely. Operating to displace the effects of anarchy is the mutual ability of states to affect each other's fate, the constant interaction and expectation of entanglement into the foreseeable future, and the gains from cooperation. When cooperation produces international institutions, it stabilizes and even enhances future cooperation.

This section examines the debate over cooperation and considers the circumstances under which cooperation can occur. In particular, we will set out those factors that support cooperation and those barriers that stand in its way. We will discuss the basics of this debate and follow it with three case studies of recent efforts at cooperation in the areas of macroeconomic policy, the management of exchange rates, and the formation of economic blocs.

## Why Nations Cooperate

Although the discussion to this point may seem to set cooperation and conflict apart as two distinct kinds of situations, the real world almost always consists of varying mixtures of the two. Harmony is both rare and uninteresting in analytical terms. Instances in which the actions of one nation have no unwanted consequences for others are simply too unlikely to warrant our attention. Perhaps especially in world politics, cooperation is not a situation in which two nations simply recognize and act in a harmonious relationship. Rather, cooperation involves bargaining between two or more nations that modify their behavior and/or preferences in order to receive some reciprocal act from each other. The aim is to arrive at a situation in which these nations coordinate their behavior so as to achieve some important purpose that they cannot achieve by themselves.[1]

There are several important implications for this way of thinking about cooperation. First, cooperation does not require that the purposes of nations be identical, but rather that some degree of parallel or overlapping interests exists such that the actions of each make some contribution to the purposes of the other. Second, the most interesting forms of cooperation are those that persist over time. These are the cases most likely to have the greatest impact. Third, when cooperation reaches the point where some type of tacit or explicit rules and regularity occurs, scholars use the term *regime* to describe it. Finally, cooperation differs in terms of its scope—that is, broad or narrow issues—and in terms of the importance of the issue. Cooperation over issues of whaling can be distinguished from those of nuclear weapons or the control of a nation's money supply.

Why should we expect cooperation to occur? What factors help bring it about? Perhaps the most obvious, but slippery, factor is the interests of the nations involved. Some degree of overlap of purpose is needed, but how much and of what kinds? No clear answers exist at this point. But from the

---

[1] This definition and the discussion that follows rely on Robert Keohane, *After Hegemony*, Princeton: Princeton University Press, 1984, 12, 51–52; Joseph Grieco, *Cooperation Among Nations*, Ithaca: Cornell University Press, 1990, 22; and Robert Putnam and Nicholas Bayne, *Hanging Together: Cooperation and Conflict in the Seven-Power Summits*, Cambridge: Harvard University Press, 1987, 2–3.

perspective of international interdependence, the interests most likely to be engaged are those affected by the benefits of coordination and/or the costs of not cooperating. National leaders must come to expect to receive significant payoffs or the avoidance of major penalties from working together. However, this process becomes much more cloudy when we remember that nations are rarely unitary actors. Rather, governments are a collection of bureaucratic interests, each of which sees the issues relating to cooperation in a quite different way. Further, governments in the advanced capitalist world generally rest on coalitions of domestic interests that may be affected in very different ways by the proposed arrangements with other nations.

Also relevant to the potential for cooperation are the relationships among the nations involved. Certainly affecting a nation's calculations is the prior existence of regimes or institutions facilitating cooperation. Previous experience of cooperation, especially if successful and routinized in institutions, can pave the way for more in the future. Why might institutions, such as the European Union, matter? Institutions, especially in a context of anarchy and uncertainty, frequently supply information that can positively influence national decisions to continue and/or expand cooperation with other states. Institutions can help attenuate concerns for relative gains and worries about cheating and can bring closure to choices among alternative procedures and arrangements. Through provision of "unbiased" information, institutions clarify the distribution of gains from cooperation and legitimize this distribution. These activities can increase the chance of reciprocity in bargaining and can improve the climate for cooperation.[2] Finally, successful institutions generate for participants gains that cannot be had without cooperation. Among similarly situated states this can produce costs from not cooperating that may demonstrate the value of participation.

Of equal or even greater importance for understanding cooperation is the power relationship among nations. The existence of a single powerful state, with significant economic resources and a strong commitment to international cooperation, can play a key role in whether nations are able to work together. The power advantages of this hegemon can be used to win, or even coerce, support from other states that otherwise might be reluctant to participate in cooperative ventures. There are two important corollaries to this argument. First, cooperation among states of relatively equal power is somewhat difficult because no state is in a position to bear the costs of promoting and encouraging cooperation. Second, when the power of the hegemon begins to wane, cooperation may also decline unless the institutions created have continuing value to the nations involved.[3]

---

[2] Robert Keohane and Lisa Martin, "The Promise of Institutionalist Theory," *International Security*, 20.1, Summer 1995, 39-51. A critical view of the efficacy of international institutions in promoting cooperation is John Mearsheimer, "The False Promise of International Institutions," *International Security*, 19.3, Winter 1994/95, 5-49.

[3] The ideas of this paragraph draw on Putnam and Bayne, *Hanging* . . . , 3-12.

What then are the main barriers to cooperation? Perhaps the greatest is the fact that nations operate as sovereign entities that must provide for their own security within an environment of anarchy. The absence of any central political authority capable of making and enforcing peace among nations makes international politics quite different from politics within (most) nations. The result is that national leaders must be wary about the ultimate consequences of agreements with other nations. They must pay attention not only to whether an arrangement produces a gain or a loss for themselves, but also whether it leads to a greater gain for other nations. The conditions of anarchy in the system mean that nations must be concerned about whether the gains of another nation might be used to augment that nation's power and to direct it toward some coercive or military purpose. One of the clearest patterns of the past 150 years is the tightening of connections among economic, technological, military, and political dimensions of national power. In a world where anarchy and self-help are the defining features, the fear of relative gain by other states may block cooperation that otherwise would prove beneficial.[4]

A second barrier to cooperation results from the fact that a nation's interests are rarely unified and that any agreement may well help some groups while harming others. Understanding cooperation means that we need to inquire into the politics of interest representation in national decisions and how domestic needs can be linked to international agreements.[5] For example, choosing to lower tariffs and join a free trading system will benefit those producers who are competitive within this new marketplace, probably damage those producers who are not competitive, and improve the choices for consumers. Whether the nation will drop its tariff protection depends in considerable part on the relative political strength of these three groups. If noncompetitive groups have control of the government or veto power over any policy change, cooperation that is in the interests of the nation as a whole will still not take place.

A further barrier to cooperation lies in the structure of the incentives available to a nation. Using the example of participating in a free trade system again, each nation that joins can expect to receive some important benefit. But an even greater benefit, at least in political terms, may come from selling in the open markets of other nations while maintaining protected markets at home. Thus nations may fail to reach agreement because they want to have

---

[4] For a debate about the effects of anarchy on cooperation in the newly emerging system in Europe, see John Mearsheimer, "Back to the Future: Instability in Europe After the Cold War," *International Security*, 15.1, Summer 1990, 5–56; and Jack Snyder, "Averting Anarchy in the New Europe," *International Security*, 14.4, Spring 1990, 5–41. An example of worries about the positional effects of cooperation is described in Charles Kupchan, *The Persian Gulf and the West: The Dilemmas of Security*, Boston: Allen and Unwin, 1987, 166–167. Also see Michael Mastanduno, "Do Relative Gains Matter?" *International Security*, 16.1, Summer 1991, 73–113.

[5] For a set of case studies considering this question, see Peter Evans et al. (eds.), *Double-Edged Diplomacy*, Berkeley: University of California Press, 1993.

their cake and eat it, too, or because they fear that others will try to accomplish this for themselves. These fears and opportunities for profit inhibit cooperation, even when there are significant benefits available to all. But even here we can turn this point around and see how cooperation can still take place. If all nations refuse to cooperate and protectionism becomes the norm, then the costs of this failure may press nations to agree to cooperate. If those that defect can be punished, then the expectation of a continuing need for cooperation to maintain free trade may be sufficient to make this happen.[6]

The question of the extent and degree of cooperation among nations depends on whether they focus more on the absolute gains they receive or on the relative gains, on the presence and success of existing institutions, on whether the domestic politics of nations contribute to or detract from cooperation, and on whether the costs of not cooperating are sufficiently painful for nations to overcome the inclination toward defection. To help illustrate these arrangements, we will now consider three cases of efforts at cooperation: one concerning macroeconomic policy coordination, a second involving attempts to manage flexible exchange rates, and a third looking at the formation of economic blocs. The first focuses on the economic summits beginning in 1975, the second focuses on the agreements to bring down the value of the dollar in 1985, and the last examines cooperation to promote economic integration in Europe, North America, and East Asia.

## MACROECONOMIC POLICY COOPERATION

As we discussed in Chapter 2, macroeconomic policy involves government efforts to manage the overall level of economic activity through fiscal and monetary policy. Traditionally, this means decisions regarding taxes and spending (usually made jointly by chief executives and legislatures) and decisions on expansion and/or contraction of the money supply and interest rates (usually made by central banks). Cooperation among nations on these decisions would include efforts to adjust and coordinate fiscal and monetary policy so as to produce some desired economic outcome that would otherwise prove elusive. In examining the economic summit process, we are interested in understanding the factors that promoted and inhibited cooperation and the outcomes of these efforts.

The fact that economic summits began in 1975 is not an accident.[7] Over the preceding four years, several events combined to produce incentives for

---

[6] For a discussion of the varying sides of this issue, see Keohane, *After* . . ., and Grieco, *Cooperation* . . . . The central question here is the problem of collective action. See Mancur Olson, *The Logic of Collective Action*, Cambridge: Harvard University Press, 1965.

[7] This discussion of economic summits draws heavily on Putnam and Bayne, *Hanging* . . . ; Richard N. Cooper et al., *Can Nations Agree? Issues in International Economic Cooperation*, Washington, D.C.: Brookings, 1989; and Martin Feldstein, *International Economic Cooperation*, Chicago: University of Chicago Press, 1988.

cooperation at the level of heads of state. The collapse of the Bretton Woods system of fixed exchange rates, the expansion of the EEC to ten members, the oil crisis of 1973–74, and the world economic recession in 1974–1975 all created circumstances in which cooperation could improve many nations' positions. Elections in advanced industrial economies had increasingly come to depend on the fate of the economy. When the prosperity of virtually all was swept by external events, this gave national leaders a very good reason to become directly involved in managing the trade-offs associated with the resulting discussions and agreements with other nations. Finally, U.S. leadership, traditionally the linchpin in coordinating the world economy, seemed to fail in the early 1970s as the United States tried to solve its problems through efforts that frequently forced adjustment on other nations.

Perhaps the two most important factors promoting cooperation were the manifest ties of interdependence and the shared experience of working together under the Bretton Woods system. The leadership of the Western world had developed a strong recognition and understanding of their common fate since at least 1945. The events of 1971–1975, even as they often produced conflicting policies, nonetheless acted to reinforce that understanding. Later events helped to bring home the consequences of not cooperating. In 1977 the United States pursued an expansionist macroeconomic policy but paid an important price when that policy resulted in a much larger current account deficit. This deficit came about when other nations failed to stimulate their economies, resulting in a poor showing for U.S. exports even as foreign goods were moving to the United States to take advantage of growth there. A similar fate befell France in 1981, when it, too, expanded alone. Eventually this helped force a socialist government to devalue the franc twice and to adopt a deflationary fiscal policy. Clearly, nations needed the export markets of each other in order to pursue policies of balanced growth.

The economic summits, which began at Rambouillet, France, in 1975, can be divided into three groups. The first four summits, 1975–1978, were driven by the need to recover from the 1974–1975 recession. As such, they focused on the level and timing of economic stimulus and the management of demand, with secondary interests in protectionism and exchange rates. By 1978, after several years of discussion about coordinated fiscal stimulus, a genuine agreement was reached. It called for additional budget stimulus by Germany and Japan in return for a pledge by the United States to reduce its dependence on external oil. Although less than successful in the end, the 1978 Bonn agreement was perhaps the best example of nations adjusting their policies in ways that would not have happened in the absence of cooperation.[8]

The 1979 oil crisis and subsequent inflation and recession from 1980 to 1982 not only scuttled the Bonn agreement, but also shifted the tone and

---

[8] The best detailed discussion of the Bonn Summit is found in Robert Putnam and C. Randall Henning, "The Bonn Summit of 1978: A Study in Coordination" and Gerald Holtham, "German Macroeconomic Policy and the 1978 Bonn Economic Summit," both in Cooper et al., *Can Nations . . .*, 12–177.

substance of the economic summits. The hammer blows produced by these events prompted many nations to search for ways to protect themselves, either by securing oil supplies or by finding domestic economic solutions.[9] Between 1979 and 1983 several nations shifted their efforts toward attacking inflation through applying monetary brakes and raising interest rates and making structural changes that transferred economic responsibility to their private sectors. The most nationalist-oriented in its policies was the United States, which combined a very restrictive monetary policy with a strong fiscal stimulus. The results were a massive federal budget deficit, rising interest rates, and a rising dollar. Following the dollar's rise was a rapidly increasing deficit in the U.S. current account. The summits of this period, reflecting the situation created by U.S. policies, involved limited efforts at coordination coupled with criticism of the looming imbalances in the world economy.[10]

By 1985 the enormous size of the U.S. current account deficit forced the United States to acknowledge these imbalances, and the summits shifted back toward international cooperation. The primary focus was management of a realignment of exchange rates, with the dollar falling and other currencies rising. The major agreements (to be discussed later) were made outside the summits, but these agreements were the core of the discussions there, along with increasing recognition of the need for a new round of trade negotiations under GATT. The Uruguay Round began in 1987 as a result of the endorsement of the 1986 Tokyo Summit.

Taken together, the summits have only a spotty record of accomplishment. Probably the greatest barrier to success lies in the domestic politics of each nation. Although all are tied together by interdependence, this has not yet created a politics that will produce decisions based on this interdependence. The formation of political power is based on interests that remain inward-looking. At most, about one third of the GNP of most nations is based on exports (the United States is closer to one tenth), and the combination with internationalized capital has not yet formed a dominant political bloc in any nation. Political institutions represent national interests and their own bureaucratic interests, both of which reinforce the concept of sovereignty. Leaders of these groups will be very reluctant to surrender power to international institutions or systems of international cooperation. Further, the policy predispositions of nations reflect their domestic politics. Germany has consistently resisted inflationary policies, while the United States has frequently supported them. These differences have often prevented agreement on macroeconomic coordination.

---

[9] Somewhat contrary to this trend was the Tokyo Summit, which served to produce agreement on targets for controlling oil imports. However, these targets were inflated and were achieved mostly as a result of the recession. See Putnam and Bayne, *Hanging . . .*, 110–118.

[10] Criticism was somewhat muted after 1982, when the United States relaxed its monetary policy and experienced an economic boom produced by the stimulus of the budget deficit. This, in conjunction with the rising dollar, pulled in record levels of imports and helped to stimulate the economies of Europe and Japan.

At best, economic summits may work much like nuclear arms control negotiations in the 1970s: Leaders exchange information about policy, build a sense of common purpose, and occasionally produce agreements with limited but desirable results. The key factors in such agreements over the 1975–1995 cycle have been the convergence of domestic political developments and the ability of the United States to assume the task of leading other nations to cooperate. When these agreements take place, as in 1978 and 1985, cooperation of some significance is the result. Otherwise, much more limited results are the outcome.[11]

## EXCHANGE RATES

Does this somewhat gloomy conclusion bear out when we examine efforts to deal with the wild swings in currencies in the 1980s? Cooperation over exchange rates is much more substantial and continuous in some respects. At the same time, many of the same barriers to macroeconomic coordination can be found here. Perhaps the best conclusion is that the tension between cooperation and conflict may be more intense over exchange rates than over macroeconomic policy. Exchange rates engage internationally minded domestic interests more clearly than does macroeconomic policy, but the level and intensity of cooperation required are also much greater and more identifiable.

Exchange rates, whether under fixed or flexible systems, affect the interests of politically organized groups in a direct and intense manner. The prices that exporters charge are greatly influenced by a falling or rising currency, especially for those who operate using the nation as a home base to manufacture goods for sale abroad. A currency that rises by 10 percent confronts an exporter with the choice of absorbing the change and reducing profits or raising prices and risking lower sales. (Review the discussion in Chapter 2 if this does not make sense.) Meanwhile, importers must face the same choice when the currency falls in price. Banking interests engaged in overseas investments prefer a rising currency because this reduces the price of assets abroad and increases their buying power. The impact of exchange rates on domestic interests is reflected in the choices of a government concerned about its international accounts and about the votes of those interests.

Cooperation among nations over exchange rates engages a common interest in stability because this is the arrangement that strikes a balance between the different domestic interests involved. In a system of fixed exchange rates, this cooperation takes the form of establishing an initial price relationship of currencies and governmental intervention in foreign exchange markets to maintain the currency's value. Whenever a currency becomes out of line with the nation's balance of payments, cooperation is required to adjust the fixed rate of exchange.[12] The same circumstances in a flexible system may call for

---

[11] Putnam and Bayne, *Hanging* . . . .

[12] This was the major role of the IMF under the Bretton Woods system.

governmental intervention to move the exchange rate more into line with a current account balance. Flexible systems may also result in such rapid swings in a currency's rate that governmental intervention is needed.

Any significant effort to manage exchange rates under the flexible system since 1973 cannot hope to succeed unless the major economic powers cooperate. No nation acting alone can possibly control its currency. Without the combined resources and the overt and coordinated efforts of other nations, a single nation is essentially at the mercy of the market. Along with these powerful incentives for cooperation is the fact that exchange rates contain an inherent and substantial dimension of conflicting interests. A fall in one nation's currency and subsequent improvement in its current account are always matched by a general or more focused rise in the currencies of other nations, which then must suffer a worsened current account. At the same time, a failure to act invokes the immediate costs associated with price swings generated by the market. Indeed, one nation might coerce others into cooperation by acting to exacerbate market moves. These other nations will act to prevent an even worse outcome from inaction.

This interesting mixture of cooperative and conflictual dimensions associated with exchange rates is complicated further by several structural realities. Exchange rate markets are driven by many factors of supply and demand for currency in addition to those created by exports and imports. Differences in interest rates among nations can generate capital movements that move exchange rates up or down.[13] Thus decisions about monetary or fiscal policy that affect interest rates can also influence the exchange rate. Markets are further affected by speculators trying to anticipate and profit from fluctuations in exchange rates. A currency's price sometimes changes as a result of perceptions of the nation's economic strength: Stronger economies are expected to have stable or higher exchange rates and thereby attract those who want a stable store of value. What is clear is that exchange rates very often do not move in such a way as to adjust a nation's current account imbalances.

When intervention does take place, governments recognize that markets are simply too big for even coordinated action to control over extended periods of time. The hope from intervention is to move markets in the direction of fundamental forces and to stabilize movements that might prove damaging if left alone. In pursuing these goals, central banks can rely on a market tendency toward a herd instinct whereby traders play "follow the leader." This makes it possible for small amounts of actual intervention, when coupled with clear signals of cooperation and resolve by major nations, to produce major moves in exchange rates. The risk, of course, is that the herd instinct will go too far and lead to precipitate changes or even panic selling.

A final and perhaps most crucial feature of government involvement in foreign exchange markets is the role of market confidence in government policies and leaders. Fiscal, monetary, and exchange rate policies must be

---

[13] Generally, higher or rising interest rates cause a currency to rise, whereas lower or falling rates cause a currency to decline.

made with an eye toward how they will be received in world markets for equities, bonds, and foreign exchange. A clear negative reaction to a nation's policies can act to veto those decisions before they have an opportunity to succeed or fail. Because money markets are the main suppliers of credit to governments, the latter cannot ignore how these entities respond collectively to their actions.[14]

## Managing Exchange Rates: 1985–1987

The context for international cooperation on exchange rates in 1985 was more than a decade of floating rates following the collapse of the Bretton Woods system of fixed rates and severe imbalances in the world economy created by the U.S. budget and trade deficits. This meant that leaders needed to create a system for coordinating their behavior in the midst of serious economic difficulties.

Before 1981 U.S. international accounts were in equilibrium, while U.S. fiscal accounts were at historically high deficit levels. The tax cuts of 1981, coupled with increases in government defense and welfare spending, produced massive increases in the budget deficit. Between 1983 and 1986 deficits hovered around $200 billion, nearly three times the level in 1980. A tight monetary policy pushed interest rates to record levels, and this served to attract foreign funds, driving up the exchange rate of the dollar. The dollar rose from about 200 yen in 1981 to 270 yen in 1983 and moved between 230 and 250 for the next two years. The dollar rose much more against other currencies. It moved up about 60 percent against a weighted average of currencies and rose steadily from 2 German marks to 3.3 from 1981 to 1985.[15] The consequence was to put great pressure on U.S. exporters to raise their prices, while importers enjoyed the luxury of keeping prices low. U.S. merchandise exports, which had been growing at the same pace as imports from 1976 to 1981, stagnated and even declined from 1981 to 1986. Merchandise imports rose from $260 billion in 1981 to more than $340 billion in 1986.[16]

The United States had two basic alternatives for dealing with this problem: The policies of the 1980s could have been reversed and efforts made to make the United States more competitive internationally, or price levels could have been readjusted through a lower dollar without altering basic policy. Adopting the first alternative would have meant a rejection of the basic premises of the Reagan administration. Attacking the budget deficit through higher taxes would have permitted lower interest rates and thereby a lower

---

[14] An excellent discussion of this process is found in Jeffrey A. Frieden, *Banking on the World*, New York: Harper & Row, 1987, 112–122.

[15] I. M. Destler and C. Randall Henning, *Dollar Politics: Exchange Rate Policy Making in the United States*, Washington, D.C.: Institute for International Economics, 1989, 17, 23–25.

[16] John Pool and Steve Stamos, *The ABC's of International Finance*, Lexington: D. C. Heath, 1987, 77.

dollar, but it also would have meant undermining both the administration's political position with upper-income groups and its image with others. Further, this policy almost surely would have produced a serious recession.[17] A corollary policy would involve lowering costs and increasing savings, investment, and spending on research and development to improve U.S. competitiveness.

Rather than take on the political dynamite of this option, the Reagan administration actually pursued two contradictory policies between 1981 and 1989.[18] For the first half of this period, the administration chose to ignore (sometimes referred to as *benign neglect*) the international consequences of its policies and concentrated instead on the domestic economic boom that resulted. Officials simply accepted the large deficits, the rising dollar, and the subsequent growth of U.S. debt that was needed to finance the boom. But after the 1984 election, a policy of reducing the dollar while preserving existing fiscal policy emerged. Exporters were provided with price incentives to attempt to regain lost overseas markets, and importers were forced to raise prices. Domestically, the costs of adjustment were borne by consumers but were disguised by the intricacies of the connections between the dollar and imported goods.

Beginning in 1985 the new U.S. Secretary of the Treasury, James Baker, and his assistant, Richard Darman, moved to organize an international effort to lower the value of the dollar.[19] In a meeting at the Plaza Hotel in New York, the finance ministers and central bank heads of the G-5 (United States, Germany, Japan, France, and Great Britain) orchestrated a collective effort to increase the exchange value of the main nondollar currencies. This was to be accomplished by coordinated market intervention and other signals of determination to see this achieved.[20] Each country pledged a substantial sum of foreign exchange for this operation. Although initially scheduled for six weeks and a 10 to 12 percent drop, the dollar's fall actually extended until December 1987. Much of this period involved something other than smooth cooperation, as there was considerable disagreement over the wisdom of the continuing fall in the dollar.

Between the Plaza Accord in September 1985 and the Louvre Agreement in January 1987, the dollar fell from 240 to 140 yen and 2.8 to 1.8 deutsche

---

[17] Instead, the United States experienced a continued income recession for middle and lower wage groups, who have not had any significant growth in real income since 1973. Although jobs were being created at record levels, they were primarily at low wages. Households were often forced to maintain purchasing power by increasing the number employed. See Phillips, *The Politics of Rich and Poor,* New York: Random House, 1989.

[18] There is no evidence that anyone in the Reagan administration contemplated anything resembling this strategy, although Richard Darman indicated sympathy for some of its elements.

[19] The discussion of the events of this effort at cooperation draws heavily on Yoichi Funabashi, *Managing the Dollar: From the Plaza to the Louvre,* Washington, D.C.: Institute for International Economics, 1989; and Destler and Henning, *Dollar* . . . .

[20] *Market intervention* means entering the foreign exchange markets to sell dollars and to buy one or more of the other four main currencies: the pound, the deutsche mark, the yen, and the franc.

marks.[21] The German government was ready to stop after a 7 percent mark appreciation. The Japanese became concerned at 180 yen. At the Louvre in February 1987, the United States reversed its position and supported a stabilization of its currency. This proved ineffective until after the stock market crash in October of that year.

How can we understand this effort to manage exchange rates and the taut mixture of cooperation and conflict involved? In terms of interests, the Reagan Administration by 1985 was being subjected to a barrage of complaints about the high dollar from U.S. exporters, and sentiment in Congress, which also received these concerns, was increasingly protectionist. Some in the Administration who were most committed to letting markets set exchange rates were replaced by more pragmatic officials. From the U.S. perspective, the ideal arrangement would have been to engineer a coordinated effort to push dollar values down while preserving the levels of foreign investment needed to sustain the budget deficit.

For the Germans, concerns centered on the importance of removing the imbalances in the world economy produced by the U.S. deficits without generating a dollar collapse. Further, a rising deutsche mark would help hold down inflation in Germany—always a key element of policy choice in that country. But German leaders also thought the imbalances were largely a U.S.-Japanese problem and preferred that most of the exchange rate adjustment come between the dollar and the yen. Perhaps most important, from the German perspective, was preservation of the European Monetary System (EMS). This was an arrangement among ten European states in the EEC to fix exchange rates for their currencies with each other and to coordinate fiscal and monetary policies. The German central bank—the Bundesbank—played the key role in this system, setting the standard for conservative policies and using its resources to maintain currency parities. German leaders feared that a precipitous decline of the dollar would put intense pressure on the EMS for realignment and might even force its breakup.[22]

By contrast, the Japanese were more receptive to dollar depreciation. They worried about the consequences of rising protectionist sentiments in Congress much more than did the Germans. Japanese financial sectors hoped to benefit from a higher yen, while some political figures saw exchange rate adjustment as preferable to structural changes in terms of openness to the world. Even so, the massive appreciation of the yen eventually led to the disintegration of the domestic political coalition favoring this policy. Small- and medium-sized exporters were battered, and even large firms found themselves

---

[21] Eventually the dollar fell to 120 yen and 1.6 deutsche marks in December 1987. See Destler and Henning, *Dollar . . .*, 23–24.

[22] The Germans often repeated to the Americans what they saw as the basic structural difference between themselves and the Japanese. Germany was much more closely tied to Europe, with over half its foreign trade there, compared to 10 percent with the United States and 3 percent with Japan. Funabashi, *Managing . . .*, 120–121.

pressed to deal with the trade-off between raising prices and accepting lower profits. But the United States seemed determined to allow or to cause the dollar to fall and used noncooperation to prevent stabilization.

We should remember that the strategy of a lower dollar had the effect of rescuing the Reagan Administration from acknowledging the costs of its economic policies. Japan and Germany were being forced to bear most of the politically difficult costs of adjustment. These countries (especially Japan) had simply taken advantage of a situation created by the United States. But as the dollar continued to fall, the United States refused to participate in a stabilization effort. Instead, it attempted to hold out the possibility of sanctioning additional decline unless these countries agreed to stimulate their economies and/or make structural changes. The United States pressed this position because of the very slow improvement in the U.S. current account deficit. Only when fears of an end to foreign investment in the United States became intense did the United States reverse its position.

## Conclusions

What conclusions can we reach about the process of cooperation in the two case studies? The study of international political economy has not developed a clear understanding of the sources of cooperation, nor can we predict its future direction. This brief review points out both the weakness of cooperation in macroeconomic coordination and the coercive elements of cooperation in managing exchange rates. The most interesting and important theoretical question raised by the exchange rate case concerns the behavior of the United States as hegemon. For much of the postwar period, the United States accepted the burdens of world leadership. Providing grants and loans, maintaining open markets for foreign goods, and supplying military security are but a few of many examples. The United States behaved as a liberal, somewhat benevolent, hegemon. The exchange rate case of the 1980s continues a trend beginning in 1971 to emphasize a much more narrow and nationalistic definition of U.S. interests. The United States has been willing to use its continuing power to force adjustments onto other, often allied, states. The implications of this pattern for multilateral cooperation may turn out to be very negative and to support the view that cooperation can diminish in the wake of a declining hegemon.

At the same time, the globalization of finance has profound effects for macroeconomic and exchange rate decisions. When we look more closely, cooperation and coordination may be greater than the case studies initially suggest. Much of this cooperation may derive from pressure generated by the structural power of capital: Mobile capital frequently punishes states whose policies conflict with market expectations. There are three different contexts in which cooperation may occur on macroeconomic and exchange rate policies: among national leaders, among central bankers, and during times of crisis. Efforts by national leaders to set and coordinate policies at annual summits have had limited success. Because the politics of matters such as spending and taxes is overwhelmingly domestic, agreement on timing and outcomes will usually be difficult. Punishment of outliers by global markets may be the most effective pressure on domestic policy makers. But this can take a long time.

A second context is the coordination of national monetary policy by central bankers and midlevel officials. Here it is possible on a daily, weekly, and monthly basis to make interest rate, monetary, and exchange rate decisions that follow markets and operate to coordinate results. Although mostly acting to ratify market shifts and coordinate responses to markets, these fine-tuning operations occasionally succeed in making marginal adjustment to global markets. The forums for this cooperation are periodic meetings of G-7 finance ministers, central bankers, and deputy finance ministers (sometimes known as "sherpas"); and regular meetings of national and supranational officials at the Bank for International Settlements, International Monetary Fund, and Organization for Economic Cooperation and Development (OECD).

A third context, which somewhat recombines the first two, involves crisis situations that threaten or potentially threaten the stability of the world economy. On several occasions—the 1982 debt crisis, the 1987 stock market crash, the 1994-1995 Mexican peso crisis, and the 1985-1987 dollar exchange rate misalignment—national leaders and financial officials have been able to act together to resolve serious problems. Often this is a result of the ongoing contact among lower-level officials. These efforts sometimes yield actions to establish arrangements that anticipate crises. For example, in 1995 the United States' central bank—the Federal Reserve—worked out a procedure to purchase large amounts of U.S. government securities from Japanese banks in the event that these banks are experiencing liquidity problems. And, on a multilateral level, members of the G-7 have proposed creating an emergency reserve of money that could be used to support a country facing severe but temporary financial difficulties in paying its debts.

From the early 1970s and the breakup of the Bretton Woods system, the incentives for cooperation on economic policies have increased, but its incidence is less consistent. Although a calamity has not happened and stability has eventually occurred, no real institutions for macroeconomic or exchange rate cooperation have developed. The interests that produce stability seem ad hoc and uncertain. Perhaps most disturbing is the role of the United States, which has taken an increasingly nationalistic and even bullying posture in its international economic negotiations. The United States retains the power to force adjustments on other states while avoiding making difficult adjustments itself. This behavior may have undermined the ability of the major economic powers to work together effectively and may account in part for the movement toward economic blocs.[23]

---

[23] For evidence that interests remained opposed, see Leonard Silk, "Bonn's Contrasts with Washington," *New York Times*, May 17, 1991; Jonathan Fuerbringer, "Weak Effort to Aid Yen," *New York Times*, March 10, 1990; and Clyde Farnsworth, "U.S. Resists Japan Plea to Aid Yen," *New York Times*, March 24, 1990.

At the same time, institutional manifestations of, and efforts at, cooperation are much more substantial than at any previous time. A massive array of cooperative activities sustains the world economy every day.[24] Undoubtedly, the most important and far-reaching effort at international cooperation is the European Union. Less developed, but also significant, are other economic blocs, including the bloc between the United States, Canada, and Mexico and a potential bloc in Asia.

# ECONOMIC BLOCS

## Globalization or Regionalization?

Does the evidence of globalization presented in Chapter 5 really represent greater international activity, but confined to nations in close geographical proximity? Are we seeing not the integration of a global economy, but instead an acceleration of ties within several separating regions of the world? Should we be talking about the regionalization of the world economy instead of globalization? Is the future of the world economy one of fragmentation into exclusionary blocs?

These are some of the questions raised by the growth of regional economic blocs like the European Union and the North American Free Trade Agreement. Unfortunately, at present there are few clear answers to what is essentially a prediction about the future. We need to understand better whether increasing regional integration leads to an expansion of intraregional trade that comes at the expense of trade with the rest of the world. This may have much to do with how open the regional arrangement is to the world and with how much it participates in multilateral trade agreements; in other words, with how much its rules and practices discriminate against outside goods and investment.

We believe that globalization and regionalization, at present, are not conflicting processes. Financial flows and trade destinations may have a regional bias, but the terms on which regionalization occurs are global. Competitive standards are global; tariff levels and trading rules are mostly established globally; capital is raised in global markets; technology and innovation meet global standards; and communication and innovation systems are globally based. At the same time, economic blocs have an inherently discriminatory bias: They involve the reduction of trade barriers only for members. The greatest threat to world trade could come if protectionist forces gain control of governments involved in economic blocs and use the machinery of the blocs to raise barriers.

## The European Union

The European Union (EU) is by far the most significant and extensive effort at international economic cooperation. It is the focal point of the most radical

---

[24] See Stephen Krasner (ed.), "International Regimes," *International Organization*, 36.2, Spring 1982.

effort to shift political and economic responsibility to a transnational level; the EU seeks to expand its geographical scope even as it increases the scope of issues under its jurisdiction; and the EU is the most far-reaching effort to achieve monetary cooperation. The European Union is something of a real-life experiment in studying international cooperation, and its fate will help scholars judge the future of world politics.

Established in 1958, the European Economic Community (EEC) has successfully promoted the reduction of tariffs and quotas among its members. The motives of its founding members contained an interesting mixture of political and economic thinking. France, in particular, wanted to incorporate Germany into a European system and tame any aggressive tendencies. Also important was the desire to expand the size of the market in which firms could sell their products. Reducing tariffs across the six original states was designed to reap the benefits of freer trade and to improve the position of European firms in world markets. When economies of scale exist—that is, when the cost per unit of production falls as output rises—the costs of a firm would fall and global competitiveness would improve if the firm could sell in a larger market. The 1970s and 1980s produced expansion of the EEC from six to twelve members (see Table 6.1). But after the early 1970s there was little additional progress toward economic integration. This changed in December 1985, when the twelve EEC members signed the Single European Act (SEA).[25] This agreement moved integration beyond tariffs and sought to remove the myriad nontariff barriers created by having twelve countries enacting different laws.

The goal of the 1985 agreement was the free movement of trade, people, and money, and a specific timetable (December 31, 1992) was established for states to adopt more than three hundred rules and procedures that would establish common standards throughout a newly named European Community (EC). The consequence has been more uniform standards, free banking across all EC nations, and lower costs of doing business. A single market of 340 million persons makes it much easier for companies to lower costs by expanding production to sell to many more consumers. Progress toward a single market has been substantial but remains incomplete. In most (but not all) of Europe, passport controls have ended, and more than 93 percent of the three hundred specific measures have been adopted. Beyond specific rules, the SEA also made important advances in decision-making procedures within the EC Council of Ministers (see later for more detail). Previously, the Council of Ministers operated with a national veto rule; with the SEA, many decision arenas were now to be decided by majority vote of the nations. This innovation greatly increased the policy flexibility of the EC.

In late 1991 the EC took steps to expand its membership and to shift its cooperation to a much more intense and significant level. In October the EC reached agreement with the seven members of the European Free Trade Area

---

[25] A useful compendium of events and arrangements for 1992 is found in Nicholas Colchester and David Buchan, *Europower*, New York: Times Books, 1990.

**FIGURE 6.1**
**Expansion of the European Union**

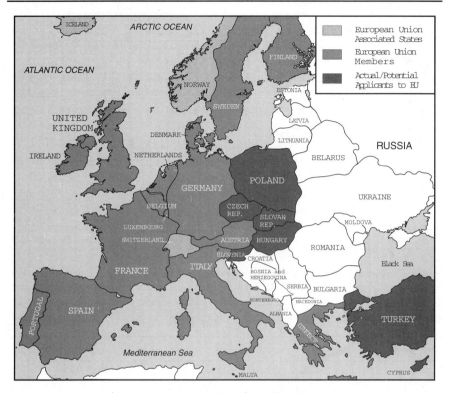

SOURCE: Organization for Economic Cooperation and Development.

(EFTA) to bring them into the new trading system after 1992. EFTA nations would initially participate only as associated states and later apply for full membership. In January 1995 Austria, Finland, and Sweden were admitted as members.[26] Several other nations are now lining up to become members.

In December 1991, at Maastricht, the European Community reached agreement on a broad set of goals that would bring about a much greater degree of integration. The Treaty on European Union increased the range of issues subject to majority vote in the Council of Ministers, added to the responsibility of the European Parliament, called for a common foreign and security policy, and defined a timetable and criteria for establishment of economic and monetary union (EMU). The result of this last process would be a common

---

[26] In addition to Austria, Finland, and Sweden, the former members of EFTA are Norway, Switzerland, Iceland, and Liechtenstein. In November 1994 Norway voted not to join the EU. The remaining four former EFTA states have an arrangement with the EU as associated states. They gain access to EU markets but cannot participate in decision making.

TABLE 6.1
**Expansion of the European Union**
*Original Members*

| COUNTRY | POPULATION | PER-CAPITA INCOME INCOME (PPP) | PERCENT EXPORTS TO EU STATES |
|---|---|---|---|
| Belgium | 10.1 | 18,600 | 74.9 |
| France | 58.0 | 19,440 | 62.7 |
| Germany | 81.6 | 20,700 | 54.4 |
| Italy | 58.1 | 18,070 | 57.8 |
| Luxembourg | .4 | 21,500 | n.a. |
| Netherlands | 15.4 | 18,000 | 76.1 |
| *1973 Additions* | | | |
| Denmark | 5.2 | 16,400 | 54.4 |
| Ireland | 3.6 | 12,420 | 74.3 |
| United Kingdom | 58.2 | 16,400 | 56.0 |
| *1981/1986 Additions* | | | |
| Greece | 10.5 | 8,360 | 64.1 |
| Portugal | 9.4 | 9,890 | 75.1 |
| Spain | 39.2 | 13,310 | 71.2 |
| *1995 Additions* | | | |
| Austria | 7.8 | 18,700 | 66.1 |
| Finland | 5.0 | 15,500 | 53.2 |
| Sweden | 8.7 | 18,000 | 55.8 |

*Population in millions*            *PPP=purchasing power parity*
*Per-capita income in U.S. dollars*     *n.a.=not available*

currency. Implementation of the TEU in 1993 led to renaming the EC as the European Union (EU).

# Organization of the European Union

The governing structure of the European Union, especially after passage of the Single European Act (SEA), is a complex system of overlapping responsibility, decision making, and representation. There are four main units to the EC: one executive, two legislative, and one judicial. These are:

## EUROPEAN COMMISSION

The Commission holds the executive power, vested in a president of the Commission (currently Jacques Santer). The Commission, composed of

TABLE 6.1 (CONTINUED)

**Expansion of the European Union**

| COUNTRY | POPULATION | PER-CAPITA INCOME INCOME (PPP) | PERCENT EXPORTS TO EU STATES |
|---|---|---|---|
| *Associated States* | | | |
| Iceland | .3 | 17,400 | 66.8 |
| Norway | 4.3 | 18,600 | 66.5 |
| Switzerland | 6.9 | 22,000 | 58.9 |
| *Actual/Potential Applicants* | | | |
| Cyprus | .7 | 15,470 | 40.8 |
| Czech Republic | 10.3 | 7,770 | 49.5 |
| Hungary | 10.3 | 6,260 | 49.5 |
| Malta | .4 | 8,280 | 74.4 |
| Poland | 38.5 | 5,010 | 55.6 |
| Slovak Republic | 5.4 | 6,450 | 49.5 |
| Slovenia | 2.0 | 8,100 | n.a. |
| Turkey | 57.7 | 5,550 | 51.7 |
| *Aspirants* | | | |
| Albania | 3.1 | 900 | n.a. |
| Bulgaria | 8.6 | 4,470 | 40.8 |
| Estonia | 1.6 | 3,200 | n.a. |
| Latvia | 2.7 | 5,400 | n.a. |
| Lithuania | 3.7 | 5,000 | n.a. |
| Romania | 23.2 | 2,370 | 32.5 |

SOURCES: OECD, World Bank, *The Economist*, IMF.

the president and sixteen other commissioners appointed by the fifteen heads of government (two commissioners each from the four largest nations) of the EU nations and supported by a staff of fifteen thousand, is located in Brussels. The commissioners, though appointed by member governments, are pledged to act in the interest of the EU. The Commission has the responsibility for initiating legislation and legal action against member nations.

## COUNCIL OF MINISTERS

The Council is composed of representatives of member states. The Council has final legislative authority. The Single European Act of 1985 broadened the scope of majority-rule decisions in the Council to include all actions required for creation of a single market. This enhances the ability of the Council to act, as compared with a single state veto system. Voting is weighted by national population, which creates a complex system of coalition building.[27]

## EUROPEAN PARLIAMENT

The Parliament is composed of members elected by the populations of individual states for five-year terms. Traditionally limited to a restricted power over the budget, the Parliament could well gain wider authority over the budget, the right to initiate legislation, and the ability to approve the Commission.

## EUROPEAN COURT OF JUSTICE

The Court is composed of justices nominated by member states. Its responsibility is to render final decisions on disputes among EU institutions, member states, or on suits against EU institutions.[28] The process of political decision making in the EU is very complex but mainly involves the initiation of legislation by the Commission, its modification by the Parliament, and a final decision by the Commission.[29]

Many important issues are raised by expansion of the European Union. Perhaps the most significant include problems brought about by incorporating several small and sometimes quite different countries. Voting in the European Commission is directly affected by expansion such as that in 1995. Already the distribution of votes gives much greater weight to smaller countries, but the locus of real decision making is with the four largest states.[30] Whatever arrangement is made, expansion creates new dynamics of coalition building. Expanding membership also raises questions about political and economic compatibility. Some postcommunist states, such as the Slovak Republic, retain vestiges of authoritarianism. Many potential members have

---

[27] There are still areas where the veto system (or unanimity) prevails, primarily in taxes and decisions on social policy.

The weighting in 1995 was as follows:

          10 votes (each)—Britain, Italy, Germany, France
          8 votes—Spain
          5 votes—Netherlands, Belgium, Greece, Portugal
          4 votes—Austria, Sweden
          3 votes—Finland, Denmark, Ireland
          2 votes—Luxembourg

[28] See Colchester and Buchan, *Europower*, 131–143. For a detailed discussion of the European Court and its impact on international cooperation, see Ann-Marie Burley and Walter Mattli, "Europe Before the Court: A Political Theory of Legal Integration," *International Organization*, 47.1, Winter 1993, 41–76; and Geoffrey Garrett and Barry Weingast, "Ideas, Interests, and Institutions: Constructing the European Community's Internal Market," in Judith Goldstein and Robert Keohane (eds.), *Ideas and Foreign Policy*, Ithaca: Cornell University Press, 1993, 173–206.

[29] The best description is in Colchester and Buchan, *Europower*, 40–41.

[30] For example, Germany has ten votes or one for each 8,000,000 persons. Luxembourg, by contrast, has two votes or one for each 190,000 persons.

per-capita incomes far below the EU average. And those states with a combination of extensive agriculture and low-cost labor present special competitive problems for existing EU states.

## Economic and Monetary Union

The incentives for cooperation can be understood even better by considering in detail the process leading toward EMU. Here again we draw on the earlier discussion of cooperation, especially the role of interests defined by the benefits and costs of cooperation, the costs of not cooperating, and the impact of existing institutions on the calculations of member states.

In important ways, an economic and monetary union can be traced to the breakup of the Bretton Woods system of fixed exchange rates in the early 1970s. The chief result of that breakup was a realignment of currencies, with the dollar falling against all others. Many in Europe (in and out of the EEC) attempted to set up a system of fixed exchange rates with each other so as to offer some protection against the falling dollar. This ultimately proved impossible because of the growth of private transactions, especially for purposes of speculation. Another round of dollar depreciation in the late 1970s helped rekindle the idea of a European system for managing exchange rates.[31] In 1978 most of the EEC (Britain was the main exception) joined in creating the European Monetary System (EMS). Its main feature was a system of linked exchange rates. Against a backdrop of fears of lost sovereignty and higher inflation, an exchange rate mechanism (ERM) was created. The ERM defined a small range of fluctuation for each currency in the system. The benchmark was a weighted average of currencies called the European Currency Unit (ECU). Each currency had a fixed rate against the ECU, plus or minus 2.25 percent, and as a nation's currency approached this limit, its central bank was obligated to intervene to preserve the parity.[32]

The EMS contributed to the movement toward monetary union through a conditioning of the interests of the major states. In other words, the EMS demonstrated both the possibility of monetary cooperation and also its benefits. Fluctuations in exchange rates narrowed considerably in the 1980s because of the EMS and the efforts to foster a greater coordination of monetary and fiscal policies. Over time, the ECU gained in credibility as an important

---

[31] This was the period of 1977–1979, when the United States, in several economic summits, tried to move West Germany to adopt an expansionary economic policy to pull the United States out of its recession and trade deficit.

[32] Several states with weaker currencies were permitted a wider range. The weighting for establishing the value of the ECU is mainly based on five currencies—those of Germany, France, Britain, Italy, and the Netherlands—which together represent 80 percent of the value of the ECU. The German deutsche mark alone accounts for more than 30 percent. For more detail on the process, including the computation of the ECU, see John Pinder, *European Community*, Oxford: Oxford University Press, 1991, 119–130; Colchester and Buchan, *Europower*, 162–165.

denominator of EC transactions. By the late 1980s several defectors from the EMS were moved by its successes to join.[33] They found that the costs of not cooperating were substantial and that the benefits of participating in the system were significant enough to warrant joining.

The key to the success of the EMS was the role played by Germany and its central bank, the Bundesbank. With Europe's strongest economy and the most intense commitment to monetary stability and low inflation, Germany offered the deutsche mark as a de facto key currency for the EMS. This role meant that participant nations used the deutsche mark for intervention in currency markets and, consequently, used German inflation rates and monetary policy as a benchmark for their decisions on these matters. The operation of this system resulted in a convergence of macroeconomic policies and inflation rates over the decade of the 1980s and opened the door for closer monetary cooperation.[34]

The decision to move toward an open market for goods in the European Community created a powerful momentum for a closer monetary union. Free trade also required the free movement of money. Permitting money to move freely, allowing banks to establish branches across the EC, and promoting the development of an integrated market for financial services contained a set of robust incentives for political cooperation designed to extend the EMS.

Also important as a conditioning factor was the further globalization of finance during the 1980s. Prompted by the massive U.S. trade and budget deficits, this process accelerated with the computer and telecommunications advances that made global financial markets possible.[35] European firms that were engaged in global trade demanded new financial services, and financiers saw new profit opportunities. The Single European Act of 1985 created free capital movement and an integrated market for financial services throughout the EC. This tapped into the interests of these firms and provided an enormous boost for monetary union.

## The Maastricht Agreement

The most important step toward EMU was taken at the meeting in Maastricht, the Netherlands, in December 1991. The goal established there was nothing less than creation of a single currency to replace the national currencies of the EU members. Perhaps more than any other action in the integration of Europe, a single currency would require the surrender of national sovereignty. Consequently, this is the most difficult move in the integration process.

Why take such drastic action? As with other events, the decisions for EMU and a common currency are a result of political and economic factors. The EU

---

[33] In particular, Britain, Greece, and Portugal joined EMS. Pinder, *European . . .*, 130.

[34] For more detail on the Bundesbank and its role in the EMS, see Ellen Kennedy, *The Bundesbank*, London: Pinter, 1991, 79–103.

[35] See "Ebb Tide," *The Economist*, April 21, 1991, 7.

states share powerful interests in the success of the integration venture. At the same time, there is a complex mixture of complementary and conflicting interests that sometimes moves countries toward opposing views on the shape of future cooperation. And reaching agreement involves a process of negotiation whereby countries modify their preferences in order to gain an agreement. Germany—now the key player in the EMS and the strongest advocate of financial stability—has pressed for a rapid transition to a system modeled on the Bundesbank. This means a bank largely independent of control by politicians and capable of acting effectively to manage inflation. Ironically, many other EU states also prefer an independent bank because that would reduce German influence as compared to the EMS. Decisions on interest rates would no longer be set by the Bundesbank. The Maastricht agreement means that the Germans will ultimately give up the deutsche mark itself in return for a powerful European central bank. Other EU states likewise surrender an important element of their sovereignty, gain some additional role in policymaking, and must lower their inflation rates and budget deficits.

Beyond this, interests begin to diverge and re-form in interesting ways. Many in France see closer cooperation in Europe as an essential element in establishing a new political and economic entity capable of dealing effectively with the United States and Japan. French influence within a strengthened EU would be important, whereas dealing alone with the United States and Japan puts France in a position of weakness. Others in France take a more traditional view and see a renewed EU as the best means of containing German power.[36] Many British, especially among the Conservatives, fear the implications for national sovereignty of moves toward common monetary, economic, foreign, and social policies. British Prime Minister John Major has urged delay in the timetable and less power for a central bank.[37] Several EU countries with a tradition of an easy monetary policy, large budget deficits, and high inflation have expressed concern over the deflationary implications of a central bank. Some, including Spain, Greece, Portugal, and Ireland, have pressed for more economic aid from the wealthier EU countries as the price for entering the new system.[38] Although some of these countries may not make it into the late 1990s monetary union, they have nonetheless accepted the responsibility to work toward these goals.[39]

The economics of European integration also created powerful incentives for EMU and a single currency. Throughout the 1970s and 1980s, goods and especially capital moved more freely throughout Europe. And the SEA

---

[36] Alan Riding, "France Pins Hopes on European Unity," *New York Times*, December 1, 1991.

[37] "A Dangerous Passage," *The Economist*, November 2, 1991, 49–50.

[38] Alan Riding, "The 'Poor Four' of Europe Are Demanding More Aid," *New York Times*, December 5, 1991.

[39] For discussion of some of the additional problems associated with negotiation of the Maastricht agreement, see Alan Riding, "With No Thatcher to Assail, Europe's Unity Stalls," *New York Times*, March 17, 1991; Alan Riding, "The New Europe of 1992 Is Closer in Economics Than in Politics," *New York Times*, June 16, 1991.

provided for an end to all capital restrictions and for free banking across the EC. As we have seen earlier, capital mobility forces states to choose between exchange rate stability and an independent monetary policy. The globalization of finance undermines the ability of all states to pursue an independent monetary policy, so states concentrate on the costs of floating exchange rates. These are substantial, especially as trade and capital flows increase. One important cost is the resources that businesses devote to protecting themselves from exchange rate risks. Just the cost of foreign exchange transactions in Europe is estimated at $30 billion. Uncertainty in calculations of long-term investment due to periodic realignment of exchange rates in EMS made this only a partial solution. Thus a single currency is the most efficient solution that would support closer integration.

How does the process of achieving a single currency work, and how has it worked since 1991? The Treaty on European Union and subsequent agreements call for the formation of supranational institutions, a timetable of events, and a set of economic criteria that nations must meet to join the single currency. An independent European central bank—the European Monetary Institute—was created in 1994. The bank is governed by a fifteen-person board, with members nominated by, but not recallable by, each country. The European Council, after consulting the parliament, picks the chairman. The responsibilities of the European Monetary Institute will likely include a shared control with the Bundesbank over interest rates, broad direction for monetary policy, and a narrowing of the bands for exchange rate fluctuations. Movement toward a single currency and a genuine central bank (the current name for which is Eurofed) is dependent on success in achieving convergence in macroeconomic policy.

For a nation to participate in the last stage of this process, its inflation rate, interest rates, public debt, currency stability, and budget deficit must conform to certain standards. This is because currency unity can work only if monetary and fiscal policies are closely related. Inflation must be within 1.5 percent of the average of the three lowest in the EU, and long-term interest rates must be no more than 2 percent higher than the three best. The exchange rate must have remained within the narrow EMS band for the preceding two years without realignment. The budget deficit cannot be more than 3 percent of GDP, and public debt cannot be more than 60 percent of GDP. The Maastricht agreement commits those that meet these standards to establish a common central bank on January 1, 1998, and to lock exchange rates and establish a single currency on January 1, 1999.[40] Those that initially do not qualify may join later

---

[40] The criteria for inflation are that a country must not exceed the average inflation rate of the three lowest EU nations by more than 1.5 percentage points and that its interest rates must be within 2 percentage points. A country's budget deficit cannot exceed 3 percent of its gross domestic product (GDP), nor can its public debt exceed 60 percent of GDP. Its currency must not have been devalued within the previous two years and must not have exceeded the normal 2.25 percent margin. In late 1991 only two countries—France and Luxembourg—actually met these criteria. See "The Deal is Done," *The Economist*, December 14, 1991, 52.

**TABLE 6.2**
**EU Single-Currency Criteria**

| COUNTRY | 1995 DEFICIT AS % GDP (MAX.=3.0%) | 1995 DEBT AS % GDP (MAX.=60.0%) |
|---|---|---|
| *Currently Meet Both Criteria* | | |
| Germany | 2.9 | 59.5 |
| Luxembourg | 0.4 (surplus) | 6.3 |
| *Close to Meeting Criteria* | | |
| Austria | 5.5 | 68.0 |
| Britain | 5.1 | 52.5 |
| Denmark | 2.0 | 73.6 |
| Finland | 5.4 | 63.2 |
| France | 5.0 | 51.5 |
| Holland | 3.1 | 78.4 |
| Ireland | 2.7 | 85.9 |
| Portugal | 5.4 | 70.5 |
| Spain | 5.9 | 64.8 |
| *Far from the Mark* | | |
| Belgium | 4.5 | 134.4 |
| Greece | 9.3 | 114.4 |
| Italy | 7.4 | 124.9 |
| Sweden | 7.0 | 81.4 |

SOURCE: *The Economist*, December 9, 1995, 20.

after they meet the requirements.[41] The outlook is not altogether positive that many EU nations will meet these requirements. Table 6.2 provides a focused look at two of the most easily measured criteria: deficits and debt.

The goals associated with a single currency are not entirely consistent. For a single currency to work to generate efficiency gains, it must have wide membership. At the same time, locking exchange rates and establishing a credible and stable currency require that entrance criteria be tough and rigid. As we see from Table 6.2, this will sharply reduce the number that can join. There is increasing fear that the single currency will be delayed or that it can begin with only a few participants, thereby creating different categories of EU membership. Germany is the key actor in this process. The traditional strength and stability of the deutsche mark means that many Germans are hesitant to substitute an untried currency linked to countries with less commitment to currency stability. Germans must be convinced that the conversion of

---

[41] Britain won the option of deciding later whether it will participate, known as "opting out."

the deutsche mark for the European currency will work and that they will receive money just as strong as the deutsche mark. Several German leaders have taken the strictest position on the Maastricht criteria, defining an unswerving adherence to these standards. The effort to make the grade pushes states to contract government spending, in some cases with drastic results.

In late 1995 the French effort to cut spending by reducing benefits to public employees sparked a wave of strikes and demonstrations. The French government was prepared to accept these very large domestic political costs because it sees entry into a single currency as essential to the continuation of French power in Europe. The unification of Germany and its continued economic prosperity with low inflation, combined with French problems with budgets, inflation, and economic growth, threaten the power and influence of France in Europe. The ability to meet the single currency criteria and to carry out the timetable is viewed by French leaders as a fundamental measure of national power and credibility and as an indicator of the future direction of integration and unity in Europe. French President Jacques Chirac publicly argued that "we cannot proceed with a change of this magnitude from a position of weakness vis-à-vis Germany."[42] Consequently, Chirac was prepared to engage in a very difficult policy of tax increases and spending cuts. The ability and willingness of other European Union countries to take the painful steps to meet the single currency criteria may depend on an equally complex mixture of economic and political motives. The march toward EMU can be littered with the fallout from higher interest rates, higher taxes and unemployment, and political unrest as EU countries adjust to the new demands of globalization.

Also casting a shadow on progress toward EMU were serious problems in the operation of the exchange rate mechanism of the European Monetary System during 1992 and 1993. Several currencies came under speculative attack to such an extent that the continuation of the ERM was in doubt. Remember that the ERM works to keep the currencies of the members of the EMS within very narrow bands and pegged to the ECU. For several years before 1992, traders in global markets reached the conclusion that monetary union in Europe would occur and that exchange rate fluctuations would decline. Between 1987 and 1992 there was essentially no realignment of currencies in the ERM. Dramatic increases in cross-border investment took place as expectations were confirmed by the 1991 Maastricht agreement. Working to shatter this placid environment was the reunification of West and East Germany after 1990 and a persistent recession throughout Europe. This led to important conflicts over fiscal and monetary policies among several European states.

The Germans, largely ignoring their traditional role as monetary leader in the ERM, focused attention on a smooth integration of the formerly communist East Germany. This was a very expensive process—more than $100

---

[42] *New York Times*, May 22, 1995, A3.

billion annually—and budget deficits ballooned. The fears of inflation prompted the Bundesbank to raise interest rates. Other European countries, faced with rising unemployment and stagnant growth, were unwilling to follow the Bundesbank in raising interest rates because this would further restrict economic growth. These conflicts led currency traders to anticipate currency realignments, primarily a drop in the value of most currencies against the deutsche mark. The resulting speculative sales of pounds and lira, for example, forced these governments to choose among the unpleasant alternatives of raising interest rates, expending foreign exchange reserves, or accepting currency realignment. Britain and Italy eventually chose to withdraw from the ERM, while France maintained the franc only with help from Germany. A second round of this tug-of-war between governments and currency traders in 1993 led to a dramatic widening of the bands of currency fluctuation. This crisis was prompted mainly by the conclusion of currency traders that France was not in a position to defend the franc within the narrow band of fluctuation. What followed was waves of speculation against the franc and the decision to widen the bands for most currencies in the ERM.[43]

The exchange rate crises hang over the effort to achieve a single currency. The ERM now works less effectively to constrain exchange rates, and the problems of inconsistent monetary policies remain. But testimony to the strength of the interests in a single currency is the fact that the crises have not blocked or even delayed the effort. In a series of meetings after 1993, EU states have reaffirmed their commitment to move ahead with a single currency.[44] In an important sense, the currency crises demonstrate very clearly the problems produced by conflicting monetary policies in a context of deep integration and free capital movement. Equally, the crises show the disadvantages of trying to maintain independent yet linked exchange rates and move toward tighter integration. The exchange rate crises confront EU states with the choice of moving forward to a single currency or moving backward to less integration. Few states are willing to take the risks of disintegration.

## Conclusions

Developments in the EC and EU after 1985 are certainly the most far-reaching efforts in international cooperation. Given the history of conflict in Europe in the twentieth century, the possibility of a politically and economically united

---

[43] Short but readable reviews of the ERM crises of 1992 and 1993 can be found in Bank for International Settlements, *Annual Report*, Basel, 1993; and *Annual Report*, Basel, 1994.

[44] In December 1995 the EU leaders agreed unanimously on a name for the new currency—the *Euro*—and accepted a timetable for its introduction. In 1998 a decision will be made about which countries qualify for participation in the Euro; on January 1, 1999, the exchange rates for these countries will be set, and the European Central Bank will take responsibility for monetary policy; and in 2002 the Euro will begin to circulate and become the sole legal tender.

Europe is an extraordinary accomplishment. The driving forces behind these recent moves are powerful structural changes in the world economy, including the decline in U.S. economic leadership, the explosion of globalization, and the new competitive climate in the 1980s and 1990s. The SEA decisions should be seen as a response by elements of the European political and economic elite to changes in the world economy of the 1980s. Most important were the decline of the United States as the primary source of cutting-edge technologies and the most innovative production techniques and the U.S. abdication of responsibility for the international monetary system. Wide elements of the political and economic elites of Europe concluded that they could no longer rely on a U.S.-based system for economic organization. Relying on the Japanese for technological developments—much as the Europeans had done on the United States for thirty years—was not seen as a viable option. The Europeans did not have common security or cultural interests with Japan, a country that many saw as an economic predator. Contributing to these conclusions was the failure of individual national economic strategies of the 1975–1985 period. The decision was to establish a system that could be much more self-sufficient. A single large market would justify bigger research and development expenditures and would promote cost savings from economies of scale. A single monetary system could also help protect from the vagaries of U.S. exchange rate policies, and the newly competitive European firms could defend Europe from the Japanese.[45]

The Maastricht decisions to move toward a European Union are closely related to the end of the Cold War in Europe in 1989–1990. For approximately forty years the integration process in Europe was bolstered by common European and American need to deter and counter Soviet power in Europe. Though separate institutions, the EEC and the North Atlantic Treaty Organization (NATO) had similar origins and derived from similar purposes. The fear of the Soviets helped overcome deep and historical conflicts in Europe. With the Soviet threat receding, many felt that maintaining progress toward integration was needed to avoid losing the gains from closer integration. It is significant that the response of European states to structural changes in the international security and economic environment is to increase cooperation.

## A North American Trade Bloc?

Building on prior trade arrangements, the United States, Canada, and Mexico negotiated a North American Free Trade Agreement (Nafta) with the purpose

---

[45] This and the subsequent paragraph rely on Wayne Sandholtz and John Zysman, "1992: Recasting the European Bargain," *World Politics*, 62.1, October 1989, 95–128. For another view of the politics of the negotiation process that established SEA, see Andrew Moravcsik, "Negotiating the Single European Act: National Interests and Conventional Statecraft in the European Community," *International Organization*, 45.1, Winter 1991, 19–56. A summary of different perspectives is Jeffrey Anderson, "The State of the (European) Union," *World Politics*, 47, April 1995, 441–465.

of eliminating virtually all barriers to trade among the three nations.[46] The first step was a free trade agreement between Canada and the United States, which took effect in January 1989. By 1999 essentially all tariffs on all goods and services will be eliminated between these nations. Nafta was signed by Mexico, Canada, and the United States in December 1992 and was ratified by the U.S. Congress in November 1993 after additional side agreements were reached. The terms of the massive document call for reduction of trade barriers spread over a fifteen-year period, with different schedules for different products. But most of the reductions come quickly, and the consequences for trade growth could be seen almost immediately. Concerns by the United States that Mexico would be used as a production platform by third parties to the agreement were restricted, and Canadian worries about the onslaught of U.S. cultural products and the Mexican desire to retain control of its energy production led to these areas being treated as exceptions to the agreement. The principal institution established by Nafta is the North American Trade Commission, which is designed to settle trade disputes.[47]

The motivations for the United States in pursuing these agreements stem primarily from difficulties in multilateral trade negotiations in GATT and from the competitive pressures generated by the movement toward 1992 in the EC.[48] Urged on by its own trade problems—the need to expand markets for exports and to close a yawning trade deficit—the United States in the early 1980s pushed for a new round in GATT to reduce barriers to trade even more. For much of the decade this was a slow and frustrating process. Negotiating FTAs proved to be a quicker way of establishing trade relationships more to the liking of U.S. political leaders. These leaders also hoped that bilateral agreements involving preferential access to the large U.S. market would spur negotiations in GATT. One additional purpose of extending free trade to Mexico was to reinforce the liberalization of that country's economy undertaken after 1985.[49]

---

[46] A free trade agreement (FTA) can be distinguished from the cooperation in the European Union in terms of the scale and scope of the system. An FTA generally does not have a common external tariff and, aside from arrangements for settling trade disputes among the parties, does not have significant institutions for further economic or political cooperation. For example, the North American Free Trade Agreement (Nafta) is unlikely to produce anything resembling the linked currencies and moves toward monetary union in the EU.

[47] A useful overview of Nafta is Robert Pastor, "The North American Free Trade Agreement: Hemispheric and Geopolitical Implications," *The International Executive*, 36.1, January/February 1994, 3–31.  For an analysis of free trade agreements in general, see Jeffrey J. Schott (ed.), *Free Trade Areas and U.S. Trade Policy*, Washington, D.C.: Institute for International Economics, 1989. A more specific discussion of the U.S.-Canadian agreement is in Jeffrey J. Schott, *United States-Canada Free Trade: An Evaluation of the Agreement*, Washington, D.C.: Institute for International Economics, 1988.

[48] More detail on GATT can be found in Chapters 4 and 6.

[49] See Jeffrey J. Schott, "More Free Trade Areas?" in Schott (ed.), *Free Trade . . .*, 1–58.

**FIGURE 6.2**

**North American Trade: 1995**
*(Billions of U.S. Dollars)*
*(Figures in Parentheses = Percent of Total Trade)*

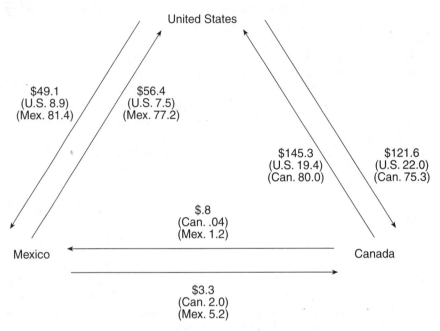

United States

$49.1
(U.S. 8.9)
(Mex. 81.4)

$56.4
(U.S. 7.5)
(Mex. 77.2)

$145.3
(U.S. 19.4)
(Can. 80.0)

$121.6
(U.S. 22.0)
(Can. 75.3)

$.8
(Can. .04)
(Mex. 1.2)

Mexico

Canada

$3.3
(Can. 2.0)
(Mex. 5.2)

SOURCE: International Monetary Fund, *Direction of Trade Statistics Quarterly*, December 1995.

For Canadians, preserving access to the U.S. market and developing a clear set of mechanisms for settling trade disputes constituted the main considerations. Canada and the United States represent the world's largest bilateral trading relationship, and Canada is very dependent on the United States for markets and investment. Much of this trade was in automobiles and auto parts, spurred by the 1965 agreement that established free trade in cars. American firms employ one million Canadians, while Canadian firms employ 740,000 American workers. Canadian leaders wanted to stabilize and improve access to the United States. Some also saw Mexico as a potential market and production site.[50]

---

[50] Stephen Thomsen, "Regional Integration and Multinational Production," in Vincent Cable and David Henderson (eds.), *Trade Blocs? The Future of Regional Integration*, London: Royal Institute of International Affairs, 1994, 112. Schott, "More Free Trade Areas?" in Schott, *Free Trade Areas and U.S. Trade Policy.* For a series of articles considering Nafta from a Canadian perspective, see Ricardo Grinspun and Maxwell Cameron (eds.), *The Political Economy of North American Free Trade*, New York: St. Martin's Press, 1993.

Mexico's decisions relating to an FTA with the United States are conditioned by the size of its trade with the United States and similar fears of U.S. protectionism. Further, the acceptance of free trade represents a radical departure in Mexico's foreign economic policy. In 1985 Mexico adopted a strongly liberal policy in trade, thereby casting aside a long tradition of protectionism. Reacting to an enormous foreign debt, a collapse in oil prices, and years of low increases in productivity, the Mexican government moved toward opening its markets to foreign competition and toward stimulating exports of manufactured goods. By 1987 tariff rates had been cut in half, quantitative restrictions drastically reduced, and price controls virtually eliminated.[51] This strategy accentuated the importance of access to the U.S. market. Perhaps the clearest result of the liberal trend was the expansion of the *maquiladoras*, or export processing zones in Mexico. Here imports of parts and exports of assembled goods took place without tariffs. These zones expanded dramatically after 1985—to the point that nearly 500,000 Mexican workers were directly employed in *maquiladora* factories before Nafta took effect.

Each country has significant political opposition to freer trade. In Canada the 1988 agreement became the major issue in national elections, with opponents warning that jobs would be lost to the United States. There was significant resistance in the United States to the deal with Mexico, due mostly to the substantial differences between the two economies. Labor unions objected strongly, as did many environmentalists, producers in low-tech, low-skills industries, and some agricultural interests—such as citrus growers. These groups are bound together by fears of a loss of sales and jobs to imports from Mexico or from the transfer of production to what they see as a low-wage, environmentally lax Mexico. In Mexico, opposition centered on nationalistic fears of U.S. corporations overwhelming Mexican-based businesses. Many worried about the loss of economic sovereignty.

Recall that in the discussion of free trade in Chapter 2 we argued that free trade is on balance beneficial but that it can produce major adjustments and restructuring that are very difficult for some groups. Free trade usually undermines the economic position of owners and workers in sectors that are not competitive in global terms. Businesses in these areas will go bankrupt, and workers will lose jobs as resources are shifted to areas of the economy enjoying a comparative advantage. The psychological and cultural costs of this process can be very great. The benefits of free trade come in the form of higher-quality and lower-priced imports that replace domestic production. Those groups in a country that is able to compete effectively in global or regional markets will be strong supporters of free trade, as they were in the case of Nafta. The strongest supporters of Nafta in the United States and Canada were multinational firms and investment capital, which were eager to

---

[51] Ignacio Trigueros, "A Free Trade Agreement Between Mexico and the United States?" in Schott (ed.), *Free Trade . . .* , 255–267.

consolidate and take further advantage of a regional production and investment system.[52]

The short-term consequences of Nafta have been much as expected. Perhaps the clearest beneficiary is Canada, where exports to the United States have risen sharply and have helped increase support for free trade.[53] Trade between the United States and Mexico has grown but has been adversely affected by the peso crisis. The 50 percent drop in the peso's value against the dollar has hurt U.S. exports and benefited Mexican exports. Nevertheless, there is evidence that the restructuring based on efficiency gains is proceeding. Taking advantage of the power of global communications, firms have begun to locate different parts of the production process where the combination of cost and productivity is the greatest. This often means low-technology production and assembly in Mexico and high-technology manufacturing and research and development in the United States. The regionalization of automobile production, already developed before Nafta, fits this pattern. A large proportion of the trade crossing borders is intrafirm or affiliated firm trade in automobiles and parts. This pattern has spread to other industries as falling tariffs combine with global finance and communications to permit regionalization of production for smaller and smaller firms.[54] The employment consequences of the regionalization of production are unclear, especially for the United States. Because Mexican tariffs were much higher than for the United States, several years may be needed to determine the net results.

Perhaps the most significant overall effect of Nafta is the boost given to liberal tendencies throughout Latin America. In Mexico the severe peso crisis led not to nationalism and protectionism but rather to accelerating privatization of state enterprises. In 1994 Chile reached an agreement with Nafta states to negotiate full membership in the FTA. Other Latin American states have already moved substantially toward free trade. As part of establishing and invigorating small regional free trade agreements, Latin American states have cut tariffs for the rest of the world from an average of 56 percent to 12 percent between 1984 and 1994. A series of sometimes crosscutting free trade agreements now structures much of the trade relationships within Latin America: Group of Three (Mexico, Venezuela, and Colombia), Caricom (Trinidad and

---

[52] A useful theoretical perspective on the domestic politics and regional free trade is Marc Busch and Helen Milner, "The Future of the International Trading System: International Firms, Regionalism, and Domestic Politics," in Richard Stubbs and Geoffrey Underhill (eds.), *Political Economy and the Changing Global Order,* New York: St. Martin's Press, 1994, 259–276. More detail can be found in Richard Stevenson, "Selling a Free-Trade Pact With Mexico," *New York Times,* November 11, 1990; Keith Bradsher, "Last Call to Arms on the Trade Pact," *New York Times,* August 23, 1993; Kirk Victor, "Trading Away Jobs," *National Journal,* April 27, 1991; Anthony DePalma, "Mexico's Hunger for U.S. Goods Is Helping Sell the Trade Pact," *New York Times,* November 7, 1993.

[53] Trade growth was especially large in those areas liberalized by the U.S.–Canada FTA. *The Economist,* January 14, 1995, 26–27.

[54] Lorraine Eden and Maureen Appel Molot, "Continentalizing the North American Auto Industry," in Grinspun and Cameron, *The Political Economy . . .,* 297–313; James Sterngold, "In NAFTA's Complex Trade-Off, Some Jobs Lost, Others Gained," *New York Times,* October 9, 1995.

Tobago, Jamaica, Suriname, and several microstates), Andean Pact (Venezuela, Colombia, Peru, Ecuador, Bolivia), Mercosur (Brazil, Argentina, Uruguay, Paraguay), and the Central American Common Market (Guatemala, Costa Rica, El Salvador, Honduras, and Nicaragua). Basic agreements have been reached to establish a Free Trade Area of the Americas by 2005. Many states see the advantages that Mexico has through privileged access to the U.S. market, including the attraction this provides to global capital. Nafta's existence and success appear to demonstrate the costs of not cooperating in establishing free trade and thereby generate additional cooperation among states.

## An East Asian Trade Bloc?

East Asia is the most complex and dynamic of the three regions and is the least organized in political terms. The dominant power in Asia—the United States—has not pushed for regional economic cooperation, preferring instead to work out bilateral relationships. The natural leader of the integration process is Japan because of the size and level of development of its economy. But Japan carries significant political burdens from World War II. Back then Japan organized what it called the Greater East Asian Co-Prosperity Sphere at the point of a gun, and many Asians have negative memories of Japanese imperialism. This limits the ability to organize any formal political framework for economic integration. Unlike Europe and North America, Asia has no region-wide institutions and has only very limited panregional agreements or subregional institutions. The Association of South East Asian Nations (ASEAN) has historically operated as a political forum for seven nations and in 1992 took steps to organize a free trade area.[55] The Asia-Pacific Economic Cooperation Conference (APEC) has existed as a broad forum for discussion and limited coordination of data collection. But APEC shows no signs of advancing toward a regional political and economic institution to regulate trade.[56]

Even a brief consideration of the complexity of East Asia quickly reveals some of the problems for broad cooperative arrangements similar to those in Europe and North America. East Asia lacks the similarity of economic development of Europe or even Nafta. There is one large developed state (Japan), four small states with high incomes (Australia, Hong Kong, Singapore, and New Zealand), several small states of middle- to lower-level incomes (Korea, Taiwan, Malaysia, Thailand, the Philippines, and Indonesia), one very large but poor state (China), and several small and very poor countries (Burma, Cambodia, Laos, Vietnam). East Asia is the fastest-growing region in the world, with many countries achieving sustained GDP growth above 6 percent. The dynamic properties of globalization may be affecting this region in significant ways,

---

[55] The membership of ASEAN includes: Brunei, Indonesia, Malaysia, the Philippines, Singapore, Thailand, and recent addition Vietnam.

[56] The members of APEC are Australia, Brunei, Canada, China, Hong Kong, Indonesia, Japan, Korea, Malaysia, New Zealand, the Philippines, Singapore, Taiwan, Thailand, and the United States.

producing new forms of economic integration.[57] The creation of complex production networks, based around information technology and different aspects of the production value chain and located in countries at very distinct levels of development, may require unprecedented mechanisms for integration.

East Asia contains many actual and potential poles of economic power, and this diversity may undermine the capacity for cooperation. In addition to Japan, the newly industrialized economies (NIEs) of Korea and Singapore have become important actors in their own right. A Chinese economic area (CEA) consisting of China, Taiwan, and Hong Kong unites advanced industrial capabilities and substantial capital resources with a huge labor pool. And ASEAN states have developed to the point that they have begun to formulate independent economic ambitions. Laced through each of these subregional situations is Japanese foreign direct investment, but also present are U.S. investors and sometimes a very large presence by Korea, Hong Kong, and Taiwan. Japanese FDI directed toward manufacturing production is mainly a result of the rising yen that followed the Plaza Agreement in 1985 and expanded rapidly until 1990. Since 1990 Japanese FDI has leveled off and even begun to decline. The economic links across East Asia established by Japan are important and have resulted in emulation of the Japanese system at the governmental and firm level. But there is little evidence of bloclike activity here.[58] The diversity of levels of development and the number of actors in East Asia make the political organization of economic integration quite difficult.

## Economic Blocs and the Future of the World Economy

Regional economic blocs are significant focal points for cooperation among economically advanced states. In the European Union, real and important transfers of sovereignty have taken place, and more are in sight. The persistence of the EU following the end of the Cold War, and especially its moves toward greater integration and expansion of membership, provide strong support for the view that cooperation is possible and that institutions enhance cooperation.[59] Although Nafta has few institutional parallels, and cooperation is far less important, it, too, is moving toward expansion of membership. Once begun, economic blocs generate a logic of expansion. Those outside the bloc want to gain the benefits of cooperation and to avoid the costs of not cooperating. This process is evident in Europe and in the Western Hemisphere.

---

[57] Mitchell Bernard and John Ravenhill, "Beyond Product Cycles and Flying Geese: Regionalization, Hierarchy, and the Industrialization of East Asia," *World Politics*, 47.2, January 1995, 171–209.

[58] For an argument emphasizing Japanese capabilities for integrating East Asia through technology and FDI, see Mark Taylor, "Dominance through Technology," *Foreign Affairs*, November/December 1995, 15–20. For the most detailed examination of the potential for an economic bloc in East Asia, see Jeffrey Frankel and Miles Kahler (eds.), *Regionalism and Rivalry: Japan and the United States in the Pacific Area*, Chicago: University of Chicago Press, 1993.

[59] For a contrary view, directed at the situation in Europe, see Joseph M. Grieco, "The Maastricht Treaty, Economic and Monetary Union and the Neo-realist Research Programme," *Review of International Studies*, 21, 1995, 21–40.

**TABLE 6.3**

**Intra-bloc and Inter-bloc Trade**
*(In Percent of Total Exports and Imports)*

|  |  | WITH: EU | NORTH AMERICA | EAST ASIA |
|---|---|---|---|---|
| EU | 1975 | 51.2 | 8.7 | 3.7 |
|  | 1992 | 59.8 | 8.0 | 8.0 |
| Nafta | 1975 | 18.8 | 34.8 | 15.7 |
|  | 1992 | 17.0 | 38.9 | 27.4 |
| East Asia | 1975 | 11.5 | 22.6 | 30.6 |
|  | 1992 | 14.3 | 22.9 | 45.0 |

SOURCE: Adapted from Masami Yoshida et al., "Regional Economic Integration in East Asia: Special Features and Policy Implications," in Cable and Henderson , *Trade Blocs* ..., 62–63.

The main concern generated by economic blocs is the potential for fragmentation in the world economy. The guiding trade principle since 1945 has been multilateralism—meaning the establishment of a widening arc of states, all of which participate in the world economy on basically the same terms. Thus nations negotiate together the terms for access to each other's economies and extend these terms to virtually all nations. Economic blocs represent discrimination and exclusion and suggest the possibility of economic struggle extending to political and even military hostility. Economic blocs establish the institutional framework for much greater discrimination and separation, should the political basis within nations shift in this direction.

At present, the chances of this are remote; such an outcome would require a revolutionary political change within states over free trade and protection. This political transformation would not only need to construct a plausible strategy for bloc self-sufficiency but also would need to overcome the very large interests that each bloc has in access to other areas of the world. A rough measure of this interdependence across blocs is Table 6.3.

The evidence indicates a growing tilt toward intraregional trade in each area, with the most pronounced internal shift coming in East Asia. But there are other significant trends: an increasing interdependence between North America and East Asia and growing connectedness between the EU and East Asia. Further, notice the absolute levels of trade: 40 percent of EU trade is with non-EU members, 16 percent of EU trade is with North America and East Asia, 55 percent of East Asian trade is outside the region, and more than 60 percent of North American trade is with other parts of the world. The largest and most powerful states are the most interdependent with the world outside their region. For example, Germany, Italy, France, and Britain have more than the EU average of 40 percent of non-EU trade, the United States conducts only 28.6 percent of its trade with other Nafta states, and more than one third of Japanese exports are to the United States and Germany alone. Any move toward significantly exclusionary blocs would need to overcome the substantial interdependence among regional blocs indicated by this data.

Perhaps the most convincing evidence that regional blocs are unlikely to lead to global fragmentation is the successful conclusion of the Uruguay Round of GATT in December 1993.[60] Long delayed by conflict, the Uruguay Round attempted to deal with several important exceptions and areas of exclusion from previous GATT agreements, in addition to reducing tariffs. Since the 1940s GATT has been a very important multilateral forum because of its membership of more than one hundred nations and the significance of the ability to gain global agreement on substantial tariff reductions. The new GATT agreement extends its jurisdiction to agriculture, services, intellectual property, investment, and textiles. But most important is the establishment of the World Trade Organization (WTO) as the successor to GATT, with new authority for managing and enforcing the rules of international trade. The WTO and the new Uruguay Round agreement significantly undermine the ability of regional blocs to engage in additional discrimination and strengthen the forces of multilateralism. The most important consequence of regional blocs is to increase market access, and, for now, regionalization and globalization are complementary not contradictory processes.

## CONCLUSIONS

Cooperation among advanced industrial states has become both more essential and more difficult over the past two decades. The ability of these states to bargain over concessions and thereby to produce a mutually beneficial coordination of behaviors is much more important now because of the growth of globalization. Failure to coordinate macroeconomic policies can have sudden and rude consequences; ignoring exchange rate effects can result in enormous and persistent international imbalances. Nonetheless, the political relationships needed for cooperation to succeed are problematic.

Much of this can be traced to the decline of U.S. hegemony. The United States can no longer create the cooperative structures of the world economy and gain acceptance for them. For perhaps twenty years, U.S. officials have been much more conscious of the costs of leadership, especially a growing current account deficit and the burdens of defense spending. The considerable power remaining to the United States has sometimes been used to push other states to accept some of these costs. But U.S. weaknesses, measured by the relative decline in its weight in the world economy and by large budget and trade deficits, undermine the capacity for creating order. U.S. power is big enough to be an essential element of any multilateral system and big enough that other states will sometimes have to cooperate (exchange rate cooperation in the 1980s is a good example). And yet the U.S. ability to fashion a multilateral system of cooperation has largely vanished. The era of U.S.

---

[60] For more detail on GATT, see Chapters 4 and 7.

hegemony has been replaced by a system of U.S. dominance in which genuine bargaining and meshing of interests are prerequisites for cooperation. Frequently, cooperation has required disproportionate concessions by the Japanese and Europeans.

The European Union is certainly the best example of an effective system of cooperation responding to the ties of interdependence. This is a result of efforts to cope with the rush of connectedness in the 1980s, the need to protect member nations from some of the unfavorable consequences of U.S. decline, and the rise of Japan and the end of the Cold War. Along with the North Atlantic Treaty Organization, the EU provides a powerful institutional context promoting cooperation in Europe. Circumstances favor incorporating additional members into the EU and establishing closer economic and political union by the end of the century.

The record of cooperation in the EU has not always extended to multilateral arrangements among the EU, United States, and Japan. Interdependence here has advanced enough to matter significantly in national political life, but not enough to generate frequent and effective cooperation. Powerful incentives for cooperation exist, but very strong barriers frequently prevent this from taking place. When we remember that interdependence also has uncomfortable consequences—competition, involvement of other nations in what once were domestic political choices, and constant adjustment to external demands—we are reminded that conflict is often a partner in efforts at cooperation.

## ANNOTATED BIBLIOGRAPHY

Vincent Cable and David Henderson (eds.), *Trade Blocs? The Future of Regional Integration*, London: Royal Institute, 1994.
> A collection of very insightful articles discussing different aspects of regional trade blocs.

Nicholas Colchester and David Buchan, *Europower*, New York: Times Books, 1990.
> A detailed and excellent, but dated, description of the European Community.

Richard N. Cooper et al., *Can Nations Agree? Issues in International Economic Cooperation*, Washington, D.C.: Brookings, 1989.
> A series of excellent case studies in international macroeconomic coordination.

I. M. Destler and Randall Henning, *Dollar Politics: Exchange Rate Policy-making in the United States*, Washington, D.C.: Institute for International Economics, 1989.
> A very useful case study of the domestic politics of efforts to manage the value of the dollar in the 1980s.

Wendy Dobson, *Economic Policy Coordination: Requiem or Prologue?*, Washington, D.C.: Institute for International Economics, 1991.
> A broad assessment of international economic cooperation.

Jeffrey Frankel and Miles Kahler (eds.), *Regionalism and Rivalry*, Chicago: University of Chicago Press, 1993.
> A detailed examination of the existence of an economic bloc in East Asia.

Yoichi Funabashi, *Managing the Dollar: From the Plaza to the Louvre*, Washington, D.C.: Institute for International Economics, 1989.
> A detailed description of the process of cooperation in the operation of the international financial system in the 1980s.

Joseph M. Grieco, *Cooperation Among Nations*, Ithaca: Cornell University Press, 1990.
> A theoretically informed study of cooperation in international trade.

Lisa Martin, *Coercive Cooperation: Explaining Multilateral Economic Sanctions*, Princeton: Princeton University Press, 1992.
> Considers the impact of institutions on economic cooperation.

John Pinder, *European Community*, Oxford: Oxford University Press, 1991.
> The best study of the European Community.

Robert Putnam and Nicholas Bayne, *Hanging Together: Cooperation and Conflict in the Seven Power Summits*, Cambridge: Harvard University Press, 1987.
> One of the best studies of cooperation relating to macroeconomic coordination.

John G. Ruggie (ed.), *Multilateralism Matters*, New York: Columbia University Press, 1993.
> A collection of sophisticated studies of different aspects of postwar multilateralism.

Jeffrey Schott (ed.), *Free Trade Areas and U.S. Trade Policy*, Washington, D.C.: Institute for International Economics, 1989.
> A series of detailed studies of free trade areas.

Arthur A. Stein, *Why Nations Cooperate*, Ithaca: Cornell University Press, 1990.
> A game-theoretic analysis of international cooperation.

Stephen Thomsen and Stephen Woolcock, *Direct Investment and European Integration*, New York: CFR Press, 1993.
> A detailed look at the impact of foreign direct investment on cooperation in Europe.

Michael Webb, *Global Capital and Policy Coordination: International Macroeconomic Adjustment Since 1945*, Ithaca: Cornell University Press, 1995.
> Sees growing international cooperation on macroeconomic policy, even after the decline of U.S. hegemony.

# Chapter 7

# COMPETITION AND CONFLICT AMONG ADVANCED INDUSTRIAL STATES

One of the main themes of the preceding chapter is worth repeating, namely that discussions of conflict and competition cannot be far removed from an analysis of cooperation. The world economy simply could not function without the manifold layers of international cooperation.[1] The notion of a global marketplace existing outside a framework of cooperative political relations among nations is as mythological as the bloodless world of perfect competition. Thus we need to remember that competition among firms or nations is possible only in a context in which the rules for trade, investment, and profit making have been created and are maintained through international cooperation.

That having been said, competition and conflict are inherent elements of capitalism. Productive power and the military power linked to it generate an enormous prize to be won by sovereign states. Domestic political power frequently rests on economic growth and dynamism. International rivalry over at least the past two centuries has been caught up in the efforts of capitalist firms to secure markets and resources. The two great wars of the twentieth century began as conflicts among capitalist states. Late in the century, fears abound about the ability to compete in the world economy. Many of the same factors that undermine cooperation also serve to enhance competition and conflict.

The ebb and flow in the balance between cooperation and conflict has led some to express concern about a shift toward the latter. Chapter 7 offers some perspective on this possibility. We begin with a discussion of the concept of competitiveness, considering its appropriateness for understanding the economic relationships among nations. This involves showing how economic advances in one nation can harm the economic, political, and military positions of other nations. Further, governments must be able to act

---

[1] For a useful examination of many different arenas of international cooperation, see Peter Haas (ed.), "Knowledge, Power, and International Policy Coordination," *International Organization*, special issue, 46.1, Winter 1992.

effectively to improve national competitiveness to make *competitiveness* a meaningful political term. There are many strategies used to enhance the competitiveness of nations. We will review these and explain how they might succeed or fail.

The three great arenas of global economic competition are Japan, the United States, and Europe. Japan deserves a detailed look as a nation that may have established a new competitive standard for others to match. Characterizations of Japan as a predator state that engages in unfair competition are common. This section will examine the postwar rise of Japan and the special business–government relationship often cited as the source of its extraordinary growth. The United States has found itself under considerable competitive pressure in recent years as its economic and corporate strength has been challenged. These problems have been traced to weaknesses in firms, government policy, and in the economic system as a whole. Problems in Europe are even more severe than in the United States, and many trace these difficulties to the commitment to social welfare policies. Our review identifies the most troubled areas and the somewhat different strategies designed to improve Europe's competitive position.

The traditional reaction to increased competition is protectionism, whereby a government attempts to help its nation's firms by shielding them from the outside world. We will examine the nature of contemporary protectionism. In the wake of a general decline in tariffs, nontariff barriers (NTBs) and efforts at managed trade have assumed a much greater role. This "new" protectionism, along with a consideration of the political economy of decisions to adopt such a policy, receive our attention. Finally, we will look at the conclusion of the Uruguay Round of GATT and the new World Trade Organization (WTO) as the new institutional forum for dealing with matters of protection and free trade.

## THEORIES OF COMPETITIVENESS

From the beginning of the industrial era, the ability of specific industries in certain nations to achieve advantages over those industries in other nations has defined competitiveness and has distinguished nations from one another. Further, these same economic capabilities have been closely related to the capacity for producing military and political power. Whether in terms of generating wealth that facilitated a large military establishment or the technological infrastructure to support building railroads, dreadnoughts, or ICBMs, economic competitiveness has been linked with national power. Today the military, political, economic, and technological dimensions of international competition are bound together very tightly. World influence demands accomplishment in all four areas, while each increasingly depends on the other three.

For our purposes, *competitiveness* can be defined as the ability of a nation to achieve economic growth and a rising standard of living, even while exposed to international trade and capital flows.[2] Understanding this process calls for an analysis of the broad characteristics of nations along with a consideration of specific industries because it is here that actual competition takes place. Our interest lies in identifying those attributes of a nation that help or hurt an industry or industry segment in global competition. But additionally, examining competitiveness turns the economic performance of a business system, along with the general relationship of the political system to business activity, into intensely political questions.

The competitiveness debate raises questions about the type of international trading system that is most desirable. The notions of free trade and comparative advantage—now nearly two centuries old—define the most desirable system as one in which each nation should specialize in a world of open trade, based on the existing factor endowments of each nation. In this system, no nation is better off defecting and engaging in autarchy or mercantilism. Those who pursue these paths will eventually produce and consume fewer goods at higher prices (less for more). One of the key issues of competitiveness is whether important gains can be had for one nation by taking steps to boost its proportion of high-profit and knowledge-intensive industries. Although this corresponds to historical experience, such an option does not fit well with the theory of comparative advantage.

The very notion of thinking about nations as engaged in economic competition is one that divides economists from most political economists. The former, operating from a liberal perspective on trade, argue that the economic relationships among nations are positive sum. That is, the economic development of one nation helps the economic position of other nations. Growth in Nation A provides a market for the goods of Nation B and, most important, as Nation A improves its comparative advantage, it is able to supply better goods at lower prices to Nation B.[3] Scholars who approach this matter from the perspective of political economy often acknowledge the correctness of the liberal view but add that conflict is an equally important, and sometimes more important, aspect of international economic relations. Conflict arises because economic growth occurs at different rates, thereby affecting the relative strength of nations involved in international political and military

---

[2] The ability to produce rising standards of living, while maintaining a policy of autarchy or without selling in world markets, is an interesting but empirically limited experience. We are concerned here only with those nations involved in the world economy.

[3] This view is most forcefully presented in Paul Krugman, "Competitiveness: A Dangerous Obsession," *Foreign Affairs*, March/April 1994, 28–44. Critical responses are in "The Fight over Competitiveness," *Foreign Affairs*, July/August 1994, 186–202. A more scholarly analysis of the concept of competitiveness is David Rapkin and Jonathan Strand, "Is International Competitiveness a Meaningful Concept?" in C. Roe Goddard et al. (eds.), *International Political Economy: Readings on State-Market Relations in the Changing Global Order*, Boulder: Lynne Rienner, 1995.

competition. Additionally, the success rate of a nation's firms, and thus the prosperity of its citizens, depends partly on the actions of the government. Thus the citizens of a nation have an employment and income interest in the success of some firms—those operating in the nation—over that of other firms. The combination of these three factors promotes economic conflict and competition among nations.

To sustain their contention that nations don't engage in economic competition, liberals must rely on a version of reality that distorts as much as it reveals. In a world of free trade and investment, market resources are employed at their most efficient. The geography of production is irrelevant, except that production takes place in the most efficient location. When and where resources are inefficiently used, they must be redeployed to more efficient uses and locations. In the case of labor, it must move to places of greater efficiency. In such a world, nations are simply an irrelevant boundary. Each place (nation) produces goods in which it has a comparative advantage; trade allows all places (nations) to benefit from global efficiencies. Thus places (nations) don't compete but instead gain from the collective efficiencies of all places (nations). The real competitors are firms, which struggle with each other for profits and market share; the gains of one firm usually come at the expense of other firms.

In the idealized world of global perfect competition, nations cannot change the fate of their geographic area and have no purpose except collectively to provide the political rules for enforcing contracts. But in real life, nations exist and struggle with each other for power and position. Most important, a nation is a political organization whose main purpose is to advance the interests of (at least some) of its population. National leaders cannot be indifferent to the fate of their part of the world economy. Firms are but the front line of competition, the most visible part of a complex system of (mostly) nation-based institutions that support interfirm competition. Simple comparison of the firms in the United States and those in Vietnam shows clearly the dramatic differences in the capacity for competition and the contribution of national institutions to these differences.

It is also true that in their trade relations, the United States and Vietnam share complementary interests. But the same can be said for firms competing against each other. IBM and Toshiba can cooperate to each's benefit and simultaneously compete for customers. Although firms and nations both compete and benefit from each other, this is not to say the process is the same. Rising Japanese incomes do not reduce incomes in the rest of the world, but we cannot let this positive sum relationship obscure arenas and dimensions of economic conflict between nations.

A further theoretical grounding for competitiveness as a political issue depends on showing how the actions of governments can make industries grow faster or even make industries develop that otherwise would not evolve. One version of this analysis, known as *strategic trade theory*, argues that government intervention can work if one of two situations holds. First, government action targets a high-profit industry with large economies of scale, and this action helps to dissuade foreign firms from entering the market or compels them to leave. The object is to be the nation with the firms that capture a proportion of the global market large enough to reap the greatest economies of scale. This serves to drive out other competitors because they can never gain a large enough market share to bring down costs through economies of scale. The nation that establishes a position in such an industry first will come to dominate global production. A second element of strategic trade theory focuses on actions that help establish industries with important economic spin-offs or *externalities*. Here the purpose is to make sure that your nation contains its share of industries whose operations generate benefits for other industries. The best examples are those knowledge-intensive industries that generate demand for other advanced businesses. The relationship between the computer industry and the computer software industry is an obvious case. The nation containing the greatest proportion of high-externalities industries will likely produce the highest rates of economic growth.[4]

Another approach to thinking about political efforts to improve international competitiveness relates to the concept of comparative advantage (discussed in Chapter 2). Research today rejects the standard view that factor endowments controlling comparative advantage are fixed, especially in certain high-technology fields. Rather, the factors that most influence production may be created in part through government action. Again, the proportion of knowledge-intensive industries—those characterized by high research and development costs, high risk and payoff, and rapid change—in a society can be a consequence of government decisions. A combination of policies designed to develop the infrastructure for knowledge generation and application may be a necessary ingredient for the establishment of these industries. Thus education policies, efforts to enhance knowledge and technical skills in the population, and actions to assume some of the risks and costs of product development can have a major impact on where knowledge-intensive firms locate. Nations thereby compete in terms of creating comparative advantage that affects which ones will capture the largest proportion of these companies. The presence of high-tech industries makes a major contribution to wage rates, growth rates, and a nation's standard of living.[5]

---

[4] Paul R. Krugman, "Is Free Trade Passé?" in Phillip King (ed.), *International Economics and International Economic Policy: A Reader*, New York: McGraw-Hill, 1990, 91–107; Paul R. Krugman, *Rethinking International Trade*, Cambridge: MIT Press, 1990. For a critique of strategic trade theory, see J. David Richardson, "The Political Economy of Strategic Trade Policy," *International Organization*, 44.1, Winter 1990, 107–135. An effort to demonstrate that strategic trade does not yield benefits is Paul Krugman and Alasdair Smith (eds.), *Empirical Studies of Strategic Trade Policy*, Chicago: University of Chicago Press, 1994.

[5] Bruce Scott, "Creating Comparative Advantage," in King (ed.), *International Economics . . .*, 78–90; Michael Porter, *The Competitive Advantage of Nations*, New York: Free Press, 1990.

## STRATEGIES OF COMPETITIVENESS

Given that nations are in conflict over power and position, that economic development is closely related to this process, that the success of firms and governments is of vital concern to citizens and leaders, and that government actions can sometimes affect rates of growth, what strategies have governments followed to improve the competitive position of the nation and its firms? Perhaps surprisingly, nations engage in a wide variety of actions designed to expand the economic well-being of firms and citizens. Additionally, firms adopt many strategies to promote competitiveness. There are three broad categories of national competition strategies: liberalization, state investment and regulation, and protectionism. For firms, the main categories include actions affecting costs, improving quality, and expanding markets.

There are three main types of state competitiveness strategies:

1. Liberalization—The main goal is to expand the scope of markets and thereby to reap the benefits of increased firm competition, of larger markets, or to attract firms to an environment with fewer restrictions. States use deregulation, tax reduction, lower deficits, free trade agreements, and antitrust enforcement to create, expand, and promote markets.

2. State investment—The main purpose is to bolster supporting institutions and to increase opportunities for firms. Examples include: spending on infrastructure such as telecommunications, education, and other public goods; targeted aid to industries in the form of tax breaks, state purchases of production and direct and indirect subsidies; the creation and funding of research and development in a variety of institutions; business–government partnerships; and exchange rate manipulation.

3. Protectionism—The purpose is to manipulate the governmental ability to control trade access so as to increase national production and sales. This might be accomplished by tariffs, nontariff barriers, state subsidies, managed trade, coerced trade, and linking protection of the domestic market to increased exports.

The competitiveness options available to firms are equally diverse:

1. Decrease costs—When a firm faces competition, it needs to reduce costs and thereby reduce the prices of its products. This can be done by downsizing by slashing workers, including managerial workers; by engaging in foreign direct investment to relocate production so as to maximize the labor cost/productivity relationship; by adopting new production strategies such as lean production; by improving management communication capabilities; and by making strategic alliances to gain knowledge and/or to secure preferential capital and organizing suppliers.

2. Increase quality—An equally effective but sometimes more difficult strategy is to improve the quality of the product. This might be done by adopting flexible production techniques to increase the ability to offer customers greater variety; by intensifying quality control to reduce defects; by investing in new technology; and by making strategic alliances to gain knowledge.

3. Expand markets—Firms often compete to gain market share and to expand into new markets. These can be done by foreign direct investment to produce and sell in new markets; by new product development; by the purchase of an existing firm and its markets; and by strategic alliances to gain market access, cartelize markets, or stabilize sales.

As we examine the competition practices of nations and firms, the strategies will become clearer. However, the success or failure of these activities may be more difficult to determine.

## THE RISE OF JAPAN

At the end of World War II Japan was devastated, with 40 percent of its industrial system in ruins, and occupied by the United States. For the next two to three years, U.S. officials used their special powers to make important economic and political changes. Japan's immense economic conglomerates, *zaibatsu*, were broken up; many persons associated with the war were purged from positions of responsibility; the military establishment was dismantled; and the economic system was liberalized. The harshest policies began to change in 1947. As the Cold War between the United States and the Soviet Union intensified, pressure on Japan was relaxed and replaced by a policy emphasizing economic recovery. Concern over the Soviet ability to exploit instability around the world prompted a shift of U.S. policy in Europe and Asia. The revival of the Japanese economy and its integration into the rest of East Asia became the primary means for establishing an economic and political bulwark against Soviet expansion there. Perhaps the most important by-products of this were the 1951 U.S. commitment to Japanese security and Japan's complete dependence on the United States for military protection. From the U.S. perspective, this arrangement bound Japan to a U.S.-based definition of international order. For Japan, this opened the door to economic recovery and security by using to its advantage this U.S. economic and security umbrella.[6]

The political system that emerged from the U.S. occupation represented a complex mixture of new democratic institutions and traditional oligarchical

---

[6] The best discussion of the occupation period is Michael Schaller, *The American Occupation of Japan*, New York: Oxford University Press, 1985. Also helpful is Bruce Cumings, "Power and Plenty in Northeast Asia: The Evolution of U.S. Policy," *World Policy Journal*, 5.1, Winter 1987-88, 79-106.

**FIGURE 7.1**

**Comparative GDP Growth: 1961–1995**

**U.S./Germany/Japan**

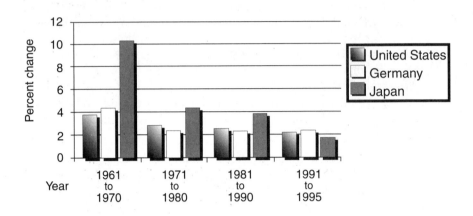

practices. In 1947 the United States imposed a constitution establishing a representative democracy elected by universal adult suffrage and requiring, through Article 9, that Japan renounce the right to use military force for national ends. By the mid-1950s, a dominant political coalition had been formed composed of the bureaucracy, big business and finance, and a conservative political organization, the Liberal Democratic Party. Business interests provided the money, and the bureaucracy supplied much of the political leadership. Genuinely liberal or radical political interests were systematically excluded from political power.[7] This coalition was able to establish a very strong state based on its institutional resources and a consensus on the need for economic growth.

## The Strategy of Growth

In the 1950s and 1960s Japan faced a situation not unlike that of the nineteenth and early twentieth centuries: catch-up. Almost from the beginning of the postwar era, Japan's political and economic leaders were determined to move into the ranks of the major industrial nations. They were unwilling to rely on the obvious comparative advantage of low wages and instead aimed

---

[7] A detailed analysis of the postwar Japanese political system is found in T. J. Pempel, "Japanese Foreign Economic Policy: The Domestic Bases for International Behavior," *International Organization*, 31.4, Autumn 1977, 723–774. Also important is Chalmers Johnson, *MITI and the Japanese Miracle*, Stanford: Stanford University Press, 1982, 50–51. Between 1956 and 1986, seven of ten prime ministers had also served as minister of international trade and industry. See W. G. Beasley, *The Rise of Modern Japan*, New York: St. Martin's Press, 1990, 246. Additional detail on the Japanese political system can be found in Gerald Curtis, *The Japanese Way of Politics*, New York: Columbia University Press, 1988.

to make Japan a nation of capital-intensive and high-technology production. This came in spite of capital deficiencies and poor resources and the great advantages of Western nations. The government acted to move the economy in these directions by establishing economic priorities, organizing large and economically powerful cartels, protecting certain industries, managing the foreign trade process, and providing guidance for investment. This industrial policy was designed to direct economic development and to compensate for Japanese backwardness and economic weakness.[8]

The Japanese were extremely successful in promoting economic growth, as demonstrated in Figure 7.1. Until recently, Japan's GDP growth rate (remember that this excludes exports) has consistently exceeded that of the United States and Germany by a wide margin. Over time, the gap has narrowed along with an overall decline in the rate of increase. Especially during the 1980s, Japan's advantage came from greater consistency of growth. The German and U.S. patterns were subject to greater fluctuation, with much sharper swings in the business cycle than in Japan. Since 1991 Japan has generated much slower growth due mainly to the bursting of the "bubble economy." This developed in the late 1980s when bank lending exploded, leading to excessive increases in stock and real estate prices.

The initial strategy of development in the 1950s was to reestablish the textile industry, long the mainstay of the economy. But this moved quickly into building infrastructure and the strategic targeting of industries expected to expand rapidly as incomes around the world grew. The Japanese government was unwilling to accept the "natural" position indicated by Japan's comparative advantage: concentrate on low-wage and low-technology industries. Instead, a series of capital-intensive and relatively high-technology industries was given special support by the government. These industries included: steel, electric power, shipbuilding, chemical fertilizers, petrochemicals, synthetic textiles, plastics, autos, and electronics. Because capital, especially equity capital, was scarce, the Japanese government acted to mobilize resources for these industries. The Bank of Japan guaranteed loans made by private banks to designated industries, and government-controlled bank resources were used as supplements. Over time, private loans were available to certain industries when the government made clear its priorities. The nurturing of special industries was accompanied by strict protection of the Japanese market for finished goods. The need for foreign technology was satisfied through licensing production by Japanese firms. Thus rather than import goods based on advanced—but foreign—technology, the Japanese used the attractiveness of their market to obtain licensing and patent agreements that allowed Japanese firms to gain the knowledge and production experience. Not only was Japan helped by a large and protected domestic market; it also benefited from

---

[8] Daniel Okimoto, *Between MITI and the Market*, Stanford: Stanford University Press, 1989, 23.

relatively open access to large foreign markets. This permitted Japanese industries to reap the cost advantages of high-volume production. Between 1955 and 1970 Japan was able to move beyond production of low-wage, technologically limited goods into much more advanced areas.[9]

By the 1960s the emphasis on exports resulted in a current account surplus and the beginnings of significant outward foreign direct investment. Initially this investment was concentrated in raw materials and in low-tech manufacturing facilities located in developing countries, and it had the effect of providing inputs that would result in Japanese exports to third countries. The great boom in Japanese foreign direct investment came after 1980 and especially after 1985, in conjunction with large Japanese international surpluses, corresponding U.S. deficits, and the Plaza Agreement and rising yen. Accumulating foreign resources permitted Japan to invest abroad. Annual outflows of FDI peaked in 1989 at almost $68 billion and by 1994 had fallen to $41 billion. This was increasingly focused on advanced countries and on industries where Japan was exporting. Protecting export markets, only a modest motive in the 1960s, became a much more important factor in the 1980s. Recently Japanese FDI has been increasingly directed toward other Asian states in order to take advantage of lower manufacturing costs.[10]

The role of international trade in Japanese economic growth is sometimes misunderstood. The recent rise in U.S. imports from Japan and concern over this would suggest that Japan lives and dies from this relationship. Although quite important, foreign trade has a more limited impact on the Japanese economy. Table 7.1 provides a comparison of the role of international trade in the economies of four major industrial nations. Clearly Japan's dependence on foreign trade is much less than that of the United Kingdom or Germany and is somewhat less than that of the United States.

But this obscures some important elements in Japanese international trade policy. Japan, more than most other countries in the U.S.-organized world economy, has rejected the notion of mutual gains from free trade. Although Japan joined GATT in 1955, it was slow in removing restrictions on imports because of fears of backwardness and the dependence on external resources. The Kennedy Round of tariff negotiations in the mid-1960s represented an important shift in viewpoint, with Japan accepting the need

---

[9] Access to foreign markets was made possible by U.S. pressure on its Western allies to admit Japan to full status in GATT. Several countries had resisted this. Ryutaro Komiya and Motoshige Itoh, "Japan's International Trade and Trade Policy, 1955–1984," in Takashi Inoguchi and Daniel Okimoto (eds.), *The Political Economy of Japan, Volume 2: The Changing International Context*, Stanford: Stanford University Press, 1988, 174–179. For a discussion of Japan's economic strategy, see Johnson, *MITI . . .*, 198–304.

[10] Note the similarity of motivation with U.S. MNCs in the 1958–1975 period discussed in Chapter 4. See Young-Kwan Yoon, "The Political Economy of Transition: Japanese Foreign Direct Investments in the 1980s," *World Politics*, 43, October 1990, 1–27; and Makihiro Matsuoka and Brian Rose, *The DIR Guide to Japanese Economic Statistics*, Oxford: Oxford University Press, 1994, 144–149; *The Economist*, May 20, 1995, 7.

**TABLE 7.1**
**Ratio of Exports and Imports to GNP**

| COUNTRY | 1984 | 1994 |
|---|---|---|
| Japan | | |
| Exports | 15.1% | 9.7% |
| Imports | 12.6 | 7.6 |
| United States | | |
| Exports | 7.7 | 10.4 |
| Imports | 10.6 | 11.9 |
| United Kingdom | | |
| Exports | 28.1 | 26.0 |
| Imports | 28.5 | 26.9 |
| Germany | | |
| Exports | 29.4 | 26.9 |
| Imports | 32.2 | 26.2 |

SOURCE: International Monetary Fund, *International Financial Statistics Yearbook*, Washington, D.C., 1995.

for lower tariffs. This was due to the increasing competitiveness of Japanese exports and the expectation that lower world tariffs would spur these exports. By the early 1980s Japanese tariff rates were generally as low as those of the EEC and somewhat lower than those of the United States.[11] At the same time, many countries continue to charge that substantial nontariff barriers to imports still exist. These barriers include restrictions based on fear of disease, special regulations, and cultural resistance to foreign products. Further, as a result of legal restrictions and the structure of Japanese business, foreign direct investment in Japan has been very small. Although many of the legal barriers were lifted after 1982–1984, inward FDI typically represents less than 10 percent of outward FDI.[12]

The combined effects of export strength and restrictions on imports and inward FDI have skewed Japan's international trade. Most advanced industrial states exchange manufactured goods, often the same kinds of manufactured

[11] For data comparing these countries and the ratio of tariff revenue to imports, see Komiya and Itoh, "Japan's International Trade . . .," 193.

[12] The data (in billions of U.S. dollars) from 1987 to 1992 are:

| | 1987 | 1988 | 1989 | 1990 | 1991 | 1992 |
|---|---|---|---|---|---|---|
| Outward FDI | 33.4 | 47.0 | 67.5 | 56.9 | 41.6 | 34.1 |
| Inward FDI | 2.2 | 3.2 | 2.9 | 2.8 | 4.3 | 4.1 |

SOURCE: Matsuoka and Rose, *The DIR Guide . . ., 145.*

goods, in their trade with each other. Japan, by contrast, looks much more like a nineteenth-century state. It exports manufactured goods and imports raw materials. Roughly 70 percent of all world trade is in manufactured goods. And Japan, like most, has three fourths of its exports in manufactured goods. It is in imports that Japan looks unusual. At best, about 50 percent of Japan's imports are manufactured goods, whereas nearly one half of Japan's imports are raw materials, foodstuffs, and various mineral fuels.[13] Part of this distinctiveness can be explained by Japan's extreme resource dependency on the rest of the world. But much also is due to governmental and business policies.

Perhaps the greatest test of the Japanese economy came in the 1970s with the collapse of Bretton Woods and with the oil shocks. The combination of a rising yen and a massive jump in oil imports put pressure on Japan's international accounts and on its domestic inflation rates. Oil imports rose from 20 percent of total imports in 1970 to more than 50 percent by 1981. Wholesale prices rose by 35 percent in 1974, which also saw a large current account deficit, which recurred in 1980.[14]

Although the oil shocks slowed Japanese growth, the bursting of the "bubble economy" in 1989–1990 has brought on the longest and most painful period of low growth since 1950. The rise of the yen after the Plaza Agreement in 1985 produced significant dislocations and imbalances in the Japanese economy. In conjunction with the liberalization of Japanese finance, the rising yen helped fuel enormous growth in equity issues, bank lending, and the money supply. The proceeds were used to purchase stocks and real estate, and prices jumped dramatically. Expectations of rising asset values led many companies to put much of their resources into similar investments. The cycle of higher borrowing, speculation, and rising prices fed on itself and produced a price "bubble" until 1989, when the government tightened money and the bubble burst as everyone tried to sell at once. Between 1985 and 1989 bank lending rose as much as 25 percent per year, feeding annual growth of as much as 11 percent in the money supply, and this fueled a tripling of stock prices and a near-doubling of land prices. After 1989 stock prices fell by more than one half, and money supply growth dropped into negative territory. Growth rates for the Japanese economy also took a nosedive. Between 1992 and 1995, real GDP growth averaged only 1.0 percent.[15]

---

[13] Matsuoka and Rose, *The DIR Guide . . .*, 132; David Yoffie, *Beyond Free Trade: Firms, Governments, and Global Competition*, Boston: Harvard Business School Press, 1993, ix.

[14] Komiya and Itoh, "Japan's International Trade . . .," 198–200; and M. Stephen Weatherford and Haruhiro Fukui, "Domestic Adjustment to International Shocks in Japan and the United States," *International Organization*, 43.4, Autumn 1989, 600, 613–617.

[15] "The Japanese Economy: From Miracle to Mid-life Crisis," *The Economist*, March 6, 1993, has a detailed examination of the "bubble economy" and its collapse. Another very useful account of the "bubble economy" is George Lodge, *Japan Confronts an Interdependent World*, Harvard Business School Case, March 1994. Growth data are from IMF, *World Economic Outlook, May 1995*, Washington, D.C.: IMF, 1995.

# Explanations for Japanese Growth

Although growth rates for the Japanese economy have declined over time, only recently have they fallen below those for other industrialized countries. Setting aside the most recent period, Japan clearly has produced a miraculous feat of economic recovery and growth. Efforts to explain this record have emphasized a wide variety of factors. Not surprisingly, economists have traced Japan's success to market relationships. Here the generally accepted ability of the market to sort out the most efficient producers suggests that Japanese entrepreneurs were adept at responding to market incentives. But this approach fails to explain why the Japanese possessed this special market sensitivity.[16] Other economists have pointed to unusual features of the Japanese economy and culture, such as the harmony of labor and management and the high savings rate, or to the benefits of free riding on the open world economy and the security system provided by the United States.[17]

Perhaps the strongest argument, at least for many students of international and political affairs, is made by tracing the Japanese market perspicacity to the role of the government and its relationship with the economy. From the beginning of the modern era in 1868, the state has played a special role in rearranging Japanese society and politics so that Japan could compete effectively with the West. The focus of that effort in the post–World War II era has been the Ministry of International Trade and Industry (MITI). MITI and other important bureaucracies, such as the Ministry of Finance (MOF), helped provide "domestic producers with the support and guidance they needed to achieve competitive advantages in global markets."[18] This "developmental state" sought to create or at least to shape the incentives—market and otherwise—that directed the actions of Japanese firms.[19] Sometimes this took the form of subsidies to young or ailing industries, which is also somewhat common in the West. More important were efforts at organizing industries to achieve lower costs, defining national priorities in technological development, and developing national plans to share the risks associated with corporate decisions.

The texture of the relationship of MITI to the Japanese economy is not constant over time. Rather, it is affected in important ways by the nature of the external environment and the level of development of the business system. Shifts in the world economy and increasing strength of Japanese business have forced MITI bureaucrats to change their style and strategies for national economic management. Moreover, close analysis reveals that structural charac-

---

[16] David Friedman, *The Misunderstood Miracle: Industrial Development and Political Change in Japan*, Ithaca: Cornell University Press, 1988, 4–6.

[17] Johnson, *MITI . . .* , 11–17.

[18] Friedman, *The Misunderstood Miracle*, 3.

[19] Chalmers Johnson has used the term "developmental state" in *MITI and . . . .*

teristics of the Japanese enterprise not only make it an effective partner for government, but also offer numerous points of access for MITI influence.

The role of MITI reflects a long-standing judgment in the Japanese government about the proper role of the market in directing the economy. Although respecting the power of market forces, MITI officials have rejected the view that a policy of laissez-faire would necessarily produce the best possible use of Japanese economic resources. Left alone to follow the signals from the market, investors could easily direct resources toward areas such as real estate that would do little for the nation's international competitive position. Acutely conscious of Japan's backward status and fearful of the effects of weakness on the country's security and independence, MITI designed a strategy for making Japan an industrial power. It sought to identify specific industries in which Japan might make major gains, anticipate changes in the world economy, and organize the Japanese economy to make it competitive in areas that market forces, left alone, would likely avoid.[20]

As we have seen, in the 1950s MITI used control over foreign exchange, technology imports, financial support, and tax breaks to target certain industries for development. In steel, shipbuilding, machine tools, plastics, petrochemicals, and automobiles—traditionally the province of countries with large natural resources or a big domestic market—MITI moved to establish a Japanese presence. The basic objectives were to drive down costs, improve productivity, protect the domestic market from foreign competition, and expand market share abroad. The long production runs permitted by a large market share would take advantage of economies of scale that would further reduce costs.

Two aspects of the Japanese industrial structure assisted in this process. First, MITI was able to reconstitute the large business conglomerates (*zaibatsu*) of the prewar period into similar systems (now known as *keiretsu*) whereby banks, industrial firms, and trading companies functioned much like a cartel. The *keiretsu* distinguish the Japanese business system from that of most other advanced capitalist states. *Keiretsu* can be organized around a large bank, or they can involve bringing together most of the aspects of the manufacturing of a particular product. There is usually a mixture of intra-*keiretsu* relationships, from lending and borrowing capital, interlocked ownership, and stable trading arrangements. Ownership of stock is more of a long-term partnership than in the West, often involving participation in management of the firm, trade relationships, and loans. *Keiretsu*-like relationships often exist between large firms and suppliers, with very close forms of technology transfer, management, and trade. The result is a system of giant enterprises alongside a large number of small firms. What distinguishes Japan is the complex web of intrafirm cooperation.[21]

---

[20] Okimoto, *Between MITI . . .* , 11–12, 23–24, 29–36; Johnson, *MITI and . . .* , 81.

[21] Michael Gerlach, *Alliance Capitalism: The Social Organization of Japanese Business*, Berkeley: University of California Press, 1992.

Second, the reliance on debt rather than equity as the chief source of capital helps focus firms on MITI-style goals. Firms tend to look to the longer term and to growth of market share rather than to short-term profits. Supporting this was the Japanese central bank, which acted to guarantee the debt of preferred industries. The combination of *keiretsu* organization and dependence on guaranteed debt was to cushion the downside risks for certain businesses and thereby direct them toward national goals.[22]

Changes in these arrangements began in the early 1960s with external pressure for liberalization of trade and, later in the decade, for loosening controls on Japanese capital markets. Both efforts were prompted by the spectacular success enjoyed by the Japanese economy and the seemingly free ride created by the strict policy of protection. These events had several important consequences. The pressures for liberalization eventually produced results, with trade and capital barriers gradually falling between 1960 and 1982. Largely in response to these changes, MITI was forced to adopt a new strategy for internal economic management. It surrendered direct control over allocating scarce resources and began to rely more on persuasion and the adaptive skills of the *keiretsu* themselves.[23]

Perhaps the most significant recent developments came as a result of the two great changes in the world economy in the early 1970s—the collapse of the Bretton Woods system of fixed exchange rates and the price revolution in oil. Also important were growing domestic political concerns over pollution and the increasing independence of Japan's very successful and powerful business empires. The result was a lengthy debate within MITI that brought a new bureaucratic faction into power, one more cosmopolitan and international in outlook. This led to a major policy shift toward energy conservation, reduction of pollution and overcrowding, and a drive to develop knowledge-intensive, high-technology industries.[24]

Japan's move into the realm of high tech has been immensely successful and has produced a dramatic shift in the competitive environment around the world. The once-comfortable lead enjoyed by the United States has evaporated in many areas, and other nations have been both encouraged and threatened by Japan's achievements. The primary impetus behind these developments has been a combination of government and private industry efforts. MITI contributed research subsidies, and Japanese firms devoted a much larger proportion of company resources to research and development and capital investment than did similar U.S. firms. During the 1970s Japan worked to develop and adapt its production capabilities to certain areas, but especially in semiconductors, computers, and consumer electronics. In the 1980s Japan caught up in

---

[22] Johnson, *MITI and* . . . , 199–212. Of special significance in this process was access to the U.S. market, which offered an enormous opportunity to utilize economies of scale, cut costs, and raise productivity.

[23] Johnson, *MITI and* . . . , 249–272.

[24] Johnson, *MITI and* . . . , 275–301.

computers, surged ahead in semiconductors, consumer electronics, and robotics, and redirected research and development toward supercomputers, optoelectronics, and next-generation fighter planes.[25] At the beginning of the 1990s Japan had established itself as a powerful international force in high technology. A 1990 report by the U.S. Defense Department acknowledges a Japanese lead in five high-technology industries crucial to U.S. national security: semiconductors, superconductivity, robotics, supercomputers, and photonics.[26]

MITI's role in this process has continued to evolve as its control over the Japanese economy has waned. This is due, in large part, to the size and economic strength of Japan's private business enterprises. The largest corporations now have the resources to support high levels of research and development and to absorb investment risks. Further, the most intense competition for many of these corporations is other Japanese firms, thereby undermining their interest in cooperation sponsored by MITI. Funds for research and development continue to flow from MITI, and it still provides an important sanction for investment decisions and supports businesses involved in strategically vital technologies. However, MITI's ability to command has decreased with the maturing of the Japanese economy.[27]

Some scholars find the emphasis on the role of Japan's government excessive in trying to explain rapid economic growth. In particular, this view pays too little attention to Japan's firms and gives too much credit to the directive power of the state.[28] According to this view, the combination of the developmental state and complex system of Japanese firms created a special kind of environment that generated especially innovative firms. The developmental policies of the Japanese government (mostly targeted subsidies and protection of the home market) produced an unexpected response from Japanese businesses. Rather than become satisfied and inefficient producers, firms engaged in a fierce investment-driven competition for market share in anticipation of rapid growth in demand. Business leaders understood the large economies of scale (costs fall as output rises) to be won from increasing output. Preserving or increasing market share would permit a firm to reap the economies of scale and cost competitiveness. Market share required a capital investment race to increase production capabilities. The major uncertainty in the system was the impact of foreign (and, later, domestic) technology. Unable to control or predict the pace and direction of technology change, Japanese firms focused much of their competition on continuous innovation in the way

[25] Okimoto, *Between MITI* . . . , 55–85.

[26] Martin Tolchin, "Pentagon Says It Lags in Some Technologies," *New York Times*, March 22, 1990.

[27] David Sanger, "Mighty MITI Loses Its Grip," *New York Times*, July 9, 1989. For a discussion of the role of MITI in the early stages of Japanese entry into the computer market, see Marie Anchordoguy, "Mastering the Market: Japanese Government Targeting of the Computer Industry," *International Organization*, 42.3, Summer 1988, 509–543.

[28] The following discussion draws on Okimoto, *Between MITI* . . . ; Friedman, *The Misunderstood* . . .; and Laura D'Andrea Tyson and John Zysman, "Developmental Strategy and Production Innovation in Japan," in Chalmers Johnson et al. (eds.), *Politics and Productivity*, New York: Harper & Row, 1989, 59–140.

goods were produced. These firms developed new forms of production that were much more efficient and led to goods of much higher quality, making them very competitive in global markets.

Japanese firms (first in the machine tool and auto industries) generated a new form of production: one that combines very high quality control, organizational innovations (such as teams of producers), "just in time" inventory control, and flexibility of production. The cumulative effect was to introduce a dynamic flexibility into the Japanese economy as the production externalities of lead industries were fed into associated industries. The consequences were dramatic. In the late 1980s Japanese automotive firms were able to produce a vehicle in 33 percent less time than U.S. producers and 55 percent less time than European producers. But Japanese autos were made with much higher quality control: 27 percent fewer defects than U.S. autos and 38 percent fewer defects than European cars. This was accomplished with smaller plants and less than 10 percent of the average inventory size of U.S. firms.[29]

Although initially dependent on foreign technology, Japan has made tremendous strides in becoming a major competitor of the United States. One important review of the technology position of these two states concluded:

> [W]hile the United States retains leadership in software and in some other areas, Japan's technological capability across a wide spectrum of commercially significant fields is formidable and growing relative to that of the United States.[30]

This prowess is especially significant in production technology and in translating basic research into successful commercial products. The combination of capital investment, export orientation, and intense competition has moved Japan and Japanese firms to become major players in global markets.

One need not choose between a state-centered and a firm-centered explanation of Japan's success. The effectiveness of the Japanese economy comes from the ability to organize resources in such a way that firms were able to gain comparative advantages in world markets and generate new arrangements of learning and innovation. Innovation was encouraged by institutional arrangements (government and industry) that absorbed risk and provided incentives for adaptive behavior. The key to understanding Japan lies in focusing not on the state or on corporations, but rather on the way that many institutions—markets, firms, government, and industry organizations—relate to each other to create a particular and very successful national innovation system. In Japan, markets are powerful and mold economic decisions; the state shows dexterity in targeting industries for special support; and firms

---

[29] Stephen S. Cohen, "Geo-Economics: Lessons from America's Mistakes," in Martin Carnoy (ed.), *The New Global Economy in the Information Age*, University Park: Pennsylvania State University Press, 1993, 107.

[30] Thomas Arrison et al., *Japan's Growing Technological Capability: Implications for the U.S. Economy*, Washington, D.C.: National Academy Press, 1992, 1.

have an unusual mixture of intense competition and cooperation that makes them juggernauts in the world economy.[31]

## Future Prospects

While thinking about the future, we should keep in mind some of the important differences between Japan and Western nations that may act to temper a continuing pattern of spectacular economic success. Many Japanese pay a high price for their economic prosperity, as much of it does not filter down to the average consumer. High savings rates are the positive side of much lower rates of consumption. This is another way of saying that the forbearance of Japanese consumers allows the nation to devote more resources to investment. Moreover, the prices of many consumer goods are at a large premium compared to those in other countries. Prices for many goods may be as much as one-third higher in Japan.[32] Housing in Japanese urban areas is extremely expensive, and the country tolerates major inefficiencies in food production and processing. Much of the competitive advantage of some Japanese industries derives from the economic subjugation of a large portion of the female work force. The rationale of weakness or national poverty can no longer serve as a justification for many of these practices. A stronger consumer orientation may well undercut future national investment priorities and trade surpluses.

Some liberals (remember that these people emphasize the power and efficacy of markets) argue that recent trends generate strong pressures toward the convergence of Japan with the West, especially the United States and Britain.[33] According to this argument, prosperity helps breed individualism, globalization produces an internationalist perspective in Japanese corporations, technology and competition undermine harmony between worker and manager and between "salarymen" and company, and the rising cost of capital leads to a much more short-term approach to profits. Persistently low economic growth has intensified the potential for change. The political result of these trends has been increased pressure to deregulate the Japanese economy, demands to open the system to foreign (lower-priced) goods, the decreasing ability of MITI to manage the economy, political turmoil, and electoral reform. Changes in Japan are undeniable and significant, but Westerners for many decades have often seen more change than was really there.[34]

---

[31] This view is taken in different forms by: Richard Samuels, *The Business of the Japanese State*, Ithaca: Cornell University Press, 1987; Jeffrey Hart, *Rival Capitalists*, Ithaca: Cornell University Press, 1992; and Richard Nelson, *National Innovation Systems*, Oxford: Oxford University Press, 1993.

[32] Richard J. Samuels, "Consuming for Production: Japanese National Security, Nuclear Fuel Procurement, and the Domestic Economy," *International Organization*, 43.4, Autumn 1989, 625–626. Much of this is due to high costs of raw materials, an antiquated distribution system, and protectionist barriers to imports of lower-priced foreign goods.

[33] This argument is found in "Japan: Death of a Role Model," *The Economist*, July 9, 1994.

[34] A more sober analysis of economic and political change in Japan is Michael Blaker, "Japan in 1994: Out with the Old, in with the New?" *Asian Survey*, 35.1, January 1995, 1–12.

However we assess the potential for change, the rise of Japan to the world's second-largest economic power in less than forty years is a stunning accomplishment with many important consequences. Perhaps the most important is that U.S. efforts in the 1980s to revitalize its economy have led to budget deficits, trade deficits, and (after 1985) a falling U.S. dollar, all of which have acted to transfer massive financial power to Japan. Between 1981 and 1988 the cumulative U.S. trade deficit with Japan totaled more than $300 billion.[35] In conjunction with the 50 percent appreciation of the yen after 1985, this has given the Japanese an immense financial surplus for investment abroad. The result has been a rapid movement into direct and portfolio investment that mirrors the pattern of financial outreach of Britain in the nineteenth century and of the United States between 1948 and 1980.[36] By 1990 Japanese foreign direct investment totaled $311 billion and, when combined with Japan's portfolio investment, made Japan the largest creditor nation in the world.[37]

Japanese financial power is both large enough and concentrated enough to affect global markets in substantial ways. Financial decisions in Japan are blamed for the collapse of world bond and stock prices in 1987 and also credited for their subsequent recovery.[38] Long an important presence in Asia, Japan has lately begun to assume the role of economic hegemon, especially in East and Southeast Asia. Japanese money, technology, and business strategy have started to play a key role in economic development in Thailand, Indonesia, Malaysia, Singapore, and mainland China. More than 10 percent of the Thai work force is employed by Japanese firms, and the figure is rising. Japanese companies have moved beyond a traditional interest in low-tech/low-wage manufacturing toward production of sophisticated equipment for local markets and for export. The result is a growing trend toward the organization of Asian markets and production by the Japanese.[39]

Beyond the strictly financial realm, Japan has begun to assume a much larger political role in the world. Even as late as the 1970s, Japan maintained a foreign posture that was "hesitant and withdrawn." This reflected the fact that after 1945 Japan was dependent on the United States for its security, access to world markets, and technology. By the mid-1980s, however, the Japanese government had developed a much greater consciousness of its power

---

[35] Robert Pear, "Confusion Is Operative Word in U.S. Policy Toward Japan," *New York Times*, March 20, 1989; and Susan Chira, "U.S. Currency Policy Speeds Japan in Vast Economic Role," *New York Times*, November 28, 1988.

[36] *Direct investment* refers to the purchase of productive assets abroad, and *portfolio investment* refers to the purchase of financial instruments, such as stocks and bonds.

[37] "America and Japan," *The Economist*, November 30, 1991, 23.

[38] R. Taggert Murphy, "Power Without Purpose: The Crisis of Japan's Global Financial Dominance," *Harvard Business Review*, March–April 1989, 73–74.

[39] David Sanger, "Behind Thai Boom: The Japanese," *New York Times*, May 10, 1990; James Sterngold, "Japan Builds East Asia Link, Gaining Labor and Markets," *New York Times*, May 8, 1990; James Sterngold, "Japan Stakes Out Nearby Markets," *New York Times*, January 24, 1990; and Nicholas D. Kristof, "Japan Winning Race in China," *New York Times*, April 29, 1987.

and a willingness to apply that power to Japanese-defined goals.[40] Events of that decade have rearranged the power relationship between the United States and Japan. The collapse of Soviet power greatly alters the question of Japanese security, even as the United States has become dependent on Japan for financial assistance, borrowing to support its consumptive lifestyle, and increasingly for high technology. In important respects, the tables have been turned. The result shows up in a more independent, and even assertive, foreign policy, greater international thinking in such areas as foreign aid, and growing defense capabilities. Even so, Japan is still searching for a clear international role, as witnessed by its difficulty in responding to the war against Iraq in 1990-1991.[41] The decision to participate in U.N. peacekeeping operations in Cambodia suggests progress in removing the stigma of World War II.

Japan is the most spectacular example of postwar economic growth fueled by the extraordinary development of the ties of international economic interdependence. But most other advanced capitalist states have also experienced dramatic economic growth and are likewise caught up in the expanding web of international interchange. Such an environment contributes to deepening relations of cooperation, competition, and even conflict among nations. We turn now to a consideration of the capabilities of the United States in global economic competition.

## THE UNITED STATES AND COMPETITIVENESS

Not surprisingly, discussion of the question of competitiveness in the United States has expanded dramatically in the 1980s and 1990s, and several perspectives have emerged. When considering competitiveness it is important to keep in mind that it is a politically charged issue and that information and argument are frequently skewed toward the interests of the source. Several schools of thought can be simplified as: (1) the U.S. economic system has serious problems that require major national efforts, (2) the United States is basically healthy, with perhaps the need for some adjustments around the edges, and (3) the real problems are located in Japan, which unfairly blocks U.S.

---

[40] Bruce Stokes, "Who's Standing Tall?" *National Journal*, October 21, 1989, 2568-2573; Susan Chira, "Newly Assertive Tokyo," *New York Times*, September 6, 1989; Lawrence Summer, "What to Do When Japan Says No," *New York Times*, December 3, 1989; Clyde Farnsworth, "Japan's Maneuvering for a Big Global Voice," *New York Times*, October 24, 1989; Steven Weisman, "Japan Takes a Leading Role in the Third-World Debt Crisis," *New York Times*, April 17, 1989.

[41] A more theoretical treatment of Japan's position in the international system is found in Richard Rosecrance, "Japan and the Theory of International Leadership," *World Politics*, 42.2, January 1990, 184-209; and Henrik Schmiegelow and Michele Schmiegelow, "How Japan Affects the International System," *International Organization*, 44.4, Autumn 1990, 553-588. For a discussion of Japan's response to the war against Iraq in 1990-1991, see Steven R. Weisman, "Japan Counts the Costs of Gulf Action—or Inaction," *New York Times*, January 27, 1991.

exports.[42] Our viewpoint is closer to the first group, but we will give you information drawn from all sides of the argument. We will consider U.S. competitiveness from the standpoint of broad macroeconomic indicators and from the perspective of the capabilities and weaknesses of firms. We will also weigh the merits of the strategy of managed trade as a way to improve competitive outcomes.

One important approach to thinking about competitiveness is to relate national strengths to the major technological developments of the preceding two centuries. This approach argues that it is Japan, through its policies and performance, that appears to have established a new global competitive standard in the same way that Britain did in the early nineteenth century and that the United States did throughout most of the twentieth century. The preeminent position of the United States was the result of its strengths in creating and managing large, mass-production systems based on plentiful energy. American firms dominated global markets for mass-produced goods from 1920 to 1975 because of managerial innovations in controlling large enterprises, because of the ability to reap large economies of scale in the immense American market, and because of access to huge supplies of cheap energy. But rising energy prices after 1974 intersect with the emergence of information-based manufacturing to alter the technology of production. Japan presents such a major challenge because it has succeeded in mastering and perfecting this technology.[43]

## Macroeconomic Measures of Competitiveness

A related perspective considers changes in the overall ability of a nation's economic relationships to support sustained growth in output and income. Often this means comparative measures of trade, savings, investment, productivity, and income growth. The standard measure of a nation's competitiveness in world markets is its balance of trade. We have described the dramatic collapse in the U.S. position during the first half of the 1980s and the effort to reverse this collapse through a policy of dollar depreciation. Did it work? Table 7.2 provides detailed information about the trade balance, the balance on services, and income. The picture is not very favorable. Although the trade balance did improve after 1987, it has since returned to levels of the mid-1980s. The best that can be said is that the trade deficit is now much lower as

---

[42] The political orientation of different industries may be generally related to these schools. Those industries that are less competitive may be more inclined to seek government help and to support a major national effort. Those industries that are competitive or have the alternative of moving operations abroad or that are unaffected by international competition may be indifferent to or oppose such efforts, especially if the efforts require higher taxes and/or a more intrusive role for government.

[43] John Cantwell, "Japan's Industrial Competitiveness and the Technological Capabilities of the Leading Japanese Firms," in Arrison et al., *Japan's Growing . . .*, 165-188.

**TABLE 7.2**

**U.S. Trade, Services, and Investment Income Balances, 1981–1994**
*(Billions of Dollars)*

| YEAR | 1981 | 1984 | 1987 | 1990 | 1991 | 1992 | 1993 | 1994 |
|---|---|---|---|---|---|---|---|---|
| Exports: Goods | 237.1 | 219.9 | 250.2 | 389.3 | 416.9 | 440.4 | 456.9 | 502.7 |
| Imports: Goods | 265.1 | 332.4 | 409.8 | 498.3 | 491.0 | 536.5 | 589.4 | 669.1 |
| Trade Balance | -28.0 | -112.5 | -159.6 | -109.0 | -74.1 | -96.1 | -132.5 | -166.4 |
| Exports: Services | 57.3 | 70.9 | 97.7 | 147.1 | 163.1 | 176.4 | 184.6 | 195.1 |
| Imports: Services | 44.9 | 66.8 | 89.4 | 115.9 | 116.5 | 119.7 | 126.6 | 133.9 |
| Services Balance | 12.4 | 14.1 | 8.3 | 31.2 | 46.6 | 56.7 | 58.0 | 61.2 |
| Balance: Goods and Services | -15.6 | -108.4 | -151.3 | -77.8 | -27.5 | -39.4 | -74.5 | -105.2 |
| Investment Income (net) | 32.4 | 29.2 | 7.2 | 19.7 | 13.8 | 3.5 | 3.8 | -16.4 |
| Balance on Trade, Services, and Investment Income | 16.8 | -79.2 | -144.1 | -58.1 | -13.7 | -35.9 | -71.7 | -121.6 |

SOURCE: IMF, *International Financial Statistics Yearbook*, 1995.

a percent of GDP. Nevertheless, the trade deficit is large and persists through time, suggesting important weaknesses in the competitive position of the United States. The most favorable data are from the services accounts, where the United States runs a continuing and growing surplus. However, the services surplus, combined with the declining net return on foreign assets, is too small to compensate for the trade deficit.

The globalization of production (discussed in Chapter 5) complicates the use of trade balances as a measure of national competitiveness. Multinational corporations based in the United States (or elsewhere) now locate production and other facilities around the world using calculations of wage rates, productivity, and market access. Indeed, the ability of MNCs to compete in global markets depends on the global organization of production. The fact that IBM is based in the United States has only limited bearing on which facilities will be located in the United States This means we need to distinguish between those processes that make multinational firms competitive and those that make the United States attractive as a site for production, research, or distribution facilities. Indeed, at the same time that the trade deficits of the United

States have expanded, U.S.-based MNCs have remained very competitive on a global basis, as indicated by an expanding share of world trade.[44] Thus U.S. multinational corporations show competitive strength at the same time that the United States as a geographical area shows weaknesses. Which measure of U.S. competitiveness is the most accurate in an age of globalization? The answer is not clear.

Another facet of the competitiveness issue can be seen by comparing the U.S. economy's response to the rising dollar from 1981 to 1985 with the Japanese economy's response to the rising yen from 1985 to 1990. For the United States, the 60 percent rise in the dollar produced a flat line for exports from 1981 to 1986 and an explosion of imports, resulting in an enormous trade deficit. The Japanese, on the other hand, have adjusted to the high yen with remarkable speed. The higher yen prompted efforts to cut costs, increase efficiency, accept more imports, and increase domestic consumption. Although the trade surplus has shrunk, it remains quite high. Japanese exports have been boosted by consumer perception of high-quality goods and by the dominance of certain markets by Japanese products. Even though the yen rose by almost 100 percent against the dollar between 1985 and 1990, the Japanese trade surplus with the United States declined only from about $56 billion to $41 billion.[45] The remarkable contrast between the weakness of the U.S. response to shifts in the dollar exchange rate and the strength of the Japanese response to the rising yen suggests that we need to look deeper into the competitiveness question.

Perhaps the most important broad economic measure of a nation's competitiveness involves its productivity, savings, and capital investment. These represent the ability to withhold resources from present consumption and devote them to investments that permit production of more and better goods in the future. It is this capacity for improving and innovating that makes an economy competitive and makes possible rising incomes and living standards.

The evidence on U.S. savings and investment is generally negative, whereas that on productivity is more mixed. Table 7.3 indicates the similarity of the British and U.S. economies, with the lowest levels of savings and investment of six advanced economies. Germany, France, and Canada save and invest 3 to 4 percent more of their GDP than do the United States and British.

---

[44] Dennis Encarnation, *Rivals Beyond Trade: America versus Japan in Global Competition*, Ithaca: Cornell University Press, 1992, 191. Encarnation also makes a very strong case that the trade imbalance between the United States and Japan results because the United States is much more open to Japanese FDI than Japan is to U.S. FDI. This means that Japanese MNCs are much better able to locate production in the United States and to engage in intracorporate shipments that result in exports to the United States. Japan's relative closure to FDI blocks this process to U.S. firms.

[45] David Sanger, "How Japan Does What It's Doing to Keep Its Economy in Top Gear," *New York Times*, November 27, 1988; James Sterngold, "Japan Poised for Postwar Boom," *New York Times*, January 28, 1991; Clyde Farnsworth, "U.S. Is Asked to Review Japanese Trade," *New York Times*, March 25, 1991.

**TABLE 7.3**

**Comparative Savings and Investment as a Percent of GDP**
*(Average for 1970–1992)*

|                  | U.S. | BRITAIN | GERMANY | FRANCE | JAPAN | CANADA |
|------------------|------|---------|---------|--------|-------|--------|
| Gross Investment | 18.5 | 18.4    | 21.6    | 23.1   | 32.0  | 21.7   |
| Gross Savings    | 17.8 | 17.0    | 23.6    | 23.4   | 34.0  | 20.0   |

SOURCE: *The Economist,* June 24, 1995, 73.

The real exception is Japan, with much higher levels of savings and investment than any other advanced state.

When all industrial countries are combined, the gross savings rate for 1994 was 20 percent, making the United States and Britain look even less effective in providing for future growth.[46] More-refined measures indicate much the same thing. Astonishingly, with an economy less than two thirds the size of the United States', Japan actually spent $750 billion for gross investment in 1989 compared to $500 billion for the United States.[47]

In spite of the poor showing in savings and investment, productivity measures have given rise to encouragement. This concept measures the quantity of output per worker, and its growth is usually tied closely to growth in income. During the 1970s U.S. manufacturing productivity grew at only 1.4 percent, whereas that of other industrial nations grew at nearly 4 percent. The 1980s led to a turnaround in U.S. productivity growth. Between 1979 and 1989 the United States matched these same nations at 3.6 percent growth. Much of this gain came from downsizing U.S. plants, laying off workers, and increasing the productivity of those who remained.[48] Aside from changes in productivity, the absolute level of output per worker considered on a comparative basis provides a useful measure of a nation's competitiveness. Table 7.4 offers such data organized by industry.

These data show the United States enjoying a broad lead over Germany and Japan in average productivity and especially over Germany in most manufacturing industries. The massive U.S. lead in areas such as food is offset by Japanese advantages in manufacturing productivity. Less clear is whether recent U.S. productivity gains can be sustained in the face of low savings and investment levels.

---

[46] *The Economist,* May 6, 1995, 78. The U.S. savings weakness comes mainly from low and declining household savings. In 1973 the household savings rate (as a percent of disposable income) was over 9 percent; by 1994 it was 4 percent. See *The Economist,* January 21, 1995, 19.

[47] David Sanger, "Japan Keeps Up the Big Spending to Maintain Its Industrial Might," *New York Times,* April 11, 1990.

[48] Sylvia Nasar, "American Revival in Manufacturing Seen in U.S. Report," *New York Times,* February 5, 1991; Lawrence Klein, "Components of Competitiveness," *Science,* 241, July 15, 1988, 308–313. For a detailed and generally favorable picture of U.S. productivity, see William J. Baumol et al., *Productivity and American Leadership: The Long View,* Cambridge: MIT Press, 1991.

**TABLE 7.4**

**Comparative Productivity in Manufacturing**
*(Index Based on U.S. Productivity=100)*

| INDUSTRY | UNITED STATES | GERMANY | JAPAN |
|---|---|---|---|
| Computers | 100.0 | 90.0 | 95.0 |
| Automobiles | 100.0 | 62.0 | 113.0 |
| Consumer Electronics | 100.0 | 58.0 | 110.0 |
| Auto Parts | 100.0 | 75.0 | 122.0 |
| Steel | 100.0 | 100.0 | 145.0 |
| Metalworking | 100.0 | 100.0 | 117.0 |
| Food | 100.0 | 74.0 | 34.0 |
| Average | 100.0 | 77.0 | 82.0 |

SOURCE: *The Economist*, October 23, 1993, 88.

Somewhat more negative is the fact that U.S. productivity growth for manufacturing has not extended to services industries. And productivity gains have not been translated into higher real earnings. The median family income in real terms has been essentially stagnant since the early 1970s. Figure 7.2 shows rapid and significant growth from 1960 to 1970 and peaks and valleys producing very small gains since. Even in manufacturing, real wages have been dropping since 1977, making some analysts skeptical about the genuineness of the productivity growth.[49]

## Competition in Chips

Perhaps the aggregate measures have disguised more-favorable trends in specific industries, such as high technology.[50] Unfortunately, the trends are mixed and firm conclusions hard to reach. Surely the most spectacular and far-reaching shift of the 1980s was the decline of U.S. preeminence in high technology. Nothing demonstrates this decline more clearly than the rapid erosion of U.S. firms' dominance of the global semiconductor market and the emergence of Japanese firms as an equal competitor.

This story relates to our earlier discussion of government–business ties in Japan, with some interesting twists. The semiconductor industry began in the United States, reflecting the immense technological advantages enjoyed after World War II. For almost two decades the U.S. government (through the

---

[49] Louis Uchitelle, "Not Getting Ahead? Better Get Used to It," *New York Times*, December 16, 1990.

[50] Three good overviews of competitiveness issues at the level of industries are: Michael L. Dertouzos et al. (eds.), *Made in America*, Cambridge: MIT Press, 1989; Jean Claude Derian, *America's Struggle for Leadership in Technology*, Cambridge: MIT Press, 1990; and Martin Starr (ed.), *Global Competitiveness*, New York: Norton, 1988. An older but still useful volume is Bruce Scott and George Lodge (eds.), *U.S. Competitiveness in the World Economy*, Boston: Harvard Business School Press, 1985.

**FIGURE 7.2**

**Median Family Income—United States**
*(Index: 100=1950)*

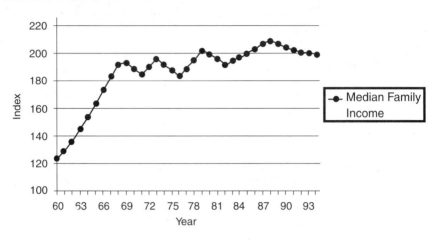

SOURCE: "American Business," *The Economist,* September 16, 1995, 12.

Defense Department) was the major customer for semiconductors. This provided stable demand even when consumer demand was limited and when production and research costs were so high that government purchases amounted to an industry subsidy. In the 1970s commercial demand surged, and many new corporations were started to supply semiconductors and to take advantage of technological breakthroughs. By 1975 U.S.-based firms produced over 60 percent of all the semiconductors in the world.[51]

In Japan the Ministry of International Trade and Industry supported a crash effort to catch up and then surpass the United States in product development. Even though United States' firms possessed overwhelming advantages, MITI realized the importance of semiconductors to high-technology production and innovation. MITI's support, plus closing the Japanese market for a time to foreign-made semiconductors, gave Japanese producers the opportunity to develop production experience and an assured market. The production wizardry of Japanese firms soon enabled them to surpass U.S. producers in quality. These same Japanese firms took large losses by selling below cost in order to capture a large segment of the U.S. market (a strategy frequently used by firms in an industry with large economies of scale). The combination of quality and price led to rapid sales growth, to falling costs of production (economies of scale), and to additional price cuts. The results were catastrophic for U.S. firms. As we see from Figure 7.3, between 1981 and

---

[51] The story of the semiconductor industry is ably told in Laura D'Andrea Tyson and David Yoffie, "Semiconductors: From Manipulated to Managed Trade," in Yoffie (ed.), *Beyond Free Trade . . .,* 29–48; and Timothy O'Shea, *The U.S.-Japanese Semiconductor Problem,* Washington, D.C.: Pew Case Studies, 1994.

**FIGURE 7.3**

**U.S. and Japanese Semiconductor Firms Global Market Share**
*(in percent)*

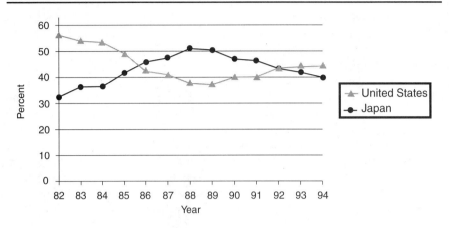

SOURCE: *New York Times*, April 17, 1994, C7.

1989 the share of the global semiconductor market held by U.S.-based firms declined from 51 percent to 35 percent. Japanese-based firms mirrored this change, rising in world market share from 35 percent to 50 percent. Since 1989 American firms have recovered as Japanese firms have slipped.

Stabilization of global competition was the product of large investment efforts by U.S.-based firms and of a major R&D partnership between the U.S. government and several semiconductor firms that permitted improvements in manufacturing technology. Created in 1987, this partnership, Sematech, is a consortium of firms organized and partially funded by the U.S. government. Motivated by the tremendous losses suffered by U.S. companies and by the possibility of dependence on Japan for semiconductors, government and industry officials focused their efforts on improving manufacturing capabilities. With $100 million supplied by the Defense Advanced Research Projects Agency (DARPA) and matched by $100 million from the industry partners, Sematech became a catalyst for improving the precision and quality of semiconductor manufacturing technology. And, by most measures, this goal was accomplished. By early 1993 Sematech had achieved a level of production tolerance unmatched in the world. But U.S. firms, most notably Intel, have also engaged in a binge of investment and research and development that has contributed much to their revival.[52]

---

[52] Steve Lohr, "Suiting Up for America's High Tech Future," *New York Times*, December 3, 1995, 3.1. For details about Sematech, see "Uncle Sam's Helping Hand," *The Economist*, April 2, 1994, 77–79; and David Gibson and Everett Rogers, *R&D Collaboration on Trial*, Boston: Harvard Business School Press, 1994, 467–533. Plans are for Sematech to continue its efforts, but without government funding after 1997.

Once again, reaching firm judgments about competitiveness is complicated by globalization. The revival after 1989 has been in U.S.-based firms, not so much in the United States as a production platform. Although many firms are establishing new plants in the United States, only about 50 percent of semiconductor production by U.S. firms occurs in the United States Further, Sematech's goal was to provide support to U.S. firms, but it found that the globalization of production and technology makes that quite difficult. Many of the U.S. firms involved in Sematech are engaged in strategic alliances for sharing technology with Japanese, Korean, and European firms. And some of the small U.S. firms receiving Sematech support have been bought by Japanese firms. Creating and capturing competitive advantages within national boundaries is a very difficult task in a world of globalization.

The semiconductor case illustrates many of the important features of competitiveness among advanced industrial states. It is a vital technology that affects many aspects of the emerging information-based economic system. Having successful firms in the semiconductor industry provides many positive consequences for other high-technology industries; failing to have such firms can mean dependence on foreign sources, which creates the risk of falling behind in more than semiconductors. The military applications of semiconductors and other high technology add to the competitive element of this industry. And the development and production of semiconductors are extraordinarily dynamic processes, requiring very strong firms, plentiful capital, and occasional government support to create and re-create competitive advantages. Semiconductors point out that the quality and strength of national innovation systems greatly affect the success of firms based in that nation.[53] At the same time, globalization undermines the national focus of high-technology innovation and the ability of nations to capture the benefits of their investments.

## Strengths and Weaknesses of U.S. Firms

The combination of ballooning trade deficits, sluggish productivity growth, and the surging Japanese economy led many analysts in the 1980s to evaluate the performance of U.S. firms as a major element in competitiveness. Many analysts found much to criticize in U.S. corporations. But many corporations in the United States have since made major efforts to overcome past deficiencies, resulting in better recent ratings.

Most of the criticisms of U.S. firms focus on structural weaknesses that generate incentives for bad decisions. That is, deeply embedded practices and arrangements in the U.S. economy and enterprise system are thought to push and pull executives toward choices that hurt American competitiveness. These include:

- The past successes of firms in focusing on mass production for the U.S. market made many ignore opportunities in foreign markets and

---

[53] If you doubt this, imagine trying to establish a successful semiconductor industry in Vietnam.

especially innovations in production technology developed in Japan. U.S. firms clung to mass production and found very difficult any shift toward flexible, lean, intense quality-control manufacturing.

- Because most firms depend heavily on equity sales of stock for capital needs and because investors were quick to sell stock based on the most recent earnings report, executives had a very short-term time horizon for decisions. Firms would avoid investments with a long-term payoff and look instead to seemingly more assured quick returns.
- Because global competition was so weak in the 1950s and 1960s, firms were able to rely on "breakthrough" technology with less attention to the more mundane problems of converting innovations into commercial products and producing these in the most effective manner.
- Mass-production techniques required workers with a minimal education and who were susceptible to intense control by managers. This led U.S. firms to ignore continuous investment in worker training and shifting power over production decisions to on-line workers.
- The emphasis on competition and antitrust laws against collusion made cooperation among U.S. firms difficult. But in an environment of rapid technological change, with innovation occurring at all levels of the production process, no firm acting alone can keep up with changes that generate competitive advantage.[54]

Together, these problems present a damaging indictment of U.S. business.

At the same time, U.S. enterprises have made major adjustments to improve their competitive position. Exports, prodded by large declines in the dollar, have grown substantially, and an international emphasis has increased throughout the U.S. business system. The rapid rise of international strategic alliances, the new emphasis on production and commercialization R&D, and the increasing use of new manufacturing systems show the ability to borrow from abroad and to cooperate. Less clear is whether time horizons have expanded because a company's stock price is still battered when earnings don't match or exceed analysts' expectations. And the most common (and controversial) competitiveness strategy—downsizing by making large cuts in the work force—suggests that companies still don't understand the value of investing in employees.

Several U.S. industries recently in deep trouble have staged dramatic recoveries. We have seen the role of large corporate investment and government support in the semiconductor industry. U.S. automakers have adopted flexible, lean manufacturing, improved quality control, and benefited from "voluntary" restraints on Japanese imports. This has made it possible for American-based companies to stabilize and even improve slightly their position in global markets. And U.S. steel producers have generated significant productivity gains, received protection from foreign imports, and engaged in savage

---

[54] This list draws on Michael Dertouzos et al., *Made in America*, Cambridge: MIT Press, 1989; and "American Business: Back on Top?" *The Economist*, September 16, 1995.

downsizing to return to profitability and increased global market share. What is less clear is how many other industries can tout these success stories and whether the improvements have found their way into broad-based improvements in incomes. As shown in Figure 7.2, measures of median family income indicate stagnation for more than a quarter century. Although downsizing, a declining dollar, and globalization produce competitive advantages for corporations, these also lower incomes for many U.S. workers.

## EUROPEAN APPROACHES TO COMPETITIVENESS

The Europeans have not been unmindful of the new competitive environment. As we noted in Chapter 6, both the decision to move toward a single market in the EC and the incorporation of some EFTA states into the EU have been designed to increase the competitiveness of European firms. The removal of nontariff barriers to trade is being advanced through the development of 282 measures drafted by the European Commission, passed by the European Parliament, and sent on to national governments for enactment into law. The effect is to create a single set of rules across the EU for commercial transactions. There are mainly two results for competitiveness: reducing costs made unnecessary by the elimination of various trade barriers and encouraging the creation of EU-wide firms capable of operations in all of these markets. This will lead to additional cost savings from economies of scale and firms large enough to afford the investments needed to compete in world markets. Beyond these results, the elimination of internal trade barriers still leaves external barriers in place. The consequence is to force many non-European firms to locate facilities within the EU in order to sell in this market. Although this strategy displaces imports and maintains employment, it may also present European firms with significant competition in their home market.

The free-market approach, embedded in the new single market in Europe, contrasts sharply with more traditional industrial and competitiveness policies in the countries of the EU. All of these countries have made extensive use of subsidies and other state aid in agriculture and manufacturing have substantial experience in state-owned firms, and many have supported development of cartels for industries in distress.[55] The movement toward the Single European Act and deregulation has prompted the European Commission to press for an end to subsidies, cartels, and other forms of market distortions.[56] However, the clash between these competing perspectives has not been sorted out. In the electronics and computer industries—areas of major importance to advanced industrial economies—EU states have acted to support

---

[55] See Colchester and Buchan, *Europower* . . . , 147–148; Richard E. Foglesong and Joel D. Wolfe (eds.), *The Politics of Economic Adjustment*, New York: Greenwood Press, 1989, contains several excellent articles on industrial policy in France, Germany, and Britain.

[56] See Colchester and Buchan, *Europower* . . . , 144–158.

**TABLE 7.5**
**Comparative Competitiveness Indicators**

|  | GERMANY | FRANCE | BELGIUM | ITALY | U.S. | JAPAN |
|---|---|---|---|---|---|---|
| Manufacturing Wages $/Hour 1994 | 27.00 | 17.70 | 22.50 | 17.00 | 18.00 | 21.00 |
| Total Tax Revenues % GDP 1994 | 39 | 44 | 46 | 45 | 30 | 29 |
| Budget Deficits % GDP 1994 | 3.5 | 6.8 | 6.0 | 9.0 | 2.7 | 2.9 |
| Unemployment in 1994 % Total Labor Force | 7.4 | 12.8 | 10.4 | 12.0 | 5.8 | 2.9 |

SOURCE: *The Economist*, various issues.

private firms. And pressure from these same firms—especially in computers and semiconductors—to do more is increasing.[57] Nonetheless, the states in the EU are sufficiently different to make a common competitiveness policy unlikely for the moment. Some, like France and Italy, are much more interventionist than are Germany and Britain. Equally relevant is the fact that industries are not always in the same position in every country; some are competitive, and some are not. This makes it difficult for the EU to opt for anything other than freeing up the market to improve competitiveness.

Despite these qualifications, the states and firms of the European Union possess many competitive disadvantages in the world economy. These derive mainly from the relative cost of production in Europe, which generally is quite high. Several of the largest and most developed European states are areas of high wages, high taxes, high welfare expenditure, and low productivity. Table 7.5 provides comparative data on several indicators relating to this problem. One factor contributing to high wage costs in Germany is the large expenditure for social welfare benefits and for vacations. Together, these make up $12 or 44 percent of the $27 per-hour wage rates in German manufacturing. By comparison, the figure for the United States is $5 or 28 percent of the $18 rate, and for Japan the figure is $7.50 or 36 percent of the $21 rate. Alone, wage rates do not necessarily indicate the actual costs of production; we must also include worker productivity to generate a unit labor cost—that is the cost of labor in producing one unit. Since 1980 unit labor costs in the United States have fallen by 20 percent, while in Germany they have risen by 30 percent. The costs of welfare and unemployment also show up in budget deficits, which are much higher in Europe than in the United States or Japan.[58]

Specific European industries also show important weaknesses. European automobile firms have been slow to adopt flexible, lean manufacturing and consequently have trouble competing in global markets. European producers take more than twice as long to make a car as the Japanese, but this product

---

[57] Steven Greenhouse, "Europe's Electronics Rescue Plan," *New York Times*, September 5, 1991.
[58] *The Economist*, January 15, 1994, 66.

is plagued by two-thirds more defects. When Porsche shifted to a Japanese-based system of flexible, lean manufacturing, production time dropped by 40 percent, defects by 50 percent, and inventory levels by 81 percent. However, the barriers to accepting such a system have been formidable. Flexible manufacturing requires changes in work rules, downtime, and worker–manager relations that conflict with traditional European practices.[59]

High-technology industries are also a major problem for European competitiveness.[60] This is especially true for semiconductors, computers, and consumer electronics. Somewhat brighter conclusions can be reached about telecommunications. In semiconductors, European producers were the main losers in the struggle between U.S. and Japanese firms in the 1980s and 1990s. World market share for European firms has fallen to 10 percent and shows little signs of recovery. Even inside Europe, domestic producers maintain only a 40 percent market share. European firms control even less of their market for computers, only 34 percent, and seem to be falling behind in the capacity to innovate and gain competitive advantage. Consumer electronics is somewhat better, with European firms stronger than U.S.-based firms but still weaker than the Japanese. Only in telecommunications do European firms dominate their home markets and compete effectively in global markets. But some part of this strength derives from protected markets and preferential policies by home governments. Liberalization of telecommunications markets on a global scale in the 1990s provides a good test of the long-term capabilities of European firms.

Individual governments and the European Union have made efforts to reverse the competitive weaknesses of European high-technology firms. Business and government elites across Europe have understood quite well the strategic nature of many of these industries. They have recognized that strength in high technology shapes the trajectory of economic development and growth for entire economies; weakness closes off possibilities that can limit growth in many areas. In the past, these concerns led to national policies designed to promote a national firm capable of competing in world markets. These efforts failed because the scale of such enterprises and markets was too small. EU leaders realized that only when the European market was a genuine reality could scale problems be overcome. This helped propel the decision for a single market in 1992. Additionally, the EU has moved to support interfirm cooperation through large-scale R&D projects. Four of these projects deserve

---

[59] Nathaniel Nash, "Putting Porsche in the Pink," *New York Times*, January 20, 1996, 17.  Cohen, "Geo-Economics . . . ," 107.

[60] The discussion of European high technology draws on John Zysman and Michael Borrus, *From Failure to Fortune? European Electronics in the Changing World Economy*, Berkeley, BRIE Working Paper, 1994; Laura D'Andrea Tyson, *Who's Bashing Whom? Trade Conflict in High-Technology Industries*, Washington, D.C.: Institute for International Economics, 1992, 217–251; Wayne Sandholtz, *High-Tech Europe: The Politics of International Cooperation*, Berkeley: University of California Press, 1992; and Kirsty Hughes (ed.), *European Competitiveness*, Cambridge: Cambridge University Press, 1993.

mention. The European Strategic Programme for Research and Development in Information Technology (ESPRIT) was created by the EEC in 1984 to provide funds for collaborative R&D. Nearly $10 billion was allocated to this program by 1994, half from government sources. R&D in Advanced Communications-Technologies in Europe (RACE) is a somewhat smaller program established in 1985 to promote collaboration in such areas as high-definition television. The European Research Coordination Agency (EUREKA), established in 1985, sponsored such projects as Joint European Semiconductor Silicon (JESSI) to catch up in semiconductor manufacturing. And Basic Research for Industrial Technology in Europe (BRITE) was directed at special materials related to superconductivity.[61] The results of these efforts remain unclear but are testimony to the intense concern in Europe over lagging behind in high technology.

The terms of international competition have changed, making obsolete the advantages that once propelled Europe, and then the United States, to world economic preeminence. There is good reason to question whether either can respond effectively to the new competitive standard being set by Japan. A much wider hearing needs to be given to the call for policies designed to create comparative advantage through investments in infrastructure supporting, knowledge-intensive industries, higher levels of national savings, and actions to cushion or even assume risks for certain key industries.[62] But beyond these proposals lies the traditional strategy for responding to the new climate of international competition: protectionism.

## PROTECTIONISM

Ironically, the acceleration of the world economy toward freer trade and even greater interdependence since the early 1970s has also led to a revival of pressures for protectionism. This should not come as too much of a surprise because more interdependence means that the most competitive and innovative foreign producers have more opportunities to sell their goods. Those who cannot meet this competition invariably begin to call for government help. But in an international climate where GATT has led to very low tariffs, protectionism has become somewhat more sophisticated.[63]

### Protectionism Without Tariffs

These "new" protectionist measures are typically designed to help a particular industry. In the broadest sense, these measures are designed to "manage"

---

[61] The best discussion of these programs is found in Sandholtz, *High-Tech Europe* . . . . A related area of European support for high-tech industry is Airbus, which is discussed in Chapter 1.

[62] An example is Robert Reich, "The Real Economy," *The Atlantic Monthly*, February 1991, 35–52.

[63] For a useful but somewhat dated overview of protectionism, see David Greenaway, *Trade Policy and the New Protectionism*, New York: St. Martin's Press, 1983.

trade outcomes without regard to the results of (seemingly) free markets. Examples of managed trade include efforts to use the threat of legally mandated restrictions to compel importers to restrict the sale of their goods "voluntarily" and negotiated arrangements that establish quotas to limit imports. A second form involves efforts to arrange a quota for exports of a particular product and in this sense might be understood as trade promoting rather than trade restricting.

Sometimes known as *voluntary export restraints* (VERs) and *orderly marketing agreements* (OMAs), these arrangements have been used to establish quotas for the sale of goods in the United States.[64] In 1981 the Japanese government acted "voluntarily" to restrict the number of automobiles sold in the United States so as to reduce pressure in the U.S. Congress for much more restrictive protectionism.[65] The Reagan administration did not want to violate its free trade ideology but could not ignore the rapid growth of Japanese auto sales in the U.S. market. Subtle pressure on Japan led it to choose the least worst option and to announce that no more than 1.68 million cars per year would be shipped to the United States. The arrangement remained in place for more than ten years, with several interesting consequences. Japanese penetration of the U.S. auto market was slowed but not stopped, with the share of the U.S. auto market rising from less than 19 percent in 1980 to 23.1 percent in 1994. Automakers in Japan have modified the mix of cars sold in the United States toward more expensive models, and prices for autos have risen much more rapidly than for other goods.[66]

From the perspective of U.S. autoworkers and executives, the VER was insufficient. Much more needed to be done to restrain the competitive pressure generated by Japan. From the position of U.S. consumers, qualitative improvements (and some jobs) were purchased at a very high cost.[67] In effect, U.S. consumers, through higher prices, subsidized both the U.S. and the Japanese auto industries. From the position of a political leader, the VER can be a relatively quiet way to provide relief to a threatened industry without challenging

---

[64] Others include countervailing duties (CVD) and antidumping arrangements, which result from what are thought to be unfair trading practices. When foreign firms sell below "fair value" or receive a state subsidy, these methods are used to raise prices to establish a "level playing field." A useful overview of protectionist trends in the United States is found in I. M. Destler, *American Trade Politics: System Under Stress*, Washington, D.C.: Institute for International Economics, 1986. Also helpful for its detailed examination of multiple case studies is Gary C. Hufbauer et al., *Trade Protection in the United States*, Washington, D.C.: Institute for International Economics, 1986.

[65] A similar agreement exists between the EU and Japan.

[66] The machine tools industry is another area where VERs have been used with very mixed results. Those producers whose resources make them uncompetitive, even in the near term, support this policy. Those who are better able to remain competitive oppose VERs. See Steve Lohr, "A Split Over Machine Tool Imports," *New York Times*, October 7, 1991.

[67] One estimate is that each job saved cost consumers $110,000 to $145,000. See Charles Collyns and Steve Dunaway, "The Cost of Trade Restraints: The Case of Japanese Automobile Exports to the United States," in King (ed.), *International Economics . . .* , 13–21.

the concept of free trade either at home or abroad. Of course, this works only so long as the exporting country cooperates.[68]

Perhaps the best example of managed trade is in the same semiconductor industry discussed earlier. In 1985, after several years of losing market share to Japanese firms, the Semiconductor Industry Association (a cooperative alliance of U.S. semiconductor firms) filed a petition under Section 301 of the Trade Act of 1974.[69] This petition and subsequent legal actions charged that Japanese firms were "dumping" semiconductors (selling in the United States at prices below the cost of production) and that the Japanese semiconductor market was closed to U.S. firms. The main purpose of this action was to force the Japanese government to begin negotiations on a division of market share between U.S. and Japanese firms. The result was an agreement reached in 1986 in which Japanese firms promised to stop dumping semiconductors in the United States and to increase the Japanese market share for U.S. firms to 20 percent within five years. After punitive tariffs were imposed in 1987 to force compliance, the U.S. share of the Japanese market began to increase. An extension of the agreement was needed in 1991 to give Japan time to meet the 20 percent quota, which it did in 1993.[70]

The longest-standing VER is the Multi-Fibre Arrangement (MFA), which can be traced back to the early 1960s. The textile and apparel industry— where the industrial revolution began two hundred years ago—is a good example of a labor-intensive, low-capital investment, low-technology industry in which comparative advantage comes largely from relative wage levels. High-wage nations have typically been unable to compete with low-wage nations in the absence of some form of protectionism. The MFA is a multilateral agreement designed to place quantitative limits on imports of textiles and apparel into high-wage countries. Associated with it is a series of bilateral agreements designed to serve the same purpose. Well over one half of all world trade in

---

[68] The best review of the auto VERs is Simon Reich, *The Reagan Administration, the Auto Producers, and the 1981 Agreement with Japan*, Washington, D.C.: Pew Case Studies, 1992; and Simon Reich, *Restraining Trade to Invoke Investment: MITI and the Japanese Auto Producers*, Washington, D.C.: Pew Case Studies, 1992. Another round of trade conflict over autos occurred from 1993 to 1995. The United States threatened to impose 100 percent punitive tariffs on Japanese luxury cars sold in the United States unless Japan opened its markets to U.S. autos and auto parts. A last-minute agreement called for Japan to increase parts purchased and for the Japanese government to encourage dealers in Japan to sell more U.S. cars. See David Sanger, "U.S. Settles Trade Dispute, Averting Billions in Tariffs on Japanese Luxury Vehicles," *New York Times*, June 29, 1995.

[69] Section 301 and its successor, Super 301 from the Trade Act of 1988, give the president the authority to impose punitive tariffs on countries engaging in "unfair" trade practices.

[70] Detailed discussion of the semiconductor case can be found in O'Shea, *The U.S.-Japanese . . .*; Krauss, *U.S.-Japan . . .*; and Tyson, *Who's Bashing Whom? . . .*, 85-154. An excellent analysis of trade conflict is John Conybeare, *Trade Wars: The Theory and Practice of International Commercial Rivalry*, New York: Columbia University Press, 1987; and David Rowe, *Trade Wars and International Security: The Political Economy of International Economic Conflict*, Cambridge: Olin Institute for Strategic Studies, 1994.

this industry is subject to one of these agreements.[71] The 1994 GATT agreement in the Uruguay Round of negotiations (discussed next) phases out the MFA to the great benefit of low-wage, high-productivity countries.

Important variations on protectionism in the West can be found in Japan, which has increasingly become the target of those who are harmed by its exports. Many have argued that Japan continues to operate as a free rider—benefiting from free trade while blocking the import of many goods. Documenting this charge is difficult because overt barriers to trade in Japan—tariffs and quotas—are generally lower than in most other advanced capitalist countries.[72] Rather, Japan retains a number of cultural and structural arrangements that effectively stand in the way of many imports. The result is a skewing of Japanese imports toward raw materials and semiprocessed manufactures and away from high-value-added and high-tech goods, as compared with other advanced capitalist states.

In general, barriers in Japan fit into one of several categories. They include:

1. Product standards (more important before 1980 than today), which indirectly or directly discriminate against foreign products
2. A distribution system—with many small retailers linked through exclusive arrangements with manufacturers and protected by price fixing—that blocks foreign firms[73]
3. Government favoritism toward Japanese firms in its purchases
4. A predominant form of business organization—*keiretsu*—that effectively creates a closed system of intrafirm purchases and suppliers that blocks entry by foreign firms
5. Cultural and business structural barriers to foreign direct investment, especially the foreign purchase of Japanese firms
6. A strong cultural preference for Japanese goods and a bias against foreign goods that makes Japan a difficult market requiring a substantial investment of time and resources
7. Substantial overt protection of Japanese agriculture that is tied to political support for the predominant party, the Liberal Democratic party[74]

---

[71] William R. Cline, "The Evolution of Protection in Textiles and Apparel," in King (ed.), *International Economics* . . ., 34–40.

[72] But it is true that in the recent past Japan has had much higher barriers and has also raised tariffs in an industry targeted by MITI for special development.

[73] This situation may be in for a change. See "Japan's Next Retail Revolution," *The Economist*, December 21, 1991, 79–80. The distribution system for automobiles is less subject to criticism. It involves an extraordinary system of individual selling in which each adult in Japan is personally contacted by a dealer to learn his or her car needs for the next year. This makes any effort to set up a distribution system for foreign cars very expensive.

[74] For the link between the Liberal Democratic party and farmers, see Gerald L. Curtis, *The Japanese Way of Politics*, New York: Columbia University Press, 1988, 49–61. A more general review of trade barriers is in Dorothy Christelow, "Japan's Intangible Barriers to Trade in Manufactures," in King (ed.), *International Economics* . . ., 41–56.

The large Japanese trade surplus, the special Japanese government–business system, and the large Japanese consumer market help draw attention to these trade barriers. Many in the U.S. Congress have called for trade retaliation unless Japan opens its markets and reduces the trade surplus by a specified amount. And these sentiments have been responsible for various VERs and managed trade agreements. This may make good politics, but it fails to deal with the fact that many of these same practices exist in the United States and most other nations.[75]

The Common Agricultural Policy (CAP) in the European Union also represents one of the most formidable systems of protection. As with many other things in the history of the EEC, EC, and EU, the Common Agricultural Policy was originally part of a compromise between France and Germany. French farmers were permitted to sell in Germany, while German farmers were protected from world prices. CAP established a free internal market for food within the EEC, a system of price supports through purchases of foodstuffs when prices fall below world levels, and a tariff and internal tax to pay for the program. Further, surplus food was often exported at subsidized prices. Because European farmers have consistently been inefficient relative to the rest of the industrialized world and because plans for modernization of agricultural production have been blocked, the gap between world prices and community support prices has widened over time. This meant that the budget for support payments also had to grow and by 1991 totaled $135 billion. The political basis for this system was the close relationship between farmers' organizations and the agricultural ministry in each state, which maintained effective control over CAP. Additionally, CAP is woven into the many political compromises and agreements that sustain the EU. This makes it a difficult arrangement to change.[76] Even so, the distortion of world trade caused by CAP is substantial because the EU should be a major importer and instead is a major exporter of food. Prices inside the EU are much higher and world prices lower because of the oversupply of food.[77]

## Why Do Nations Choose Protection?

Why should we expect protectionism to take place? The politics of the decision to place barriers on imports in any particular industry or as a general national policy is linked to a maze of interests, power relationships, and institutions. Political economists at this point can provide only a list of the main

---

[75] Keith Bradsher, "Mosbacher Joins Critics of Japan," *New York Times*, December 20, 1991.

[76] To date, only modest reforms designed to establish limits on the overall level of support payments have been adopted. There is great resistance to more dramatic reform, including slashing these payments and opening EC markets. We should note that the United States also subsidizes some exports of food, ostensibly only to offset the advantages gained by the EC.

[77] For more detail on CAP, see Pinder, *European . . .*, 77-93, and Colchester and Buchan, *Europower*, 106-117.

forces at work and cannot specify the circumstances under which protection-ism will succeed or fail.[78]

1. Because the benefits of protection are concentrated in a small number of owners and workers in the affected industry while the costs of pro-tection are spread across many consumers, political organization for protection is easier than for free trade.[79]

2. A nation's position in the world economy affects its foreign economic policy. That is, its relative proportion of world trade and the competi-tiveness of its products generate incentives and opportunities that largely define whether it pursues free trade or protection or some combination. Very large and competitive states—hegemons—will pre-fer a multilateral free trade system. Middle-ranking states will mix de-sire for free trade in the system with desire for some level of domestic protection, but they also realize that too much free riding on their part can lead to a collapse of the system. Small and/or uncompetitive states are likely to prefer protectionism at home and to hope for free trade in the system.[80]

3. The fate of the world economy—depression or prosperity—intersects with the structure of a nation's domestic interests—the relative power of protectionist versus free trade groups—to affect national decisions on foreign economic policy. It is much more difficult to sustain free trade in a depressed world economy.[81]

4. As a variation of number 3, the growth of global interdependence and extensive participation of a nation in the world economy lead to more and more firms with interests in promoting free trade. As these firms depend on global markets, they actively oppose efforts to increase protection for other industries because of fear of retaliation.[82]

---

[78] For an overview of some of the approaches discussed next and two case studies, see Richard Friman, "Rocks, Hard Places, and the New Protectionism: Textile Trade Policy Choices in the United States and Japan," *International Organization*, 42.4, Autumn 1988, 689-723. Another overview is Benjamin J. Cohen, "The Political Economy of International Trade," *International Or-ganization*, 44.2, Spring 1990, 261-281.

[79] Real P. Lavergne, *The Political Economy of U.S. Tariffs*, New York: Academic Press, 1983.

[80] The best statement of this approach is found in David Lake, *Power, Protection, and Free Trade*, Ithaca: Cornell University Press, 1988, 1-65. We have omitted two of Lake's categories: the large and uncompetitive state that probably pursues imperialism and protectionism and the small but competitive state that pursues free trade.

[81] Peter Gourevitch, *Politics in Hard Times: Comparative Responses to International Economic Crises*, Ithaca: Cornell University Press, 1986; and Ronald Rogowski, *Commerce and Coalitions: How Trade Affects Political Alignments*, Princeton: Princeton University Press, 1989.

[82] Helen Milner, *Resisting Protectionism*, Princeton: Princeton University Press, 1988; Helen Mil-ner, "Resisting the Protectionist Temptation: Industry and the Making of Trade Policy in France and the United States," *International Organization*, 41.4, Autumn 1987, 639-665; Helen Milner, "Trad-ing Places: Industries for Free Trade," *World Politics*, 50.3, April 1988, 350-376; I. M. Destler and John Odell, *Anti-Protection: Changing Political Forces in United States Trade Politics*, Washing-ton, D.C.: Institute for International Economics, 1987.

5. Choices about free trade and protection are constrained by ideas and institutions framed during particular historical periods. After ideas come to permeate elite thinking and institutions are established, the institutions create rules for the evaluation of policy.[83]

6. Likewise, when a particular set of ideas and institutions achieves predominance at the international level, it also structures choices in bilateral and multilateral negotiations. The extension of free trade ideas and institutions after 1945 conditions the nature and extent of protectionist policies.

7. Finally, protectionist or free trade proposals or policies may be used as part of a bargaining strategy designed to alter the preferences of other states. The efforts by U.S. presidents to negotiate trade outcomes with Japan violate the principles of free trade. But these agreements are partly designed to alter the Japanese trading system and to appease protectionist forces in the United States.

The new protectionism just described is often an effort to strike a political balance between a general commitment to freer trade and the genuine economic damage that such a policy can have on inefficient domestic producers and their workers.[84] The leadership of advanced industrial nations understands that withdrawal from the world economy would have disastrous economic and political consequences. The incentives to keep an open system functioning are simply too great to permit its demise.[85] At the same time, this viewpoint is politically viable only as long as the system produces a rising standard of living, and this requires that nations continually adjust to its inherent dynamism. Prolonged recession would surely unravel the political supports that make such a system possible. The recent growth of protectionism, the difficulties in GATT, and the rise of economic blocs do not clearly portend the end of an open system. But in a stagnant or shrinking world economy, these developments certainly could serve as a basis for fragmentation and even disintegration.

[83] Judith Goldstein, "The Political Economy of Trade: Institutions of Protection," *American Political Science Review*, 80.1, March 1986, 161–184; Judith Goldstein, "The Impact of Ideas on Trade Policy: The Origins of U.S. Agricultural and Manufacturing Policies," *International Organization*, 43.1, Winter 1989, 31–71.

[84] Jagdish Bhagwati, *Protectionism*, Cambridge: MIT Press, 1988, 47–59. In this and a subsequent book, *The World Trading System at Risk*, Princeton: Princeton University Press, 1991, Bhagwati offers a spirited attack on the new protectionism. A response is in Paul Krugman, *The Age of Diminished Expectations*, Cambridge: MIT Press, 1990, 101–113.

[85] For the view that the structures and interests of interdependence are simply too powerful to permit any significant shift toward protectionism, see Susan Strange, "Protectionism and World Politics," *International Organization*, 30, Spring 1985, 233–259.

# THE URUGUAY ROUND AND THE WORLD TRADE ORGANIZATION

It is fitting that we close a chapter on competitiveness with a discussion of perhaps the most important institution of international cooperation—the General Agreement on Tariffs and Trade (GATT). This serves to remind us that competition can take place only in a framework of cooperation created largely by nations. Tariff reductions, new trade rules, and new trade institutions derive from and amplify cooperation; at the same time, these actions not only provide the context for competition among nations and firms, but also actually accelerate competition. The competitive process associated with nations and firms depends on the common rules and open system created by GATT and its successor, the World Trade Organization.

In important ways the future of the free-trade order erected after World War II has focused on the success of the latest negotiating session of GATT, the Uruguay Round. Throughout the postwar era, the United States has served as the chief instigator and supporter of GATT, and the substantial decline in tariff levels can be attributed to its leadership. But the Uruguay Round was beset by problems from the outset in 1982. Its purpose was to move GATT regulations into new areas and to deal with long-standing trade barriers and problems. These include tariffs and issues of trade in financial services, tourism and construction, trade involving copyrights and patents, and regulations restricting foreign direct investment. Although eventual success was delayed by the difficult issues being addressed, the Uruguay Round was concluded with a comprehensive agreement among 117 nations reached in December 1993 and signed in Marrakesh, Morocco, in April 1994.

The greatest stumbling block to an agreement came over agricultural trade—an area of U.S. strength and European and Japanese weakness. The United States has pressed Europe (with its CAP) for thirty years to lower subsidies and tariff barriers on food products; it has pushed Japan to end its total ban on rice imports and to replace that with tariffs. Because of the political power of farmers in these countries and the likelihood that freer trade would put many out of business, governments in Europe and Japan have resisted liberalization. The price of these actions is a high cost of agricultural products for consumers there and lost markets for U.S. producers. The United States was ready to open its markets (and thereby damage its producers) in textiles, sugar, and dairy products. But on several occasions the talks collapsed when the United States and Europe could not agree on the level of tariff reductions in agriculture.[86]

---

[86] Steven Greenhouse, "Industrial Nations Agree to Push for Trade Accord," *New York Times*, June 5, 1991; Peter Passell, "Adding Up the World Trade Talks: Fail Now, Pay Later," *New York Times*, December 16, 1990; Bruce Stokes, "*Apres* GATT, *le Deluge?*" *National Journal*, January 12, 1991.

The Uruguay Round also took up the Multi-Fibre Arrangement and its restrictions on textiles and apparel. Proposed changes included replacing the MFA and its many bilateral agreements with a global quota. Dismantling this protectionist system for developed states' textile and clothing industries will be a boon for many Third World states. In return, developed states looked to gain better protection in the Third World for intellectual property, especially patents and brand names. Another arena for expanding GATT is trade in services like shipping, banking, tourism, and investment. Proposals involved removing various restrictions such as requirements for local content in production facilities owned by foreigners and shipping that must take place only in containers owned by the host nation.[87]

From the beginning, the Uruguay Round faced the problem of confronting the most difficult and entrenched trade barriers. Furthermore, the threat of a U.S. pullout unless U.S. terms were met has also hung over negotiations. The deadline of December 1990 failed to produce an agreement, and the talks moved into overtime. The main obstacle was the difficulty over CAP. The United States and other agricultural exporters wanted a dismantling of the CAP subsidies, while the Europeans resisted making anything but minor changes. The talks continued throughout 1991 with oscillating moods of optimism and pessimism about their ultimate success. In December, after another breakdown, the director general of GATT moved to break the impasse by confronting the parties with a "take it or leave it" set of compromises. But even this was met with much hostility in both Europe and the United States. In April 1992, further efforts to reach agreement failed, leading to a delay of serious negotiations until after the 1992 U.S. elections. Settlement of a trade dispute between the EU and the United States over oil seeds in late 1992 helped pave the way to compromise proposals and a final agreement.[88]

The difficulties in achieving a GATT agreement can be seen better if we think of this process as a complex and multilayered bargaining game. This is a game with a set of domestic winners and losers in each nation. Further, this game is being played without a hegemon with the ability to make concessions, dispense rewards, and punish defectors across the system. The trick to a successful outcome is to gain international terms through agreement among

---

[87] H. B. Junz and Clemens Boonekamp, "What Is at Stake in the Uruguay Round?" *Finance and Development*, June 1991, 10–15; Sylvia Ostry, "The Uruguay Round: An Unfinished Symphony," *Finance and Development*, June 1991, 16–17; "World Trade," *The Economist*, September 22, 1990.

[88] Keith Bradsher, "Bush and Europe Fail to Bridge Gap on Trade Barriers," *New York Times*, April 23, 1992; Steve Greenhouse, "A Move to Break the World Trade Deadlock," *New York Times*, December 21, 1991; Keith Bradsher, "Trade Plan Criticized, Stalling World Talks," *New York Times*, December 24, 1991. The talks can be followed in: "Rocking a Lifeboat Can Be Dangerous," *The Economist*, December 8, 1990, 69–70; "GATT Reprieved?" *The Economist*, October 19, 1991, 15. "GATT: The Eleventh Hour," *The Economist*, December 4, 1993, 23–26. The best overall discussion of the Uruguay Round is Valerie Brown and Louis Wells, *The Uruguay Round of the GATT: Choices in U.S. Policy*, Cambridge: Harvard Business School Case, 1994.

many nations (adjustment and compromise) that will provide domestic winners with strong enough incentives to back the agreement and overcome the resistance of losers. This becomes a series of simultaneous bargaining games—at the international and domestic levels—in which national political leaders try to manage toward a favorable conclusion. They are subject to pressure at home from a shifting balance of winners and losers based on the terms of the international agreement. And these leaders are also subject to pressure from abroad owing to the need to make concessions and adjustments in order to reach an agreement. Among the most powerful and advanced states, the national executive and other political leaders have a varying commitment to the postwar institutions of free trade and international cooperation. We should not be surprised when such negotiations frequently seem to reach an impasse, especially when a hegemon is absent. But also constraining choices is the importance of preserving the global economic order itself and fear of the consequences of a decline in cooperation.[89]

The Uruguay Round agreement signed in 1994 made important advances in many areas. Average tariff levels will be cut by one third, from just over 5 percent to 3 1/2 percent The problems of nontariff barriers and trade conflicts have been addressed by clarifying the standards for dumping, quotas, VERs, and subsidies. In agriculture, tariff levels will be slashed, subsidies cut, and the use of quotas restricted. And the Japanese and Korean rice markets will be partially opened to imports. The quota system of the MFA will be phased out over ten years, leaving tariffs in this area similar to those for other goods. Standards were also established for intellectual property. A General Agreement on Trade in Services was reached. It contains a statement of broad principles, but the lack of clarity and the exemption of areas such as shipping limit its impact.[90]

The most important part of the new agreement is the establishment of the World Trade Organization. GATT was never more than a limited institution to coordinate the negotiation of agreements; it never had the ability to adjudicate disputes or to enforce the rules. The WTO is a much more formal and robust international organization, similar to the World Bank and International Monetary Fund. High-level national representatives will meet at the WTO twice each year. Most significant is the new role in settling trade disputes among nations. Fact-finding bodies will issue reports to the WTO council that will serve as the basis for decisions. These outcomes may be taken to an appellate body, whose decisions are binding. Failure to comply with WTO rulings will result in fines and/or punitive actions by the aggrieved nation(s). The creation of WTO shifts the process of managing trade relations from bilateral

[89] The best statement of the intersection of international and domestic politics is Robert Putnam, "Diplomacy and Domestic Politics: The Logic of Two-level Games," *International Organization*, 42.3, Summer 1988, 427–460. Extension of these ideas with case studies is in Evans et al. (eds.), *Double-Edged Diplomacy* . . . .

[90] Detail on the agreement can be found in Brown and Wells, *The Uruguay Round* . . .; and *New York Times*, December 15, 1993, C18, and December 16, 1993, C6.

conflicts to a strong international organization, using rules established by multilateral agreement. One analyst has called the WTO "an International Court of
Justice for world trade, with the institutional strength and legal mandate to ensure fair trade and global economic integration."[91]

Completion of the Uruguay Round demonstrates the continued viability
of multilateral support for free trade. This marks a significant step away from
protectionism and reduces the momentum toward regional trade as a basis for
trade restriction. Protectionism is blocked by the tremendous web of global
trade and financial interdependence and the domestic political interests and
transnational coalitions tied to this connectedness. The balance of power still
remains with this political bloc and, except in the case of a prolonged global
downturn, protectionism will not win the day.

## CONCLUSIONS

Even in the context of an open world economy, competition among nations
and among firms takes place. The global system of relatively free trade generated in large part by GATT makes substantial and mutual gains from trade possible. Nonetheless, nations and firms compete for additional gains from trade:
Nations compete by supporting their own firms, national and multinational;
nations compete to attract firms and business from around the world; and
firms compete with each other for market share and profits. Finally, nations
see economic competition as intimately linked to political and military competition in the international system.

Economic competition and conflict rarely get out of bounds because nations and firms understand the mutuality of gains from the present world economy and the potential damage from its demise. This helps sustain the immense
effort that nations must also make to cooperate in creating a political context
for competition. And when different national practices or unpleasant outcomes
produce conflict, nations typically moderate their demands to resolve the differences. The international institutions for resolving trade conflict have been
weak and the rules sometimes unclear. But trade conflict, such as between the
United States and Japan, is unlikely to lead to real political hostility.

What is the future direction for competition? First, there is some limited
merit in the criticisms leveled at Japan, primarily in the areas of barriers to
trade and investment. The Japanese retain a legacy from 250 years of isolation.
Their leadership has never accepted the Western rationale for free trade, and
their trading practices still retain some elements of a warlike posture.
But Japan's success comes mostly from marshaling its national resources to
compete in global markets. It is as silly to condemn Japan for this achieve-
ment as it would be to condemn the United States and Germany for unfair

---

[91] Salil Pitroda, "From GATT to WTO: The Institutionalization of World Trade," *Harvard International Review*, 17.2, Spring 1995, 47.

competition in their successes in the late nineteenth century. Attacking Japan for subsidizing industries or selling below cost to win market share is little more than sour grapes directed toward a nation that succeeds in these strategies where others have failed. The greatest part of the rhetoric attacking Japan comes from those who cannot, or will not, adjust to the new competitive environment.

Although protectionism has been increasing in the wake of Japan's success and the new climate of global competition, more energy has been directed toward other strategies. These usually involve aid directed toward increasing the productive capabilities of specific, high-value industries; improving the national infrastructure of competition (such as in education and training); creating larger markets through free-trade agreements; and attracting firms by making markets freer of regulation or through regulations that help firms operate effectively.

Perhaps the greatest uncertainty in understanding competition is the impact of globalization. This makes identifying the nationality of firms more difficult, disperses the benefits of national investments throughout the world through technology transfer and strategic alliances, and places the locus of competitive power in the hands of geographically mobile multinational corporations. In the near and long term, globalization may have its greatest effect by incorporating the Third World into the competitive process on much more equal terms. The globalization of production, investment, finance, and communications transfers to the Third World much of the infrastructure of competition formerly located exclusively in rich nations. The emergence of Newly Industrialized Countries (NICs) and many other candidate NICs expands dramatically the scope of competition. It is to this arena of rapid change and development that we now turn our attention.

## ANNOTATED BIBLIOGRAPHY

Bela Balassa, *Japan in the World Economy*, Washington, D.C.: Institute for International Economics, 1988.

An overview with considerable data.

William J. Baumol, *Productivity and American Leadership: The Long View*, Cambridge: MIT Press, 1991.

Provides a detailed study of U.S. productivity.

Jagdish Bhagwati, *Protectionism*, Cambridge: MIT Press, 1988.

Jagdish Bhagwati, *The World Trading System at Risk*, Princeton: Princeton University Press, 1991.

Both books offer a spirited and convincing case against the new protectionism.

Jean Claude Derian, *America's Struggle for Leadership in Technology*, Cambridge: MIT Press, 1990.

A very useful examination of competitiveness in technology looking at several industries.

I. M. Destler, *American Trade Politics*, Washington, D.C.: Institute for International Economics, 1986.
> A detailed study of the political economy of trade during the early to mid-1980s.

I. M. Destler and John Odell, *Anti-Protection: Changing Political Forces in the United States*, Washington, D.C.: Institute for International Economics, 1987.
> A rich set of analytical case studies.

Dennis Encarnation, *Rivals Beyond Trade: America versus Japan in Global Competition*, Ithaca: Cornell University Press, 1992.
> Traces the imbalance in U.S.-Japanese trade to asymmetries in foreign direct investment between these two countries.

David Friedman, *The Misunderstood Miracle*, Ithaca: Cornell University Press, 1988.
> Counters the MITI thesis and focuses on the impact of small- and medium-sized manufacturing in Japan.

Otis Graham, Jr., *Losing Time: The Industrial Policy Debate*, Cambridge: Harvard University Press, 1992.
> A detailed look at the political debate regarding an active governmental policy in supporting specific industries.

Jeffrey Hart, *Rival Capitalists*, Ithaca: Cornell University Press, 1992.
> Examines competitiveness in terms of differing forms of relationships between states and society.

Takashi Inoguchi and Daniel Okimoto (eds.), *The Political Economy of Japan, Volume 2, The Changing International Context*, Stanford: Stanford University Press, 1988.
> A very insightful collection of essays.

Chalmers Johnson, *MITI and the Japanese Miracle*, Stanford: Stanford University Press, 1982.
> An essential book on the evolution of Japan's business–government system.

Paul Krugman, *Rethinking International Trade*, Cambridge: MIT Press, 1990.
> A very important critique of free trade.

Helen Milner, *Resisting Protectionism*, Princeton: Princeton University Press, 1988.
> An essential source for understanding the political economy of support for free trade.

Theodore Moran, *American Economic Policy and National Security*, New York: CFR Press, 1993.
> Links economic competitiveness to military strength.

Joseph Morone, *Winning in High-Tech Markets*, Boston: Harvard Business School Press, 1993.
> Provides an analysis of competition in high technology from the firm perspective.

Michael Porter, *The Competitive Advantage of Nations*, New York: Free Press, 1990.
> An essential study of the competitiveness of firms as they operate in a national context.

Daniel Okimoto, *Between MITI and Market*, Stanford: Stanford University Press, 1989.
> Brings the analysis of changes in MITI into the 1980s.

David Rapkin and William Avery (eds.), *National Competitiveness in a Global Economy*, Boulder: Lynne Rienner, 1995.
> An excellent collection of essays.

Wayne Sandholtz et al. (eds.), *The Highest Stakes*, New York: Oxford University Press, 1992.
> Offers an analysis of mercantilist tendencies in competitiveness thinking.

F. M. Scherer, *International High-Technology Competition*, Cambridge: Harvard University Press, 1992.

An economist examines high-technology competition, using several case studies.

Gilbert Winham, *International Trade and the Tokyo Round Negotiations*, Princeton: Princeton University Press, 1986.

A very detailed study of the negotiations.

Karel van Wolferen, *The Enigma of Japanese Power*, New York: Vintage Books, 1990.

Presents a very critical view of Japanese government and politics.

John Zysman and Laura Tyson (eds.), *American Industry in International Competition*, Ithaca: Cornell University Press, 1983.

A dated but very helpful study of the political economy of firm competitiveness.

# *Chapter 8*

# RICH AND POOR STATES IN THE WORLD ECONOMY

During the first forty years of the post–World War II era, world politics largely revolved around the ideological chasm between the East and the West. With the waning of the Cold War, however, coming decades seem likely to bring growing attention to the development gap between the North and the South.[1] In the words of former Secretary-General of the United Nations Javier Perez de Cuellar: "We cannot forget that while the iron curtain has been brought down, the poverty curtain still separates two parts of the world community."[2]

The present level of international social and economic inequality is historically unprecedented. Before this century living standards had never diverged so widely across different countries and regions of the world. The moral and political issues raised by this inequitable distribution of resources take on added urgency when one considers the persistence of absolute poverty and hunger, runaway population growth, and the prospects of ecological disaster in many of today's poorer countries. Most disturbingly, despite

---

[1] Scholars, journalists, and politicians have invented many labels to distinguish the richer and poorer countries of the world from one another. Some use the terms *North* and *South* because most of the wealthier countries of the world are located in the northern latitudes, whereas the poorer countries tend to be south of the equator. The term *Third World* originated in an effort to distinguish the world's poor countries from the industrialized capitalist countries, called the First World, and from the industrialized communist countries, called the Second World. Southern countries are sometimes referred to as *developing, less developed,* or *underdeveloped* to contrast them from the advanced industrialized or developed countries. In general, these labels attempt to distinguish between relatively high-income countries that have undergone extensive industrialization and lower-income countries that remain at the earlier stages of industrialization. The latter countries often also share the experience of colonization. None of these labels is terribly precise. Some countries are difficult to classify. This is not surprising because development is a continuum, not an either-or proposition. Moreover, the use of these terms to place large numbers of states into broad categories often misleadingly implies a unity and a commonality among them that do not exist in reality. The label of "Third World" is particularly anachronistic given the end of the Cold War. Nevertheless, in deference to common usage, we shall employ these terms interchangeably throughout the text.

[2] Quoted in Julius O. Ihonvbere, "The Third World and the New World Order in the 1990s," in Robert J. Griffths (ed.), *Developing World 95/96* (6th ed.), Guilford, Conn.: Dushkin, 1995, 6.

improvement in Southern living standards and the rapid economic growth of a handful of developing countries, the divide between rich and poor appears stubbornly resistant to amelioration. Indeed, the divide between the richest 20 percent of the world's population and the poorest 20 percent has doubled in size over the past thirty years.[3]

This development gap poses moral, political, and economic challenges for the relatively wealthy countries of the North. Although the rhetorical fireworks of the seventies have since dimmed, Third World countries continue to press the North to agree to reforms in the international economic order that might help spur Southern development. Issues of great concern to the North, such as Third World debt, illegal immigration, the destruction of the world's rain forests, and the illegal drug trade, can be traced indirectly to continuing Third World poverty. Failure to reach agreement between North and South on such problems could lead to serious consequences for countries on both sides of the divide. Inequality and economic deprivation can also contribute to the outbreak of violence and war, both within and among countries. Conflicts between North and South, as well as among Southern countries themselves, over the control of important resources, such as oil and strategic minerals, are likely to persist. Northerners also possess a direct economic stake in the success of Southern development efforts. Over one third of U.S. exports, for instance, are destined for Southern countries.[4]

To cope more readily with the serious repercussions that the development gap holds for both rich and poor countries, we need to understand the political economy of North–South relations. This chapter and the five that follow will provide the background necessary to understand the nature of these relations by focusing on two related issues. The first of these concerns North–South bargaining over the distribution of gains from the economic ties between them. The development gap has rendered North–South economic relations more conflictual than the links among Northern countries. There is less agreement between North and South over the basic rules and norms that should structure the world economic system. As a result, relations have rested less upon shared values than upon the exercise of political and economic power. We will examine the ways in which North–South bargaining has been influenced by asymmetries in power and the efforts of Third World states to offset the enormous power advantages of the North.

The second major focus is on the struggle of Third World governments to devise workable strategies of development in the international system. In particular, countries have varied in the degree to which they are willing to open their economies to trade and investment with the North. We argue that such choices are heavily influenced by the particular political and economic

---

[3] Barbara Crossette, "U.N. Parley Ponders Ways to Stretch Scarce Aid Funds," *New York Times*, March 7, 1995.

[4] Steven Greenhouse, "Surging Growth in Third World Gives an Economic Lift to U.S.," *New York Times*, August, 19, 1993.

circumstances, both domestically and internationally, faced by given Third World states.

The debate over appropriate strategies of development is, however, partly driven by disagreements over the origins and continuing sources of the development gap between North and South. Why did the North develop first? Can the South succeed by following the pattern established by the North? Or do the differing international conditions faced by Third World countries today dictate an altogether different path (or paths) to development? Do extensive economic ties with the North help or hinder Third World development efforts? These are some of the questions this chapter seeks to explore by examining alternative theoretical perspectives on the development gap.

To better set the stage for this discussion, however, it may be instructive to investigate the dimensions of the economic inequalities between North and South. We begin, therefore, by examining different methods for measuring development and by reviewing various statistical data relating to the development gap.

## INDICATORS OF DEVELOPMENT

Economists have long sought a single, simple measure of economic development and human welfare. This sort of yardstick should, ideally, provide some sense of how far a society has progressed over time and how different nations compare with one another in economic performance. This is, however, an inherently difficult task. The concepts of "development" and "human welfare" are multidimensional and subject to varying interpretations. Overall averages calculated for societies as a whole tell us nothing about the status of particular groups or individuals and may hide gross inequities in the distribution of resources. Economic figures cannot capture the psychological, spiritual, cultural, or other nonmaterial aspects of human welfare. Even after a given measure has been selected, its meaningfulness can be called into doubt by the difficulty of collecting accurate and reliable data, particularly for Third World countries where mechanisms for gathering economic information are less developed than in the North.

Because, however, governments, international agencies, and businesses require clear and comparable measures of development for planning and decision-making purposes, the issue cannot be easily sidestepped despite the difficulties involved. The most commonly cited statistical measure of economic development is per-capita income. This figure is calculated by adding up the value of all of the market transactions conducted within a given society over the course of a particular year and dividing by total population. Because inflation can appear to boost income without any real change in the standard of living, its effects are typically canceled out by recalculating income figures in terms of a given base year. To make comparisons over time in "real," inflation-adjusted income, measurements from years prior to the chosen base year are raised by the amount of intervening inflation, and figures for later years are lowered.

To allow for international comparisons, income figures for any given country are stated in terms of U.S. dollars. One way to accomplish this is to use exchange rates in the conversion. If, for instance, Mexico's yearly per-capita income is calculated at thirty thousand pesos and the exchange rate is six pesos per dollar, then Mexico's annual per-capita income expressed in dollar terms would be $5,000 (these figures are hypothetical).

Using exchange rates to accomplish the conversion of income figures from local currencies into dollars does, however, introduce important distortions. Exchange rates may vary significantly, even over brief periods of time. These gyrations produce artificial and misleading shifts in comparative calculations of national income when exchange rates serve as the basis for conversion. When the value of the dollar falls vis-à-vis the Japanese yen, for instance, the same yen will be able to purchase more dollars than before. Although Japan's per-capita income level may not change at all—when calculated in yen—it will appear to rise when translated into dollars at the new exchange rate.

Also, local price levels vary significantly from country to country. Exchange rate–based income comparisons tell us, in effect, how well the average person from another country could live if all of his or her income were converted to dollars and spent in the United States on American goods and services. In reality, a haircut that costs $15 or $20 in the United States may cost only a fraction of that amount in most Third World countries due to lower labor costs. In other words, a given income level, stated in dollars, will go much further in a Third World country, where the overall price level is much lower, than it would in the United States. This distortion tends to understate the living standards of most Third World countries when comparisons with the North are accomplished via exchange rate conversions.

Economists have developed a new measure of per-capita income that attempts to correct for these problems. This new method of calculating income levels is called *purchasing power parity* (PPP). Income figures are adjusted to account for differences in local price levels. When PPP conversion is used to compare income, the gap between North and South, while still large, noticeably narrows. In particular cases, the different estimates produced by these two methods for calculating average national income can be striking. Using exchange rate conversion, for instance, the World Bank estimated China's per-capita GDP at $370 in 1990. But China's per-capita income jumps to over $2,000, by the World Bank's estimate, when income conversion is accomplished by the PPP method. This astounding difference stems from vastly lower price levels in China as compared with the United States. When PPP figures are substituted for exchange rate figures, the World Bank's estimate of the Third World's share of total global output for 1990 jumped from 18 percent to 34 percent.[5]

---

[5] Steven Greenhouse, "New Tally of World's Economies Catapults China into Third Place," *New York Times*, May 20, 1993.

Whichever conversion method is used, however, per-capita income has a number of disadvantages as a measure of development or welfare. It reflects only current income, not the amount of wealth accumulated over previous years. It provides us with no clue as to how equitably or inequitably income is distributed across the population. It does not reflect the value of goods and services that are not exchanged for money in the legal economy. Thus, for instance, household work, barter, illegal exchange, and subsistence production (for one's own use) are not measured by income figures.[6] Because all market transactions are treated the same, purchases of staple foods and housing are given the same weight as the money spent on cigarettes, junk food, or tanks, even though most people would agree that these various items make very different contributions to human welfare. The environmental costs of economic activity are ignored, no matter how real. The sale of timber obtained by clear-cutting a forest shows up as an addition to total income even if one result is to impose costs on nearby communities in the form of flooding during rainy seasons.[7]

The Human Development Index (HDI) was devised by researchers at the United Nations Development Program as a means for capturing some of the social dimensions of a nation's socioeconomic development that are neglected by income measures alone.[8] The HDI includes three components of human development: longevity (measured by life expectancy), knowledge (measured by a combination of adult literacy and mean years of schooling), and standard of living (measured by per-capita GDP, adjusted for the local cost of living by means of PPP conversion).

For each component, a nation's rating is determined along a scale ranging from 0 to 1. Zero represents the lowest possible measure for that component, and one represents the highest. So, for instance, a country with an adult literacy rate of 75 percent would score .75 on that component of the HDI. The scores from all three components are then averaged to produce an overall measure of human development that can be compared across countries. Table 8.1 shows HDI scores for a range of countries, as well as aggregate scores for all developing countries, the least-developed countries, and industrialized countries. Notice that industrialized countries score three times as high as the overall average for the least-developed countries.

The HDI is a useful way to compare the overall quality of life across different countries. Life expectancy, for instance, reflects on a country's overall nutrition level, the quality of its health care, and the type of sanitary conditions under which people live. Adult literacy and mean years of schooling capture

---

[6] As a result, income figures for some Third World countries may be misleadingly low because some parts of the South still rely more on barter or subsistence production than do Northern countries.

[7] For an interesting discussion of the deficiencies of GDP measures and alternative ways to measure economic welfare, see Clifford Cobb, Ted Halstead, and Jonathan Rowe, "If the GDP Is Up, Why is America Down?" *Atlantic Monthly*, October 1995.

[8] For a description of how the HDI is compiled, see United Nations Development Program, *Human Development Index, 1994*, New York: Oxford University Press, 1994, 90–93.

TABLE 8.1

**Three Measures of Development: Selected Countries**

|  | HUMAN DEVELOPMENT INDEX 1992 | REAL GDP PER-CAPITA (PPP$) 1991 | GNP PER-CAPITA (US$) 1991 |
|---|---|---|---|
| United States | 0.925 | 22,130 | 22,340 |
| Hong Kong | 0.875 | 18,520 | 13,580 |
| Korea, Republic of | 0.859 | 8,320 | 6,350 |
| Costa Rica | 0.848 | 5,100 | 1,870 |
| Mexico | 0.804 | 7,170 | 3,080 |
| Brazil | 0.756 | 5,240 | 2,920 |
| Saudi Arabia | 0.742 | 10,850 | 7,900 |
| Botswana | 0.670 | 4,690 | 2,580 |
| Cuba | 0.666 | NA | NA |
| China | 0.644 | 2,946 | 370 |
| Philippines | 0.621 | 2,440 | 740 |
| Indonesia | 0.586 | 2,730 | 610 |
| Nicaragua | 0.583 | 2,550 | 400 |
| Egypt | 0.551 | 3,600 | 610 |
| Vietnam | 0.514 | NA | NA |
| Zimbabwe | 0.474 | 2,160 | 670 |
| Kenya | 0.434 | 1,350 | 340 |
| Pakistan | 0.393 | 1,970 | 400 |
| Ghana | 0.382 | 930 | 420 |
| India | 0.382 | 1,150 | 330 |
| Zambia | 0.352 | 1,010 | 420 |
| Zaire | 0.341 | 469 | NA |
| Tanzania | 0.306 | 570 | 120 |
| Ethiopia | 0.249 | 370 | 120 |
| Guinea | 0.191 | 500 | 500 |
| All Developing Countries | 0.541 | 2,730 | 880 |
| Least-Developed Countries | 0.307 | 880 | 240 |
| Industrial Countries | 0.918 | 14,860 | 14,920 |

*Source:* United Nations Development Program, *Human Development Index, 1994,* New York: Oxford University Press, 1994, 95, 129–133.

both the quality and the breadth of a nation's educational system. The HDI can reveal cases where relatively high income levels fail to translate into a commensurate quality of life, or, conversely, where the population of a country with a relatively low per-capita income nevertheless enjoys relatively good health and education. Costa Rica, for instance, outscores both Mexico and Saudi Arabia on the HDI, even though Mexico's average income (using PPP figures) is 40 percent higher and Saudi Arabia's is double that of Costa Rica.

Another way to measure development is to focus on wealth rather than on income. Traditionally, wealth has been measured by estimating the market value of a nation's physical capital, including such things as factories, machinery, and buildings. This figure provides some sense of the size of the productive base upon which future economic returns depend. Yet a nation's future economic potential rests upon more than these so-called "produced assets." Both natural resources and the level of human skills possessed by members of a society are as important, and often moreso, than the available stock of machines and factories.

For this reason, researchers at the World Bank are in the process of compiling a broader measure of national wealth that includes natural and human resources alongside manufactured capital.[9] For each nation, the World Bank attaches estimated monetary values to a set of natural resources, such as land, minerals, and water. Much the same is done for human or social resources, including education and skills. Adding the value of physical, natural, and human resources together and dividing by population, World Bank researchers hope to arrive at overall estimates of per-capita wealth for each nation.

This research, still in progress, has yet to produce definitive results. The methodology for attaching monetary values to human and natural resources is complex and contentious. The World Bank has, however, released preliminary estimates that show the relative proportions of wealth accounted for by human resources, produced assets, and natural capital (see Table 8.2).

This method for calculating wealth shows that, on a global basis, the value of the world's natural resources exceeds the total value of all manufactured wealth and that both of these together are far outweighed by the combined economic value of the world's human and social resources. This suggests that, from the standpoint of maximizing long-term economic health, nations are better served by focusing on ways to preserve and exploit scarce natural resources on a sustainable basis and on investing in human resources, such as education, than by placing sole priority on enhancing the nation's stock of factories, machines, and other hardware.

Notice also, however, that the relative weight of these different sources of wealth varies considerably from one set of countries to another. In India, China, and the countries of East and Southeast Asia, an overwhelming majority of wealth is accounted for by human resources while these countries are relatively poorer in natural capital. Africa's wealth, by contrast, is heavily dependent upon natural capital while its human resources contribute far less to the overall total. Latin America falls in between these extremes. These differences in the composition of wealth have important implications for each country's development strategy and help to determine where a nation's comparative advantage lies in world trade.

---

[9] Peter Passell, "The Wealth of Nations: A 'Greener' Approach Turns List Upside Down," *New York Times*, September 19, 1995. For a more extended discussion on the topic of "green" accounting, see James Robertson and Andre Carothers, "The New Economics: Accounting for a Healthy Planet," *Greenpeace*, January/February 1989.

**TABLE 8.2**
**Sources of Wealth by Region**
*(percentage of total)*

|  | HUMAN RESOURCES | PRODUCED ASSETS | NATURAL CAPITAL |
|---|---|---|---|
| World | 64 | 16 | 20 |
| High-income countries | 67 | 16 | 17 |
| Developing countries |  |  |  |
| Sub-Saharan Africa | 31 | 17 | 52 |
| Eastern and Southern Africa | 33 | 14 | 52 |
| Western Africa | 25 | 25 | 50 |
| India and China | 73 | 18 | 9 |
| Other Asia | 75 | 13 | 12 |
| East Asia and Pacific | 75 | 13 | 12 |
| South Asia | 76 | 16 | 9 |
| Latin America and the Caribbean | 50 | 15 | 35 |
| Middle East and North Africa | 39 | 29 | 32 |
| Eastern Europe | 41 | 16 | 43 |

*Source:* The World Bank. *Monitoring Environmental Progress: A Report on Work in Progress,* Washington, D.C.: The World Bank, 1995, Table 8.1, 63.

This new way of measuring wealth also underlines the need for sustainable development strategies. Countries that rapidly deplete their mineral resources, cut down forests or undermine the value of their land through short-sighted agricultural practices may increase their income in the short run or even translate revenues from these activities into physical capital. This will, however, only create the illusion of greater wealth. In the long term, such a pattern of development cannot be sustained and will erode the environmental basis for economic activity. Using traditional measures of wealth, these risks are undetectable. The World Bank's new measuring stick promises to aid in capturing such costs.

## MEASURING THE DEVELOPMENT GAP

Northerners often find it tempting to adopt a fatalistic attitude toward the enormous development gap between North and South, based on the assumption that such disparities have always existed and therefore always will. Yet Latin America, Africa, and Asia each has served as the home of civilizations that once rivaled or surpassed European society in science and technology, culture, and economic productivity. In fact, the present concentration of global wealth and income is of quite recent origin.

It has been estimated, for instance, that per-capita GDP in what we now refer to as the North exceeded that of the South by only 50 percent in the mid-nineteenth century. Table 8.3, based upon data calculated by Paul

**TABLE 8.3**
**Relative Shares of World Manufacturing Output: 1750–1900**

|               | 1750 | 1800 | 1830 | 1860 | 1880 | 1900 |
|---------------|------|------|------|------|------|------|
| Europe        | 23.2 | 28.1 | 34.2 | 53.2 | 61.3 | 62.0 |
| United States | 0.1  | 0.8  | 2.4  | 7.2  | 14.7 | 23.6 |
| Japan         | 3.8  | 3.5  | 2.8  | 2.6  | 2.4  | 2.4  |
| Third World   | 73.0 | 67.7 | 60.5 | 36.6 | 20.9 | 11.0 |

*Source:* Adapted from Paul Bairoch, "International Industrialization Levels from 1750 to 1980,"
*Journal of European Economic History,* 11, 1982, 296.

Bairoch, shows just how recently development in the North began to outrace
that in the South. In 1830 what is now the Third World accounted for over 60
percent of world manufacturing production as compared with 34 percent for
Europe as a whole. Matters changed rapidly over the next thirty years, however, as the industrial revolution allowed Europe's share to rise to over 53 percent, while the Third World's share declined to just under 37 percent.

The North continued to expand its lead through the remainder of the
nineteenth century and well into the twentieth century. In contemporary
times, the social and economic contrasts between North and South have become truly stark. In 1992 the average per-capita GNP in the 109 countries
that the World Bank classifies as low- and middle-income came to $1,040. The
corresponding figure for the twenty-three high-income countries—$22,100—
was more than twenty-one times larger.[10] In terms of income, the gap has
recently grown wider, both relatively and absolutely. Between 1980 and
1992 per-capita GNP grew at an average annual rate of 0.9 percent in less-
developed countries, while Northern countries averaged per-capita GDP
growth of 2.3 percent per year.[11] It is estimated that 70 percent of world income is produced and consumed by 15 percent of the world's population, the
vast majority residing in Northern countries.[12]

The gap shows up as well, although less starkly, in more-direct measures
of social and physical well-being. In 1992 the typical Northerner could expect
to live seventy-seven years—thirteen years longer than the average South-
erner.[13] The average Third World citizen must make do on a diet consisting of
20 percent fewer calories than the average Northerner consumes daily. In
1990 the World Bank estimated that 950 million of the world's 5.2 billion people suffered from chronic malnutrition.[14] The overwhelming majority of the
hungry are to be found in the South. In 1990 Northern countries averaged
one physician for every 420 persons. The corresponding figure for the South

[10] *World Development Report, 1994,* Table 1. Note that these figures differ from those that appear
in Table 8.1 due to differences in which countries are counted in various categories.

[11] *World Development Report, 1994,* Table 1.

[12] Ihonvbere, "The Third World and the New World Order in the 1990s," 8.

[13] *World Development Report, 1991,* Tables 1 and 28.

[14] Robin Broad, John Cavanaugh, and Walden Bello, "Development: The Market Is Not Enough," *Foreign Policy,* Winter 1990–91, 145.

was one doctor for every 4,810 people (in sub-Saharan Africa, the ratio is 1:19,690). Whereas seven infants out of every one thousand born in the North die within their first year of life, the corresponding figure for the South is sixty-five. Yet despite this high infant mortality rate, the South's population growth rate is almost three times that of the North. These rapidly growing populations place difficult strains on the environment, lead to overcrowding in large cities, and force economies and agricultural systems to race to provide adequate jobs and food. Whereas 99 percent of Northern citizens meet minimal standards of literacy, only an estimated 64 percent of Southerners can read and write at a basic level. In the North, secondary school enrollment amounts to 93 percent of total secondary school-age youths. The figure for the South is only 45 percent. Finally, whereas 78 percent of Northerners live in cities, the same is true for only 36 percent of Southerners.[15]

These aggregate figures hide the fact that the South's meager resources are not shared equally by the members of those societies. Glaring gaps between rich and poor exist within Third World societies. In fact, inequities in income, wealth, and landholding are typically much more pronounced in the South than in the North.[16] On average, for instance, 50 percent of all income in Southern societies goes to the richest 20 percent of the population.[17]

Nevertheless, if one looks at measures other than per-capita income, it is apparent that the gap between living standards in the North and those in the South has narrowed over recent decades. Table 8.4. shows that Southern performance across a range of social indicators has improved relative to the North since the sixties and early seventies. Indeed, over the past thirty years, infant mortality has been cut in half, fertility rates have declined by 40 percent, and life expectancy has risen by ten years across the Third World as a whole.[18]

The structure of Southern economies and their relationship to the global economy differ markedly from those of the North. Forty-seven percent of Southern merchandise exports consist of fuels, minerals, metals, and other primary commodities, with the rest comprised of manufactured goods. Though Asian countries tend to count a high percentage of manufactured goods among their exports, Africa still relies upon primary commodities for 76 percent of its exports, while such goods account for 62 percent of Latin American exports. Only 18 percent of Northern exports, by contrast, consist of primary commodities as opposed to manufactured goods.[19]

---

[15] All data from *World Development Report, 1994*, Tables 1, 26, 27, 28, and 31.

[16] See Montek S. Ahluwalia, "Income Inequality: Some Dimensions of the Problem," in Mitchell Seligman (ed.), *The Gap Between Rich and Poor: Contending Perspectives on the Political Economy of Development*, Boulder: Westview Press, 1984, 14–21.

[17] "Down the Rathole," *The Economist*, December 10, 1994, 69.

[18] Lawrence H. Summers and Vinod Thomas, "Recent Lessons of Development," in Jeffrey Frieden and David Lake (eds.), *International Political Economy: Perspectives on Global Power and Wealth* (3rd ed.), New York: St. Martin's, 1995, 423.

[19] All data from *World Development Report, 1994*, Table 15.

**TABLE 8.4**

**Narrowing the North–South Gap**
*Development Indicators*

| | REAL GDP PER CAPITA 1960 1990 | LIFE EXPECTANCY 1960 1992 | ADULT LITERACY 1970 1992 | DAILY CALORIE SUPPLY 1965 1988–90 | ACCESS TO SAFE DRINKING WATER 1975–80 1988–91 | UNDER-FIVE MORTALITY 1960 1992 |
|---|---|---|---|---|---|---|
| All LDCs as % of North | 18  17 | 67  84 | 41  71 | 72  81 | 36  70 | 80  92 |

*Source:* United Nations Development Program, *Human Development Report, 1994*, New York: Oxford University Press, 1994, 140-143.

Agriculture plays a larger role in Third World economies—where it accounts for 19 percent of total GDP on average—than it does in the North, where agriculture comprises only 3 percent of total production.[20] The terms of trade deteriorated for the South throughout the eighties. In other words, the average prices of Southern exports fell relative to the average prices of the goods the South imported. The same quantity of Southern exports, which could buy $100 worth of Northern goods in 1980, could buy only $89 worth of the same products in 1988.[21] The Third World debt crisis severely hampered the Third World's ability to import additional goods during the eighties. After rising at an annual rate of 5 percent between 1965 and 1980, Third World imports grew by only 1.4 percent per year from 1980 to 1989.[22] Overall, Third World economies are less diversified and more vulnerable to international shocks than those of the North.

## CONTENDING PERSPECTIVES ON DEVELOPMENT

Scholars disagree over both the sources of the development gap and the likelihood that it can be narrowed in the future. There is also extensive debate over whether the South benefits from its extensive economic ties with the North. These disagreements revolve around much more than how to interpret the data. Fundamentally, they stem from differing assumptions about the nature of the development process itself. Here we identify and compare two contrasting theories about the problems of Third World development and North–South political economy.

These two theories, labeled *modernization* and *dependency,* are primarily scholarly in nature. As such, they provide a necessary conceptual introduction

---

[20] *World Development Report, 1990*, Table 3.

[21] *World Development Report, 1990*, Table 14.

[22] All data from *World Development Report, 1991*, Table 14.

to some of the issues and debates that we will examine in a more substantive way in later chapters. Ultimately, this necessarily abstract discussion will provide us with the tools needed to sort through the complex and messy realities of North–South political economy.

Yet it is worth noting that these ideas have found their way from the sanctuaries of academia to the stormy citadels of the political world. In debates between representatives of the North and the South in the United Nations and elsewhere, arguments drawn from these two perspectives are often featured in the political rhetoric of the respective sides. Northern spokespersons often appeal, implicitly, to modernization theory, which emphasizes the benefits to the South of openness to trade and investment from the North. In the past, though less so today, Third World representatives have invoked dependency theory as a basis for demanding the reform of an exploitative world economic system. Therefore, aside from the merits of these two differing perspectives as explanations for the development gap, the modernization and dependency theories are worth examining for the insights they provide into the intellectual bases of political debates between North and South.

## Modernization Theory

Modernization theory views the obstacles to Third World development through the prism of the North's own development experience. The North grew rich, according to this theory, not by exploiting the South, but rather by discovering the secrets of sustained economic growth. The cultural values and social, political, and economic institutions that provided the keys to Northern development are embodied in the notion of modernity. The modernization of Europe involved the gradual shedding of traditional ways of organizing society. Although little of this process was planned, simultaneous trends in a number of different spheres of social life converged to create the basis for dynamic economic growth and industrialization.

What are the principal elements of modernity? The list of traits provided by different authors varies enormously.[23] But among the most commonly cited are secularization (or the declining centrality of religion in social and cultural life), urbanization, the rise of science and technology, increased social mobility,

---

[23] A partial list of works in the modernization tradition would include: Alex Inkeles and David H. Smith, *Becoming Modern: Individual Change in Six Development Countries*, Cambridge: Harvard University Press, 1974; David McClelland, *The Achieving Society*, Princeton: Van Nostrand Co., 1961; Henri Avjac, "Cultures and Growth," in Christopher Saunders (ed.), *The Political Economy of New and Old Industrial Countries*, London: Butterworth's, 1981; Kalman Silvert, "The Politics of Social and Economic Change in Latin America," in Howard Wiarda (ed.), *Politics and Social Change in Latin America: The Distinct Tradition*, Amherst: University of Massachusetts Press, 1974; Myron Weiner (ed.), *Modernization: The Dynamics of Growth*, New York: Basic Books, 1966; Cyril Black, *The Dynamics of Modernization*, New York: Harper & Row, 1966; Gabriel Almond and James S. Coleman, *The Politics of Developing Areas*, Princeton: Princeton University Press, 1960; and Daniel Lerner, *The Passing of Traditional Society*, New York: Free Press of Glencoe, 1958. For a critique of the modernization school, see Alajandro Portes, "On the Sociology of National Development: Theories and Issues," *American Journal of Sociology*, July 1976.

a system of social rewards based upon merit rather than upon inherited status, a tolerance for social innovation and intellectual diversity, the limitation of controls placed by political authorities on social and economic life (i.e., the emergence of a "private" sphere), the ascendance of rule by law, and the development of an extensive division of labor within society. All of these traits complement the development of modern market-based economies in which economic decision making is decentralized among large numbers of producers, consumers, and laborers and is relatively free of direct control by political or religious authorities.

Traditional societies are dominated by religious authority, revolve around rural life, lack the capacity to generate scientific and technological discoveries, suffer from rigid social structures allowing little mobility, distribute social rewards based upon inherited status rather than upon merit, discourage innovation and new ideas, place few controls on the arbitrary exercise of political authority, and feature little social differentiation. The economies of traditional societies often rest upon either subsistence agriculture—in which extended families produce only for their own needs—or feudal or semifeudal landholding arrangements, in which relatively small numbers of large landowners live off of the surplus produced by an indentured peasantry. Northern societies were once characterized by the traits associated with traditionalism, but they gradually made the transition to modernity over a period of centuries. According to modernization theorists, many Southern societies continue to be dominated by traditional values and institutions, though most have begun to embrace some elements of modernity.

The most critical element in the transition from a traditional society to a modern one, from the standpoint of economic development, is the emergence of a system of rewards for innovation. The society must not only come to expect and welcome change and to embrace the notion of progress, but also willingly tolerate the inequalities that result from allowing individuals to reap handsome private returns for innovations that have high social value. For this to be possible, the state must devise means of organizing and protecting private property. By *property*, we refer not just to material possessions, but also to the propriety that innovators must have over their own original ideas if others are not to profit from them instead. Although the state must protect property rights, it must at the same time allow economic decisions to be made in at least partial autonomy from political oversight and intervention. This is necessary because innovation is most likely to occur if decision making is decentralized through competitive market arrangements that encourage and reward new ideas while punishing inefficiency and stagnation. As this discussion suggests, the development of capitalist institutions lies at the heart of modernization, although the rise of capitalism in the North would not have been possible without the simultaneous transformations already mentioned in the noneconomic spheres of society.

Economists cite other factors, besides the rate of innovation, that may influence a country's potential for economic development. These factors include overall rates of savings and investment, the skill level of the work force, the relative abundance of natural resources, and the degree to which market prices are allowed to steer available resources to their most efficient uses.[24]

Modernization theorists suggest that before sustained and self-generating economic growth can become possible in the South, Third World societies must undergo the same transition from traditionalism to modernity previously undergone by the North. The path to development thus lies through emulation of the North. The principal obstacle to modernization arises from the persistence of traditional cultural values and institutions in the South that are incompatible with economic growth and industrialization.

Adherents to this school of thought disagree over just how likely it is that Third World societies will progress smoothly toward modernity. Perhaps the majority believe that the modernization of the Third World is an inevitable process. The agents of progress, in this view, are many. They include the modernizing political elites (often Northern educated) to be found in many Third World countries. Multinational corporations serve as transmitters of modern skills and values while also providing close-up examples of modern forms of economic organization. Exposure to international trade offers Southern societies with incentives to embrace reform and change if they are to compete effectively. The penetration of Third World societies by European or U.S. culture through books, films, advertising, consumer products, and the media also helps Southerners to assimilate modern values and beliefs.

North–South economic interdependence is to be valued, according to modernization theorists, not simply for the mutual gains that routinely flow from market transactions, but also for the beneficial impact that such ties have in helping to erode and undermine the traditional social values and structures that hold back development. Over time, both external and internal pressures will tend to shrink the traditional sector of the economy and society while the growth of the modern sector proceeds apace. Evidence of these trends at work, according to modernization theorists, can be found in growing urbanization, the development of a wage labor force, and broadened educational opportunities.

A minority of modernization theorists accept the distinction between traditionalism and modernity but question the assumption that Southern societies will necessarily modernize over time, leading eventually to a convergence between the social and economic structures of North and South. These authors instead see traditionalism as deeply embedded in the cultures and institutions of many Third World countries. Change may come slowly and not necessarily in the direction of a European-inspired ideal of modernity. Others

---

[24] For a brief but accessible discussion of neoclassical growth theory and some of its recent variants, see "How Does Your Economy Grow?" *The Economist*, September 30, 1995, 96. For scholarly works exemplifying so-called new or endogenous growth theory, see Paul Romer, "Increasing Returns and Long-Run Growth," *Journal of Political Economy*, October 1986; Paul Romer, "Endogenous Technological Change," *Journal of Political Economy*, October 1990; and Paul Romer, "The Origins of Endogenous Growth," *Journal of Economic Perspectives*, Winter 1994.

who question the inevitability of modernization and convergence between North and South go further to suggest that economic development may well be possible in societies that embrace some elements of modernity but not others. There may be, in other words, multiple paths of development.

Modernization theory has been criticized on a number of grounds. It has been pointed out, for instance, that the concept of traditionalism is quite nebulous. In practice, the *traditional* label has been applied to virtually any social practices and institutions that are not modern, or in other words, not characteristic of present-day European and North American societies. To bundle all of the many varied Third World cultures that do not meet the criteria for modernity under the label *traditional* perhaps serves to obscure more than to illuminate.

Some critics also charge that modernization theory springs from an ethnocentric viewpoint. Certainly it is not difficult to deduce that most modernization theorists consider modernity good and traditionalism bad. This obviously reflects a Eurocentric bias. Whatever the merits of Northern societies, they are certainly not above reproach, and Southerners who embrace modernity in a general way may well hope to avoid some of the less-appealing aspects of Northern societies even while seeking to match Northern living standards. Moreover, modernization theorists may be too dismissive of traditional societies, ignoring the possibility that they might contain redeeming traits worth preserving.

Some critics point out that modernization theory incorrectly assumes that the obstacles to Third World development lie solely in the persistence of the traditional sector of the society. This ignores the possibility that the modern sector itself may be subject to contradictions and distortions that slow growth. Moreover, the movement from traditionalism to modernity is likely to be anything but smooth. Modernization in Europe proceeded in fits and starts, and the process often generated enormous dislocations such as war, revolution, unemployment, mass immigration, and class conflict. There is little reason to expect modernization to be any less disruptive as it transforms Third World societies.

Modernization theorists are quite sanguine about the benefits of North–South economic exchange for Southern development. Whether it is true in general that links with the North spur modernization, most modernization theorists ignore the potential conflicts of interest between North and South. This is apparent in their tendency to downplay the North's potential economic power over the South. As we will discuss, the South's dependence upon the North offers the latter with political leverage that can be used to capture a disproportionate share of the benefits flowing from North–South economic exchange.

Despite these criticisms, modernization theory offers important insights into the development experience of the North. It would be surprising indeed, despite the changed context, if these insights did not hold useful lessons for those seeking to promote Southern development. Perhaps the most important of these is that capitalism, as a distinctive way of organizing economic relationships within a society, is a powerful mechanism for producing wealth. The development of capitalism, in turn, is dependent upon the evolution of supportive social, political, and cultural institutions in the noneconomic spheres of society. Whether these innovations can be successfully transplanted to a society from without or whether they must evolve indigenously is a crucial question in assessing the prospects for capitalist-led development in the Third World. This is, in fact, the central question raised by dependency theory, our second perspective on Third World development.

## Dependency Theory

Dependency theorists reject modernization theory's optimistic prediction that Third World states who imitate the cultural attitudes, institutions, and policies of the North can follow the same path toward development previously trod by present-day rich countries.[25] They point out that the international context facing developing societies today is vastly different from that which confronted the early industrializers. Capitalism developed largely indigenously in Europe, and the first wave of industrializers faced no competition from already developed rivals. Moreover, industrialization in Europe was helped along by the access that conquest provided Europeans to the raw materials and cheap labor of colonized lands.

Present-day developing countries face an entirely different set of international realities. Third World efforts to industrialize must cope with the formidable competition provided by the already well-established manufacturing capacities of the North. Moreover, the infrastructure needed to support scientific and technological innovation is overwhelmingly located in the North. In general, capitalism was introduced to Southern societies from the outside on terms largely set by, and favorable to, Northern governments, merchants, and investors. Southern economies remain heavily dependent upon external trade with the North, and Northern multinational corporations often dominate the most dynamic industries in many Third World countries.

---

[25] Among the major works in the dependency school are Theotonio Dos Santos, "The Structure of Dependence," in K. T. Fann and Donald Hodges (eds.), *Readings in U.S. Imperialism*, Boston: Porter Sargent Publisher, 1971; Fernando Henrique Cardoso and Enzo Falleto, *Dependency and Development in Latin America*, Berkeley: University of California Press, 1979; Fernando Henrique Cardoso, "The Consumption of Dependency Theory in the United States," *Latin American Research Review*, 12, no. 3, 1977; Susanne Bodenheimer, "Dependency and Imperialism," *Politics and Society*, May 1970; Samir Amin, *Accumulation on a World Scale*, New York: Monthly Review Press, 1974; Andre Gunder Frank, *Capitalism and Underdevelopment in Latin America*, New York: Monthly Review Press, 1967; Andre Gunder Frank, *Latin America: Underdevelopment or Revolution*, New York: Monthly Review Press, 1969; C. Furtado, *Development and Underdevelopment*, Berkeley: University of California Press, 1964; A. Emmanuel, *Unequal Exchange*, London: New Left Books, 1972; Paul Baran, *The Political Economy of Growth*, New York: Monthly Review Press, 1957; and Immanuel Wallerstein, *The Modern World-System: Capitalist Agriculture and the Origins of the European World-Economy in the Sixteenth Century*, New York: Academic Press, 1976.

Dependency theorists contend that these differences (and others) between early and late developers mean that the development experiences of the North hold little relevance for assessing the present-day prospects for Southern development. These distinctions are considered so important, in fact, that dependency theory locates the primary obstacles to Third World development in the international system rather than in the domestic political, cultural, and social characteristics of particular states. In other words, the international system, rather than the nation-state, is viewed as the appropriate unit of analysis.

Capitalism is the most important defining feature of the contemporary international system, according to dependency theorists. Capitalism is a distinct set of economic relations defined by the private ownership of property, wage labor, and market exchange. The capitalist world system, which some dependency theorists believe has existed since the sixteenth century,[26] involves two sets of exploitative relationships. Within firms, the owners of capital exploit workers by profiting from their labor. The second relationship of exploitation, and the more relevant one from our standpoint, exists between core and peripheral states in the world economy. Capitalism does not develop evenly. Instead, it tends to concentrate development in certain areas, called the *core,* which are characterized by advanced industrialization, rapid technological development, and high wage rates and living standards. Peripheral areas, which constitute the geographic bulk of the world economy, instead feature limited industrialization, little technological innovation, and relatively low wages and living standards.

The development of core countries is linked to the underdevelopment of the peripheral countries. The workings of the capitalist world system tend to perpetuate and reinforce economic inequalities among countries. As two prominent advocates of dependency put it: "Both underdevelopment and development are aspects of the same phenomenon, both are historically simultaneous, both are linked functionally and, therefore, interact and condition each other mutually."[27]

Third World countries were drawn into the capitalist world economy through colonialism as well as through the expansion of European trade and investment. European countries used their political domination to create and enforce a division of labor that reserved the most dynamic segments of the world economy for themselves. North–South trade was built around the movement of manufactured goods from North to South and the transfer of primary products, including minerals, raw materials, and agricultural goods, from South to North.

---

[26] For an interpretation concerning the origins of the capitalist world system, see Wallerstein, *The Modern World-System.*

[27] Quoted in J. Samuel Valenzuela and Arturo Valenzuela, "Modernization and Dependency: Alternative Perspectives in the Study of Latin American Underdevelopment," in Heraldo Munoz (ed.), *From Dependency to Development: Strategies to Overcome Underdevelopment and Inequality,* Boulder: Westview Press, 1981, 25. Translated from Osvaldo Sunkel and Pedro Paz, *El Subdesarrollo Latinoamericano y la Teoria del Desarrollo,* Mexico, 1970, 6.

Moreover, whereas Northern countries traded extensively with one another, Southern countries traded almost exclusively with the North. Colonialism left the economies of Southern countries geared more toward the needs of Northern markets than the domestic needs of their own societies. This set of economic relationships, dependency writers point out, outlived colonialism itself.

This position of Southern subordination to, and dependence upon, the North is captured in Theotonio dos Santos's widely cited definition of *dependency:* "Dependency is a situation in which a certain number of countries have their economy conditioned by the development and expansion of another . . . placing the dependent country in a backward position exploited by the dominant country."[28]

Dependency theorists offer a number of mechanisms by which dependency hampers Southern development. Some cite changes in relative export prices as the primary means by which Northern societies extract surplus wealth from the South. The prices of the primary goods exported by the South, it is argued, tend to decline over time relative to the prices of the manufactured goods that Southern societies must import from the North. A country that finds itself in this situation—where, over time, a given quantity of the country's exports can purchase less and less of the imports it desires—is said to be suffering from declining terms of trade.

Northern multinational corporations are also viewed as instruments of exploitation. Foreign firms bring inappropriate technology, use their mobility and transnational links to evade taxes and regulations, drive out local competitors, manipulate Southern governments, refuse to hire and train top management drawn from the host country, and repatriate their profits rather than invest them locally.

Dependency theory asserts that these forms of Northern exploitation, along with others such as foreign aid, commercial bank lending, and the influence of multilateral lending agencies, hinder Southern industrialization and development.

Dependency theorists differ over how severe and universal are the constraints that dependence places on Third World development. Some, especially among the early writers, argued that dependence allowed little latitude for development and was likely to continue to produce growing misery and poverty among most Southerners. The principal beneficiaries of dependence in the South would be a "*compradore*" class of elites who benefited from their privileged ties with the North, whether they be political or economic, and who acted as the local agents of imperialism.

Some dependency authors concede that dependency is not incompatible with economic growth and development, even including a degree of industrialization. Moreover, some countries are likely to progress further than others.

---

[28] Quoted in Valenzuela and Valenzuela, "Modernization and Dependency," 25–26. Also see Theotonio Dos Santos, "The Structure of Dependence," in K. T. Fann and Donald Hodges (eds.), *Readings in U.S. Imperialism*, Boston: Porter Sargent Publisher, 1971.

These authors nevertheless maintain that dependence constrains develop-ment in most Southern countries, rendering economic growth and industrial-ization slower and less substantial than might otherwise be the case. They also generally argue that the overall relative position of the periphery in compari-son with the core is unlikely to improve even where absolute gains are made.

A third set of authors argues that although dependency is sometimes com-patible with vigorous economic growth, it nevertheless produces a myriad of undesirable "distortions" that are peculiar to dependent Southern societies and economies. Among these distortions are growing income inequality, wasteful consumption, cultural degradation, and political repression. The main concern of these authors is not with whether "development" is occurring, but rather with the type of development produced under conditions of dependence.

Dependency theorists differ widely over the appropriate remedy for Third World dependence upon the North. Some favor inwardly directed develop-ment strategies that emphasize production for the domestic market. This would imply a curtailment of economic ties with the North through high pro-tectionist barriers designed to nurture domestic industry and the strict regula-tion of foreign investment.

Others advocate some form of collective bargaining strategy, whereby Southern states pool their political and economic resources to press for re-forms in the international economic order, much as trade unions attempt to ameliorate capitalist exploitation of workers. This can take the form of re-source cartels, such as OPEC, which are designed to reverse the declining terms of trade, or broad coalitions that demand Northern assent to various specific reforms such as the lowering of Northern protectionist barriers to Southern manufactured goods, commodity stabilization plans, or mandatory codes of conduct for multinational corporations. Those who advocate this strategy often stress the importance of improving economic ties, including the development of regional common markets, among Southern countries as a means of lessening dependence upon the North.

Finally, some dependency theorists argue that Third World states can es-cape dependence upon the capitalist world system only through socialist rev-olution and reconstruction. Such a strategy would involve the elimination of private capital and the development of nonexploitative links with other like-minded countries.

In short, although modernization theory asserts that Southern economic ties with the North are desirable because they transfer needed technology and skills, foster efficiency through competition, and break down cultural and institutional barriers to development, dependency theory views Northern economic and political penetration of the South as exploitative, producing a transfer of resources from the poor to the rich.

In order to evaluate dependency theory, we must distinguish between two lines of argument, each of which can be found, together or separately, in the writings of different authors. The first strain of dependency theory focuses pri-marily on economics. The concern here is with the way in which Third World states have been incorporated into the world capitalist system and the effects this process has had on their prospects for development. The second strain focuses on politics. In particular, this strain of dependency theory explores the asymmetries in power and interdependence that influence bargaining between North and South over the rules of the international economic system. Although both the economic and political dimensions of dependency theory derive from the same body of thought, each deserves separate treatment in any effort to assess the strengths and weaknesses of the dependency approach to Third World development and North–South relations.[29]

The economic dimension of dependency theory revolves around the suggestion that dependent capitalism, introduced to the South via Northern colonialism, trade, and investment, differs from the homegrown variety. The dependence of Third World economies on trade and investment with the North and their subordinate position in the international division of labor constrain the prospects for Southern development and lead to imbalances and distortions.

Critics of dependency theory have pointed to several difficulties with these claims.[30] One of these is that many of the features that are associated with dependency, such as penetration by multinational corporations and heavy reliance on external trade and technology, are also characteristic of many developed countries. Canada, for instance, is more dependent upon direct foreign investment than is India. Moreover, as any reader of Dickens can surmise, the extreme social and economic inequalities that are painful features of most developing countries today were not unknown to the European societies of 150 years ago. This suggests that some of the inequities and distortions that have been attributed to external dependence may instead be characteristic of the early stages of capitalist development more generally.

Dependency writers might respond that the nature of North–North trade differs substantially from North–South trade. Northern countries trade principally in manufactured goods with one another. Southern trade with the North, by contrast, rests to a much larger degree upon the exchange of raw materials for manufactured goods. If, as dependency theorists assert, the latter

---

[29] Our discussion of these two strains in dependency theory draws upon a similar distinction made in James Caparaso and Behrouz Zare, "An Interpretation and Evaluation of Dependency Theory," in Heraldo Munoz (ed.), *From Dependency to Development: Strategies to Overcome Underdevelopment and Inequality*, Boulder: Westview Press, 1981, 44–45.

[30] For critical reviews of dependency theory, some more sympathetic than others, see David Ray, "The Dependency Model of Latin American Underdevelopment: Three Basic Fallacies," *Journal of Interamerican Studies and World Affairs*, February 1973; Sanjaya Lall, "Is Dependence a Useful Concept in Analyzing Underdevelopment?" *World Development*, November 1975; Richard Fagen, "Studying Latin American Politics: Some Implications of a Dependencia Approach," *Latin American Research Review*, Summer 1977; Raymond Duvall, "Dependence and Dependencia Theory: Notes Toward Precision of Concept and Argument," *International Organization*, Winter 1978; Tony Smith, "The Underdevelopment of the Development Literature: The Case of Dependency Theory," *World Politics*, January 1979; and Bill Warren, "Imperialism and Capitalist Industrialization," *New Left Review*, September-October 1973. For an effort to subject dependency propositions to empirical testing, see Vincent Mahler, *Dependency Approaches to International Political Economy: A Cross-National Study*, New York: Columbia University Press, 1980.

form of trade is subject to deteriorating terms of trade for the kinds of goods that Third World countries typically export, then this division of labor works to the disadvantage of the South.

Yet, while recent years have indeed witnessed a deterioration in the South's terms of trade with the North, studies that have examined longer time periods have reached different conclusions. The prices of primary goods, such as raw materials and agricultural goods, do tend to fluctuate more widely than do the prices of manufactured goods—a pattern that leads to cycles of feast or famine for countries that depend upon only a few primary products for the bulk of their exports. The empirical evidence, however, shows no long-term tendency for the prices of primary goods to fall relative to manufactured goods over the course of the twentieth century. Even if trends in the terms of trade did favor manufactured goods, however, the implications of this would be complicated by the fact that some core countries, such as the United States, Canada, or Australia, depend upon primary goods for a substantial portion of their exports, while some developing countries, especially in East Asia, have become substantial exporters of manufactured goods.

As we will discuss in a later chapter, multinational corporations often hold superior bargaining positions vis-à-vis Third World host states. This allows them to extract considerable benefits from their Third World operations and to escape some forms of regulation. Yet this does not establish that direct foreign investment stymies Third World development. The economic benefits that multinational corporations bring Third World societies vary depending upon the nature of the investment. Manufacturing investments likely offer the host state more than do extractive investments, such as mining or agricultural production. Yet the package of assets that foreign firms bring to the country, including capital, technology, managerial expertise, and global marketing networks, often cannot be matched by local firms, whether private or state-owned. In any case, the ability of Third World countries to maximize the benefits of direct foreign investment while minimizing the negatives varies across countries and across time.

Perhaps dependency theory's greatest shortcoming is that it has trouble explaining the enormous diversity of Third World development experiences. Whereas many Third World countries remain locked in poverty and show few signs of narrowing the gap with the North, a growing handful of countries have displayed impressive economic dynamism. Located primarily in East Asia, these so-called newly industrializing countries (NICs) have grown at rates far exceeding those in the North. As we will discuss more thoroughly in the next chapter, they have also developed diversified economies that rest increasingly upon the production and trade of manufactured goods. Some have even become the originators of new technology.

Moreover, these countries have succeeded not by asserting greater autonomy from the North, but rather by integrating themselves ever more thoroughly into the international economic system. Although the strategies pursued by these countries do not necessarily suggest a blueprint for success by other Southern nations, it does seem clear that the nature of the international economic system does not preclude the possibility of development for all Third World countries. Indeed, because the external constraints faced by the NICs did not differ radically from those facing many other Southern states, these cases of success should shift our attention toward those internal or domestic characteristics that can account for such different outcomes. This requires close attention to factors that are not typically included in dependency analysis.

The other strain of dependency theory emphasizes the disparities in political power between North and South. The most obvious power advantage possessed by the North lies in its preponderance of military resources over that of the South. Because economic conflicts are rarely resolved through the use of coercion, however, North–South bargaining is more directly influenced by other forms of power.

Northern leverage depends principally upon asymmetries in the relations of economic interdependence between North and South. Simply put, asymmetrical interdependence exists when two countries depend upon trade, investment, and other economic ties with one another, but one country is significantly more dependent upon the relationship than is the other. If the relationship were for some reason suddenly cut asunder, the more dependent trade partner would be hurt far more than the less dependent partner. The less dependent country can therefore play upon the weakness and vulnerability of the more dependent country as a source of power or leverage.

A hypothetical case may help to clarify this point. Let us imagine that two countries, A and B, engage in trade with one another. For country A, its trade with country B constitutes only a small share of its overall trade with all countries and a much smaller proportion of its total national income. Were trade between A and B to be curtailed, country A would be only marginally hurt and could probably substitute for the losses by expanding its trade with alternative partners. Country B, however, is much smaller and less well-developed than country A. Trade with A constitutes a large portion of country B's overall trade and a significant increment of its national income. The loss of trade with country A would be devastating to country B's economy. Moreover, as a less developed nation dependent upon a narrow range of exports, country B might find it difficult to locate alternative buyers for its goods. This, in extreme form, is a relationship of asymmetrical interdependence. Country B's vulnerability to a rupture in trade provides country A with a source of power over B. Should political or commercial conflicts arise between the two countries, country A can reliably compel concessions from country B by threatening to withhold trade.

Dependency theorists point out that this hypothetical case conforms rather closely to the actual realities of economic ties between many Northern states and many Southern states. As a result, the North's interests dominate in bargaining between the two.[31]

---

[31] For a seminal discussion of how asymmetries in economic dependence can provide one party with potential power over another, see Albert Hirshman, *National Power and the Structure of Foreign Trade*, Berkeley: University of California Press, 1969.

Dependency theorists are on much firmer ground with this line of argument than with their critique of dependent capitalism. Southern dependence upon the North may not pose an insuperable obstacle to development, but it does clearly give rise to disparities in power and influence both in relations between particular states and in collective negotiations over the rules and institutions of the international economic order.

Before we embrace these conclusions, however, several caveats are in order. It should be noted that the recognition that power flows from asymmetrical interdependence is not unique to dependency theory. Indeed, the concept of asymmetrical interdependence can, with appropriate modifications, be applied to the analysis of power in many different spheres of social, political, and economic life. Moreover, asymmetries exist not just between North and South but also among Northern countries themselves, although the resulting disparities in power are unlikely to be as wide in the latter instances as in the former. Finally, power relationships among states are not static. OPEC, for instance, managed to turn the tables on the North during the seventies when it took advantage of the industrial world's enormous dependence on a particularly crucial resource.

## CONCLUSIONS

What seems clear from our overview of modernization and dependency theories is that neither provides an entirely adequate, overall understanding of the problems facing Southern countries as they attempt to close the development gap with the North. Modernization theory ignores some of the less appealing aspects of economic development under capitalism. It is also vague on some key theoretical points, such as the concept of traditionalism. Moreover, modernization theory overlooks the importance of power disparities between the North and the South. Dependency theory has weaknesses as well, especially in its tendency to exaggerate the constraints that the international system places on development. The concept of dependence is vague, and the links between it and underdevelopment are tenuous. Dependency theory also provides us with few means for understanding why some Third World countries are rapidly developing while others are falling further behind. These shortcomings in the two principal alternative perspectives on development are perhaps a measure of the limits to our knowledge about the complex process of economic development.

Nevertheless, both modernization theory and dependency theory offer useful insights. Modernization theory provides a convincing account of the factors that contributed to the development of the North, and it points to a number of present-day obstacles to development in the cultures and institutions of Southern societies. It also makes a strong case for the proposition that the spread of capitalism and the incorporation of Third World states into the international economic system provide an overall positive contribution to Southern economic development. Dependency theory, on the other hand, reminds us that great power disparities flow from Southern dependence upon the North.

In general, we suggest that modernization theory is closer to the mark in contending that the gains to the South from North–South economic ties outweigh the losses. Indeed, as one might expect from market exchanges, both North and South tend to benefit. Yet this does not imply that both sides benefit equally. The gains from mutual trade and investment may accrue to both North and South, yet not in equal proportions. As dependency writers point out, market relations are not free from the exercise of power. Asymmetrical interdependence provides the North with leverage over the South. The use of this leverage can, as we will see in later chapters, allow the North to bend the rules of the game in its favor to ensure that the benefits of North–South economic relations flow disproportionately its way. These insights, drawn from both modernization and dependency theories, will structure much of the discussion that follows. The South has been attracted toward greater involvement with the world economy by the promise of economic gain and accelerated modernization through exchange with the North. Yet it has also been repelled due to the dangers posed by overreliance upon the North and the risk that this dependence holds for exploitation.

Although modernization and dependency remain the principal general perspectives on development and North–South political economy, recent years have brought a shift in the terms of debate. New questions are being raised. Increasingly, scholars are turning to comparative studies that ask why countries facing similar international circumstances pursue differing development strategies. These policy choices, in turn, are seen as critical to economic outcomes.

Neither dependency theory nor modernization theory is well adapted to answering these sorts of questions. Dependency theory's emphasis on external constraints rules out domestically generated variation across countries. Modernization theory does look at domestic factors but emphasizes broad social and cultural traits that change slowly and are only loosely connected to specific policy choices. The newer literature, by contrast, pays close attention to the roles that political coalitions, as well as bureaucratic, institutional, and political structures, play in determining which development path a particular state is likely to choose. These sorts of factors are used to help explain, for instance, why the large countries of Latin America, including Brazil and Mexico, have generally pursued inward-looking development strategies stressing autonomy, whereas a number of successful East Asian countries, such as South Korea and Taiwan, have opted for outward-looking strategies based upon export expansion. We will explore the issues raised by this recent literature at length in the following chapter.[32]

---

[32] Two recent examples of research in this vein are Stephan Haggard, *Pathways from the Periphery: The Politics of Growth in the Newly Industrialized Countries*, Ithaca: Cornell University Press, 1990; and Sylvia Maxfield, *Governing Capital: International Finance and Mexican Politics*, Ithaca: Cornell University Press, 1990.

## ANNOTATED BIBLIOGRAPHY

Cyril Black, *The Dynamics of Modernization,* New York: Harper & Row, 1966.
A widely cited statement of modernization theory.

Fernando Henrique Cardoso and Enzo Falleto, *Dependency and Development in Latin America,* Berkeley: University of California Press, 1979.
An important study of Latin American political and economic development from a dependency perspective. Cardoso and Falleto offer a less deterministic and more historical and contextual approach to the study of dependency than do many of the earlier authors in this tradition.

Vincent Mahler, *Dependency Approaches to International Political Economy: A Cross-National Study,* New York: Columbia University Press, 1980.
An attempt to subject dependency theory to empirical testing.

Kurt Martin (ed.), *Strategies of Economic Development: Readings in the Political Economy of Industrialization,* New York: St. Martin's Press, 1991.
A collection of theoretical essays on development.

Robert Packenham, *The Dependency Movement,* Cambridge: Harvard University Press, 1992.
A critical overview and assessment of the dependency school.

Alajandro Portes, "On the Sociology of National Development: Theories and Issues," *American Journal of Sociology,* July 1976.
A critique of modernization theory.

Tony Smith, "The Underdevelopment of the Development Literature: The Case of Dependency Theory," *World Politics,* January 1979.
A critique of dependency theory from a liberal perspective.

United Nations Development Program, *Human Development Report*, New York: Oxford University Press, 1995.
Issued annually, these reports focus on the social, cultural, and economic aspects of development. Especially useful is the Human Development Index, which provides a composite measure of the quality of life in various countries. Contains ample charts and data.

J. Samuel Valenzuela and Arturo Valenzuela, "Modernization and Dependency: Alternative Perspectives in the Study of Latin American Underdevelopment," in Heraldo Munoz (ed.), *From Dependency to Development: Strategies to Overcome Underdevelopment and Inequality,* Boulder: Westview Press, 1981.
Perhaps the best and most concise comparison of the modernization and dependency perspectives.

Bill Warren, "Imperialism and Capitalist Industrialization," *New Left Review*, September–October 1973.
A critique of dependency theory from a Marxist perspective.

Charles Wilbur (ed.), *The Political Economy of Development and Underdevelopment* (5th ed.), New York: Random House, 1992.
A collection of classic and contemporary essays on Southern development, most written from a left perspective.

World Bank, *World Development Report, 1995*, New York: Oxford University Press, 1995.
Issued annually, these reports contain a wealth of information on all aspects of Southern economies. Each report focuses upon a different theme related to Third World development. In addition to the tables, charts, and boxes scattered throughout the text, an appendix titled "World Development Indicators" is provided at the end of each volume. This section contains comprehensive social and economic data on each country displayed in thirty or more tables.

# Chapter 9

## STRATEGIES OF SOUTHERN TRADE AND DEVELOPMENT

Third World development strategies have varied across nations and over time. Some countries have enjoyed enormous success, whereas others have stumbled along the path to a better life for their citizens. Various models of economic growth and industrialization have shifted in and out of fashion. This chapter examines the diverse ways in which Southern states have managed the process of development and their nations' ties to the international economy. We distinguish between national and collective strategies for overcoming underdevelopment and closing the gap between North and South. National strategies involve policies designed to spur growth in a particular country. Collective strategies revolve around the coordinated efforts of multiple Third World countries to enhance their bargaining power vis-à-vis the North, to shift the rules of the international economic order to the South's advantage, and to enhance South–South economic ties.

## NATIONAL STRATEGIES OF TRADE AND INDUSTRIALIZATION

Development strategies in the Third World have followed a rough historical progression. Under colonialism, Third World economies were forcibly oriented toward trade patterns dictated by the colonial powers. The colonized lands provided raw materials and agricultural commodities to the imperial center, which, in turn, sold consumer and industrial goods to the colonies.

For the most part, this arrangement precluded the possibility of industrialization in the South. Indeed, the colonial powers intentionally discouraged the development of manufacturing industries that might compete with their own. The British, for instance, dismantled thriving textile and handicraft industries in India when they arrived. The legacies of colonialism made it difficult for Southern countries to break free of this pattern even after the colonists departed. The colonial powers built infrastructures designed to service the colonial trading system. Roads and railways, for instance, linked mines or plantations with ports, bypassing population centers in the interior of the country. Although natives were often incorporated into the colonial bureaucracy, they were given few opportunities to learn entrepreneurial skills. Vast agricultural regions were converted from the production of staple foods for domestic consumption to cash crops designed for export. Without a domestic manufacturing capability of their own, the former colonies remained dependent on the revenues earned from these exports in order to finance consumer good imports. Many countries, in Africa, for instance, remain entrenched in the colonial trading pattern, reliant upon the export of a narrow range of agricultural goods or raw materials.[1]

Beginning in the 1930s, however, a number of countries, especially in Latin America, began to develop a substantial manufacturing sector based upon a strategy known as *import substitution industrialization* (ISI). This strategy was forced upon Latin American countries during the thirties and early forties when the Great Depression first eroded traditional export markets while World War II later interrupted the flow of consumer goods from the North. Initially as a necessity and then, after World War II, as a matter of conscious choice, Latin American countries began to seek greater self-sufficiency and domestic industrialization.

The difficulty in pursuing such a course, after the war had ended, was that Southern firms were generally too small and inexperienced to withstand direct competition from Northern exporters. In an effort to nurture these infant industries and to substitute domestic production for previously imported goods, Third World governments raised protectionist barriers to stymie foreign competition. The first industries to be offered protection were producers of consumer goods because the technical barriers as well as the capital requirements to this sort of production were lower. Due to the lack of experienced entrepreneurs, these firms were often created and owned by the state. Besides tariff protection, the new firms were offered other forms of assistance, including subsidized financing and preferential access to foreign exchange with which to purchase imported inputs. Where domestic industry lacked the knowledge or the capital to engage in certain types of production, Northern multinational corporations were encouraged to jump protectionist barriers and to serve local markets through domestic production rather than through exports.

Other policies were associated with ISI. Local currencies were kept overvalued. This cheapened the price of imported inputs such as oil, raw materials, and capital goods for ISI industries. Wage rates were allowed to rise, and social spending increased so as to encourage the growth of a domestic market for the consumer goods produced by ISI industries. Although the export of cash crops remained necessary in order to secure the foreign exchange

---

[1] For a brief discussion of colonialism, see Paul Harrison, *Inside the Third World* (2nd ed.), New York: Penguin Books, 32–46.

needed for imported industrial inputs, the agricultural sector was generally squeezed. Investment was shifted from agriculture to industry, and surplus rural labor was channeled toward urban areas.

ISI produced impressive growth and industrialization during the fifties in much of Latin America and elsewhere.[2] Yet by the sixties ISI began to run out of steam due to contradictions inherent to the strategy. After the potential for further growth in the consumer goods sector slackened, governments began to pursue the "deepening" of ISI by encouraging the development of manufacturing capabilities in basic and intermediate industries such as steel and capital goods. For the most part, these investments involved larger-scale commitments of capital and more-sophisticated technologies than had been the case in the consumer goods industries. This required foreign borrowing or massive government spending. Moreover, because the domestic market for such goods remained small in many countries, new factories could not operate at efficient economies of scale, leading to high prices and large government subsidies.

These were not the only problems encountered by countries pursuing ISI. The justification for protecting the initial ISI industries from foreign competition was that they needed a breathing spell until they attained sufficient size and experience to compete successfully on their own. In fact, many firms became dependent on protectionism and lobbied hard against lifting barriers. With little effective competition, moreover, these firms had few incentives to maximize efficiency or to carry out innovation. They were also free to charge monopoly prices.

Financial difficulties also characterized the late stages of ISI. Government subsidies to industry and high social spending led to large budget deficits. Foreign borrowing, the repatriated profits of multinational corporations, and the discouragement of exports due to overvalued currencies also led to external deficits and a growing debt, despite the substitution of domestically produced goods for imports. Growing wage levels, large budget deficits, and the high prices associated with inefficient and monopolistic ISI industries created severe inflationary pressures.

Among development experts, ISI is now largely in disrepute. Although ISI may once have played a necessary role in jump-starting the process of industrialization in Latin America and elsewhere, many observers have concluded that the rigidities and inefficiencies that ISI policies produce have more recently served to hinder growth and development. The past two decades have brought great interest in an alternative path to development often referred to as *export-led industrialization* (ELI). This strategy entails an emphasis on the growth of manufacturing production aimed at the international market, in contrast to ISI, which focused on producing for the domestic market. ELI is

---

[2] For a discussion of Latin America's experience with ISI, see Robert Alexander, "Import Substitution in Latin America in Retrospect," in James L. Dietz and Dilmus D. James (eds.), *Progress Toward Development in Latin America: From Prebisch to Technological Autonomy*, Boulder: Lynne Rienner, 1991, and other essays in the same volume.

rooted in theories of international trade that emphasize that countries are best off specializing in those goods for which they possess a comparative advantage while opening their economies to the import of goods that can be produced more cheaply elsewhere. Although the goal of ISI was to develop a well-rounded and relatively self-sufficient industrial economy, the goal of ELI is to exploit a country's particular advantages by finding a narrower, but profitable, niche in the world economy.

The most successful examples of export-led industrialization can be found in East Asia, a region where the total number of poor people fell from 400 million to 180 million between 1970 and 1990 despite a two-thirds increase in population.[3] Leading the surge among East Asian developing countries have been the "Four Tigers"—South Korea, Taiwan, Singapore, and Hong Kong.[4] These countries have sustained astonishingly high rates of economic growth over the past several decades and stand poised to join the ranks of the world's most highly developed nations.

A statistical portrait of these four nations underscores their economic dynamism.[5] Over the past four decades, Taiwan has averaged real GNP growth exceeding 8 percent per year. Life expectancy in Taiwan jumped from fifty-nine years in 1952 to seventy-four in 1988. Forty-five percent of young Taiwanese go on to gain some higher education. In 1988–89, one third of all college students were pursuing degrees in engineering, while 10 percent of the work force as a whole has had some engineering training. In 1988 Taiwan had an unemployment rate of 1 percent. The last time unemployment exceeded 2 percent was 1964.

South Korea's real per-capita income has grown at an average rate exceeding 8 percent per year since the early sixties. South Korean life expectancy reached seventy-one years in 1992, up from fifty-eight in 1965. Thirty-seven percent of Korean students go on to higher education after graduating high school, and unemployment levels have ranged between 2 percent and 4 percent over the past twenty-five years. South Korea has moved well beyond the

---

[3] "A Survey of Asia," *The Economist*, October 30–November 5, 1993, 3.

[4] For general treatments of the East Asian NICs, see Richard P. Appelbaum and Jeffrey Henderson (eds.), *States and Development in the Asia Pacific Rim,* Newbury Park: Sage Publications, 1992; Ezra Vogel, *The Four Little Dragons: The Spread of Industrialization in East Asia,* Cambridge: Harvard University Press, 1991; Bela Balassa, *Economic Policies in the Pacific Area Developing Countries,* New York: New York University Press, 1991; Roy Hofheinz, Jr., and Kent E. Calder, *The Eastasia Edge,* New York: Basic Books, 1982; and Jon Woronoff, *Asia's "Miracle" Economies* (2nd ed.), Armonk: M. E. Sharpe, 1992.

[5] Unless otherwise cited, data on Taiwan and South Korea in the next four paragraphs are taken from "The Economies of South Korea and Singapore," *The Economist,* February 23, 1991; "Korean GNP Up a Brisk 9 Percent," *New York Times,* April 1, 1991; Sheryl WuDunn, "Taiwan Sets Course for Modernity," *Des Moines Register,* October 27, 1991; "South Korea," *The Economist,* August 18, 1990; Damon Darlin, "Taiwan, Long Noted for Cheap Imitations, Becomes an Innovator," *Wall Street Journal,* June 5, 1990; "Taming the Little Dragons," *The Economist,* July 14, 1990; "South Korea," *The Economist,* May 21, 1988; "Taiwan and Korea: Two Paths to Prosperity," *The Economist,* July 14, 1990; and World Bank, *World Development Report, 1994,* New York: Oxford University Press, 1994.

simple, labor-intensive industries in which it initially specialized. South Korea's shipbuilding industry is now the world's largest. The country is a major producer of semiconductor chips, and its thriving auto industry enjoyed a 40 percent rise in exports during 1993.[6]

In much of Latin America, economic development has been accompanied by extreme and growing inequalities in income and wealth. Data from 1980 show that in Brazil, for instance, the top 10 percent of the population accounted for 50.9 percent of the national income, whereas the earnings of the bottom half amounted to only 12.6 percent.[7] In Latin America as a whole, the bottom 20 percent of income earners receive just 4 percent of all income.[8] This unfortunate pattern has been avoided among the East Asian newly industrializing countries (NICs). In Taiwan, for example, growth has generally brought more, not less, equity. The combined income of the top 10 percent of Taiwanese households amounted to fifteen times the bottom 20 percent in the early fifties. By 1980 this ratio had fallen to 4.2:1 (below that of many Northern countries, including the United States, Sweden, and Japan). Although inequality worsened slightly during the eighties, Taiwan remains highly egalitarian by comparative standards. Income distribution is even more equitable in South Korea, where the income of the top 10 percent is only 3.7 times that of the bottom 20 percent.

Both Taiwan and South Korea have based their strategies of development on rapid export growth and international specialization. South Korea is the world's twelfth-largest trading nation, and trade accounts for over one half of Korean GNP. After years of large trade surpluses, Taiwan had accumulated $90 billion in official foreign exchange reserves by 1995—among the largest in the world. From 1950 to 1991 Taiwan averaged annual export growth of 21 percent, while the comparable figure for South Korea exceeded 27 percent. These two countries plus Hong Kong and Singapore accounted for over 60 percent of all Southern exports of manufactured goods in 1990.[9]

Singapore and Hong Kong,[10] both small city-states and centers of Asian finance and commerce, boast per-capita incomes exceeding those of Spain and Ireland. A consulting group known as the Business Environment Risk Information Corporation has rated Singapore's work force the best in the world, an important factor in explaining the large waves of direct foreign investment that Singapore has succeeded in attracting.[11]

---

[6] Andrew Pollack, "Strong Yen Aids Japan's Asian Rivals," *New York Times*, May 23, 1994.

[7] Francis Hagopian and Scott Mainwaring, "Democracy in Brazil: Problems and Prospects," *World Policy Journal*, Summer 1987, 490.

[8] "Easing the Pain of Market Forces," *The Economist*, December 11, 1993, 43.

[9] Stephan Haggard, *Developing Nations and the Politics of Global Integration*, Washington, D.C.: Brookings, 1995, 47, 48.

[10] Hong Kong's future remains cloudy. Presently a British colony, Hong Kong will revert to the control of mainland China in 1997. Although China has pledged to respect Hong Kong's autonomy in many respects, many Hong Kong residents and business firms fear Chinese interference in the island's traditionally laissez-faire economy.

[11] See "Business in Singapore: A Snappy Little Dragon," *The Economist*, June 9, 1990.

A group of export-oriented states in Southeast Asia has begun to follow the path blazed by the Four Tigers (and before them, by Japan). While world export growth averaged 5 percent from 1980 through 1992, Malaysia's exports jumped 11.3 percent per year, and Thailand achieved annual export growth of 14.7 percent.[12] In 1993 Malaysia's economic growth exceeded 8 percent for the sixth straight year.[13] Over the past 15 years, Indonesia has experienced an eighteenfold increase in electrical output and a doubling of paved roads, while economic growth has averaged 7 percent per year since 1965. The proportion of Indonesia's population living in abject poverty has fallen from 60 percent in the early sixties to 15 percent today, and the nation's infant mortality rate has declined 60 percent since the early seventies.[14]

Success has brought new challenges for the East Asian NICs. South Korean wage levels doubled from 1987 to 1990 in the wake of that country's transition to democratic rule, though wage growth has slowed more recently. Wages rose by 40 percent in Taiwan between 1986 and 1990. As a result of higher labor costs, both countries face increasing competition from the fast-growing, lower-wage countries of Southeast Asia. Taiwan's trade surplus has narrowed in recent years, while South Korea's large surpluses of the mid- to late eighties have given way to renewed trade deficits in the early nineties.[15]

Each of the Four Tigers has responded by encouraging the growth of high-technology manufacturing and information-based service industries. Seeking to become a high-tech innovator rather than an imitator, Taiwan doubled private and public spending on research and development from 1985 to 1990. Taiwan's many small manufacturing firms, which are highly efficient but lack the capacity to engage in large-scale research or investment projects, have begun to forge new links with bigger Japanese and American firms. The Hsinchu Science-Based Industrial Park, formed in 1980, offers an example of Taiwan's commitment to technological development. The government has channeled over $500 million into the development of Hsinchu, which is home to thirteen thousand researchers, 150 high-tech firms, and four national laboratories. Researchers at Hsinchu helped launch Taiwan's national semiconductor industry in the early eighties. It also serves to attract Taiwanese scientists, technicians, researchers, and entrepreneurs back from overseas jobs.[16] The payoff from this attention to high technology has been impressive. In 1994 Taiwan produced more than two million notebook computers, making it the world's largest portable computer producer. Taiwan now ranks third in the world as a producer of computer equipment.[17]

---

[12] *World Development Report, 1994*, 187.

[13] "Malaysia: Still Striving," *The Economist*, October 30–November 5, 1993, 36.

[14] Philip Shenon, "As Indonesia Crushes Its Critics, It Helps Millions Escape Poverty," *New York Times*, August 27, 1993.

[15] "The Economies of South Korea and Singapore," *The Economist*, February 23, 1991.

[16] "Yin and Yang in Asia's Science Cities," *The Economist*, May 21, 1994.

[17] "Taiwan's Big Prize," *The Economist*, April 15, 1995.

Taiwanese firms are also moving their low-wage production to surrounding countries. China, Indonesia, Malaysia, and Thailand received a combined $5 billion in Taiwanese investment capital in 1988 and 1989. The same is true of South Korea's large industrial conglomerates, whose combined overseas investments doubled in 1994–95.[18]

South Korea and Taiwan have also begun to reduce their states' role in directing economic growth and to shift away from mercantilist trade policies. Between 1986 and 1990, average tariff levels fell from 28 percent to 10 percent in Taiwan and from 24 percent to 13 percent in South Korea. The South Korean government is engaged in efforts to loosen restrictions on foreign investment, raise social welfare spending at home, and increase the availability of credit to small businesses in an effort to curb industrial concentration, and it has allowed the Korean currency, the won, to appreciate against the dollar and other foreign currencies.[19]

The East Asian NICs have some important commonalities that help to explain their success.[20] South Korea and Taiwan each received large sums of aid from the United States during the 1950s, a factor that helped jump-start the drive toward industrialization. U.S. aid financed 80 percent of South Korean imports in the fifties.[21] Each carried out extensive land reform in the early post–World War II period. These steps broke the political and economic power of conservative landholding elites while establishing the necessary conditions for relatively egalitarian growth patterns. Organized labor has been politically weak in both countries. Each was ruled, over much of the postwar era, by strong, centralized authoritarian states who governed largely autonomous of control by particular social groups.

South Korea and Taiwan passed through relatively brief phases of import substitution industrialization before switching to export-led strategies in the early sixties. Each developed powerful economic ministries staffed by skilled technocrats who have used tax incentives, subsidies, credit, and regulatory policies to promote favored industries. State industrial policies have sought to push

---

[18] James Brooke, "South Korea Strives for a Market in Latin America," *New York Times*, April 6, 1995.

[19] "Taming the Little Dragons" and "Korea's Anti-Mercantilists," *The Economist*, June 11, 1988.

[20] For discussions of the East Asian development model and the political conditions that underlay it, see Stephan Haggard, *Pathways from the Periphery: The Politics of Growth in the Newly Industrializing Countries*, Ithaca: Cornell University Press, 1990; a special issue of *International Studies Notes*, Winter 1990, on the East Asian development model; various essays in Frederic C. Deyo (ed.), *The Political Economy of the New Asian Industrialism*, Ithaca: Cornell University Press, 1987; Bela Balassa, *The Newly Industrializing Countries in the World Economy*, New York: Pergamon Press, 1981; Leroy Jones and Il Sakong, *Government, Business, and Entrepreneurship in Economic Development: The Korean Case*, Cambridge: Harvard University Press, 1980; David Yoffie, *Power and Protectionism: Strategies of the Newly Industrializing Countries*, New York: Columbia University Press, 1983; Alice Amsden, *Asia's Next Giant: South Korea and Late Industrialization*, New York: Oxford University Press, 1989; Robert Wade, *Governing the Market: Economic Theory and the Role of Government in East Asian Industrialization*, Princeton: Princeton University Press, 1990; and David C. Kang, "South Korean and Taiwanese Development and the New Institutional Economics," *International Organization*, Summer 1995.

[21] Waldo Bello and Stephanie Rosenfeld, *Dragons in Distress: Asia's Miracle Economies in Crisis*, San Francisco: Institute for Food and Development Policy, 1992, 4.

development along a path of increasing technological sophistication. Both South Korea and Taiwan have carefully screened direct foreign investment.

Singapore and Hong Kong began their paths to prosperity as regional financial and marketing centers before broadening their economies to encourage manufacturing growth and exports. Each has nondemocratic political systems, skilled bureaucracies, and weak labor unions.

Each of the Four Tigers has achieved stunningly high rates of domestic savings and investment. The overall savings rate in East Asia (excluding Japan) reached 36 percent in the early nineties, double the average rate in Latin America. Singapore raised its savings rate from 1 percent in 1965 to 40 percent in the early 1990s.[22] All have placed great stress on education. In South Korea, college enrollment rose from 142,000 in 1965 to 1.4 million by the late eighties.[23] Yet whereas other Third World countries, such as those in Latin America, place a large share of their educational resources into higher education, the main emphasis in East Asia is on good quality primary education and on the widespread proliferation of knowledge and skills. This focus on basic education promotes higher worker efficiency and allows for greater equity.[24]

Some interesting differences distinguish the East Asian NICs from one another. South Korea, the most statist of the four, has relied heavily upon large industrial conglomerates, both state-owned and private, whose growth has been fueled by cheap credit and heavy borrowing. Sales of the top four South Korean industrial groups, called *chaebols*, equaled one third of all sales of Korean firms in 1993. The top thirty *chaebols* combined to account for 75 percent of the country's GDP.[25] South Korea has also accumulated a substantial foreign debt, although its creditworthiness is considered far stronger than those of Latin American countries with similar debt loads.

Taiwan's economy, by contrast, rests upon a collection of many small equity-based companies. Unlike South Korea, Taiwan has avoided extensive foreign borrowing. Hong Kong is alone among the four East Asian NICs in relying almost solely upon market mechanisms rather than aggressive state intervention to steer economic growth and development. Unlike South Korea and Taiwan, Singapore has depended heavily upon foreign direct investment to stimulate growth, even to the point of favoring foreign firms over local firms.

The World Bank and other development agencies have held up the success of the East Asian NICs as examples to be copied by other Third World nations. Indeed, dozens of countries in Latin America, Asia, and Africa have abandoned the ISI strategies of previous decades in favor of more-liberal, open, and export-oriented economies. The recent experience of the Southeast Asian countries suggests that some of the nations seeking to emulate the Four

[22] Michael Prowse, "Miracles Beyond the Free Market," in Christian Soe (ed.), *Annual Editions: Comparative Politics, 95/96* (13th ed.), Guilford, Conn.: Dushkin Publishing, 1995, 223.

[23] Paul Kuznets, *Korean Economic Development: An Interpretative Model*, Westport, Conn.: Praeger, 1994, 120.

[24] "A Survey of Asia," *The Economist*, October 30–November 5, 1993, 6.

[25] "South Korean Cars: Three's a Crowd," *The Economist*, June 11, 1994, 63.

Tigers will succeed. Yet it is far from certain that the East Asian model of industrialization can be generalized to large numbers of Third World countries.

For one thing, the so-called neoliberal version of ELI now being urged upon Third World countries by the World Bank and many development experts differs in subtle but important ways from the more mercantilistic strategy pursued by the East Asian NICs in the early stages of their economic takeoff. In South Korea and Taiwan, industrialization involved a heavy dose of state economic management and intervention. A recent World Bank study of East Asian development summed up the government's role in the South Korean economy: "From the early 1960s, the government carefully planned and orchestrated the country's development. . . . [It] used the financial sector to steer credits to preferred sectors and promoted individual forms to achieve national objectives. . . . [It] socialised risk, created large conglomerates (chaebols), created state enterprises when necessary, and moulded a public–private partnership that rivaled Japan's."[26]

Both East Asia and Latin America experienced extensive state intervention. They differed, however, in whether industrial production was directed toward the domestic market or external markets. Contemporary advocates of ELI have typically embraced the export orientation of the East Asian countries while ignoring or rejecting the heavy state economic role that was characteristic of such nations until recent years. Whether the neoliberal version of ELI now being pursued by many Third World countries can match the accomplishments produced through the more mercantilist strategies adopted by the early export-oriented industrializing countries is an interesting but as yet unanswered question.

It is also important to note that the successes of South Korea and Taiwan seem to be associated with a number of characteristics peculiar to the historical development of these societies. These characteristics include the rule of strong authoritarian governments, the development of skilled bureaucracies, the weakness of the landowning class, and low levels of labor mobilization. Each also enjoyed favored relations with the United States, bringing considerable economic aid as well as military protection during the early stages of their industrialization drives.

The issue of historical timing also deserves attention. The East Asian NICs adopted ELI at a time when most other Third World countries were pursuing inward-looking strategies. Northern markets were growing at a brisk pace, while trade barriers were falling rapidly. Conditions were ripe for the success of a strategy built around the targeting of Northern markets with manufacturing goods built by low-wage workers. In today's climate, by contrast, many Third World nations are competing to service the same Northern markets, and growth in Northern demand is sluggish.

Those who seek to emulate countries such as South Korea and Taiwan must also reckon with the less-appealing consequences of rapid industrializa-

---

[26] Prowse, "Miracles Beyond the Free Market," 223.

tion in East Asia. In South Korea, for instance, growth has brought staggering levels of industrial pollution. In one highly publicized incident, a large chemical leak on March 14, 1991, contaminated a major reservoir that provided drinking water to nearby communities. Hundreds, perhaps thousands, of people became violently ill after drinking the sullied tap water. This episode led to an emotional debate among South Koreans over the environmental costs of development.[27]

The rush to development has also led to shortcuts that have compromised the quality of the region's infrastructure. During 1994 and 1995 South Korea witnessed a series of deadly disasters, including the collapse of a highway bridge (leading to thirty-two deaths), the explosion of a gas pipeline (one hundred deaths), the sinking of a ferry (twenty-nine deaths), and the disintegration of a major department store (400 deaths and 900 injuries).[28] South Korea also has the world's highest rate of industrial accidents and occupation-related illnesses.[29] In some respects, development has been directed by skewed priorities. Despite the success of South Korean manufacturing firms, for instance, the number of housing units nationwide in 1988 fell 40 percent short of the number of households. South Korea's capital, Seoul, was home to two million squatters out of a population of nearly ten million.[30]

Although South Korea and Taiwan have recently moved tentatively toward democracy, the East Asian NICs have traditionally featured repressive authoritarian regimes who squelched political opposition and severely limited the rights of labor. In 1990 and 1991, for instance, the new democratic government of South Korea carried out a major crackdown on labor, declaring one major union illegal and arresting 140 union leaders.[31]

## TRANSITIONS TO EXPORT-LED INDUSTRIALIZATION: THREE COUNTRY STUDIES

Many Third World countries may find it difficult or impossible to duplicate the supportive domestic and international conditions that launched the East Asian nations along their path to prosperity or, if successful, to avoid the serious social and environmental drawbacks of rapid industrialization. The challenge that such countries face is to find ways of adapting an export-oriented strategy to their own unique circumstances.[32]

---

[27] David Sanger, "Chemical Leak in Korea Brings Forth a New Era," *New York Times,* May 1991.

[28] Sheryl WuDunn, "Koreans Ponder: Are Pillars of Postwar Miracle Shaky?" *New York Times,* July 18, 1995.

[29] Bello and Rosenfeld, *Dragons in Distress,* 25.

[30] Bello and Rosenfeld, *Dragons in Distress,* 39.

[31] Bello and Rosenfeld, *Dragons in Distress,* 45.

[32] For an argument that the success of the East Asian NICs cannot be duplicated by other Third World countries, see Robin Broad and John Cavanaugh, "No More NICs," *Foreign Policy,* Fall 1988.

Three of the largest Third World countries to recently attempt the transition from inward- to outward-oriented development are China, India, and Brazil. This section examines the successes and failures that these three countries have experienced in their attempts to apply the lessons of the East Asian model to the special problems that each faces.

# China

Beginning in 1979 a group of reformers in the Chinese communist leadership, led by Deng Xiaoping, undertook a dramatic turnabout in China's strategy of economic development. Until this point, China's largely self-contained economy had been steered by traditional communist state planning and ownership. During the eighties, however, Chinese leaders introduced a series of market reforms designed to speed up the process of economic modernization and open China to the world economy. Although the state-owned sector of the economy remained in place, a thriving private sector sprang up alongside it. At first, this economic experiment was limited to several special economic zones located along China's southern coast, but similar policies were later extended to other parts of the country. Chinese leaders gradually freed prices from state control, decentralized economic decision making, and encouraged foreign trade and investment. Reflecting the ideological tensions created by China's pragmatic turn, state officials contend that China is building a "socialist market economy." Somewhat more bluntly, Chinese leader Deng Xiaoping has succinctly declared that "development at a slow pace is not socialism."[33]

China's economy has responded with enormous vitality to the economic reforms introduced since 1979. Indeed, China's economic growth rate was the world's highest during the eighties and early nineties. Per-capita income in China rose at a rate of 7.8 percent per year from 1980 through 1991.[34] Overall growth averaged over 12 percent per year from 1992 through 1994.[35] Incredibly, average per-capita income in China shot up over 50 percent from the beginning of 1992 through the end of 1995.[36] Much of this growth has been fueled by rapid export expansion, propelling China in rank from the thirty-first-largest world trading country in 1980 to the eleventh-largest in 1993.[37] Between 1979 and 1994 Chinese exports grew at a rate of 16 percent per year.[38]

---

[33] Patrick Tyler, "Chinese End Austerity Drive in Favor of Yet More Growth," *New York Times,* November 23, 1993.

[34] Nicholas Kristoff, "Riddle of China: Repression as Standard of Living Soars," *New York Times,* September 7, 1993.

[35] "The Outlook for China," *New York Times,* October 13, 1993.

[36] Lester Brown, Nicholas Lenssen, and Hal Kane, *Vital Signs, 1995: The Trends That Are Shaping Our Future,* New York: W. W. Norton (Worldwatch Institute), 1995, 70.

[37] "China Wants to Join the Club," *The Economist,* May 14, 1994, 35.

[38] "Survey: China," *The Economist,* March 18, 1995, 17.

China's growth has been aided by a massive influx of foreign direct investment. China attracted over $44 billion in foreign direct investment between 1979 and mid-1993, more than half of it originating from Hong Kong. Foreign investment boomed in 1994, when $30 billion entered the country—accounting for one half of all foreign direct investment flowing to the Third World as a whole for that year. China was home to an estimated 450,000 expatriate business managers in 1995.[39]

Economic reform has ushered in an age of revolutionary social and economic change for the Chinese people. The lives of many Chinese citizens have been fundamentally transformed in a span of less than two decades. Whereas in 1970, for instance, one third of all Chinese lived at or below the basic subsistence level, by 1990 this figure had fallen to 10 percent. Child mortality, which stood at 210 out of every 1,000 children under age five in 1960, declined to 43 by 1990. Life expectancy has risen from forty-three in 1969 to sixty-nine in 1990. As a result of government inoculation programs, in fact, a baby born in Shanghai is likely to live longer than a baby born in New York City. Overall, the Chinese consumed 2.5 times more meat, eggs, and milk in 1994 than they did in 1982. Per-capita housing space more than doubled in the eighties. In 1978 China possessed roughly eight bicycles, eight radios, and 0.3 televisions for every one hundred people. By 1990 these figures had risen, respectively, to thirty-four, twenty-two, and sixteen.[40] Since 1978 the number of washing machines in China has risen from virtually zero to over ninety-seven million.[41]

Yet despite recent gains, China remains a relatively poor society, especially in the rural areas, where three quarters of the population live. China has only two telephones for every one hundred people. Increasing this figure to ten per one hundred by the year 2000 will require an investment of $100 billion.[42] Fifty million rural people cannot afford the price of daily tea.[43] Only 40 percent of urban residents and one in seven rural Chinese have access to safe drinking water.[44]

Moreover, China's rapid economic growth has produced enormous social disruption and many unappealing side effects. One hundred million rural laborers are unemployed, and many are migrating to the cities in search of

---

[39] "China's Diaspora Turns Homeward," *The Economist*, November 27–December 3, 1993, 33; "Survey: China," *The Economist*, March 18, 1995, 10; and "Multinationals: A Survey," *The Economist*, June 24, 1995, 13.

[40] Data in this paragraph are drawn from Kristoff, "Riddle of China," "A Survey of Asia," 12; Robert Benjamin, "Big Changes in Diet Challenge the Chinese," *Des Moines Register*, February 27, 1994; Peter Nolan, "Introduction: The Chinese Puzzle," in Qimiao Fan and Peter Nolan (eds.), *China's Economic Reform: The Costs and Benefits of Incrementalism*, New York: St. Martin's Press, 1994, 11, 13.

[41] "Survey: The Global Economy," *The Economist*, October 1, 1994, 28.

[42] "Hanging on a China Line," *The Economist*, August 27, 1994, 54.

[43] Jack Goldstone, "The Coming Chinese Crisis," *Foreign Policy*, Summer 1995, 47.

[44] Robert Benjamin, "Rapidly Developing China Faces Environmental Catastrophe," *San Francisco Chronicle*, August 4, 1994.

work. Urban–rural inequality has risen over the past decade, with average urban incomes reaching three times rural levels. In 1993 twenty Chinese provinces experienced peasant protests, 830 of which involved over five hundred people and 21 of which involved more than five thousand participants. Even urban areas have experienced increasing labor unrest, with 1993 witnessing over twelve thousand significant labor disputes at Chinese factories.[45]

Many unwelcome social changes are also evident. Crime has increased tenfold since 1979. Divorce rates have doubled. Most troubling to many Chinese is the pervasiveness of corruption in public life. In 1993 Chinese leader Deng Xiaoping warned that China had become "dominated by corruption, embezzlement and bribery." Chinese Premier Li Peng has stated that the fight against corruption among government officials has become a "life or death" struggle for China and its political leadership.[46]

These serious problems pale, however, in comparison to the threats posed by environmental degradation and potential agricultural shortages. Due to a heavy reliance on coal in power production, sulfur dioxide levels far exceed international standards in virtually every major Chinese city. Air pollution has become the leading cause of disease in China. Indeed, the air in Beijing is so dirty that local entrepreneurs have mounted a thriving business in "oxygen bars"—places where wheezy patrons stop off on their way home from work to purchase a whiff of fresh air delivered via oxygen canisters.[47] Other environmental problems have reached disastrous proportions as well. As a result of agricultural expansion and urban development, for instance, China's forest cover has shrunk to 13 percent of its total land area (compared with 31 percent for the world as a whole).[48]

China's grain output rose from 150 million tons in 1960 to 456 million tons in 1993, with most of the increase occurring during the eighties as a response to agricultural reforms.[49] Yet despite recent gains, China faces a serious agricultural crisis. China's ratio of arable land per farm worker is among the lowest in the world. Yet China has lost one third of its farmland to industrialization, soil erosion, salinization, and other causes over the past forty years. Agricultural land is expected to shrink another 10 percent over the next fifteen years. Providing food for China's growing population will pose the most important challenge of the next several decades. Increased food demand will stem from two sources. China's population, already 1.2 billion people, is expected to rise by 25 percent, or 300 million people, over the next twenty years. As incomes rise, moreover, the Chinese people will continue to increase and to upgrade their diets. Even without considering increased population,

[45] See "Survey: China," 19, and Goldstone, "The Coming Chinese Crisis," 48.

[46] See Orville Schell, "China—The End of an Era," *The Nation*, July 17/24, 1995; and Seth Faison, "In China, Rapid Social Changes Bring a Surge in the Divorce Rate," *New York Times*, August 22, 1995.

[47] BBC World Service broadcast, October 6, 1995.

[48] Benjamin, "Rapidly Developing China Faces Environmental Catastrophe."

[49] "Survey: China," 20.

this factor alone will generate tremendous demand. If, for instance, the Chinese people increased their grain consumption to match the levels of South Koreans, China would need 600 million tons of grain each year. Assuming present Chinese grain production levels, China would have to import an amount of grain equal to all international shipments worldwide in 1994 in order to satisfy this level of consumption. If Chinese fish consumption rose to Japanese levels, China would consume all of the fish harvested worldwide.[50]

How China will manage this rising demand for food remains uncertain. With the major improvements registered during the eighties, Chinese grain yields have already neared the limits of what appears possible, given present methods and technology.[51] As mentioned, presently cultivated land is expected to shrink in the coming years, and very little unexploited arable land remains available. Agriculture's share of total investment in the Chinese economy has, moreover, been declining in recent years.[52] Most likely, China will become a major food importer in future years, using industrial exports to pay for grain shipments from abroad.

One of the biggest puzzles facing China in the coming years concerns what to do about the hugely inefficient state-owned sector of the economy. Although the private economy has experienced explosive growth, state-owned enterprises (SOEs), concentrated in heavy industry, have not shared the same dynamism. The proportion of economic output accounted for by SOEs has fallen from 78 percent in 1978 to 43 percent in 1994. Despite tentative reforms, SOEs continue to act as a drag on the rest of the economy. Ten percent of such firms are virtually inactive, and one third of the work force in the state-owned sector are deemed "unproductive." Forty percent of SOEs showed a loss in 1994, and most carry heavy debt loads, cumulatively equal to one third of China's GDP. One half of the central government's budget is taken up by subsidies to SOEs.[53]

Chinese authorities have allowed a few SOEs to go bankrupt and have sought, with limited success, to attract foreign partners to help invigorate others. Officials have been reluctant to cut off subsidies, close down unprofitable firms, or engage in wholesale privatization for fear that such steps would lead to massive unemployment and social unrest. One quarter of the Chinese population is dependent upon people employed by SOEs. It is estimated that 30 to 40 percent of all workers employed by SOEs would lose their jobs if such firms were run by commercial standards.[54]

---

[50] See Goldstone, "The Coming Chinese Crisis," 36; "Survey: China," 20–21.

[51] Goldstone, "The Coming Chinese Crisis," 36.

[52] "Survey: China," 19.

[53] See "China Stirs Its Sleeping Giants," *The Economist,* August 17, 1994; Patrick Tyler, "China's Industries Battle Bankruptcy by Diversification," *New York Times,* May 5, 1994; Patrick Tyler, "Overhaul of China's State Industry at a Standstill," *New York Times,* December 16, 1994; "Survey: China."

[54] "Shrinking the Chinese State," *New York Times,* June 10, 1995; "Out of Work, on the Move," *The Economist,* October 14, 1995.

China has approached the transition from socialism to capitalism much differently than have many of the former Soviet bloc countries. China—rejecting the "shock therapy," or rapid and thorough transformation, adopted by Poland and several other Eastern European countries—has followed a gradualist path that has, nevertheless, brought spectacular results.[55] Yet alongside the undeniable economic gains, China's dramatic experiment has produced many negative side effects, including growing crime, inequality, corruption, and environmental devastation. These outgrowths of economic progress were certainly not foreign to the experiences of today's developed countries as they passed through a similar stage of development. But whereas the process of development was spread over many decades, or even centuries, in the West, the speed of China's economic transformation is unprecedented. Can the world's most populous nation, ruled by an aging and politically inflexible elite, manage the stresses and contradictions loosened by rapid modernization without inviting a social and political explosion of some sort? The answer to this question will have important implications stretching far beyond China itself.

## India

Almost fifty years after gaining independence, India remains a country plagued by grinding poverty. In 1993 India ranked 134th of the 173 nations on the U.N. Human Development Index. India is home to 27 percent of the world's desperately poor, and one half of the population live in absolute poverty. More than one half of India's people are illiterate, only 10 percent have access to adequate sanitation, 63 percent of India's children under age five are malnourished, and 142 babies of every 1,000 born die before the age of five. This huge country possesses only six million telephones and thirty-five million television sets for 950 million people.[56]

For decades India was among the most devoted practitioners of an inward-looking strategy of development. The state controlled and directed strategic sectors of the economy; foreign investment was strictly limited and highly regulated; import substitution policies were designed to protect and nurture domestic industrialization; and India's currency, the rupee, was purposefully overvalued.

After traveling to East Asia and expressing admiration for South Korea's model of development, however, newly appointed Finance Minister Mohammed Singh announced a dramatic shift in economic strategy in the summer of 1991. India would abandon ISI policies in favor of liberalization and a focus on exports. This turnabout was prompted by India's worsening financial

---

[55] For comparisons between the Chinese model and the "shock therapy" programs adopted in some Eastern European countries, see Nolan, "Introduction: The Chinese Puzzle."

[56] For data in this paragraph, see Edward Gargan, "Shackled by Past, Racked by Unrest, India Lurches Toward Uncertain Future," *New York Times*, February 18, 1994; "Survey: India," *The Economist*, January 21, 1995, 1; and United Nations Development Program, *Human Development Report, 1994*, New York: Oxford University Press, 1994, 73.

straits, including persistent balance of payments deficits, dwindling foreign reserves, and a burdensome foreign debt that had risen from $20.5 billion in 1980 to $72 billion by 1991. India's predicament was exacerbated by a precipitous decline in previously significant levels of Soviet foreign aid as well as by the shrinkage of Soviet demand for Indian goods.

Following Singh's initiative, the Indian government pledged to devalue the rupee, eliminate the state budget deficit, cut subsidies to public firms while closing those that were particularly unprofitable, remove restrictions that discourage foreign investment, and reduce many barriers to imported goods. The World Bank and the IMF quickly rewarded India's shift from ISI toward a more liberal economic strategy by granting extensive new credits designed to relieve the immediate financial strains plaguing the country. Domestic reactions were more mixed, with many groups and individuals expressing worry and dismay that the new policies would produce increased unemployment and hardship among those reliant upon state support.[57]

India's reforms have brought a number of positive results. By 1993 economic growth had recovered to an annual rate of 4 percent, with rising industrial output leading the way. Exports jumped by 21 percent in 1993–94, erasing India's trade deficit and allowing its once-depleted foreign exchange reserves to reach $17 billion. Foreign capital began flowing into Indian stock markets, while foreign direct investment rose to $5 billion in 1993–94.[58]

Nevertheless, economic liberalization runs against India's historic tradition and has drawn fierce domestic opposition. The principal winners have been among India's relatively small middle class. Many others, especially those dependent upon state protection or vulnerable to growing international competition, feel threatened by India's turn toward greater reliance on the market mechanisms. The public sector still accounts for one half of India's industrial stock. The government has set aside plans to carry out widespread privatization or to allow unprofitable firms to go bankrupt. Indeed, large Indian companies, whether private or public, cannot lay off workers or close plants without government permission. Subsidies to rural farmers for water and power remain a substantial drain on government revenues. So, too, does interest on the public debt, which consumes 45 percent of the central government budget each year.[59]

Foreign investors still face widespread hostility and distrust. In 1995 the regional government of Maharashtra, India's main industrial state, rejected the

---

[57] See Bernard Weintraub, "Economic Crisis Forcing Once Self-Reliant India to Seek Aid," *New York Times*, June 29, 1991; Bernard Weintraub, "India Is Now in a New Ballgame," *New York Times*, July 8, 1991; "Indian Economy: Pepsi Generation," *The Economist*, June 9, 1990; and "India's Plan Is Backed," *New York Times*, September 23, 1991.

[58] "The State of Reform in India," *The Economist*, August 6, 1994, 29; "How to Keep Investors Out," *The Economist*, June 11, 1994; "The Lure of India," *The Economist*, February 26, 1994; and Gargan, "Shackled by Past, Racked by Unrest."

[59] Gargan, "Shackled by Past, Racked by Unrest"; "How to Keep Investors Out"; "The State of Reform in India"; and "India's Economic Nationalists," *The Economist*, August 12, 1995.

largest foreign investment project ever proposed for India—a $2.8 billion power plant to be built by the Enron Corporation. Political instability has cast further doubt upon India's long-term commitment to liberalization. Support for the ruling Congress Party has weakened, and the 1996 elections brought an unwieldy coalition government to power.[60]

Indeed, India possesses a set of traits that seems likely to make the successful transition to an outward-looking strategy of development especially difficult: a weak central government, extreme poverty, entrenched vested interests, cultural fragmentation, and a traditional distrust of the outside world. When one adds to these India's enormous size and still-burgeoning population, the prospects for a rapid improvement in the standard of living of most Indians appear slim.

## Brazil

Brazil's ISI strategy, spectacularly successful at generating economic growth during the sixties and seventies, was derailed in the eighties.[61] ISI succeeded in producing a diverse industrial structure in Brazil. Growth in GNP averaged 9 percent per year from 1965 to 1980. Yet much of this expansion was fueled by massive foreign borrowing. This accumulation of debt harmed Brazil's creditworthiness and led to a sharp contraction of foreign bank lending to the country in the eighties. Brazilian industry also became increasingly inefficient as it remained sheltered from international competition and was nursed along with government subsidies. Before March 1990, imports were simply prohibited in one thousand categories of goods, while quotas restricted many other sorts of imports. Tariffs averaged 78 percent in 1984, and the central bank strictly controlled access to foreign exchange. Imports represented only 5 percent of Brazilian GNP in 1989, compared with 28 percent for South Korea and 33 percent for Taiwan. The eighties witnessed the failure of Brazil's ISI strategy. Per-capita income stagnated, the number of Brazil's hungry rose from twenty-five million to thirty-five million, and inflation averaged 260 percent per year.[62]

Brazil's turn toward economic liberalization began in 1990. Since then import bans have been lifted on hundreds of items, and average tariffs have fallen to 14 percent. Between 1992 and 1994 imports rose by 50 percent. Yet exports grew even more quickly, allowing Brazil to post a $10 billion trade

---

[60] "India's Economic Nationalists"; John F. Burns, "India Project in the Balance," *New York Times*, September 6, 1995.

[61] For an overview of the history and development of the Brazilian economy, see Werner Baer, *The Brazilian Economy: Growth and Development* (3rd ed.), New York: Praeger, 1989. On contemporary issues, see Werner Baer and Joseph S. Tulchin (eds.), *Brazil and the Challenge of Economic Reform*, Washington, D.C., and Baltimore: Woodrow Wilson Center Press and Johns Hopkins University Press, 1993.

[62] "Brazil's Economy: The Right Stuff," *The Economist*, June 9, 1990; James Brooke, "Brazil Opens Its Borders to Goods from Abroad," *New York Times*, August 16, 1993; James Brooke, "A Hard Look at Brazil's Surfeits: Food, Hunger and Inequality," *New York Times*, June 6, 1993.

surplus in 1994, along with accumulated foreign reserves of $42 billion. GDP growth jumped to 5 percent in 1993.[63]

After years of negotiations, Brazil reached an agreement to reschedule its huge foreign debt to Northern commercial banks in 1993.[64] This paved the way for a vast wave of new foreign investment into the country. In 1994 it was estimated that an average of three hundred American business representatives per day visited Sao Paulo, Brazil's largest industrial city.[65] New foreign direct investment flows to Brazil reached $5 billion in 1995. Portfolio investment, in the form of stock and bond purchases, has also risen dramatically. Sectors of the economy that were previously forbidden to outsiders, such as oil, mining, telecommunications, banking, and insurance, have been opened to foreign investors.[66]

Some sectors of Brazilian industry have responded with alacrity to the increasingly competitive environment brought about by trade and investment liberalization. Brazil's automobile industry, for instance, experienced a 46 percent improvement in productivity between 1990 and 1993. Auto manufacturers introduced ten new car models in 1993, compared with the usual two. Multibillion-dollar expansion plans promised to double Brazil's automobile output by the year 2000. Similar changes have occurred elsewhere. Average prices for electronic goods fell by 40 percent between 1989 and 1993. The processed food sector introduced six hundred new products in 1992, compared with three hundred in 1991.[67]

Brazil's most intractable economic problem throughout the eighties and early nineties was an inflation rate of mind-boggling proportions. Successive anti-inflation plans failed to cure this malady until 1994, when new President Fernando Henrique Cardoso instituted a new initiative that included the issuance of a new currency and a sharp reduction in government spending. From a rate of 40 percent per month (the equivalent of 2,500 percent per year) in the first half of 1994, Brazilian inflation subsided to 1.5 percent by September.[68]

Cardoso's economic reforms extended to other areas as well. His government promoted the privatization of state enterprises, the reorganization of the social welfare system, the reduction of paperwork for imports, the transfer

---

[63] Brooke, "Brazil Opens Its Borders to Goods from Abroad"; James Brooke, "Brazil Cuts Its Tariffs on Many Goods," *New York Times*, September 12, 1994; James Brooke, "For Brazil, New Praise and Potential," *New York Times*, October 10, 1994.

[64] "Brazil Signs Foreign Debt Agreements," *New York Times*, November 30, 1993.

[65] James Brooke, "U.S. Businesses Flocking to Brazilian Ventures," *New York Times*, May 9, 1994.

[66] Brooke, "For Brazil, New Praise and Potential"; James Brooke, "Mexican Crisis Depressing Brazil and Argentina Stocks," *New York Times*, February 20, 1995.

[67] Brooke, "Brazil Opens Its Borders to Goods from Abroad"; "Brazil's Car Industry: Party Time," *The Economist*, September, 17, 1994; James Brooke, "Car Makers Shift to High Gear in Brazil," *New York Times*, March 28, 1995.

[68] James Brooke, "Brazil's Mythic Inflation Under Full Scale Attack," *New York Times*, March 3, 1994; Brooke, "For Brazil, New Praise and Potential."

of health and education programs to the states, and the encouragement of foreign investment.

Cardoso's own personal odyssey reflected the dramatically changed economic and ideological climate in Brazil and elsewhere in Latin America during the nineties. Cardoso first gained fame as a left-wing sociologist who co-authored one of the seminal works in the dependency school[69] and who was a vocal critic of Brazil's right-wing military dictatorships of the sixties and seventies. Cardoso was drawn into mainstream politics beginning in the late seventies as Brazil gradually moved toward democracy. After serving as finance minister during the early nineties and presiding over Brazil's ultimately successful debt negotiations, Cardoso became the darling of international financiers. By 1994 this once-radical sociologist could be quoted as saying: "Whoever tries to make decisions against the market is going to fail."[70]

The depth of neoliberal sentiment within the Brazilian political class, and within those of other Latin American countries as well, is evident in the reflections of Augusto Carvalho, a Brazilian congressman affiliated with the former Brazilian Communist Party, now known as the Popular Socialist Party: "I have changed, the left has changed, the Congress has changed. We're not against foreign capital that can create jobs and bring technology to the country."[71]

The biggest challenge facing Brazil today, however, is to find some way to reconcile this newfound commitment to free markets with the imperative of improving the life chances of those who lack the skills or resources to compete in this new economic environment. Brazil remains a country where the richest 20 percent of the population earns twenty-six times more than the poorest 20 percent. Regional disparities are striking. Compared with relatively prosperous southern Brazilians, residents of Brazil's largely rural northeastern region live seventeen fewer years, suffer an adult literacy rate one third lower, and receive average incomes of 40 percent less. One half of Brazil's seventy million workers have less than four years of schooling, and 15 percent have less than one year.[72]

In 1994 U.S. Undersecretary of Commerce for International Trade Jeffrey Garten predicted that "there is a very big chance that looking back from the end of this century, Brazil could be the big success story."[73] If this success is to be shared by all Brazilians, however, its economic managers must find a way

---

[69] Fernando Henrique Cardoso and Enzo Falleto, *Dependency and Development in Latin America*, Berkeley: University of California Press, 1979.

[70] Brooke, "For Brazil, New Praise and Potential."

[71] Brooke, "Brazil's Mythic Inflation Under Full Scale Attack." For an interpretation of how neoliberal ideas came to gain dominance in most Third World countries, see Thomas J. Biersteker, "The 'Triumph' of Liberal Economic Ideas in the Developing World," in Barbara Stallings (ed.), *Global Change, Regional Response: The New International Context of Development*, Cambridge: Cambridge University Press, 1995.

[72] Jacqueline Mazza, "Argentina, Brazil, Chile: Democracy and Market Economics," *Great Decisions*, Washington, D.C., Foreign Policy Association, 1994, 68; Paul Lewis, "U.N. Lists 4 Lands at Risk Over Income Gaps," *New York Times*, June 2, 1994; "Survey: Brazil," *The Economist*, April 29, 1995, 1.

[73] Brooke, "For Brazil, New Praise and Potential."

to spread the benefits of renewed economic growth in a more inclusive manner than has been done in the past. Otherwise, an observation made by one of Brazil's military presidents during the boom years of the seventies will once again hold true for this most recent economic upturn: "Brazil is doing fine. It's the people who are doing poorly."[74]

## COLLECTIVE STRATEGIES OF DEVELOPMENT

Some Third World countries have sought development not through industrialization and diversification of their economies but instead through attempts to turn the tables of traditional colonial trade patterns against the North. During the seventies there existed great interest in the potential of resource cartels to enhance Southern wealth. The aim of this strategy was to exploit the North's dependence upon various Southern raw material or agricultural exports. Although no single Third World country controlled a sufficient market share to manipulate world prices for the commodities it exported, the major Southern producers acting collectively might successfully coordinate production and pricing decisions so as to maximize their joint revenues.

Although, for reasons we will discuss later, most such efforts failed, this strategy produced one spectacular success story: the Organization of Petroleum Exporting Countries (OPEC). The history of how the oil-exporting states gained control over their petroleum resources from Northern oil companies and accumulated enormous riches during the seventies and early eighties is a fascinating one. Yet this Third World success story is not unblemished. OPEC has been plagued by serious internal divisions, some resulting in war and violence, while, since the early eighties, the oil-exporting nations have witnessed a humbling fall in oil prices and revenues.

Prior to the 1970s, relations between the oil-exporting countries and the major Northern oil companies worked decidedly to the advantage of the latter. Seven large oil firms (sometimes called the Seven Sisters) came to dominate the world oil market. These included five U.S. firms (Esso, Mobil, Standard of California, Gulf, and Texaco), one British (British Petroleum), and one Anglo-Dutch (Shell). A French company, CFP, later became a major player as well. These large firms pioneered the global search for new oil reserves, striking major finds in most of the present-day OPEC countries during the period from World War I through the early fifties.[75]

The oil-producing countries initially found themselves almost entirely dependent upon the seven major firms for the development of their oil resources. None had the skills, technology, or marketing networks necessary to

---

[74] Brooke, "A Hard Look at Brazil's Surfeits."

[75] For readable accounts concerning the relationship between the major oil firms and producing countries, consult Anthony Sampson, *The Seven Sisters: The Great Oil Companies and the World They Created* (rev. ed.), London: Coronet, 1988; Daniel Yergin, *The Prize*, New York: Simon and Schuster, 1991; and John Blair, *The Control of Oil*, New York: Pantheon, 1976.

exploit its oil riches without outside help. Relations between oil-producing states and firms revolved around the concession system. Contracts negotiated between these parties gave particular firms or groups of firms the exclusive right to explore for oil in an agreed-upon territorial area within the country. Whatever oil was found belonged to the firm, which controlled all exploration, production, refining, and marketing decisions and activities. In return for these rights, Northern oil companies agreed to turn over a share of their revenues to the producing state in the form of taxes or royalties. This system gave the seven major firms control over production and pricing, although producing states sometimes attempted to influence such decisions.

Challenges to these arrangements were met with resistance, not only from the oil firms themselves, but also from Northern governments who saw the major oil companies as agents of the national interest and key guarantors of the Northern access to a critical resource. In the early fifties, for instance, the seven major oil firms organized a boycott of Iranian oil after the nation's prime minister, Mohammed Mossadegh, ordered the nationalization of assets belonging to the Anglo-Iranian oil company. When the boycott failed to lead to a reversal of the nationalization decision, the United States helped to organize a coup d'état that toppled Mossadegh and returned Mohammed Reza Pahlavi to his previous position as Shah.

As time went on, the major oil-producing states increasingly chafed under the traditional arrangements. Each found it difficult, however, to bring about fundamental change acting on its own. The oil companies adopted a united stand in negotiating with host countries and played oil producers off against one another.

In 1960, at the initiative of Venezuela, five major oil-producing countries (the other four were Iran, Iraq, Saudi Arabia, and Kuwait) attempted to improve their collective bargaining position by forming the Organization of Petroleum Exporting Countries.[76] The immediate precipitating factor was the decision by the major oil firms to lower prices in the face of a global glut of petroleum. Their revenues threatened, the oil-producing countries denounced the price cut and set out to gain greater control over the production and pricing of oil.

OPEC achieved relatively little of major significance during its first decade of existence. Beneath the surface, however, several trends were setting the stage for a revolution in the world of oil. Northern oil consumption rose at a rapid rate during the sixties. At the same time, the growth of U.S. oil production began to slow and, by the early seventies, had reached a plateau. The juxtaposition of these two trends led to a tightening of world oil supplies, especially after the United States began importing increasing amounts of foreign oil to compensate for the stagnation of domestic production.

---

[76] On the origins and evolution of OPEC, see Ian Skeets, *OPEC: Twenty-Five Years of Prices and Politics*, Cambridge: Cambridge University Press, 1988.

Other important factors contributed to OPEC's fortunes. A growing number of independent oil companies began to challenge the seven major firms for access to foreign oil reserves. These newcomers were often willing to strike bargains more favorable to the oil-producing countries, undermining the unity of the major oil firms. The oil-producing countries themselves came to acquire increasing competence in matters relating to oil, thus enhancing their confidence that they could manage their own industries with less reliance upon Northern firms. Also, OPEC absorbed a number of new members over the course of the sixties, including Libya, Indonesia, Algeria, Qatar, Nigeria, and Abu Dhabi. By 1970 OPEC members accounted for 90 percent of world oil exports.[77] Finally, the emergence of radical nationalist regimes, such as in Libya, upset old arrangements between traditional rulers and the firms while increasing the aggressiveness of oil-producing states in their efforts to revise the old order.

With these elements in place, the dominant position of the major oil companies quickly eroded, and events conspired to magnify OPEC's power over world oil markets. In 1970 Libya compelled Occidental Petroleum, an independent oil company, to raise the price of its Libyan-produced crude oil. OPEC moved quickly to exploit Libya's triumph. At an unprecedented meeting in Caracas during February 1971, twenty-three oil firms acceded to OPEC demands for an across-the-board price increase. The next two years brought further OPEC-dictated price rises along with the beginning of a widespread movement on the part of oil-producing states to nationalize all or part of oil company assets within their nations. Indeed, whereas in 1970 the Seven Sisters controlled 60 percent of world oil production outside of the Soviet-controlled bloc, this figure had fallen to 14 percent by 1995, largely due to the effects of nationalist measures by the producing countries.[78]

In the midst of the October 1973 Arab–Israeli war, the Arab members of OPEC cut production by 5 percent and announced an embargo on deliveries of oil to Western supporters of Israel. In an already tight oil market, these actions led to a quadrupling of oil prices to almost $12 a barrel the following December. These high prices were sustained over the next five years, although inflation eroded the real value of OPEC oil revenues. The OPEC revolution triggered an economic recession in the North while generating a massive transfer of wealth from oil-importing countries to the oil-exporting countries. The United States largely failed in its efforts to organize a counter-cartel of oil-importing countries, although modest levels of cooperation among the principal Northern countries were institutionalized through the creation of the International Energy Agency.

OPEC again engineered a massive hike in oil prices in 1979 after the onset of the Iraq–Iran war removed 5 percent of world oil supplies from

[77] Robert Mortimer, *The Third World Coalition in International Politics* (2nd ed.), Boulder: Westview Press, 1984, 44.

[78] "Oil: A Very Crude Form of Politics," *The Economist*, May 6, 1995, 64.

the market. The price of oil tripled to roughly $35 per barrel. Again, the drain of more-expensive oil, combined this time with tight monetary policies in the United States that were designed to reduce inflation, tipped much of the world economy into a major downturn.

Many Third World countries drew inspiration from OPEC's success during the seventies despite the fact that Southern oil import bills rose along with those of the North. Countries who relied heavily upon natural resource exports viewed OPEC as a model for their own development efforts. Producers of bauxite, copper, tin, coffee, bananas, and other Third World commodities formed associations similar to OPEC in hopes of managing supply and driving up both prices and revenues. These ventures enjoyed little success. Beginning in the late seventies and early eighties, slowing demand in the North led instead to declining prices for many Southern raw material and agricultural exports. OPEC's exceptional success stemmed from the critical role of oil in Northern economies, the concentration of vast oil reserves in a relatively small group of Southern oil-producing countries, and, most importantly, the fact that market forces worked in OPEC's favor during the seventies.

OPEC's achievements also invigorated Third World efforts to negotiate a New International Economic Order (NIEO) with the North.[79] Beginning in the sixties, Southern countries worked collectively through the United Nations and informal coordinating mechanisms such as the Group of 77 to hammer out a set of common demands for the reform of North–South relations.[80] The NIEO called for a variety of changes in the rules of the existing global economy: coordinated efforts to raise and stabilize commodity prices, the lowering of Northern barriers to Southern manufactured exports, increased Northern aid and financial assistance to the South, greater Third World voting power in institutions such as the International Monetary Fund and the World Bank, a global code of conduct for multinational corporations, debt relief, and greater Southern access to Northern technology. The Third World coalition counted upon OPEC's demonstrated power, along with its own unity, to provide the South with sufficient leverage to extract Northern concessions.

Indeed, fears that a stalemate in North–South bargaining might prompt desperate Southern responses harmful to the world economy prompted some prominent Northern commentators to embrace a strategy of compromise. Others in the North argued that wealthy countries shared an interest in reforms that might spur Southern growth and stimulate greater North–South trade.[81] For its part, OPEC endorsed Third World demands, pushed for the

---

[79] On the negotiations surrounding the NIEO, see Robert Mortimer, *The Third World Coalition in International Politics* (2nd ed.), Boulder: Westview Press, 1984; Jeffrey Hart, *The New International Economic Order*, New York: St. Martin's Press, 1983; Stephen Krasner, *Structural Conflict: The Third World Against Global Liberalism*, Berkeley: University of California Press, 1985; Jagdish Bhagwati and John Gerard Ruggie (eds.), *Power, Passions and Purpose*, Cambridge: MIT Press, 1984.

[80] Despite its title, the Group of 77 eventually grew to include over 120 Third World countries.

[81] For statements of this viewpoint, see Independent Commission on International Development Issues, *North-South: A Programme for Survival*, Cambridge: MIT Press, 1980; and the Brandt Commission, *Common Crisis, North-South: Cooperation for World Recovery*, Cambridge: MIT Press, 1983.

North to expand negotiations with the South, and increased its own aid to Southern countries harmed by rising oil prices.

Although the South's leverage proved sufficient to force the North into a series of global bargaining rounds over the NIEO proposals during the seventies and early eighties, it remained inadequate to bring about real change. Northern countries, particularly the United States, rejected the bulk of Third World demands. Northern leaders perceived the redistributive aspects of the NIEO as contrary to their own nations' interests. Moreover, Northern spokespersons argued that many NIEO provisions would hamper global economic growth by interfering with market mechanisms.[82] Ultimately, negotiations failed also because the South, as well as some in the North, had overestimated the Third World's true power. Southern nations often warned that the North's failure to accept reform would lead to radical Third World responses, such as the proliferation of resource cartels, debt repudiation, nationalization of multinational corporate assets, and political upheaval. In fact, however, few of these consequences followed from the failure of the NIEO negotiations. The underlying reality was that the South remained more dependent upon the North than vice versa. A serious break in economic relations between the two would hurt the South far more than the North. Southern power thus proved a chimera.

The 1980s were a difficult decade for OPEC. The high oil prices of the late seventies and early eighties stimulated successful conservation measures in the North, fuel-switching to alternative sources of energy, and increased production from non-OPEC sources. Due to investments in energy efficiency, the amount of oil that OECD countries needed to produce an extra dollar of GNP fell by 45 percent between 1973 and 1988. This contributed to a 20 percent drop in OECD oil consumption between 1979 and 1988. At the same time, the production of oil from non-OPEC sources, such as Mexico, the North Sea, and Alaska, grew by 20 percent from 1979 to 1986. Northern countries also began to diversify their sources of supply and to build up strategic stockpiles of oil in an attempt to rob OPEC of its power to control the oil market. Thus OPEC countries lost market share and became marginal producers—serving only that portion of world demand left unsatisfied after non-OPEC sources of supply had been exhausted.[83] OPEC's share of the world oil market (excluding the Soviet Union) fell from 63 percent in 1972 to 38 percent in 1985.[84]

OPEC responded to these challenges by attempting to limit production in an effort to bolster prices. Each member country was allotted a production quota to ensure that overall OPEC production did not breach agreed-upon ceilings. In practice, OPEC remained too divided to sustain this sort of cooperation. As prices softened, many countries attempted to sustain falling

---

[82] For a critical assessment of the NIEO, see Robert Tucker, *The Inequality of Nations*, New York: Basic Books, 1977.

[83] All data in this paragraph are from "The Cartel That Fell Out of the Driver's Seat," *The Economist*, February 4, 1989.

[84] Joseph Stanislaw and Daniel Yergin, "Oil: Reopening the Door," *Foreign Affairs*, September/October 1993, 83.

revenues by producing more oil than called for by their allotments. At first, Saudi Arabia compensated for this overproduction by reducing the rate of its own oil extraction and sales while attempting to persuade other OPEC producers to honor their quota agreements. The Saudis served, in other words, as a swing producer. By 1986, however, Saudi Arabia's market share and revenues had fallen precipitously, and jawboning had failed to curb widespread cheating within OPEC. At that point, the Saudis chose to discipline other OPEC members and to recapture lost market share by dramatically increasing their own oil production. This flood of oil onto world markets sent prices spiraling downward, falling, by early 1988, to between $12 and $13 per barrel. In real terms (discounting for inflation), the price of oil now stood below the levels prior to the price hikes of the early seventies. The economic effects on OPEC were disastrous: Between 1979 and 1988, per-capita income fell by 27 percent among OPEC countries taken together, while imports shrank by half.[85] Saudi oil revenues, which peaked at $19,000 per person in 1980, fell precipitously to $3,000 per person by 1994.[86]

By some indicators, OPEC would appear well-positioned to reassert dominance over world oil markets in the decade ahead. During the late eighties and early nineties, oil prices fell too low to sustain expensive oil exploration projects or to spur additional investments in energy conservation. In the United States, virtually all gains in energy efficiency took place prior to 1986. By some measures, such as the fuel efficiency of new cars, progress toward greater energy efficiency has been reversed. Production by some non-OPEC sources is likely to fall in future years. U.S. oil production fell by 25 percent between 1986 and 1993, while imports rose from 28 percent of U.S. oil consumption in 1985 to 45 percent in 1994. The major oil companies cut expenditures on oil exploration by one third between 1985 and 1988. Although U.S. oil producers spent $14 billion per year on exploration in the early eighties, that figure had declined to $5.3 billion in 1992. Declining investment and growing domestic demand have sharply cut Mexican oil exports in the last decade. British and Norwegian production will decline in future years as the North Sea fields are exhausted. Falling investment levels, backward technology, and political instability have recently brought about a precipitous decline in oil production in the former Soviet Union. Russian production, which totaled 11.5 million barrels per day in 1988, had fallen to 7 million barrels by 1993 and declined a further 12 percent in 1994. Due to declining production and rising demand, some OPEC oil exporters, such as Qatar, Gabon, Nigeria, and Ecuador, are likely to produce only enough oil for their own consumption by the turn of the century. Thus the balance of power within OPEC seems likely to shift even more decisively in favor of the Persian Gulf states that possess enormous oil reserves. In 1990 five Persian Gulf states accounted for two thirds of the world's proven oil reserves. OPEC as a whole possessed 76 per-

---

[85] "The Cartel That Fell. . . ."

[86] Agis Salpukas, "Long-Term Oil Strain Seen," *New York Times*, October 31, 1994.

cent of global reserves, a figure that is expected to rise to 80 percent by the year 2000.[87]

Yet while OPEC's share of world oil production and sales seems destined to rise, this factor alone is unlikely to return OPEC to its glory days of the seventies and early eighties, when the organization engineered the massive transfer of wealth from oil-consuming countries to its member states through dramatic price hikes. Not only are prices expected to remain soft over the next decade, but also OPEC's ability to control overproduction by its own member states is in doubt.

Most observers predict that world demand for oil will grow only sluggishly through the end of the century and beyond. During the decade from 1993 to 2003, oil demand was expected to rise a total of 15 to 20 percent.[88] Economic growth is projected to proceed at a modest pace in the mature economies of the major oil-importing countries. What growth that does occur is unlikely to be associated with rising levels of energy consumption. As in recent decades, the share of energy-intensive, heavy-manufacturing industries in the overall economies of Northern countries will continue to dwindle, while the shift toward industries requiring relatively low inputs of energy, such as services and high technology, will continue apace.

Perhaps most importantly, ecological concerns about global warming are likely to spur efforts to reduce dependence upon fossil fuels. Carbon dioxide, a major product of burning hydrocarbons such as oil or coal, has been found to play a major role in exacerbating the greenhouse effect. Northern nations have pledged to stabilize or reduce carbon dioxide emissions over the next decade. Both conservation and fuel switching will be relied upon to achieve these goals. There remains great potential for conservation through the production of more-energy-efficient cars (including the growing use of electric-powered automobiles), appliances, homes, and factories.[89] Environmental concerns (along with security concerns about overreliance on foreign oil in the wake of the Persian Gulf War) have already renewed interest in renewable and nonfossil energy sources, including nuclear, solar, wind,[90] hydroelectric,

---

[87] The information in this paragraph has been taken from Mathew Wald, "Gulf Victory: An Energy Defeat?" *New York Times*, June 18, 1991; Saleh Billo, "Six OPEC Nations Have 70.5% of World's Proven Oil Reserves," *Oil and Gas Journal*, February 5, 1990; "The Cartel That Fell . . ."; Salpukas, "Long-Term . . ."; Agis Salpukas, "Oil Companies Shifting Exploration Overseas," *New York Times*, November 8, 1993; and Stanislaw and Yergin, "Oil: Reopening the Door."

[88] Stanislaw and Yergin, "Oil: Reopening the Door," 90.

[89] To offer but one example, sales of energy-efficient compact fluorescent lamps jumped fourfold between 1989 and 1995. These bulbs are four times more efficient than incandescent bulbs and last ten times longer. The increased use of fluorescent rather than incandescent bulbs over the six years cited saved a quantity of energy equal to the output of twenty-eight large coal plants. See Lester Brown, Nicholas Lenssen, and Hal Kane, *Vital Signs, 1995: The Trends That Are Shaping Our Future*, New York: W. W. Norton (Worldwatch Institute), 1995, 58-59.

[90] To cite two examples, production of wind power increased 22 percent in 1994 alone. Shipments of energy-producing photovoltaic solar cells rose 15 percent during the same year, while costs for such cells have declined 50 percent since 1985. See Brown, Lenssen, and Kane, *Vital Signs*, 54-55, 57-58.

biomass, and geothermal as well as natural gas, which is a relatively clean-burning hydrocarbon.[91] Moderate demand for additional oil in the North will, however, be partially offset by the increased energy needs of certain rapidly growing Southern countries. Oil demand in Asia, for instance, is expected to grow by five billion barrels per year over the next decade.[92]

On the supply side, onetime fears that the world might be running out of oil have been proven unfounded, at least for the foreseeable future. Indeed, between the early seventies and the early nineties, proven oil reserves doubled to over one trillion barrels.[93] New technology has expanded the potential for exploiting known, but previously inaccessible, oil resources. It is estimated, for instance, that the tar sands in the Alberta province of Canada contain oil deposits larger than the entire Middle Eastern oil reserves. Recent technological advances now suggest that it may be possible to extract oil from this dense, rocklike source at economically competitive prices.[94] The major constraint to expanding oil production lies in the huge investments required, combined with the weak incentives provided by low prices. Nevertheless, Western oil companies have begun to expand their activities in the many countries—such as Venezuela, Argentina, Colombia, Brazil, China, Vietnam, and Russia—that have recently lowered barriers to foreign investment in their oil industries or even begun to privatize formerly state-owned companies.

Thus although OPEC's share of the world oil market may indeed rise, overall energy demand is likely to grow only slowly, while oil use may actually fall as it fills a declining proportion of total energy needs. The supply of oil, meanwhile, is plentiful, assuming that the needed investment is forthcoming. Oil prices are unlikely to rise dramatically in this climate. In contrast with the eighties, however, when declining oil prices removed incentives for additional investments in conservation or alternative energy development, Northern governments will be inclined to mandate continued progress in these areas through the use of tax and regulatory policies.

OPEC's economic power is also threatened by serious internal division among member states. As they often have in the past, these deep fractures may well hamper future efforts to coordinate production and pricing policies—both prerequisites to maximizing the cartel's overall revenues. The most obvious divisions are political. There exist deep ideological and political differences between the conservative monarchical regimes of the Persian Gulf region, the radical Arab nationalist governments of Libya and Iraq, and the fundamentalist Islamic republic of Iran, a non-Arab country.

---

[91] A conservative estimate is that known natural gas reserves represent 145 years of supply at present levels of production, though actual reserves are probably much higher given that exploration has not been carried out in many parts of the globe. Some observers expect that natural gas will gradually replace oil in many uses and that gas production will exceed oil production by the year 2010. See Brown, Lenssen, and Kane, *Vital Signs*, 48–49.

[92] Stanislaw and Yergin, "Oil: Reopening the Door," 90.

[93] Stanislaw and Yergin, "Oil: Reopening the Door," 88.

[94] T. R. Stauffer, "Canada Is Ready to Exploit Huge Oil Reserves Locked in Sands," in Robert Jackson (ed.), *Annual Editions: Global Issues, 95/96* (11th ed.), Guilford, Conn.: Dushkin Publishing, 1995, 132.

The recent past has witnessed two instances of armed conflict among OPEC members, both instances involving Iraq. In each case, Iraqi aggression was partly motivated by considerations related to oil. The Iraqi invasion of Iran in 1980 was stimulated by Iraq's desire to gain exclusive control over a strategic waterway that lies astride the Iraqi–Iranian border. Lacking an adequate port along its short Persian Gulf coastline, Iraq sought a secure means by which it could off-load greater quantities of oil into tankers bound for Northern markets through the gulf. Iraq's violent attempt to solve this problem touched off an inconclusive eight-year war that claimed one million lives.

Oil also played a key role in Iraq's ill-fated decision to invade Kuwait in the summer of 1990. In the wake of its deadly war with Iran, Iraq faced huge reconstruction costs as well as an enormous foreign debt. Because the country exported little else aside from oil, Iraq's hopes for economic revival rested almost exclusively on its ability to obtain higher oil revenues. Kuwaiti behavior presented a serious obstacle to this goal. In the first half of 1990 Kuwait consistently produced more oil than allowed by its OPEC quota. The failure of Kuwait and several other OPEC members to observe agreed-upon limitations on their oil production frustrated Iraqi efforts to engineer a hike in the world price of oil. Kuwait also angered Iraq by refusing to compromise over a dispute in which Iraq charged that Kuwait pumped more than its fair share of oil from a major field straddling the border between Iraq and Kuwait. Finally, Kuwait refused to forgive the $10 billion debt that Iraq accumulated from loans used to finance its war with Iran.[95]

The conflict between Iraq and Kuwait over production and pricing policies reflects broader and more-enduring divisions among OPEC producers. OPEC has long been split between price "hawks" and price "doves." The former countries consistently push for higher oil prices, whereas the latter lobby for price moderation. With some exceptions, the doves, who include OPEC's most important member, Saudi Arabia, among their ranks, have generally won out in recent years.

The countries who favor higher prices share one or more of the following characteristics:

1. Dwindling oil reserves that are likely to be exhausted in the near- to medium-term future at historical levels of production
2. Large and growing populations
3. Relatively modest levels of investment in the wealthy oil-consuming countries of the North

---

[95] For more on the political divisions within the Arab world, as well as the factors that led to Iraq's invasion of Kuwait, see Yahya Sadowski, "Revolution, Reform or Regression? Arab Political Options in the 1990 Gulf Crisis," *The Brookings Review*, Winter 1990/91; Geraldine Brooks and Tony Horwitz, "Brotherly Hate: Gulf Crisis Underscores Historical Divisions in the Arab 'Family,'" *Wall Street Journal*, August 13, 1990; and "The Middle East: New Frictions, New Alignments," *Great Decisions*, New York: Foreign Policy Association, 1991. On the implications of the Gulf War for future energy security, see Robert Lieber, "Oil and Power After the Gulf War," in David N. Balaam and Michael Veseth (eds.), *Readings in International Political Economy*, Upper Saddle River, N.J.: Prentice-Hall, 1996.

These nations seek to maximize short-term revenues from a rapidly depleting resource while satisfying the demands for industrialization and a higher standard of living from large numbers of still relatively poor citizens.

OPEC members with abundant reserves, small populations, and extensive investments in the North have very different interests. For these countries, high prices would stimulate oil exploration, conservation, and fuel switching in the oil-consuming countries and thereby reduce the demand for oil in future decades. With small populations, these countries have a less urgent need to maximize present income. Moreover, as an increasing share of these nations' revenues comes from returns on foreign investment, they must worry that high oil prices might damage Northern economies and interrupt the flow of repatriated profits from abroad.

This division within OPEC overlaps with another: the split between integrated and nonintegrated producers. Several OPEC countries, including Venezuela, Saudi Arabia, Kuwait, and, to a lesser extent, Nigeria, have begun to aggressively integrate their oil production with the ownership of downstream operations, such as refining and retail sales, located in oil-consuming countries. Integrated producers not only desire the revenues from these downstream investments, but also seek to lock up outlets for the sale of their own crude oil, thus reducing future uncertainties over foreign demand.

Nonintegrated OPEC producers, such as Iran, Iraq, and Libya, who lack these downstream connections face the risk that they may become marginal producers in the future. In other words, these countries would service only that portion of demand left over after the integrated producers have disposed of their output through refineries and marketing networks abroad. Integrated producers can use their control of downstream operations to assure steady, predictable levels of production and sales, whereas nonintegrated producers are likely to find themselves unable to locate buyers for all of their output if supply should exceed demand.[96]

The aftermath of the Gulf War has left Saudi Arabia in a position of dominance within OPEC. Among the price hawks, Iraq has been defeated in war while Iran is eager to curry Saudi favor. Saudi Arabia vastly increased its oil output during the war in an effort to compensate for lost Iraqi and Kuwaiti production. Since the war's conclusion, Saudi leaders have been eager to maintain these high levels of production and the corresponding market share. In September 1991 the Saudis compelled other OPEC countries to agree to raise the official overall ceiling on OPEC production while rejecting proposals that Saudi exports be reduced in order to bolster oil prices. Saudi leaders appear to look forward to a long period of price moderation and stability in world oil markets as well as to closer cooperation with oil-importing countries.[97]

---

[96] Bob Williams, "OPEC Ventures Downstream: Industry Threat or Stability Aid?" *Oil and Gas Journal*, May 16, 1988.

[97] Youssef M. Ibrahim, "Oil Output Is Raised by OPEC," *New York Times*, September 26, 1991.

## Global and Regional Trade Agreements

Another form of collective effort to promote Southern development involves multilateral bargaining over the removal of barriers to mutual trade and investment. Southern countries pursue this path through both global and regional forums. In the global forum, groups of Third World countries often coordinate their demands in negotiations with the North over trade liberalization. In regional forums, Southern countries form smaller groupings that are intended to promote economic integration among member economies.[98] The following discussion addresses both settings.

## The Uruguay Round Agreement

The Uruguay Round global trade accord, signed in April 1994, will benefit Third World countries by lowering Northern barriers to Southern exports in the areas of agriculture, textiles, and clothing. On average, Third World exports to Japan and the European Union are expected to rise by 15 percent as a result of the Uruguay agreement.[99] Greater openness to trade may also force Third World producers to increase productivity as a means of remaining competitive on world markets. A study conducted jointly by the World Bank and the OECD Development Center claims that the Third World as a whole will experience yearly gains of $213 billion by 2002 as a result of changes brought about by the Uruguay Round. These gains are not, however, spread equally across the Third World. The study also concludes that Africa and the Caribbean, for instance, are likely to lose from the accord.[100]

A number of Third World countries have specific reasons for concern. Food importers might have to pay higher food prices as Northern countries withdraw agricultural subsidies and reduce the surpluses previously sold on world markets. The poorest Southern countries enjoyed privileged access to Northern markets prior to the Uruguay Round. This competitive advantage vis-à-vis wealthier Third World exporters has now been erased. Also, Third World countries will have to pay more to gain access to Northern technology as a result of tougher rules for protecting intellectual property rights.[101]

## Regional Free Trade Agreements

The trend toward regional economic integration among Southern countries has moved most quickly in Latin America. Free trade agreements among Latin

---

[98] Although the following discussion focuses on Latin America and Asia, some movement toward regional economic cooperation is also evident in Africa. See Robert Browne, "How Africa Can Prosper," in David N. Balaam and Michael Veseth (eds.), *Readings in International Political Economy*, Upper Saddle River, N.J.: Prentice-Hall, 1996.

[99] "China Wants to Join the Club," *The Economist*, May 14, 1994, 35.

[100] "For Richer, for Poorer," *The Economist*, December 18, 1993, 66.

[101] "For Richer, for Poorer," 66.

American countries are not new. The Andean Pact—comprised of Bolivia, Colombia, Ecuador, Peru, and Venezuela—and Caricom, which encompasses eight Caribbean nations, both date back to the 1970s. Recent agreements, however, are more comprehensive and far reaching. Mercosur, an accord that lowers trade and investment barriers among Brazil, Argentina, Uruguay, and Paraguay, went into effect on January 1, 1995. In anticipation of the agreement, trade between Brazil and Argentina tripled from 1990 to 1993. Mexico, Venezuela, and Colombia, the so-called Group of Three, have recently agreed to phase out trade barriers among their economies over the coming decade.

The movement toward economic integration in Latin America shows no signs of slowing. The Andean Pact countries are seeking a trade agreement with the Mercosur group. Ecuador is soon expected to join the Group of Three. Colombia plans to sign a free trade agreement with Caricom. Chile may soon become a member of Mercosur. And bilateral free trade arrangements have been concluded between Mexico and Bolivia, Chile and Peru, and Chile and Ecuador.

Led by Brazil, nineteen Latin American countries agreed in 1994 to seek to merge these various commercial arrangements into a single trade pact covering virtually all of the Latin American continent. The Latin American Integration Association and the United Nations Economic Commission on Latin America have been charged with the task of comparing and reconciling the complex provisions of the existing accords so as to pave the way for full Latin American integration. At the Miami Summit of the Americas in December 1994, the United States agreed to join these efforts with the aim of eventually creating a free trade regime spanning the entire hemisphere, North and South.[102]

Even before many of these plans are put into effect, Latin America's recent conversion to the gospel of free trade has reshaped the continent's economies. Between 1991 and 1993 average tariff levels in Latin America dropped from 26 percent to 12 percent. For ten South American countries and Mexico, intraregional exports increased from 11 percent of total exports in 1989 to 19.2 percent in 1993. Between 1987 and 1992 Latin American exports grew an average of 10 percent per year in real terms. Economies that were selectively sheltered from international competition and trade are being transformed and restructured as they are increasingly integrated into the global economy.[103]

The most controversial regional trade agreement involving Latin America has been the North American Free Trade Agreement (NAFTA), which provides

---

[102] Information contained in the previous three paragraphs has been drawn from James Brooke, "The New South Americans: Friends and Partners," *New York Times*, April 8, 1994; James Brooke, "Latins Envision a Single Trade Zone," *New York Times*, June 17, 1994; James Brooke, "On Eve of Miami Summit Talks, US Comes Under Fire," *New York Times*, December 9, 1994; and Haggard, *Developing Nations and the Politics of Global Integration*, 75-99.

[103] "Reforming Latin America," *The Economist*, November 26, 1994; Shahid Javed Burki and Sebastian Edwards, "Consolidating Economic Reforms in Latin America and the Caribbean," *Finance and Development*, March 1995.

for the gradual removal of most barriers to the movement of trade and investment among the United States, Canada, and Mexico. NAFTA, which took effect on January 1, 1994, after contentious ratification debates in all three countries, represented an extension of the earlier U.S.-Canada trade agreement completed in 1988. Besides addressing trade and investment, NAFTA and associated side agreements address issues such as intellectual property rights, the treatment of labor, and environmental standards.

Mexican President Carlos Salinas served as the driving force behind NAFTA. Salinas believed that Mexico's traditionally inward-looking and nationalistic development strategy had led to the economic crisis of the 1980s, featuring a crushing debt load and a sharp economic contraction. He therefore embraced and accelerated the neoliberal, or market- and export-oriented, policies of his predecessor, President Miguel de la Madrid. Salinas hoped that NAFTA would establish Mexico as a magnet for foreign investment, thus spurring economic recovery. A rebounding economy, in turn, would allow Mexico's longtime ruling party, the Institutional Revolutionary Party (PRI), to regain the prestige and authority that it had lost over the previous decade. In particular, Salinas sought to fend off the challenge posed by an invigorated Mexican left, which mounted a strong electoral showing in the 1988 presidential election. NAFTA would galvanize popular support around the image of a new, more "modern" Mexico. It would also serve to "lock in" the neoliberal policy shift championed by Salinas and make it difficult for successors to undo his legacy.

During the first year of NAFTA's implementation, U.S.-Mexican trade boomed, and foreign investors flocked to Mexico. The biggest beneficiaries were those associated with Mexico's manufacturing export industries, located mostly along the border in the North. Mexicans from the poorer, rural southern part of the country, however, suffered from an influx of cheaper American grain and other agricultural goods. The anger of Mexico's peasants caused by this threat to their livelihood was symbolized by the opening of a guerrilla campaign launched by the Zapatista National Liberation Front, based in the southern state of Chiapas. The Zapatistas carried out their first armed attacks on Mexican authorities on the day that NAFTA took effect, underlining the central role that the agreement played in spurring rebellion.

The long-term effects of NAFTA on Mexico are difficult to discern at present. Roughly one year after NAFTA was implemented, Mexico suffered a severe financial crisis, involving a steep drop in the value of the peso and massive capital flight (see Chapter 12). The austerity measures taken to restore financial stability plunged Mexico into a deep economic recession, from which it was still emerging a year later. Although NAFTA did not cause Mexico's peso crisis, it may have played a contributing role by encouraging unrealistically large flows of capital into the country, thus allowing authorities to mask Mexico's large trade imbalance and the overvaluation of its currency.

Most economists expect that NAFTA will bring positive benefits to most Mexicans in the long run, after the present crisis is past. Still, it is clear that

NAFTA represents neither a magic cure for Mexico's underlying economic troubles nor a guarantee against economic instability.

Economic integration has occurred more slowly in East Asia.[104] The greatest progress has been made by subregional groupings. The most important of these is the Association of Southeast Asian Nations (ASEAN), which includes Thailand, Indonesia, the Philippines, Malaysia, Brunei, and Singapore. In 1992 ASEAN members agreed to gradually reduce or remove trade barriers among their economies. Other bilateral or subregional trade liberalization arrangements have been concluded among various East Asian nations.

It appears unlikely, however, that an exclusively Asian economic bloc encompassing the entire region will emerge.[105] In 1993 Malaysia advanced a proposal for such an organization, to be called the East Asian Economic Grouping. Notably, this bloc would have excluded the United States, Australia, and New Zealand. The United States expressed sharp disapproval, and most Asian nations, including Japan, showed little enthusiasm for the idea. The proposed members settled instead for a much looser East Asian Economic Caucus, which would serve as a consultative group to coordinate bargaining demands in global trade negotiations.

The cool response to Malaysia's proposal reflected several factors. Many East Asian nations depend heavily upon exports to markets outside the region, especially the United States. A free trade arrangement that excludes these target markets holds limited appeal. Also, a purely East Asian trade bloc would likely be dominated by Japan, raising historically based fears among those Asian nations who once suffered under Japanese colonial rule.

The largest and perhaps most promising regional trade organization to encompass East Asia is the Asian-Pacific Economic Cooperation (APEC) forum, created at Australia's initiative in 1988. In addition to Asian nations such as Japan, China, South Korea, Hong Kong, Taiwan, Australia, and New Zealand, APEC includes Pacific Rim countries from the Western Hemisphere, including the United States, Canada, Mexico, and Chile. Largely ineffectual during its initial years, APEC gathered momentum when a series of initiatives was passed at its 1993 and 1994 summit meetings. At the 1994 event, APEC members agreed to move toward full free trade by the year 2020. APEC nations also agreed to explore other integration measures, such as a regional investment code and the harmonization of product and environmental standards.

At APEC's 1995 meeting, member nations agreed to pursue the lowering of trade barriers through voluntary measures, forgoing the legal commitments involved in a more formal agreement. By the 1996 meeting, each government was to have unveiled a set of unilateral trade measures designed to bring about greater economic openness. This unique method for pursuing

---

[104] The following discussion of Asian regional economic cooperation relies upon Haggard, *Developing Nations and the Politics of Global Integration*, 62-74; and Richard Higgott and Richard Stubbs, "Competing Conceptions of Economic Regionalism: APEC versus EAEC in the Asia Pacific," *Review of International Political Economy*, Summer 1995.

[105] For a similar conclusion, see Karl J. Fields, "Circling the Wagons: The Trend Toward Economic Regionalism and Its Consequences for Asia," 1

multilateral liberalization promises to lead to speedier progress that would be possible through the slow and tortuous negotiation of a formal treaty. Yet this nonbinding approach will allow states to continue protection of politically sensitive sectors and may result in uneven progress across countries. Liberalization is likely to be less universal than a more formal approach might produce. Ultimately, APEC's future success will be determined by its ability to bridge the vast cultural, political, and economic differences among its members. It remains uncertain whether such a large, diverse, and geographically far-flung grouping can function as a unified or coherent economic bloc.[106]

The movements toward economic integration in Latin America and Asia have given rise to very different conceptions about the rationale and goals underlying these developments. For some, the goals of Southern regional cooperation are to encourage South–South trade, lessen dependence upon the North, gain greater Southern leverage in global economic negotiations, improve the South's bargaining position vis-à-vis Northern corporations, and promote Southern political unity. Others advocate a form of integration that ties groups of Southern countries to regionally dominant Northern countries, so as to facilitate Northern investment flows and ensure greater and continuing access to Northern markets.

The first model, represented by the Andean Pact in Latin America and by Malaysia's proposal for an East Asian Economic Grouping, seeks to weaken the ties of Southern dependence upon the North and to encourage greater Southern autonomy. The second model, represented by NAFTA in Latin America and by APEC in Asia, reinforces such dependence, though on terms that its advocates promise will be more favorable to the South. Although both models share some features, they lead to potentially different patterns of trade, investment, and political cooperation. Which vision prevails will help to determine the nature of North–South ties in the twenty-first century.

## CONCLUSIONS

As is evident from this overview, Third World states have pursued a variety of development paths. It should also be clear that no single model or strategy of development is appropriate for all countries or all times. Progress toward economic prosperity is dependent upon the right fit or mix among three sets of factors:

1. The internal economic, political, and cultural attributes of a given country
2. The opportunities and constraints provided by the international political economy
3. The policy choices made by governing elites

---

[106] Andrew Pollack, "In a Move to Open Its Markets, China Pledges to Cut Tariffs on 4,000 Items Next Year," *New York Times*, November 20, 1995.

Analysts are often led astray by focusing on the latter of these three, the choice of development strategy, in isolation from the first two. Yet policies that lack domestic political support or that are poorly tailored to a country's specific mix of economic resources are unlikely to succeed. Similarly, the continuing evolution of the international economic system means that policies that are feasible and desirable during one period may become less so as time goes on.

**TABLE 9.1**
**Strategies of Development**

|                          |                           | Orientation | |
| ------------------------ | ------------------------- | --------------------------- | --------------------------- |
|                          |                           | Inward | Outward |
|                          | Raw Materials/ Agriculture | Pre-colonial/ Subsistence | Colonial Trade Resource Cartels |
| Type of Production       |                           | | |
|                          | Manufacturing             | ISI | ELI |

The notion that policy success is dependent upon supportive domestic and international conditions is reinforced by the evidence reviewed in this chapter. Among major Latin American countries, the shift to ISI was prompted by the disruptions in international trade produced by the Great Depression and World War II. These policies were sustained after the war by the rise of nationalist political movements at home. The initial stage of ISI proved successful until its growth potential was exhausted due to the limited domestic market for consumer goods. The deepening phase of ISI was accompanied by the emergence of authoritarian governments and growing international indebtedness. The internal contradictions of ISI, combined with unfavorable international economic conditions during the late seventies and early eighties, set the stage for a lost decade of economic stagnation in Latin America. The harsh realities of the eighties prompted the abandonment of ISI in many countries by the end of the decade and initiated a trend toward more-liberal economic strategies with still-uncertain consequences.

The East Asian NICs passed through brief ISI stages before shifting to ELI strategies in the early sixties. Domestic and international conditions proved favorable to the success of such strategies. Rising wage levels in the North made it possible for the first wave of export-led industrializers to target Northern markets for labor-intensive goods. The growing openness of the world economy combined with rapid economic expansion in the North also offered a congenial environment for ELI. Domestically, the East Asian countries featured strong, autonomous states free of serious challenges from either organized labor or landed elites. Technocratic bureaucracies were given the power to orchestrate state intervention so as to upgrade the levels of technology and skills in the economy and to target capital toward promising export industries. International and domestic factors thus supported a strategy of ELI. Whether other countries now attempting to emulate the success of the East Asian NICs will enjoy similar supportive internal and external conditions remains to be seen.

For decades, the oil-producing countries proved unable to fully exploit the economic potential of their vast petroleum reserves. Domestically, these countries lacked the skills, capital, and political will necessary to curb their dependence upon the major international oil companies. Internationally, the lack of coordination among producing countries, the glut of oil on world markets, and the political influence of Northern consuming countries all weighed against the efforts of producing countries to boost oil revenues. These circumstances began to change in the sixties, leading to OPEC's spectacular successes of the seventies. Shifting market conditions, combined with disunity among oil producers during the eighties, partially eroded the gains made during the seventies.

This suggests that it can be misleading to think of Third World development in terms of "models" that can be evaluated in the abstract and adopted or abandoned at will by given states. Instead, development strategies evolve historically, and their success or failure must be considered in light of the particular circumstances facing particular countries. It is not policy alone, but rather the fit between an overall strategy of development and the domestic, as well as international, factors confronting public and private decision makers, that determines the path of economic development.

## ANNOTATED BIBLIOGRAPHY

Robert Alexander, "Import Substitution in Latin America in Retrospect," in James L. Dietz and Dilmus D. James (eds.), *Progress Toward Development in Latin America: From Prebisch to Technological Autonomy*, Boulder: Lynne Rienner, 1991. Provides a historical overview and evaluation of Latin America's experience with import substitution industrialization.

Bela Balassa, *Economic Policies in the Pacific Area Developing Countries*, New York: New York University Press, 1991. Balassa, a well-known liberal economist, attributes the success of the East Asian newly industrializing countries less to government industrial policy than to sound macroeconomic policies and high savings rates. He thus differs from those writers who characterize the economic strategies of these countries as mercantilist.

Waldo Bello and Stephanie Rosenfeld, *Dragons in Distress: Asia's Miracle Economies in Crisis*, San Francisco: the Institute for Food and Development Policy, 1992. The authors explore the less favorable aspects of rapid growth in the East Asian newly industrializing countries. These include environmental destruction, political authoritarianism, and the repression of labor. They criticize the view that East Asia should serve as a model for other parts of the South.

Robin Broad and John Cavanaugh, "No More NICs," *Foreign Policy*, Fall 1988.

The authors argue that the success of the export-oriented industrializers of East Asia will not be easily duplicated by other Third World countries. They outline an alternative path of development.

Thomas M. Callaghy and John Ravenhill (eds.), *Hemmed In: Responses to Africa's Economic Decline*, New York: Columbia University Press, 1993.

A collection of essays, including both country and sectoral studies, focusing on how African governments and firms have attempted to cope with the prolonged economic downturn of the past two decades.

Frederic C. Deyo (ed.), *The Political Economy of the New Asian Industrialism*, Ithaca: Cornell University Press, 1987.

An excellent collection of essays on the political factors underlying the economic strategies of the East Asian newly industrializing countries.

Stephan Haggard, *Pathways from the Periphery: The Politics of Growth in the Newly Industrializing Countries*, Ithaca: Cornell University Press, 1990.

An informative and provocative comparison of the development strategies pursued by the newly industrializing countries of East Asia and Latin America. Haggard emphasizes the role of external crises, state-society relations, and development ideas in determining the policy choices made by state officials, as well as their consequences.

Stephan Haggard, *Developing Nations and the Politics of Global Integration*, Washington, D.C.: Brookings, 1995.

Examines the political dynamics underlying the formation of regional trade and investment pacts among Southern nations.

Robert Mortimer, *The Third World Coalition in International Politics*, Boulder: Westview Press, 1984.

A comprehensive and detailed history of the rise and fall of the Third World's quest for a New International Economic Order.

Barbara Stallings (ed.), *Global Change, Regional Response: The New International Context of Development*, Cambridge: Cambridge University Press, 1995.

A collection of essays that examines how countries in different Third World regions have adapted their development strategies in response to recent global changes, including the end of the Cold War, increased competition among the developed countries, new patterns in trade and production, the globalization of international finance, and new ideological currents.

Robert Wade, *Governing the Market: Economic Theory and the Role of Government in East Asian Industrialization*, Princeton: Princeton University Press, 1990.

Wade credits government intervention as a significant cause of rapid economic development in the East Asian newly industrializing countries. A very sophisticated and lucid treatment of the topic.

Marc Williams, *Third World Cooperation: The Group of 77 in UNCTAD*, New York: St. Martin's, 1991.

A historical account of the efforts of Third World countries to bring about a New International Economic Order.

Daniel Yergin, *The Prize*, New York: Simon and Schuster, 1991.

This is a classic study of the politics and economics of oil. Written by a noted historian and energy analyst, this especially well-written and accessible treatment makes for fascinating reading. Contains an extensive discussion of OPEC.

# Chapter 10

# FOREIGN AID AND THIRD WORLD DEVELOPMENT

Conceived of a marriage between idealism and self-interest, the world heralded the birth of foreign aid almost half a century ago.[1] Great things were expected of aid, not least of which was the conquest of world poverty. At present, however, foreign aid has settled into a beleaguered middle age, marked by unfulfilled dreams and scaled-down expectations. Sapped of their youthful spirit, many aid agencies find themselves engaged in a lonely battle to defend their very existence against legions of critics.

The high hopes that once surrounded foreign aid stemmed from its early accomplishments. Seeking to kick-start a slumping world economy and contain the spread of communism and Soviet influence, the United States poured 2.5 percent of its GNP into the reconstruction of Western Europe between 1947 and 1951.[2] Dubbed the Marshall Plan, U.S. assistance proved critical in hastening Western European recovery from the devastation of World War II.

Motivated by humanitarian impulses as well as pragmatic economic and security interests, the United States sought to replicate this success by expanding foreign aid to the developing world during the fifties. The Point Four program, established in 1951 to provide technical assistance, was followed by the creation of the Development Loan Fund (a precursor of the present-day Agency for International Development), extending concessional financing for development projects and programs in Third World countries.

Meanwhile, the International Bank for Reconstruction and Development (IBRD), or World Bank, also began to shift its emphasis from European reconstruction to Third World development. A World Bank affiliate called the International Development Agency (IDA), which provided long-term, interest-free loans to finance development in the world's poorest countries, was created in

---

[1] Foreign aid takes many different forms. Some are beyond the scope of this chapter. We give little attention, for instance, to foreign military aid or to assistance provided by private voluntary organizations. Our focus is on official economic assistance.

[2] World Bank, *World Development Report, 1985*, New York: Oxford University Press, 1985, 94.

1960. The specialized agencies of the United Nations, such as the Food and Agricultural Organization and the World Health Organization, also grew in number and size during the fifties and sixties.[3]

Alongside the expansion of these multilateral agencies came the establishment of aid organizations in the developed nations of Western Europe and elsewhere. During the next twenty years, the bilateral assistance programs of these donors grew much faster than that of the United States. Whereas the United States accounted for 60 percent of the bilateral assistance provided by all member countries of the Development Assistance Council (DAC) at the time of the organization's founding in 1961, the U.S. contribution dropped to 17 percent of the total by 1993.[4] The seventies also brought tremendous growth in the foreign assistance provided by a number of newly wealthy OPEC countries. During the eighties, Japan rapidly expanded its foreign assistance, surpassing the United States to become the world's largest aid donor by the end of the decade.[5] By the early nineties, official development assistance to the South had grown to over $60 billion per year.[6] An immense network of organizations and bureaucracies had evolved to administer this large flow of funds. Many of the world's poorest nations had become inextricably dependent upon outside aid.

Yet, faith in aid has diminished even while the flow of assistance has increased. Early hopes that the success of the Marshall Plan could be duplicated in the Third World were soon dashed by the realization that Southern countries lacked not only capital and financing, but also a myriad of other necessary prerequisites to development, including economic infrastructure, skilled and educated populations, competent bureaucracies, stable governments, and experienced entrepreneurs. A greater appreciation of the enormous challenges of Third World development dictated a more modest and reserved set of expectations toward foreign aid.

Yet, this was not the only source of disappointment. Critics increasingly questioned the purposes, philosophy, and methods of those who dispensed and received development assistance. Some charge that aid is a tool for

---

[3] On the United Nations agencies, see Douglas Williams, *The Specialized Agencies and the United Nations: The System in Crisis*, London: C. Hurst & Co., 1987. Note that aid is dispensed through both bilateral and multilateral agencies. Each major donor country runs its own bilateral aid program, which provides money, food, and technical advice directly to individual recipient nations. A number of multilateral agencies, including the World Bank; the three major regional development banks in Latin America, Africa, and Asia; and the specialized agencies of the United Nations, provide development assistance funded through member contributions and other means. Bilateral aid accounts for almost two thirds of overall foreign assistance, with multilateral programs making up 22 percent. The remaining 14 percent is funneled through nongovernmental organizations that raise many of their funds privately. *World Development Report, 1990*, 128.

[4] The DAC is an affiliate of the Organization for Economic Cooperation and Development (OECD), which includes most major donor countries. *World Development Report, 1985*, 94; and "Trends in Development Assistance," *AID Fact Sheet*, 1995.

[5] Anthony Rowley, "Flush with Funds," *Far Eastern Economic Review*, December 29, 1988, 52; and "Foreign Aid: Stingy Sam," *The Economist*, March 25, 1989, 26.

[6] "Trends in Development Assistance," *AID Fact Sheet*, 1995.

serving the political and economic interests of donor countries. Moreover, aid props up repressive Third World governments, worsens inequality, and destroys the environment.[7] Others attack aid as a needless and costly subsidy that sustains bloated Third World bureaucracies and discourages recipient governments from carrying out needed policy reforms or supporting private sector growth.[8] Both left and right condemn the inefficiency and corruption that too often plague foreign aid.

The American public holds decidedly mixed views toward foreign aid. A survey conducted in January 1995 revealed that a large majority of respondents felt that the U.S. government spends too much on foreign aid and favored cuts in aid spending. The same survey also found, however, that Americans vastly overestimate the proportion of federal spending devoted to foreign assistance. Although in fact development aid constitutes only 0.4 percent of government spending in the U.S., the median estimate offered by survey respondents placed aid expenditures at 15 percent of the budget. Over 86 percent of respondents believed that the U.S. spent more than other countries on aid. Yet the U.S. actually ranks last among 24 major donor countries in aid as a percentage of GDP. When informed as to the actual share of government spending accounted for by aid, only 18 percent of respondents still thought existing aid levels were too high.

The survey also discovered that humanitarian rationales for aid attract the strongest support. Americans are less inclined to favor aid programs that are designed to reward friendly countries or to win economic benefits for U.S. business. Military aid is also quite unpopular. But majorities ranging from 74 percent to 91 percent want to maintain or increase aid devoted to ends such as child survival, humanitarian relief, repairing the environment, family planning, and long-term economic development. There exists strong support for targeting aid toward the poorest countries. Americans are skeptical, however, that aid actually reaches those who need it or achieves humanitarian aims. Roughly 80 percent of respondents believed that too much aid went to undemocratic regimes, that aid is plagued by waste and corruption and that foreign assistance programs often foster dependence on the part of recipients.[9]

Systematic data on Third World attitudes toward foreign aid are scarce, but anecdotal evidence of frustration abounds. Popular movements have arisen to protest the social dislocations and environmental destruction that have

---

[7] For two examples among many, see Theresa Hayter and Catherine Watson, *Aid: Rhetoric and Reality*, London: Pluto Press, 1985; and Frances Moore Lappe, Joseph Collins, and David Kenley, *Aid as Obstacle: Twenty Questions About Our Foreign Aid and the Hungry*, San Francisco: Institute for Food and Development Policy, 1981.

[8] See, for instance, P. T. Bauer, *Reality and Rhetoric: Studies in the Economics of Development*, Cambridge: Harvard University Press, 1984, especially Chapters 3 and 4, 38–72; and Nick Eberstadt, "The Perversion of Foreign Aid," *Commentary*, June 1985.

[9] All public opinion data from Steven Krull, *Americans and Foreign Aid: A Study of American Public Attitudes*, College Park: Program on International Policy Attitudes, 1995. Also see Christine Contee, *What Americans Think: Views on Development and U.S.-Third World Relations*, Interaction and Overseas Development Council, 1987.

accompanied huge aid-funded projects in Brazil, India, and Indonesia. Widespread resentment over the suspected misuse and theft of aid funds played a role in the political upheavals that forced Ferdinand Marcos from power in the Philippines. The unpopular policy reforms demanded of major debtor countries in recent years by bilateral and multilateral donors as a condition for further funding have prompted rioting in various countries. In a small, but perhaps symbolic, incident which occurred in 1985, Haitian peasants waved machetes in an attempt to fend off U.S. helicopters attempting to deliver food aid. These farmers acted out of fear that cheap foreign food would depress prices and undermine their livelihood.[10]

These critical responses to the growth of foreign aid are not surprising. Indeed, the emotionally charged debate over aid may flow inevitably from the fundamental nature of foreign assistance. Aid's very existence can be traced to the persistent gap between rich and poor in the world economy. From a Third World standpoint, aid is often viewed as a poor substitute for structural reforms in the international economic order, which might more directly reduce this inequality between the haves and have nots of the world. Moreover, stark contrasts inevitably arise between the humanitarian declarations used to justify aid and the political as well as economic motives that govern the allocation of assistance. This clash between rhetoric and reality leaves aid-givers vulnerable to charges of hypocrisy. Finally, although aid may, on the whole, make a modest contribution to Third World development and poverty reduction, it also fosters dependence. The relationship between donor and recipient, never an equal one, is almost certain to provoke resentment and provide opportunities for manipulation.[11]

The remainder of this chapter examines various controversies surrounding the relationship between aid and development. After a brief discussion of the different types and strategies of aid giving, we explore the effectiveness of foreign assistance in spurring economic growth, reducing poverty, and enhancing environmental sustainability in the Third World.

## THE RATIONALE FOR AID

The rationale for aid rests upon its presumed superiority, in some respects, over private financial flows as an instrument for furthering Third World development. The World Bank cites the advantages foreign assistance offers in promoting both efficiency and equity.[12]

---

[10] Lloyd Timberlake, "The Politics of Food Aid," in Edward Goldsmith and Nicholas Hildyard (eds.), *Earth Report: Monitoring the Battle for Our Environment*, Mitchell Brazley, 1988, 24.

[11] For a general discussion of the tensions between aid givers and recipients, see the chapter entitled "Donors, Recipients and the Aid Giving Process" in Jeffrey Pressman, *Federal Programs and City Politics*, Berkeley: University of California Press, 1975.

[12] See *World Development Report, 1985*, 99–100.

**TABLE 10.1**

**Official Development Assistance by OECD Countries, 1991**

|  | MILLIONS OF U.S. DOLLARS | AS PERCENTAGE OF DONOR GNP |
|---|---|---|
| Ireland | 72 | 0.19 |
| New Zealand | 100 | 0.25 |
| Australia | 1,000 | 0.38 |
| United Kingdom | 3,248 | 0.32 |
| Italy | 3,352 | 0.30 |
| Netherlands | 2,517 | 0.88 |
| Canada | 3,604 | 0.45 |
| Belgium | 831 | 0.42 |
| Finland | 930 | 0.76 |
| France | 7,484 | 0.62 |
| Austria | 548 | 0.34 |
| Germany | 6,890 | 0.41 |
| United States | 11,262 | 0.20 |
| Norway | 1,178 | 1.14 |
| Denmark | 1,200 | 0.96 |
| Sweden | 2,116 | 0.92 |
| Japan | 10,952 | 0.32 |
| Switzerland | 863 | 0.36 |

SOURCE: World Bank, *World Development Report, 1994*, New York: Oxford University Press, 1994, 196.

Official aid, according to the World Bank, finances certain types of projects that promise large social and economic returns but, nevertheless, seldom attract the interest of private capital. These include investments in health, education, agricultural research, and basic infrastructure. Many such projects pay off only over thirty- to forty-year periods, a time frame longer than most private investors are willing to accommodate. Moreover, some types of technical assistance and policy advice provided by official aid institutions are simply unavailable through private sources. Aid's principal role in development is to complement, rather than substitute for, the private sector. The desired result is a more well-rounded and efficient pattern of economic growth. Aid is also justified on equity grounds. Because most aid is provided on concessional terms, poorer countries gain access to resources that they would otherwise find unaffordable. Similarly, without the subsidies made possible by concessional assistance, the poor within recipient countries would be unable to pay the full costs for the services they receive.

## STRATEGIES OF FOREIGN ASSISTANCE

The basic strategies and philosophies of development underlying foreign aid have shifted markedly over time. We can distinguish among five major approaches. A top-down model, pursued most vigorously during the fifties and sixties, sought to stimulate Third World development through the provision of infrastructure and technical advice. The seventies brought a more egalitarian "bottom-up" strategy, designed to combine "growth with equity" through investment in the poor. During the eighties, attention shifted to the strengthening of market mechanisms. New conditions placed on aid encouraged governments to remove barriers to trade and foreign investment, encourage private sector growth, and adopt more orthodox economic policies. The nineties have witnessed an emphasis on sustainable development and preservation of the environment. Finally, aid agencies have begun to incorporate democracy promotion programs alongside their traditional missions.[13]

Early approaches to foreign aid were consistent with the theories of modernization then in vogue. Development was equated with industrialization and the expansion of the largely urban-based "modern" sectors of Third World economies at the expense of the "traditional" rural sectors. Most lending went to state-owned infrastructural projects, including such items as dams, roads, electrical grids, communications networks, and port facilities. The inadequacy of infrastructural development was considered a critical bottleneck to Third World growth and industrialization. Once this constraint had been overcome, economic growth would proceed according to the comparative advantage of various Third World countries.

This strategy relied heavily upon the creation of conditions likely to attract foreign investment. Multinational corporations would be enticed by cheap labor, abundant raw materials, and a growing Third World consumer market. Technical advice played a key role in providing state bureaucrats and local entrepreneurs with the skills and knowledge needed to manage a modern economy.

Agriculture took a back seat to industry, and the rural population was viewed primarily as an enormous reserve of potential wage labor, to be tapped gradually over time according to the expanding demands of the modern sector. Nevertheless, traditional agricultural exports were counted upon to generate foreign exchange that, in turn, could be put toward the importation of needed capital goods. Thus subsistence farmers producing basic food

---

[13] For useful overviews of the history of foreign aid and the shifting strategies of assistance, see Robert Packenham, *Liberal America and the Third World: Political Development Ideas in Foreign Aid and Social Science*, Princeton: Princeton University Press, 1973; *World Development Report, 1985*, 94–99; Robert Wood, *From Marshall Plan to Debt Crisis: Foreign Aid and Development Choices in the World Economy*, Berkeley: University of California Press, 1986; Stephen Hellinger, Douglas Hellinger, and Fred M. O'Regan, *Aid for Just Development: Report on the Future of Foreign Assistance*, Boulder: Lynne Rienner Publishers, 1988, 13–32; and Brice Nissen, "Building the World Bank," in Steven Wasserman (ed.), *The Trojan Horse: A Radical Look at Foreign Aid*, Berkeley: Ramparts Press, 1974.

staples for their own consumption were encouraged to switch to specialized commodities that could be marketed abroad.

Although this strategy succeeded in stimulating industrialization in many countries, it became apparent, by the late sixties, that the benefits of modernization were not trickling down to the poor majority as its proponents had hoped and had promised. In some countries, such as Brazil, income inequality worsened considerably, and the bottom 40 percent to 60 percent ended up both relatively and absolutely worse off than before.

These considerations led to a rethinking of traditional wisdom during the seventies. Under the leadership of Robert McNamara (1968–81), the World Bank, working particularly through its "soft" loan affiliate, the International Development Agency, began to focus more directly on eliminating the sources of Third World poverty.[14] This orientation was often referred to under the label of "growth with equity." Around the same time, the U.S. Congress passed "New Directions" legislation designed to refocus the work of the Agency for International Development (AID) toward the needs of the poor majority. The Foreign Assistance Act of 1973 directed that AID place greatest emphasis on "countries and activities which effectively involve the poor in development. . . ."[15] Many European countries followed suit.[16]

Concerns about equity were not the only ones driving this new attention to the plight of the poor. It was expected that poor people, if given the proper training and resources, could become productive contributors to development rather than drags upon it. This belief undergirded the two principal components of the new growth with equity strategy. The first was an emphasis on satisfying the basic needs of poor rural and urban dwellers. Proponents of this approach argued that the poor cannot become economically productive as long as they are afflicted by illness, malnutrition, illiteracy, inadequate shelter, and the lack of access to clean water supplies. Without these basic needs, the poor become locked in a continuing cycle of poverty, unable to earn a livelihood or to improve their economic circumstances.[17]

The second component of the strategy followed from the first. After the poor were secure in their basic needs, they required new opportunities to begin providing for themselves and contributing to the remainder of society. The role of aid was to fund expanded education programs, agricultural extension schemes, rural cooperatives, small business development, and other projects designed to enhance the economic productivity of the poor.

---

[14] For an examination of the World Bank policies toward the poor during the McNamara years, see Robert L. Ayres, *Banking on the Poor: The World Bank and World Poverty*, Cambridge: MIT Press, 1983.

[15] Hellinger, Hellinger, and O'Regan, *Aid for Just Development*, 22. Also on the impact of the "New Directions" legislation, see Robert L. Curry, "The Basic Needs Strategy, the Congressional Mandate, and U.S. Foreign Aid Policy," *Journal of Economic Issues*, December 1989.

[16] See Steven Arnold, *Implementing Development Assistance: European Approaches to Basic Needs*, Boulder: Westview Press, 1982.

[17] For a discussion of basic needs, see Paul Streeten and Chahid Javed Burki, "Basic Needs: Some Issues," *World Development*, vol. 6, no. 3, 1978.

Aid officials who embraced this growth with equity strategy rejected calls for more far-reaching efforts to redistribute wealth and income. The emphasis remained on growth. New-style investments were expected to produce economic returns as high or higher than more traditional projects.[18] Greater equity would emerge as a by-product of this strategy, however, as the retargeting of investment priorities allowed the poor to lay claim to larger increments of future growth.

This bottom-up approach to development drew criticism from a number of different directions. Some argued that, despite rhetoric about investing in human resources, the new lending programs did little more than subsidize consumption by the poor. Such "welfare" programs created only dependence, without providing the poor with the means to provide for themselves.

Others suggested that the aid community's new emphasis on aiding the poor amounted to less than met the eye. Poverty-oriented lending by the World Bank increased from 5 percent to 30 percent of total disbursements during the seventies. Yet this left 70 percent of the bank's funds devoted to traditional projects. Moreover, some critics charged that much of the money allocated for the poor actually benefited those who were already relatively well-off in Third World societies, either because elites found ways of siphoning off aid for their own uses or because aid agencies used too sweeping a definition of who counted as poor.

In any case, enthusiasm for the new focus on poverty waned with the replacement of McNamara as head of the World Bank and the election of Ronald Reagan as president in the United States. Both the World Bank and AID shifted priorities during the eighties.[19] Previous approaches to foreign aid, it was argued, placed too little emphasis on the encouragement of free markets and private enterprise. The centerpiece of the new strategy designed to correct this oversight became known as "policy dialogue."

The World Bank began to expand program and structural adjustment lending. These loans were not tied to specific projects, as in the past, but instead provided budgetary or balance of payments support. To qualify for such loans,

---

[18] A study by the Overseas Development Council, based upon World Bank data through the early eighties, suggests that poverty-oriented World Bank projects performed better than nonpoverty projects along a variety of economic criteria, including overall return on investment. Moreover, repayment rates were as high for poverty projects as for nonpoverty projects. Education directed at the poor offered the highest gains. See Sheldon Annis, "The Shifting Grounds of Poverty Lending at the World Bank," in Richard Feinberg (ed.), *Between Two Worlds: The World Bank's Next Decade*, New Brunswick: Transaction Books, 1986.

[19] For discussions of these changing priorities at the World Bank and AID during the eighties, see Clive Crook, "The World Bank," *The Economist*, September 27, 1986; John Sewell and Christine Contee, "U.S. Foreign Aid in the 1980s: Reordering Priorities," in John Sewell, Richard Feinberg, and V. Kallab (eds.), *U.S. Foreign Policy and the Third World*, New Brunswick: Transaction Books, 1985; Christopher Madison, "Exporting Reaganomics–The President Wants to Do Things Differently at AID," *National Journal*, May 5, 1982; Christine Contee, "U.S. Foreign Aid in the 1980s," *Policy Focus* (published by the Overseas Development Council), no. 4, 1985; Joel Johnson, "Foreign Aid: The Reagan Legacy," *Policy Focus* (published by the Overseas Development Council), no. 2, 1988.

however, governments were required to agree to policy reforms designed to reduce the state's role in the economy. These policy adjustments included the privatization of state-owned enterprises, decreased social welfare subsidies, trimmer government budget deficits, lower trade barriers, and the elimination of regulations that discouraged foreign investment. These demands were justified on the grounds that heavy state intervention stifled economic growth and that aid provided leverage to correct such impediments to development.[20] Indeed, as traditional aid has declined in relative importance as a source of new capital for Third World countries, aid agencies have begun to emphasize their role as consultants and sources of information and advice to Southern governments. Lynn Spire, World Bank research director, explains that in the future: "The bank will become more of a knowledge-based institution, advising countries on developing their private sector."[21]

Alongside this emphasis on policy dialogue came a renewed effort to strengthen the roles of foreign investment and the private sector in Third World economies. The World Bank expanded funding for the International Finance Corporation, which, unlike other branches of the Bank, made equity investments in partnership with private firms. Likewise, during the Reagan administration, a new entity known as the Bureau for Private Enterprise was created within AID with much the same mission.[22] World Bank Director James Wolfesohn has argued that the bank's key role is to "create the conditions for private capital to flow into all these countries."[23]

The nineties have brought two new programmatic objectives for foreign assistance: sustainable development and democracy promotion. The so-called Earth Summit, held in Rio de Janeiro, Brazil, in June of 1992, challenged both Northern and Southern governments to give greater attention to environmental sustainability when devising development plans. Although little additional money has been devoted to environmental programs, aid agencies have reallocated some existing funds toward environmental projects and have begun to screen traditional projects more carefully for their environmental impacts.[24]

The eighties and early nineties witnessed a wave of democratization in the Third World and the former Soviet bloc. Northern countries, led by the United States, have directed a small but growing proportion of aid to programs designed to nurture and strengthen these fledgling democracies. USAID, for instance, has embraced democracy promotion as one of its four principal goals. This so-called political aid is devoted to promoting a democratic culture within the civil societies of targeted countries and often flows to

---

[20] For a report on one such effort to link aid with policy reform, see John Felton, "Egypt: Aid Payments Used to Spur More Economic Reforms," *Congressional Quarterly*, August 26, 1989.

[21] Paul Lewis, "A New World Bank: Consultant to Third World Investors," *New York Times*, April 27, 1995.

[22] See Madison, "Exporting Reaganomics . . . ."

[23] Lewis, "A New World Bank."

[24] The topic of sustainable development is addressed at greater length in Chapter 13.

nongovernmental organizations, such as labor unions, political parties, civic organizations, and educational institutions. Although democracy promotion is not directly tied to economic development, it has a number of indirect effects on the economic assistance programs that constitute our principal concern. Most obviously, democracy promotion projects compete for limited funds with traditional economic assistance programs. Moreover, many Northern countries have begun to condition economic assistance on the recipient country's respect for democracy and human rights.

Aside from the merits of any one approach, these frequent shifts in the assumptions and strategies favored by the aid community deserve further comment. The movement from one approach to another is less the result of steadily accumulating knowledge and insight into the process of development than a function of shifting political winds in the North. The top-down approach of the fifties and sixties must be understood in the context of the Cold War. The United States and its allies hoped that the emphasis on infrastructure would provide quick, tangible evidence of Western largess, strengthen friendly governments, and, by stimulating rapid growth, inoculate Third World societies against the appeals of socialism. The poverty-oriented focus of the seventies reflected the liberal political climate of that era. In particular, the Vietnam War brought home for many the dangers of supporting narrowly based Third World elites without attention to the needs of the poor majority. The emphasis on markets and private enterprise during the eighties stemmed from the conservative philosophy of newly elected Northern leaders such as Ronald Reagan and Margaret Thatcher. The focus on sustainable development during the nineties was spurred by the growth of the global environmental movement, while democracy promotion reflected interest in nurturing the newly founded and still fragile democracies of Eastern Europe and the Third World.

What difference does it make which approach to development is embraced by the aid community? Most obviously, the assumptions underlying foreign assistance affect project selection and design as well as the allocation of funds. Yet far more significant is the broader influence these ideas exert over the policies of the recipient countries themselves. The World Bank is one of the key sources of data and analysis on development issues. Its reports, publications, and activities are widely followed and play a pivotal role in debates among experts and government officials. As we have seen, the Bank, along with other institutions, such as AID and the IMF, actively seeks to shape the economic policies of Third World states. Changes in approach and philosophy at the largest aid agencies thus ripple through the entire Third World, altering, in both approach and emphasis, the development choices made by Southern governments.

This has been particularly true during the eighties and nineties, when the World Bank and other agencies have sought to expand and strengthen the scope of policy dialogue with recipient nations. Thus World Bank President Barber Conable's remark, in February 1990, about changing strategies of development in the Third World could be read as a measure of the Bank's success in gaining acceptance for ideas it aggressively sponsored in recent years: "If I were to characterize the past decade, the most remarkable thing was the generation of a global consensus that market forces and economic efficiency were the best way to achieve the kind of growth which is the best antidote to poverty."[25]

## THE EFFECTIVENESS OF AID

Does aid work? Has it contributed to efficient and equitable Third World development? Measuring the effectiveness of aid is a challenging task. It is difficult, for instance, to know what might have happened in the absence of aid. Moreover, success can be defined in different ways, depending upon whether one chooses to emphasize overall economic growth, poverty reduction, equity, or environmental impact. In addition, many factors besides aid affect a country's economic performance. Singling out aid's contribution is therefore tricky at best.[26]

Clearly, however, success stories are available, whether we are speaking of projects that have brought real benefits to targeted recipients or nations that have used aid as a tool for stimulating overall development. Among other things, foreign assistance programs have helped Southern countries to eliminate smallpox, immunize children against disease, spread family planning, reduce illiteracy, and increase grain yields. One study covering a ten-year period examined the economic rate of return for 504 World Bank projects where results could be estimated. On average, these investments brought a return of 18 percent, quite healthy by any standard.[27] The World Bank also points to South Korea and Indonesia as countries where aid played a major role during the formative stages of development to both spur growth and reduce poverty.

Many countries, however, such as Tanzania, the Sudan, Zaire, Mozambique, Niger, Togo, Zambia, and Haiti, have been, and remain, heavily dependent on external aid but show disappointing economic results. The difference between success or failure, the World Bank argues, has to do with a country's willingness to pursue sound, market-oriented policies. Aid works within a conducive policy setting but cannot compensate for the deleterious effects of poor economic decision making.[28]

Yet, aid's critics suggest that foreign aid itself possesses inherent shortcomings stemming from the structure of the aid process as well as the priorities and motives of the donors. We take up seven of these criticisms in the sections that follow.

---

[25] Robin Broad, John Cavanaugh, and Walden Bello, "Development: The Market Is Not Enough," *Foreign Policy*, Winter 1990-91, 144. Broad, Cavanaugh, and Bello offer a critique of the overwhelming emphasis on markets in the approach described by Conable.

[26] For a detailed survey that attempts to assess aid's effectiveness, see Robert Cassen and Associates, *Does Aid Work?*, Oxford: Clarendon Press, 1986.

[27] *World Development Report, 1985*, 103.

[28] For the World Bank's views on aid's effectiveness, see *World Development Report, 1985*, 101-105; and *World Development Report, 1990*, 128-33.

## Poverty and the Misallocation of Aid

Perhaps the most widely accepted rationale for foreign aid lies in its potential for reducing Third World poverty. Indeed, as we have seen, public support for aid rests principally upon its purported humanitarian purposes, yet aid's success in ameliorating poverty is far from proven. After three decades of aid flows, the World Bank estimates that one third of the Third World's population, or 1.1 billion people, continue to live in absolute poverty (defined as annual income below $370).[29] Indeed, in a report reviewing the history of foreign aid between 1969 and 1985, the DAC concluded that "the most troubling short-coming of development aid has been its limited measurable contribution to the reduction—as distinguished from the relief—of extreme poverty, especially in the rural areas of both middle-income and poor countries."[30]

Part of the explanation for aid's disappointing record in attacking poverty is that political and economic considerations have influenced the allocation of foreign assistance. Substantial amounts of aid do not go to the countries that are most in need. To be sure, aid accounts for a significant portion of the income and investment in some of the world's poorest countries. Forty-seven countries count upon aid for 5 percent or more of their national income.[31] Yet in 1988, 41 percent of aid was distributed to middle- and high-income countries.[32] Aid receipts per capita bear little relation to average income. Indeed, Israel, a relatively wealthy country, received more than twice as much aid per capita as the next highest nation on the list. Overall, the richest 40 percent of all people living in the Third World receive twice as much aid per person as the poorest 40 percent.[33]

This misplacement of priorities is evident in the allocation of foreign assistance devoted to education. A disproportionate share of educational aid goes to higher education rather than primary schooling. In sub-Saharan Africa during the eighties, for instance, ODA to primary school education amounted to $1 per student while aid to higher education equaled $575 for every student. Much the same pattern exists with respect to heath care, where rural clinics receive less aid than urban hospitals that cater to the middle class.[34]

The diversion of aid from poorer to relatively better-off Third World countries stems principally from the political and economic interests of donor countries. Historically, the influence of nondevelopmental considerations on aid allocation decisions has been most pronounced in the case of the United States. In 1986, according to the World Bank, development assistance to low-income countries accounted for only 8 percent of the overall U.S. aid

---

[29] *World Development Report, 1990,* 1.

[30] *World Development Report, 1990,* 127.

[31] "Foreign Aid: The Kindness of Strangers," *The Economist,* May 7, 1994, 20.

[32] *World Development Report, 1990,* 127.

[33] "Foreign Aid: The Kindness of Strangers," 19.

[34] "Foreign Aid: The Kindness of Strangers," 20.

**TABLE 10.2**
**Top Recipients of Official Development Assistance, 1991**

| RANKED BY: TOTAL AID RECEIPTS IN MILLIONS OF US $ | | PER-CAPITA RECEIPTS IN U.S. $ | | AS % OF GNP | |
| --- | --- | --- | --- | --- | --- |
| Egypt | 4,988 | Israel | 352.5 | Mozambique | 69.2 |
| India | 2,747 | Jordan | 247.1 | Nicaragua | 47.6 |
| China | 1,954 | Nicaragua | 219.0 | Guinea-Bissau | 43.4 |
| Indonesia | 1,854 | Namibia | 124.1 | Tanzania | 33.8 |
| Israel | 1,749 | Gabon | 121.4 | Bhutan | 25.4 |
| Turkey | 1,675 | Zambia | 110.2 | Malawi | 22.6 |
| Bangladesh | 1,636 | Mauritania | 102.9 | Jordan | 22.2 |
| Pakistan | 1,226 | Botswana | 102.5 | Burundi | 21.6 |
| Ethiopia | 1,091 | Guinea-Bissau | 101.3 | Rwanda | 21.5 |
| Tanzania | 1,076 | Papua New Guinea | 100.1 | Uganda | 20.5 |

Source: World Bank, *World Development Report, 1994*, New York: Oxford University Press, 1994, 198–199.

budget.[35] One study found that among seventeen donor countries, the United States ranked last in the degree to which it allocated aid according to the poverty-related needs of recipient countries.[36] Another study found that U.S. aid to relatively high income countries amounted to $250 per person while American assistance to very poor countries came to only $1 per person.[37] In 1994, only 26 percent of bilateral U.S. economic aid went to Asia, Africa, and Latin American combined. The remainder was allocated to the Middle East, Western Europe, and the former Soviet bloc.[38]

A substantial portion of U.S. aid is channeled through the Economic Support Fund (ESF), which is administered by AID. ESF aid is explicitly intended to reward friendly countries and to promote political stability in areas considered important to U.S. interests. Roughly 40 percent of all U.S. economic aid takes the form of ESF assistance to Israel and Egypt as a reward for their willingness to enter into the Camp David Accords. Other countries, such as the Philippines, have received ESF funds as compensation for their willingness to allow U.S. military bases on their soil. Although some ESF aid goes to fund development projects, most provides general balance of payments support or finances commodity imports.

---

[35] *World Development Report, 1990*, 127–28.

[36] Mark McGillivray, "The Allocation of Aid Among Developing Countries: A Multi-Donor Analysis Using a Per Capita Aid Index," *World Development*, vol. 17, no. 4, 1989, 565.

[37] "Foreign Aid: The Kindness of Strangers," 20.

[38] "What Is USAID?" *AID Fact Sheet*, 1995.

# The Ironies of Food Aid

Food aid is among the most widely misunderstood forms of foreign assistance.[39] Sending food to hungry Southerners is popularly viewed in the North as a particularly humanitarian act. In fact, however, food aid sometimes does more harm than good.

The least controversial form of food aid is emergency assistance designed to compensate for shortfalls during times of drought and famine. Under these circumstances, outside food can save hundreds of thousands or even millions of lives. The need for such assistance has grown, rather than lessened, over time, particularly in the case of many African countries that have experienced repeated food shortages over the last two decades. In mid-1994 the United Nations Food and Agricultural Organization estimated that over twenty million people in fifteen sub-Saharan African countries were in danger of starvation. Yet only one half of the food donations required to avert famine had been pledged by donor countries.[40]

Yet in practice, emergency food efforts have been plagued by problems. Famine is rarely the result of natural factors alone. It is often exacerbated by government policies that discourage food production, the failure to set aside adequate food reserves during good years, slowness on the part of the government and outside donors in reacting to signs of impending shortages, and, as in the recent case of Somalia, the dislocations caused by war or political instability. These essentially political sources of hunger not only serve to heighten the probability of famine, but also hinder efforts to assist the hungry after outside help is needed. Conflicts between the local government and international relief agencies are common. Government authorities are often slow to acknowledge the prospect of famine for fear of shouldering the political blame for the country's desperate condition. Moreover, the distribution of food and medical supplies is fraught with political implications in severely divided societies. This often gives rise to intense bargaining between local governments and outside donors over the control of distribution activities.

These complexities are illustrated in the case of the recent famine in the Sudan. In 1990 Sudanese authorities repeatedly denied the prospect of food shortages despite increasingly urgent warnings of impending famine by outside observers and international relief agencies. The Sudanese government refused to request special assistance, effectively limiting donor access to the hungry. Moreover, aid personnel already working in the southern part of the country, where government troops were engaged in the suppression of an ethnic revolt, were forced to leave after authorities accused them of assisting

---

[39] For a brief survey and evaluation of various forms of food aid, see *World Development Report, 1990*, 135. Also see Edward Clay and Olav Stoke (eds.), *Food Aid Reconsidered: Assessing the Impact on Third World Countries*, London: Frank Cass, 1991; and Vernon Ruttan (ed.), *Why Food Aid?*, Baltimore: Johns Hopkins Press, 1993.

[40] "African Nations Face Famine as World Tires of Offering Aid," *Des Moines Register*, June 5, 1994.

the rebels.[41] This disturbing case is not unique. Almost identical events disrupted famine relief efforts in Ethiopia during 1984 and 1985.[42]

With some variations, a similar pattern repeated itself in Somalia in 1992-93, where the collapse of any functioning government and the outbreak of intense clan warfare both exacerbated a worsening famine and interfered with the efforts of international aid agencies to feed a starving population. In this case, outside military intervention, in the form of United Nations and then American troops, was required to restore some semblance of order and provide protection for relief efforts.

Emergency aid often arrives too late or fails to reach those in greatest need. The European Community pledged food assistance in 1984 when much of sub-Saharan Africa faced famine conditions. Yet, actual food deliveries did not begin until four hundred days later. The slow response of the international community as well as that of local governments prompted many African farmers to abandon their land and migrate to enormous famine camps. Many who survived failed to return to their farms in time to sow new crops after the rains returned.[43]

After aid began arriving in 1985, the huge quantities of food overwhelmed port, storage, and transportation facilities. Only 75 percent of the food delivered to Ethiopia was distributed, while the figure for the Sudan was 64 percent. Moreover, food aid failed to end when the famine finally lifted. Aid continued to pour into Kenya after returning rains allowed a record harvest in 1985. The overabundance of food flooded markets, depressed prices and lowered rural incomes.[44]

A more ironic case of misdirected food aid occurred in the wake of the 1976 earthquake in Guatemala. Large quantities of food were delivered despite the fact that agricultural production remained unaffected by the quake and no food shortages existed.[45]

Despite the problems that surround emergency food programs, virtually all observers agree that such relief efforts are both necessary and useful. Yet

---

[41] "African Famine: Yet Again," *The Economist*, January 5, 1991, 33; and Alyson Pytte, "Congress Is Using Aid as a Lever to Protest Rights Abuses" and "Somalia and the Sudan: Two Countries Plagued by Poverty, Famine and War," *Congressional Quarterly*, May 13, 1989, 1132–35. In March of 1991, Sudanese officials finally decided to make a formal appeal for emergency food aid and allow relief workers freer access to the country.  Lewis, "Sudan Will Allow New Famine Relief."

[42] See the epilogue to William Shawcross, *The Quality of Mercy: Cambodia, Holocaust and Modern Conscience*, New York: Simon and Schuster, 1985.

[43] Timberlake, "The Politics of Food Aid," 24.

[44] Timberlake, "The Politics of Food Aid," 23–24.

[45] Timberlake, "The Politics of Food Aid," 24. For extended treatments of emergency and disaster assistance programs, see Randolph Kent, *Anatomy of Disaster  Relief: The International Network in Action*, London: Pinter Publishers, 1987; and Lynn H. Stephens and Stephen J. Green (eds.), *Disaster Assistance: Appraisal, Reform and New Approaches*, New York: New York University Press, 1979. For a readable and interesting case study of international famine  relief operations in Cambodia during the early eighties, see Shawcross, *The Quality of Mercy*.

emergency assistance accounted for only 5 percent of all food aid in 1985.[46] The remainder is divided between project and program aid, both of which are the subject of controversy.

Project aid, which accounted for 25 percent of all food assistance in 1985, targets food toward specific purposes and populations. Examples include "food for work" schemes such as the enormous World Food Program project in Ethiopia where thousands of rural dwellers are given food in exchange for work. In this case, recipients planted trees and terraced slopes in an effort to improve soil conservation. A different form of project aid provides supplemental food for populations considered at risk. Although useful in many instances, project aid may simply substitute for, rather than supplement, government social service assistance. Moreover, some projects go awry. One study of a child nutrition program found that the children's health actually improved after the project ended. While aid was available, mothers fed their children only the free grain and butterfat available through the program. Afterward, they reverted to a more balanced diet, including locally available fruits and vegetables.[47]

Program aid made up 70 percent of all food aid in 1985. Food is simply provided free or sold at subsidized prices to governments to do with what they please. Governments generally resell the food within their own country, using the resulting revenue for other purposes. The motives behind this form of food assistance have less to do with altruism than with the political and economic interests of donor countries. Sir William Ryrie, former head of the British Overseas Development Administration, has observed that the bulk of food aid "is frankly more a means of disposing of European agricultural surpluses than of helping the poor."[48] The same, of course, is true of the United States Food for Peace program.[49]

Food aid is often distributed to friendly countries as a political reward. Owen Cylke, former acting director of the U.S. Food for Peace program, has commented that "it's used as a slush fund of the State Department to meet political requirements around the world."[50] In 1983, six of the top ten recipients of U.S. food aid were net food exporters. Egypt, a U.S. ally, received 20 percent of all cereal aid to the Third World in 1985–86 and 50 percent of all such aid to Africa. This was despite the fact that Egypt's average caloric intake was 28 percent higher than necessary for a healthy diet. Because Egypt subsidizes food sales, bread is cheaper than chicken feed and is often fed to livestock. Patterns such as these prompted one World Bank study to conclude that "the

[46] Timberlake, "The Politics of Food Aid," 22.

[47] Timberlake, "The Politics of Food Aid," 24–26.

[48] Timberlake, "The Politics of Food Aid," 27.

[49] Martha Ann Overland, "Lawmakers Seek to Remove Politics from Foreign Aid," *Des Moines Register*, July 22, 1990.

[50] Overland, "Lawmakers Seek to Remove Politics from Foreign Aid."

distribution, quantity and nature of food aid sometimes bears little relation to dietary deficiency."[51]

The influx of cheap, subsidized, Northern food into poor Third World countries can encourage dependence and vulnerability. Insecure governments prefer to keep food prices low so as to appease politically active urban populations. However, this practice denies rural farmers adequate revenue, thus discouraging agricultural investment and production as well as perpetuating rural poverty. The result is that cities swell with rural immigrants, while the country becomes vulnerable should food aid levels fall due to poor harvests and dwindling surpluses in the North.[52] Food aid is therefore often resisted by rural residents who make up the majority of the population in many Third World countries. In 1990, Indonesian officials appealed to the U.S. ambassador to stop the shipments of 700,000 tons of U.S. grain after local farmers protested that they would be forced out of business due to the influx of aid.[53]

## Growth Versus the Environment

Over the past decade, aid agencies have experienced enormous pressure from groups in both the North and the South to give greater attention to the environmental, social, and cultural impacts of the projects they sponsor. The World Bank, in particular, has come under attack for a series of controversial projects that critics charge have brought devastating consequences to the environment and local inhabitants. Although the Bank has taken steps to revise its lending practices, many environmental groups remain skeptical about its commitment to reform.[54]

The environmental and social costs associated with the Bank's emphasis on economic growth are plainly evident in the case of the Super Thermal Power Plant and coal mine in India's Singrauli region. Funded by an $850 million World Bank loan, the project led to the forcible resettlement, with little compensation, of twenty-three thousand local inhabitants. Ash from the coal-fired plant has polluted neighboring cropland and a nearby reservoir, leading to the growing incidence of tuberculosis and malaria among local residents.

---

[51] Timberlake, "The Politics of Food Aid," 27–28. Also see Overland, "Lawmakers Seek to Remove Politics from Foreign Aid."

[52] Timberlake, "The Politics of Food Aid," 29.

[53] Overland, "Lawmakers Seek to Remove Politics from Foreign Aid." For a defense of food aid, see H. W. Singer, "Food Aid: Development Tool or Obstacle to Development?" *Development Policy Review*, vol. 5, 1987.

[54] For a discussion of bargaining between environmental advocacy groups and the World Bank, see Pat Aufderheide and Bruce Rich, "Environmental Reform and the Multilateral Banks," *World Policy Journal*, Spring 1988. Also see Bruce Rich, *Mortgaging the Earth: The World Bank, Environmental Impoverishment, and the Crisis of Development*, Boston: Beacon Press, 1994, which offers a critical evaluation of the World Bank's environmental record.

The World Bank and Indian authorities were, moreover, slow to provide assistance to resettled villagers.[55]

A migration project in Indonesia, financed by a $1 billion Bank loan, has led to the resettlement of three million poor people from Java and Bali to outlying islands. Authorities hoped to relieve overcrowding and provide peasants with small plots of new farmland. Millions of acres of tropical rain forest have been cleared to make room for new settlers. The land of traditional local inhabitants has also been seized, leading to violent confrontations with the Indonesian army. Yet only one half of the new farms have succeeded, due largely to poor soils that are unsuitable for agriculture. Many settlers have migrated back to the cities in search of work.[56]

A World Bank funded colonization scheme in Brazil known as "Polonoroeste" has brought similar results. Hundreds of thousands of poor peasants have poured into the Rondonia and Mato Grosso provinces of the Amazon region along a highway constructed with World Bank financing. Huge tracts of virgin rain forest have been cleared and indigenous Indian populations displaced. Yet due to the leaching of minerals from the soil caused by heavy rains, most farms prove productive for only a few years. Many resettled peasants have responded by burning and clearing additional forest acreage. In 1987 it was estimated that the Amazon basin as a whole was afflicted by six thousand forest fires, the great majority man-made.[57]

In May 1987, World Bank President Barber Conable conceded the Bank's poor environmental record and promised a better performance in the future: "If the World Bank has been part of the problem in the past, it can and will be a strong force in finding solutions in the future."[58] The Bank subsequently created a new environmental division staffed by sixty specialists. Some pending projects, including dams in India, Brazil, and Nepal, have been rejected on environmental or social grounds. New projects that exclusively address environmental problems have been approved, and environmental concerns have played a larger role in the planning of traditional projects. By 1990 the World Bank claimed that nearly one half of all Bank projects had environmental concerns built into them.[59] World Bank lending for free standing environment projects increased to $2.4 billion in 1994, up thirtyfold from 1989 levels.[60]

---

[55] See Art Levine, "Bankrolling Debacles?" *US News & World Report*, September 25, 1989, 43–44; and Graham Hancock, *Lords of Poverty: The Power, Prestige and Corruption of the International Aid Business*, New York: Atlantic Monthly Press, 1989, 130-31.

[56] See Levine, "Bankrolling Debacles?" 46—47, and Hancock, *Lords of Poverty*, 133-38.

[57] Hancock, *Lords of Poverty*, 131-33.

[58] Aufderheide and Rich, "Environmental Reform and the Multilateral Banks," 301.

[59] On the Bank's reforms, see Philip Shabecoff, "World Bank Stressing Environmental Issues," *New York Times*, September 24, 1990; Jeremy Warford and Zeinab Partow, "Evolution of the World Bank's Environmental Policy," *Finance and Development*, December 1989, 5-9; and Bruce Rich, "The Emperor's New Clothes: The World Bank and Environmental Reform," *World Policy Journal*, Spring 1990.

[60] Hilary F. French, *Partnership for the Planet: An Environmental Agenda for the United Nations*, Worldwatch Paper no. 126, July 1995, 36-37.

In 1991 the Bank established the Global Environmental Fund (GEF), a new lending facility devoted to addressing environmental problems. In 1994, donor nations agreed to replenish the GEF with substantial new resources. Nevertheless, the World Bank has now been forced to share administrative responsibility over the GEF with the United Nations Development Program and the United Nations Environmental Program due to distrust of the Bank on the part of Third World governments and private environmental groups.[61]

Despite the World Bank's new "green" image, critics argue that the Bank's conversion has been less than complete. Peggy Hillward, director of forestry research for Probe International, for instance, charges that the World Bank is sponsoring "the same old projects with a few trees planted around the edges."[62] A congressionally mandated report issued in June 1990 by the U.S. Agency for International Development cited twenty-seven Bank projects that posed environmental or social dangers.[63] As of January 1990, an estimated 1.5 million people had been forcibly displaced by ongoing Bank projects, and proposed plans threatened to displace a similar number.[64]

The serious environmental and social costs associated with some forms of development are not easily accommodated within the traditional models of economic growth embraced by most aid agencies. For this reason, the World Bank and other development organizations have begun to experiment with new models that include measures of ecological and resource depletion alongside long-accepted yardsticks of development (see Chapter 8).[65] These innovative measurements can reveal the hidden trade-offs underlying development. This new thinking about sustainable growth must be incorporated into project selection and design, however, before it will produce any widespread practical effect.

## The Overreliance on Outside Experts

Development agencies have been criticized for relying too heavily on foreign experts in the design and implementation of aid projects while failing to take advantage of local talent or to consult with the poor about the plans that affect their lives. These tendencies often lead to poorly designed projects and feed resentment among recipients. Even worthwhile projects may wither over time if local people are not given the training, incentives, or responsibility necessary to sustain them.

---

[61] "Greened," *The Economist*, December 4, 1993; Paul Lewis, "U.S. and Other Donor Nations Plan $2 Billion for Environment," *New York Times*, March 17, 1994.

[62] Shabecoff, "World Bank Stressing Environmental Issues."

[63] Levine, "Bankrolling Debacles?" 43.

[64] Rich, "The Emperor's New Clothes," 313.

[65] For a brief discussion of these issues, see James Robertson and Andre Carothers, "The New Economics: Accounting for a Healthy Planet," *Greenpeace*, January/February 1989. On how these ideas have crept into World Bank thinking, see Warford and Partow, "Evolution of the . . . ."

The proclivity of aid agencies to manage aid projects through the use of imported expertise is pervasive. It has been estimated that at least 150,000 foreign-aid workers and consultants are employed in the Third World at any given time. The expense of keeping expatriate personnel in the field is considerable—$100,000 or more per year for each employee—and usually much greater than that associated with the use of local labor.[66]

Not all of these foreign experts originate from the North. Many multilateral agencies, such as the United Nations Development Program, hire substantial numbers of Third World personnel. Yet these employees are often assigned to foreign postings. Only 10 percent of United Nations professionals, for instance, work in their home country.[67] Paul Streeten, a consultant to the World Bank, notes that "a mediocre Indian, who might be useful within his competence in India, is recruited by the UN to work in Sierra Leone at ten times the salary he would earn at home, on a job for which he is ill-qualified, while a Sierra Leonean advises India."[68]

Foreign-aid workers are often clustered in separate project units, outside of the recipient country's normal bureaucratic structure. This inhibits the accumulation of skills and learning experiences on the part of local officials and leaves aid projects without a strong constituency inside the regular bureaucracy. As a result, projects are often abandoned once outside aid is terminated.[69]

The work of this vast legion of aid emissaries is seldom effectively coordinated by various donor agencies. Some countries suffer from "aid overload." The proliferation of aid projects from a multitude of donors simply overwhelms the capacity of the local bureaucracy to cope. In one recent year, for instance, Burkina Faso was visited by 350 separate aid missions. Project duplication is common and little standardization in equipment or design takes place. Donors provided Kenya, for instance, with eighteen different varieties of water pumps for the country's rural water-supply system.[70]

Nor are the intended beneficiaries of aid typically given significant roles in designing or implementing aid projects. A study completed in 1988 by the World Bank's Operations Evaluations Department candidly concluded that "the principles guiding beneficiary participation in Bank-financed projects have been quite abstract and of limited operational impact. Beneficiaries were not assigned a role in the decision-making process, nor was their technical knowledge sought prior to designing project components."[71]

---

[66] Hancock, *Lords of Poverty*, 115.

[67] Hancock, *Lords of Poverty*, 117.

[68] Hancock, *Lords of Poverty*, 115.

[69] *World Development Report, 1990*, 132.

[70] Cassen, *Does Aid Work?*, 221, 223.

[71] Hancock, *Lords of Poverty*, 125-26. For more on this problem, see Hellinger, Hellinger, and O'Regan, *Aid for Just Development*.

The consequences of failing to consult local knowledge can be devastating to project success. Three examples may help to illustrate this point. AID experts relied upon a local irrigation canal to provide water to a fish farm project in Mali. Yet, it was later discovered that the canal carried water for only five months out of the year. To prevent the fish pond from going dry during the remainder of the year, an expensive diesel powered pump was installed to bring water from a source over two kilometers away. Moreover, fish food had to be imported because no suitable local source could be found. The increased costs of capital and inputs soon rendered the fish farm absurdly uneconomical. In a second such experiment, this time in the southern African nation of Malawi, a fish farm was located next to a bird sanctuary, providing the nearby population of fish-eating fowl with a tasty diet.[72] A third project, cited by AID as a model, involved the planting of rows of trees as windbreaks in the Majjia Valley of Niger. The purpose was to limit soil erosion by blocking destructive wind currents. In fact, however, the trees depleted the already low water table and attracted birds and insects that pillaged nearby field crops. Moreover, the project brought on tensions between aid administrators and local herders over land rights.[73] The mistakes associated with these projects, and others like them, might have been avoided had local expertise been tapped in the first place.

## The Costs of Tied Aid

The common Northern practice of "tying" bilateral aid to the purchase of exports from the donor country substantially reduces the real value of such assistance to Third World countries. The purpose of tied aid is to allow manufacturers in the donor's own country to capture a larger share of the sales stimulated by foreign aid. Tied aid also promotes future orders for donor country exporters. Once an aid recipient installs machinery or equipment purchased from a particular supplier, it is likely to go back to that same firm for parts, supplies, and replacements. Thus tied aid generates a stream of business.

When aid is tied in this way, however, recipient countries are forbidden to shop around for the least expensive or most appropriate equipment. On average, tying aid reduces its value by roughly 20 percent.[74] Moreover, Northern firms that benefit from tied aid serve as vested interests, lobbying for aid projects requiring heavy Northern inputs, whether or not these projects are the most appropriate from the recipient's point of view.

Japan, France, and Germany each tie much of their bilateral aid. Of the $1.4 billion in bilateral aid Germany provided in 1986, 86 percent returned to

---

[72] Both cases are discussed in Hancock, *Lords of Poverty*, 123–24.

[73] Stryk Thomas, "Milk Shakes in the African Desert," *This World,* July 3, 1994, 9.

[74] C. J. Jepma, "The Impact of Untying Aid of the European Community Countries," *World Development,* vol. 16, no. 7, 1988, 804.

the country through the purchase of German products.[75] Similarly, 80 percent of Japanese aid went to pay for Japanese exports. Overall, two thirds of the bilateral aid provided by major donor countries is fully or partially tied. In 1990, tied aid financed an estimated one third of the $25 to $30 billion in annual capital goods exports worldwide.[76]

## The Preference for Bigness

Some of the most persistent criticisms of aid have to do with the size and type of projects that donors typically sponsor.[77] Aid agencies tend to prefer large-scale, capital-intensive investments that require a sizable import component over smaller, labor-intensive projects relying principally upon locally produced inputs. Thus, in competition for the same funds, a single expensive infrastructure project, such as a dam, road, or port facility, will often win out over multiple smaller and less costly projects, such as rural health clinics or agricultural extension programs. These biases in project lending tend to skew development toward the modern urban sector of the economy to the detriment of the poorer rural areas and often contribute to an overdependence on imports.

The sources of this behavior stem from various bureaucratic needs of the aid agencies themselves. Most foreign assistance programs, for instance, finance only the foreign currency component of the projects they sponsor. This encourages recipient nations to maximize the proportion of total project costs that depend upon imported goods and favors reliance upon foreign suppliers over local firms. Future orders of parts and replacement equipment are likely to go to these same foreign companies as well. Another consequence is that projects relying heavily on "hardware," such as imported capital equipment, are favored over those involving heavy labor costs that must be paid in local currency.

The preference for "bigness" is also related to bureaucratic factors. Aid agencies are under enormous pressure to "move money." Success is defined less in terms of the quality of projects or their contributions to development or poverty alleviation than in the total amount of funds dispersed. Within the agency, a good administrator is viewed as one who can lend the most money at the least cost in terms of bureaucratic overhead. Large projects are most efficient in this regard. The paperwork and man-hours required to initiate and review the progress of a small project are scarcely less than those needed to administer a large project. An overworked bureaucrat who seeks to impress his/her superiors with his/her productivity will thus find the oversight

---

[75] "Playing the Aid Game," *World Press Review*, February 1989, 51.

[76] Clyde Farnsworth, "US Will Tie Aid to Exports in Bid to Curb the Practice," *New York Times*, May 14, 1990.

[77] The discussion that follows in this section is drawn principally from Judith Tendler, *Inside Foreign Aid*, Baltimore: Johns Hopkins University Press, 1975.

responsibilities associated with a single large loan far more manageable and rewarding than those that accompany many small loans. These incentives to think big become even more intense when the quantity of funds available to lend suddenly rises faster than the agency's work force, as in 1988 when donors approved a $75 billion jump in World Bank capital, almost doubling the Bank's resources.

This syndrome is reinforced in the case of bilateral agencies that must spend their aid allocations within a given time period or lose access to the funds altogether. Moreover, if funding for a particular year is not fully dispersed, legislative overseers may conclude that future aid appropriations can be safely cut. These external funding constraints typically lead to an end-of-the-fiscal-year frenzy to spend all remaining funds. Under these circumstances, even marginal projects may be considered more favorably than before, particularly if they promise to move money quickly.

## Recipient Country Corruption

Corruption, entrenched inequality, and the insensitivity of elites to the plight of the poor in many Third World countries seriously hamper even sincere efforts on the part of outside agencies to reach those in need. According to Volkmar Kohler, West German secretary for development, "We have to work with elites who have no interest in seeing the poorer classes in their societies advance."[78] Unrepresentative political regimes are many times plagued by officially sanctioned corruption. One World Bank staffer has admitted that Third World governments often demand financial kickbacks from firms involved in aid projects: "We know that it happens all the time. Its how business is done in those countries."[79] For these reasons, democracy is increasingly viewed by many economists as a prerequisite to equitable development.[80] A recent United Nations study rated countries according to their achievements in "human development." It noted that twenty of the twenty-five nations scoring lowest on the human development scale were African dictatorships.[81] Donor countries have begun to take such considerations into greater account when allocating aid budgets. In 1991, several Western governments canceled or scaled back assistance programs to Kenya in the wake of revelations that large amounts of aid money were regularly lost to government sanctioned corruption.[82] Canada and Britain, along with other donor countries, have conditioned their foreign aid on the recipient country's respect for human rights.[83]

---

[78] "Playing the Aid Game," 51.

[79] Levine, "Bankrolling Debacles?" 44.

[80] "Democracy and Growth," *The Economist*, August 27, 1994.

[81] Paul Lewis, "Poorest Countries Seek Increases in Aid," *New York Times*, July 3, 1990.

[82] Jane Perlez, "Citing Corruption in Kenya, Western Nations Cancel Aid," *New York Times*, October 21, 1991.

[83] "Summit Leaders Link Human Rights to Foreign Aid," *Des Moines Register*, October 17, 1991.

## LEARNING FROM FAILURE

The controversies dogging the major aid agencies have grown more frequent and intense in recent years. In 1992 an internal World Bank staff report found that over 37 percent of the Bank projects completed in 1991 could be judged failures using the Bank's own criteria. This represented a 150 percent increase in the Bank's failure rate over the previous decade.[84] Another internal World Bank report prepared in 1992 by the Bank's Operations Evaluation Department reviewed project completion reports through 1991 for ninety-nine structural adjustment loans in forty-two countries. The report found that two thirds of the countries suffered declines in both public and private sector investment during the loan periods.[85] A similar internal International Monetary Fund review of structural adjustment programs in nineteen low-income countries found that current account deficits and foreign debt loads actually worsened during the periods in which the IMF programs were in effect.[86] A report submitted by former World Bank employee David Knox has criticized the African Development Bank, arguing that it is bloated by bureaucracy, subject to political manipulation and poorly organized to evaluate and monitor the projects that the Bank funds.[87] A study conducted by Peter Boone, an economist at the London School of Economics, examined aid flows to ninety-six countries between 1971 and 1990. He concluded that the vast majority of aid financed consumption and that aid had little impact on overall economic growth rates.[88]

Japan has become a vocal critic of the neoliberal, free market policies espoused by the World Bank and the International Monetary Fund. Japanese officials argue that Third World countries need strong states to steer investment patterns, screen imports and foreign investment and encourage the acquisition and development of technology. The activist state role favored by Japan is based upon that country's own experience, as well as those of other East Asian NICs, including South Korea and Taiwan. Japanese officials are therefore skeptical about the advice offered Third World countries by the World Bank and other aid agencies, which tends to discourage state intervention in the process of economic development. This issue came to a head in 1993, when the World Bank published a study titled *The East Asian Miracle*. Although Japanese officials had originally requested the study, they were unhappy with its conclu-

---

[84] "World Bank's Failure Rate," *New York Times*, April 14, 1993; Pratap Chatterjee, "World Bank Failures Soar to 37.5% of Completed Projects in 1991," in Kevin Danaher (ed.), *50 Years Is Enough: The Case Against the World Bank and the International Monetary Fund*, Boston: South End Press, 1994.

[85] Cameron Duncan, "Internal Report Card Looks Bad for Structural Adjustments," in Kevin Danaher (ed.), *50 Years Is Enough: The Case Against the World Bank and the International Monetary Fund*, Boston: South End Press, 1994.

[86] "Foreign Aid: The Kindness of Strangers," 22.

[87] "Development Banking: Double Trouble," *The Economist*, May 14, 1994.

[88] "Down the Rathole," *The Economist*, December 10, 1994, 69.

sions, which attributed East Asia's success to financial discipline rather than government industrial policy. Japan, a major contributor to both the World Bank and the IMF, has become increasingly bold in pressing for a reorientation of the development policies and models embraced by these institutions.[89]

These critical assessments, along with the problems reviewed earlier in this chapter, raise the important question of whether aid can be reformed. Can aid agencies learn from past mistakes and failures? Our earlier discussion has identified some evidence of institutional flexibility. As we saw, outside criticism of the World Bank's environmental record has led to significant (though, by some standards, still insufficient) progress toward a more ecologically sensitive method of operation.[90]

This is not the only evidence of greater responsiveness in the aid community. One sign of innovation is movement by several major donor agencies, including the World Bank and AID, to provide credit to the poor. Traditionally, aid agencies funded large-scale projects undertaken, in most cases, by governments. Critics argued that this form of assistance rarely benefited the poor directly. Indeed, most poor people lacked access to credit of any type, except through black-market lenders who charged usurious rates of interest. Commercial banks typically view the poor as bad credit risks. The fallacy of this has been demonstrated by the Grameen Bank of Bangladesh. Founded twenty years ago by a visionary economist named Muhamad Yunus, Grameen lends small amounts of money, often equivalent to only a few hundred dollars, to small scale cooperatives, most composed of poor women. These funds are used to establish small businesses, usually handicraft or livestock enterprises. Two million families in Bangladesh have received such loans. Loan volume approached $500 million in 1995, with a repayment rate of 97 percent. Following Grameen's lead, other microbanks have been established elsewhere in the Third World over the past decade, providing loans to an estimated ten million poor borrowers worldwide.[91]

Encouraged by this success, the World Bank recently announced plans to set a microbanking program designed to funnel $200 million in funds to over one million borrowers each year in amounts as little as $100. These small-scale loans, to be paid back within one year, would be accompanied by training and advice to help the poor to start their own businesses.[92] AID has supported the creation of similar microbanking programs in Indonesia, Senegal, and the Dominican Republic.[93]

---

[89] John Judis, "World Bunk," *In These Times*, December 13, 1993.

[90] For an examination of how institutional learning took place in the World Bank as it grappled with criticisms of its environmental record, see Phillipe Le Prestre, *The World Bank and the Environmental Challenge*, Cranbury, N.J.: Associated University Presses, 1989.

[91] Patrick E. Tyler, "Banker Is Star at Parley on Women," *New York Times*, September 14, 1995; David Bornstein, "The Barefoot Bank with Cheek," *The Atlantic Monthly*, December 1995.

[92] Christopher Wren, "World Banks Seeking Funds for Small Loans to the Poor," *New York Times*, July 17, 1995.

[93] "Supporting Economic Growth," *AID Fact Sheet*, 1995.

Long criticized for its secrecy, the World Bank has become somewhat more open about its operations, allowing greater public access to internal documents. It has also created a new appeals panel which will consider complaints about Bank projects from citizens of recipient countries.[94]

Another recent reform is AID's move to channel a larger proportion of U.S. bilateral assistance through nongovernmental organizations (NGOs) rather than Third World governments. Called the New Partnerships Initiative, the program's objectives are to empower small businesses and entrepreneurs, strengthen local NGOs and foster greater grassroots democracy. By working through NGOs, AID hopes to reach the poor more directly and bypass the corruption and red tape often involved in working through governments.[95]

Improvements can be cited in other areas as well. By 1994, the World Bank had succeeded in bringing its failure rate down to 18 percent, still high, but a considerable improvement over a few years earlier.[96] Tied aid has declined as a proportion of the total. Over time, a larger proportion of assistance has been given in the form of grants rather than loans that must be repaid. An increasing share of aid has been funneled through multilateral institutions, which are less subject to direct political manipulation than bilateral programs and where Southern countries have somewhat greater representation. Some donors have reduced or cut off aid to particularly repressive or inegalitarian regimes.[97] World Bank lending for health and education programs has tripled since 1990.[98]

These examples suggest that reform is possible. Like most bureaucracies, however, aid agencies prefer incremental change to wholesale shifts in policy and practice. Most of the reforms discussed above have resulted when Northern governments and aid agencies have experienced outside political pressures and the glare of publicity from failed projects or programs. Only when the media, nongovernmental organizations, Third World governments, academic observers or national legislatures take steps to expose serious problems has serious movement toward reform been forthcoming.

## THE FUTURE OF FOREIGN AID

The prospect of significant future increases in Northern aid to the South seems slight. After rising during the early eighties, U.S. foreign aid has declined since then. Seeking to allocate its dwindling funds more effectively, USAID chief Brian Atwood announced plans in 1994 to restructure his agency over the coming few years. This reorganization would close missions in

---

[94] Lewis, "A New World Bank."

[95] Barbara Crossette, "Private Groups to Get More Foreign Aid," *New York Times*, March 13, 1995.

[96] Lewis, "A New World Bank."

[97] For data relating to these points and a generally optimistic perspective on the willingness and ability of aid agencies to undertake reform, see David Lumsdaine, *Moral Vision in International Politics: The Foreign Aid Regime, 1949–1989*, Princeton: Princeton University Press, 1993.

[98] Lewis, "A New World Bank."

roughly one half of the over one hundred nations in which AID previously operated, cut 1,200 employees and reduce AID's list of priority goals from thirty-three to four (promoting democracy, protecting the environment, fostering sustainable development and controlling population growth).[99] Despite these reforms, the Republican majority in the U.S. Congress mounted a major attack on USAID in 1995, seeking to cut funding substantially and to undercut the agency's independence by folding it into the State Department.[100] The United States is not alone in reducing aid. Overall ODA flows fell from a peak of $61.9 billion in 1991 to $54.5 billion in 1994 and are expected to continue falling.[101] Moreover, a rising proportion of aid—from 2 percent in 1989 to 7 percent in 1994—is being diverted from long-term development projects to short-term disaster relief.[102]

The lessening of Cold War tensions between East and West and the fall of Communist regimes in Eastern Europe seem likely to have profound effects on aid flows to the South as well. During the Cold War, the United States. and the Soviet Union used aid as an inducement in their competition for Third World allies. With the waning of this rivalry, the United States will see less need to use aid as a tool for countering Soviet influence, while Third World countries will no longer find it as easy to win assistance by appealing to Cold War fears. The breakup of the Soviet Union and the economic turmoil that has plagued its successor states has virtually eliminated the flow of aid to former Soviet allies, such as Cuba and Vietnam.

Moreover, Third World countries have expressed alarm at the prospect that new and existing aid funds will be diverted to Eastern Europe.[103] Although referring to private capital flows, World Bank President Barber Conable, nevertheless did little to quiet these fears with his remark that developing nations "must work harder to attract investment or money will go to Eastern Europe."[104] Indeed, the World Bank has in recent years extended billions of dollars in loans to Eastern European nations. In addition, the European Bank for Reconstruction and Development, capitalized at $12 billion by Western governments, is designed to provide financing for Eastern European development with a focus on the promotion of private enterprise.[105]

---

[99] "Foreign Aid: The Kindness of Strangers;" Steven Holmes, "State Department Seeks Funds of Other Agencies," *New York Times*, November 11, 1993; "U.S. Agency for Development Plans to Cut Aid to 35 Nations," *New York Times*, November 20, 1993; Andrew Cohen, "Clinton Doctrine: The Help That Hurts," *The Progressive*, January 1994; "Creating a New USAID" and "USAID Mission Closeouts," *AID Fact Sheet*, 1995.

[100] Steven Greenhouse, "Foreign Aid and G.O.P.: Deep Cuts," *New York Times*, December 21, 1994; and Paul Lewis, "Rubin Says World Economy in 'a Pause,'" *New York Times*, October 4, 1995.

[101] "Trends in Development Assistance," *AID Fact Sheet*, 1995.

[102] "Foreign Aid: The Kindness of Strangers," 19.

[103] Paul Lewis, "Poorest Countries Seek Increases in Aid," *New York Times*, July 3, 1990.

[104] "Conable Advice to Third World," *New York Times*, June 14, 1990.

[105] Pamela Fessler, "Eastern Europe: Republicans Scramble to Meet Democrats' Aid Challenge," *Congressional Quarterly*, February 10, 1990; and John Granford, "Aid Plan for Eastern Europe," *Congressional Quarterly*, February 24, 1990.

The decline in aid from other sources may be partially offset by the rapid growth of Japanese assistance to Third World countries. Japan's share of the official development assistance provided by all members of the Development Assistance Council rose from 2 percent in 1962 to 18 percent in 1987. Japan is now the world's largest provider of foreign aid, and its spending levels seem likely to rise still further in the near future.

Although recipient countries may welcome Japan's growing commitment to foreign aid, they have less reason to cheer the conditions attached to such funds. Three quarters of Japan's assistance is directed to countries in Asia and Oceania, where Japanese trade and investment levels are also high. Comparatively little finds its way to Africa or Latin America. Moreover, Japanese aid to the world's least-developed countries carries hard terms and contains a greater proportion of loans (versus grants) than is true for other aid donors. As we have seen, Japan ties a high proportion of its aid to the purchase of Japanese goods. Finally, a relatively large share of Japanese funds go toward infrastructural projects that bring few immediate benefits to the poor.[106]

## CONCLUSIONS

This chapter has struck a largely pessimistic note regarding the effectiveness of aid in promoting development and alleviating poverty in the Third World. Such a conclusion does not imply that all aid is bad or useless. Indeed, as we have also emphasized, aid comes in many shapes and forms. Not surprisingly, aid can claim many successes alongside its failures. Most projects probably have mixed effects, with costs and benefits spread unevenly across the affected population. Overall, aid may well provide measurable, and sometimes significant, economic benefits in many Third World countries. Indeed, it would be puzzling if the billions of dollars in aid that flow to the Third World each year did not have some positive impact.

Yet aid has surely failed to perform up to the hopes of its early proponents or, perhaps, even to the standards of its more modest defenders within the aid community today. We have surveyed a variety of specific criticisms that have been directed at aid. Three broader, more general points take us to the roots of aid's shortcomings.

The contribution foreign aid can make to Southern development is limited in part by the modest size of aid flows. In 1992, foreign assistance from all sources amounted to 1.3 percent of overall Third World GNP, or roughly

---

[106] For data on Japanese aid, see Rowley, "Flush with Funds" and Anthony Rowley, "On Toyko's Terms," *Far Eastern Economic Review*, March 9, 1989, 78. More extended treatments include Shafiqul Islam (ed.), *Yen for Development: Japanese Foreign Aid and the Politics of Burden-Sharing*, New York: Council on Foreign Relations Press, 1991; Bruce M. Koppel and Robert M. Orr, Jr. (eds.), *Japan's Foreign Aid: Power and Policy in a New Era*, Boulder: Westview Press, 1993; Margee M. Ensign, *Doing Good or Doing Well? Japan's Foreign Aid Program*, New York: Columbia University Press, 1992.

$11 for each Southerner.[107] To bring the limited contributions of aid into even clearer perspective, it has been estimated that the total value of Northern aid is exceeded by the costs to the Third World of Northern protectionism against Southern exports.[108] Although aid totals in the tens of billions of dollars may appear impressive, they seem less so when placed in the context of overall Third World needs. Moreover, as noted earlier, present aid levels seem likely to fall still further.

Another fundamental source of aid's limited success has to do with the poor state of our knowledge about the process of economic development. What seems clear is that there are many potential routes to development rather than a single model that can be successfully applied under all circumstances. This rather messy reality, however, makes it only more difficult to fashion aid strategies appropriate to each country. Changing academic and political fashions have combined with the inherent complexity of the development problem to produce a series of wrenching shifts in the strategies and philosophies embraced by the aid community. This inconsistency itself has detracted from aid's effectiveness.

Yet the most important constraints on aid are political. Why does aid often fail to reach the poor or to benefit them more directly? The fundamental answer is rather simple: the crucial decisions regarding aid are made by governments, over the heads of the poor themselves. Although aid is certainly not free of humanitarian motives and purposes, these often take a back seat to other concerns, including the pursuit of political power.

Donor governments use aid to reward friends and woo neutrals, to exercise leverage over the internal and external policies of recipients, to strengthen threatened allies, to pry open foreign markets, and to enhance the donor country's image at home and abroad. From the standpoint of the recipient government, aid provides resources that help bolster the political power and legitimacy of the existing leadership. Political elites in these nations often use aid to reward supporters, while denying resources to opponents, and sometimes indulge in direct corruption. Aid also encourages certain patterns of development that benefit different elements of society unevenly, perhaps, for instance, strengthening the modern, urban sector at the expense of the traditional, rural sector.

Seeing aid in terms of its effects on the political power of both donor and recipient governments helps us to understand why Third World political elites sometimes express ambivalent attitudes toward external assistance. Although aid may strengthen political leaders in relation to their domestic rivals, it also places them and their countries in a position of dependence upon aid donors. And dependence, of course, means increased vulnerability and the greater potential for external manipulation. This same aspect of the relationship makes

---

[107] United Nations Development Program, *Human Development Report, 1994*, New York: Oxford University Press, 1994, 167.

[108] "Foreign Aid: Stingy Sam," 26.

the continuation of aid attractive to donor country leaders, even when foreign aid is unpopular among taxpayers and when evidence of its success in promoting development is ambiguous.

Given the political stakes associated with aid, the poor's lack of participation in the aid process is hardly accidental. Indeed, were aid to be reformed to focus more directly and effectively on the poor and to provide them with substantial input and control, aid would undoubtedly lose much of the appeal it presently holds for political elites in both donor and recipient nations. Ironically, taking the "politics" out of foreign aid might simply undercut the motivation for governments to go on spending and receiving foreign aid, leading to a massive contraction of such programs. This likelihood merely underscores the close association between politics and economics in North–South relations.

## ANNOTATED BIBLIOGRAPHY

Robert L. Ayres, *Banking on the Poor: The World Bank and World Poverty*, Cambridge: MIT Press, 1983.
   A detailed examination of the World Bank's poverty lending programs during the 1970s.

P. T. Bauer, *Reality and Rhetoric: Studies in the Economics of Development*, Cambridge: Harvard University Press, 1984.
   Chapters three and four present a conservative critique of foreign aid.

Edward Clay and Olav Stoke (eds.), *Food Aid Reconsidered: Assessing the Impact on Third World Countries*, London: Frank Cass, 1991.
   A collection of essays, mostly case studies, on the effects of food aid.

Robert Cassen and Associates, *Does Aid Work?*, Oxford: Clarendon Press, 1986.
   A detailed, thorough, and balanced effort to measure the contributions of foreign aid to Third World development and poverty reduction.

Kevin Danaher (ed.), *50 Years Is Enough: The Case Against the World Bank and the International Monetary Fund*, Boston: South End Press, 1994.
   A collection of short essays that, taken together, offer an impassioned critique and condemnation of the policies and effects of the world's two largest multilateral financial organizations.

Graham Hancock, *Lords of Poverty: The Power, Prestige and Corruption of the International Aid Business*, New York: Atlantic Monthly Press, 1989.
   A biting critique of foreign aid written by a journalist with extensive experience in the Third World. Criticizes the hypocrisy and ineffectiveness of the foreign aid bureaucracy.

Theresa Hayter and Catherine Watson, *Aid: Rhetoric and Reality*, London: Pluto Press, 1985.
   A radical critique of foreign aid.

Stephen Hellinger, Douglas Hellinger, and Fred M. O'Regan, *Aid for Just Development: Report on the Future of Foreign Assistance*, Boulder: Lynne Rienner Publishers, 1988.
   Presents proposals for reforming foreign aid.

David Lumsdaine, *Moral Vision in International Politics: The Foreign Aid Regime, 1949-1989*, Princeton: Princeton University Press, 1993.

A unique book. Lumsdaine argues that foreign aid has been chiefly motivated by altruism rather than self interest and that the humanitarian thrust of aid has become stronger over time. Aid is submitted as an illustration that morality does matter in international affairs.

Paul Mosley, Jane Harrigan, and John Toye, *Aid and Power: Policy-Based Lending* (vols. 1 and 2), New York: Routledge, 1991.

A sophisticated and comprehensive history, analysis and evaluation of the World Bank's shift to policy based lending during the 1980s. Published in two volumes. The first volume examines the rationale and goals of policy based lending, using quantitative data. The second volume examines various country cases.

Judith Tendler, *Inside Foreign Aid*, Baltimore: Johns Hopkins University Press, 1975.

Although dated, Tendler's book continues to offer important insights into how bureaucratic factors influence and hamper the performance of foreign aid agencies.

Sarah Tisch and Michael Wallace, *Dilemmas of Development Assistance: The What, Why and Who of Foreign Aid*, Boulder: Westview Press, 1994.

A basic primer on foreign aid.

Robert Wood, *From Marshall Plan to Debt Crisis: Foreign Aid and Development Choices in the World Economy*, Berkeley: University of California Press, 1986.

A theoretical and empirical examination of the post–World War II foreign aid system. Links foreign aid and the debt crisis with an approach drawing upon both dependency theory and regime analysis.

Robert Zimmerman, *Dollars, Diplomacy, and Dependency: Dilemmas of U.S. Economic Aid*, Boulder: Westview Press, 1993.

A balanced assessment of U.S. foreign aid written by a former aid official.

# Chapter 11

# MULTINATIONAL CORPORATIONS IN THE THIRD WORLD

The growth of the multinational corporation (MNC) is one of the most revolutionary and controversial phenomena in the development of the world economy during this century. MNCs are business firms that own or control production in more than one country. In practice, the largest MNCs orchestrate an ensemble of investments scattered across dozens of countries. Tied together by a vast communications web, these firms match various corporate functions, such as research and development, production, and marketing, with locales around the globe that feature the right mix of necessary ingredients, whether these be the skills and wage rates of local labor, the tax and regulatory policies of governments, the availability of needed infrastructure, or the supply of natural resources. The sheer size of many MNCs, combined with their economic efficiency and international mobility, not only provides such firms with a key place in the world economy, but also endows them with considerable political power and influence.

In recent decades, MNCs have expanded in numbers, size, and economic clout. Over the past several decades, the rate of growth in global foreign direct investment has outpaced both domestic growth and international trade. The number of MNCs based in the world's fourteen richest countries has more than tripled over the past twenty-five years, from seven thousand in 1969 to twenty-four thousand in 1994. The world's two hundred largest corporations now account for 25 percent of all global economic activity. U.S. MNCs earn twice as much in revenue from manufacturing operations abroad as from exports. Indeed, one third of all world trade takes place on an intrafirm basis—among different units of the same global company. The yearly sales of the largest MNCs dwarf the annual GNPs of a vast majority of Third World countries.[1]

---

[1] Data in this paragraph taken from Richard Barnet, "Lords of the Global Economy," *The Nation*, December 19, 1994, 754; and "The Discreet Charm of the Multicultural Multinational," *The Economist*, July 30, 1994.

The large-scale movement of modern foreign direct investment (FDI) to the Third World dates from the turn of the century. The earliest MNCs to invest in the developing countries focused on agricultural goods and the extraction of raw materials. The demands of rapidly growing Northern industries as well as the rising affluence of European and North American consumers created a healthy market for Southern resources and cash crops. Very little Northern investment in the South flowed into manufacturing at this stage. In 1914, for instance, mining, oil, and agriculture accounted for 70 percent of all U.S. FDI located in developing countries, whereas manufacturing amounted to only 3 percent.[2]

The composition of FDI in the Third World began to change during the interwar period. U.S. firms, in particular, established growing numbers of manufacturing subsidiaries in Latin America. By 1939 Latin America was the home of two hundred foreign-owned manufacturing operations, two thirds of the total for all developing countries.[3] Yet foreign investment in Third World manufacturing did not really take off until after World War II. Today the subsidiaries of Northern-owned MNCs account for substantial shares of invested capital, employment, and output in the manufacturing sectors of most Third World countries. Their dominance is greatest in the most technologically advanced types of products and manufacturing processes.

Nevertheless, despite growth in the absolute levels of foreign investment in the South, FDI has expanded even more quickly in the North. On the eve of World War I, FDI located in the developing countries accounted for 60 percent of the total worldwide. By the early sixties, the Third World share of FDI had fallen to one third. This proportion fell further to roughly one quarter in the mid-1980s.[4] By this latter period, over one half of all U.S. FDI was located in only five developed countries (Britain, Canada, Germany, Switzerland, and the Netherlands).[5]

The relative significance of FDI to Third World economies has varied considerably over time. MNC investment in the South grew from an annual average of $2.6 billion during 1967–69 to $12.8 billion in 1979–81. Largely due to rising levels of commercial bank lending, however, the share of FDI in overall private financial flows to the Third World declined from over 50 percent in 1970 to 20 percent in 1985. Indeed, levels of new foreign investment fell absolutely during the early eighties, dropping to an annual average of roughly $10 billion. A modest turnaround began in 1986 as the flow of FDI to developing countries increased to $12.5 billion. During the same year, FDI

---

[2] Rhys Jenkins, *Transnational Corporations and Uneven Development: The Internationalization of Capital and the Third World,* New York: Methuen, 1987, 5.

[3] Jenkins, *Transnational Corporations and Uneven Development,* 5–6.

[4] Jenkins, *Transnational Corporations and Uneven Development,* 5 and 13.

[5] John R. O'Neal, "Foreign Investment in Less Developed Regions," *Political Science Quarterly,* vol. 103, no. 1, 1988, 137–38.

again accounted for almost 50 percent of private financial flows. This was largely due, however, to a collapse in bank lending to the Third World.[6]

The nineties have witnessed a major resurgence in FDI flows to the Third World, reaching $70 billion in 1993. If portfolio investment, in the form of stocks and bonds (see Chapter 12 for a discussion of portfolio investment), and bank lending are included, total private investment flows from North to South reached $150 billion in 1993. Yet these foreign investments are highly concentrated in a handful of relatively prosperous Southern countries. In 1993, for example, four fifths of all private investment to the Third World was targeted at twelve Asian and Latin American countries.[7]

This revival of FDI flows to the Third World has been prompted by a variety of factors: falling interest rates in the North, the loosening of regulations on foreign investments in the South, rapid economic growth rates in some of the principal host countries, the emergence of debt–equity swaps as a tool for transforming Third World debt into equity investments (see the discussion of debt–equity swaps in Chapter 12), and new opportunities to purchase previously state-owned firms recently privatized by Third World governments.

## MOTIVES FOR FOREIGN DIRECT INVESTMENT IN THE THIRD WORLD

Northern firms have a variety of motives for investing in Third World countries. Some seek access to Southern resources. Extractive industries, such as mining, oil, or timber, are attracted by the presence of raw materials or mineral deposits. Many Southern countries, by virtue of their climate or geography, are particularly well suited to the production of cash crops desired in the North, such as sugar, coffee, cocoa, or tropical fruits. Northern agribusiness firms invest in the production, processing, and packaging of such agricultural commodities in the South.

Manufacturing firms have greater freedom over where they locate their investments than do natural resource producers. The former often have a choice between servicing foreign markets through export or foreign investment. Decisions to invest in the Third World are influenced both by competitive pressures in particular industries and by the incentives created by government policies. One school of thought, known as *product life-cycle theory*, suggests that firms that gain a monopoly position as a result of successful innovation will move abroad in search of new markets or lower costs as a

---

[6] Gerald Pollio and Charles H. Riemenschneider, "The Coming Third World Investment Revival," *Harvard Business Review*, March/April 1988, 114; and Stephen Krasner, *Structural Conflict: The Third World Against Global Liberalism*, Berkeley: University of California Press, 1985.

[7] "Coping with Capital," *The Economist*, October 29, 1994, 86; "Multinationals: A Survey," *The Economist*, June 24, 1995, 12.

means of preserving higher-than-normal profits after imitation has begun to erode their initial advantage over rivals at home.[8]

Most manufacturing FDI in the Third World produces commodities aimed at the local market. This sort of investment is most common in the larger, more prosperous Southern countries that have sizable and therefore attractive consumer bases. MNCs may decide to produce in such countries rather than export in order to better adjust to local tastes or to take advantage of lower labor or capital costs.

Often, however, the decision to invest abroad is prompted by the necessity of jumping protectionist barriers in order to gain access to Third World markets. Southern governments may erect tariffs or other sorts of barriers precisely in order to discourage imports while encouraging local production of the protected goods. The aim of this strategy, often referred to as *import substitution*, is to spur industrialization. Many MNCs have discovered ways to benefit from such policies. A single large factory can service the entire local demand for a given product in many Third World countries. Thus the first foreign firm to gain entry can profit handsomely. Freed from competition due to the umbrella of protection and the limited size of the domestic market, the local subsidiary can establish an effective monopoly, allowing it to charge higher prices and earn greater-than-normal profits. This very fact has engendered local resentment toward foreign firms.

For some firms, the primary incentive to invest in the Third World is to escape environmental regulations or higher taxes in their home country. Indeed, those Southern countries with a particularly urgent need for foreign investment have often explicitly molded their tax and regulatory policies to attract the interest of Northern multinationals.

Finally, foreign-owned assembly operations have been established in many Third World countries in order to take advantage of the low wage rates characteristic of Southern labor markets. Typically, products assembled in such factories are exported back to Northern markets, where they can be priced competitively vis-à-vis similar goods produced by other firms with more-expensive Northern labor.

## THE BENEFITS OF FOREIGN DIRECT INVESTMENT TO THIRD WORLD HOST COUNTRIES

Our primary concern in this chapter is with the impact of foreign direct investment on the Third World and the relationship between MNCs and host

---

[8] For elaboration, see Charles Kindleberger, "The Monopolistic Theory of Direct Foreign Investment," and Raymond Vernon, "The Product Cycle Model," both in George Modelski (ed.), *Transnational Corporations and World Order: Readings in International Political Economy*, San Francisco: W. H. Freeman & Co., 1979.

countries. Considerable debate surrounds these topics. Defenders of MNCs argue that FDI stimulates economic growth and development. MNCs augment scarce local resources and bring with them a package of assets that can seldom be matched by indigenous firms.[9] Elements of this package include:

## CAPITAL

Many Third World countries are characterized by low rates of domestic savings. As a result, their economies are dependent upon external capital flows to finance new investment. FDI offers one means by which scarce local capital can be supplemented. To be sure, MNCs demand a price for injecting fresh capital into the host country's economy. Specifically, foreign investors prefer to repatriate a large portion of the profits they earn abroad. Yet the terms of FDI often compare favorably with those accompanying other sources of external financing. Commercial loans from Northern banks, for instance, carry interest charges that must be paid regardless of whether the local investment they finance proves profitable. In contrast, although MNCs share in the benefits from FDI, they also bear much of the risk. If one of its Third World subsidiaries loses money, an MNC will find that there are no profits to repatriate. Indeed, the headquarters of the firm may well choose to inject new capital into the failing subsidiary in an attempt to turn the operation around and salvage its initial investment. FDI also offers certain advantages over foreign aid. Although foreign assistance may be provided on favorable financial terms, it often comes with political strings attached, whether implicit or explicit. This is seldom the case for FDI.

## TECHNOLOGY

Although some Third World countries have managed to establish impressively modern manufacturing sectors, the vast majority of the new technology created worldwide still originates in the laboratories and universities of the North. MNCs provide one mechanism by which Northern technology is transferred to the Third World. MNCs tend to invest in the most technologically advanced sectors of Third World economies, supplying goods and services that are beyond the technological capacity of local firms to produce efficiently. MNCs also aid in technological diffusion through means such as licensing technology to other firms or passing along knowledge, skills, and techniques to local partners through joint ventures.

## MANAGEMENT EXPERTISE

The Third World subsidiaries of MNCs often organize production more efficiently than do local firms due to superior management skills and techniques.

---

[9] For a detailed empirical comparison between foreign and local firms in one country, see Larry N. Willmore, "The Comparative Performance of Foreign and Domestic Firms in Brazil," in Sanjaya Lall (ed.), *Transnational Corporations and Economic Development*, New York: Routledge, 1993.

MNCs possess great experience in managing large-scale enterprises. Branch plant managers can draw upon the vast storehouse of information and expertise contained within the corporation as a whole. Knowledge of modern management methods is spread through the training of indigenous personnel, whose representation in the ranks of management typically grows at the expense of expatriates the longer the MNC subsidiary is in place.

## MARKETING NETWORKS

Even where local firms can match MNCs in price and product quality, they may lack easy access to the extensive foreign marketing networks available to Northern firms. MNCs often possess long-standing relationships with, or even control over, Northern wholesale and retail outlets, enjoy greater information about market demand and consumer tastes, and command larger advertising resources.

# THE COSTS OF FOREIGN DIRECT INVESTMENT TO THIRD WORLD HOST COUNTRIES

Critics argue that the economic and political costs of FDI often outweigh the benefits.[10] Many criticisms center around differences between foreign and domestic firms and the ways they do business.

MNCs are accused of earning excessive profits in Third World countries, made possible by their oligopoly position in local economies.[11] The largest proportion of these profits is repatriated to shareholders in the firm's country of origin rather than reinvested locally. According to some studies, MNCs also overcharge for technology transfer to their own subsidiaries and rely more heavily upon imported parts and machinery than do domestic firms. Each of

---

[10] For critical treatments of MNC operations in the Third World, see Richard Barnet and Ronald Muller, *Global Reach: The Power of the Multinational Corporations*, New York: Simon and Schuster, 1974; Volker Bornschier and Christopher Chase-Dunn, *Transnational Corporations and Underdevelopment*, New York: Praeger, 1985; John Cavanaugh and Frederick Clairmonte, *The Transnational Economy: Transnational Corporations and Global Markets*, Washington: Institute for Policy Studies, 1982; Stephen Hymer, "The Multinational Corporation and the Law of Uneven Development," in Jagdish Bhagwati (ed.), *Economics and World Order*, New York: Macmillan, 1972; Richard Newfarmer, "Multinational and Marketplace Magics in the 1980s," in Jeffrey Frieden and David Lake (eds.), *International Political Economy: Perspectives on Global Power and Wealth*, New York: St. Martin's Press, 1991; Osvaldo Sunkel, "Big Business and 'Dependencia,'" and Johan Galtung, "A Structural Theory of Imperialism," both in Modelski, *Transnational Corporations;* and Jeremy Brecher and Tim Costello, *Global Village or Global Pillage*, Boston: South End Press, 1995.

[11] Business concentration is especially high in many extractive sectors. Data from the seventies indicate that three MNCs shared 70 percent of the world production, marketing, and distribution of bananas. Six firms controlled 70 percent of world aluminum production capacity. Fewer than ten corporations dominated the global production and processing of the following commodities: copper, iron ore, lead, nickel, tin, tobacco, and zinc. Garrett Fitzgerald, *Unequal Partners*, New York: United Nations, 1979, 11–12.

these practices tends to reflect negatively in the host country's balance of payments position.

Critics contend that MNCs often borrow from the already scarce supply of local capital rather than bring new investment funds into the country. Because of their size and resources, foreign firms typically receive preferential terms from local banks when borrowing money, as compared with local firms. Another criticism is that MNCs discourage local entrepreneurship by often entering a country through the acquisition of an existing Third World firm or using superior resources to drive native competitors out of business.

Third World governments particularly object to a common MNC practice known as "transfer pricing." MNCs resort to this technique in an attempt to lower their overall tax burden or to evade restrictions on the repatriation of profits. Transfer pricing is essentially an accounting practice applied to intrafirm trade. Different branches or subsidiaries of the same firm, located in different countries, often exchange goods. A U.S.-based manufacturer, for instance, might produce parts in a factory located in Texas but ship these parts to a plant in Mexico for assembly. In turn, the assembled product is transported back to the United States for final sale. The price that the home firm charges the Mexican subsidiary for the parts or that the subsidiary charges the home firm for the assembled product is essentially arbitrary because these transactions take place within the same company and are not exposed to market forces. If, let us say, Mexico imposes a higher tax on corporate profits than does the United States, then the MNC can lower its overall tax bill by overpricing the parts shipped to Mexico while underpricing the assembled products that are "sold" back to the home firm in the United States. By manipulating the prices on intrafirm trade in this way, the Mexican subsidiary will show little profit on its books, thus avoiding the high Mexican tax rate, while the profit of the home firm will be artificially boosted—allowing it to be taxed at the low U.S. rate. This sort of practice is hard to detect because it is difficult to know what the products might have sold for in arm's-length transactions among independent firms. Because most Third World countries tax the profits of foreign corporations at relatively high rates, they are often targets of transfer pricing schemes and suffer a loss of potential tax revenue as a result.

Some forms of FDI represent attempts to export pollution from Northern countries, where environmental enforcement is stringent, or to exploit reserves of cheap labor. In Ilo, Peru, for instance, local villagers suffer from serious respiratory and other health problems stemming from the air and water pollution produced by a nearby copper smelter plant owned by three large American corporations. The plant emits up to two thousand tons of sulfur dioxide into the air each day—ten to fifteen times the legal levels for similar operations in the United States—as well as streams of toxic wastes that make their way into the local water supply.[12]

---

[12] Calvin Sims, "In Peru, a Fight for Fresh Air," *New York Times*, December 12, 1995.

Mexico is host to 1,800 U.S.-owned product assembly plants located along the border. Called *maquiladoras*, some of these plants relocated to Mexico to take advantage of lax Mexican environmental laws and to break free of stricter regulations in the United States. A study by the American National Toxic Campaign found that of twenty-three such factories sampled, seventeen were responsible for significant toxic waste discharges. Much of southern California's furniture industry has moved across the border to escape severe air pollution controls on solvent emissions. Mexico has recently taken steps to tighten its environmental laws and to crack down on polluters, but its enforcement mechanisms remain inadequate.

In addition to the environmental problems associated with *maquiladoras*, critics point out that the jobs created through these factories are extremely low paying and that work conditions as well as health and safety standards are far below those in the United States. Moreover, *maquiladoras* have developed few backward linkages to the rest of the Mexican economy. Of the $23 billion in physical inputs consumed by the *maquiladora* industries yearly, only 2 percent is supplied by Mexican sources.[13]

FDI also carries political risks. MNCs may appeal to their home government to exert pressure on a host state when disputes arise. The Hickenlooper Amendment, passed by the U.S. Congress in 1962, requires that aid be denied to countries that nationalize the assets of U.S. corporations without prompt and adequate compensation. The law has been applied, or its use threatened, on several occasions. More dramatically, the United States, through the use of CIA covert operations and economic pressure, took part in the overthrow of governments in Iran (1953), Guatemala (1954), and Chile (1973) after the assets of firms from the United States and other Northern countries were nationalized. Although other factors influenced these decisions, the desire of U.S. officials to defend U.S. corporate interests abroad played an important role in all three instances.

## A BARGAINING FRAMEWORK FOR ANALYZING MNC–HOST COUNTRY RELATIONS

Are MNCs a boon or a burden to Third World host countries? The answer is more complex than either of the two perspectives just outlined would suggest. Whether the benefits of FDI outweigh the costs depends substantially upon the balance of bargaining power between the firm and the host state. This bargaining relationship determines whether a state will have the capacity to control the activities of foreign investors and thus limit negative impacts. In this section, we first review the various types of regulation that Third

---

[13] See William Burke, "The Toxic Price of Free Trade in Mexico," *In These Times*, May 22-29, 1991; Robert Reinhold, "Mexico Says It Won't Harbor U.S. Companies Fouling Air," *New York Times*, April 18, 1991; and "Survey: Mexico," *The Economist*, October 28, 1995, 16.

World states have attempted to impose upon MNCs in the past. We then examine the sources of bargaining power available to each party.

## Regulating MNC Behavior

During the seventies, in particular, Third World states adopted a variety of regulations designed to control and channel the activities of MNCs. Many countries exclude foreign investment in certain crucial sectors of the economy such as public utilities, mining, steel, retailing, insurance, and banking. In some cases, foreign investors are required to form joint ventures providing majority control to local partners. A number of Latin American countries limit profit repatriation and technology payments by foreign-owned subsidiaries. Requirements that a stated percentage of production must be exported are common. Some countries require that indigenous labor be hired into middle- and upper-level management positions. Several countries have placed limits on MNC access to local capital markets in an effort to encourage greater contributions of external financing for new investments. Finally, attempts have been made to encourage MNC subsidiaries to carry out local research and development.[14]

These controls have been imposed most successfully by the larger, more prosperous Third World countries, which are in a relatively strong position to bargain over the terms of FDI. In addition to the risk that demanding regulations will simply scare away foreign investors, smaller, less-developed countries have a more difficult time enforcing investment rules.

Indeed, impressively strict regulations designed to enhance local control often have surprisingly little effect on MNC operations in practice.[15] Consider the common stipulation that MNCs must enter into joint ventures providing majority ownership to local partners. Compliance with this regulation is often achieved through fictitious means. A foreign firm will simply lend to the local partner the capital needed to acquire majority ownership. Or the original equity investment in the project is held artificially low so as to make it possible for the local partner to come up with the required money. The enterprise then funds its operations through debt rather than equity, often borrowing funds from the parent company of the foreign partner. These sorts of nominal shareholding arrangements create the illusion, without the reality, of a large local stake in the enterprise.

---

[14] For general discussions of Third World efforts to regulate FDI, see Jenkins, *Transnational Corporations and Uneven Development*; Krasner, *Structural Conflict*; Robert Cohen and Jeffrey Frieden, "The Impact of Multinational Corporations on Developing Nations," and Robert Kurdle, "The Several Faces of the Multinational Corporation: Political Reaction and Policy Response," both in Kendall Stiles and Tsuneo Akaha (eds.), *International Political Economy: A Reader*, New York: HarperCollins, 1991; Francisco Orrago Vicuna, "The Control of Multinational Corporations," in Modelski, *Transnational Corporations*; and Stephen Guisinger, "Host Country Policies to Attract and Control Foreign Investment," in Lall, *Transnational Corporations and Economic Development*.

[15] The material in this and the next two paragraphs relies upon Franklin B. Weinstein, "Underdevelopment and Efforts to Control Multinational Corporations," in Modelski, *Transnational Corporations*.

Even where local partners legitimately put up the majority of capital to fund a project, they seldom exercise real control. The MNC typically provides raw materials, equipment, spare parts, financing, technology, managerial skills, and marketing services. Because the keys to the success of the enterprise are in the hands of the foreign partner, so is effective control over how it is run. Foreign control may in fact be formalized in basic agreements concluded at the outset of the venture that reserve key functions to the MNC.

Many countries attempt to ensure that MNCs hire, train, and promote local workers into management positions or require that a certain proportion of the final product consist of locally produced parts. Yet the first restriction is often waived when foreign subsidiaries attest that people with the requisite skills and experience are not available locally. In some cases, local managers are hired but given little responsibility. Local content rules can be circumvented by using creative accounting to inflate the value of the portion of the overall product accounted for by local inputs.

The Andean Pact represents one attempt to overcome the poor bargaining position of small countries. In December 1970 Bolivia, Colombia, Chile, Ecuador, and Peru (Venezuela was added in 1973, while Chile abandoned the group in 1976) announced Decision 24—an agreement on "common treatment for foreign capital, trademarks, patents, licensing agreement, and royalties." This agreement imposed a common set of new regulations on MNCs operating in pact countries. These regulations included the exclusion of FDI from certain economic sectors, limits on profit repatriation and access to local lending, a phased-in reduction of foreign ownership in MNC affiliates to a maximum of 49 percent, and controls on technology transfer and royalty payments. The impact of these regulations has been mixed. Technology payments were renegotiated downward after implementation of the pact, and local participation in MNC operations increased. Due to incomplete data, however, the effect of Decision 24 on flows of new FDI is difficult to judge with precision. Investments by U.S. MNCs in pact countries continued to increase during the late seventies, but at a slower pace than in the rest of Latin America.[16]

The difficulty with national, or even regional, controls is that MNCs can reallocate their investment flows toward countries that offer less interference. Thus many Third World countries have long called for a strict, binding global code of conduct for MNCs.[17] Northern countries, however, have resisted these demands. Instead, in 1976 the OECD sponsored a weaker, voluntary code that lacked Third World approval.[18] In the late eighties, negotiations

---

[16] Jenkins, *Transnational Corporations and Uneven Development*, 173–75; Cohen and Frieden, "The Impact of Multinational Corporations on Developing Nations," 169; R. N. Gwynne, "Multinational Corporations and the Triple Alliance in Latin America," in C. J. Dixon, D. Drakakis-Smith, and H. D. Watts, *Multinational Corporations and the Third World*, London: Croom Helm, 1986, 128.

[17] See United Nations, "Resolution Establishing the Commission on Transnational Corporations and Charter of the Economic Rights and Duties of States," in Modelski, *Transnational Corporations*.

[18] OECD, "Declaration on International Investment and Multinational Enterprises and Guidelines for Multinational Enterprises," in Modelski, *Transnational Corporations*.

over international regulation of MNC activities resumed under the auspices of the United Nations Center on Transnational Corporations (UNCTC). After several years of North–South stalemate, however, these negotiations were quietly set aside, and the UNCTC was itself disbanded.

## The Determinants of Relative Bargaining Power

MNCs and Third World states are engaged in an interdependent relationship. Each party wants something from the other. The principal concern of the MNC is to maximize profits. To accomplish this, it must gain access to the resources, markets, or cheap labor of the Third World country where an investment opportunity presents itself. The goals of the host state are diverse. Third World political leaders are attracted to the jobs, skills, output, technology, and global marketing power that MNCs have to offer.

Although the goals and interests of the two parties are potentially compatible, the MNC's desire to maximize profits may, as we have seen, lead it to engage in practices that reduce the benefits accruing to the host country. Third World countries are therefore often inclined to regulate and control MNC behavior so as to maximize host countries' share of benefits from the investment.

The host country's ability to successfully set the terms under which foreign investors do business in that country is constrained by its relative bargaining power. The country's principal bargaining advantage is its capacity to control access to the country and to exert legal control over foreign business operations after an investment has been made. The MNC, however, is far from helpless. Its power derives both from the package of assets it has to offer the host country and from its mobility. If the host state drives too hard a bargain, imposing regulations so onerous as to substantially erode the profit-making potential of foreign-owned subsidiaries, MNCs may take their business elsewhere or, less drastically, simply devise ways of evading regulations.

The balance of bargaining power between foreign firms and host countries may vary according to: (1) the characteristics of the host country, (2) the characteristics of the investment, and (3) changes in the international economic environment.[19] We review each of these factors in the following sections.

### CHARACTERISTICS OF THE HOST COUNTRY

Host countries possessing characteristics that render them attractive to foreign investors are likely to find themselves in a relatively strong bargaining position. The more lucrative the investment, the more likely it is to be made in

---

[19] This section relies heavily throughout on Theodore Moran, "Multinational Corporations and Dependency: A Dialogue for Dependentistas and Non-Dependentistas," *International Organization*, Winter 1978. Also see Franklin Weinstein, "Underdevelopment and Efforts to Control Multinational Corporations," in Modelski, *Transnational Corporations*; and John Stopford and Susan Strange, *Rival States, Rival Firms: Competition for World Market Shares*, New York: Cambridge University Press, 1991.

spite of heavy host state regulation. Thus Third World countries with large domestic markets, skilled and disciplined work forces, bountiful natural resources, and well-developed infrastructures can afford to drive hard bargains with foreign firms that, presumably, will be eager to gain access to the country and its many economic opportunities.

The host country's position is also strengthened to the extent that it has available alternatives to foreign investment. If, for instance, the country already possesses a strong industrial structure, whether public or private, or is able to accumulate capital locally due to a high domestic savings rate, then its dependence on FDI is lessened. The price that the host state can demand of foreign investors for the right of entry is likely to go up.

Finally, states with large, sophisticated, and honest bureaucracies will be in a better position to bargain on an equal basis with highly skilled MNC negotiators. They will also possess a greater capacity to gather critical information, monitor MNC behavior, and enforce relevant laws and regulations.

Some Third World countries, such as Brazil, Mexico, and South Korea, possess many, though not all, of these characteristics. Yet most Southern countries lack, in varying degrees, a considerable number of the crucial characteristics that might place them in a favorable bargaining position with foreign firms.

## CHARACTERISTICS OF THE INVESTMENT

The bargaining relationship between governments and firms may vary across different investment projects within the same country. Some types of industry are more easily regulated than others. Bargaining leverage shifts to the host state when projects involve well-known and slowly changing technologies. In such cases, it is well within the capacity of state- or locally owned private firms to manage the production facility in question or to establish competing projects. Low-technology foreign investment is therefore often subject to heavy regulation, intense local competition, or even outright nationalization.

Investment projects resting upon more-sophisticated or rapidly changing technology are less vulnerable to state demands. In these cases, the local skills and knowledge needed to manage the project or to create competitive local alternatives may not exist. Moreover, the success of such ventures depends upon continuous infusions of new technology from the home firm. This increases the host state's dependence upon a foreign firm and places the latter in a strong bargaining position.

Much the same logic applies with respect to the foreign marketing requirements associated with production for export. Products marketed through complex networks, especially when the latter are controlled by the multinationals themselves, may require the cooperation of foreign firms if they are to be exported successfully. When products can be more readily sold abroad by state- or locally owned private firms, it is easier for Third World governments to escape dependence on foreign capital and to assert control over local production.

Capital-intensive projects typically require large fixed investments in factories and machinery. After these are in place, the foreign firm is hostage to state control due to high sunk costs. Only continued production and sales will possibly allow the firm to recoup its sizable initial outlay. Where fixed investment is low, however, a firm can more easily close up shop and relocate to a different country should state demands prove intolerable. Thus the size of the initial investment influences relative bargaining power.

Related to this point is the fact that potential foreign investors have greater bargaining power before a project is established than after. Knowing that the host state may be eager for additional investment, the firm will seek explicit pledges of favorable treatment prior to committing to a project. MNCs often attempt to play countries off against one another in an effort to strike the best and most reliable deal. After the project is in place, however, the firm's threat to relocate becomes less credible, and further concessions will be difficult to obtain. Indeed, Third World states often seek to alter the original bargain in their own favor.

In general, Third World bargaining power has been greatest with respect to mining and raw materials investments. These projects typically involve well-known and slowly changing technologies, simple marketing requirements, and high fixed investments. Owing to these factors, many foreign-owned extractive operations were nationalized by Third World governments during the seventies.

MNCs usually have greater leverage in manufacturing industries, especially those involving sophisticated and changeable technologies, complex foreign marketing requirements, and low fixed investments. Indeed, it is in just such industrial sectors that the concentration of MNC ownership is highest in the Third World.

## CHANGES IN THE INTERNATIONAL ECONOMIC ENVIRONMENT

The balance of bargaining power between states and firms can vary over time due to a changing international economic environment. During the seventies, for instance, external conditions tended to strengthen Third World states relative to MNCs. Growing competition among MNCs made it easier for governments to play firms off against one another in an attempt to achieve a more favorable bargain. In particular, previously dominant U.S. firms now faced growing competition from European and Japanese MNCs. After falling from a high of over 60 percent during the sixties, the U.S. share of the total world stock of foreign direct investment declined further from 46 percent in 1980 to 35 percent in 1988. Although the United States accounted for 31 percent of new FDI flows from 1980 through 1984, this proportion fell to 17 percent from 1985 through 1989.[20] Moreover, European and Japanese firms often proved more tolerant of state regulation than did U.S. corporations.

---

[20] United Nations Center on Transnational Corporations, *World Investment Report, 1991: The Triad in Foreign Direct Investment*, New York: United Nations, 1991, 32.

Another international economic factor that favored Third World states during the seventies was the growing availability of commercial bank lending. This provided an alternative source of capital and lessened Third World dependence upon FDI. Able to do without MNCs more easily, governments of developing countries tightened regulations and funneled borrowed funds into state-owned corporations that sometimes served as direct competitors to existing foreign firms.

Finally, the seventies were a time of relative growth and prosperity for many Third World countries. Manufacturing exports expanded rapidly. Moreover, world prices for raw material commodities were high during the first half of the decade. The wave of Third World nationalizations of foreign investments in extractive industries was largely prompted by host state efforts to ensure that the benefits of these soaring prices would be captured locally rather than carried abroad in the repatriated profits of MNCs.[21]

These favorable conditions changed rapidly during the eighties. A Northern recession led to declines in both Southern manufacturing exports and commodity prices. This, combined with higher oil prices and rising interest rates, led to a financial squeeze that culminated in the Third World debt crisis. As many countries teetered on the brink of insolvency, Northern banks drastically contracted their lending operations in the Third World.

Suddenly, many Third World countries came to view increased flows of FDI as one of the few available options that might allow them to sustain economic growth while simultaneously digging their way out from under a mountain of debt. Yet just when it was most needed, flows of FDI to the South entered a period of absolute decline. This was prompted in part by the dire economic circumstances in most Third World countries, but it was also a result of the strict regulations and controls that many MNCs confronted in developing nations.

Most Third World states, facing an unfavorable international economic environment and chastened by declining investment flows, were led by their weakened bargaining position to loosen controls on foreign investment as the eighties progressed. Mexico entirely revamped its foreign investment codes, removing many of the restrictions imposed during the seventies. Venezuela has done the same and has recently decided to invite back many of the same international oil companies whose assets it nationalized in 1976 to help with the exploitation of the Orinoco Belt.[22] Many developing nations, especially in Asia, now offer special incentives to MNCs willing to set up assembly operations in so-called export processing zones. Governments seek to attract export-oriented production by offering tax, tariff, and regulatory concessions to foreign firms that agree to establish factories in these special areas.[23] Other

---

[21] Pollio and Riemenschneider, "The Coming Third World Investment Revival."

[22] John McClean, "Venezuela Reverses Economic Course," *Chicago Tribune*, May 27, 1991.

[23] Joseph Grunwald and Kenneth Flamm, *The Global Factory: Foreign Assembly in International Trade*, Washington: Brookings, 1985.

common elements of deregulation include guarantees of unrestricted profit repatriation, tax breaks, special electrical rates, the removal of export and local input requirements, and streamlined approval procedures.

These relaxed controls and new incentives have contributed to the renewed interest of multinational corporations in the Third World and have stimulated new investment flows. They also reflect, however, the weakened bargaining positions that most Third World states possess vis-à-vis foreign firms. The terms of the typical investment deal have swung decidedly in favor of the latter during the past decade.

This bargaining framework approach to understanding the relationship between host states and foreign firms offers considerable advantages over treatments that exaggerate either the virtues or the villainy of MNCs in the Third World. Southern states can potentially influence the balance between the costs and benefits of FDI by setting the terms under which the subsidiaries of MNCs must operate. Whether a given government can do so effectively without discouraging desired flows of investment depends upon the relative bargaining strengths of the state and the firm. This, in turn, varies across countries and industries as well as across time.

A bargaining approach does, however, contain one major drawback. This sort of analysis is based upon the assumption that state managers in developing societies are motivated only by the desire to serve the national interests of their own country. The primary goal of the political leadership is to maximize the economic welfare of the society as a whole through the bargains it strikes with foreign investors. In some cases, however, this is an unrealistic assumption. Some observers argue that although political elites in Third World countries may sometimes possess the capability to bargain effectively with foreign corporations, they often lack the political will to do so.

This is most obviously the case when MNCs use their considerable resources to win favors through bribery and corruption. In one example, five nations banded in 1974 to form the Union of Banana Exporting Countries. Each government agreed to place an export tax on banana exports. One of the affected corporations, United Brands, paid a $1.25 million bribe to the Honduran minister of economics. In return, the Honduran government partially reneged on its agreement with other banana-exporting countries by cutting its export tax from fifty cents to twenty-five—a move that would have saved United Brands from $6 to $7 million yearly. In this case, United Brands's efforts backfired. Unlike most such episodes, news of the deal leaked to the public, and the Honduran government was overthrown.[24]

Corruption is not the only threat to host state autonomy. Some Third World elites maintain power in part through close military, economic, and political relationships with the home governments of local MNC affiliates. Vigorous efforts to control MNC activities may threaten to sour these relationships.

---

[24] Not long afterward, the chairman of United Brands committed suicide by leaping from the forty-fourth floor of a New York skyscraper. Paul Harrison, *Inside the Third World*, Middlesex, England: Penguin Books, 1981, 349.

Political motives also may prompt some Third World leaders to adopt an overly restrictive stance toward MNCs, purposely discouraging investments that could bring considerable benefits to the country. This might be the case, for instance, when the legitimacy of a government rests upon its nationalist appeal. Under these circumstances, MNCs may provide convenient scapegoats, perhaps diverting attention from government responsibility for other pressing national problems. Finally, some Third World governments may be divided on the question of foreign investment and thus unable to adopt any consistent bargaining position.

These considerations suggest the need for caution in applying a bargaining analysis to host state–MNC relations. Nevertheless, considerable evidence suggests that host states have in fact proven eager, in most instances, to strike better deals with MNCs when their bargaining position so allows. The extremes of co-optation or destructive defiance appear the exceptions rather than the rule.

## RECENT TRENDS IN MNC–HOST COUNTRY RELATIONS

Several important trends are reshaping the nature of foreign investment in the Third World. The geographic locus of investment flows has shifted from Latin America and the Middle East to Asia. Three long-term shifts in the sectoral orientation of MNC activities in the Third World are also continuing. Manufacturing investments are increasingly favored over those in the extractive industries, while, within the manufacturing sector, export-oriented production is growing faster than production for the domestic markets of the Southern host countries. Recently, however, FDI growth has been swiftest in the service sector of Third World economies. Finally, the terms of MNC entry into Third World countries are changing dramatically, with foreign firms increasingly shedding the risks of outright ownership in favor of more-limited and indirect forms of involvement in the Third World.

East Asia's share of global foreign direct investment rose from 3 percent in 1987 to 12.5 percent in 1992.[25] The redirection of foreign direct investment toward East and Southeast Asia is both a response to, and a partial source of, the rapid economic growth rates experienced in recent years by many countries of the region, including China, South Korea, Singapore, Taiwan, Hong Kong, Thailand, Malaysia, and Indonesia. By contrast, many other parts of the Third World remain mired in the economic doldrums that began in the eighties, rendering them unattractive to foreign investors. A number of Latin American countries, such as Chile, Mexico, Brazil, and Argentina, have, however, recently begun to attract large quantities of FDI after experiencing a sharp reduction in such flows during the eighties.

---

[25] "The Gorgeous East," *The Economist*, July 16, 1994, 56.

The emphasis on Asia reflects the growing foreign role of Japanese corporations—the most active foreign investors in the region. The internationalization of Japanese firms has stemmed in part from their accumulation of vast financial resources as a result of Japan's export successes. These firms have also been prompted to search for low-cost manufacturing sites abroad as a way of compensating for increasing Japanese wage levels and the rise of the yen. Between 1985 and 1989 the flow of Japanese capital, including FDI, to other Asian economies grew sixfold in dollar terms. Japanese firms have focused on countries with well-educated and disciplined work forces. These include Thailand, where one new Japanese factory was opened for each workday in 1989, and Malaysia, which received $25 billion in FDI, most from Japanese investors, over the six years ending in 1991.[26]

The shift in the sectors targeted by foreign investors from extractive industries to manufacturing and from production for domestic consumption to exports is illustrated by data on U.S. MNC affiliates located in the Third World. Between 1950 and 1984 the share of U.S. Third World FDI located in extractive industries fell from over one half to less than 40 percent, while the proportion accounted for by manufacturing rose from 15 percent to 37 percent.[27] The share of exports in the total sales of U.S. MNC subsidiaries in the South grew from 8.4 percent in 1966 to 18.1 percent in 1977 and has continued to rise.[28] In addition to the manufacturing export sector, multinational corporations have increasingly been attracted to the Southern service industries, including banking, insurance, transportation, shipping, tourism, construction, retail sales, advertising, and telecommunications. Service industries are likely to capture an increasing share of North–South investment flows over the coming decade.

Perhaps the most important trend in Third World host country–MNC relations during the recent years has been the development of new, more flexible forms of investment.[29] Traditionally, foreign investment entered the Third World in the form of a tightly integrated package under the ownership and control of the MNC. Elements of this package included capital, technology, managerial expertise, and marketing. Foreign investors typically resisted pressures from the host country to break up this package by allowing greater local control over various elements. Third World governments often responded by attempting to steer the behavior of foreign firms through the imposition of external legal and regulatory controls.

---

[26] See "Asia's Emerging Standard-Bearer," *The Economist*, July 21, 1990; and David Sanger, "Power of the Yen Winning Asia," *New York Times*, December 5, 1991.

[27] Jenkins, *Transnational Corporations and Uneven Development*, 7.

[28] United Nations Center on Transnational Corporations, *Transnational Corporations and International Trade: Selected Issues*, New York: United Nations, 1985, 6.

[29] This discussion relies upon Lapper, "Dressed for Designer Deals," Pollio and Riemenschneider, "The Coming Third World Investment Revival," and C. P Oman, "New Forms of Investment in Developing Countries," in Lall, *Transnational Corporations and Economic Development*.

Out of these conflicting perspectives emerged a set of arrangements that satisfied neither party. Third World governments argued that foreign control over all aspects of investment concentrated too much economic power in foreign hands, especially in critical sectors; limited the spin-off of skills, technology, and other benefits to the rest of the local economy; and led to abuses such as those surveyed earlier in this chapter. MNCs, for their part, became increasingly frustrated by government regulations that raised costs, cut profits, and hemmed in their autonomy. The result was a standoff: Governments resorted to more-extreme measures of control, such as outright nationalization, while MNCs increasingly steered clear of new commitments in the Third World.

In recent years, however, each side has begun to abandon previously rigid positions and to seek out more-cooperative arrangements designed to reconcile conflicting interests. As we have seen, Third World governments have begun to dismantle the unwieldy system of regulatory controls that served to discourage new foreign investment. MNCs, meanwhile, have begun to abandon their insistence on formal ownership and control over all phases of investment, thus removing one of the concerns that prompted Third World governments to impose onerous controls in the first place.

Although the older forms of MNC investment in the Third World continue to persist, a host of new ventures involves foreign firms as limited partners in projects often initiated and largely controlled by Third World businesses or governments. Typically, foreign firms provide only those elements of the overall project that local participants can't provide for themselves. The once-monolithic packaging of capital, technology, management, and marketing has given way to a new division of labor in which local and foreign partners perform different functions, depending upon the particular strengths they bring to the project.

These partnerships take many forms. In joint ventures, local and foreign firms team up to provide capital and management while dividing up profits. Or Third World firms may subcontract to provide components of a larger product or to carry out assembly operations for a foreign firm. In some cases, foreign firms provide the missing ingredients for a project that is predominantly controlled by Third World partners. For instance, a foreign firm may, in return for a fee, license technology to a Third World firm to be used in the production or design of a particular product. Foreign firms may also provide managers for a project that is locally owned. Turnkey contracts call for foreign firms to construct factories that are then turned over to a Third World firm for operation. Product-in-hand contracts are like turnkey contracts, except that the foreign partner also trains local managers in how to operate the plant. Finally, some Third World businesses act as franchisees, putting up the capital or paying royalties and providing management while the franchiser provides technology and trademarks along with direction in how the operation is to be run.

Malaysia's effort to develop a domestic automobile industry provides one example of the new flexibility in MNC–host country relations. The government forged a partnership with the Japanese firm Mitsubishi to produce a small economy car called the Proton. In return for one-third ownership, Mitsubishi provided the necessary design, technology, and machinery. When difficulties plagued the plant after it opened under Malaysian management, Mitsubishi was called in to provide managerial expertise as well. The operation has become profitable and has begun to generate exports on top of healthy domestic sales.[30]

These new arrangements satisfy many Third World concerns about foreign involvement in their economies. Much greater control is vested in local parties. This limits the potential for MNC abuses while contributing to the local accumulation of skills, knowledge, and experience. Third World governments, which often take a direct role in such ventures, gain greater say over which projects are initiated and how they are run, thus lessening the need for indirect controls and regulations. At the same time, some of the benefits that foreign investment can provide are preserved, such as access to skills and technology unavailable locally. Another benefit is less obvious. Many of the Northern firms involved in such deals are small- to medium-sized businesses and have little prior experience in Third World markets. Their growing presence opens new channels for foreign investment in the Third World and presents established MNCs with greater competition. Overall, this improves the bargaining climate for Third World countries in their relations with foreign capital.

These new "designer deals" do, however, hold potential drawbacks for the Third World. By gaining greater control, Third World governments and private firms also shoulder higher risks. When the role of MNCs is lessened, MNCs give up responsibility for assessing the wisdom of investment decisions. If a project fails, the losses are felt much more directly in the Third World itself and much less in the bottom line of MNC spreadsheets. A related problem is that these arrangements provide only limited infusions of foreign capital into Third World host countries. Capital, a precious commodity in most Third World countries, must be raised locally or borrowed from abroad.

This shift of responsibility, risk, and uncertainty to the Third World partners is precisely what makes the new forms of involvement attractive to many MNCs. Often they profit by providing services under contract without the necessity of putting their own capital at risk. The lower profile of these new investment forms also removes the political spotlight from foreign business involvement in the Third World, lessening the prospect of populist and nationalist agitation against their presence.

## CONCLUSIONS

Many MNCs make handsome profits on their Third World operations. Southern countries often benefit from the capital and know-how that accom-

---

[30] "New Car for Malaysia, New Influence for Japan," *New York Times*, March 6, 1991.

pany such investments. The potential for mutual gain has indeed perpetuated the ongoing relationship between Northern firms and Southern host governments. Yet although each party is, in varying degrees, dependent upon the other, the interests, purposes, and perspectives of MNCs and Third World states diverge in some essential respects. These differences have given rise to a history of conflict. The "rules of the game" governing foreign investment in various Third World countries have changed greatly over time, often in response to changes in relative bargaining power. Efforts to devise a lasting and mutually acceptable framework for MNC-Third World relations have generally produced disappointing results.

The fundamental source of MNC-Third World conflict stems from the varying attributes of the two parties. MNCs are economic entities that seek to maximize profits on a global scale. Though, in practice, FDI may contribute to the development of a host country's economy, this is, from the firm's perspective, an incidental result, not the primary purpose of the investment. Changes in corporate practice that might maximize the benefits to a host country appeal to corporate executives only if the changes also happen to make sense in terms of overall profitability—a circumstance that is probably rare.

Third World states are political entities bounded by territorial borders. The principal concerns of Southern leaders are to promote economic development while also reducing their countries' vulnerability to foreign manipulation. From the Third World perspective, MNCs represent both opportunity and threat. FDI brings economic assets that are scarce in most Third World countries. Yet in the absence of effective regulation, these assets are subject to foreign control. Decisions made outside the country's borders ultimately determine both the economic and political effects of FDI.

MNCs would prefer a world without borders. Yet they must operate in a system of sovereign states. MNCs cannot escape the realities of fragmented political authority in the international system, but they can and do attempt to minimize the interference of national regulation on their global operations by translating their mobility, knowledge, and resources into bargaining power.

Short of outright nationalization, host states cannot alter the global or transnational character of the MNC. They can, however, use their legal and territorial control to impose regulations designed to ensure that FDI takes place on terms that further national development goals. Their ability to do so, without disrupting the stream of foreign investment, depends upon the stringency of the regulatory regime that the state seeks to impose as well as upon its relative bargaining power.

The tensions between Northern MNCs and Southern host states may tighten or relax over time. The outcomes of bargaining between them may vary as well. But the fundamental character of their relationship is likely to persist. Conflicting interests and desires will continue to weigh against the mutual dependence of firms and states upon one another, ensuring a stormy marriage between the two.

## Annotated Bibliography

Volker Bornschier and Christopher Chase-Dunn, *Transnational Corporations and Underdevelopment*, New York: Praeger, 1985.
    A conceptual analysis of international capital flows employing world systems theory—a school of thought that is closely related to the dependency perspective.

Jeremy Brecher and Tim Costello, *Global Village or Global Pillage*, Boston: South End Press, 1995.
    A radical critique of globalization and the spread of multinational corporations written for a general audience.

Peter J. Buckley and Jeremy Clegg (eds.), *Multinational Enterprises in Less Developed Countries*, New York: St. Martin's Press, 1991.
    A collection of theoretical and empirical essays on the role that multinational corporations play in Third World countries.

Rhys Jenkins, *Transnational Corporations and Uneven Development: The Internationalization of Capital and the Third World*, New York: Methuen, 1987.
    A comprehensive treatment of MNCs in the Third World written from a dependency perspective. Contains a wealth of data, history, and theoretical analysis.

Sanjaya Lall (ed.), *Transnational Corporations and Economic Development*, New York: Routledge, 1993.
    An excellent collection of essays, new and old, on the economic dimensions of foreign direct investment in the Third World.

George Modelski (ed.), *Transnational Corporations and World Order: Readings in International Political Economy*, San Francisco: W. H. Freeman & Co., 1979.
    Although dated, this reader contains a number of classic theoretical works on the politics and economics of foreign direct investment.

Theodore Moran, "Multinational Corporations and Dependency: A Dialogue for Dependentistas and Non-Dependentistas," *International Organization*, Winter 1978.
    A seminal source on the bargaining approach to analyzing MNC–host country relations.

John Stopford and Susan Strange, *Rival States, Rival Firms: Competition for World Market Shares*, New York: Cambridge University Press, 1991.
    Examines interfirm competition among multinational corporations and bargaining between firms and states.

United Nations Center on Transnational Corporations, *World Investment Report, 1991: The Triad in Foreign Direct Investment*, New York: United Nations, 1991.
    A fact-filled review of trends and patterns in foreign direct investment.

Van Whiting, *The Political Economy of Foreign Investment in Mexico: Nationalism, Liberalism and Constraints on Choice*, Baltimore: Johns Hopkins University Press, 1991.
    A detailed case study focusing on Mexican efforts to regulate foreign direct investment.

# *Chapter 12*

# THIRD WORLD DEBT AND NORTH–SOUTH FINANCE

Over the past two decades, Mexico's economy has served as an uncanny barometer of the North–South financial climate. During the heady days of the 1970s, Northern bankers often made Mexico City the first stop on their itinerary as they peddled loans to one Third World country after another. When the bubble of debt-led Southern growth burst in the early eighties, it was Mexico that first approached the precipice of national default. The ensuing Mexican bailout, organized by the U.S. Treasury Department and the International Monetary Fund (IMF) in 1982, established a pattern for subsequent debt rescheduling agreements with dozens of Third World countries over the following years.

More diligently than most other Southern debtors, Mexico closely followed Northern policy prescriptions for nursing its economy back to health and restoring its international creditworthiness. When, despite seven years of austerity, this painful remedy failed to bring relief to either Mexico or other Southern countries, Mexico negotiated the first Brady Plan deal with its commercial creditors in 1989. The Brady Plan offered Mexico, and subsequently other debtor nations, the first measure of genuine debt reduction since the beginnings of the debt crisis.

Mexico led the way in the early nineties when Northern financial resources again began flowing to Latin America in the form of burgeoning portfolio investments. Coming full circle, however, it was Mexico that first slipped back into financial crisis in late 1994, when a plummeting peso sparked massive international capital flight.

Like so many other Third World countries, Mexico has a recent history that has been profoundly shaped by the quality of its relationship to the international financial system. Periods of feast, such as the seventies and early nineties, have been followed by cycles of crisis and financial famine. The Third World debt crisis of the eighties and the recent topsy-turvy movement of Southern stock markets serve to underline the instability and unpredictability of North–South financial relations.

With the Mexican case providing a central focus, this chapter explores the political economy of Third World debt and North–South financial ties. We begin by inventorying the dimensions and costs of Third World debt. Next, we introduce the principal players in this continuing drama. In the heart of the chapter, we outline the origins and evolution of the debt problem, with special attention to the dynamics of North–South bargaining. Finally, we examine the contemporary growth of portfolio investment in the Third World and the causes of Mexico's most recent financial meltdown.

## THE COSTS OF THIRD WORLD DEBT

Hovering menacingly over much of the Third World, a dark cloud of debt dimmed prospects for Southern economic growth and development for most of the 1980s and continues to cast a shadow over some economies even today. In 1970 Third World debt to Northern banks, governments, and multilateral lending institutions totaled $70 billion. In 1979 overall Third World debt came to $400 billion. By 1993 the latter figure had more than quadrupled to a sum of $1.66 trillion.[1]

The burden of paying the stream of principal and interest due each year on this enormous debt has imposed severe costs on people throughout the Third World. Forced to squeeze domestic consumption in order to free the resources needed to satisfy the debt burden, governments have adopted measures that invariably produce economic hardship. As Jamaica's former Prime Minister Michael Manley observed in 1980, officials in debtor countries often face a cruel choice between "using your last foreign exchange to pay off Citibank and Chase Manhattan or buying food and medicines for your people."[2]

Between 1980 and 1985, two thirds of Third World countries experienced negative or negligible economic growth rates.[3] From the mid-1970s onward, sub-Saharan Africa entered into what former World Bank President A. W. Clausen called "the worst economic crisis any region has faced since World War Two."[4] The real incomes of workers in Mexico and Venezuela declined by 40 percent over the course of the eighties. Per-capita GNP in Latin America as a whole, which had risen by 40 percent during the seventies, fell by 7 percent in the following decade.[5]

---

[1] Edward R. Fried and Philip H. Trezise, *Third World Debt: The Next Phase,* Washington: Brookings, 1989, 5; and Steven Greenhouse, "Third World Markets Gain Favor," *New York Times,* December 17, 1993. These figures include only medium- and long-term debt. Third World countries owe many additional billions of dollars in short-term debt.

[2] Quoted in Michael Moffitt, *The World's Money: International Banking from Bretton Woods to the Brink of Insolvency,* New York: Simon and Schuster, 1983, 127.

[3] Robin Broad and John Cavanaugh, "How to Approach Third World Debt," *New York Times,* March 3, 1988.

[4] Quoted in Kari Polanyi Levitt, "Linkage and Vulnerability: The 'Debt Crisis' in Latin America and Africa," in Bonnie Campbell (ed.), *Political Dimensions of the Debt Crisis,* New York: St. Martin's Press, 1989, 15.

[5] For data on changes in Latin income levels, see Tom Wicker, "The Real Danger of Debt," *New York Times,* December 2, 1988; Alan Riding, "Rumblings in Venezuela," *New York Times,* March 7, 1989; and Clyde Farnsworth, "U.S. Falls Short on Its Third World Debt Plan," *New York Times,* January 9, 1990.

No less shocking are the social consequences of the debt crisis. From 1980 to 1984, government spending on health care fell in fourteen Latin American countries, while education outlays declined in ten.[6] Other areas of the Third World, particularly Africa, were hit even harder. In its 1989 *State of the World's Children* survey, UNICEF focused on what it referred to as "children in debt." Its findings are disturbing:

> [I]n the thirty-seven poorest countries (most of which are in Africa), per capita spending on health has fallen by half over the last few years, and on education by a quarter. Malnutrition is rising in Burundi, Gambia, Guinea-Bissau, Niger, Nigeria, and other African countries. Some 350,000 more African children died last year due to reduced health budgets, deteriorating sanitation, and the lack of foreign exchange to import even basic medicines.[7]

Although low-income debtor countries pay an average of $43 per person in debt repayment each year, only $35 per person is spent in these countries each year on health and education. Although not solely responsible for these gloomy developments, the debt crisis was an important contributor to each.[8]

The debt crisis also engendered social and political instability in many countries. In 1989 "IMF riots," so called because they followed announcements of new government austerity policies demanded by the IMF in return for new loans, broke out in a number of Latin American countries. These incidents of unrest left fourteen dead in Argentina, two hundred dead in the Dominican Republic, and three hundred dead in Venezuela, not to mention the many injured and the millions of dollars in losses from supermarket looting and vandalism. Wrenching economic reforms launched by Brazil during 1990, designed in part to prepare the country for renewed debt negotiations, led to severe economic recession and immense political and social turmoil. In June of that year an estimated 1.5 million workers participated in 330 separate strikes in protest of spreading unemployment and a declining standard of living. Striking workers at a Ford plant demolished cars and computers, while a peasant organization announced a "massive and radical offensive" of land occupations.[9] The story is similar in many parts of Africa. Urban insurrection in Sudan following the introduction of IMF reforms in 1985 toppled the government of Gaafar al-Nimeiry, while similar policies have led to rioting in Nigeria, Tunisia, and Morocco.[10]

---

[6] "Latin American Debt: Living on Borrowed Time?" *Great Decisions, '89*, New York: Foreign Policy Association, 1989, 30.

[7] Ernest Harsch, "After Adjustment," *Africa Report*, May/June 1989, 47.

[8] Barbara Crossette, "U.N. Planning Ambitious, and Risky, Conference on Poverty," *New York Times*, January 23, 1995. Also see Fran Hosken, "Austerity's Human Toll," *The Humanist*, January/February 1989.

[9] James Brooke, "Brazil's Costly Trip to a Free Market," *New York Times*, August 6, 1990; George de Lama, "Latin World Teeters on Edge of an Abyss," *Chicago Tribune*, June 4, 1989. Also see Riding, "Rumblings in Venezuela."

[10] Harsch, "After Adjustment," 48.

The costs of the debt crisis were not limited to the South. Some groups in the United States and other Northern countries also paid a heavy price. In an effort to reduce the outflow of foreign exchange, the four largest Latin American countries reduced their imports by from one third to one half between 1981 and 1986.[11] As a result, the U.S. trade balance with Latin America dropped from a small surplus in 1980 to an $18 billion deficit in 1985.[12] U.S. exports to the region fell from $42 billion in 1981 to $30 billion in 1988, costing an estimated one million jobs in U.S. export industries.[13] The economies of cities on the U.S. side of the border with Mexico were so devastated by the loss of cross-border business after the Mexican financial crisis of 1982 that then-California Governor Edmund Brown, Jr., requested that federal economic disaster relief funds be sent to the area.[14]

At the close of the 1980s, these enormous costs prompted movement in negotiations between North and South over methods for coping with the debt problem. Announced in the spring of 1989, the so-called Brady Plan, named after its sponsor, U.S. Secretary of the Treasury Nicholas Brady, signaled the North's newfound willingness to embrace limited debt forgiveness as a response to the burdens of the most heavily indebted countries. Northern governments have also offered debt relief to the poorest debtor nations, especially those in Africa.

In other respects as well, the debt crisis has eased. At its height, many feared that if one or more of the largest debtor countries defaulted on their international obligations, proving either unable or unwilling to continue payments on their debts, the entire world banking system could be threatened. After all, the world's largest banks were heavily exposed in Third World lending. In 1982 the nine largest U.S. banks held Third World debt in the seventeen largest debtor countries equal to 196 percent of their primary capital. Since the mid-1980s, however, Northern banks have lowered their exposure to Third World debt by selling off loans, diversifying their portfolios, and setting aside financial reserves against the possibility of Third World losses. By 1992, developing country debt had fallen to roughly one half of capital assets for the nine largest U.S. banks. The danger of a global financial meltdown from defaults on Third World debt has been substantially eliminated.[15]

Nevertheless, the problem of Third World debt will remain a serious one for some time. The following sections examine the origins and evolution of the debt crisis. We begin by surveying the principal actors and the roles that they have played.

---

[11] Clyde Farnsworth, "Debts of Latins Making Trade Links Tortuous," *New York Times*, December 26, 1987.

[12] Broad and Cavanaugh, "How to Approach Third World Debt."

[13] "Latin American Debt: Living on Borrowed Time?" 27.

[14] Wayne King, "Peso's Turmoil Shakes Economies of Cities on Mexican-U.S. Border," *New York Times*, August 22, 1982.

[15] William Cline, "Managing International Debt: How One Big Battle Was Won," *The Economist*, February 18, 1995, 18.

# ACTORS

The largest Third World debtors are generally located in Latin America, with Brazil, Mexico, and Argentina heading the list. Latin America as a whole owes over $500 billion to Northern creditors. Outside of Latin America, debt levels in Indonesia and India are each approaching $100 billion. Sub-Saharan African countries collectively bear a debt burden of close to $200 billion.[16]

Among heavily indebted middle-income countries, the average debt-to-GNP burden is just over 40 percent. This figure rises to over 110 percent for a group of thirty-two severely indebted low-income countries, most of which are located in Africa. Although commercial bank debt constitutes a significant share of the total for middle-income countries, the great majority of low-income country debt is owed to official creditors, including bilateral aid agencies and multilateral lending organizations.[17]

Although a variety of Third World entities holds Northern loans, the public or state sector accounted for the bulk of Southern borrowing during the seventies. Governments often relied upon foreign funds to finance their budget deficits. State-owned industrial firms or public utilities also borrowed heavily from abroad. PEMEX, Mexico's publicly owned oil company, alone borrowed $15 billion from external sources in 1981.[18] Governments often funneled foreign loans into national development banks, which then relent the money to private firms. When governments did not borrow money directly, they nevertheless commonly provided guarantees for loans undertaken directly by private corporations or banks.[19]

Most commercial lending to Third World countries is organized through bank syndicates. Many banks working together contribute, in varying proportions, to large "syndicated" loan packages to a given Third World country. The big banks that put up the largest amount of money negotiate with borrower countries on behalf of all of the other banks. These deals often involve an enormous number of banks. Six hundred banks were party to negotiations over rescheduling agreements with Mexico in 1983, while similar negotiations

---

[16] Kenneth Gilpin, "New Third World Fear: Investors Could Walk Away," *New York Times*, April 24, 1994; "Indonesia: Up to Its Ears," *The Economist*, March 25, 1995.

[17] "Poor Country Debt: A Never-Ending Story?" *Overseas Development Institute Briefing Paper*, March 1, 1995.

[18] The Debt Crisis Network, *From Debt to Development: Alternatives to the International Debt Crisis*, Washington: Institute for Policy Studies, 1985, 26.

[19] The mix of borrowing by public or private actors varied from country to country. In Brazil, and to a lesser extent Mexico and Venezuela, most of the debt was contracted by public sector entities. In Chile, private firms accounted for most of the borrowing, whereas Argentina was a mixed case. See Jeffrey Frieden, "Winners and Losers in the Debt Crisis: The Political Implications," in Barbara Stallings and Robert Kaufman (eds.), *Debt and Democracy in Latin America*, Boulder: Westview Press, 1989, 26–28; and Jeffrey Frieden, "Third World Indebted Industrialization: International Finance and State Capitalism in Mexico, Brazil, Algeria and South Korea," *International Organization*, Summer 1981.

**TABLE 12.1**

**Most Heavily Indebted Developing Countries, 1992**
*Ranked by:*

| TOTAL EXTERNAL DEBT IN MILLIONS OF U.S. $ | | AS % OF EXPORTS | | AS % OF GNP | |
| --- | --- | --- | --- | --- | --- |
| Brazil | 121,110 | Guinea-Bissau | 6,414.2 | Nicaragua | 750.3 |
| Mexico | 113,378 | Nicaragua | 3,161.7 | Mozambique | 494.8 |
| Indonesia | 84,385 | Sudan | 2,961.8 | Guinea-Bissau | 200.5 |
| India | 76,983 | Mozambique | 994.5 | Côte d'Ivoire | 191.0 |
| China | 69,321 | Uganda | 906.5 | Tanzania | 177.7 |
| Argentina | 67,569 | Tanzania | 784.4 | Congo | 166.0 |
| Egypt | 40,018 | Madagascar | 649.4 | Jordan | 163.2 |
| South Korea | 42,999 | Sierra Leone | 574.0 | Mauritania | 158.4 |
| Thailand | 39,424 | Côte d'Ivoire | 473.7 | Sierra Leone | 158.3 |
| Venezuela | 37,193 | Argentina | 449.8 | Jamaica | 131.7 |

SOURCE: World Bank, *World Development Report, 1994*, New York: Oxford University Press, 1994, 200–201, 206–207.

with Brazil during the early nineties involved 750 creditors.[20] Yet although many banks have some stake in the debt crisis, Third World lending has been overwhelmingly concentrated with a very few large banks. In the mid-1980s, nine large institutions together accounted for 63 percent of all Third World lending by U.S. banks.[21]

Northern governments are major creditors to the Third World through their foreign aid programs. Much Northern aid is given in the form of loans rather than outright grants, although usually at less than market interest rates. The major Northern creditor governments hammer out common strategies in their negotiations over debt issues with Third World countries through an informal consultative arrangement known as the "Paris Club."

Northern governments play other roles in the debt crisis as well. They provide capital to the International Monetary Fund and the World Bank and control the policies of those organizations through their preponderance of voting power. Government authorities in the North regulate the behavior of banks falling under their jurisdiction. Northern governments have provided temporary financing designed to help debtor countries avoid default. And, finally, the United States, in particular, has intervened in the relationship between debtor countries and their creditors with comprehensive proposals for managing the debt problem.

---

[20] Vinod K. Aggarwal, *International Debt Threat: Bargaining Among Creditors and Debtors in the 1980s*, Policy Papers in International Affairs, no. 29, Berkeley: University of California Press, 1987, 16; "Reforming Latin America," *The Economist*, November 26, 1994, 40.

[21] Harold Lever and Christopher Huhne, *Debt and Danger*, Boston: Atlantic Monthly Press, 1985, 17.

The International Monetary Fund is the multilateral lending agency most directly involved with Third World debt, although the role of the World Bank has grown in recent years. The principal purpose of the IMF is to lend money to countries experiencing shortfalls in their current accounts. Fund loans must be repaid within one to three years. Each member country gains the right to borrow foreign exchange from the IMF by contributing a combination of the country's own currency and gold to the IMF's reserves. Each member's contribution is roughly proportional to the size of its economy.

Beyond certain credit limits (which vary according to the country's original contribution), however, IMF authorities may set conditions on additional borrowing. Before lending large amounts to a member country, in other words, the IMF extracts promises from the government that it will undertake various policy reforms that the IMF believes are necessary to correct existing current account deficits and to earn the foreign exchange needed to repay loans issued by the IMF. The terms of IMF policy reform packages are generally based upon the assumption that countries that run large deficits or borrow heavily abroad are living beyond their means by consuming more than they produce. Fund-supported "stabilization programs," as they are commonly known, are designed to reduce domestic consumption and consequently to lower the country's demand for imported goods and foreign loans.

The specific package of policy reforms sponsored by the IMF usually includes a number of the following measures: abolish or liberalize foreign exchange and import controls; reduce growth in the domestic money supply and raise interest rates; increase taxes and reduce government spending; abolish food, fuel, and transportation subsidies; cut government wages and seek wage restraint from labor unions; dismantle price controls; privatize publicly owned firms; reduce restrictions on foreign investment; and depreciate the currency.

The economic hardships that these policies typically produce make them politically unpopular. The IMF's ability to compel governments to pursue these reforms stems less from the size of the loans that the IMF itself has to offer (which are typically only a portion of the country's overall needs) than from the fact that Northern banks will not extend new credits or reschedule old debts with a country that has not reached an agreement with the IMF. A debtor country's international credit standing rests upon its ability to obtain an IMF seal of approval. An accord with the IMF signals to private lenders that, in the IMF's view, a debtor country is pursuing the appropriate course necessary to correct past and present financial imbalances.

The World Bank has played an increasingly important role alongside the IMF in managing the Third World debt crisis. Although the World Bank once focused overwhelmingly on "project" lending, whereby loans were tied to specific investments such as a hydroelectric dam or a new road, more recently the Bank has shifted a large portion of its resources toward "structural adjustment" loans. This latter type of lending links balance of payments financing to reforms in broad sectors of the economy. The sorts of reforms supported by the Bank are similar to those sponsored by the IMF; indeed, the two institutions often coordinate the advice they give client countries.

# The Origins and Evolution of the Third World Debt Crisis

The fundamental origin of the debt crisis lies in the dependence of many Third World countries on external capital rather than on internal savings to finance economic growth. During the fifties and sixties, outside capital flowed to the Third World principally through Northern aid and foreign direct investment. Beginning in the late sixties, these sources declined in relative importance as commercial banks stepped up their lending to Third World countries. While official development assistance from the North dropped from 58 percent of total Third World financial receipts in 1960 to 30 percent in 1978, the share accounted for by bank lending rose from 2 percent to 33 percent during the same period. Real private bank lending to the Third World grew by 144 percent from 1970 to 1973.[22]

This change in the composition of financial flows from North to South was perhaps as important as the dramatic increase in the total volume in contributing to financial crisis in the Third World. From the recipient's standpoint, foreign aid and foreign direct investment offer advantages over bank borrowing. Foreign aid normally includes a concessionary element, sometimes taking the form of outright grants. Even when assistance must be paid back, aid funds come with little or no interest attached. As for foreign direct investment, the physical assets transferred to a host country through foreign investment are unlikely to be dismantled and removed. Foreign direct investment often produces a transfer of skills and technology as well. Although a stream of profits from the investment may leave the country, this will occur only so long as the investment is productive and generating output, wages, and tax payments locally. If the investment goes sour, the outward flow of profits ceases, and the costs of coping with a bad business decision are shared between the multinational and the host nation.

The terms attached to commercial bank loans are more strenuous. Unlike foreign aid, all commercial bank lending must be repaid at market interest rates. In contrast to foreign direct investment, the principal and interest on these loans fall due on a regular basis regardless of whether the investment financed by the loan is generating revenue.[23] Indeed, the cost of the debt may rise for reasons beyond the control of the debtor. Two thirds of the Third World loans issued from 1973 to 1983 carried variable rather than fixed interest rates, meaning that Southern debt payments rise or fall with changes in Northern interest rates.[24] Commercial borrowing places much of the risk on the borrower.

---

[22] Esmail Hosseinzadeh, "The Crisis of Third World Debt: Is There a Way Out?" Roger Oden (ed.), *Proceedings of the Fifteenth Annual Third World Conference*, Chicago: TWCF Publications, 1991, 27.

[23] For a comparison of bank borrowing and foreign direct investment, see Hosseinzadeh, "The Crisis of Third World Debt."

[24] Sarah Bartlett, "A Vicious Circle Keeps Latin America in Debt," *New York Times*, January 15, 1989. It was estimated in 1988 that every point rise in the rate of interest charged on Third World debt cost Southern debtors $3.5 billion annually. See Steven Greenhouse, "Third World Tells IMF that Poverty Has Increased," *New York Times*, September 29, 1988.

The demanding and inflexible terms of commercial bank lending thus played a role in the origins of the Third World debt crisis. But why were the risks that accompanied the explosion of bank lending to the South so clearly underestimated by both the banks and the Third World borrowers?

Despite its rigorous conditions, there is no inherent reason why borrowing money from a bank should lead to economic ruin. Indeed, large corporations routinely borrow from banks to finance expansion plans. The key to assessing the riskiness of any given loan is to ask whether the productive activities financed by the loan are likely to generate revenues sufficient to allow the borrower to pay back the principal, with interest, over an agreed-upon time period. If so, then both lender and borrower will be well served by the transaction. If not, then the results are likely to be less happy.

## The Misplaced Optimism of the Seventies

The debt crisis of the eighties was built upon the misplaced optimism of the seventies. Banks lent money to Third World countries based upon hopes that the ambitious development schemes espoused by government planners would fuel rapid Southern growth and export expansion. This faith, shared by bankers and borrowers alike, was eventually shattered when it became clear that too few of the funds borrowed from the North found their way into projects capable of paying for themselves.

There were several reasons why bankers took such imprudent risks. The first is a lack of historical memory. Latin American debt crises were common in the nineteenth and early twentieth centuries. Prior to the current crisis, the most recent such episode occurred in the 1930s, when many Latin American countries defaulted on their outstanding loans. Few bankers, unfortunately, took serious note of such cautionary precedents.[25]

Why, though, did Northern banks suddenly rediscover the Third World in the seventies? Many found themselves awash with lendable funds early in the decade but experienced great difficulty attracting creditworthy borrowers in the North. With no place else to turn, the banks sent the surplus south. These surplus funds came from two sources. During the sixties and early seventies, the United States routinely ran balance of payments deficits. Many of these dollars remained overseas, finding their way into dollar-denominated accounts at banks abroad. Because the bulk of these dollars ended up in European banks or in the subsidiaries of American banks located overseas, they came to be referred to as Eurodollars.

This accumulation of overseas dollars expanded dramatically when OPEC nations, finding themselves with far more money than they could possibly spend after the quadrupling of oil prices in 1973, also began to make huge

---

[25] On the historical precedents for the international debt crisis of the 1980s, see Barry Eichengreen and Peter Lindert (eds.), *The International Debt Crisis in Historical Perspective*, Cambridge: MIT Press, 1989; Albert Fishlow, "The Debt Crisis in Historical Perspective," in Miles Kahler (ed.), *The Politics of International Debt*, Ithaca: Cornell University Press, 1985; and John Makin, *The Global Debt Crisis: America's Growing Involvement*, New York: Basic Books, 1984, 36–53.

deposits of their largely dollar-denominated oil revenues in Western banks. These developments allowed the Eurodollar market to grow from $315 billion in 1973 to $2 trillion in 1982.[26] For the banks to profit from these new deposits, of course, they had to find customers willing to borrow the funds they contained. Yet, partly as a consequence of the OPEC-engineered oil price rise, most Northern nations slipped into economic recession during 1975. Businesses cut back plans for expansion, and consumers put off big-ticket purchases. With money to lend and few prospects in the North, banks began to look south.

There they discovered many eager customers. The newly industrializing countries of the Third World, particularly those in Latin America, found themselves amidst an explosion of manufacturing production and exports. To sustain this growth, Third World countries needed financing to pay for increasingly expensive oil imports as well as for the purchase of imported capital goods, such as the machinery used in newly built Southern factories. Rapid Third World growth was fueled not only by increased manufacturing exports, but also by the strong prices that most Third World commodities fetched on world markets early in the decade. Commodity prices rose by 13 percent in 1972 and a further 53 percent in 1973.[27] Overall, the Third World's share of world exports increased from 18 percent to 28 percent during the seventies.[28]

Normally reserved bankers expressed an almost giddy sense of elation at the growth and promise of the profitable new markets of the South. Some portrayed commercial lending as a magical cure for underdevelopment. Foreign debt was seen as a badge of honor and success, not shame, for Third World countries. This bravado is reflected in the comments of G. A. Costanzo, then vice president at Citibank, on Mexico's economic prospects: "Mexico . . . is in a particularly favorable position as it enters the 1980s. . . . Mexico's external debt may surpass that of Brazil during this decade, reflecting not an uncontrolled deficit but the recognition of unparalleled investment opportunities."[29] Southern borrowers shared this optimism. From their perspective, moreover, Northern loans looked like bargains. Due to high inflation levels, real interest rates were remarkably low, while the dollar's weakness made dollar-denominated loans seem cheap.

Alongside these economic motivations, Third World governments welcomed bank financing for political reasons as well. Nationalist sentiment ran strong in many countries. Seeking to harness these passions to their own benefit, many Third World politicians directed nationalist agitation toward multinational corporations—the most obvious and intrusive forms of Northern penetration in Southern societies. Moreover, Southern governments chafed against the superior bargaining power that many MNCs derived from their

---

[26] The Debt Crisis Network, *From Debt to Development*, 25.

[27] Lever and Huhne, *Debt and Danger*, 36.

[28] Andre Gunder Frank, "Can the Debt Bomb Be Defused?" *World Policy Journal*, Spring 1985, 729.

[29] William Greider, *Secrets of the Temple*, New York: Simon and Schuster, 1987, 434.

mobility. Particularly in Latin America, therefore, governments sought to create alternatives to the MNCs by buttressing state-owned firms. A strong publicly owned sector of the economy strengthened the hand of Southern governments in bargaining with MNCs while also providing political leaders with greater direct control over the economy and with a means of asserting their nationalist credentials. Because reducing dependence upon MNCs required access to alternative sources of capital, Third World governments looked to Northern banks that, in a relatively low-profile and unobtrusive manner, provided funds subject to the direct control of state bureaucrats and politicians.[30]

For a variety of reasons, therefore, both Northern lenders and Southern borrowers were well motivated to deepen their relationships with one another, and favorable conditions made international lending seem a good bet for all concerned. The eagerness of the banks to cash in on this huge and profitable new market was, moreover, relatively unrestrained by normally cautious Northern government bank regulators. Eurodollar funds were largely beyond the reach of government regulations designed to limit risky lending behavior. U.S. dollars deposited overseas escaped the jurisdiction of U.S. banking officials, while European bank regulations applied only to local European currencies, not to foreign currency–denominated accounts. This lack of normal oversight contributed to overlending.[31]

Northern banks found overseas lending quite profitable for a time. Earnings from the foreign operations of the seven biggest U.S. banks climbed from 22 percent of total profits in 1970 to 60 percent in 1982. Many bankers waved aside the concerns of those who questioned whether the large buildup of foreign debt by still-poor Third World societies was sustainable. Citibank chief Walter Wriston, whose bank epitomized the frenetic climate of international banking in the seventies, predicted that "this fear that banks have reached a limit will turn out to be wrong tomorrow, as it always has in the past."[32]

## The Bottom Falls Out:
## The Fickleness of the World Economy

Yet the economic conditions that nurtured the growth of Third World borrowing during much of the seventies shifted dramatically as the decade drew to a close. After several years of relative stability in oil markets, OPEC managed to engineer a trebling of world oil prices in 1979. The oil bill of oil-importing Third World countries leapt from $7 billion in 1973 to almost $100 billion in 1981.[33] This proved a bitter pill to swallow for the newly industrializing

---

[30] Frieden, "Third World Indebted Industrialization."

[31] See Miles Kahler, "Politics and International Debt: Explaining the Crisis," in Kahler (ed.), *The Politics of International Debt*; and Mary Williamson, "Banking Regulation and Debt: A Policy of Flexible Response," *Policy Focus*, Overseas Development Council Policy Paper no. 1, 1988.

[32] Greider, *Secrets of the Temple*, 433.

[33] Moffitt, *The World's Money*, 100.

countries of the Third World, whose appetite for additional oil was rising just as prices rocketed skyward.

Far more devastating in the long run, however, was the North's reaction to OPEC's price hike. In the United States, the Federal Reserve clamped down on the U.S. money supply in an effort to wring inflation from the economy. This had several undesirable effects from the standpoint of Third World borrowers. Interest rates climbed to an average of 15.5 percent from 1979 to 1982. This meant higher payments on most commercial bank loans to the Third World. The U.S. economy, along with those of other Northern countries, entered the worst economic downturn since the Great Depression. Global growth averaged only 1.1 percent from 1979 to 1982, and world trade actually shrank. Slow growth hurt Southern exports to the North. Commodity prices fell by one fourth between 1980 and 1982 as demand slackened.[34] Southern manufacturing exports were dampened not only by the economic slowdown itself, but also by increased Northern protectionism as economic hardship in the North pushed governments to attempt to save jobs in industries threatened by Southern imports.[35] The dollar, strengthened by high interest rates in the United States, rose to record highs, forcing Third World governments to expend more in their local currency to obtain the dollars necessary to pay back the banks.

Peter Nunnenkamp has estimated that external factors over which Third World governments had little or no control accounted for $570 billion in new debt accumulation between 1974 and 1981.[36] By 1982 debt payments consumed 70 percent of the export revenues of the twenty-one largest nonoil-exporting debtors, up from 36 percent in 1973, and the overall current account balance for all nonoil-exporting Third World countries reached a deficit of $97 billion.[37]

## Southern Mismanagement and Capital Flight

Unfavorable international developments were not the only forces working to transform Third World debt from a problem into a crisis. Internal factors such as poor policy choices and capital flight served to further aggravate matters.[38]

---

[34] Lever and Huhne, *Debt and Danger*, 38.

[35] By 1988 the cost to the Third World in lost export revenues due to Northern protectionism amounted to twice the value of Northern aid to the South. Greenhouse, "Third World Tells IMF that Poverty Has Increased."

[36] Hosseinzadeh, "The Crisis of Third World Debt: Is There a Way Out?" 9.

[37] The Debt Crisis Network, *From Debt to Development*, 32. Moffitt, *The World's Money*, 101.

[38] Corruption also played a role in the worsening of the debt problems of some countries. Funds ostensibly borrowed to finance development often found their way into the pockets of Third World government officials or businessmen. Ferdinand Marcos is said to have stolen and funneled into overseas investments $10 billion during his long reign. This compares with a Philippine foreign debt of $26 billion at the time Marcos stepped down in 1986. Similarly, it has been charged that $3 to $4 billion of Zaire's $5 billion external debt was diverted by President Mobutu Sese Seko for his own uses. See Graham Hancock, *Lords of Poverty*, New York: Atlantic Monthly Press, 1989, 175–79. For a general discussion of mismanagement and corruption as sources of the debt crisis, see George B. N. Ayettey, "The Real Foreign Debt Problem," *The Wall Street Journal*, April 8, 1986, 28.

Many Third World governments, particularly in Latin America, supported artificially high exchange rates during the late seventies and early eighties in an effort to control inflation without recession.[39] Overvalued currencies badly hurt exports, encouraged import growth, and led to large trade deficits that were covered by further borrowing from abroad.[40]

As conditions worsened, it became clear that these overvalued currency rates could not be sustained and that severe currency depreciation lurked just around the corner. Holders of liquid assets in these countries feared that the value of their cash holdings might take a nosedive. In response, the wealthy began converting their assets into dollars in massive amounts and sent the proceeds abroad. As further incentive for this so-called capital flight, interest rates in many Third World countries were held artificially low by legal ceilings even as rising inflation rendered the real rate of return on savings accounts negative. Just the opposite was true in the United States, of course, where monetary policies were at the same time producing skyrocketing real interest rates.

This combination of factors led to a hemorrhaging of foreign exchange toward the North. For the years 1976 to 1984, the World Bank estimated that Mexico experienced $54 billion in capital flight (57 percent of Mexican external debt), that Argentina saw an outflow of $28 billion (60 percent of external debt), and that $35 billion fled Venezuela (a sum greater than Venezuela's entire external debt).[41] In 1985 IMF estimates put total Third World capital flight at $200 billion—a figure that, by 1989, would rise to $340 billion for the fifteen largest debtors alone.[42]

With high interest rates, a buoyant stock market, and a stable political system, the United States attracted roughly one half of all Latin American flight capital. Between 1977 and 1985, deposits by Mexican investors in U.S. banks increased 570 percent; for Argentineans, the increase in deposits was 450 percent; and Peruvian deposits rose 750 percent.[43]

Capital flight exacted a steep price from Third World debtors. During the years 1983 and 1984, Northern banks accepted more money in deposits from Southern sources than they dispersed to Third World countries in new loans. Capital flight took a toll on foreign exchange reserves, domestic investment, and tax revenues in Third World countries. Mexico lost an estimated $3.2 billion in taxes between 1977 and 1984 due to capital flight.[44]

Staggered by these blows, Third World governments attempted to maintain the momentum of growth by continuing to borrow. The banks, again flush

---

[39] Remember that high exchange rates tend to reduce the price of imports, which then act to keep other domestic prices from rising.

[40] Rudiger Dornbusch, "The Latin American Debt Problem: Anatomy and Solutions," in Stallings and Kaufman (eds.), *Debt and Democracy in Latin America*, 8.

[41] "Latin American Debt: Living on Borrowed Time?" 28.

[42] Hosseinzadeh, "The Crisis of Third World Debt: Is There a Way Out?" 9; and Mike McNamee and Jeffrey Ryser, "Can This Flight Be Grounded?" *Businessweek*, April 10, 1989.

[43] Frank Riely, "Third World Capital Flight: Who Gains? Who Loses?" *Policy Focus*, no. 5, Overseas Development Council, 1986.

[44] Riely, "Third World Capital Flight: Who Gains? Who Loses?"

with deposits from OPEC nations, proved willing to accommodate Third World demands for additional funds; however, they began to exact higher spreads, premiums tacked onto base interest rate levels, as compensation for the greater riskiness of the new loans.[45] Ominously, most of the new lending during this period went not to finance promising development projects but instead to allow debtors to make payments on past debts. This expedient succeeded in staving off default for a time. Meanwhile, bankers and Third World governments hoped that the newly unfavorable world economic climate would change again for the better and allow the resumption of Third World growth.

## The World Holds Its Breath: The Mexican Crisis

These hopes proved illusory. The bubble of optimism burst in August 1982 when Mexican officials announced that their country, then the world's second-largest debtor, lacked the funds to cover scheduled loan payments and stood on the verge of involuntary default. Ironically, given the role of the 1979 OPEC oil price hike in worsening the indebtedness of so many Third World countries, the first large debtor to approach default was a major oil exporter. In addition to the external circumstances mentioned earlier, such as higher interest rates and Northern recession, the Mexican predicament was exacerbated by unrealistic government economic policies.

The Mexican economy grew at the explosive rate of 8.1 percent per year between 1978 and 1981. This growth curve was clearly unsustainable in the face of an unfavorable international economic climate. Most significantly, oil prices began to slide during the early eighties, causing a $6 billion drop in Mexican oil revenues in 1981 as compared with oil revenues in 1980.[46] Yet officials attempted to maintain a feverish pace of economic growth through massive government spending. By 1982 the government budget deficit, largely financed by foreign borrowing, reached a stupendous 16.3 percent of Mexican GNP. Seeking to quickly exploit large, newly discovered oil deposits, Mexico also borrowed heavily to finance the import of capital equipment for expansion of the oil industry. Lastly, Mexican officials maintained an overvalued exchange rate, thereby encouraging imports and discouraging exports.[47]

Mexico's day of reckoning arrived when Northern banks balked at providing enough additional financing to cover the large payments falling due on old debts plus the continuing demand for new funds needed to pay for the excess of imports over exports. The prospect of Mexican default set off alarm

---

[45] By pushing interest payments still higher, these added premiums worsened matters by increasing the burden placed on the many debtor countries already experiencing difficulties in servicing their loans. The Debt Crisis Network, *From Debt to Development*, 33, and Moffitt, *The World's Money*, 110.

[46] Robert Bennett, "Mexico Seeking Postponement of Part of Its Debt," *New York Times*, August 20, 1982.

[47] Lever and Huhne, *Debt and Danger*, 40–41.

bells in Northern governmental and banking circles as the stark realization finally sank in that the stability of the entire Northern financial system stood in jeopardy. Mexico owed the Bank of America and Citibank roughly $3 billion each.[48] Citibank's Mexican exposure equaled two thirds of its net corporate assets.[49] A long-term interruption of Mexican debt payments could have spelled disaster for a number of the largest U.S. banks.

At this point, the U.S. government, abandoning its previously aloof stance toward Third World debt, stepped in to provide emergency short-term financing designed to keep Mexico solvent until a longer-term solution could be found. As part of the deal, the United States also made an immediate $1 billion advance payment for discounted Mexican oil and provided Mexico with $1 billion in credits toward the purchase of surplus U.S. grain. Mexico subsequently entered into negotiations with the IMF and its private bank creditors, during which debt payments were suspended for 120 days. Ultimately, the IMF provided almost $4 billion and the banks $5 billion in new financing, while payments on almost $19 billion in old debt were stretched out over a longer time period. In return, Mexico agreed to follow a stabilization plan designed by IMF officials that, among other things, required the government to close its budget deficit and devalue the peso.[50]

The most difficult phase of the negotiations revolved around the bankers' reluctance to lend new money to Mexico. Additional money was needed in order to finance necessary imports, complete ongoing investment projects, and roll over old debt. Without new funds, Mexican default seemed assured. Collectively, of course, the Northern banks all had an interest in avoiding this outcome. Yet individually, many bankers feared that Mexico would never pay its debts in full, and none wished to throw good money after bad. The Mexican deal almost came apart because many banks, especially the smaller ones, wished to benefit from a successful conclusion to the negotiations without, however, putting up new money of their own. If enough banks had maintained this attitude, of course, a successful deal would have proven impossible.

Drawing upon powers it had never previously exercised, the IMF provided the solution by compelling banks into involuntary lending. IMF officials, supported by the United States, threatened to withdraw their portion of the loan package, as well as their oversight of Mexican reforms, unless each bank contributed new funds proportionate to its previous stake in Mexico.[51] This persuaded the banks to follow the IMF's lead in the short run, but it failed to resolve the longer-term problem of the banks' newfound reluctance to provide even prudent amounts of new lending to Third World debtors.

---

[48] Alan Riding, "Mexican Outlook: Banks Are Wary," *New York Times,* August 17, 1982.

[49] "Latin American Debt: Living on Borrowed Time?" 28.

[50] For a chronology of the Mexican debt rescheduling negotiations, see Aggarwal, *International Debt Threat,* 66–67.

[51] Robert Bennett, "Bankers Pressured to Assist Mexico," *New York Times,* August 21, 1982.

# The IMF Takes Charge

The IMF quickly assumed a role at the center of the debt crisis as more debtor countries experienced problems similar to Mexico's. During the seventies, the IMF typically found itself drawn into negotiations with a few troubled debtors each year. In the wake of Mexico's troubles, dozens of countries on the verge of default, seeking to secure new loans and renegotiate the terms of old ones, approached the IMF and the banks. By 1983 the IMF had conditional lending programs in forty-seven countries.[52]

The IMF's cure for the problems of Third World debtors flowed from its diagnosis of the illness. Michel Camdessus, executive director of the IMF, attributed the debt crisis to "the criminal conduct" of "politicians who neglect to take care of urgent problems and prefer to wait for a miracle."[53] Having identified the cause of the debt crisis as economic mismanagement by debtor country governments, the IMF, supported by Northern governments and banks, placed the burden of adjusting to the crisis on the debtor countries themselves. Third World officials were expected to adopt correct economic policies, such as those previously discussed, and their citizens, having earlier lived beyond their means, would now have to swallow the medicine of austerity, no matter how unpleasant its taste.

In its deal with Mexico, for instance, the IMF demanded that subsidies on basic foodstuffs be reduced and that wages be restrained. As a result, authorities raised the prices of corn tortillas by 40 percent and bread by 100 percent. Wages were allowed to grow by only one third the inflation rate.[54]

The IMF prescription for Third World debtors generally led to substantial improvement in debtor country trade balances, but the price was frightening in lost economic growth and deteriorating social conditions. As a result, the IMF's remedy for Third World debt problems came under severe criticism. Many of these criticisms had to do with the economic soundness of the fund's policy prescriptions. One study found that low-income countries that followed IMF programs during the seventies performed no better by a variety of economic measures than did countries not under the fund's guidance.[55] Another survey conducted by the IMF itself found that IMF-sponsored programs in sub-Saharan African countries met preestablished targets for growth, inflation, and trade in only a minority of cases.[56]

Some critics maintained that the IMF focused too exclusively on reducing Third World imports by dampening demand while neglecting supply-side measures that might stimulate debtor country exports. Domestic investment

---

[52] "Latin American Debt: Living on Borrowed Time?" 29.

[53] James Brooke, "Zaire Dispute with IMF Centers on Capital Flows," *New York Times*, September 29, 1988.

[54] "Latin American Debt: Living on Borrowed Time?" 29.

[55] John Loxley, *The IMF and the Poorest Countries*, Ottawa: North-South Institute, 1984.

[56] Cited in John Loxley, "IMF and World Bank Conditionality and Sub-Saharan Africa," in Peter Lawrence (ed.), *World Recession and the Food Crisis in Africa*, London: James Currey, 1986, 96.

levels slumped during the eighties in most Third World countries, declining, for instance, by 25 percent in Latin America between 1980 and 1988.[57] Among the fifteen most heavily indebted countries, domestic investment plummeted from an average of 24 percent of GNP from 1971 to 1981 to 18 percent from 1982 to 1987.[58] With insufficient investment in export industries, Third World countries found themselves limited in their ability to increase their export capacity or to enhance the efficiency and competitiveness of their products.

The effectiveness of another IMF tool—currency devaluation—proved a subject of controversy as well.[59] One undesirable consequence of devaluing a nation's currency is higher domestic inflation as the prices of imported goods rise. Moreover, devaluation can produce effects contrary to its intended purposes. Some imported goods, such as oil, are so necessary that the increased prices caused by devaluation lead to only small declines in import volumes.[60] In such cases, the net effect of devaluation is to widen, rather than to narrow, the nation's trade deficit. Much the same is true with regard to export industries that rely heavily upon imported inputs, such as raw materials, parts, or capital goods. Part of the advantage that devaluation offers such industries by allowing them to sell their products more cheaply abroad is taken away by the higher costs that these same firms incur due to domestic inflation and more expensive imported inputs—both also consequences of devaluation.[61]

The widespread perception that IMF austerity policies often brought political instability also increased the reluctance of some governments to cooperate with the IMF. Perhaps the most feared element of the typical IMF package involves the removal of government subsidies for basic foodstuffs and other necessities, such as fuel oil and public transportation. Price rises in these sensitive areas have provoked unrest in many Third World countries.

## Smoke and Mirrors: The Baker Plan

By 1985 the flaws in the case-by-case strategy devised during the initial phase of the debt crisis were evident even to policymakers in Washington, who,

---

[57] Greenhouse, "Third World Tells IMF that Poverty Has Increased."

[58] Eduardo Borensztein, "The Effect of External Debt on Investment," *Finance and Development*, September 1989, 17.

[59] For a critique of the effectiveness of devaluation, see "When Devaluation Breeds Contempt," *The Economist*, November 24, 1990, 71.

[60] Technically, economists refer to the demand for such products as *price inelastic*: A change in price produces a relatively small shift in the volume of sales.

[61] IMF policies have also had unintended effects on South-South trade. Though the great majority of Southern exports are targeted toward Northern markets, the seventies witnessed considerable growth in trade among Southern countries. This encouraging trend reversed itself in the eighties due to the fact that so many Southern debtors were simultaneously pursuing IMF-imposed austerity policies and thus cutting back on imported goods from all sources. Especially hurt by this phenomenon was Brazil, 40 percent of whose exports in 1981 went to other less-developed countries such as Argentina, Mexico, Chile, Venezuela, and Nigeria. See "Resurgent Inflation Ruins Brazil's Plan," *New York Times*, August 9, 1982.

since the Mexican bailout of 1982, had adopted a relatively passive stance toward the debt problems of the Third World. The signs of failure were numerous. Mexico again found itself approaching default, and another debt rescheduling agreement was required to pull it back from the brink. Interest rates were on the rise, and most major debtor countries remained mired in the economic doldrums despite the return of steady, if unspectacular, economic growth in the North. Northern exports to the South also remained depressed.

U.S. policymakers feared that Southern debtor governments, alarmed by political instability, might begin to explore radical solutions if the painful adjustments they had undertaken failed to bring either economic growth or renewed access to international credit markets. This concern prompted the United States to announce a new initiative called the Baker Plan, named after U.S. Treasury Secretary James Baker.

The purpose of the Baker Plan was to revive growth among a group of fifteen heavily indebted Third World countries while also enhancing these countries' long-term capacity to service their debts. Baker argued that austerity alone failed to provide the new investment needed for continued growth, especially in the crucial export industries, and only worsened the problem of capital flight. The Baker Plan's answer to this problem was three-pronged:

1. Although debtor countries were still asked to restrain domestic demand, Baker favored greater emphasis on supply-side measures designed to stimulate export growth.
2. Commercial banks were urged to provide additional new lending to finance investments in Southern export industries.
3. The United States supported expanded lending by the IMF and the World Bank.

Although many Third World debtors welcomed Baker's shift in emphasis from austerity to growth, they remained disappointed with the Plan's rejection of debt reduction, the failure of the U.S. government to offer new resources of its own, and Baker's vagueness about just how he proposed to persuade bankers to voluntarily expand their Third World lending.

Experience over the next several years bore out the Third World's pessimism and exposed the faulty assumptions upon which the Baker Plan was based. Baker's plea to the banks that they supply $7 billion in new money annually over the next three years fell upon deaf ears. In fact, 1986 and 1987 together brought only $2 billion in new lending, while lending actually fell short of repayments by $4 billion in 1988. Adding interest payments to repaid principal, the flow of funds from the South to the North far exceeded new bank lending for all three years. Bank financing was also highly concentrated, with only a few countries having access to funds during this period. A number of nations that had followed strict adjustment policies found themselves unable to gain new credit.[62]

---

[62] Fried and Trezise, *Third World Debt*, 4.

Much the same was true of official credit. Net lending by official creditors amounted to only 87 percent of Southern interest payments in 1986—a figure that fell to 38 percent in 1988.[63] The debt crisis continued to drain funds from the South, making it difficult, if not impossible, for Southern countries to make the investments needed to spur additional growth.

It is doubtful, however, that the Baker Plan could have fully succeeded even had the banks proven more cooperative. Northern economies continued to experience sluggish rates of economic growth during the eighties as compared with the sixties or seventies. Global prices for most Southern commodities remained dismally low. In early 1985, for instance, world sugar prices hovered around five to six cents per pound, while production costs in the Philippines averaged twelve to fourteen cents per pound.[64] By 1990 coffee prices had fallen one third and cocoa prices two thirds from 1979 levels.[65] Nor is it clear whether Northern markets were ready to absorb large increases in Southern manufactured exports. Under these conditions, it is quite possible that increased bank lending to the South may have increased the Third World debt bill without proportionately enhancing the debtor countries' ability to pay.

## Facing Reality: The Banks Take Cover

In 1987 and 1988 the behavior of Northern banks began to reflect the uncertainties that surrounded the repayment of Third World debt. Partly due to increased pressure from government bank regulators, banks began to make large additions to their loan loss reserves. These are funds designed to cushion a bank's reported profits should debtors default on their existing loans to the bank. Implicitly acknowledging that not all of the money they had lent to Third World countries was likely to be repaid, virtually all of the large American banks involved in Third World lending followed the lead of Citibank, which set aside $3 billion against potential losses in May 1987.[66]

Seeking to reduce their overall exposure to Third World debt, the banks also began to diversify their loan portfolios. This led to the development of a so-called secondary market for Third World debt. Losing confidence that debtor countries would ever repay their debts in full, many banks became willing to sell their Third World loans to other banks or investors at less than the loans' face value. A bank fearful of future Mexican default, for instance, might sell a $1,000,000 Mexican loan to another investor for only $700,000. Even though the bank will take a loss when it sells the loan, it does so in the expectation

---

[63] Ishrat Husain, "Recent Experience with the Debt Strategy," *Finance and Development*, September 1989, 14. Also see Paul Lewis, "3rd-World Funds: Wrong Way Flow," *New York Times*, February 11, 1988.

[64] The Debt Crisis Network, *From Debt to Development*, 9.

[65] Steven Greenhouse, "Oil Shock Squeezing Third World," *New York Times*, August 18, 1990.

[66] Jaclyn Fierman, "Fast Bucks in Latin Loan Swaps," *Fortune*, August 3, 1987.

that the loss would be greater still if it held onto the loan only to see the debtor country default. The "discount" offered on loans traded in the secondary market reflects the judgments of both buyers and sellers about the likelihood that the debt will be repaid. A very risky loan—one for which the chances of full or partial default seem high—will typically carry a steep discount.

A number of big banks turned to the secondary market in 1988 as a means of reducing their exposure to Third World debt. Citicorp sold off $1.2 billion in loans; Chase Manhattan sold off $1 billion; and Manufacturer's Hanover sold off $656 million.[67] Most of these transactions did nothing to reduce the obligations of the debtor countries. After a sale, the debtor still owed the full amount of the original loan, only now to a new creditor.

In some instances, however, the willingness of banks to sell risky loans on the secondary market worked to the benefit of Third World countries. When debtor countries had sufficient foreign exchange on hand, they sometimes simply purchased their own debts at a discounted price. Bolivia, for instance, reduced a $650 million debt to $300 million in 1988 through this means.[68] The principal constraint on such cash buy-backs lies in the scarcity of foreign exchange for most Third World countries.

Southern countries also extinguished some of their debt through so-called debt-for-equity swaps. Typically this arrangement might work like this: A bank sells its Mexican loans to a Northern electronics company for seventy cents on each dollar. The electronics company then exchanges the debt with the Mexican central bank in return for pesos at a rate equivalent to perhaps eighty cents on each dollar of the original face value on the loan. The company invests these pesos in constructing a new assembly plant in Mexico.

Notice how the benefits are distributed among the partners in this deal. Although the bank takes a loss, it also rids itself of a risky loan and improves the quality of its portfolio. The electronics company profits by purchasing the loan at 70 percent while later selling it at 80 percent of its face value. It also, of course, ends up with the pesos it needs to make the assembly plant investment. The Mexican government erases some of its debt at a 20 percent discount without the use of precious foreign exchange. In place of foreign bank debt, the country now has an equity investment that, while owned by a foreign firm, produces employment, taxes, and products locally.[69]

Despite these benefits, debt-for-equity swaps proved limited in their potential to solve the Third World debt crisis. There were, for instance, only so many Third World investment opportunities that could lure foreign firms into such deals, even with the attraction of subsidies. Indeed, in some degree the

---

[67] Merril Collett, "Brady's Debt Plan Is Short on Principle," *In These Times*, April 12–18, 1989, 2.

[68] Peter Kilborn, "Debt Reduction: Ways to Do It," *New York Times*, April 6, 1989.

[69] New rules issued by the Federal Reserve in 1987 made it possible for banks to increase their equity investment in nonfinancial companies from 20 percent to 100 percent. This made it easier for banks to swap debt for equity among themselves, without the need for the participation of multinational corporations. Pamela Sherrid, "The Brave New World of Swaps," *U.S. News & World Report*, August 31, 1987, 41.

incentives offered to multinational firms through debt-for-equity swaps did little more than shift foreign investment from one country to another without adding to aggregate investment in the Third World as a whole. Another problem was that the printing of additional local currency needed to buy back the debt often swelled the money supply and led to inflation.[70] For these and other reasons, some of the enthusiasm that accompanied the expansion of debt-for-equity swaps in 1988 diminished thereafter.

Debt-for-debt swaps provided a final mechanism for translating secondary market discounts into debt reduction for Third World countries. In these transactions, old unguaranteed loans are swapped at a discount for new securities carrying some form of partial or full guarantee of repayment. For instance, in a deal fashioned by Morgan Guaranty, Mexico exchanged $3.6 billion in old debt for $2.5 billion in new securities for a total debt reduction of $1.1 billion. Banks that participated in the deal were willing to trade the old loans for the new loans at a discount because the principal (though not the interest) on the new bonds was backed by U.S. government-guaranteed securities. Although the new bonds were worth less than the old, the bankers were assured repayment in full on the newer securities.[71]

Altogether, cash buy-backs, debt-for-equity swaps, and debt-for-debt deals eliminated $25 billion in Third World debt from 1985 through 1988.[72] Although this might seem a rather modest figure when compared with the overall size of the Third World debt burden, these transactions helped to ease acceptance of an important principle: that Third World countries should benefit from the lowered values that the secondary market placed on Third World debt. This principle was at least partially embraced by the Brady Plan—the most important Northern initiative toward solving the debt crisis.

## Inching Toward the Inevitable: The Brady Plan

Named after U.S. Treasury Secretary Nicholas Brady and presented in the spring of 1989, the Brady Plan included the first U.S. acknowledgment that debt reduction and forgiveness would have to comprise a part of any successful scheme for coping with the Third World debt crisis. The Brady Plan aimed at reducing Third World debt to private creditors. Brady originally set a goal of $70 billion in debt forgiveness for fifteen heavily indebted countries to be achieved over several years. This would constitute roughly a 20 percent reduction in outstanding bank debt.

The heart of the Brady Plan consisted of a set of incentives designed to induce banks to forgive part of the debt owed them. Banks were offered the opportunity to exchange their old loans for new bonds carrying either a

---

[70] Fierman, "Fast Bucks in Latin Loan Swaps."

[71] Kilborn, "Debt Reduction: Ways to Do It."

[72] Kilborn, "Debt Reduction: Ways to Do It"; and Robert Bennett, "Lesson on Mexican Debt," *New York Times*, March 1, 1988.

reduced principal or lower interest rates. The attraction of the new bonds, despite their discount, was that, unlike the old loans, they included guarantees of repayment secured by special funds set aside for the purpose. The new bonds thus carried a much lower risk of default than did the old debt. As with the Baker Plan, only nations agreeing to adopt IMF-sponsored policy reforms were eligible for participation in Brady Plan deals.

The special funds set aside as security for the new bonds were financed through new loans issued by the IMF, the World Bank, and Northern governments, especially Japan. Banks reluctant to provide interest or principal reduction were offered the option of lending new money. All private creditors were expected to accept one of these three forms of sacrifice (or a combination of them) in degrees proportional to their stake in the country's debt. Banks that initially refused experienced considerable pressure to participate from other banks and Northern governments.[73]

Mexico was the first country to reach an agreement with its bank creditors under the Brady Plan. The negotiations proved complex and arduous. Although the broad outlines were accepted in July 1989, the precise details of an agreement were not worked out until the following February. Roughly equal numbers of banks chose to reduce the principal on their loans by 35 percent or to accept a lower interest rate of 6.25 percent. A relatively small group of banks offered to extend new funds equal to 25 percent of their old loans. Mexico managed to lop $7 billion in principal off its total debt of $95 billion through the deal while also gaining reduced interest payments on a portion of the remainder and $1.5 billion in new lending. Mexico borrowed $5.7 billion, however, from the IMF, the World Bank, and Japan to finance the collateral fund set up to guarantee interest payments for a period of eighteen months. Overall, Mexico reduced its yearly debt service burden by roughly 10 to 20 percent. By 1994 eighteen large debtor countries had achieved similar Brady Plan deals with private creditors covering $191 billion in debt. Total debt reduction amounted to $61 billion.[74]

In late June 1990 President Bush announced an extension of the Brady Plan to cover official as well as private credit. In his "Enterprise for Americas" initiative, Bush offered to begin negotiations with Latin American countries, which could lead to reductions totaling $7 billion in the debt they owe the U.S. government. The United States also promised to expand its support for collateral funds designed to guarantee payment on private bank debt and to increase U.S. assistance (contingent upon matching funds from Europe and Japan) in support of policy reforms designed to privatize publicly owned firms or to remove restrictions on foreign direct investment or currency

---

[73] For descriptions of the Brady Plan's provisions, see Clyde Farnsworth, "World Bank and IMF Approve Plan to Cut Debt of Poorer Lands," *New York Times*, April 5, 1989; and Shafigul Islam, "Going Beyond the Brady Plan," *Challenge*, July–August 1989, 39–45.

[74] On the Mexican deal, see Sarah Bartlett, "Reservations Expressed About Mexican Debt Accord," *New York Times*, July 27, 1989; and Larry Rohter, "Pact Is Signed to Cut Mexico's Debt," *New York Times*, February 5, 1990. Also see Cline, "Managing International Debt: How One Big Battle Was Won," 18.

exchange. Bush coupled these announcements with a call for negotiations on the creation of a hemispheric free-trade pact.[75] Latin American reaction was positive. Uruguayan President Luis Lacalle declared: "When, after years of our complaining of neglect, the most important man in the world offers his hand, then, I think we should grab it—and the arm and the elbow and the shoulder, too." Carlos Andres Perez, president of Venezuela, called Bush's plan "the most advanced proposal the United States has ever proposed for Latin America. It's revolutionary, historical."[76]

The Brady Plan, combined with renewed economic growth in Latin America, has helped to ease the debt burden of the largest debtor countries. For a group of seventeen highly indebted middle-income countries, their ratio of net international debt to exports fell from 384 percent in 1986 to 225 percent in 1993. For these same countries, net external debt relative to GNP declined from 67 percent in 1986 to 42 percent in 1993. Nevertheless, debt repayments continue to absorb a substantial portion of export earnings and to render these countries vulnerable to negative external shocks.

There is concern that Brady Plan deals have accelerated a trend in which bank debt is replaced by debt owed to official creditors, especially multilateral agencies. Of total Third World debt, the share owed to official multilateral lenders increased from 36 percent in 1985 to 45 percent in 1993.[77] As a result, the quality of the loan portfolios held by official multilateral creditors has declined. Indeed, arrears on the loans issued by the IMF reached a historic high of $4 billion in 1990, forcing the IMF to consider selling some of its gold holdings in order to replenish its liquid reserves.[78] More troubling, from the perspective of Third World countries, is that the bylaws of international lending agencies prevent them from forgiving outstanding loans. Thus a growing proportion of the remaining Third World debt is nonnegotiable.[79]

Also, some critics have complained that the Brady Plan pushes the burdens of others' misjudgments onto Northern taxpayers. Not only are taxpayers asked to help fund increases in the lending resources of the IMF and the World Bank, but also, in the United States, they compensate for the revenues lost when U.S. banks deduct losses on foreign loans from their overall tax liabilities.[80]

Alongside the Brady Plan, which addresses itself to the largest debtor countries, have come a variety of Northern initiatives designed to reduce the burdens of the poorest debtor nations, particularly those in sub-Saharan

---

[75] Andrew Rosenthal, "President Announces Plan for More Latin Debt Relief," *New York Times*, June 28, 1990.

[76] Quotes cited in Robert Pastor, *Whirlpool: U.S. Foreign Policy Toward Latin America and the Caribbean*, Princeton: Princeton University Press, 1992, 97.

[77] Doug Henwood, "What Happened to Third World Debt?" in Kevin Danaher (ed.), *50 Years Is Enough: The Case Against the World Bank and the International Monetary Fund*, Boston: South End Press, 1994, 39.

[78] Clyde Farnsworth, "IMF Is Urged to Sell Gold as Hedge Against Bad Loans," *New York Times*, February 1, 1990.

[79] Jorge Castaneda, "Mexico's Dismal Debt Deal," *New York Times*, February 25, 1990.

[80] Albert Fishlow, "Coming to Terms with the Latin Debt," *New York Times*, January 4, 1988.

Africa. At a 1988 summit in Toronto, the major Northern donor countries decided to provide debt relief for low-income countries willing to agree to policy reforms overseen by either the IMF or the World Bank. In 1989 the World Bank created a new Debt Reduction Facility designed to help poor countries repurchase their debt at a discount.[81] Additional steps toward debt relief for the poorest countries were agreed to in 1991 and 1994. Although these moves should help the poorest debtor countries in the long run, the short-run benefits have been modest. Net external debt still hovers at levels far above the ability of low-income countries to pay. Indeed, a group of thirty-two severely indebted low-income countries accumulated arrears on scheduled debt payments reaching $56 billion in 1993—a year in which these same countries managed to meet only 42 percent of their debt payment obligations. As a group, these low-income debtors could afford fewer imports in the early nineties than they purchased in 1980.[82]

What is the future of the Third World debt crisis? Notwithstanding the progress made in improving debtor country trade balances and the recent moves toward debt reduction and forgiveness, the Third World debt problem remains far from resolved. Although the debt problem is more manageable now than it was during the eighties, Third World debtors remain quite vulnerable to unfavorable internal or external shocks. This will become evident in our later discussion of the Mexican peso crisis of 1994–95.

## THE POLITICS OF THIRD WORLD DEBT

In the late seventies and the early eighties, many analysts predicted that Third World debt would provide these countries with enormous political leverage over the North—power that the Third World could use to wrest concessions from Northern nations on the reform of the international economic order. The reasoning behind this argument was captured by a well-worn saying: "If you owe the bank a thousand dollars, you have a problem. If you owe the bank a million dollars, the bank has a problem."

In fact, however, it is the North that has gained leverage from the debt crisis. Early on, the nature, origins, and solutions to the debt crisis were defined largely by the North. The burden of adjustment fell upon the Third World in the form of IMF-administered austerity programs. Northern governments, the United States in particular, refused to alter related policies, such as those concerning interest rates or market access, to accommodate debtor country concerns. Nationalistic strategies of development in the South, meanwhile, gave way during the eighties to policies long favored by the North, such as the lowering of barriers to Northern goods and investments.

---

[81] Stanley Fischer and Ishrat Hussain, "Managing the Debt Crisis in the 1990's," *Finance and Development*, June 1990, 25–26.

[82] "Poor Country Debt: A Never-Ending Story?"

By the early nineties, the failure of earlier Northern-sponsored approaches had compelled Northern governments and bank officials to accept the prospect of limited debt reduction. Yet what remains striking about the history of the debt crisis during the eighties has been the inability of the Third World to wrest greater concessions from the North and the reluctance of Southern officials to contemplate radical strategies for responding to the debt crisis. Before we turn to contemporary developments in North–South finance, it may be useful to reflect in greater depth upon the political dynamics of North–South bargaining over Third World debt issues during the eighties.

## Why Not Repudiation?

The costs of attempting to repay their foreign debt have been high for many Third World countries, while the benefits have been few. Why, then, have more countries not simply repudiated their debts, refusing to pay on the grounds that their citizens have sacrificed enough? Although no major debtor country has flatly repudiated its foreign debt, several, including Peru, Brazil, and Argentina, have suspended or limited their debt payments for periods of time. These measures have been typically intended both to gain breathing space during periods when foreign reserves have run low and to be a bargaining tactic designed to force Northern banks to offer concessions in return for resumed debt payments.

Although debt moratoria can provide short-term relief and may bring concessions from creditors, they also involve costs for the debtor country itself. In particular, wayward debtors sacrifice their international creditworthiness. Countries fear that a defiant stance on debt repayment could result in a loss of access to short-term trade credit. Short-term credits, consisting mostly of loans issued for periods of days or weeks between the time of sale and the actual delivery of traded goods, are heavily relied upon to lubricate the wheels of international commerce. Without them, a nation must face the difficult prospect of conducting its trade with the outside world on a cash-only basis. The denial of trade credits is perhaps the ultimate sanction that banks have available for disciplining defiant debtors. Brazil accumulated $6 billion in arrears during its most recent payments moratorium. However, according to John Reed, chairman of Citibank, Brazil also lost access to some $3 billion in normal short-term lending.[83]

Actual debt repudiation might lead to even sterner sanctions, such as legal moves by bank creditors to seize a debtor country's assets abroad in fulfillment of its debt. The risk for any single country that decides to pursue a radical strategy is that it may rupture the entire web of relationships it holds with the international economic community. These calculations make clear the dependence of many, if not most, Third World states on the world economy. This reality is captured in Finance Minister Silva Herzog's recollection of

---

[83] "Brazil's Plan for Its Debt," *New York Times*, August 20, 1990.

deliberations among Mexican policymakers as they attempted to formulate a strategy for coping with the country's financial crisis in 1982: "We asked ourselves the question what happens if we say, 'No dice. We just won't pay.'? There were some partisans of that. But it didn't make any sense. We're part of the world. We import 30 percent of our food. We just can't say, 'Go to Hell.'"[84]

## Bargaining Power and the Debt: Southern Disunity and Northern Unity

If Third World debtors find it difficult to go it alone in defying Northern creditors, then why don't they pool their leverage through cooperation? The possibility of a debtors' cartel was a much-discussed topic among bankers, academic observers, and government officials beginning in the early eighties, when the idea was first seriously broached. Third World debtors indeed made sporadic attempts at cooperation in negotiating with the North during the eighties. Latin American countries were the most vigorous in their efforts to forge greater unity. Representatives from the region's major nations gathered frequently throughout the eighties to discuss their common debt problems.

These meetings typically produced declarations calling upon creditor governments and banks to share some of the burden of easing the debt crisis. Meeting in Ecuador in 1984, Latin American representatives appealed to creditors to "harmonize the requirements of debt servicing with the development needs of each country."[85] In November 1987 eight Latin American presidents meeting in Acapulco, Mexico, called for "mechanisms that will allow our countries to benefit from discounts in the value of the respective debts in the market and from the consequent reduction in the servicing of such debts" and for the establishment of "interest rate limits, in accordance with procedures decided upon between the parties."[86] This was followed in 1989 by a meeting of the twenty-six nations of the Latin American Economic System (SELA) to continue consultations on a common debt bargaining strategy.[87] Beyond Latin America, UNCTAD, the Third World trade organization, issued a call in September 1988 for commercial banks to forgive 30 percent of the debt owed by the fifteen most heavily indebted countries.[88]

The results of these consultations among debtor countries, however, seldom progressed beyond verbal expressions of unity. Latin American debtors rejected the notion of forming a true debtors' cartel. Even lesser forms of cooperation, such as coordinating the timing of debt renegotiations or agreeing on common terms, demands, and objectives in bargaining with the North, generally eluded debtor countries.

---

[84] Greider, *Secrets of the Temple*, 484.

[85] "Latin American Debt: Living on Borrowed Time?" 31.

[86] Mike Tangeman, "Safety in Numbers: Latin American Looks at Unity to Solve Debt Crisis," *In These Times*, February 3–9, 1988.

[87] Collett, "Brady's Debt Plan Is Short on Principle."

[88] Wicker, "The Real Danger of Debt."

This disunity among debtors stood in contrast to the generally high degree of coordination among banks, Northern governments, and international organizations. Why, then, did debtor country cooperation prove so feeble? Part of the reason is that, despite their common interests, debtor countries were, and remain, in competition with one another for Northern funds. This rivalry can lead countries to seek the favor of creditors by adopting a more cooperative stance than their neighbors.[89] Governments may be slow to associate themselves with the radical positions sometimes taken by other debtors, on the other hand, for fear that their own creditworthiness will be marred.

This was the case in 1984 when President Raul Alfonsin of Argentina called for debtor country unity in confronting the IMF and the banks. Instead of rallying around Argentina in its time of need, other Latin American countries sided with Northern creditors and persuaded Argentina to back down from its confrontational stance. Neighboring debtor nations even went so far as to provide Argentina with the short-term financing needed to pay its overdue debt bill.[90] Commenting on this episode, one Mexican Foreign Ministry official pointed out, "We have a lot of incentives to convince the other nations to be cautious. We have suffered a lot to get where we are, and we don't want to see them upset it."[91]

A related obstacle to greater unity has to do with the differing timing of the countries' respective financial crises. When Argentina moved toward a more radical strategy in 1984, as we have seen, it was discouraged by Mexico and Brazil; both of these countries had reached agreements with their creditors and therefore felt less urgency about their debt problems. Peru unilaterally declared that it would devote no more than 10 percent of its export earnings toward debt payments in 1985. Still fearful of damaging their access to international credit, Mexico, Brazil, and Argentina refused Peru their support. Brazil and Argentina had new stabilization programs in place in 1986 when Mexico came close to suspending payments, and, again, they refused to contemplate a more unified and confrontational course. Much the same was true in 1987, when Brazil declared a moratorium on payments to its private creditors. Mexico, by that time, had initiated a new stabilization plan in cooperation with its creditors, and Argentina was in no mood to rock the boat.[92]

Differences in size also impede cooperation. Small debtor countries have often been more supportive of a radical course than have larger debtor countries. Large countries receive more-favorable treatment by Northern creditors than do small countries, precisely because the big debtors pose a greater threat to the world financial system. Large debtors also have better prospects of gaining renewed access to international credit markets in the future than

---

[89] Aggarwal, *International Debt Threat*, 31.

[90] Richard Feinberg, "Latin American Debt: Renegotiating the Burden," in Richard Feinberg and Ricardo French-Davis (eds.), *Development and External Debt in Latin America: Bases for a New Consensus*, Notre Dame: Notre Dame University Press, 1988, 59.

[91] Aggarwal, *International Debt Threat*, 32.

[92] Alan Riding, "Brazil's Reversal of Debt Strategy," *New York Times*, February 22, 1988.

do their smaller brethren, and thus have more reason to protect their credit-worthiness. For reasons of image and pride, moreover, large and relatively well-developed countries like Brazil and Mexico do not wish to be lumped together with small poverty-stricken countries like Bolivia or Peru.[93] Finally, large debtor countries resent the prospect that small countries would be free riders on the efforts of the large countries in any cooperative endeavor. Small countries would benefit alongside large debtors from any favorable outcomes gained in bargaining with the North while contributing very little to the success of such a venture.[94]

Indeed, movement toward a debtors' cartel raises the problem of cheating. The North would inevitably seek to split any debtors' cartel by offering some countries special incentives to defect. This sort of obstacle has often stymied cooperation. Mexican officials, for instance, have at times believed that they could gain a better deal by relying upon their country's special relationship with the United States rather than by joining other debtor countries in a stance of defiance.[95]

Domestic factors also inhibit movement toward a radical strategy. The economic interests of the middle and upper classes in many Southern countries serve to sap governing elites of the will needed to confront the North over the debt issue. The well-to-do in many debtor countries invested substantial portions of their assets abroad during the eighties. With large amounts of money in Northern banks, these individuals have little interest in endorsing methods that might wreak havoc on Northern financial institutions.[96]

Related to this is the presence of many technocrats in the economic ministries of most Third World countries. Often trained in the North, these internationalist-oriented bureaucrats share much of the ideology and outlook of organizations such as the IMF. They may lobby for compliance with IMF- or World Bank-sponsored reforms because they are convinced that such policies are conducive to long-term economic growth, regardless of the short-term costs. The outcome of internal battles between these policymakers and their more nationalist-oriented colleagues varies across countries and across time. IMF and World Bank officials sometimes attempt to strengthen their allies in such conflicts so as to smooth acceptance of the policies they advocate. They do so indirectly by training Third World financial and development officials at special schools run by the IMF and the bank.[97] More directly, one study has documented efforts by World Bank officials to bypass and isolate nationalist bureaucrats, while cooperating with international technocrats, in

---

[93] Feinberg, "Latin American Debt: Renegotiating the Burden," 59.

[94] Aggarwal, *International Debt Threat*, 52–53.

[95] Feinberg, "Latin American Debt: Renegotiating the Burden," 59.

[96] Feinberg, "Latin American Debt: Renegotiating the Burden," 60.

[97] These are the IMF Institute and the World Bank's Economic Development Institute. Robin Broad, *Unequal Alliance: The World Bank, the International Monetary Fund, and the Philippines*, Berkeley: University of California Press, 1988, 26, 31.

the development and implementation of a structural adjustment program in the Philippines during the early eighties.[98]

Northern banks also face a number of obstacles to mutual cooperation in their negotiations with debtor countries. Perhaps the largest of these obstacles stems from the sheer number of banks whose assent must be gained in any given deal. This is true of even relatively small-scale loans. A 1983 rescheduling agreement concerning Ecuador's $1.2 billion in overdue loan payments required the participation of over four hundred banks.[99]

Coordination among this many actors would be difficult under most circumstances. But cooperation is rendered even more problematic by conflicting interests. Banks involved in international lending differ widely in their size and their proportional exposure to Third World debt. Smaller and less-heavily exposed banks are typically more reluctant than are larger and more deeply committed banks to lend new money to help troubled debtors keep current on payments stemming from previous loans. Bankers are also divided by national origin. During the early eighties, conflicts arose over the fact that U.S. banks were more heavily involved in lending to Latin America than were European banks, while the latter had lent more to Poland and other Eastern European countries than had those in the U.S. Banks of different nationality also face varying regulatory requirements from their home governments.[100]

The relationship between banks and Northern governments has at times presented problems as well. Tensions have arisen over the distribution of burdens between the two in coping with the debt crisis. Moreover, whereas banks are primarily concerned with profits, governments are motivated by broader political concerns, such as the maintenance of political stability or the spread of democracy in debtor countries. The potential for conflict between these outlooks is captured in a statement attributed to a Citicorp vice chairman: "Who knows which political system works? The only test we care about is: Can they pay their bills?"[101]

During most of the debt crisis, however, Northern banks have been remarkably successful in maintaining unity among themselves, despite these obstacles, and in securing the cooperation of other actors. The difficulties of sustaining cooperation among large numbers of banks have been eased by the rules and practices of syndicated lending as well as by the web of ties that binds banks together. Most syndicated loan agreements, for instance, require two-thirds approval before a debtor can be declared in default. Because voting is weighted according to each bank's share of the total loan, this rule effectively provides the big banks with veto power over such decisions.

---

[98] Broad, *Unequal Alliance*.

[99] Charles Lipson, "International Debt and International Institutions," in Kahler (ed.), *The Politics of International Debt*, fn. 14, 223.

[100] Aggarwal, *International Debt Threat*, 15–21.

[101] Aggarwal, *International Debt Threat*, 38.

Less formally, large banks have developed procedures for monitoring small bank behavior and for pressuring them to cooperate in rescheduling deals. An advisory committee of fourteen major banks carried out the bulk of negotiations with Mexico, for instance, in 1982. After a deal was reached, each of these banks took responsibility for bringing ten regional banks on board. Each regional bank, in turn, sought to secure the cooperation of ten nearby smaller banks. This arrangement became standard operating procedure in subsequent rescheduling negotiations. The major banks, as well as the debtor countries themselves, nudged recalcitrant banks toward cooperation in new lending by threatening to exclude the latter from future syndication deals. Due to their need to protect long-term business relationships with larger banks, small banks often found such threats compelling.[102]

Gaps in private cooperation are often filled in by the actions of public authorities. If pressure from the large banks is insufficient to induce cooperation on the part of a small bank, for instance, the latter might become the subject of informal pressure from Treasury Department or Federal Reserve authorities. The regulatory power that government agencies hold over banks provides authorities with a powerful means of influencing bank behavior.

The large banks have found the IMF and the World Bank generally responsive to their concerns and quite useful in protecting overall bank interests. The reasons for this are simple. Both institutions have weighted voting schemes that give the North far more voting power than the South. The top officials of both institutions are invariably drawn from the North and often have roots in the banking world. The IMF and the World Bank also raise funds by issuing securities in Northern financial markets. Finally, both institutions are influenced by prevailing economic doctrines, which are predominantly shaped by Northern intellectuals.

These factors generally incline the IMF toward policies favored by the banks. Indeed, bankers treat the IMF's relationship with a Third World country as an indicator of the latter's creditworthiness. A country unable to resolve its differences with the fund will likely be snubbed by the banks as well. Banks find it too costly and difficult to develop detailed economic and political data concerning each Third World country. They instead rely upon the expertise and judgment of the IMF. The IMF is also in a much better position to impose, administer, and monitor policy reform programs in troubled debtor countries than are the banks. The IMF, as a public institution that lends only to member countries, has an authority that is more legitimate than that of a private bank. Moreover, with the IMF in the lead, debtor countries find it more difficult to divide the bank coalition by striking special deals with some creditors but not with others. Finally, the fund sometimes defends the collective interests of all

---

[102] On private cooperation, see Aggarwal, *International Debt Threat*, 21–29; and Charles Lipson, "Bankers' Dilemma: Private Cooperation in Rescheduling Sovereign Debts," *World Politics*, October 1985.

banks by compelling reluctant individual banks to share their part in the burden of new lending.[103]

In general, Northern actors have been far more unified in bargaining over the debt than have their Southern counterparts. The resources at their disposal have also been greater. Yet, although still favoring the North, the balance of bargaining power has shifted somewhat in favor of debtor countries since 1989. Debtor countries began to pursue bolder tactics in their search for concessions from the North in the late eighties. Banks, by allowing their new lending to the South to dwindle, diluted one of the incentives that previously had induced a more cooperative stance on the part of debtor countries. Conflicts intensified, moreover, between the banks and Northern governments. The Brady Plan called upon banks to make sacrifices not altogether to their liking. It was motivated in part by fears that lack of progress in defusing the debt crisis might lead to political instability in Latin America. This risk was driven home when left-wing candidates came close to winning the presidencies of both Mexico and Brazil in the late eighties. Broader political considerations, along with continuing pressure from U.S. export interests harmed by Latin American austerity, came to partially outweigh U.S. government responsiveness to banker preferences. These considerations serve as a reminder that power relationships, such as those that govern North–South economic ties, are never static and can shift for a variety of reasons.

## NORTH–SOUTH FINANCE IN THE NINETIES: THE GROWTH OF PORTFOLIO INVESTMENT

The early nineties brought a dramatic revival in North–South financial flows after the prolonged slump of the eighties. The movement of all kinds of Northern capital to the Third World tripled between 1990 and 1993, reaching a level of $150 billion in the latter year.[104] The composition and destination of these new financial resources differed substantially, however, from the recent past.[105]

Portfolio investment came to replace bank lending as the dominant source of foreign financing for many Third World countries. Bank loans accounted for 77 percent of all foreign capital that flowed to the Third World in 1981. By 1993 portfolio investment had come to represent 74 percent of such flows, overshadowing both bank lending and foreign direct investment. Whereas the bank loans of the seventies and early eighties went primarily to

---

[103] On the relationship between the fund and the banks, see Aggarwal, *International Debt Threat*, 35–44.

[104] "Coping with Capital," *The Economist*, October 29, 1994, 86.

[105] For an excellent overview of recent trends in North-South financial relations, see Stephany Griffith-Jones and Barbara Stallings, "New Global Financial Trends: Implications for Development," in Barbara Stallings (ed.), *Global Change, Regional Response: The New International Context of Development*, Cambridge: Cambridge University Press, 1995.

Southern governments or state-owned firms, 60 percent of the portfolio funds of the nineties went to the private sector.[106]

Portfolio investment takes two principal forms. In the first, foreign pension funds, mutual funds, investment banks, and individuals purchase stocks or equities in Third World firms. Typically, such investments are too small to provide actual control over the firm in question. Foreign investors take on a passive ownership role, forgoing participation in management of the company. This sort of stake differs from direct investment, where a foreign firm sets up its own operations in a host country or purchases a controlling interest in a local firm and takes on direct management responsibilities. A second form of portfolio investment involves the purchase of corporate- or government-issued bonds. This is a type of loan, extended directly from an investor to the bond-issuing firm. Investors receive a stipulated interest rate on the bonds they possess, with the principal to be paid back by a specified date.

The portfolio investment flows of the early nineties were stimulated by (1) the attraction of higher interest rates in the South as compared with those in the North, (2) growing investor confidence in the economic reforms being carried out by many Southern states, (3) more-successful management of Third World debt under the guise of the Brady Plan, (4) a loosening of Third World restrictions on many forms of foreign investment, and (5) the lure of investing in a growing number of previously state-owned firms that were sold off to private ownership by many Third World governments during this period.[107]

This new wave of portfolio investment has been concentrated in a handful of Latin American and East Asian countries. Since 1989 two thirds of all portfolio investment in the Third World has gone to only five countries (Mexico, Brazil, Argentina, South Korea, and Turkey), while 80 percent of all foreign investment to the South was targeted at twelve countries between 1990 and 1993. Latin America, in particular, has been a prime recipient of portfolio funds. Although only 18 percent of North–South portfolio investment went to Latin America in 1989, the region's share jumped to 56 percent by 1992. Between June 1988 and June 1993, Argentina's stock market grew by 86 percent per year, while the annual growth in the value of Mexican stocks averaged 37 percent.[108]

Portfolio investment has provided some Third World countries with a ready and welcome new source of international financial resources. As noted earlier, however, most Third World countries have been bypassed by Northern investors. Moreover, the drawbacks of portfolio investment are substantial. Many

---

[106] Kenneth Gilpin, "New Third World Fear: Investors Could Walk Away," *New York Times*, April 24, 1994; Greenhouse, "Third World Markets Gain Favor."

[107] Masood Ahmed and Sudarshan Gooptu, "Portfolio Investment Flows to Developing Countries," *Finance and Development*, March 1993.

[108] "The Boom in Portfolio Investment," *Latin American Weekly Report*, April 15, 1993; "Coping with Capital," *The Economist*, October 29, 1994, 86; Stijn Claessens and Sudarshan Gooptu, "Can Developing Countries Keep Foreign Capital Flowing In?" *Finance and Development*, September 1994, 62; Greenhouse, "Third World Markets Gain Favor."

Northern investors know little about the firms in which they put their money. Most of these funds are provided on a short-term basis and do not offer the sort of "patient" or long-term capital that Third World countries most need. Portfolio funds are relatively liquid. They can be easily withdrawn at the first sign of trouble in a country's economy, quickly transforming a manageable problem into a deteriorating crisis as large quantities of capital flee the country.[109]

These dangers are clearly illustrated in the recent Mexican peso crisis. As 1994 dawned, Mexico was widely touted as a model of neoliberal transformation and as an example for other Latin American countries to follow. Over the previous decade, Mexican presidents had committed their country to a strategy of thorough liberalization, abandoning the traditionally dominant role played by the state in the Mexican economy. The once-vast state-owned sector of the economy had been largely privatized. Hewing closely to IMF and World Bank policy prescriptions, Mexico was the first country to enjoy the debt reduction made possible by the Brady Plan. Mexico dramatically lowered import barriers during the early nineties and entered into the North American Free Trade Agreement (NAFTA) with the United States and Canada. Once viewed with suspicion, foreign investors were now welcomed. Indeed, over $90 billion in foreign investment entered Mexico from 1990 through 1993, two thirds of it in the form of portfolio investment. Following the deep economic downturn of the eighties, GDP growth resumed at an average rate of 3.1 percent per year between 1988 and 1994, while annual inflation fell from nearly 145 percent to only 6 percent.[110]

By the end of 1994, this dreamy picture of economic health had given way to a nightmarish financial panic. Following a year of political upheaval and economic mismanagement, Mexico's peso crisis of December 1994 sent the economy into a tailspin and cast doubt upon both the wisdom of relying so heavily upon fickle international financial flows and the neoliberal policies that Mexico so well exemplified.

A number of factors prompted the wave of foreign investment that entered Mexico during the early nineties. The Brady Plan deal of 1989 and more-prudent government fiscal policies helped to restore a measure of faith in Mexico's creditworthiness. Investors welcomed Mexico's new market-oriented economic strategy, and many believed that the impending NAFTA accord would spur Mexican exports and growth. The sell-off of state-owned enterprises created new opportunities for foreign investors to gain equity stakes in a set of large and stable firms at bargain prices. Moreover, low U.S. interest rates combined with recession north of the border prompted investors to look elsewhere, including to Mexico, for profits.

---

[109] Gilpin, "New Third World Fear"; Gooptu, "Can Developing Countries Keep Foreign Capital Flowing In?" 64.

[110] "Survey: Mexico," *The Economist*, October 28, 1995, 4-5; Peter Passell, "Economic Scene," *New York Times*, January 12, 1995.

Many of the funds that flowed to Mexico from the United States in the early nineties represented repatriated flight capital. Wealthy Mexicans who had deposited massive sums abroad during the depths of the Mexican debt crisis of the eighties brought these same funds back to Mexico after economic conditions there improved in the early nineties.[111]

Although Mexico briefly benefited from the renewed flow of international investment following the drought of the eighties, the gains were more apparent than real. Little of the huge torrent of portfolio investment that Mexico attracted in the early nineties found its way into new physical investments, such as factories or machinery. Most was geared toward short-term financial speculation on Mexican stocks and other securities. Moreover, the increased availability of foreign funds was substantially offset by a large drop in Mexico's own domestic savings rate—from 22 percent of GDP in 1988 to 16 percent in 1994.[112]

In fact, the main effect of increased foreign investment was to finance Mexico's uncontrolled import consumption binge of the early nineties. Although Mexican exports grew strongly in this period, the country's import bill rose even more rapidly, producing a current account deficit of nearly $30 billion, equivalent to a whopping 8 percent of Mexican GDP, in 1994. This enormous trade deficit sapped Mexico's official reserves, which fell from $25 billion at the beginning of 1994 to only $6 billion by the end of the year. By early 1995 the government had issued $29 billion in short-term, dollar-denominated bonds, called *tesebonos*, to cover Mexico's foreign exchange shortfall.[113]

Mexico's worsening financial situation was exacerbated by both international and domestic factors. Internationally, rising interest rates in the United States, along with an economic recovery, attracted relatively liquid portfolio investment funds from Mexico and other Latin American countries back to U.S. financial markets.[114]

Domestically, Mexico suffered a series of political crises that undermined investor confidence. January 1994 brought an armed rebellion by a peasant organization called the Zapatistas in the southern state of Chiapas. Protesting NAFTA, Mexico's neoliberal economic policies, and the lack of genuine democracy, the rebels battled police and Mexican army forces for two weeks before both sides agreed to a tense cease-fire and subsequent on-and-off-again negotiations over rebel demands. In March a presidential candidate, Luis Donaldo Colosio, representing Mexico's longtime ruling party, the PRI, was assassinated. This was followed in September by the assassination of another high-ranking PRI official, Party Secretary General Jose Francisco Ruiz Massier. Both assassinations triggered allegations that they were the product

---

[111] "The Boom in Portfolio Investment."

[112] "Survey: Mexico."

[113] "Survey: Mexico," 5–6; "Survey: Latin American Finance," *The Economist*, December 9, 1995, 19.

[114] "Survey: Mexico," 6.

of infighting and rivalries within the PRI hierarchy. In December renewed violence flared up in Chiapas.[115]

During this period, Mexico's financial authorities put off measures that might have eased the country's precarious financial circumstances. Despite a growing current account deficit, the government defended an overvalued peso out of fear that a devaluation might prompt so much pain as to endanger the election of the PRI's new candidate, Ernesto Zedillo, in August's presidential election.[116]

After he was elected, Zedillo's government finally moved to devalue the peso by 15 percent on December 20. Coming on the heels of such a turbulent year, this move panicked investors and immediately set into motion a major financial crisis. Over the next two days, $5 billion fled the country. Mexican authorities proved unable to halt the free-fall of the peso, which plunged in value from 3.5 pesos to the dollar in early December to 7.5 pesos to the dollar by March 1995. The Mexican stock market lost one half of its value over the three months following the December 20 devaluation. The crisis quickly spread to other countries, such as Argentina and Brazil, where stock markets fell precipitously.[117]

Mexican interest rates briefly peaked at over 80 percent before settling back to a still-astronomical level of between 40 and 50 percent. Such high interest rates choked off domestic investment by Mexican firms. Later in the year, confidence in Mexico's currency dropped so low that many Mexican businesses refused to accept pesos in payment, insisting upon dollars instead. In January and February of 1995, at least 750,000 Mexican workers lost their jobs, and more cuts followed in succeeding months. The real wages of Mexican workers fell by 30 percent over the course of 1995.[118]

As during the 1982 crisis, Mexican authorities looked to the United States for relief. With its reputation tied to the success of the NAFTA treaty, the Clinton administration quickly responded. By the end of January 1995, with Mexico only days away from defaulting on its international debts, the United States had assembled a $50 billion international line of credit to Mexico, with $20 billion promised by the United States and the remainder pledged by the IMF, the World Bank, and other industrialized nations. Mexico offered its future oil export income as collateral for the borrowed U.S. funds, which were to be paid back within three to five years. The Mexican government drew upon

---

[115] "Survey: Mexico," 6.

[116] "Survey: Latin American Finance," 6.

[117] "Survey: Mexico," 5-6; James Brookes, "Mexican Crisis Depressing Brazil and Argentina Stocks," *New York Times*, February 20, 1995.

[118] Anthony DePalma, "In Land of the Peso, the Dollar Is Common Coin," *New York Times*, November 21, 1995; Anthony DePalma, "Mexicans Reach New Pact on the Economy," *New York Times*, October 30, 1995; Anthony DePalma, "Mexico Eager to Celebrate End to Crisis Despite Hardships," *New York Times*, April 27, 1995.

over $12 billion of U.S. credit during 1995, most of it used to retire short-term *tesebono* bonds as they fell due.[119]

In mid-March, President Zedillo announced an austerity plan, including higher taxes and cuts in public spending, designed to restore international confidence in Mexico's creditworthiness. Higher interest rates were encouraged in an effort to attract investors and strengthen the peso.[120]

Although Mexico's economy shrank during 1995, many financial indicators showed improvement. The current account deficit virtually disappeared as a falling peso stimulated exports and dampened imports. Mexico's foreign reserves rose through the year, and the stock market partially rebounded. Still, the peso again came under attack late in 1995. The Zedillo government responded by announcing a pact with Mexican business and labor designed to restrain price increases, bolster wages, increase domestic savings, and spur public investment. Foreign investors have nevertheless reacted with caution, and it remains unclear how soon Mexico will regain lost confidence and again resume the path of economic growth.[121]

The Mexican crisis has led to international efforts to avert future episodes of this kind. In June 1995 a group of industrialized nations announced the creation of a $50 billion fund that could be used to stabilize Third World currencies and financial markets in response to rapid speculative movements of international capital. Only countries committed to strict fiscal and monetary policies would be eligible for assistance. The IMF simultaneously announced more sweeping requirements for financial and economic data from borrower countries so as to allow creditors a more accurate picture of each nation's financial health.[122]

This most recent Mexican crisis offers a number of important lessons. Most obviously, the Mexican case illustrates the dangers of relying upon volatile, short-term financial flows to finance unsustainable current account deficits. More broadly, there is no substitute for a strong domestic savings rate. Foreign capital can supplement domestic resources, but it is too unreliable to provide the basis for long-term growth in the absence of sustained domestic capital formation. In contrast to East Asia, this is a lesson that has yet to be fully absorbed in much of Latin America.

---

[119] "Putting Mexico Together Again," *The Economist*, February 4, 1995; "Survey: Mexico"; Julia Preston, "Markets Skeptical, the Peso Falls Again," *New York Times*, November 9, 1995.

[120] "Survey: Mexico."

[121] DePalma, "Mexico Eager to Celebrate End to Crisis Despite Hardships"; "Survey: Mexico"; Julia Preston, "Intervening, Mexico Halts Slide in Peso," *New York Times*, November 10, 1995; Keith Bradsher, "Mexico: Absent from the White House Crisis List," *New York Times*, November 10, 1995; Preston, "Markets Skeptical, the Peso Falls Again"; DePalma, "Mexicans Reach New Pact on the Economy."

[122] Paul Lewis, "IMF to Require More Data from International Borrowers," *New York Times*, October 6, 1995.

## CONCLUSIONS

The Third World debt crisis dramatically illustrates the politics of asymmetrical interdependence. With the stability of many Third World governments and the soundness of the world financial system both at stake, political bargaining quickly displaced market mechanisms as the primary conduit for coping with Third World debt problems. Governments and public agencies assumed major roles, alongside the banks, in crafting responses to the difficulties that have grown from Southern indebtedness in the years since the Mexican crisis of 1982. This strongly political dimension of the debt crisis has highlighted the significant role that power relations play in determining the distribution of benefits and burdens from North–South economic links.

The fact that the principal burden of coping with the debt crisis has fallen on Third World countries is the expected outcome of an international order in which political power and economic power are distributed unequally among countries. In this case, the South's dependence upon the North for finance, trade, and technology has provided Northern policymakers and bankers with the leverage needed to impose their own solutions to the debt crisis. To be sure, Third World debtors have at times managed to slow or moderate the pressures for debt repayment, but their ability to deflect such pressures has proven limited. This is due in large part to the fact that it is the South, not the North, that would be harmed the most by the severing of the economic ties that bind the First and the Third Worlds. The weakness that this relationship of asymmetrical interdependence imposes upon the South has only been compounded by the relative lack of unity among debtor countries in their bargaining with the North.

As a direct result of the debt crisis, many Southern countries have submitted to a degree of Northern supervision (via the IMF and other agencies) of their domestic and international economic policies that would have been unthinkable less than two decades ago. The recent Mexican crisis, which illustrated the costs to governments that pursue policies unpopular with Northern investors, seems likely to enhance the degree of Northern oversight and to further narrow the range of policy options available to Southern policymakers.

## ANNOTATED BIBLIOGRAPHY

Vinod Aggarwal, *International Debt Threat: Bargaining Among Creditors and Debtors in the 1980's*, Policy Papers in International Affairs, no. 79, Berkeley: University of California Press, 1987.
   A brief but valuable conceptual treatment of North–South bargaining over solutions to the debt crisis.
Barry Eichengreen and Peter Lindert (eds.), *The International Debt Crisis in Historical Perspective*, Cambridge: MIT Press, 1989.
   A collection of essays that explores whether previous historical episodes of international debt crises hold lessons for coping with recent Third World indebtedness.

Miles Kahler (ed.), *The Politics of International Debt*, Ithaca: Cornell University Press, 1985.

Although somewhat dated, this collection features a number of excellent political analyses of the evolution of the Third World debt crisis. Particularly useful as a source for relevant theories and concepts.

Howard Lehman, *Indebted Development: Strategic Bargaining and Economic Adjustment in the Third World*, New York: St. Martin's Press, 1993.

Examines bargaining relationships among Southern states, Northern banks, and Northern governments over management of the debt crisis.

E. Wayne Nafziger, *The Debt Crisis in Africa*, Baltimore: Johns Hopkins University Press, 1993.

Examines sources, consequences, and solutions to debt crisis in Africa.

David Woodward, *Debt, Adjustment and Poverty in Developing Countries* (vols. 1 and 2), London: Pinter Publishers, 1992.

A detailed two-volume study of the effects of the debt crisis on Third World economies.

# *Chapter 13*

# HUNGER, POPULATION, AND SUSTAINABLE DEVELOPMENT

The entire edifice of global economic activity rests upon a fragile natural ecosystem. The demands that humans place upon their natural environment have risen to unprecedented and destructive proportions in recent decades. The global population level is expected to nearly double over the next century, while rising incomes will lead to increased consumption. These trends raise questions about whether nature can accommodate ever-increasing resource demands for food, water, energy, minerals, and timber. Already, scientists warn that our massive appetite for fossil fuels may have altered the earth's atmosphere and set in motion an irreversible pattern of global warming, with dire consequences for future generations.

Biologists use the notion of carrying capacity to measure the limits of nature's ability to sustain increasing numbers of a given species. When nature's carrying capacity is breached, resource scarcity serves to correct excess population levels in a most brutal manner. Humans differ from other species, of course, in that they possess the ability to manipulate their natural environment and thus to extend its carrying capacity in various ways. Still, this biological metaphor aptly serves to raise the question of limits. How many people can the earth support? Where do the limits to rising consumption lie? What are the consequences should we overshoot the earth's carrying capacity?

These questions pertain in different ways to North and South. Northern societies today contribute to global environmental strains in far greater degree than do those in the South. Northern countries are home to less than one quarter of the world's population, yet they account for five sixths of global resource consumption. Rich countries also contribute 80 percent of global greenhouse gas emissions.[1] One estimate suggests that the average American will, during his or her lifetime, account for 13 times the

---

[1] "Green Justice: The Facts," in Robert Jackson (ed.), *Annual Editions: Global Issues, 95/96* (11th ed.), Guilford, Conn.: Dushkin Publishing, 1995, 98–99.

environmental damage of the average Brazilian, 35 times that of an Indian, and 280 times that of a Haitian.[2]

Yet Southern resource consumption is expected to grow at a rapid pace over coming decades, due both to quickly rising populations and increasing income levels. Moreover, whereas Northern societies possess the technology and wealth needed to cope with, reverse, or compensate for environmental threats in some degree, Southern societies are less capable of countering the effects of increasing air and water pollution.

These considerations have led many development specialists to recast notions of Southern development from visions of limitless increases in consumption to more environmentally friendly notions of sustainability. Increasing consideration is being given to methods for limiting population growth and reconciling rising living standards with environmental protection. This rethinking of the development process is complex and multifaceted. This chapter examines selected issues related to the challenge of sustainable development. The first two sections explore the relationships among population, hunger, and poverty. The final section discusses international efforts to support the movement toward sustainability, focusing on the 1992 Rio Earth Summit.

## POPULATION

As Table 13.1 shows, human population growth has accelerated at an alarming pace over the past two centuries. It took over a million years for the world's population to pass the one billion mark. Yet the passage from five billion to six billion in population, currently underway, will be accomplished in just over a decade. Much of this increase is concentrated in societies already too impoverished to provide the schooling, jobs, and social services that are necessary to offer a decent standard of living for rapidly growing numbers of claimants. Runaway population growth holds back economic development, contributes to social and political frictions, strains scarce resources, and triggers sometimes-destabilizing cross-border immigration flows. In a myriad of ways, rising population pressures are likely to play the dominant role in the political, social, and economic lives of many societies across the globe in the twenty-first century.

A variety of data sheds light on the dimensions of the present population explosion. The rate of annual population growth peaked in 1963 at 2.2 percent and has since fallen, descending to 1.54 percent in 1994. Nevertheless, the absolute number of people added to the world's population continued to climb through the seventies and eighties, reaching a peak of eighty-eight to ninety million per year in the early nineties. This figure should begin to decline as well, however, before the end of the century. In 1995 the

---

[2] Paul R. Ehrlich and Anne H. Ehrlich, *The Population Explosion*, New York: Simon and Schuster, 1990, 134.

**TABLE 13.1**
**World Population Milestones**
*World Population Reached:*

| LEVEL | YEAR |
| --- | --- |
| 1 billion | 1804 |
| 2 billion | 1927 (123 years later) |
| 3 billion | 1960 (33 years later) |
| 4 billion | 1974 (14 years later) |
| 5 billion | 1987 (13 years later) |

*Projections:*

| | |
| --- | --- |
| 6 billion | 1998 (11 years later) |
| 7 billion | 2009 (11 years later) |
| 8 billion | 2021 (12 years later) |
| 9 billion | 2035 (14 years later) |
| 10 billion | 2054 (19 years later) |
| 11 billion | 2093 (38 years later) |

SOURCE: Population Information Network Gopher of the United Nations Population Division, Department for Economic and Social Information and Policy Analysis. Table titled: "World Population Milestones."

world's population stood at roughly 5.7 billion. United Nations projections suggest that population levels will grow to around ten billion people by the year 2050, although the actual figure will depend upon the speed of progress in lowering birth rates. Because birth rates in much of the developed world are already at or even below replacement levels, 95 percent of additional population growth in the years ahead will occur in the Third World. Overall, Third World populations are expected to double in the next thirty years. Although the South's share of total world population stood at 68 percent in 1950, this proportion is expected to rise to 84 percent by 2025. Over the next two decades, Third World countries will face the challenge of finding jobs for 730 million new workers.[3]

Why are Southern populations expanding at such a rapid rate? Population experts believe that the Third World is passing through the same sort of demographic transition that led to growing population levels in Europe and North America from the late eighteenth through the early twentieth centuries. According to this theory, rapid population growth is essentially a by-product of the early stages of economic development. Prior to industrialization and economic development, population levels are generally stable. High birth rates are

[3] Lester Brown, Nicholas Lenssen, and Hal Kane, *Vital Signs, 1995: The Trends That Are Shaping Our Future*, New York: W. W. Norton (Worldwatch Institute), 1995, 94-95; William Stevens, "Feeding a Booming Population Without Destroying the Planet," *New York Times*, April 5, 1994; "New Era of Human Migration Has Begun, Experts Say," *San Francisco Chronicle*, August 9, 1994.

matched by high death rates. After development produces rising incomes and increased wealth, however, death rates begin to fall dramatically. Better nutrition and sanitation, combined with less physical toil and improved access to increasingly sophisticated medical care, lead to reduced infant mortality rates and rising life expectancy. Because birth rates are initially unaffected, a declining rate of death produces an imbalance that results in a population explosion.

As incomes continue to rise, birth rates begin to decline as well (for reasons explained later) and may eventually catch up with still-falling death rates. After birth rates and death rates are equalized at low levels, population stability again appears, only now on a much higher plateau. The sequence posited by the demographic transition theory is thus: (1) high death rate/high birth rate, (2) falling death rate/high birth rate, (3) falling death rate/falling birth rate, and (4) low death rate/low birth rate.[4]

Due to a phenomenon known as *population momentum*, however, population growth will persist for a lengthy period even after couples begin to limit family size to the long-run replacement level of roughly two children each. Following a rapid burst of population growth, younger generations will account for a disproportionately large share of the overall population as compared with older generations. As these younger people move through their childbearing years, they will produce children at a faster rate than the comparatively small number of elderly people reach the end of their lives. Thus for birth rates to fall far enough to match death rates at low levels, two things must happen: Family size must decline, *and* the age distribution must even out as the first generations produced by the population boom move past their childbearing years.[5]

This theory fits Europe's experience well. It also appears to explain trends in the Third World, although the South's population explosion has been far more intense than Europe's earlier boom. Due to the spread of antibiotics and other medical advances originating in the North, Southern death rates fell at a far steeper rate during the initial stages of development. Birth rates also fell more slowly in the South, thus extending the transitional period of high growth. Nevertheless, fertility rates have fallen across most Third World regions since the sixties. Even areas such as Africa, where birth rates remain stubbornly high, have begun to witness declining fertility levels in recent years.[6]

The spread of modern contraceptives is helping to bring down birth rates in many places. In 1960 an estimated 10 percent of married women in Third World countries used some method of fertility control. By 1994 this figure had risen to 51 percent, as compared with 75 percent for Northern women.[7]

---

[4] Charles Kegley, Jr., and Eugene R. Wittkopf, *World Politics: Trend and Transformation* (5th ed.), New York: St. Martin's Press, 1995, 305

[5] For a discussion of population momentum, see Kegley and Wittkopf, *World Politics,* 299–300.

[6] Population Information Network Gopher of the United Nations Population Division, Department for Economic and Social Information and Policy Analysis, "New Fertility Declines in Sub-Saharan Africa and South-Central Asia."

[7] William Schmidt, "U.N. Population Report Urges Family-Size Choice for Women," *New York Times,* August 18, 1994; "Population: Battle of the Bulge," *The Economist,* September 3, 1994, 24.

**TABLE 13.2**

**Third World Population and Growth Rates, by Region**

|  | TOTAL POPULATION IN MILLIONS, 1992 | AVERAGE ANNUAL GROWTH (%) 1980–1992 |
|---|---|---|
| Sub-Saharan Africa | 543 | 3.0 |
| East Asia and Pacific | 1,689 | 1.6 |
| South Asia | 1,178 | 2.2 |
| Middle East and North Africa | 253 | 3.1 |
| Latin America and Caribbean | 453 | 2.0 |

SOURCE: World Bank, *World Development Report, 1994*, New York: Oxford University Press, 1994, 210–211.

Still, contraceptives help to avoid only unplanned births. Yet the vast majority of children born in Southern countries are conceived by choice. World Bank economist Lant Pritchett notes that "desired levels of fertility account for 90 percent of differences across countries in total fertility rates."[8] In some cases, the desire for large families is influenced by culture or religion. By and large, however, the incentives that most powerfully affect preferences about family size are economic. It is here, in the household economy of the family, that we can discover clues as to how best to go about restraining population growth.

Research has shown that the three most important factors affecting family size choices are income, education, and rural or urban status. Counterintuitively, poorer, less-educated rural families are likely to prefer larger numbers of children than are high-income, better-educated urban families. The reasons for this finding have to do with the economic costs and benefits of having additional children for families in differing circumstances.[9]

Poor, rural couples have two strong incentives to prefer a large family. In Third World countries, agriculture is typically very labor intensive. On small farms, children provide a relatively cheap source of added labor from a relatively early age. Their contributions can help to expand production and thereby augment family income. The costs of an additional child are relatively small for such households; chiefly, the expense is associated with food and clothing. At low income levels, moreover, it may be impossible for parents to save money for their old age, and few such families have access to the type of social security benefits that are available to elderly people in the North. For parents, then, a large number of offspring increases the chances that enough children will survive to adulthood and prosper sufficiently to take care of their parents after the latter are unable to provide for themselves.

As incomes rise, however, the incentives for rural families to prefer more children begin to diminish. A wealthier farmer may now have the means to hire skilled adult labor to help with the farm or to acquire labor-saving

---

[8] "Population: Battle of the Bulge," 25.

[9] The following discussion is based upon William W. Murdoch, The *Poverty of Nations: The Political Economy of Hunger and Population*, Baltimore: Johns Hopkins University Press, 1980, 15–58.

machinery. This lessens the family's degree of dependence upon the children's contribution. Better-off rural families are also more capable of setting aside savings for the parents' later years.

As households move from the countryside to the city, the incentives shaping choices about family size change still further. In urban areas, compulsory education laws are better enforced, and educational opportunities are more readily available. Thus children are more likely to be in school for longer periods rather than contributing to the family income through work. In any case, paid employment for children is scarce in urban areas, particularly where child labor laws are strict. The costs associated with each additional child, on the other hand, tend to rise in urban settings. Housing is more expensive. Moreover, urban parents are more likely to work at a distance from the home, increasing the costs of supervising a large number of children.

Education, particularly that of women, also plays a role in reducing family size. Better-educated parents are more likely to use modern contraceptives. Education is also associated with delayed marriage, reducing the opportunities for adding more children during a woman's childbearing years. As women gain more education and skills, they become more likely to engage in work outside the home, making a large family less attractive. Better-educated women also possess greater power within the marriage and are more likely to challenge traditional gender roles and expectations.

Indeed, the social status and education of women have been found to constitute the most powerful predictor of fertility rates. In societies where women have made progress against legal and social discrimination and where educational and economic opportunities are open to them, fertility rates are dramatically lower than in societies that offer women little social or economic power. India is a case in point. In southern regions of India, women enjoy much greater socioeconomic security than do women in northern parts of the country. Studies have found that women in southern India bear an average of only two children during their lifetimes, whereas northern Indian women give birth to an average of five children. A recent World Bank study highlights the importance of women's education in curbing population growth. In parts of the Third World where women are excluded from secondary education, the average fertility rate is seven. Where at least 40 percent of women go on to the secondary level, the average number of children born drops to three. The task of improving women's lives will be a huge one. Seventy percent of the world's poor are women. Twice as many women as men are illiterate. Many societies and cultures devalue women and continue to deny them access to education, the right to own property, or the freedom to engage in political life.[10]

The foregoing analysis suggests that population pressures are greatest among the rural poor. Bottom-up development strategies that seek to improve

---

[10] William Stevens, "Green Revolution Is Not Enough, Study Finds," *New York Times*, September 6, 1994; "Population: The Battle of the Bulge," 25.

the income and status of the poor majority will also be the most effective at bringing down birth rates. Inequitable, top-down strategies that concentrate benefits at the top of the income scale will, on the other hand, fail to alter the incentives that give rise to exploding populations.[11]

At the 1994 U.N.-sponsored International Conference on Population and Development held in Cairo, 180 nations endorsed a twenty-year Program of Action on population control. In addition to traditional population control measures, such as family planning outreach and the distribution of contraceptives, the conference focused on efforts to improve the socioeconomic and educational status of poor Third World women. In addition to their intrinsic value, such measures promise to bring down birth rates most quickly. The U.N. hopes that the $6 billion presently spent worldwide on population control will grow to $17 billion by the year 2000, with $5.5 billion of that figure provided by Northern aid agencies and the remainder by Third World governments.[12]

## FOOD AND HUNGER

The Green Revolution, launched in the sixties, harnessed modern science to the challenge of feeding a hungry world. Through cross-breeding techniques, scientists developed new varieties of wheat, rice, and other food crops that offered higher yields, better resistance to pests and disease, increased tolerance to environmental stresses, and quicker crop rotation. As a result, world grain production increased 2.6 times between 1950 and 1984. Global rice production jumped from 257 million tons in 1965 to 468 tons in 1985.[13]

Bountiful harvests helped to reduce the incidence of hunger in many parts of the world. India, a country repeatedly plagued by famine over the centuries, became self-sufficient in food. Across the Third World as a whole, the daily caloric intake per capita rose 21 percent between 1965 and 1990. The absolute number of malnourished people in the South fell by 20 percent between 1975 and 1994, despite massive population increases. Although the world's population is roughly 5.7 billion, it is estimated that present levels of agricultural output could feed seven billion people, assuming vegetarian diets and ideal distribution.[14]

Yet despite these heartening statistics, the world food system has failed to provide for everyone, and its future effectiveness is even more uncertain. Roughly 800 million people remain undernourished, lacking sufficient calories

---

[11] See Murdoch, The *Poverty of Nations*, 59-83.

[12] Schmidt, "U.N. Population Report Urges Family-Size Choice for Women."

[13] Paul Kennedy, *Preparing for the Twenty-First Century*, New York: Random House, 1993, 65–66.

[14] Henry Kendall and David Pimentel, "Constraints on the Expansion of the Global Food Supply," *Ambio*, May 1994, 199; John Bongaarts, "Can the Growing Human Population Feed Itself?" *Scientific American*, March 1994; Brown, Lenssen, and Kane, *Vital Signs*, 146–147.

or nutritional content in their diet to sustain health. One third of all Third World children are underweight for their age. Most disturbingly, fifteen million people, most of them children, die of hunger-related causes each year.[15]

The tragedy behind these figures is caused not by an inadequate quantity of food in the world, but rather by its inequitable distribution. Like other commodities, food is mainly allocated through the market. Using what income they have at their disposal, consumers bid for the food that is available. Those able to pay the market price receive the food they need, and sometimes more. Those lacking either the means to grow their own food or the money needed to purchase it in sufficient quantities simply go hungry. In short, the principal cause of hunger is poverty. Although nutritional programs run by governments or international agencies provide some relief, these efforts reach only a fraction of the chronically malnourished.

Yet although poverty and inequality account for much of the hunger in today's world, the future could bring genuine scarcity if food production fails to keep pace with population growth. Recent trends are troubling. After rising at a relatively steady pace of 3 percent per year throughout much of the post–World War II period, grain harvests have expanded at the anemic rate of only 1 percent per year since 1984. With the world's population growing at a much faster clip, this means that global per-capita grain production has been falling for over a decade. By the mid-1990s, global grain carryover stocks, as measured by days of consumption, stood at their lowest level in several decades, with the exception of a brief dip in the early seventies. This trend is especially worrisome because grain is a staple of diets around the world and accounts for the majority of the food consumed by humans.[16]

Using median population projections, food production must double by the year 2050 in order to maintain present levels of per-capita consumption. If the goal is to improve diets enough to eliminate malnutrition, then food production will need to triple in volume.[17]

Predictions as to whether this challenge can be met vary enormously. The director-general of the International Food Policy Research Institute, Per Pinstrup-Anderson, has declared that: "Our estimates show that the world is perfectly capable of feeding 12 billion people 100 years from now."[18] To the contrary, population experts Paul Ehrlich and Anne Ehrlich argue in their book *The Population Explosion* that "Human numbers are on a collision course with massive famines. . . . If humanity fails to act, nature will end the population explosion for us—in very unpleasant ways—well before 10 billion

[15] Brown, Lenssen, and Kane, *Vital Signs*, 146–147; Anne Ehrlich and Paul Ehrlich, "Why Do People Starve?" *The Amicus Journal*, Spring 1987, 44.

[16] Debra MacKenzie, "Will Tomorrow's Children Starve?" *New Scientist*, September 3, 1994, 27; Brown, Lenssen, and Kane, *Vital Signs*, 26–27, 36–37, 42–43; "The Food Crisis That Isn't, and the One That Is," *The Economist*, November 25, 1995.

[17] Bongaarts, "Can the Growing Human Population Feed Itself?"

[18] "Will the World Starve?" *The Economist*, June 10, 1995.

is reached."[19] That such knowledgeable and respected observers could reach such opposed conclusions provides some clue as to the complexity of the issues involved in charting the future relationships among food, hunger, and population. Many factors—political, economic, biological, and demographic— must be taken into account. The following discussion highlights some of the principal issues that are central to an analysis of world hunger in the coming decades.

One certainty is that much more food will be required in the future than is presently produced. Even if population control efforts are relatively successful, the number of consumers will continue to grow and, as living standards rise, they will seek enhanced diets. Where will this additional food come from?

One way to increase food production is to expand the total land under cultivation. Growth in agricultural land was rapid between 1850 and 1950. The expansion of new farmland slowed considerably after World War II, however, and has actually reversed in the developed world and some Southern countries over the past decade. Between 1972 and 1989, the total land area harvested increased only 3.6 percent, and the amount of arable land per capita has been declining for decades. Since the early sixties, 80 percent of increased food production has come as a result of higher yields, with the expansion of land under cultivation playing only a minor role in raising output.[20]

Nor is there much prospect that the growing food demands of coming decades can be met by opening new fields to production. Little arable land remains unexploited in Asia. There exists greater potential for expanding agriculture in Africa and Latin America, but the best land is already under production. Much of the arable land that remains is only marginally suited to support agriculture and is incapable of sustaining high yields. Indeed, the environmental costs of clearing new farmland are considerable because new land is typically obtained by burning or clear-cutting forests. Seventy to eighty percent of deforestation worldwide is a result of agricultural expansion. At most, it is estimated that the amount of land under cultivation could be expanded by one third over the coming years.[21]

Against this, however, must be set the farmland lost to urbanization and the harmful effects of modern agricultural practices. Nearly 1 percent of all irrigated land is lost each year due to salinization or waterlogging, both attributable to poor drainage. If this rate of loss continues, nearly 50 percent of all presently irrigated land will be lost by 2050. Land is also lost to chemical pollution, a result of the overuse of fertilizers and pesticides. The greatest threat, however, comes from soil erosion. Topsoil is currently being lost at a rate

---

[19] Quoted in Bongaarts, "Can the Growing Human Population Feed Itself?"

[20] Bongaarts, "Can the Growing Human Population Feed Itself?"; Margaret R. Biswas, "Agriculture and Environment: A Review, 1972-1992," *Ambio*, May 1994, 192-193; Donald L. Plucknett, "International Agricultural Research for the Next Century," *BioScience*, July/August 1993, 433.

[21] Bongaarts, "Can the Growing Human Population Feed Itself?"; Kendall and Pimentel, "Constraints on the Expansion of the Global Food Supply," 199.

many times faster than it is being replaced. If current trends persist, the world will be robbed of 30 percent of its global soil inventory by 2050.[22]

If the net gain in agricultural land is likely to be small in coming decades, then the main burden for increasing food supplies must be placed on techniques designed to raise the productivity of existing land. This was the aim of the Green Revolution of the sixties. Since then, scientific research into ways to enhance Third World food production has been conducted under the auspices of an informal international regime. International cooperation in this field began with the founding of the International Rice Research Institute (IRRI) in the Philippines in 1961. The IRRI developed new rice strains that dramatically raised yields throughout Asia. The Centro Internacional de Majoramiento de Maiz y Trige (CIMMYT), located in Mexico, soon duplicated this success by devising new wheat varieties that served to stimulate the Green Revolution in India, Pakistan, and elsewhere.

The Consultative Group on International Agricultural Research (CGIAR), founded in 1971, has meshed the efforts of a growing number of agricultural research organizations. CGIAR today encompasses eighteen research centers and draws funding from forty public and private sources, including Northern and Southern governments, development banks, private foundations, and international agencies. Although CGIAR's initial emphasis was on enhancing productivity through higher yields, it has since broadened its research into sustainable agriculture, including environmental concerns and resource management.[23]

In many ways, the work of implementing the Green Revolution is still unfinished. As of the mid-1980s, less than one third of grain-producing farms in the Third World planted high-yielding Green Revolution varieties of grain. Bringing high-yield seeds into more common use throughout the Third World could lead to substantial gains in food output. Unfortunately, this goal is not easily met. Green Revolution grain varieties achieve their high yields by virtue of their responsiveness to liberal quantities of fertilizer and water. Irrigation is particularly important. Although only 16 percent of the world's grain-producing lands are irrigated, these fields produce 36 percent of all the grain harvested each year.[24]

But irrigation is expensive. The most bountiful and affordable sites for irrigated agriculture have already been exploited. Future expansion of irrigated land will require large investments. As previously mentioned, existing irrigated lands are threatened by salinization and waterlogging. In some cases, the dams and reservoirs upon which many irrigation systems depend are becoming clogged with silt. In other instances, underground water tables are being depleted much faster than they are being replenished. This is true of

---

[22] Kendall and Pimentel, "Constraints on the Expansion of the Global Food Supply," 200.

[23] Plucknett, "International Agricultural Research for the Next Century."

[24] Laura Tangley, "Beyond the Green Revolution," *BioScience*, March 1987; MacKenzie, "Will Tomorrow's Children Starve?"

the aquifer that lies beneath India's bountiful Punjab wheatfields, which is falling by one meter per year. Overall, the per-capita quantity of irrigated farmland has declined by 6 percent since 1978.[25]

Fertilizers can boost yields substantially, especially if used in conjunction with modern seed varieties. Lacking either self-generated capital or access to credit, many owners of small farms in the Third World simply cannot, however, afford the expense of purchasing commercial fertilizers for their fields. In many places where fertilizer use is already heavy, farmers have begun to experience declining marginal returns. Additional quantities of fertilizer produce increasingly smaller enhancements to yield.[26]

Africa is one part of the Third World that has been almost entirely bypassed by the Green Revolution and other modern farming advances. As of the mid-1980s, only 1 percent of Africa's grain-producing fields were planted with high-yield Green Revolution varieties of seed. The fertilizer use rate in Africa is only 3 percent that of the United States. Due to the devastating effects upon livestock of diseases spread by the tsetse fly, only 16 percent of African farms rely upon animal power. Only 3 percent have access to modern farm machinery. Cereal yields in Africa are less than one quarter those achieved in the United States, one third of those in the Far East, and less than one half those of Latin America. Moreover, the output of African farms has failed to keep up with the region's rapid population growth. As a result, per-capita grain production has declined by 22 percent in Africa since 1967.[27]

When provided with adequate resources, African farmers are capable of substantially improved performance. Norman Borlaug, one of the fathers of Asia's Green Revolution, helped to transplant Green Revolution techniques to 150,000 African farms between 1986 and 1992. These farms realized average increases in yield of 3.5 times previous levels.[28] A combination of factors, including general economic stagnation, rising debt burdens, repeated drought, and, in many countries, civil violence, robs African agriculture of the investments needed to realize these sorts of results on a broad-scale basis. Should the necessary resources become available in the future, however, it is clear that Africa's farmland has the potential to produce far greater quantities of food than it does at present. This, then, offers some hope for the future.

Even where the Green Revolution has been pursued most vigorously, however, its effects have not been entirely positive. In many places, large farmers who could afford the investments required to reap the benefits from

---

[25] MacKenzie, "Will Tomorrow's Children Starve?"; Bongaarts, "Can the Growing Human Population Feed Itself?"; Kendall and Pimentel, "Constraints on the Expansion of the Global Food Supply."

[26] MacKenzie, "Will Tomorrow's Children Starve?"

[27] Richard Critchfield, "Bring the Green Revolution to Africa," *New York Times*, September 14, 1992; Tangley, "Beyond the Green Revolution"; Kendall and Pimentel, "Constraints on the Expansion of the Global Food Supply"; Biswas, "Agriculture and Environment: A Review, 1972-1992"; Bongaarts, "Can the Growing Human Population Feed Itself?"

[28] Critchfield, "Bring the Green Revolution to Africa"; "Ethiopia: A Green Revolution?" *The Economist*, November 25, 1995.

the new varieties of seed gained power and economic status relative to small farmers who lacked sufficient resources to undertake such investments. In the Punjab region of India, this led to an increasing concentration of land ownership, with nearly a quarter of all small farms disappearing between 1970 and 1980.[29]

The Green Revolution has also had negative environmental impacts that limit its sustainability, including increased soil erosion, the depletion of water tables, and chemical pollution. Moreover, because farmers in some regions have abandoned the plethora of traditional varieties of wheat or corn in favor of a small handful of new high-yielding varieties, a disturbing loss of genetic diversity is occurring. Native crops that may have useful characteristics, such as resistance to certain diseases, are threatened with extinction before scientists can even ascertain and exploit their beneficial qualities. The genetic uniformity of modern grain production also increases the risk that new diseases might wipe out entire crops or that pests will become increasingly resistant and invulnerable to modern pesticides. Traditional farming practices guarded against these risks by planting a variety of grains, each with different vulnerabilities. This diversity reduces the chances that one disease will damage the entire crop.[30]

Despite these cautionary notes, scientific advances will undoubtedly play a role in boosting future food production. If, as seems possible, genetic engineering helps to reduce problems with pests and disease, an estimated 1 to 3 percent of the world's crops would be saved. Indeed, the new science of biotechnology is being rapidly embraced by many Third World countries and could bring substantial benefits in the future, although its promise has yet to be realized in great degree.[31] New rice varieties created by the International Rice Research Institute could raise total rice production by as much as one quarter after they are planted on a widespread basis after the turn of the century. Many such breakthroughs must be realized, however, if food production is to keep pace with growing populations. Yet funding for agricultural research and improvement has declined in recent years. The amount of Official Development Assitance (ODA) targeted toward agriculture dropped from $12 billion to $10 billion between 1980 and 1990, while funding for CGIAR fell by 7 percent in real terms from 1992 to 1994.[32]

There exist other measures that can help make more food available in the future. Better management should be able to save much of the 6 percent of all grain that is presently lost through poor storage and distribution practices. In some places, land that presently produces only one crop per year could support two or more crops if properly managed. The world's farms could feed far more people if a large proportion of the grain presently fed to livestock were

[29] Vandana Shiva, "The Green Revolution in the Punjab," *The Ecologist*, March/April 1991.

[30] Shiva, "The Green Revolution in the Punjab"; Kendall and Pimentel, "Constraints on the Expansion of the Global Food Supply"; Bongaarts, "Can the Growing Human Population Feed Itself?"

[31] Anne Simon Moffat, "Developing Nations Adapt Biotech for Own Needs," *Science*, July 1994.

[32] MacKenzie, "Will Tomorrow's Children Starve?"

instead consumed directly by humans. Livestock, such as cattle and sheep, now graze roughly one half of the earth's total land area. One quarter of the world's cropland is devoted to the production of grain and other feeds for livestock. These animals consume 38 percent of the grain produced worldwide. Although the grain fed to livestock is converted to meat, which is eventually consumed by humans, the process is most inefficient. It takes seven kilograms of grain, for instance, to produce one kilogram of beef. A decline in meat consumption would free up much grain for direct human consumption and help the world's agricultural system to accommodate the demands of a growing global population. Unfortunately, proportional meat consumption is more likely to rise than to fall in the coming years. Experience suggests that as Southern incomes rise, people who had previously been able to afford only a vegetarian diet will begin to consume larger quantities of meat.[33]

Much will depend upon policy reform as well. If Southern agriculture is to modernize quickly enough to provide for rapidly growing populations, then the development priorities of many Third World governments must change. Three sets of policy biases common to many governments work against producers of basic staple food crops: an industrial bias, an urban bias, and a cash crop bias. Policymakers often equate development with industrialization. As a result, scarce capital is marshaled toward the manufacturing sector, while agriculture suffers from a scarcity of investment. Indeed, some governments deliberately manipulate food prices downward so as to please politically potent urban constituencies. The results of this urban bias are to depress rural incomes and to undermine both the ability and the incentive for farmers to modernize and expand production. Even within the agricultural sector, crucial inputs such as credit, infrastructure, and the best land are targeted principally at cash crops, such as coffee, tea, cocoa, or sugar, which can be exported to the North in return for scarce foreign exchange.

On balance, it seems possible, despite the obstacles, that the world can achieve sufficient increases in food production to avoid any dramatic lowering of present consumption levels and perhaps even to improve the diets of the millions of malnourished. Four factors appear critical to achieving this outcome: (1) continued progress must be made in reducing the rate of population growth, (2) ongoing scientific research must continue to devise increasingly reliable and higher-yielding staple crop varieties, (3) increased economic investment must be directed to agricultural modernization, particularly in the Third World, and (4) greater efforts must be made to bring about the more equitable distribution of food supplies. To say that these challenges can be met, however, is not to assume that they will be. Much will depend upon the priorities of political leaders in both North and South. What does seem apparent, however, is that the margin of error is slim when it comes to organizing the world's agricultural resources over the coming decades.

---

[33] Kendall and Pimentel, "Constraints on the Expansion of the Global Food Supply"; MacKenzie, "Will Tomorrow's Children Starve?"; Bongaarts, "Can the Growing Human Population Feed Itself?"

# SUSTAINABLE DEVELOPMENT

The most ambitious effort to date to chart a road map toward sustainable development has been the United Nations Conference on Environment and Development (UNCED), held June 3-14, 1992, in Rio de Janeiro, Brazil.[34] Popularly known as the Earth Summit, this meeting brought together representatives from over 150 nations, including 118 heads of state, to focus on the connections between threats to the global environment and economic development. The U.N. General Assembly resolution authorizing UNCED established that its purpose was to: "elaborate strategies and measures to halt and reverse the effects of environmental degradation in the context of increased national and international efforts to promote sustainable and environmentally sound development in all countries."[35]

Rio was also the site of a parallel meeting of 1,400 nongovernmental organizations called the Global Forum. Private environmental and citizens groups from around the world shared ideas, built ongoing networks, and lobbied government representatives on behalf of a more environmentally sustainable future.

The 1992 Earth Summit was modeled upon a similar conference held in 1972 in Stockholm, Sweden. That meeting, called the U.N. Conference on the Human Environment and attended by 114 nations, helped to stimulate development of the modern environmental movement. The earlier meeting also gave rise to the U.N. Environment Program and led to tighter environmental legislation in many Northern countries.

The Rio conference produced five major documents:

- The **Rio Declaration** established twenty-seven basic principles of sustainable development.
- The **Convention on Biodiversity** sought to address three major goals: (1) to commit governments to the preservation of endangered plant and animal species and habitats, (2) to encourage the sustainable use of biological resources, and (3) to establish the right of Southern nations to compensation from Northern commercial exploitation of products based upon Southern gene stocks.
- The **Climate Convention** addressed the problem of global warming, brought on by the emission of so-called greenhouse gases, such as carbon dioxide. One hundred and fifty-three nations committed themselves to curbing the emission of such gases to 1990 levels by the year 2000.

---

[34] Much of the information given next on UNCED has been culled from Edward Parson, Peter Haas, and Marc Levy, "A Summary of the Major Documents Signed at the Earth Summit and the Global Forum," *Environment*, October 1992; Peter Haas, Marc Levy, and Edward Parson, "The Earth Summit: How Should We Judge UNCED's Success?" *Environment*, October 1992; and Jerald Schnoor, "The Rio Earth Summit: What Does It Mean?" *Environment, Science and Technology*, vol. 27, no. 1, 1993.

[35] Haas, Levy, and Parson, "The Earth Summit: How Should We Judge UNCED's Success?" 8.

- The **Forest Principles** document specified seventeen nonbinding principles of sustainable forest management.
- **Agenda 21,** an eight hundred-page document, provided a work plan or agenda for action covering all major areas of sustainable Southern development.

The most important new international institution to emerge from the Earth Summit was the Sustainable Development Commission. This organization was given responsibility for integrating the planning and activities of all U.N. bodies responsible for projects related to both environmental protection and economic development. The commission was also given the job of monitoring and reporting on progress toward fulfillment of the aims and programs spelled out in Agenda 21. National governments were invited to provide annual reports to the commission on the state of environmental and development goals within their countries. The Sustainable Development Commission will periodically hold high-level conferences on topics related to its mandate and will bargain with governments and international organizations on issues of mutual concern.

In many ways, the Earth Summit was a success. Never before had so many of the world's people and governments focused such concentrated attention on the major environmental challenges of modern life. With eight thousand journalists in attendance, media coverage was extensive. Broad agreement was reached on the critical importance of coupling environmental and economic issues and on many of the principles and strategies necessary to move in the direction of sustainability. The national reports prepared by most governments for submission at the summit enhanced the information base regarding environmental conditions in many parts of the globe. The creation of new institutions, such as the Sustainable Development Commission, will ensure continued international attention and regularized consultation regarding environmental problems. The Global Forum helped to strengthen cooperation among hundreds of nongovernmental environmental organizations from all parts of the world and illustrated the potential political clout of citizen-based groups.

Nevertheless, the Earth Summit fell short of its ambitious mandate in other ways. Disagreements plagued the deliberations surrounding many important issues. Due to differing interests and perspectives, final drafts of the forestry and climate change agreements were considerably watered down. Northern and Southern countries clashed over the assignment of responsibility for various environmental problems.

The most significant conflict emerged over how to finance the expensive programs elaborated in Agenda 21. UNCED's secretariat estimated that comprehensive implementation of the provisions of Agenda 21 in the South would cost $600 billion per year. The suggested share of this amount to be provided by Northern countries was $125 billion, with the remainder to be allocated by developing countries themselves. Yet there is little or no likelihood that either Northern or Southern countries will devote sums even approaching these recommended amounts to the pursuit of sustainable development. All of Northern foreign aid to the South amounted to roughly $60 billion in the early nineties. Even if all of this aid were reprogrammed toward sustainable development projects (an unlikely prospect), it would still amount to less than half of the suggested total. In fact, the Rio conference produced Northern pledges of increased aid for environmental programs in the South amounting to only an estimated $6 to $7 billion. Nor are Southern states likely to come up with the hundreds of billions of dollars in annual funding necessary to implement Agenda 21 at a time when most are busy cutting public expenditures.

At best, Agenda 21 outlines a set of goals and strategies that can be realized only slowly through an incremental process. In the meantime, however, existing patterns of development will continue to inflict environmental damage to the land, sea, and air, sometimes in irreparable ways.

## CONCLUSIONS

The model of economic development pioneered and pursued by Northern societies over the past two centuries has been premised upon visions of limitless growth. Nature has been viewed as an infinite provider. This vision has given rise to a set of affluent, highly industrialized economies located in North America, Western Europe, and Japan. The allure of these mass-consumption societies has spread across the world, with Southerners seeking to emulate the attractive living standards of the North. As Southern countries themselves embarked upon the initial stages of economic development, falling death rates helped to spark a population explosion. It is this combination—of ever-rising consumption for a rapidly growing number of people—whose viability is now in doubt.

In recent decades, the costs and limitations of the world's present economic and demographic course have become clearer and better understood. Many scientists and ecologists doubt that nature can sustain a doubling of the world's population over the coming century combined with a continuation in present rates of economic growth. Only recently, however, have serious efforts begun to work out the implications of these concerns for Southern development strategies. UNCED represented a breakthrough of sorts in promoting the idea that development must be judged not by growth alone, but also by long-term environmental sustainability. Yet practical efforts to move toward sustainability have been modest thus far, and much evidence suggests that traditional thinking about development remains deep seated.

The stunning economic success of many East Asian countries, for instance, has led many to offer them as models for other Southern countries seeking to break free from poverty. Yet the example of these societies does little to suggest that the desire for rapid industrialization and rising mass consumption in the South can be reconciled with environmental sustainability. Indeed, the environmental costs of East Asian growth have been as impressive as the economic gains. A World Bank study recently concluded that the amount of sulfur dioxide, nitrogen dioxide, and total suspended particulates in the air increased by a factor of 10 in Thailand, 8 in the Philippines, and 5 in Indonesia between 1975 and 1988. Of the seven cities in the world with the worst air pollution, five are located in Asia. In Taiwan, asthma cases quadrupled during the eighties due to severe air pollution, and 20 percent of the island's farmland is fouled with industrial waste. A 1985 survey showed that 59 percent of Taiwanese favored increased environmental protection over economic growth. Conditions in Asia are likely to worsen over the coming years because energy consumption in the region is doubling every twelve years, and the number of motor vehicles in use is doubling every seven years.[36]

Although a rethinking of both the means and the ends of Southern development may be desirable in its own right, any real progress in promoting environmental sustainability on a global scale must focus most intently on changes in the mass-consumption habits of Northern societies, which presently use far more resources and contribute to problems such as global warming in far greater degree than does the South. Ultimately, the notion of limits will increasingly come to exert an ever-larger influence on all aspects of global economic relations.

## ANNOTATED BIBLIOGRAPHY

Lester R. Brown, Nicholas Lenssen, and Hal Kane, *Vital Signs, 1995: The Trends That Are Shaping Our Future*, New York: Worldwatch Institute and W. W. Norton, 1995. Revised yearly, this collection of reports on the state of the global environment is loaded with facts and figures. It is the best and most accessible source for those seeking a quick overview of current environmental issues.

Paul R. Ehrlich and Anne H. Ehrlich, *The Population Explosion*, New York: Simon and Schuster, 1990. A pessimistic and alarming perspective on runaway population growth and its consequences.

Al Gore, *Earth in the Balance: Ecology and the Human Spirit*, Boston: Houghton Mifflin, 1992. A broad survey of the threats currently facing the global ecosystem.

Frances Moore Lappe and Joseph Collins, *Food First*, Boston: Houghton Mifflin, 1977. A radical critique of the global food system.

William W. Murdoch, The *Poverty of Nations: The Political Economy of Hunger and Population*, Baltimore: Johns Hopkins University Press, 1980. An accessible look at the connections among population, hunger, and poverty. The author argues that structures of international and domestic inequality lie at the root of both rapid population growth and global hunger.

---

[36] "Pollution in Asia: Pay Now, Save Later," *The Economist*, December 11, 1993, 36l; Robin Broad, John Cavanagh, and Walden Bello, "Development: The Market Is Not Enough," in Jeffrey Frieden and David Lake (eds.), *International Political Economy: Perspectives on Global Power and Wealth* (3rd ed.), New York: St. Martin's, 1995, 436.

Bruce Rich, *Mortgaging the Earth: The World Bank, Environmental Impoverishment, and the Crisis of Development*, Boston: Beacon Press, 1994.
More than a damaging critique of the World Bank's environmental impact, this book offers a philosophical meditation on the sources and implications of modern materialism. Rich challenges common assumptions about development, progress, and the relationship of human society to the ecosystem.

# Chapter 14

## THE POLITICAL ECONOMY OF POST-COMMUNIST STATES

On November 8, 1917, Vladimir Ilyich Lenin appeared before the All-Russian Congress of Soviets. The previous day Bolshevik forces had seized power from the Provisional Government in a coup. Proclaiming the goal of the revolution, Lenin concluded his speech with, "We shall now proceed to construct the socialist order."[1]

Less than seventy-four years later, on August 19, 1991, the former communist Boris Yeltsin—the first elected president of the Russian republic—stood on a tank outside the Russian Parliament to beseech his followers and all people in the Soviet Union to resist a coup launched by members of the Communist Party against the president of the Soviet Union, Mikhail Gorbachev. Yeltsin's pleas helped to rally elements of the military to resist the coup, which was defeated shortly. Within days the Communist Party had its activities suspended. Within four months, the Soviet Union had disintegrated, and Gorbachev himself had resigned. In January 1992 the newly independent states of the former Soviet Union adopted a policy of rapidly shifting toward free markets and something resembling capitalism. Lenin's "socialist order" was in tatters.

Over the next several years, a political struggle for control of the economic direction of Russia was waged between the government and groups hurt by change. Economic reform moved forward even as the forces resisting change mounted a ferocious battle against liberalization. Dramatic bouts of economic disintegration coupled with periods of feeble economic stability helped generate a popular political base for those whose interests were harmed by reform. The ultimate outcome of this conflict remains unclear.

Equally dramatic was the fall of communism in Central Europe, symbolized best by the destruction of the Berlin Wall in November 1989. Throughout central Europe, from Poland to Yugoslavia and Bulgaria, the collapse of communist rule was tied to changes in the Soviet Union. Here were the real dominoes, falling down after the withdrawal of Soviet military protection in

---

[1] Merle Fainsod, *How Russia Is Ruled*, Cambridge: Harvard University Press, 1963, 84.

1988–89. Between October and December 1989, communist governments throughout the region collapsed. What followed were efforts at reform, albeit of a very different character and pace in different countries. The result in Yugoslavia was catastrophe, with political breakdown and civil war. In Czechoslovakia, a more amicable split into two parts was accomplished. Romania, Bulgaria, and Albania produced a somewhat truncated reform effort, due to the rapid recovery of neocommunist forces. And, despite serious difficulties in Poland, Hungary, and the new Czech Republic, some marked progress toward economic and political reform had been made.

The drama of change in Asian communist states is of a different variety, but equally significant. In China, on October 1, 1949, Mao Zedong proclaimed the victory of the Communist Party in the twenty-two-year civil war with the assertion that "China has stood up." But the death of Mao in 1976 and the arrest one month later of his wife and three others in the "Gang of Four" marked the end of the ten-year Cultural Revolution and the beginning of a turn toward reform communism. China was psychologically traumatized, economically weakened, and politically riven by the Cultural Revolution. Even so, a reform faction led by twice-purged Deng Xiaoping maneuvered its way to power and by 1979 launched a radical reform program aimed at strengthening the position of the Communist Party and of China in the international system. This economic reform focused on dramatic increases in the role of markets and free prices and opening to foreign investment and ideas, while political reform emphasized pragmatism over ideology. The economic results have been astonishing, with very rapid growth and increasing integration of China into the world economy.

In Vietnam, on September 2, 1946, Ho Chi Minh proclaimed Vietnam's independence from French colonial rule using eighteenth-century language familiar to Americans: "All men are created equal. . . ." It was not until 1954 that the northern half of Vietnam gained independence and not until 1975 that the country was reunited. Crushing blows from economic weakness combined with radical changes in the Soviet Union and China to move the communist leadership to chart a new course in 1985–86. Following the Chinese path, Vietnam adopted market reforms and economic opening. And, as in China, economic growth has been very high. Though communist governments still rule in China and Vietnam, and vestiges of the old economic order remain, the economic changes in these societies have been profound, even spectacular.

How are we to understand the broad trajectory of development in the Soviet Union and other communist states and the eventual demise or radical change in this system of economic and political organization?[2] One approach

---

[2] The concept of post-communism needs some clarification. The shift away from communist forms of political and economic organization has been most pronounced in the former Soviet Union and in countries of central Europe. There, *post-communism* refers to the demise of communism as a political and economic option. In Asia, change is more complex. China and Vietnam have adopted radical economic reforms that jettisoned much of the command economy of communism; but these states retain exclusive communist control over the political systems. The concept of post-communism applies only to economic changes in Asia.

might emphasize the moral and political crisis of communism, another the limitations of the system, yet another an aggressive foreign policy and consequent overextension.

This chapter will sketch out an analysis consistent with the perspective offered by political economy. It will examine the problems generated by external competitive pressure on a system of political economy poorly equipped to compete. We will consider the basic characteristics of a command economy, focusing particular attention on its inherent flaws. Especially important are the problems faced by a command economy in developing institutions capable of adjustment, innovation, and dynamism in competing with the market-based system in the West. The discussion then moves on to a consideration of the efforts at reform, particularly those after 1985 in the former Soviet Union and in Central and Eastern Europe, after 1979 in China, and after 1986 in Vietnam. Finally, we will look at the process and problems of a transition to a market economy in post-communist countries. The revolutionary nature of this process, the near-term and long-term economic prognoses, the likely political difficulties, and the role of Western aid are the main topics.

## THE POLITICAL ECONOMY OF CHANGE IN COMMUNIST STATES

Any effort to conceptualize the dramatic changes in China, the former Soviet Union, central Europe, and in Vietnam is subject to important qualifications. The most obvious qualification is that we have not witnessed the end of this process, and so we must be careful not to produce an argument that can be rendered moot by a sharp turn of events. More important, any analysis can provide only a partial understanding of a multidimensional process. The insights from political economy can give us a sense of some of the broad forces at work, but because we omit the roles of such factors as ideology, leadership, and political struggle, an approach from political economy should not be taken as the final word.[3]

A central theme of this book is the importance of the competitive international environment, which we have understood as a complex process involving economic, technological, political, and military struggles. Much of the process that moved toughened communist elites to change their societies can be traced to the effects of international competition.

For much of its history, Russia has found itself hard-pressed to keep up with the nations of Europe in many areas of this competition. The sixty years before the Revolution in 1917 were a time of dramatic change. Russia's leaders sought to catch up with other states in Europe where industrialization was proceeding apace. The elimination of serfdom and substantial

---

[3] For an effort that offers a somewhat comprehensive approach to change in communist systems, see Andrew C. Janos, "Social Science, Communism, and the Dynamics of Political Change," *World Politics*, October 1991, 81–112.

industrialization did lead to significant change. But wars with Japan in 1904–1905 and with Germany from 1914 to 1917 exposed serious weaknesses. At a basic level, the capacity to produce and distribute the implements of large-scale warfare was grossly lacking. This became especially evident during the First World War when Russian military failures, brought on by ill-equipped troops, helped spark a revolutionary movement that swept first the czar and then a more democratic government from power. Between the two world wars, this competition continued but in a context of economic uncertainty and depression and institutions poorly developed for operating in the world economy.

During this very difficult era, several nations at somewhat different levels of industrial development embarked on a path of near-autarchy to ensure their security in a hostile setting. Germany and Japan, rocked by the world depression, moved toward military aggression and toward closing themselves off from economic reliance on the rest of the world. Even earlier, a radical version of this strategy was adopted by Josef Stalin for the Soviet Union. Beginning in 1928–29, Stalin dropped a more market-oriented posture and wrenched the Soviet Union toward "collectivization" and "socialism in one country." Stalin's decisions had the effect of creating a new model of political economy. After 1945 this system was imperfectly extended to the nations in Eastern Europe under Soviet military control and later to China, North Korea, Vietnam, and Cuba. This command economy became the main alternative to the world capitalist economy and was a centerpiece of the ideological struggle in the Cold War.

The development of a command economy in the Soviet Union during the 1920s and 1930s was mostly a result of the political needs of the Communist Party. In 1921 a New Economic Policy had experimented with private ownership and free markets as a strategy of economic growth. Although growth occurred, it was modest and concentrated in agriculture. Peasant producers of grain were willing to accelerate production only when more consumer goods were available. Further, expansion of the private economy led to the creation of a larger class of wealthy entrepreneurs in urban and rural areas whose interests were in conflict with those of the Communist Party. Stalin's victory in a power struggle with Leon Trotsky led to adoption of the policy of collectivization. This involved seizing control of all the means of production in the country. Resistance was met with military force, leading to millions of deaths. From Stalin's perspective, this eliminated those who might have resisted communist political domination and opened the door to a development strategy designed to correct Soviet industrial backwardness.[4]

Stalinism combined political authoritarianism, control of virtually all the means of production by the state, and exclusion of external economic

---

[4] Especially useful for understanding this era are: Merle Fainsod and Jerry Hough, *How the Soviet Union Is Governed*, Cambridge: Harvard University Press, 1979; Stephen F. Cohen, *Bukharin and the Bolshevik Revolution*, New York: Vintage, 1971; Alec Nove, *An Economic History of the U.S.S.R.*, New York: Penguin, 1989.

relations, except through a government trading company. Totalitarianism became an approximation of reality with the combination of a terroristic secret police, Communist Party control of all meaningful organizations, and state allocation of economic resources. The essence of the system was the creation of a "garrison state" in which the process of industrialization was harnessed to the military requirements of international competition.[5] Much of the motivation for this crash program of industrialization came from fear of the West, especially Germany. Stalin was very conscious of his nation's weaknesses in military capabilities.

Thought of purely in economic terms, and ignoring the horrendous human cost, collectivization initially produced a rapid growth of industrial output. By taking control of agriculture, forcibly removing peasants from the country to the city and putting them to work in heavy industry, the state was able to achieve enormous increases in the production of steel, machinery, and raw materials. At the same time, the basic elements of a command economy were put into place. Agriculture was turned into a state enterprise on large collective farms, while heavy industry was largely created through governmental effort. In addition, a large bureaucracy designed to carry out centrally designed economic plans was established. The decade after 1928 achieved some measure of success, at least in areas related to the production of war goods. Spurred by reconstruction after World War II, growth resumed and provoked the continuing shift of peasants and workers to more productive and skilled activities. But this came at an economic cost on top of the human cost: The economic system became increasingly bureaucratic and rigid and less capable of adaptation and innovation.

Difficulties began to emerge in the late 1950s. The command economy that had proven its effectiveness in moving unused and poorly used resources toward more productive activities was much less able to organize and coordinate the multifaceted processes of input and output in an increasingly complex system. Central planning simply could not issue enough orders to the many interdependent layers of production to allow them to work together smoothly. Instead, the planners in *Gosplan*—the mammoth bureaucracy that designed and implemented the Five-Year Plans—issued gross targets for production units. These targets often made little sense in terms of the needs of other economic units that required particular types of goods to reach their own targets. The primary measures of success in a command economy are total output and the maximization of the use of inputs. Efficiency in the use of inputs and the relationship of output to actual demand—essential criteria of success in a market economy—were all but irrelevant. The result was an incoherent and even irrational economic system producing the wrong quantity of frequently low-quality goods.[6]

---

[5] This is a version of Janos, "Social Science . . .," 97.

[6] Nove, *An Economic History . . .*, 357–59.

But the crisis of the command economy went even deeper, to the very fiber of political, economic, and social relations. The system was based on the political need for nearly total control of society and economy by the Communist Party. At the same time, competition with the West and the link between expanding consumer goods and the preservation and extension of regime legitimacy created great pressure for rapid but qualitatively sophisticated economic growth. This kind of growth, which requires substantial flexibility and dynamism in economic decisions, stood in sharp contradiction to the Party's need for control. Occasional efforts at reform designed to introduce more flexibility into the system came up against fears of loss of Party control.

After Khrushchev's ouster in 1964, his successors placed even greater reliance on bureaucratic modes of planning. The result was to entrench the position of groups whose interests lay with stability and routine. The bureaucratic system under Brezhnev gained such strength that central political leaders lost control of the economy. The flow of information from bottom to top became corrupted when bureaucratic layers concealed massive failures. "A pervasive campaign of lies kept both the leaders and the populace misinformed."[7] The ability of the system to produce economic growth and goods of reasonable quality and to compete with the West ceased almost completely.

The source of this systemic crisis was the destruction of politics and economics in the fusion of state and society under Stalin and his successors.[8] The collapse of normal political and economic affairs into a realm dominated by the needs of the Communist Party severely undermined the capacity of the institutions of the nation for effective adjustment and adaptation. The institutional vibrancy of nations operating in the capitalist world economy—from multinational corporations to state bureaucracies—was almost entirely absent from the communist system of state socialism.

Missing were a decentralization and autonomy of decision making and responsibility, some meaningful criteria for measuring the success and failure of economic units, a realistic chance that these institutions could be eliminated by failure and prosper through success, and a market system capable of transmitting effective price signals to those persons responsible for production decisions. Such arrangements—approximately those of a modern market economy—create strong incentives to respond rapidly and effectively to the forces of supply and demand. When managers of business units have effective decision-making power and when those units survive and prosper only if they produce goods or services that succeed in an open market with other competing units, flexibility and dynamism will emerge.

The communist command economy, because of the centralization of decisions about production and because of the absence of prices based on supply and demand, was incapable of solving its own problems. Throughout the

---

[7] Seweryn Bialer, "Gorbachev's Move," *Foreign Policy*, 68, Fall 1987, 67.

[8] This argument is made by Bartlomeij Kaminski, *The Collapse of State Socialism: The Case of Poland*, Princeton: Princeton University Press, 1991, 3–8.

economy, goods of low quality were typical; quantities produced bore no relation to actual demand; distribution was hampered by poor delivery systems; and incentives for effective change simply did not exist. The sclerosis of Soviet society and economy became so severe that even elements of the Communist Party concluded that radical reform was needed. Ironically, these efforts at change played a key role in the collapse of the system.

## GORBACHEV AND THE FAILURE OF REFORM

### The Nature of Reform

Even before Gorbachev's assumption of the position of General Secretary in 1985, some limited efforts at reform had been introduced. Half-hearted efforts at decentralization, but without meaningful price adjustments, were followed by efforts to create giant cartel-like organizations. Investment binges in areas like agriculture and attempts to plan innovation in technology had little effect on actual growth rates. Especially after Brezhnev's death in 1982, the problems of the Soviet economy and unfavorable comparisons with the West provoked a more fundamental questioning of the merits of a command economy.[9]

Over the next three years a broad consensus on the need for significant change emerged within the Party elite. The main question for this group was whether the Soviet Union could continue as a great power.[10] That is, large portions of the governing elite were beginning to doubt that the existing system could generate the material base for effective competition in the international system. Underlying this uncertainty was a recognition that the communist command economy had failed to make the transition from the development of heavy industry to high levels of mass consumption and then to the high technology and information-based economy of the late twentieth-century world. Much less clear to communist officials was what to do about this failure. Behind virtually all proposals for change lay the potential for a serious diminution and even destruction of communist power in the Soviet Union.

During his first three to four years, Gorbachev's strategy was based on loosening political controls and encouraging greater freedom of expression, combined with much discussion, but little concrete action, concerning economic restructuring. The main effect of *glasnost* was to help win public support, create a forward-looking coalition, and improve information about the real state of the Soviet economy. Only limited efforts at decentralization of decision making were attempted, while the problem of the poor quality of goods was attacked by another bureaucracy for inspection. Although some

---

[9] For efforts at reform in the period between Brezhnev and Gorbachev, see Timothy J. Colton, *The Dilemma of Reform in the Soviet Union*, New York: Council on Foreign Relations, 1986, 70–82.

[10] George W. Breslauer, "Linking Gorbachev's Domestic and Foreign Policies," *Journal of International Affairs*, 42.2, Spring 1989, 267.

autonomy was extended to local managers, nothing resembling a real price system was permitted.[11]

Aside from the threat that change posed to the Party bureaucracy, Gorbachev's desire for reform confronted a price system that had become a form of bribery for continued support of the system. The cost of basic commodities was maintained by massive subsidies, which permitted prices to remain exceedingly low. Any move toward genuine market-based prices would inevitably result in massive inflation and substantial economic hardship for many Soviet citizens. The resulting political backlash—in spite of the likely increase in the availability of goods as supplies rise to take advantage of higher prices—served as a major impediment to such radical reforms.

## Domestic and International Politics

The combination of open political debate and persistent economic weakness produced a crisis atmosphere of increasing proportions. Issues and questions that previously were taboo—the empty shelves in stores, the proper role of the Party and the KGB, elections for local and national office, nationalities, and political independence—now became topics of fierce discussion. In this climate, support for the Communist Party declined precipitously among its own membership and among the general public. The explosion of nationalism in many of the republics and the spreading demands for independence raised the specter of a disintegration of the state.

The creation of a meaningful political life after decades of domination by the Party has not yet led to a normal process of coalition formation. Not only is the tradition of open political links and trade-offs among groups missing, but also the structure of interests makes the process more difficult. Old coalitions among the great power centers of Soviet society—the KGB, the Party, the bureaucracies, and the military—frayed because of turmoil and sharp differences within these groups. Republican nationalism produced a situation in which many who supported economic transformation also wanted a form of political change that was unacceptable to the central government. At the same time, Gorbachev's personal political standing declined due to his identification with the Communist Party, economic failure, and his refusal to seek a popular mandate.

Accompanying this unraveling of the domestic system were equally dramatic shifts in foreign policy. Gorbachev engaged in important negotiations in arms control, articulated the policy of a nonthreatening defense posture, withdrew from Afghanistan, and recognized the overextension of Soviet interests abroad.[12] But domestic policy and foreign policy dovetailed most dramatically

---

[11] Marshall J. Goldman, *Gorbachev's Challenge: Economic Reform in the Age of High Technology*, New York: Norton, 1987, 77–78.

[12] Breslauer, "Linking Gorbachev's . . ."; and Seweryn Bialer, "The Domestic and International Sources of Gorbachev's Reforms," *Journal of International Affairs*, 42.2, Spring 1989, 283–97.

in 1988–89 over Eastern Europe. Here weaknesses at home and long-standing difficulties in maintaining domination of Eastern Europe combined to produce a sudden and complete collapse of Soviet power in this area. Further, the disintegrating Soviet position in this great prize from World War II merged with the political and economic crisis at home to destabilize the system even more.

The events in Eastern Europe are also important in their own right, especially as an indication of the pathways from communist autarchy to participation in the world economy. Stalinism here was a result of Soviet occupation in World War II and the determination to retain control after 1945. Intensification of the Cold War in 1947 produced an even more heavy-handed domination with direct extension of the Soviet system westward. The result was a vicious version of nineteenth-century imperialism, with the resources of Eastern Europe used on a massive scale to help rebuild the Soviet Union.[13] Stalin's death in 1953 ushered in a two-decade period of revolts against Soviet rule and some greater flexibility in techniques of control. Various forms of demonstration, riot, and revolution occurred in East Germany in 1953, Poland and Hungary in 1956, Czechoslovakia in 1968, and Poland in 1970. In 1956 and 1968 Soviet military force was used to crush independence movements in Hungary and Czechoslovakia. But alongside this intervention came an increasing recognition of the international political costs of such actions and a growing tolerance for limited economic experimentation. The Soviet hope was that economic growth would help stabilize these regimes. Restricted mainly to Hungary and Poland, this reform went beyond anything in the Soviet Union, but it did little to reshape these economic systems. In Hungary the replacement of political criteria for planning with economic criteria did produce an initial jump in output but eventually resulted in a dead end for economic growth. During the 1970s and 1980s borrowing from the West and energy subsidies from the Soviets helped close the gap between economic performance and expectations. Neither of these efforts made any real contribution to economic reform. Instead, Eastern Europe was caught in a sullen acceptance of communist rule and a growing recognition of the vast differences in living standards between themselves and the West.[14]

The first real crack in the system occurred in Poland in 1980–81. The labor union, Solidarity, created to protest rising prices and a poor economy, succeeded in carving out a significant measure of political independence. Solidarity began to operate as a public interest group—claiming to represent all of the Polish people—in negotiations with the government over prices, wages, and political rights. Eventually the Polish government and military, along with the Soviet government, found that they could not accept the political demands made by such a powerful and independent organization. In December 1981 martial law was declared, Solidarity outlawed, and its leaders

---

[13] Charles Gati, *The Bloc That Failed: Soviet-East European Relations in Transition*, Bloomington: Indiana University Press, 1990, 24.

[14] Gati, *The Bloc* ..., 29–62.

arrested. What followed was a period of several years in which the government was forced to adopt aspects of the Solidarity program (even with Solidarity officially repressed) as it tried unsuccessfully to deal with a national political paralysis and economic crisis.

The continuing stagnation and deterioration in the economy drained the government of legitimacy. The spark for political change was provided by Gorbachev's announcement in 1988 of the unilateral withdrawal of some Soviet troops from Eastern Europe. This signaled the end of Soviet military protection for communist regimes in this region. Motivated partly by the deepening crisis in the Soviet Union and partly by the adamant rejection of reform by much of the communist leadership in Eastern Europe, this announcement had major repercussions. It was followed quickly by the reinstatement of Solidarity and the creation of what amounted to a coalition government in Poland consisting of the Communist Party, the military, and Solidarity.[15]

These events opened the door to the political revolutions of 1989. The fragility of all communist regimes in Eastern Europe was demonstrated by the cascading political crisis that ensued. Stunning electoral losses by the Polish Communist Party and rapid political liberalization in Hungary were amplified in importance by another statement from Gorbachev forswearing military intervention.[16] The Hungarian Party, sensing the tenuousness of its position, decided to curry favor with its people by permitting East German citizens to travel to West Germany, where they could expect to be welcomed. The ensuing flood of refugees from East to West was symptomatic of the pathetic illegitimacy of the East German regime. But mass demonstrations and pressure by Gorbachev on communist parties in other states also led to the disintegration of communism throughout Eastern Europe between October and December 1989.[17]

## The Collapse of Communism in the Soviet Union

The biggest domino—the Communist Party of the Soviet Union—survived another twenty months but likewise met its end (or so it seemed) in a dramatic fashion. Although some efforts at political reform continued, the dominant feature of Soviet life during 1990-91 was an increasing political paralysis. Three special aspects of the Soviet situation worked against greater innovation. The continuing economic crisis, the political instability caused by independence movements in many of the republics (including Russia), and the trauma produced by the loss of Eastern Europe and Moscow's standing as a superpower all undercut efforts to forge a coherent program of change.

---

[15] Gati, *The Bloc ...*, 61-66.

[16] With this statement, Gorbachev renounced the Brezhnev Doctrine, enunciated in 1968 to justify the Soviet military intervention in Czechoslovakia. Brezhnev announced that the Soviet Union had the right to use military force to protect socialist regimes in Eastern Europe.

[17] Gati, *The Bloc ...*, 161-90.

Economic deterioration accelerated in 1990–1991, with the Soviet economy moving into a steep recession. Several plans for radical reform via a quick shift to a market economy were floated as a trial balloon only to die from the absence of a supporting consensus. Criticism from conservative circles prompted Gorbachev to backtrack and to attempt to find a compromise solution.[18] The loss of superpower status cut into the position of the KGB and military—institutions benefiting from this status. And the unremitting pressure for independence by various republics placed the economic and political viability of the state itself in doubt.

These events came to a head in late August 1991, when conservative elements of the Communist Party attempted to seize power from President Gorbachev and restore order. The rapid collapse of this effort not only revealed internal divisions within even groups like the KGB and military but also ushered in a popular attack on the Communist Party itself.[19] In a stunning set of actions, Gorbachev quit as head of the Communist Party, and the party itself was suspended from political activity.[20] Perhaps most astounding was the decision to eliminate the central government and to replace it with a government controlled by fully independent republics.[21] What did not follow, at least initially, was adoption of a plan for dismantling the existing economic system and replacing it with free markets. Instead, only fragile and uncertain efforts toward reestablishing economic union among the republics came in the wake of the failed coup.[22] The effect of the failed coup was to drain power from the central government and to increase the significance of the individual republics. Gorbachev's fate hinged on support from Boris Yeltsin, the elected president of the Russian republic, and defeat of the coup enhanced Yeltsin's stature. The weakness of the central government shifted political initiative to the republics. The two most important—Russia and Ukraine—were determined to pursue their own agendas. For Russia and Yeltsin, it was a rapid transition to market reforms; for Ukraine, it was altering the political and economic terms of its relationship with other republics. These two republics withdrew their support from the Soviet government, which meant Russia withholding tax revenues and Ukraine refusing to sign a new union treaty.

---

[18] For a sampling of the many stories of these events, see Bill Keller, "Gorbachev Turns to the Forces of Law and Order," New York Times, December 16, 1990; Serge Schmemann, "Gorbachev to Mix Plans on Economy of Left and Right," New York Times, June 22, 1991; Francis X. Clines, "Moscow Planning Tries to Sell New Plan," New York Times, August 12, 1991; "Beyond Perestroika," The Economist, June 9, 1990.

[19] Predictions of a coup by reformers can be seen in Francis X. Clines, "An Ex-Gorbachev Ally Warns of a Coup," New York Times, August 17, 1991. For the aftermath, see Bill Keller, "Soviets' Rush Toward Disunion Spreads," New York Times, August 26, 1991.

[20] Serge Schmemann, "Soviets Bar Communist Party Activities," New York Times, August 30, 1991; Serge Schmemann, "Gorbachev Quits as Party Head," New York Times, August 25, 1991.

[21] Serge Schmemann, "Soviet Congress Yields Rule to Republics to Avoid Political and Economic Collapse," New York Times, September 6, 1991.

[22] Francis X. Clines, "Soviet Republics Agree to Create an Economic Union," New York Times, October 12, 1991.

These actions effectively sealed the fate of the central government. Change came rapidly in December 1991 as eleven of the fifteen republics created the Commonwealth of Independent States (CIS), thereby eliminating the Soviet Union and Gorbachev's position as president.

The situation in 1995 is depicted in Figure 14.1 and Table 14.1.

**FIGURE 14.1**
**The Commonwealth of Independent States**

Among the newly independent states in the CIS, certainly Russia and Ukraine are the best situated to succeed in the long run.[23] Both possess large populations, large industrial complexes, and substantial natural resources. Belarus also enjoys some of the same capabilities. The Baltic states—Latvia, Lithuania, and Estonia—have not joined the CIS and look toward the European Union. Each of the Baltic states is heavily industrialized but may find access to the markets of the CIS more appealing (and more open) than those of the EU. Moldova was traditionally part of Romania and might move toward reintegration. Three small southern states—Georgia, Armenia, and Azerbaijan—have been the scene of heavy fighting and intense political conflict. The five Asian states—Kazakhstan, Uzbekistan, Turkmenistan, Kyrgyzstan, and Tajikistan—have large Muslim populations and are generally poorer than the rest. But Kazakhstan and Uzbekistan are certainly big enough and have sufficient natural resources to support economic growth.

---

[23] The commonwealth that was created in December has not taken shape. The arrangements for economic cooperation, separate currencies, disposition of Soviet military capabilities, and political coordinating bodies remain unclear.

**TABLE 14.1**

**Former Soviet Republics' GNP and Population**

| | % FORMER SOVIET GNP | POPULATION IN MILLIONS | % OF FORMER SOVIET POPULATION | % NATIONALITIES | |
|---|---|---|---|---|---|
| RUSSIA | 61.1 | 147.4 | 51.4 | 83 | Russian |
| BALTIC STATES | | | | | |
|    Estonia | 0.6 | 1.5 | 0.6 | 68 | Estonian |
|    Latvia | 1.1 | 2.7 | 1.0 | 54 | Latvian |
| | | | | 33 | Russian |
|    Lithuania | 1.4 | 3.7 | 1.3 | 80 | Lithuanian |
| | | | | 9 | Russian |
| | | | | 8 | Polish |
| SLAVIC STATES | | | | | |
|    Ukraine | 16.2 | 51.7 | 18.0 | 74 | Ukrainian |
| | | | | 21 | Russian |
|    Moldavia | 1.2 | 4.3 | 1.5 | 64 | Moldavian |
| | | | | 14 | Ukrainian |
| | | | | 13 | Russian |
|    Belarus | 4.2 | 10.2 | 3.5 | 79 | Belarussian |
| | | | | 12 | Russian |
| | | | | 4 | Polish |
| Caucasus | | | | | |
|    Georgia | 1.6 | 5.5 | 1.9 | 69 | Georgian |
| | | | | 9 | Armenian |
| | | | | 9 | Russian |
|    Armenia | 0.9 | 3.3 | 1.2 | 90 | Armenian |
| | | | | 5 | Azeri |
|    Azerbaijan | 1.7 | 7.1 | 2.4 | 78 | Azeri |
| | | | | 8 | Russian |
| | | | | 8 | Armenian |
| CENTRAL ASIA | | | | | |
|    Kazakhstan | 4.3 | 16.5 | 5.7 | 36 | Kazakhs |
| | | | | 41 | Russian |
| | | | | 6 | Ukrainian |
|    Uzbekistan | 3.3 | 19.9 | 6.9 | 69 | Uzbeks |
| | | | | 13 | Russian |
|    Turkmenistan | 0.7 | 3.6 | 1.3 | 68 | Turkmeni |
| | | | | 13 | Russian |
| | | | | 9 | Uzbeks |
|    Tajikistan | 0.8 | 5.1 | 1.8 | 59 | Tadzhiks |
| | | | | 23 | Uzbeks |
| | | | | 10 | Russian |
|    Kyrgyzstan | 0.8 | 4.4 | 1.5 | 52 | Kirghiz |
| | | | | 22 | Russian |
| | | | | 13 | Uzbeks |

SOURCE: Data are from the *New York Times*, September 1, 1991, E-2.

The collapse of the Soviet Union and the creation of the CIS were quickly followed by dramatic economic moves. On January 2, 1992, Russia moved toward free markets and prices for most goods, thereby taking the decisive step to eliminate a command economy. This came about two years after a similar action by Poland and somewhat less drastic reform policies in other central European states. We now turn to a more detailed examination of the nature of this transformation from communism to a more market-based system.

## POST-COMMUNIST STATES AND THE WORLD ECONOMY

There is no better measure of the influence of the world economy than its impact on those communist states that excluded themselves from it for more than half a century. The dazzle of high incomes, technological innovation, and rapid economic growth played a key role in drawing these nations away from autarchy. The acceleration of growth in the 1980s, the dynamism of the European Community, the economic surge of Japan, and the threat of advancing military technology helped spur efforts at economic reform. The collapse of reform communism and the Soviet withdrawal from the field of competition appear to open a new era for the world economy—one of great promise but also of new threats.

The integration into the capitalist world economy of more than four hundred million persons—located in a dozen or more states and representing even more ethnic groups, all with low levels of income and serious weaknesses in competitiveness—is a daunting task. It is fraught with danger from the likelihood that economic transformation will be accompanied by even lower incomes, much higher inflation and unemployment, and the retraining and displacement of a large proportion of the population. This will also place great demands on the political and economic systems in the West.

We have seen how private and public capital flows have expanded technology, markets, and prosperity. The significant complementarity of interests between post-communist states and the West should not obscure the competitive and conflictual dimensions of this process. Integration also means opening world markets to the goods produced by former communist societies. This will surely play havoc with labor-intensive manufacturers and agricultural producers in Europe and elsewhere. As we saw in much of our previous analysis of international political economy, this situation contains a complex balance of complementary and conflicting interests.

During the Tet Offensive in South Vietnam in 1968, a U.S. commander issued a now-famous justification for an especially brutal and destructive bombardment: "We had to destroy the town in order to save it." In many ways, this epigram of another time and place is more appropriate for Eastern Europe and the Soviet Union, because in order to save this area, much of its existing economic system must be destroyed. This will be very painful and dangerous.

**TABLE 14.2**

**Components of Transformation to Market Economy**
*I. Macroeconomic Stabilization and Restructuring*

   A. End fiscal deficits and establish monetary stability
   B. Eliminate controlled prices and state subsidies
   C. Base exchange rate on real prices
   D. Create a convertible currency
   E. Eliminate tariffs, quotas, and other trade barriers

*II. Institutional Reforms*

   A. Transfer control of state firms to private hands
   B. Establish financial system with private banks
   C. Ensure legal protection of private property and eliminate restrictions on entrepreneurial activity
   D. Create legal guarantees for foreign investment and repatriation of profits
   E. Create new tax system
   F. Protect severely disadvantaged groups
   G. Create supportive institutions, such as accounting standards and management education

SOURCE: This table is based in part on Susan M. Collins and Dani Rodrik, *Eastern Europe and the Soviet Union in the World Economy*, Washington: Institute for International Economics, 1991, 11; and "Business in Eastern Europe," *The Economist*, September 21, 1991, 6.

## Components of Economic Change

What are the main features of the economic transformation of post-communist states? Before answering this question, it is important to keep three things in mind. First, change of this sort will take a long time, perhaps two or three decades. Second, in many ways the changes have an organic quality in that developments in several areas depend on each other. Failure in any one area can therefore derail the whole process. Third, although the countries of the former Soviet bloc share the experience of command economies, there are substantial differences in history, politics, geography, and culture that will affect their development.

There is significant agreement among Western thinkers about what must be done to bring post-communist states into the capitalist world economy. Disagreement centers mainly on whether the pace of change needs to be moderate or rapid. The main lines of agreement are found in Table 14.2.

The basic and most important consequence of macroeconomic stabilization and restructuring is to create an effective market system in which prices act to transmit meaningful signals to producers about what to produce. Control of monetary and fiscal policy is needed to make sure that government actions in spending, taxing, and printing money do not distort prices through inflation. As we have seen, large budget deficits financed through an expanding money supply lead to inflation. The greatest part of government outlay in the former Soviet Union has been military spending, subsidies to firms, and price subsidies for basic commodities. Assuming a balanced set of government accounts (which also means an enormous cut in subsidies), opening the door to foreign goods and establishing a convertible currency will serve to "import world prices," and this will help ensure that production will reflect a nation's position of comparative advantage in the world economy.[24]

But even in the best of circumstances, instituting free markets and prices based on supply and demand will certainly lead to substantial inflation. This is because prices set under the old command economy, especially for basic commodities, contained no meaningful relationship to actual supply and demand. Free markets will result, at least initially, in large price increases to reflect actual scarcity and thereby produce substantial inflation.

## Economic Change in the Former Soviet Union

The problems associated with establishing free markets are especially acute in the former Soviet Union. The command economy was the strongest here, and before 1991 the least progress had been made toward actual reform. Establishing free markets confronts more than sixty years of a command economy where the culture of markets, prices, and profits had been deeply suppressed. Several years of delaying reform led to a near collapse of the old system, some development of market prices in an underground economy, and a frightening decline in actual production. Partially responsible for this state of affairs was a debilitating imbalance in government accounts and mismanagement of the money supply. The root of the crisis was the breakdown in the system of spending and taxing. The combined budget deficits of the central government and the republics totaled as much as 25 percent of GNP. Inflation reached as high as 365 percent per year in 1991, approaching the level of hyperinflation that can destroy entire economic systems. Growth in the money supply was completely out of control, limited only to the production capacity of printing presses.[25]

The beginning of the Russian "big bang" came on January 2, 1992, when prices were freed for all commodities except basic food and fuel. For these "essentials" a slower process of decontrol was used. Other former republics joined this process very reluctantly and only after it became clear that Russia planned to go ahead with it. An explosion of prices followed, with many rising as much as tenfold. For some time the price system has remained very primitive, with information and supply networks frequently nonexistent and

---

[24] Collins and Rodrik, *Eastern Europe* . . ., 12; and John Williamson, *The Economic Opening of Eastern Europe*, Washington: Institute for International Economics, 1991, 22.

[25] "Free Fall," *The Economist*, September 28, 1991, 73. These estimates in the fall of 1991 may have been too optimistic. In January 1992 inflation was estimated at 700 percent and the decline of GDP at 40 percent. G. Bruce Knecht, "From Soviet Minister to Corporate Chief," *New York Times Magazine*, January 26, 1992, 25.

commodity exchanges often little more than "flea markets." As these arrangements develop, price increases have declined but are still subject to the effects of inflating the money supply.

The consequences of the "big bang" have been decidedly mixed, with substantial growth in privatization and markets but also political chaos, rampant inflation, traumatic economic decline, and the rise of authoritarian political movements. First the good news. A market system has been created in Russia. The greatest part of the old command economy has been dismantled. Most prices are free and respond to the relationship of supply and demand. Large portions of the state economic apparatus have been privatized; estimates are that 62 percent of GDP in 1995 was in private hands and that more than 80 percent of industrial employees work in private firms. Even many large state-owned enterprises have been privatized and restructured through large reductions in workers and production based on market signals and profit orientation. And the Russian money supply, composed of rubles and dollars, now links domestic and international prices through a market-based exchange rate. The savings rate is high—33 percent of GDP—but the investment rate is only 16 percent, suggesting the reluctance to commit resources to future returns in an uncertain environment.[26]

Radical economic reform helped bring on more than free markets in Russia: The severe economic distress that followed also contributed to a political backlash. A large part of these negative results came from the extreme imbalances in the economy in 1991 and the near-breakdown of the existing political and economic system. The institutions of a market system were insufficiently developed to compensate for the decline of the old system and may have contributed to the problems. The crisis of 1991, described earlier, derived mainly from the disintegrating ability of the command economy to link supplies of inputs and outputs and from the fiscal crisis of the state. Production declined precipitously due to shortages of all manner of goods; and the massive budget deficit pumped more money into the process of trying to purchase a declining supply of goods. The explosion of inflation added to the difficulties produced by the collapse of the institutions of the Communist Party and the Soviet state. Inflation rates rose from about 200 percent annually in 1991 to more than 2,000 percent in 1992 (10,000 percent in Ukraine) but have since declined to 10 percent to 20 percent per month in 1995 (or an annual rate of about 100 percent).[27]

The government has begun to impose massive cuts in military spending and subsidies so as to balance the budget. If successful, this should help hold down inflationary pressures and contribute to stabilizing the value of the ruble. The sorting-out process that comes from creating the infrastructure of

---

[26] The best discussions of market creation in Russia are: Anders Anslund, *How Russia Became a Market Economy*, Washington, D.C.: Brookings Institution, 1995; and "Russia's Emerging Market," *The Economist*, April 8, 1995.

[27] *The Economist*, December 4, 1995, 81.

markets, importing world prices with a convertible currency, and developing production units capable of responding to price incentives will inevitably take some time. Unclear is just how much time is available.

Early reaction to the "big bang" was generally one of resigned acceptance, but scattered demonstrations and acts of violence suggested the potential for a backlash. Market systems and rising prices typically exacerbate class differences. Those with low incomes and little savings are forced to make very unpleasant choices about what to buy. These circumstances generate intense pressure for increasing wages. The central bank, acting at cross purposes with the government, continued a very expansionary monetary policy. This made granting wage demands much easier. Yeltsin has received passionate criticism, even from former supporters of his programs. Some demonstrations have been led by military officers, and former communists use their continuing institutional positions to organize a political opposition that capitalizes on the pain of economic reform. The great difficulties associated with the change from communism to capitalism present an extraordinary challenge to the fragile political order in many of the newly independent states of the former Soviet Union.[28]

The political situation in early 1996 was tense and difficult, with the fate of economic and even political reforms hanging on the outcome of the presidential election in late spring. In December 1995 elections to the Duma (Russian Parliament) produced a victory for the communists under Gennady Zyuganov. The communists won more than one-third of the seats, and various extreme nationalists and antireform groups captured enough of the remaining seats to have an absolute majority. Recent elections in Russia have produced a variety of candidates promoting a return to authoritarianism—a view that voters seem to reject in practice but embrace in theory. More likely, voters for authoritarian candidates are expressing a protest against the dismal economic and political circumstances that have developed in Russia after the demise of the communist state. Two key indicators of the decline of state power in Russia include: the rise of local gangs and organized crime, which carry on some of the same functions as the state; and the great problems encountered by the Russian military in Chechnya. The combination of a dysfunctional state and economy produces intense uncertainty that is expressed in voting for extremist parties.

Boris Yeltsin—candidate for reelection as president, hero of the attempted coup in 1991, and sometime leader of the reform forces—trailed badly in the opinion polls. Yeltsin suffered because of his identification with the economic hardships produced by reform and by the bloody stalemate in the war in

---

[28] Reaction to economic reform is found in the following reports from the *New York Times*: Francis X. Clines, "Ex-Ally of Yeltsin Demands Cabinet's Ouster Over Prices," January 14, 1992; Serge Schmemann, "5,000 Angry Military Men Gather with Complaints in the Kremlin," and "Uzbek Students Riot in Worst Violence on Prices," both in January 18, 1992; Celestine Bohlen, "New Russian Budget Is Strong Medicine," January 25, 1992; and "Ruble-Rich Ukrainians Looking for Bargains," January 29, 1992.

Chechnya. Three major groups compete for power in Russia: a reformist group with strong support among financial and economic interests (domestic and abroad); a conservative group, resisting reform at the same time that some profit from subverting its purpose, with support from heavy industry and the old military-industrial complex; and a populist-reactionary bloc, calling for any number of wild actions designed to appeal to those disaffected by change.[29] How far could a reactionary/conservative alliance, with control over the Duma and the presidency, go in overturning reform? Much of this possible outcome depends on the state of the Russian economy.

Measuring the level of economic decline in Russia is made difficult by the unreliability of statistical reporting in the country. Before the end of communism, production enterprises frequently overreported output; since then the growth of small enterprises has led to underreporting in order to avoid taxes. Figure 14.2 presents data on economic changes in several post-communist economies. The economic collapse in Russia has been profound and is comparable to the Great Depression of 1929–35 in the United States. Production has declined precipitously, and unemployment has risen dramatically. This is largely due to the breakdown of the old system by 1991 and to the difficulties in the transition from a command to a market economy. Many state-owned firms were unsalvageable; others could survive only through massive cuts in workers and major restructuring; others with viable resources have been looted by former owners. The establishment of market signals and a system of firms capable of responding to these signals took some time but seems now to be emerging. The decline has stopped, and the basis for economic growth may have started to emerge from the dustbin of communism.

## Economic Change in Central Europe

A somewhat more favorable, but still difficult, situation can be found in Poland, which carried out even more of these same macroeconomic reforms in early 1990. Faced with inflation rates worse than in the CIS, the Polish government, under Solidarity, freed prices, gained control of fiscal and monetary policies by cutting subsidies, established currency convertibility at a market rate, placed a ceiling on wage increases, and liberalized trade. This version of the "big bang" created most of the elements of a market system in one bold stroke. Given the inherent difficulties in this transition, the result has been mixed but mostly positive in economic terms. Politically, the Solidarity coalition has fallen apart. But the budget deficit was eliminated, and inflation fell. Inflation for 1995 was estimated at 25 percent, down from 600 percent in 1990 and 250 percent in 1989. Foreign trade is in balance, goods are plentiful, and the private sector has expanded considerably.

---

[29] This analysis draws on Michael McFaul, "The Dynamics of Revolutionary Change in Russia and the Former Soviet Union," in Michael Klare and Daniel Thomas (eds.), *World Security*, New York: St. Martin's Press, 1994, 63–84; "Russia and Democracy," *The Economist*, December 16, 1995, 19–21; and *The Economist*, December 23, 1995, 59–61.

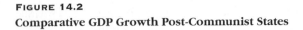

**FIGURE 14.2**

**Comparative GDP Growth Post-Communist States**

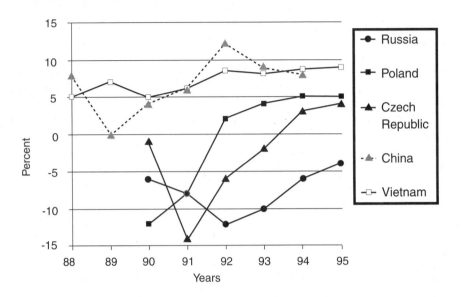

At first, the decline in state-owned firms was substantial and more than offset growth in the private sector. Industrial output fell by more than 28 percent in 1990 and another 10 percent in 1991; GDP fell by 13 percent in 1990 and another 8 percent in 1991. Unemployment has risen to more than 10 percent, and real income has fallen by as much as one quarter.[30] But since 1992 the Polish economy has grown by almost 5 percent each year (see Figure 14.2). Feeding off these initial problems is an increasingly fragmented political situation. The broad coalition established by Solidarity has come unglued, as shown by the splintered voting in the first post-communist election. Thirteen parties divided almost 90 percent of the vote, with the ex-communists taking one fifth of the parliamentary seats in an election that appeared to reject the strategy of a rapid move to free markets. The election resulted in a government headed by an avowed critic of free markets and financial discipline. In 1996 Lech Walesa, the hero of the anticommunist revolution, was defeated for president by an ex-communist. Although reform has gone too far to be reversed, forward movement may have ended and backsliding may be coming.[31]

---

[30] "Business in Eastern Europe," *The Economist*, September 21, 1991, 5; Collins and Rodrik, *Eastern ...*, 15–17.

[31] "How Many Polish Parties Does It Take to Make a Cabinet?" *The Economist*, November 2, 1991; Stephen Engleberg, "Economic Tonic Braces Poland, but Ills Remain," *New York Times*, October 25, 1991; Gabrielle Glaser, "Walesa Picks Economic Foe as Premier," *New York Times*, December 6, 1991; "Central Europe," *The Economist*, November 18, 1995.

Hungary and Yugoslavia offer some interesting variations on the Polish model. Before 1989 both countries had pursued substantial market reforms. Since then, Hungary has adopted a limited version of Poland's "big bang," with some controls remaining on foreign exchange and trade. The effects have been more moderate than in Poland, with a balanced foreign trade, inflation at 36 percent, rising unemployment, and falling industrial output. Yugoslavia, by contrast, has been torn by a civil war partly related to efforts to control inflation. Prior to 1989 Yugoslavia lacked any central monetary authority, with several units having the power to issue money. The effort to create a central bank located in Serbia clashed with the independent authorities in the economically advanced areas of Slovenia and Croatia. Policies regarding prices and convertibility, similar to those in Poland, also broke down over regional differences. This resulted in efforts to win independence by Croatia and Slovenia and in a move by a militarily superior Serbia to gain the upper hand through force. What followed was a terrible civil war lasting until 1995. The focus of the conflict was the effort by Serbia to gain control over Muslim Bosnia. Only a major diplomatic and military intervention by NATO was able to stop the war and arrange a peace agreement. The economy of the former Yugoslavia is in tatters and may take many years to rebuild.[32]

The former Czechoslovakia also presents variations on the Polish model. Czechoslovakia was the most economically advanced nation in the region and initially adopted a slower transition to a market system. The results include very favorable international balances and a less brutal economic decline. Even so, the shift toward free markets threatened many in the less developed sections of Slovakia. In 1993 the country was split into the Czech Republic and Slovakia. The Czechs have pushed forward with a moderate reform policy and have achieved the most stable economy in central Europe. Inflation and unemployment are low, and growth is comparable to that in Poland. The Czech Republic and Slovakia retain the highest per-capita GDP in central Europe.[33]

Ironically, what formerly was East Germany is in both the best and the worst of situations. It has the advantage of becoming part of a booming capitalist economy in Germany and has reaped the benefits of aid and investment. But the experience of incorporation into Germany has also had devastating effects. Industrial production fell by 50 percent, far more than in Poland, and unemployment reached one half of the work force. The reason is that East German goods simply could not compete in quality or price with those from the West. Further complicating matters has been an increase in wages, reducing competitiveness even more. For the combined Germany, a large trade surplus has been wiped out and replaced by a small deficit, and rising inflation

---

[32] Marlise Simons, "A Sign of Bad Times in Yugoslavia: Trade War Between Two Republics," *New York Times*, January 28, 1990; Stephen Engelberg, "Feuds Crippling Yugoslav Economy," *New York Times*, April 20, 1991; "Business in Eastern Europe," *The Economist*, September 21, 1991, 9; Collins and Rodrik, *Eastern . . .*, 17–18.

[33] "Business in Eastern Europe," *The Economist*, September 21, 1991, 5, 9; "Central Europe," *The Economist*, November 18, 1995.

led the Bundesbank to raise interest rates to the highest levels since the 1940s. The eastern section of Germany recovered faster than others in central Europe, and growth rates beginning in 1992 have exceeded 6 percent.[34]

An essential feature of the integration of Central Europe into the world economy is its ability to develop new and successful patterns of foreign trade. Although autarchy was central to the original view of a command economy in the 1920s and 1930s, it became a less accurate description of affairs beginning in the 1960s. The Council for Mutual Economic Assistance (CMEA) was established in the 1940s to facilitate trade within the Soviet bloc in central Europe. By 1987 as much as one fifth to one third of production in Poland and Hungary was for export. But this was heavily concentrated within the bloc, with exports to other communist bloc countries or the Soviet Union accounting for 40 to 80 percent of total exports.[35] Trade within CMEA was defined primarily by implicit Soviet subsidies resulting from Soviet sales of raw materials (mostly oil) at below world market prices and the purchase of manufactured goods from Eastern Europe that could not meet world standards. The collapse of communism in Central Europe has led to a dramatic reorientation of its trade.[36]

Well before the reforms of 1990–91, trade with the West was taking place. But by 1994 central European trade was dominated by relationships with Germany and the rest of the European Union. A de facto deutsche mark zone has already emerged in Central Europe, based on the fact that roughly one third of the trade (imports and exports) of these states is with Germany. Add in the other nations of the EU and the total is 50 to 60 percent.[37] The key next step is membership in the European Union. This is complicated by a number of factors: EU fears of competition from unit labor costs that are only about 40 percent of those in Austria; the costs from additional EU expenditures on agricultural and social subsidies; and the political difficulties of incorporating several new players into decision making.

## Privatization

We have concentrated on the process of freeing domestic markets, prices, and foreign trade. But this process will lead to economic growth only if there are

---

[34] Bruce Stokes, "Germany's Trauma," *National Journal*, May 4, 1991, 1040–43; Ferdinand Protzman, "A Cost of German Unity," *New York Times*, June 12, 1991; Stephen Kinzer, "East Germans, Nurtured by Bonn, Take Heart and Begin to Prosper," *New York Times*, September 29, 1991. Alexander Dyck, *Germany in the 1990s: Managing Reunification*, Cambridge: Harvard Business School Case, 1994.

[35] Percentages for 1988 are given in Collins and Rodrik, *Eastern* ..., 30; trade totals for 1987 are given in Williamson, *The Economic* ..., 5.

[36] John Pinder, *The European Community and Eastern Europe*, London: Pinter Publishers, 1991, 92.

[37] The main exception is Slovakia, where total EU trade is only about 30 percent. See "Central Europe," *The Economist*, November 18, 1995, 7.

entrepreneurs with control over productive assets who can respond to price signals with output. Perhaps the most difficult barrier to effective economic change in central Europe and the former Soviet Union has been the fact that command economies concentrated control of economic resources in the state. For markets to work, these assets must be in the hands of persons who are capable of effectively organizing production and competing with domestic and foreign firms.

This means that state-owned firms must be transferred to private control—a complicated and difficult process. The collapse of the central planning authority in many of these countries means that effective control of many firms has passed from the government to the workers and managers of those firms. Very often this has resulted in simply stealing firms' assets by groups who lack the incentives or knowledge to make them into profitable enterprises. Beyond this, privatizing state businesses is blocked by the lack of private capital and by the absence or weakness of institutions—such as stock markets and commercial banks—for organizing the capital that does exist. Also missing is an effective system of accounting to give some sense of the assets, profits, and losses of these entities.

Three main strategies have been used to privatize state firms: selling to anyone, including foreigners; selling only to domestic capitalists; and issuing vouchers to everyone, who can sell them or exchange them for shares of stock. Nationalism has often blocked purchase of firms by foreigners, and the "sale" to domestic buyers is often corrupted by those with special access to the process. Frequently former communist managers or other officials have used their position to gain control of firms on very favorable terms, sometimes even retaining subsidies after "privatization." Although figures for privatization are impressive—in Russia many thousands of enterprises have been sold through a voucher system; in central Europe, two thirds or more of the economy is said to be in private hands—there are good reasons to doubt whether this will generate large numbers of effective firms.[38] The most likely success stories are the owners of small stores and shops. These new entrepreneurs will have little choice but to become effective; otherwise, they will go broke. Large firms may have many more options, from political favors to market manipulation. Only in 1996 did the Russian privatization process shift its attention from small to large enterprises. Planning focused on selling off a few actual or potentially profitable firms in areas like power production and insurance.

This discussion of privatization helps to highlight the problem of the sequence of reforms. Given the organic quality of the needed changes in prices, ownership, trade, and institutions, any effort to define a precise set of stages is hopeless and even dangerous. Furthermore, these nations have already started

---

[38] Useful discussions of privatization are found in Shafiqul Islam and Michael Mandelbaum (eds.), *Making Markets*, New York: CFR Press, 1993; "Central Europe," *The Economist*, November 18, 1995; "Russia's Emerging Market," *The Economist*, April 8, 1995; Knecht, "From Soviet . . .," 25–26; and Anslund, *How Russia . . .*, 223–71.

into the process, most frequently attacking the area of prices first. Nevertheless, there are significant issues associated with deciding what to do when. If privatization cannot occur without an efficient banking system, should the government create this first? But if profitable private firms don't exist for banks to lend to, what is the mechanism for developing a viable system of private banking? In general terms, the problem confronting post-communist states involves creating an entire economic system when each of the parts can function properly only as all the other parts come into place. This is equivalent to requiring that everything be done at once or that nothing be done at all.[39]

## Aid from Capitalist States?

Much has also been made of the role that might be played by the capitalist world in promoting and assisting change in Central Europe and the former Soviet Union. However, we should be somewhat restrained in our expectations of the scale of this help and its probable impact. The two main paths for aid are trade and money. Because of the scale of needs and the contradictory interests of Western societies, neither path should be seen as a central element in supporting or easing the pain of change.

Some of the relatively easy decisions have already been made. All six East European countries are now members of GATT, the IMF, and the World Bank. Several former Soviet republics, including Russia, are to be admitted to the IMF and the World Bank. This opens the door to technical help and aid. In addition, one half of Poland's government-to-government debt of $33 billion was written off in March 1991. Both Bulgaria's and Hungary's debts are substantial but are owed to private banks.[40] In late 1991 members of the G-7 agreed to postpone the annual principal payment of $6 billion in the foreign debt of the former Soviet Union. The total of this debt may be as high as $70 billion. The deferment averted imminent default and was conditioned on the former republics assuming the debt of the former Soviet Union.[41]

But any realistic measure of possible Western aid pales when we consider the capital requirements needed to bring Central Europe and the CIS up to the same income and productivity levels as their Western neighbors. The capital needs of this area are immense due mainly to the poor quality of much of the capital stock accumulated under communism. One estimate of the requirements for a ten-year transition to raise income and productivity levels to the standards of Western Europe is more than $1.5 trillion per year.[42] An

---

[39] An excellent elaboration of the issues involved in the sequencing problem can be found in "Business in Eastern Europe," *The Economist*, September 21, 1991, 5–6.

[40] Pinder, *The European* ..., 93.

[41] Serge Schmemann, "Creditors to Let Soviets Postpone Paying Principal," *New York Times*, November 22, 1991.

[42] Collins and Rodrik, *Eastern* ..., 76–79.

optimistic estimate of the likely amounts of net capital transfers from official Western sources and private banks to both the CIS and Central Europe (excluding Germany) is $30 billion per year.[43] Clearly the source of the largest proportion of capital must be domestic savings. There is also some uncertainty as to whether aid will help or hurt the process of establishing free markets. Aid might be used to shore up the existing system or might simply be siphoned off into corruption. Most of the aid immediately following the 1989–90 period of change was to facilitate withdrawal of Soviet troops from Central Europe or to provide funds to purchase excess Western farm production.[44]

Perhaps the most important and interesting form of aid is through the International Monetary Fund and somewhat coordinated commitments from several G-7 countries. The IMF has been deeply involved in providing incentives for liberalization and reform, especially in the areas of ruble convertibility and exchange rate stability. Its commitment of funds has frequently been timed to enhance the political fortunes of reformers and sometimes to help undermine the position of reform opponents. In 1996, with Russia facing a presidential election that threatened a communist victory, the IMF approved a $10 billion loan. This was expected to increase the election chances of Boris Yeltsin. A significant portion of the funds were to be dispersed before the election to help Yeltsin pay long-overdue wages and to increase social spending. The loan commitments were preceded by a decision of the Russian government to drop plans for increases in tariffs and to end subsidies to a large natural gas firm. From 1992 to 1996, this dance between the IMF and the government has been repeated many times, often with the government retreating on reforms.[45]

Pessimistic conclusions about the process of change must be tempered by the fact that the interests of the West in a successful transition from communism to market economies are very large. High incomes in Central Europe and the CIS create natural markets for the goods of the capitalist West. Admission of some of these states to the EU will facilitate this trade. At the same time, failure generates not only a bad market but also millions of immigrants

---

[43] Collins and Rodrik, *Eastern ...*, 83–89.

[44] Thomas L. Friedman, "Ex-Soviet Lands to Get Swift Aid," *New York Times*, January 24, 1992. Estimates of actual aid include $45 billion to Eastern Europe and $80 billion to the former Soviet Union from 1989 to 1991. The overwhelming role of Germany must be noted. For example, $46 billion of the $80 billion to the former Soviet Union came from Germany, much of it designed to facilitate Soviet acceptance of reunification. See *Orlando Sentinel*, January 23, 1992, A-3; and Paul Montgomery, "Aid to Eastern Europe Estimated at $45 Billion," *New York Times*, November 12, 1991. The role of private investment has been much smaller. For this and indications of problems in German investment in Eastern Europe, see Stephen Engelberg, "Eager if Uneasy, East Europe Accepts German Investments," and Ferdinand Protzman, "Germany Curbs Trade Aid for Former Soviet States," both in *New York Times*, January 23, 1992.

[45] A detailed examination of the IMF and Russian reform is Maria Elayna Mosley, *Two-Level Game Theory: The International Monetary Fund and Post-Communist Nations*, senior honors project, Rollins College, 1993. Also see Michael Gordon, "Russia Drops Big Tariff Increase, Clearing Way for an I.M.F. Loan," *New York Times*, March 26, 1996, A-1.

and political instability. Probably the most important act by the West would be to throw open its markets to the goods of these post-communist states. The availability of a giant market would make it much easier to attract private capital for modernization. But such an arrangement is very unlikely for two reasons. First, this could drain capital from the West to the East at undesirable levels. Second, it would require that Western states accept the political consequences of displacing many of their businesses and workers who could not compete with the new imports. Indeed, there is already considerable evidence of reluctance to take these steps.[46]

## THE POLITICAL ECONOMY OF CHANGE IN CHINA AND VIETNAM

Perhaps the most important difference between the formerly communist states of Central Europe and China and Vietnam is the manner by which communism came to these nations. In Europe, communist control of national governments was almost always the result of the Soviet army, in particular through the occupation of this area during the defeat of Germany in World War II. The Soviet military was essential to eliminating opposing political groupings and to elevating communists to power. By contrast, communism in China and Vietnam emerged largely without the assistance of the Soviet Union. Here communist parties were successful in capturing the nationalist mantle as the main force for opposing international domination and imperialism. Further, communist parties in Vietnam and China tapped into revolutionary sentiments among peasants deriving from hostility to traditional feudal and even capitalist landowning systems. The result was that communist parties in Vietnam and China could claim legitimate mass support, perhaps even a majority of the nation; but communist parties in Central Europe could make no such claim. When Soviet military backing vanished, communism in Central Europe collapsed very quickly. Because Soviet support was never essential to communist power in China, the collapse of the Communist Party of the Soviet Union was important only in demonstrating the dangers in reform. The Soviet role in Vietnam expanded after 1975, mainly due to conflict between China and Vietnam. Consequently, change in the Soviet Union after 1985 contributed to the Vietnamese decision to begin economic reforms. But, communism survives in China and Vietnam because it has strong national legitimacy. Whether communism can continue in power through the process of economic reform is less certain.

The political economy of communism in China before 1978 focused mainly on the political and ideological mobilization of the enormous population to increase production and thereby to create a modern industrial

---

[46] This paragraph relies on Pinder, *The European* . . . , 3, 17; and "Business in Eastern Europe," *The Economist*, September 21, 1991, 6.

**TABLE 14.3**

**Post-Communist States**
*Comparative Data*

| COUNTRY | GDP/PPP[47] $ PER CAP. (IN MILLIONS) | POPULATION (IN MILLIONS) | AVERAGE ANNUAL INFLATION 92–95 | RURAL POPULATION % |
|---------|------|------|------|------|
| Russia | 6,220 | 153 | 1,600% | 26 |
| Poland | 4,880 | 39 | 26% | 17 |
| Czech Rep. | 7,700 | 10 | 11% | NA |
| Hungary | 5,730 | 10 | 22% | 34 |
| China | 2,000 | 1,200 | 16% | 72 |
| Vietnam | 1,000 | 72 | 12% | 80 |

SOURCE: *The Economist*, various issues.

economy. This strategy was accompanied by a strong inward orientation and an emphasis on self-reliance. Because China possessed such an abundance of underutilized resources, the strategy of mobilization and autarchy was able to produce economic growth. But this system was heavily burdened by inefficiencies and lack of dynamism, much like the Soviet economy.[48]

In Vietnam, the economic system until 1975 was dominated by the needs of a nation at war. This meant extreme hardship, ideological mobilization, and production determined by military necessity. After 1975, Vietnam's economic decisions were made in relation to the political problems associated with incorporating the hostile south—its adversary in a twenty-one-year civil war—and to the military alliance with the Soviet Union. Gaining control of the economy in the south, driving suspected enemies of communist rule out of the country, "reeducation" of other potentially antagonistic elements, and collectivizing southern agriculture, industry, and commerce were the main features of the years immediately after 1975. The result was ten years of stagnation and even deterioration in agriculture. Vietnam became a ward of Soviet aid and loans. All the while, in that first decade after reunification, China surged forward under economic reform, the Soviet Union stumbled toward reform, and many states in Southeast Asia experienced dramatic economic growth through deepening connections to the capitalist world economy.[49]

---

[47] The acronym *GDP/PPP* stands for *gross domestic product* measured in *purchasing power parity* terms. This is an effort to convert the national product of a country into comparable world prices. The normal procedure is to convert national product into a common currency using the market exchange rate. Unfortunately, this rarely translates into world prices. To understand PPP, you need to understand that the prices in a country for essentially the same goods can vary widely from world prices. For example, in Hanoi in 1994 a decent meal at a restaurant cost about $3 and a can of beer, comparable to Western beer, cost about 30 cents. In Winter Park, Florida, at the same time, a similar meal would cost about $12 and a can of beer about $1.50. A haircut in Hanoi was 25 cents; in Winter Park, $8. Purchasing power parity is an effort to treat the goods and services of a country in world prices. This tends to raise the measurement of GDP of a poor country.

[48] Readers may wish to consult portions of Chapter 9 for additional detail on China's economic development.

[49] Readers may wish to consult portions of Chapter 1 for additional detail on Vietnam.

# China

Sequentially, economic liberalization came first in China, in response to the economic and political damage done by the Cultural Revolution. A reform-oriented group led by Deng Xiaoping pushed aside antireform groups and instituted a series of actions that moved the Chinese economy toward a particular version of post-communism. Reform policies were gradual in order to avoid upsetting important political groups in China. In the same sense, reform was limited by the continuing commitment of Deng and other reformers to the ideological traditions of Marx, Lenin, and Mao, to socialism, and to the existing system of party and state control of society. But juxtaposed against this seemingly traditional orientation was acknowledgment of the importance of private ownership, the benefits of markets in directing economic activity, and the role of material incentives in motivating proper economic decisions.[50]

There are striking and significant differences between the processes of economic reform in China and Russia. The "Big Bang" in Russia focused on industry, came almost all at once, and was enacted only after the collapse of communism. The opening to the rest of the world brought in many consumer goods, some international aid, but little foreign direct investment. By contrast, in China reform is directed by the Communist Party, involves incremental changes starting first in agriculture, has produced a limited opening to the world, but has attracted enormous amounts of FDI.

In the old communist command economy in China, both agricultural production and demand were controlled by central planners. Production was organized into collectives that managed the activities and controlled the wages of peasant producers. The amount of production was based on procurement quotas set by central planners, who attempted to anticipate national demand. The reform of agriculture has emphasized changes in the organization of production, chiefly by shifting production decisions to private, individual peasants: what is termed a "household responsibility system." Individual peasants now have access to, or even long-term leases for, land and are responsible for production decisions and for profits or losses from those decisions. Free markets now exist for food products, although these markets involve only a portion of agricultural output. The state remains heavily involved at the level of subsidized inputs, such as fertilizer, in establishing procurement quotas at fixed prices, and in allocating resources for agricultural investment. Peasants are able to sell the production that exceeds procurement quotas on free markets, although this accounts for less than one half of total output. Between 1979 and 1986 this mixture of private and command economies led to dramatic increases of more than 50 percent in agricultural output and in peasant incomes. Since 1986 several factors have combined to limit growth: mainly stagnant investment in agriculture and the disincentives created by the

---

[50] Harry Harding, *China's Second Revolution: Reform After Mao*, Washington, D.C.: Brookings Institution, 1987, 91, 99–101.

remaining vestiges of central planning, but also soil erosion and peasants shifting into the industrial economy.[51] The state remains a major player in production and distribution and is especially interested in restraining agricultural price increases so as to contain inflation.

This unusual mixture of socialist command economy and market economy is also present in the reform process for industry. As with agriculture, economic reform of industry involves conflicting sentiments among communist leaders: a recognition that free markets and enterprise autonomy are essential to economic growth and a recognition that these reforms will lead inexorably to a decline in state power and to the expansion of an individualist-oriented economy. The national communist leadership has been grudging in its willingness to transfer real autonomy to enterprise managers, recognizing the very significant role that state control of these enterprises plays in establishing and preserving state power. The ability to preserve employment levels, manipulate investment, and dispense favors grows out of political management of state enterprises. And yet, the economic logic of efficiency gains and growth has moved state officials toward granting greater autonomy and freer markets.

The early successes in agriculture led communist leaders after 1984 to extend reforms to industry. The command economy still operates to require the production of an output quota, provide inputs at fixed prices, and purchase the output at fixed prices. But managers are generally able to obtain other inputs at market prices and to sell above-quota output at market prices. Additional flexibility has been introduced by distinguishing between a small number of goods considered essential—for which mandatory planning remains—and those goods thought less essential—where a looser guidance plan directs production. This has been accompanied by important but still limited price reform in the sense that some commodities can fluctuate within upper and lower limits, others are negotiated between government enterprises, and others are essentially free. Prices for goods traded in nonfree settings (such as goods under guidance planning) increasingly reflect prices for those same goods in free markets. Another version of agricultural reform has been extended to small- and medium-sized state enterprises. The state has been willing to lease the assets of these enterprises to nonstate groups in return for a fixed payment and/or proportion of profits. Lessees are able to retain the profits (after paying taxes) and operate as if they were owners: making investments, taking risks, and losing control through enterprise failure. This state–private mixture is also evident in one of the most interesting features of Chinese reform: the township and village enterprises (TVEs). Typically operating in rural areas, TVEs are profit-seeking enterprises owned and directed by local governments. They have become major industrial producers

---

[51] Harding, *China's Second Revolution* . . ., 101–08; "China," *The Economist*, March 18, 1995, 19–21; and Susan Shirk, *How China Opened Its Door*, Washington, D.C.: Brookings Institution, 1994, 89.

and employers. Township and village enterprises are like many other operations that have state ties and ownership, but operate as if they were private.[52]

Perhaps the arena of reform with the greatest potential impact on China is the proliferating links to the world economy. International trade policies provide some of the best indicators of the effort by reformers to manage incremental change. The strategy of reformers was to encircle the command economy and its related political interests with a market sector that would intersect with and eventually outgrow the planned sector.[53] Special benefits provided to various units of the economy threatened by reform—such as large state enterprises in heavy industry—helped mute their opposition, even as market dynamism and opportunities affected their actions and calculations. This strategy of incrementalism and side payments to win support for (or at least neutrality toward) reform is also present in the decentralization of authority to local governmental officials.

The terms for access to the world economy, and the many benefits that this could provide, were a key element of the strategy of decentralization. Hoping to balance the need for foreign currency and technology with the desire to contain foreign influences and to protect domestic industries, the Chinese government in 1980 established four Special Economic Zones in Shenzhen, Zhuhai, Shantou near Hong Kong, and in Xianmen near Taiwan. These are coastal enclaves where special rules apply: Raw material and capital imports are not subject to tariffs; other taxes are at a lower rate; investors, often foreign, have managerial control of their enterprises; relatively free labor markets have been established; and production is primarily for export. Provincial officials with Special Economic Zones (SEZs) were also able to keep almost all tax revenues, industrial profits, and foreign exchange. The enormous economic boom generated in Guangdong province (near Hong Kong and the site of three SEZs), including the bonanza from tax revenues and foreign exchange receipts, led other provinces to covet the same opportunities. In 1984–85 similar arrangements were extended to Hainan Island and to fourteen coastal cities; by 1988 the entire coast of China had received SEZ-like designation; and by 1995 several thousand inland areas emerged as SEZs. The success of SEZs also forced the central government to relax restrictions on which economic units could engage in foreign trade. This has resulted in an explosion in the number of foreign trade corporations established by local and provincial governments.[54]

---

[52] TVEs are estimated to generate almost 40 percent of China's industrial output and to employ one hundred and twenty million workers. "China," *The Economist*, March 18, 1995, 19. For a survey of industrial economic reforms, see Harding, *China's Second Revolution* . . ., 113–30; and Colin Mackerras et al., *China Since 1978*, New York: St. Martin's Press, 1994, 78–89.

[53] This argument is made by Shirk, *How China Opened* . . ., 27–31.

[54] Shirk, *How China Opened* . . ., 34–54; Mackerras et al., *China Since 1978*, 90–100; Nicholas Lardy, *Foreign Trade and Economic Reform in China Since 1978*, Cambridge: Cambridge University Press, 1992, 37–82.

What are the results of China's economic reforms? As we can see from Figure 14.2, China's growth has been very significant. When we expand the time horizon, Chinese GDP growth between 1980 and 1995 has averaged nearly 10 percent, the fastest in the world during that period. Accurate measures of China's GDP are made difficult by manipulated price levels and exchange rate. Per-capita GDP measures range from $425 to $3,550; a good guess is about $2,000. International trade growth and foreign direct investment have also been very important. Between 1978 and 1995, China's exports and imports have increased more than tenfold to more than $200 billion. And in both 1994 and 1995 China was the recipient of more than $30 billion in FDI, second only to the United States. The structure of the Chinese economy has been altered but not transformed by economic reform. In particular, the state-owned sector (SOE) has declined in importance. In 1985 SOEs produced almost 65 percent of China's industrial output, collective-owned enterprises (mostly TVEs) about 30 percent, and private firms about 5 percent. By 1994 SOEs were down to 35 percent, collectives up to 40 percent, and private and semiprivate firms accounted for 25 percent of industrial production.[55]

But the positive results of economic reform have sometimes been overshadowed by unpleasant consequences: corruption, inflation, growing inequality, and dispossessed masses roaming China looking for work. Inflation in China is driven by a variety of factors. The gradual enlargement of free markets in a system where prices were previously fixed at artificially low levels will produce inflation, especially when output cannot always be increased to respond to demand. In addition, China has experienced a series of investment booms and continues to provide subsidies to unprofitable SOEs. Inflation is exacerbated in both cases by large increases in the money supply. Over the years since reforms began, inflation rates have operated in cycles. Most recently, inflation rates were only about 5 percent in 1992, rising to more than 25 percent in 1994, and falling again to about 10 percent for much of 1995.[56] The growth of corruption is not surprising in a society where pay for government officials is very low, where the opportunities for entrepreneurial activity are encouraged, and where government and business are intermingled. Increasing inequality is also not surprising. With stagnating incomes in agriculture and racing growth in industry and foreign trade, those areas that are dependent on agriculture and that don't have access to foreign trade are almost certain to fall behind. This process also leads to increasing numbers of dispossessed persons who are unable to find employment in rural areas and who begin moving to urban areas to find work. One estimate places the number of such persons at one hundred million.[57]

---

[55] "Business in Asia," *The Economist*, March 9, 1996, 5, 19; *The Economist*, December 2, 1995, 64; Shirk, *How China Opened* ..., 87, 91; "China," *The Economist*, March 18, 1995, 9.

[56] *The Economist*, November 25, 1995, 33–34.

[57] See "China: The Titan Stirs," *The Economist*, November 28, 1992.

The social and political dislocation caused by rapid growth, the growth and redistribution of economic wealth, and the decentralization of economic and political power all contribute to political instability in China. Of further significance is the general absence of political reform permitting efforts to organize politically and to express grievances. The most important manifestation of the combination of the difficulties of economic reform and the failure of political reform was the events surrounding the demonstrations and massacre in Beijing and Tiananmen Square in 1989. During a forty-day period, large demonstrations that were broadcast around the world called on the communist government to respond to complaints and especially to accept greater democracy. This situation split the government into those willing to respond to the demonstrators and those committed to repression. Economic reform had always generated fears among party conservatives that change would undermine communist rule. Eventually, after much indecision, the government used the military to end the demonstrations, producing much bloodshed and several thousand deaths. After a short interregnum, even the politically conservative leaders who took power (Jiang Zemin, General Secretary, and Li Peng, Prime Minister) resumed progress toward economic reform. The long-term political consequences remain unclear.[58]

## Vietnam

In 1985–86, Vietnam faced a series of crises that generated powerful incentives for change in its domestic and foreign policies. Vietnam is a very poor country with little margin for error. And yet it confronted a combination of internal and external circumstances that presented great danger. Ten years after victory and national reunification, the economic system remained stagnant, with widespread food shortages and inflation of 500 percent. Vietnam was heavily dependent on the Soviet Union, a nation in the throes of economic reform and likely to reduce its aid. Hostile relations with China continued, and Vietnamese leaders watched warily as Chinese economic reforms produced rapid economic growth. Vietnam's economy looked even weaker in comparison with many other Asian states that had experienced twenty years of economic growth and expected more to come. And Vietnam's resources were being squandered in the morass of a military occupation of Cambodia that had produced condemnation by much of the world.

Although some economic reforms had begun in 1981, the effects had dissipated by the mid-1980s. Vietnam had adopted changes in agriculture and industry that were similar to those in China in that peasants and enterprise managers could sell above-quota production on markets. But the palpable crisis atmosphere of 1985–86 made the small gains from these changes seem insignificant. Previously dismissed from the ruling Communist Party Politburo,

---

[58] A short, but useful, discussion of the events surrounding the Tiananmen Square crisis is Mackerras et al., *China Since 1978*, 32–37, 45–62.

reformer Nguyen Van Linh became General Secretary, and the Party Congress called for *doi moi* or renovation of the economy. This was followed over the next three years by a series of liberal reforms that went beyond those in China.

By 1989 most prices in Vietnam were free of government control (exceptions were made for fuel and electricity), as was the distribution of goods. Most production was based on market-determined price signals, and this was true for both state-owned enterprises and for private enterprises. Administered prices, even for SOEs, were set near free market levels. A crisis in food production in 1988, which led to near-starvation conditions in part of the country, pushed the government to dismantle the agricultural collectives and to create a system of private, family farms producing for the market. Fiscal stabilization came in 1989–90 in conjunction with ending subsidies to SOEs and terminating any pretense of a command economy. Much government spending was directed at propping up failing SOEs, and with the tax collection system antiquated and poorly organized, revenues were far short of expenditures. Inflation continued to be a serious problem. Ending state subsidies to SOEs was essential, as was an end to Vietnam's involvement in Cambodia. Additionally, interest rates were raised to produce a return above the rate of inflation, which resulted in increased bank deposits. Foreign trade was liberalized substantially, and the exchange rate of the dong was devalued to approximate market levels.[59]

Understanding the results of Vietnamese reforms can best be gained against some background on the nature of Vietnam's economy. Vietnam is one of the twenty poorest countries in the world. Using market exchange rates, Vietnam has a GDP of about $15 billion or about $220 per person. Converting Vietnam's output to world prices raises this to about $1,000 per person. The country possesses considerable natural wealth, including a large capacity for food production and much untapped energy resources. Vietnam is essentially a rural society, with about 80 percent of the population of 75 million living in the countryside. In spite of its poverty, Vietnam has many social indicators that compare favorably with much richer countries. Its adult literacy and life expectancy at birth are similar to those in Thailand and Turkey—nations with ten or even twenty times Vietnam's per-capita income. The economy, not surprisingly, is based on agriculture: In 1993 almost 75 percent of GDP was from agricultural production, 13 percent from industry and construction, and 6 percent from services. The industrial sector is predominately light industry, and much of this is also tied to agriculture. About one half of all employment in manufacturing is in textile and food processing. A comparatively small proportion of Vietnam's GDP is derived from heavy industry. The industrialization of the Soviet Union and much of Central Europe under communism, which emphasized large, heavy industry, did not take place in Vietnam. In many ways Vietnam is a preindustrial society. The result is fewer and smaller state-owned

---

[59] The story of economic reform can be found in Michael Williams, *Vietnam at the Crossroads*, New York: CFR Press, 1992, 39–58; and "Vietnam," *The Economist*, July 8, 1995.

enterprises making a smaller contribution to the economy. Before reform, the state-owned sector generated only about one third of GDP. And much of that was small-scale cooperatives in which local governments acted as owners.[60]

Even though economic reforms in Vietnam have gone much further toward markets and liberalization than in China, approximating the "shock therapy" of Russia and some post-communist states in Central Europe, the results have been largely positive. The small size and local ownership of many SOEs and the loose collectivization of agriculture prompted much spontaneous market orientation as reform proceeded. Ending the central planning system was much easier in Vietnam because the government had never been as deeply involved in the economy as in China or the Soviet Union. The introduction of markets and economic freedom produced a quick response from peasants and a rapid growth of shopkeeper capitalism. Agricultural production rose rapidly, moving Vietnam in two years from a deficit position as a food producer to the status of a major international exporter of rice. Overall, the economy has grown an average of 8 percent beginning in 1992 and should expand by 9.5 percent in 1995. Though many state-owned enterprises collapsed and many thousands of people were left unemployed, the growth of the rest of the economy has more than compensated. Because the country was less dependent on heavy industrial firms owned by the government, Vietnam did not experience the traumatic downturn of Russia and Central Europe. Inflation has fallen dramatically, remaining below 15 percent annually after 1991.[61]

Liberal terms for foreign investment have led to large quantities of FDI, probably at levels that equal or exceed the absorptive capacities of the country. In 1993, Vietnam received $2.6 billion in FDI.[62] Foreign investors complain bitterly about the bureaucratic red tape, but this may reflect the weaknesses of the government more than any deliberate strategy. Vietnam has won praise for the extent of its economic liberalization and has been successful in obtaining as much as $2 billion in international aid and loans. Throughout the country limited political reform can be seen, much of it associated with adjusting to the needs of foreign business and tourists. By 1994, international faxes and satellite television from Hong Kong were readily available; in 1995, Internet connections and global e-mail became possible. Personal freedom for

---

[60] Details on the Vietnamese economy can be found in Dwight Perkins, "Reforming the Economic Systems of Vietnam and Laos," in Borje Ljunggren (ed.), *The Challenge of Reform in Indochina*, Cambridge: Harvard University Press, 1993, 1–18; and "Vietnam," *The Economist*, July 8, 1995. Comparison of the role of SOEs in the Vietnamese and Russian economies is instructive. In 1991 more than three fourths of the Russian labor force were employed in SOEs, a figure rising to over 83 percent if collectives are included. See Anslund, *How Russia ...*, 224.

[61] The best work available on economic reform in Vietnam is Jonathan Haughton, "Overview of Economic Reform in Vietnam," in David Dapice et al. (eds.), *In Search of the Dragon's Tail: Economic Reform in Vietnam*, Cambridge: Harvard University Press, 1996. Also see Brantly Womack, "Vietnam in 1995," *Asian Survey*, 36.1, January 1996, 73. Also very useful is Adam Fforde and Stefan de Vylder, *From Plan to Market: The Economic Transition in Vietnam*, Boulder: Westview Press, 1996.

[62] "Vietnam," *The Economist*, July 8, 1995, 13, 15; Womack, "Vietnam ...," 73.

Vietnamese citizens was also much greater, if only to engage in ballroom danc-
ing and to listen to love songs on the radio. But the government is still prepared to crack down on open political dissent.[63]

One striking difference between Vietnam and Russia and China is the fate
of state-owned enterprises. In Vietnam SOEs are actually increasing their role
in the economy. Since 1990, SOEs have increased from about one third to
about 40 percent of GDP. There are several interesting reasons for this outcome. Vietnam requires all foreign investors to have a Vietnamese partner, and
this usually means connecting to a state-owned enterprise. The number of Vietnamese SOEs has fallen from twelve thousand in 1990 to about seven thousand in 1995. But privatization has been limited, and most transfers from state
to private hands have been spontaneous and local. Remember that Vietnam's
SOEs include a large number of small enterprises, owned by local governments
and cooperatives. And these same enterprises are substantially disciplined by
market forces. Consequently, the increasing role of SOEs may not have the
same drag effect on GDP growth as in other post-communist states.[64]

What of the future for Vietnam? Rapid economic growth should continue,
fueled by FDI, growing production and export of agriculture and natural resources (mainly oil), some industrialization, and investment in infrastructure.
Though there are wide regional and urban–rural gaps, this growth will contribute to the reduction of the absolute poverty that afflicts much of the
country. But there are many impediments to economic development, especially the many and serious infrastructure gaps: The banking system has
largely failed to mobilize national savings for investment because of the deep
distrust of banks; the road system is very primitive, with a trip by car from
Hanoi to Haiphong (sixty-five miles) taking four to five hours; and the legal
system and business service sectors are quite weak, producing high transaction costs. Government corruption and ineptitude mix with the tradition of
political control to insulate the economic system from much needed changes.
But, on the bright side, the population is young and eager for change; economic globalization opens wider avenues for attracting resources and integration into production chains; and the government shows some signs of
developing into a more flexible and supportive agent of economic growth.

## PROSPECTS FOR THE FUTURE

There is no simple way to explain the origins and unfolding evolution of the
economic and political transformation of communism. However, two forces

---

[63] For a sense of events in Vietnam, see *Far Eastern Economic Review*, December 1, 1994, 77
(aid); October 26, 1995, 23 (Internet); September 7, 1995, 33, 36 (political crackdown).

[64] There are important exceptions. In several of the heavy industry areas that do exist in
Vietnam—cement, for example—the state enterprise enjoys a monopoly.  For details on SOEs in
Vietnam, see *The Economist*, December 2, 1995, 34; Perkins, "Reforming . . .", 10; and David
Dollar, "Vietnam: Successes and Failures of Macroeconomic Stabilization," in Ljunggren (ed.),
*The Challenge . . .*, 209.

working on these events are worth remembering. First, in the Soviet Union, China, and Vietnam, the main factor moving tough-minded communist elites toward economic reform was the same. In each case fears and opportunities coming from international economic, military, and political competition drove these leaders to undertake immense risks and to jettison deeply held principles and practices. Leaders in all three countries saw their nation falling behind other nations deeply involved in a much more dynamic capitalist world economy. Without much greater and more complex forms of economic growth, leaders harbored significant fears for national security. Second, and closely related to these same calculations, was the ongoing globalization of the world economy. Increasing access to capital, technology, and markets provided an opportunity that proved irresistible.

Can these dramatic changes continue? Predicting the course of events for post-communist states is an adventure for the foolhardy and naive. There are many variables that could redirect events in ways that we cannot foresee. At best, offering a short catalogue of circumstances that may shape the direction of change seems the wisest path.

In the past, neither reform nor revolutionary change has persisted very long without prompting a backlash or reaction that can stop or even reverse course. This has become an active possibility in several post-communist states, with a beleaguered population beset by the traumas of economic dislocation turning to more conservative groups who promise relief. Even after these societies successfully traverse the initial downturn and begin the process of growth, significant economic reverses can be expected. In the best of circumstances, growth is an uneven process. And given the fragility of these societies and their dependence on external markets and capital, major problems should come as no surprise. For China and Vietnam, where economic success has been much greater, the main question concerns the impact of economic change on the power and position of communist parties.

A second dimension of uncertainty involves the fact that the development of post-communist societies comes at a critical juncture for the world economy. The European Union is on the verge of its own transformation into a single market, strengthened processes of centralized decision, and expansion into Central Europe. How this will affect developments in states that are left out is unclear. In Asia no institutional structure exists to manage the incorporation of China and Vietnam into the capitalist world economy. And many points of conflict exist, from human rights to copyright laws, between Western and Asian political and economic traditions. Japan remains uncertain about its role in Asia and in global affairs. The United States may be content to let market forces "manage" the process of change in Asia. The diversity of the positions of the main actors in the world economy raises the question of whether they can cooperate with each other to deal effectively with the many problems presented by post-communism. Although the rich nations in the world economy cannot solve these problems, their actions can affect the character and pace of events.

Finally, there is the relationship of security and economic growth. Economic instability and dislocation frequently contribute to problems of military security. Remember that World War I, World War II, and the Cold War all began over Central Europe. Events in Yugoslavia and Russia have already produced military confrontation and bloodshed. And in Asia, China sometimes seems ready to translate its new economic and military power into hegemonic aspirations, creating grave security problems for many states. The main questions involve whether economic development can occur in the absence of a sense of physical security among the populations and elites in Europe and Asia and whether security systems can be developed to cope with the military consequences of economic change. Peace in Europe and Asia over the past forty years is a result of a complex mixture of bipolarity, U.S. commitment and involvement, and a variety of international institutions. Uncertainties abound about the future, but most thinking suggests that without a major commitment from the most powerful capitalist states, insecurity, disorder, and war may emerge in and among post-communist states.[65]

## ANNOTATED BIBLIOGRAPHY

Anders Anslund, *How Russia Became a Market Economy*, Washington, D.C.: Brookings Institution, 1995.
  A very insightful look at the political economy of Russian reform from an inside participant.
Susan M. Collins and Dani Rodrik, *Eastern Europe and the Soviet Union in the World Economy*, Washington: Institute for International Economics, 1991.
  An extraordinarily rich source of information and analysis.
Padma Desai, *Perestroika in Perspective*, Princeton: Princeton University Press, 1989.
  An analysis of the economic dimensions of reform.
Harry Harding, *China's Second Revolution: Reform After Mao*, Washington, D.C.: Brookings Institution, 1987.
  Although dated, by far the best single book on the first decade of reform.
Charles Gati, *The Bloc That Failed*, Bloomington: Indiana University Press, 1990.
  A very detailed study of political relations after 1985.
Bartlomeij Kaminski, *The Collapse of State Socialism*, Princeton: Princeton University Press, 1991.
  The best theoretical analysis of the internal flaws of the command economy.
Kenneth Lieberthal, *Governing China: From Revolution Through Reform*, New York: Norton, 1995.
  The best survey of China's history since 1949.
Borje Ljunggren (ed.), *The Challenge of Reform in Indochina*, Cambridge: Harvard University Press, 1993.
  An excellent collection of articles.

---

[65] For a thorough discussion of these issues, see John Mearsheimer, "Back to the Future: Instability in Europe After the Cold War," *International Security*, 15.1, Summer 1990, 5–56; Jack Snyder, "Averting Anarchy in the New Europe," *International Security*, 14.4, Spring 1990, 5–41; and Stephen Van Evera, "Primed for Peace: Europe After the Cold War," *International Security*, 15.3, Winter 1990/91, 7–57.

Michael Mandelbaum (ed.), *The Rise of Nations in the Soviet Union*, New York: Council on Foreign Relations Press, 1991.

   A useful collection of essays focusing on U.S. policy alternatives.

Alec Nove, *An Economic History of the U.S.S.R.*, New York: Penguin, 1989.

   A classic source.

John Pinder, *The European Community and Eastern Europe*, London: Pinter Publishers, 1991.

   An indispensable source.

Susan Shirk, *How China Opened Its Door*, Washington, D.C.: Brookings Institution, 1994.

   A detailed look at the politics of China's international trade and investment policy.

Graham Smith (ed.), *The Nationalities Question in the Soviet Union*, London: Longman, 1990.

   A detailed look at each former republic.

# Chapter 15

## CHARTING THE FUTURE:
## ECONOMIC INTERDEPENDENCE
## AND NATIONAL COMPETITIVENESS

Change is a pervasive theme in the history of the international political economy. Few essential attributes of the system remain static for long. Our conclusion surveys important trends along two key dimensions of the contemporary world economy and projects them into the future.

We first examine the prospects for successful management of the international economic system. The presence of conflicting interests at both the domestic and international levels precludes the possibility of harmonious economic relations among states. Instead, international economic interdependence rests upon a complex mixture of cooperation and conflict. The balance between the two shifts over time, however, depending upon political conditions within and among states.

The volatility of international economic relations is illustrated by the history of the past sixty-five years. This period can be broken into three distinct eras. The first spanned the decade of the thirties, when competitive impulses overwhelmed cooperative efforts. Under the strains produced by the Great Depression, nations erected stiff protectionist barriers and formed economic blocs in vain efforts to preserve domestic production and employment. These actions led to a painful contraction of world trade and raised political tensions. Attempts to find cooperative solutions to the breakdown of the international economic order produced only limited results, due largely to the weakness of existing international institutions and the absence of any country with the power or willingness to exercise leadership.

The next era of international economic relations, stretching from 1947 to 1973, brought more serious and fruitful efforts at cooperation. A variety of new institutions and rules was created to help manage and encourage the growth of economic interdependence. Protectionist barriers fell dramatically, and levels of international trade and investment expanded rapidly, especially during the sixties. All of this was made possible by a number of essentially political factors, including U.S. hegemony and leadership, the close security relationships forged among the United States, Western Europe, and Japan during the Cold War, and the lessons that political leaders learned from the harsh experiences of the 1930s.

The era since 1973 has brought a more even balance between the cooperative and competitive dimensions of the international political economy. Although economic interdependence has continued to expand and deepen, it has done so in an erratic manner. This era has featured three major global recessions, three episodes of oil-supply disruptions, a major bout of inflation during the late seventies, the growth of nontariff barriers and managed trade, the emergence of the Third World debt crisis, and extreme imbalances in trade among the major economic powers. International economic issues have assumed heightened political salience in many countries, and the rules and institutions designed to manage international economic relations have been subject to strains produced by changing economic realities as well as by disagreements among the major powers. With unity and common purpose difficult to achieve, political leaders from various states have, nevertheless, found ways of muddling through repeated crises and conflicts, often devising temporary fixes or papering over differences. These expedients have sufficed to avert a plunge into outright economic warfare. Indeed, the world economy has continued to move toward deeper levels of economic interdependence. Yet gaps in the system's management have grown, and serious differences in perspective have placed international cooperation under strain.

The first section of this chapter assesses the prospects for successful management of the future international economic order. Will competition spin out of control, leading to mutually destructive conflict, as during the 1930s? Or can the world's nations break free of the indecisiveness and uncertainty of the last two decades and complete the agenda of liberalization begun, but left unfinished, during the fifties and sixties?

In addition to exploring the fate of the international system as a whole, this chapter also examines possible changes in the relative economic fortunes of particular countries and regions. The competitive position of any given country is influenced by a variety of factors. Institutional change, the unevenness of technological innovation, shifting product cycles, and evolving political and economic strategies all place various countries on different trajectories of rise and decline.

The post–World War II period has witnessed significant shifts of this sort. Over the past four decades, the United States' relative position has eroded, and Japan's position has improved enormously, while Western Europe's experience falls somewhere in between. The economies of Eastern Europe and the Soviet Union failed to keep pace with those of the West during the seventies and eighties—a factor partly responsible for the dramatic political changes that have engulfed those countries in recent years. The Third World has become vastly more diverse. Industrialization surged ahead in many parts of Latin America, especially Mexico and Brazil, during the fifties, sixties, and seventies before slowing to a crawl in the eighties as a result of the debt crisis. Although a handful of OPEC countries achieved instant wealth during the seventies as a result of two steep price rises, the same nations were compelled to adapt to more-modest revenues as prices again fell over the past decade. The clearest Third World success stories are to be found in East Asia, where a number of countries, including South Korea, Taiwan, Singapore, Hong Kong, Malaysia, and Thailand, have achieved astonishing growth rates based upon export-oriented strategies of development. With only a few exceptions, the countries of South Asia and Africa, by contrast, have posted consistently disappointing results and remain mired in poverty.

How will the fortunes of various nations and regions fare over the coming decades? Any predictions of this sort are necessarily speculative. Nevertheless, we can gain insights by considering the strengths and weaknesses that different countries possess as they face future international economic competition.

## COOPERATION AND COMPETITION IN THE WORLD ECONOMY

Predicting the future balance between international economic cooperation and competition is a challenging task. The complexity of the real world and the imprecision and inconsistency of existing theory serve to cloud the crystal ball of even the most acute observer. Rather than suggest a definitive scenario, then, we instead consider the forces that may reinforce cooperation alongside those that seem to point toward conflict and competition.[1]

### Harbingers of Cooperation

The most important reason for expecting the persistence of international economic cooperation in the future stems from the growing dependence of national economies on one another for essential goods, services, and raw materials. This global web of trade and investment has arisen partly from technological advances and economic processes. Improvements in transportation have greatly lowered the cost of moving goods, raw materials, and even people from one part of the globe to another. And the communications revolution has made it possible for large corporations to manage far-flung multinational empires. Firms interested in obtaining the cheapest labor and raw materials or in expanding into new markets have exploited these new opportunities for international growth.

---

[1] On the contradictory tendencies toward both integration and fragmentation in the contemporary international system, see Benjamin R. Barber, *Jihad vs. McWorld*, New York: Times Books, 1995. For a critical appraisal of globalization, see William Greider, "The Global Marketplace: A Closet Dictator," in David N. Balaam and Michael Veseth (eds.), *Readings in International Political Economy*, Upper Saddle River, N.J.: Prentice-Hall, 1996.

These fundamental economic realities provide powerful incentives for policymakers to choose cooperative economic strategies. To be sure, interdependence threatens various values and interests, as we later suggest. As a result, states often seek to manage and regulate their relationship with the world economy. Nevertheless, policymakers are generally acutely aware that the costs of "going it alone" in today's world economy are prohibitively high. Indeed, an increasingly elaborate global division of labor has brought greater prosperity to the world economy as a whole. This trend has lent support to a key tenet of economic theory that holds that economic welfare is maximized when nations specialize in those goods that they can produce most efficiently while trading for products that they are poorly suited to produce.

There also exists a widespread understanding that the growth of trade and investment is impossible without a substantial commitment among states to openness, policy coordination, and cooperation in setting the rules and institutions needed to manage the system. The fear that spiraling political conflict could undermine the bases for international economic growth and prosperity inhibits policymakers from resorting to extreme nationalistic strategies and from pressing too hard for relative advantage. These shared perceptions do not preclude the possibility of serious differences among nations in the future, but they may set broad limits on the scope and intensity of conflict and competition.

The impact of spreading interdependence on domestic interests and coalitions is less certain but may also weigh in favor of stronger international cooperation. In most countries, economic policymaking is influenced by more than simple calculations of the national good. Political leaders are dependent upon coalitions of particular interests. In the making of foreign economic policy, two sets of groups are usually most important: nationalists, who are harmed by the growth of economic interdependence, and internationalists, who directly engage in, and benefit from, foreign trade and investment.

Rising economic interdependence tends to heighten the political mobilization of both groups and intensifies the conflicts between them. With some important exceptions, however, high levels of trade can be expected to strengthen the power of internationalists, who favor cooperation and openness, at the expense of nationalists.

Nationalist coalitions typically emerge when large numbers of domestic industries begin to experience competition from more efficient foreign producers. The affected firms and workers seek government protection in the form of import restrictions or other sorts of regulations designed to counter the economic advantages possessed by foreign competitors. Such efforts are sometimes rewarded, especially under conditions that tend to strengthen the appeal of nationalism, such as prolonged periods of economic hardship or the persistence of negative trade balances.

Yet, although economic interdependence stimulates nationalist interests to mobilize in the defense of jobs and profits, it also, in the long run, weakens the political clout of nationalists by strengthening the relative economic clout of internationalist interests in the national economy. Even if uncompetitive firms or industries succeed in gaining a degree of state protection, this seldom reverses the shrinking importance of such sectors to the national economy as a whole over time. Internationalist coalitions, on the other hand, tend to include many of the nation's largest, fastest-growing and most competitive firms. As trade and investment grow, the absolute and relative number of firms with a stake in economic openness tends to grow over time as well. The force of internationalist arguments in favor of free trade is also bolstered by two additional factors: Free trade policies not only favor consumers, who benefit from the lower prices and greater selection provided by access to foreign goods, but also draw the strong endorsement of economic theory.

Although a host of factors may influence the balance of power between nationalist and internationalist forces across countries and across time within a single country, the future spread of interdependence is likely to enhance the relative political weight of internationalist interests. Over the long term, economic success is a surer route to political influence than is failure.[2]

Optimism about the future potential for economic cooperation also rests upon a recent and rather unexpected trend: the growing convergence among nations around similar liberal economic strategies. This was not the case in the past. Indeed, only North America, Western Europe, and a handful of other countries clearly organized their economies around the precepts of economic liberalism, including the primacy of private capital, the reliance upon market forces, and relative openness to international trade and investment. Much of the Third World pursued a nationalist strategy of development, stressing heavy state intervention and import protectionism. The OPEC countries nationalized foreign oil investments and attempted to manage a resource cartel. The East Asian NICs, following Japan's example, pursued an export-oriented version of mercantilism, using the state to carve out new sources of comparative advantage. The socialist bloc countries built command economies that remained largely isolated from the remainder of the world economy.

Although, as the next section indicates, present trends are complex and somewhat contradictory, a host of recent developments may point toward the global triumph of liberalism. National economic strategies appear to be converging around market-centered models of development—a trend that, if sustained, could smooth the route toward international economic cooperation. The Third World has retreated from demands for a new international economic order in which resources would be allocated according to political rather than market criteria. Nationalist import substitution strategies of development have also lost favor. Instead, country after country has, under the

---

[2] On this point, see Robert Baldwin, "The New Protectionism: A Response to Shifts in National Economic Power," 372–373, and G. K. Helleiner, "Transnational Enterprises and the New Political Economy of U.S. Trade Policy," both in Jeffrey A. Frieden and David A. Lake (eds.), *International Political Economy: Perspectives on Global Power and Wealth* (2nd ed.), New York: St. Martin's Press, 1991. Also see Helen V. Milner, *Resisting Protectionism: Global Industries and the Politics of International Trade*, Princeton: Princeton University Press, 1988.

pressures of the debt crisis and poor economic performance, begun to privatize state industries, dismantle subsidies and price controls, lower overvalued currencies, and remove barriers to imports and foreign investment. The East Asian NICs have also begun to reduce the state's role in steering economic development. The same is true in Japan. As the Japanese economy matures and becomes more internationalized, the role of the MITI (Ministry of International Trade and Industry) and other bureaucracies has receded, while barriers to imports and foreign investment have eased. Most dramatic, of course, has been the movement of Eastern Europe and the republics of the former Soviet Union toward capitalism and reintegration with the world economy. Even socialist countries where communist parties remain strong or dominant, such as China and Vietnam, have begun to introduce market reforms and encourage greater trade, investment, and aid from the West.

The global movement toward greater market openness is also evident in the recent success of the Uruguay Round of trade negotiations. The Uruguay Accord included provisions to lower tariffs, remove barriers to trade in services, reduce agricultural protectionism and subsidies, and strengthen the protections accorded intellectual property rights. A World Trade Organization has been created to monitor compliance with these agreements and to resolve disputes that may arise.

This increasing convergence around market-centered strategies of economic management is both cause and consequence of another closely related trend: the growing power of internationalist capital vis-à-vis both states and workers. As capital has become more mobile across national borders, states have had more difficulty regulating or controlling such flows in ways that promote traditional conceptions of the national interest. Moreover, states that pursue policies that fail to meet with the approval of large financial institutions or internationally mobile firms may suffer from capital flight, declining investment, job losses, and a falling currency. This is particularly true in the area of macroeconomic policy. If financial markets perceive that an expansionist monetary policy raises the risk of inflation, currency traders and investors are likely to diversify out of that nation's currency. Capital will flow to currencies and countries that follow a firmer anti-inflationary set of policies. Globalization has altered the balance of power between states and firms in favor of the latter and increased the incentives that governments experience to maintain "business confidence" in their policies.

In much the same way, international capital mobility decreases the power of labor. Compared with capital, labor is relatively immobile internationally, despite the increased immigration flows of recent decades. Nor, in most cases, do nationally based labor movements have close transnational ties with labor organizations in other countries. The territorial constraints on labor and the weakness of international coordination among labor movements allow capital to play workers off against one another by threatening to relocate to a more hospitable country if concessions on wages, benefits, or work rules are not forthcoming. As a result, organized labor has lost clout and membership in many countries over recent years.

The increasing integration of global markets and the growing power of capital are thought by many to promote greater efficiency, productivity, and growth worldwide. Others, however, point out that these trends have been accompanied almost everywhere by a worsening inequality in income and wealth and by a fraying of the social safety nets that many nations erected after the Second World War to aid the least-advantaged groups in their midst. Moreover, some fear that the weakening of national and international regulation of capital, especially in financial markets, may bring greater instability to the world economy as huge sums of capital are carried along by speculative booms and busts. Nonmarket values, such as the environment, may also fare poorly in a world where capital reigns supreme.

The future of these trends is still uncertain. How far will market reforms go in Eastern Europe and the remaining socialist countries? Will liberalization succeed in the countries where it is being attempted for the first time? Will political backlash against the costs of liberalization (higher prices, greater unemployment, increasing inequality, and high levels of economic insecurity) stall or reverse reform in some Third World or Eastern European countries? How will Northern countries react if established industries are threatened by the cheap imports upon which Eastern Europe and many Third World countries are pinning their hopes for economic growth? Does the triumph of liberalization necessarily ensure easier economic cooperation among countries, or will it lead to growing competitive pressures and conflict?

## Competition

Despite the many factors favoring cooperation, there also exist powerful forces that could lead to heightened conflict and perhaps serve to undermine the basis for growing global interdependence. Some of these forces are quite traditional and stem from the tensions between national autonomy and economic interdependence as well as from the enduring sources of competitive rivalry among nations. Others are related to more recent trends and developments, such as shifts in relative power and the changing nature of bargaining over trade and other issues.

If it is rare for political leaders to isolate their country from the world economy, it is likewise rare for a government to permit trade and investment to take place entirely without regulation or restriction. Interdependence brings costs as well as benefits. In managing their nation's economic relationships with the rest of the world, policymakers attempt to balance the benefits and the costs of interdependence.

The most important political cost of interdependence is the erosion of national autonomy. Economic dependence can leave a country vulnerable to manipulation, as even the United States discovered during the seventies when it became dependent upon OPEC oil. In addition, interdependence can greatly complicate the task of economic policymaking as decision makers must now take into account the reactions of foreign firms and governments when choosing among national economic policies and goals. Political leaders may also seek to limit trade and investment with nations that are military rivals for fear that such exchanges might allow the transfer of militarily relevant technologies.

Moreover, although trade between two countries may benefit both, there is no guarantee that both will prosper equally. Indeed, it is often possible for one nation to gain advantages over other states or to push burdens onto other states by restricting and regulating trade and investment in various ways. Because the competitive nature of world politics ensures that national leaders are concerned about relative power and position as well as about absolute economic gains, growing interdependence is bound to lead to increased struggle for national advantage alongside efforts at cooperation.

These enduring sources of competition and conflict manifest themselves in various forms in the contemporary world economy. The first important source of uncertainty about the future of international cooperation has to do with the consequences of declining U.S. power. The theory of hegemonic stability suggests that periods of openness and growing interdependence are linked to the existence of a hegemonic power that is willing to exercise leadership by providing collective goods and creating, as well as enforcing, rules of the game. Without this sort of leadership, management of the international economic system becomes complicated by the difficulty of gaining agreement among many competitive and relatively equal states. Sanctions against cheating become less certain as well.

Although the United States remains the world's largest single economic power, its relative decline has, nevertheless, allowed the establishment of several competing power centers, each with the capacity to take independent action and to make its wishes felt in bargaining over the future of the global economy. This has rendered the United States less capable of exercising leadership than in the past. Moreover, the United States may also be less willing to champion free trade than it once was. Facing the loss of technological leadership to other advanced industrial nations along with low-wage competition from Third World countries, many U.S. firms and labor unions have begun to press for trade protection. At the same time, Congress has passed legislation designed to press the executive branch to retaliate more forcefully and speedily against other nations judged guilty of unfair trade practices.

Alongside the decline of U.S. leadership has been the rapid rise of Japan. This shift in relative power has been particularly disruptive. Japan has so far proven unable to fill the leadership vacuum left by U.S. decline. Not only does Japan still lack the power to serve as a genuine hegemon, but it also, for historical reasons, lacks both the experience and the willingness needed to accept the political demands of international leadership. Finally, despite recent changes, the Japanese economic model has rested upon a mercantilist rather than a liberal philosophy. Such an approach places only limited emphasis on international cooperation and has led to tensions between Japan and its trading partners.

In combination, the decline of the United States and the rise of Japan have lent momentum to the retreat from globalism and to the movement toward regional economic blocs. Within such blocs, international cooperation is high, and barriers to trade and investment are partially or wholly removed. Such arrangements, however, may discriminate against imports or investment originating from outside the bloc. The EU is the most significant manifestation of this trend. Another example is the North American Free Trade Agreement (NAFTA), which ties together the United States, Canada, and Mexico, but could one day come to encompass countries in South America as well. A less formal East Asian bloc centered around Japan has begun to emerge with the intensification of intraregional trade, aid, and investment patterns. Recent progress in the Asian-Pacific Economic Cooperation (APEC) forum suggests the possibility that Asian regionalism could evolve into a more formal trade bloc, although APEC also includes the United States and several other non-Asian nations.[3]

The formation of regional blocs is essentially a political response to a more competitive international economic environment. There exists a danger that nations may come to see the integration of regional blocs as a hedge against a breakdown in the rules and institutions that manage the global economy. If so, then such behavior could lead to a self-fulfilling prophecy, in which the development of blocs becomes one of the decisive factors in complicating globalist and multilateral solutions to world economic problems.

Another troubling consequence of the shifting competitive positions among states has been the emergence of serious imbalances in the world economy. In particular, Japan (and, until recently, Germany) has run persistently large trade surpluses, while the United States has suffered from large-scale, long-term deficits. These imbalances stem from fundamental economic factors, such as the contrasting savings rates in the United States and Japan, as well as lapses in monetary management and cooperation. The political effect, however, is to raise tensions and galvanize protectionist forces in deficit countries, including the United States.

Until recently, the political consequences of economic competition and rivalry were muted by the close security ties among the advanced capitalist countries. With the waning of the Cold War and the decline of the Soviet threat, this cohesive factor could well begin to weaken. Western Europe and Japan are likely to become less deferential to the United States as they become less dependent upon U.S. military protection. Indeed, it is even possible that the Cold War allies could become military competitors in the not-too-distant future. Such a development would inevitably have negative effects on economic cooperation.

The future of international economic cooperation is also clouded by the complexity of contemporary bargaining. The early stages of international cooperation in the decades after World War II, such as the Kennedy Round of

---

[3] See Jeffrey E. Garten, "Trading Blocs and the Evolving World Economy," *Current History*, January 1989, 15–16; Lester Thurow, "America, Europe and Japan: A Time to Dismantle the World Economy," *The Economist*, November 9, 1985; and Louis Uchitelle, "Blocs Seen Replacing Free Trade," *New York Times*, August 26, 1991.

trade negotiations, focused upon relatively simple goals, like the lowering of tariff barriers. Today, however, the goals are much more ambitious, the scope of the issues addressed is broader, and the intrusiveness of international commitments on the domestic sphere is much greater. Trade negotiators must deal with more varieties of protectionism, many of them less visible and more subtle than tariffs. Bargaining has come to encompass areas excluded from GATT, such as trade in agriculture and services as well as nontraditional concerns, including protections for intellectual property and the rights and obligations of foreign investors. As the Structural Impediments agreements between the United States and Japan and the recent U.S.–Mexico free trade negotiations suggest, trade agreements are coming to affect policies that were once considered purely domestic in nature. Indeed, at issue are fundamental aspects of national economic structure. All of this makes international cooperation more significant and substantial today than in the past. The issues are fundamental and the stakes higher. Yet it also suggests that cooperation at the cutting edge is becoming increasingly complex and politically salient, making agreements more difficult to reach or to implement and honor. In short, the easy part of building an open, liberal international economic order is past, and the hard part remains.

## NATIONAL COMPETITIVENESS

Whatever the fate of the world economy as a whole, political leaders and citizens care most about the prosperity and security of their own country. A country's economic performance not only determines living standards at home, but also affects its power and prestige abroad. For these reasons, nations worry about their relative position in the world economy and draw comparisons with commercial or military rivals. This section surveys the competitive strengths and weaknesses of various countries or regions, discusses some of the principal economic problems faced by each, and projects trends in power and wealth into the coming decades.

### The United States

In sheer size, the U.S. economy remains far larger than that of any other single nation. This fact alone guarantees that the United States will remain an influential political and economic power for decades to come. Moreover, the United States brings a number of important strengths to international economic competition, including continued technological leadership in many areas, an enviable system of higher education, ample natural resources, an efficient agricultural sector, and a flexible market-oriented economy. Faced with growing foreign competition, many U.S. manufacturing firms have lowered costs and improved product quality since the early eighties. The end of the Cold War has brought lower defense spending burdens, thus freeing resources for the civilian economy. The United States' considerable assets and strengths rule out a calamitous decline and probably ensure a slow but steady absolute rise in living standards in the future.

Nevertheless, the competitive challenges facing the United States are likely to grow over the long term, and its relative position in the global economy may well continue to deteriorate. The United States' large foreign debt guarantees foreign investors a claim on a portion of future U.S. production in the form of repatriated profits for years to come. U.S. technological leadership is slipping, and U.S. production of scientists and engineers considerably trails that of Germany and Japan on a per-capita basis. Several significant domestic ills—including a low national savings rate, a deteriorating infrastructure, a troubled primary and secondary educational system, high crime rates, worsening inequality, racial and ethnic divisions, and persistent federal budget deficits—continue to retard national economic performance.

The future of U.S. competitiveness will depend upon answers to a number of critical questions: Can a system of government built upon so many checks and balances marshal the political will needed to devise coherent responses to the domestic and international problems outlined? Can U.S. management and labor forge new, more cooperative relationships in the future, making possible real gains in productivity and product quality? Can U.S. corporations develop a longer-term perspective, thus freeing strategic planning from the constraints imposed by concerns about short-term profitability? Will U.S. citizens confront the difficult trade-offs posed by the challenge of retaining U.S. economic competitiveness, such as that between consumption and investment? Is it possible to develop a national consensus around any particular strategy for dealing with international competition?

## Western Europe

Over the past decade, the countries of Western Europe have undertaken a series of initiatives designed to revive anemic growth rates and reverse the region's slipping economic competitiveness. These initiatives have centered around the strengthening of cooperation through the European Union (EU).

In 1992 hundreds of barriers to the movement of goods, capital, and labor among Western European countries were removed. This step was designed to lower transportation costs and raise productivity by allowing for product standardization, greater economies of scale in production, increased competition, and greater labor mobility. The Maastricht Treaty, approved by the member states of the EU in 1992, seeks to accelerate still further the process of economic integration by providing for monetary unification, including the creation of a European central bank and a single currency by the end of the century. Alongside these movements toward "deepening" cooperation, the EU has also engaged in "broadening" its membership. Three new members, Austria, Sweden, and Switzerland, joined the EU in 1995, and several Eastern European countries have been granted associate membership, which ensures them improved access to EU markets and consideration for eventual membership at a later date.

These historic steps toward greater European economic integration and cooperation have not taken place without considerable conflict and controversy. The Maastricht Treaty generated heated debate in many countries, particularly Britain, Denmark, and France, and only narrowly met the requirement for unanimous ratification by all twelve existing member nations.

The path to monetary union was also cast in doubt by the European currency crisis of 1992–93. At the time, EU governments were pledged to keep the value of their currencies aligned within a narrow band. Beginning in 1990, however, the German government began to spend vast new sums for the reconstruction of the eastern half of the newly reunified Germany. To counter the inflationary potential of this fiscal stimulus, the Bundesbank tightened Germany's money supply and raised interest rates. These high interest rates attracted currency traders and investors, who sold other European currencies and purchased deutsche marks. In order to defend the value of their beleaguered currencies, other European governments faced the prospect of raising interest rates at home in order to stanch the flow of capital to Germany. This step would, however, choke off domestic growth. Rather than persist in such a policy, Britain and Italy chose instead to remove themselves from the EU system of fixed alignments and to allow the value of their currencies to fall.

This episode raises the question of whether national governments will ultimately be willing to sacrifice national autonomy to a unified monetary system, despite their previous pledges to do so. The main advantage of a single European currency is that it would lower the transaction costs of doing business across national borders by freeing traders from the necessity of exchanging national currencies. Yet monetary union would also make it impossible for individual governments to manipulate monetary policy so as to respond to economic shocks specific to their own countries. Europe's money supply and interest rates would move together under a centrally managed system. This would work well as long as the economic needs of all EU members converged. Should Germany prefer a tight monetary policy to counter inflation but Italy a loose one to spur growth, however, these contradictory preferences could not be reconciled under a unified monetary system.

The Maastricht Treaty specified a set of strict financial targets that must be met before any EU member can join the centralized monetary system. Currently, however, only Germany and Luxembourg qualify under these standards. This raises doubts about whether the Maastricht Treaty's preconditions will be met by the target date of 1999.

The EU project has also run into other complications. In 1994 voters in Norway rejected proffered EU membership. Other countries, including Turkey and several Eastern European states, still desire membership. Yet many worry that EU decision making will became unmanageable as its membership expands and becomes more diverse.

Moreover, neither deepening nor broadening has yet to resolve the underlying structural problems that still plague the European economy. Despite joint efforts and large government assistance, the high-technology sectors of European industry generally lag behind those of the United States and Japan. Europe as a whole continues to suffer from high unemployment and overcapacity in certain industries. Relatively high social welfare spending levels in many countries are an economic burden. European agriculture is relatively inefficient and highly subsidized. The region also depends heavily on imported oil and natural gas—a handicap should energy prices rise in coming years.

The overthrow of communism in Eastern Europe has had mixed implications for the western half of the continent. The removal of the Soviet threat has allowed for lower defense spending levels. Western Europe has benefited from greater access to Eastern markets and investment opportunities. In the short run, however, Western economic aid to Eastern Europe has proven expensive. Some Western European industries are threatened by import competition from the lower-wage economies of the East. Political unrest and ethnic violence in parts of Eastern Europe, particularly the former Yugoslavia, have led to large-scale westward migration, with disruptive social and economic effects on some EU members.

Western Europe faces many serious choices as it attempts to cope with rapid internal change and growing external competition: Should the community remain open to the world economy, or should it protect embattled economic sectors, particularly those based upon high technology? Should the EU move toward full monetary integration? If so, how rapidly, and where would control over monetary policy lie? Should the membership of the EEC be further expanded? If so, which countries should be allowed in? How fast? Under what terms? How will a larger membership affect the balance of power within the community and the effectiveness of its decision-making mechanisms? How will Western European countries cope with the underlying structural problems that they face, such as high unemployment, the lack of technological dynamism in some sectors, and a high social welfare burden?

## Russia and Eastern Europe

Will the collapse of communism bring a brighter economic future for the countries of the former Soviet Union and Eastern Europe? According to Western economists, market reforms should eventually produce substantial benefits by introducing genuine competition, forcing inefficient producers out of business, and allowing prices to determine production through the mechanisms of supply and demand. Yet the transition from centrally planned economies to market economies has thus far been filled with pain and confusion. Reform has brought inflation, bankruptcies, unemployment, and falling levels of income and production to the former Soviet bloc countries. Some nations in the region appear to have weathered the worst of these transitional hardships and to have turned the corner toward the more promising future promised by capitalism's proponents. Others have far to go and could easily become sidetracked along the way. It remains to be seen, moreover, whether the region's governments will possess the political stability, legitimacy, and will that are needed to guide their nations through this difficult and possibly prolonged period of confusion and uncertainty.

Russian economic reform began in earnest following the breakup of the Soviet Union in late 1991.[4] Despite small steps toward economic decentralization begun under Soviet leader Mikhail Gorbachev in the late eighties, the Russian economy was still largely state dominated. The bloated and heavily subsidized industrial sector emphasized the production of military and capital rather than consumer goods. The agricultural system remained hugely inefficient. Prices were still set by economic planners rather than by market forces. The fall of communist systems in 1989 and 1990 in Eastern Europe along with the division of the Soviet Union into fifteen independent states in 1991 disrupted long-standing economic ties among these entities. The challenge of transforming the Russian economy along the Western, market-centered model, as proposed by Russian President Boris Yeltsin, appeared daunting.

Yet in the four years that have passed, much has been accomplished. Prices have been freed. The ruble has been made convertible. Military spending has been slashed. Much of the formerly state-owned sector of the economy has been privatized, while new entrepreneurial enterprises have sprung up everywhere. Some of the most unprofitable firms have been allowed to go bankrupt. A new financial system, featuring hundreds of private banks and flourishing stock markets, has taken root. Trade with the outside world has been liberalized, and foreign investment has begun to flow into Russia, though not in the quantities that Russian officials had expected or hoped for.

This is not to say that all has been smooth sailing. The initial stages of reform brought wrenching changes, most still not complete, and much hardship. Industrial production plummeted. During 1992 and 1993, inflation lurched out of control, the ruble plunged in value, and a great deal of domestic capital fled the country for the safety of foreign bank accounts. Tax revenues fell sharply, leading to large budget deficits. Real wages declined, and the all-encompassing social safety net provided under communism was gradually dismantled. Despite expressions of support and sympathy, Western governments provided only modest amounts of economic assistance. Political instability was evident in the periodic confrontations between Yeltsin and his critics in the Russian Parliament.

Still, reform efforts persisted, sometimes in fits and starts. By 1995 Russians began to see some payoff from these patient efforts. The Russian government managed to whittle its budget deficit to reasonable proportions, while

---

[4] For a review of the changes discussed next, see "Survey: Russia's Emerging Market," *The Economist*, April 8, 1995; and Anders Aslund, *How Russia Became a Market Economy*, Washington, D.C.: Brookings Institution, 1995.

the central bank brought the money supply under control. As a result of these steps, inflation subsided, and the value of the ruble stabilized, though neither accomplishment is necessarily permanent. The flow of Russian capital out of the country began to slow, and foreign investment showed signs of picking up. Many private enterprises have revamped their management, shifted to new types of production, and sought out new markets. Per-capita income began to recover some of the losses of previous years. Some economists believe that the worst is over and that the economy is poised for gradual recovery.

Despite these hopeful signs, Russia faces many continuing challenges. Agricultural reform has a long way to go, as evidenced by the disastrous grain harvest of 1995. Organized crime, in the form of huge Mafialike syndicates, has spread its tentacles throughout Russian society. Market reforms have introduced widening inequality, fomenting resentment among many Russians. Highly trained scientists and other skilled personnel continue to leave the country for higher-paying jobs in the West. Russia's industrial plants and infrastructure are antiquated and have suffered from deterioration due to neglect and declining investment. The country's health system is in crisis, as evident in the astonishing fact that male life expectancy has fallen substantially in recent years. Political instability could stall or reverse the process of reform. Parts of Russia harbor strong separatist sentiments. This could lead to more internal strife and violence, along the lines of the recent civil war in Chechnya. The Russian party system remains chaotic, and centrist or liberal forces have lost ground to nationalist and communist groups.

Whatever the short-term prospects for Russia's economy, the long-term prospects appear more promising. Russia's sheer size, in population and territory—along with its bountiful natural resources and talented pool of scientific expertise—suggests that Russia may eventually stage a vigorous recovery and emerge as an economic force to be reckoned with as it becomes more deeply involved in international commerce over the coming decades.

The countries of Eastern Europe began the transition to market capitalism earlier than Russia, and several have made substantial progress. The former East Germany is a special case, due to its absorption by West Germany. After reunification, West Germany moved quickly to transplant its economic, political, and legal system to East Germany. The costs have been enormous, with western subsidies to the eastern portion of the country amounting to 40 percent of eastern income. Much of eastern Germany's uncompetitive industrial base collapsed following reunification as easterners rushed to buy western commodities. Nevertheless, eastern Germany's infrastructure is being rapidly modernized and its economy reorganized. Despite relatively high unemployment, average incomes—although still below those in the western part of the country—have risen to levels far above prereunification standards. Despite the temporary pain and confusion caused by reunification, eastern Germany's long-term economic prospects are bright.

Poland, Hungary, and the Czech Republic, although lacking the advantages possessed by the east Germans, have also begun to see the rewards of economic reform. Each has carried out thorough reforms and attracted considerable Western aid and foreign investment. In these countries, reform initially led to a sharp economic contraction and other dislocations. But each has more recently begun to experience renewed economic growth and increased stability, based upon vibrant private sectors. Slovakia, although its performance thus far has been less impressive than those of Poland, Hungary, and the Czech Republic, is also usually considered to have reasonably good prospects of making the transition to a market economy.

The southern tier of states in Eastern Europe, including Romania, Albania, and the war-torn states of the former Yugoslavia, shows far less promise. Reforms in these states have proceeded much more slowly, and Western assistance and investment have been largely lacking. Much poorer than the northern tier of states, Romania and Albania have backward infrastructural and industrial structures and poorly skilled populations. Neither has made an unambiguous commitment to Western democracy. Each is relatively insulated from the world economy. Yugoslavia, on the other hand, might have accomplished the transition to a market economy with reasonable success, had it not split apart and fallen into ethnic and religious violence. With the exception of Slovenia and possibly Croatia, however, the trauma and destruction of war, along with international economic sanctions, have doomed any prospect for near-term economic recovery in the states of the former Yugoslavia.

Western firms have channeled considerable investment sums into the northern tier of Eastern European states. The challenges they have faced in these countries have been considerable. These include an unsettled legal climate, resistance among workers to the more stringent demands of Western-style workplaces, a shortage of knowledgeable and experienced local managers, and outdated and poorly maintained production facilities that require expensive modernization. Still, these obstacles are slowly being overcome, and many Western firms appear committed for the long haul.

Eastern European leaders speak hopefully about the prospect of one day joining the EU, but Western European states have strong reasons for moving slowly in this direction. A larger number of members in the EU could well complicate EU decision making. This problem appears more serious when one considers the gap in levels of development between the two halves of Europe and the potential for political instability in the East. Also, because new rules allow for workers to migrate freely across borders within the EU, the addition of poorer Eastern cousins could lead to massive immigration to the West.

Political, social, and environmental problems also complicate Eastern Europe's economic future. Serious ethnic cleavages threaten political order in some countries. Severe air and water pollution—a legacy of the previous order—poses a serious health threat and will require massive sums to correct.

Finally, there is a larger question about what sort of role Eastern Europe will play in the world economy. Although many East Europeans look upon the highly technological, service-dominated economies of Western Europe with longing and hope, some have suggested that Latin America might provide a more realistic picture of Eastern Europe's future. Many of the firms migrating to the East are associated with technologically backward smokestack industries in search of low labor costs as well as looser environmental regulations. In neither its technological level nor its education and training is Eastern Europe yet well suited to compete in the information age.

# Japan

In many ways, Japan holds an enviable position as the twenty-first century approaches. Japan's large trade surpluses, combined with a high national savings rate, provide it with enormous economic clout. The nation's large number of scientists and engineers is pushing Japan toward global technological leadership. Japan is situated in East Asia, the world's most economically dynamic region. Its multinational firms are rapidly integrating the fast-growing economies of other states in the region under Japanese hegemony. Japan's work force is disciplined, hard working, and well educated, and Japanese management has often proven itself flexible and innovative. A cooperative relationship ties government and business in mutually beneficial arrangements. Economic management lies in the hands of a skilled and powerful bureaucracy. Taken together, these elements of the Japanese economic model suggest a potent formula for international competitiveness.

Yet Japan, too, faces challenges. Some of these, such as the country's high level of dependence upon foreign sources of raw materials, are of long standing. Most, however, derive from more recent changes in Japan's domestic and international position. Its very success, along with the uniqueness of its political and economic systems, has generated charges that Japan does not play fair in international competition. Strains between Japan and its economic partners have grown. If these strains give way to outright conflict, Japanese firms could face increasingly severe restrictions on their business activities abroad. Japan must also cope with growing competition from other East Asian countries, which combine lower wage rates with increasing technological sophistication. Domestically, Japan's population is aging, raising the prospect of labor shortages combined with a declining savings rate (as retirees draw upon their savings to finance consumption) in the years ahead. As Japan's economy matures, consumers may increasingly rebel against protectionist and collusive practices that drive up prices. Demands for social welfare spending have also increased, while members of the younger generation are less willing than were their parents to sacrifice family and leisure time for long hours at the office.

Some of these problems have contributed to the prolonged slump in which Japan's economy has been mired thus far during the 1990s. More directly, however, recent economic troubles were triggered by a sharp decline in the value of land and other economic assets, including stocks and bonds in Japan. The prices of these assets were driven to dizzying heights by the speculative "bubble economy" of the 1980s. When this financial bubble inevitably burst in 1989, firms and individuals who had borrowed heavily against the artificially high value of their land or other assets were pushed near or over the brink of insolvency. As a result, the Japanese banking system has faced huge losses on bad loans. In this climate, credit has tightened and consumers have become more cautious in their spending, thus deepening the economic recession.

Japan's recent economic downturn has been a shock to the confidence and sense of security of a people who have become accustomed to rapid growth over the past forty-five years. The repercussions have been varied. The commitment among big firms to the policy of lifetime employment has weakened, and many college graduates are, for the first time in decades, finding themselves confronted with a tight and competitive labor market. In politics, the Liberal Democratic Party (LDP) has suffered dramatic defections as new political parties have emerged on the scene. In 1993 the LDP lost power in the Diet, for the first time since the early fifties, to a coalition of opposing parties. Since then, the LDP has reentered the government through a coalition with the Socialist Party, whose leader occupies the office of prime minister. Nevertheless, the confusing and rapidly shifting nature of Japan's current political scene has made it difficult for the country's leadership to chart a coherent path out of Japan's prolonged economic troubles.

Japan looks both less formidable and less unique today than it did a decade ago. Japan's economic system is more internationalist, its policies less mercantilist, and its politics more pluralist than has been the case over most of the postwar era. Despite its recent difficulties, however, Japan is likely to remain a serious economic competitor in the coming years. History teaches us that the Japanese system is remarkably adaptable, capable of learning lessons from Japan's own experiences, as well as those of others, and of turning adversity to the country's own advantage.

## The Third World

Some analysts argue that the wave of market-oriented reforms currently sweeping the Third World will place Southern countries on the path to sustained economic growth. The East Asian NICs are often cited as beacons of the kind of future that could await other nations that follow their example. Yet these conclusions are not universally shared. Some argue that the successes of the NICs will be difficult to duplicate and that fundamental trends point toward the increasing marginalization of much of the Third World in the decades ahead.

Since World War II, the comparative advantage of most Third World countries has rested upon one of three sets of resources: strategic location, critical raw materials, and cheap labor. All three may well become less central to the functioning of the world economy in the years ahead.[5] A variety of Third World countries benefited from their perceived military and political importance to one or both superpowers during the Cold War. The United States and

---

[5] This discussion rests upon Alvin Toffler, "Toffler's Next Shock," *World Monitor*, November 1990, 34–38, 41–42, 44.

the Soviet Union carried their rivalry to the Third World by spreading vast sums of economic and military aid among scores of strategically vital allies. In some cases, these countries were compensated for their willingness to host U.S. or Soviet military bases. In others, the superpowers sought to bolster the allegiance or political stability of countries that sat astride strategic shipping lanes or provided militarily critical resources. Some countries received favor because they were located along the front lines of the U.S.–Soviet rivalry or because they had symbolic value as exemplars of capitalism or socialism.

With the end of the Cold War, the strategic and political significance of previously favored clients has evaporated. Foreign aid to many such countries has already declined and has been reallocated according to economic rather than political criteria. Spending for overseas bases has also fallen.[6]

Countries that depend upon the bulk export of a few varieties of raw materials will also suffer. In the past, the principal markets for such resources lay in the North. Yet as Northern economies become less dependent upon manufacturing and more heavily oriented toward services and the production and exchange of information, the demand for imported raw materials will fail to keep pace with overall economic growth. This trend is, in fact, already well established. Today, for instance, Japan uses 60 percent fewer raw materials to produce each unit of economic output than it did in 1973. Another important constraint on the export of Third World resources is the increasing tendency for Northern countries to devise synthetic substitutes for previously imported raw materials. Examples include artificial sweeteners and synthetic rubber.

Some types of industries will continue to shift production to the Third World in search of lower labor costs. But the most dynamic high-technology sectors are likely to remain in the North. For such industries, labor constitutes an increasingly small proportion of total costs. Far more important is access to capital, new knowledge, and a highly skilled work force. Factory managers must have direct and regular contact with Northern-based designers and engineers in order to carry out constant modifications in the production process as well as in the end product. Economic processes are also increasingly tied to communications networks and technological infrastructures that are lacking in the South.

None of this means that Third World development is at a dead end. It does suggest, however, that Third World countries must blaze different paths to development than in the past. It is tempting, under contemporary circumstances, to seek new orthodoxies or universal prescriptions to replace the old. Some experts point to the export-led strategy pursued by the East Asian NICs as a model for the remainder of the Third World. Such advice must be subjected to careful scrutiny. The development community has, in the past, often been given to faddishness. Witness the fifties, when the now-discredited strategy of ISI was widely hailed as the cure to Third World underdevelopment.

---

[6] On the consequences of the Cold War's ending for the Third World, see Fred Halliday, "The Third World and the End of the Cold War," in Barbara Stallings (ed.), *Global Change, Regional Response: The New International Context of Development*, Cambridge: Cambridge University Press, 1995.

Although some countries may well benefit by borrowing selectively from the experiences of the East Asian NICs, the capacity of most to do so is doubtful. There is, in fact, considerable controversy over just which factors are responsible for the success of countries such as South Korea and Taiwan.[7] Moreover, the development strategies devised by these nations grew out of their distinctive political, economic, and cultural institutions. It remains to be seen whether similar strategies can be successfully transplanted to the different institutional soil of other Third World countries. Finally, if a handful of East Asian NICs succeeded in targeting certain vulnerable Northern industries, there is no assurance that dozens of countries could simultaneously accomplish the same feat, particularly if each aims at much the same markets.

Nevertheless, some lessons can be learned from the experiences of countries such as South Korea and Taiwan. Although each of the Asian NICs began its route toward industrialization by developing or attracting low-wage industries, none was content to remain trapped in this particular niche of the world economy. Each sought to upgrade the skills, educational level, and discipline of its work force while also pushing the economy toward higher levels of technological sophistication and autonomy. This allowed these countries to shift upward into more-lucrative and dynamic industries, much as Japan had done in earlier decades. This suggests that the surest route to development lies less through cheap labor than through productivity increases that rely upon the application of the new knowledge and the capital accumulated during previous phases of growth.

Unfortunately, these lessons are principally relevant to the already better-off Third World countries. Such a strategy is beyond the realistic means of the poorer Third World countries. The great majority of people in these countries continue to make their living off the land. In such societies, a premature emphasis on modern industry benefits the few at the expense of the many. Scarce resources have often been directed toward showcase industrial projects that end up as white elephants, failing due to poor infrastructural support, inadequate skills, and managerial inexperience or to an inability to afford the spare parts and imported energy needed to sustain the project.

The problems of the poorest countries are so serious that quick solutions are unlikely, and advice must be offered with a large dose of humility. Nevertheless, it seems clear that the first task for such societies must be to develop a modernized, diversified, and sustainable agricultural sector. There are several keys to successful agrarian development: avoid overconcentration of land ownership, allow markets to set realistic prices that provide incentives to producers, make credit and technical information available to small farmers, and encourage environmentally sound and sustainable agricultural methods. As efficiency gains raise rural incomes, it is possible to develop small-scale local industries aimed at providing the tools and implements needed by farmers, as well as a growing supply of consumer goods.

---

[7] For a summary of the controversy, see Stephan Haggard, "The Newly Industrializing Countries in the International System," *World Politics*, January 1996.

These tasks are, of course, easier said than done. Many Third World countries face harsh climates, unfavorable geography, burgeoning populations, political instability, widespread illiteracy, gross economic and social inequalities, and foreign interference. Though progress is possible, no tidy solutions to these problems are available. What seems clear about the future is that the diversification of the Third World will continue, with some countries experiencing healthy growth and development while others, perhaps the majority, struggle to keep up.

## CONCLUSIONS

The basic themes of this book have revolved around the struggle for power and wealth among nations. Two parallel, yet interacting, structures in the international system shape the pursuit of these goals. Fundamentally, nations seek power as a guarantee of survival in a competitive and anarchic state system characterized by territoriality, legal sovereignty, and self-help. Because there exists no higher authority capable of maintaining order in the international system, nations are left to their own devices in seeking ways of promoting their own security. Nations do so primarily through the accumulation of military might, yet a nation's military potential rests upon the size and technological sophistication of its economy. The combination of these military and economic resources determines a nation's power, or ability to influence others.

The competitive aspects of the international system largely derive from the fact that power is always relative. More power for one state means less for others. The relative nature of power thus ensures a degree of rivalry. This tendency manifests itself most clearly in arms races and war, but it also takes the form of economic conflict because political leaders must be concerned that relative economic gains by competing states could one day be translated into greater military might.

Alongside this competitive state system, however, exists the global marketplace, made possible by growing economic interdependence. In this realm, states, as well as firms and individuals, seek wealth for its own sake. States can bring about a higher standard of living for their citizens by encouraging the growth of trade and investment with other countries. Although the struggle for relative power engenders conflict, the pursuit of wealth through economic interdependence more often gives rise to cooperation because all can gain simultaneously.

It is the relationship between politics and markets that informs the study of international political economy and gives rise to complex patterns of competition and cooperation among states in the world economy. Although much may change in the years ahead, the struggle for both power and wealth is likely to remain a persistent feature of the political and economic relations among states.

# GLOSSARY

**Absolute Advantage** A situation in international trade where one country is able to produce a good or set of goods at a lower cost than some other country or set of countries. *See also* Comparative Advantage.

**Agency for International Development (AID)** A bureaucratic arm of the U.S. State Department charged with dispensing and administering bilateral foreign aid funds.

**Andean Pact** An accord signed by five Latin American countries in 1970 in which each pledged to impose common regulations on direct foreign investment. This represented an attempt to increase host-country bargaining power vis-à-vis multinational corporations by limiting the ability of the latter to play small countries off against one another.

**Asian-Pacific Economic Cooperation (Conference)** A regional economic forum consisting of countries located in Asia and the Pacific Rim.

**Asymmetrical Interdependence** A form of mutual dependence between two parties in which one partner is more dependent upon the relationship than the other. The less dependent party holds potential leverage over the more dependent party.

**Autarchy** An economic policy designed to promote an extreme version of economic self-sufficiency. This leads to closing off domestic markets from external trade as well as severely restricting exports. Such a policy frequently is designed to defend the nation against political and ideological imports that accompany trade along with organization of the economy for war.

**Baker Plan** Announced in 1985, this American initiative attempted to encourage renewed bank lending to Third World debtors in hopes that these countries could then grow their way out of the debt crisis. Although its immediate objectives were not realized, the Baker Plan represented the first partial step away from the previous reliance on Third World austerity as a solution to the debt problem.

**Balance of Payments** An accounting system designed to measure all transactions a nation has with the rest of the world over some period of time. *See also* Current Account; Capital Account.

**Basic Needs** A "bottom-up" approach to Third World development designed to enhance the living conditions and earning potential of the poorest segments of Southern societies. This developmental model was popular among aid agencies during the seventies but lost favor in the eighties.

**Bilateral Assistance** Foreign economic assistance administered directly by donor country governments.

**Brady Plan** Announced in the spring of 1989, the Brady Plan was an American initiative designed to alleviate the problem of Third World debt. The significance of the Brady Plan is that it signaled, for the first time, official Northern recognition that debt reduction should play a role in the management of the debt crisis. The plan provided incentives for Northern banks to forgive a portion of the debt owed them by certain Southern countries.

**Bretton Woods**  An agreement reached in 1944 at Bretton Woods, New Hampshire, that led to the creation of the postwar international economic order directed by the United States. Centered on the dollar, fixed exchange rates, and the International Monetary Fund, this system ended in 1971.

**Capital Account**  An item in the balance of payments that measures the investment of resources abroad and in the home country by foreigners. *See also* Direct Foreign Investment; Portfolio Investment.

**Capital Controls**  Restrictions placed on the movement of capital across national boundaries. Governments impose controls in order to increase their ability to manage the domestic economy.

**Capital Liberalization**  The process of removing and/or reducing capital controls.

**Central Bank**  The government-owned and run bank designed to manage the money supply of the nation. Examples include the Federal Reserve in the United States and the Bundesbank in Germany. In a financial crisis, the central bank provides funds to the system when other lenders (usually private banks) have stopped making loans.

**Collective Goods**  Benefits that meet two strict requirements: consumption by any one person or nation does not reduce the supply of the good and no one can be excluded from consumption. An important issue in the theory of hegemony is the nature and extent to which hegemons provide collective goods to the international system.

**Colonial Trade System**  A set of trading relationships typical of the colonial era. Colonized countries exchanged raw materials and agricultural commodities for manufactured goods produced by the imperial country. In the postcolonial period, most Third World countries have sought to alter this division of labor between North and South by developing their own industrial capacities.

**Command Economy**  A system of political economy in most communist states in which decisions about what to produce and about prices for goods are made by central political authorities.

**Common Agricultural Policy (CAP)**  An important form of protectionism and income support for farmers in the European Community. Arranged in the 1950s and 1960s, CAP provides for funds to maintain high prices for farm products and for tariffs to protect these prices from external competition. *See also* European Community.

**Commonwealth of Independent States (CIS)**  The successor political organization to the Soviet Union, organized late in 1991. The character, composition, and durability of this organization remains unclear.

**Comparative Advantage**  A strict definition refers to a situation in which one country may be unable to produce different types of goods more efficiently than another, but it nonetheless produces some goods better than others. This comparative advantage justifies a policy of free trade on economic grounds. A looser usage of the term refers to a country possessing an advantage in producing some goods and a disadvantage in others.

**Competitiveness**  The capacity of a nation to generate real growth in income for most persons in the country even when its economy is open to trade with the rest of the world.

**Complex Interdependence**  A theoretical model of international relations that contrasts with traditional models of realism. Complex interdependence posits a world where economic issues are not less important than security issues, where linkages among nations reduce government control over foreign affairs, and where military power is essentially unimportant.

**Convertibility**  An arrangement in which a government permits the free exchange of its currency for that of other nations. *See also* Exchange Rates.

**Cooperation**  A situation in which two or more nations bargain over modifying their behavior and/or preferences in order to receive some reciprocal act from each other. The aim of these complementary concessions is coordination of their actions in order to gain some benefit they cannot have alone.

**Corn Laws**  Tariffs placed on food and grain products imported into Britain during the 19th century. Repeal of the Corn Laws in 1846 signaled a British turn toward free trade.

**Creditor Nation**  This is a measurement of a nation's net foreign position which indicates that it holds more assets abroad than foreigners hold of its assets. *See also* Debtor Nation.

**Current Account**  This is a summary item in the balance of payments that measures the net of exports and imports of merchandise and services, investment income and payments, and government transactions. *See also* Balance of Payments.

**Dawes Plan**  A proposal made in 1924 by a private U.S. citizen, Charles Dawes, calling for a reduction in reparation payments made by Germany to Britain and France and loans by U.S. banks to Germany.

**Debt-for-Equity Swaps**  This term refers to a set of complex schemes for converting privately held bank debt into equity investments in the Third World. These deals became popular in the late 1980s at a time when Northern banks sought to reduce their exposure to increasingly shaky Third World loans.

**Debtor Nation**  This is a measurement of a nation's net foreign position that indicates that it holds less assets abroad than foreigners hold of its assets. *See also* Creditor Nation.

**Debt Service**  The proportion of export earnings accounted for by the repayment of principal and interest on a nation's foreign debt.

**Demographic Transition**  A theory which posits that rapid population growth begins when a country enters the initial stages of economic development, but later slows as incomes reach moderate levels and the economy matures.

**Dependency**  A theory of development designed to explain the gap between living standards in the North and the South. Beginning with colonialism, Southern development has been constrained by the Third World's dependent or peripheral role in the international economy. North–South economic ties are marked by Northern exploitation of the South. Genuine, self-sustained economic development will require changes in the relationship of Southern countries to the international economic order.

**Dirty Float**  A system of floating exchange rates in which governments occasionally intervene to prevent unwanted swings in the price of their currency. *See also* Exchange Rates.

**Discount Rate**  The interest rate charged by a nation's central bank to its member banks when they borrow money. The discount rate is a major instrument used by the central bank in controlling interest rates for the economy as a whole and for influencing growth in the money supply. *See also* Central Bank.

**Doi moi**   A policy adopted by the communist government in Vietnam after 1986 calling for the creation of free markets and openness to the world economy.

**Economic and Monetary Union (EMU)**   A term that refers to the elimination of all barriers to trade in the European Community by the end of 1992 and the development of a single currency later in the decade.

**Elasticity**   A technique for being more precise in stating the relationship between a change in price and resulting changes in demand or supply. When percentage changes in the quantity of demand or supply are greater than percentage changes in price, we speak of an elastic demand (or supply) of a product. When percent changes in demand are less than percent changes in price, this is a case of inelastic demand. For purists, this can be seen in the slope of the demand (or supply) curve.

**Embedded Liberalism**   A system of domestic and international political economy developed after World War II. Arrangements emphasizing free markets were tempered by broad acceptance of limits on the ability of the world economy to influence developments in the domestic economy. Free trade was accepted only as a goal and widespread limits on capital flows permitted nations to formulate independent domestic economic policies.

**Eurocurrency (Eurodollar)**   A development in the 1950s and 1960s in which dollars were deposited in European banks and came to be bought, sold, and borrowed. In the 1970s and 1980s, this expanded to include other currencies.

**European Currency Unit (ECU)**   A weighted average of currencies in the Exchange Rate Mechanism of the European Community used as a benchmark to fix exchange rates among these nations.

**European (Economic) Community (EC, EEC)**   Officially begun in 1958, the European Economic Community established a set of stages for the elimination of tariffs and other barriers to trade. Originally composed of six nations, by 1986 the EEC expanded to twelve members and in 1991 agreed to add six additional members. In 1986, the nations of the EEC committed themselves to a single market by 1992 and to the political arrangements needed to achieve this result. After this decision, the EEC became known as the European Community. *See also* Common Agricultural Policy; European Currency Unit; Economic and Monetary Union; European Monetary System; Exchange Rate Mechanism.

**European Monetary System (EMS)**   A monetary arrangement created after the breakdown of the Bretton Woods system and designed to maintain a fixed exchange rate system among some of the countries in the European Community. *See also* European Currency Unit; Exchange Rate Mechanism.

**Exchange Rate Mechanism (ERM)**   The specific means by which a system of fixed exchange rates is maintained in the European Monetary System. Exchange rates are tied to the European Currency Unit (with small room for fluctuation). Governments act to peg interest rates to those in Germany and intervene in foreign exchange markets to maintain the fixed value of their currency.

*See also* European Currency Unit; European Monetary System.

**Exchange Rates**   The price at which one currency can be exchanged for another. The system of exchange can be fixed, with governments acting to keep exchange rates within a certain agreed-on band, or floating (also known as flexible), in which demand and supply in a free market for currencies determine the price or rate of exchange. *See also* Dirty Float .

**Export-Led Industrialization (ELI)**   Pursued most successfully by a group of East Asian newly industrializing countries, a strategy of Export-Led Industrialization focuses on the production of manufactured goods for export to Northern markets.

**Fiscal Policy**   This refers to a government's policies on taxing and spending, in particular as these affect the level of economic activity.

**Foreign Direct Investment**   An investment in a nation by foreigners in which real assets are purchased. These include real estate or plant and equipment assets and involve some effort to manage. *See also* Portfolio Investment.

**Foreign Exchange Reserves**   The amount of foreign exchange held by a government.

**Free Trade**   A particular international economic system in which barriers to trade have been eliminated. In practice, free trade exists only to a degree since some restrictions on trade across nations have always been present.

**Free Trade Agreement**   A system of economic cooperation among nations in which tariffs, quotas, and other barriers to free trade are removed. Typically, this arrangement does not extend to establishing a common external tariff nor to the development of elaborate institutions for cooperation.

**General Agreement on Tariffs and Trade (GATT)**   A system of treaties among more than 100 nations establishing rules for the conduct of international trade. Most rules relate to tariffs and quotas, though some arrangements have been made regarding other nontariff barriers. The rules are the result of a series of negotiating sessions that began in the 1940s. *See also* Free Trade; Nontariff Barrier.

**Globalization**   The process of deepening and tightening of interdependence among actors in the world economy after 1973. Much higher levels of international financial transactions and increasing international production are key features.

**Gold Standard**   An international monetary system in which gold served as the medium for defining exchange rates. International payments were thereby made in terms of gold and sometimes actually in gold. This system existed from the 1870s to 1914 and briefly after World War I.

**Gross Domestic Product/Gross National Product (GDP/GNP)**   The total of all goods and services produced by a country over some period of time is GDP. Gross National Product is derived by adding the income of nationals from foreign activity to GDP and subtracting income of foreigners from activity in the country measured.

**Hegemony**   An international system in which one dominant state takes on the role of organizing and managing the world economic system. This means supplying capital, defining the rules for international trade, promoting political and military security, and having its money operate as a key currency.

**Human Development Index**   A statistical tool for measuring and comparing national development and human welfare. Developed by the United Nations Development Program, the Human Development Index is a composite of four individual measures of human welfare: life expectancy, adult literacy, mean years of schooling and per capita income, adjusted for the local cost of living. Scores on this composite index vary between 0 (the lowest measure of human development) and 1 (the highest measure of human development).

**Import Substitution Industrialization (ISI)** An inward-directed strategy of industrialization focused on the production of manufactured goods intended for sale in the domestic market. Typically, an ISI strategy provides trade protection or other forms of state assistance to import-substituting firms and industries.

**Interdependence** A situation in world affairs in which the linkages among nations makes their fate on certain issues mutually dependent. *See also* Asymmetrical Interdependence.

**Interest Rates** Technically, this is the price of borrowing money. There are a vast array of interest rates depending on who is borrowing and the length of time required to pay the money back. *See also* Discount Rate; Prime Rate.

**International Monetary Fund (IMF)** An international financial institution funded and governed by member states. Provides financing to countries experiencing balance-of-payments shortfalls. Has played a key role in the Third World debt crisis by conditioning financial assistance upon debtor country policy reforms.

**Key Currency** Historically, this is the currency of the international hegemon that comes to be widely accepted as payment for international transactions. This acceptability depends on confidence in the stability of the value of the currency and the reputation for acceptability in payment for goods or debts. In the nineteenth century the British pound and in the mid-twentieth century the U.S. dollar served as key currencies.

**Keynesianism** An economic policy common in capitalist societies after World War II and named in honor of the British economist, John Maynard Keynes. The purpose was to reduce the severity of economic recessions through government spending, which often included deficits in fiscal accounts.

**Liberalism** A policy toward the world economy emphasizing the benefits of free markets and free trade. These views originate with Adam Smith and David Ricardo about 200 years ago and today infuse the policies of many governments, international businesses, and international economic organizations.

**Liberalization** A policy that leads to greater market freedom for firms through lower tariffs, reduced capital controls, or fewer restrictions and regulations.

**Liquidity** A term referring to the level of cash held by a nation or firm. This also refers to the ability to convert an asset to cash quickly.

**Macroeconomic Policy** A governmental policy directed toward affecting the national economy as a whole. Examples include tax policy, spending policy, and monetary policy.

**Maquiladora** Special agreements between the United States and Mexico created special export processing zones inside Mexico. Here, parts from the U.S. and finished goods assembled in Mexico could cross the border with tariffs.

**Market segmentation** A situation in which the prices for similar goods are significantly different in different areas or markets.

**Marshall Plan** A proposal by U.S. Secretary of State George Marshall in 1947 calling for massive aid to Europe. The purpose was to secure a U.S. position of strength in Europe and reduce Soviet strength.

**Mercantilism** A policy designed to maximize exports while minimizing imports so as to generate the largest possible trade surplus. This was standard practice for nations prior to the mid-nineteenth century.

**Mercosur** A regional free trade agreement among the countries of Brazil, Argentina, Uruguay, and Paraguay. Mercosur went into effect on January 1, 1995.

**Ministry of International Trade and Industry (MITI)** This is the unit of the Japanese government most responsible for planning and managing the Japanese economy. Although its powers have diminished since the 1950s, MITI continues to play an important role in encouraging risk-taking and product development by private enterprises in Japan.

**Modernization** A theory of development designed to explain the gap between living standards in the North and South. The North's economic prosperity is attributed to its successful transition from traditional to modern forms of social, political and economic life. The economic backwardness of Southern countries is traced to the persistence of traditional social values and institutions. Southern development is thus dependent upon modernizing domestic reforms.

**Monetary Policy** Decisions normally made by a nation's central bank concerning interest rates, the growth of the money supply, and exchange rates. *See also* Discount Rate; Open Market Operations.

**Multilateral Assistance** Foreign economic assistance which is channeled from donor countries through international organizations, such as the World Bank or United Nations Special Agencies.

**Multinational Corporation (MNC)** A business firm which engages in the production of goods or services in more than one country.

**New International Economic Order (NIEO)** A package of proposed reforms in the international economic order sponsored by Third World countries during the 1970s. Largely rejected by the North, these proposals were intended to direct greater economic resources toward the South while also providing Third World countries with a greater role in managing the rules and institutions of the world economy.

**Nontariff Barriers** Mechanisms, other than tariffs, used by nations to restrict trade, usually by inhibiting or blocking imports. These can include various kinds of regulations, quotas, or requirements attached to trading with a country that operate as an impediment to trade.

**North American Free Trade Agreement (NAFTA)** A regional free trade agreement among the countries of Canada, the United States, and Mexico.

**Oligopoly** A type of industry in which there are only a small number of producers and in which there are barriers preventing new firms from entering the industry. Usually, firms in an oligopolistic industry are able to affect prices and often engage in at least tacit collusion.

**Open-Market Operations** An action of a nation's central bank involving the sale or purchase of government securities in the market. The purpose is to drain funds from the economy—by selling securities, the central bank ends up with more money—or pumping funds into the economy—buying securities results in the central bank exchanging securities for money. This is a key instrument for managing the overall level of the money supply. *See also* Central Bank; Monetary Policy.

**Organization of Petroleum Exporting Countries (OPEC)**    Formed in 1960, OPEC is a cooperative arrangement among many of the world's major oil exporting countries. Its purpose is to facilitate common agreement among member states on matters relating to oil policy, such as production levels and pricing.

**Portfolio Investment**    An investment in a nation by foreigners in which debt or stock ownership is involved. The result is a claim on resources, but typically no participation in managing the company or assets is involved.

**Post-communism**    A descriptive term used to refer to nations that have dropped some or all of communist political and economic policies. In Europe and former Soviet Union, this has meant an end to communist political control and an end to command economies. In Asia, this has meant significant economic liberalization directed by communist governments.

**Prime Rate**    The interest rate charged by banks to their best customers, usually large and well-run businesses.

**Privatization**    A system for transferring control over government-owned enterprises to private hands. The focus of this effort is in post-Communist states of the Commonwealth of Independent States and Eastern Europe. Some successful transfers of government corporations to private hands took place in Great Britain during the 1980s.

**Product Cycle**    A term defining a set of stages in the development, production, and sales of a product in which the stages are associated with the comparative advantage of different countries. The creation and development of a product usually take place in advanced industrial countries with large scientific complexes, but once the method of production has matured, manufacture can take place where costs are lowest.

**Productivity**    Broadly, this is the quantity of output of a good or service measured by the amount of input. For example, the amount of a good one worker can produce in a period of time is a measure of productivity.

**Protectionism**    A policy of excluding the import of goods and/or services into a nation. Like free trade, this is always a matter of degree since total exclusion is exceedingly rare. *See also* Free Trade.

**Purchasing Power Parity**    A statistical device designed to allow for more accurate comparisons of income and living standards across nations. The conversion of national income measures into dollars is adjusted for local purchasing power, or the cost of living.

**Radicalism**    Also closely linked to Marxism, this is a way of analyzing international political economy that emphasizes the way political and economic power are used to bias economic outcomes and garner special benefits for privileged and powerful groups and classes.

**Regime**    A relationship among nations in which there is a convergence of beliefs, expectations, norms, and procedures for making decisions relating to a particular problem or issue in international affairs. A regime is important to the extent that it affects the actions and choices of nations associated with the regime.

**Rio Earth Summit**    Formally called the United Nations Conference on Environment and Development (UNCED), the Rio Earth Summit brought together representatives from 150 nations in June, 1992 with the purpose of elaborating "strategies and measures to halt and reverse the effects of environmental degradation in the context of increased national and international efforts to promote sustainable and environmentally sound development in all countries."

**Smoot-Hawley Tariff**  A tariff proposal enacted in 1930 by U.S. protectionists during the Great Depression and signed by President Hoover. This led other capitalist states to adopt similar tariffs and contributed to a crushing decline in world trade and worsening depression in the U.S. and elsewhere.

**Strategic Alliance**  An arrangement between two or more firms that creates some continuing cooperative relationship. This could involve production, marketing, and/or research and development, such that the sharing and transfer of information, products, and/or production takes place.

**Strategic Trade**  An international trade policy in which various forms of governmental aid are directed at a specific industry or industries so as to boost their competitive advantages in global markets. The industries selected for targeting typically have substantial positive consequences for the economy or have a cost or market structure that promotes a small number of producers.

**Structural Adjustment**  In contrast with traditional project loans, which finance particular development investments or activities, the World Bank began shifting part of its lending to structural-adjustment financing in the 1980s. Typically, this newer type of financing provides balance-of-payment support to countries which have committed themselves to Bank-sponsored policy reforms.

**Sustainable Development**  The term "sustainable development" was first brought into common use by the World Commission on Environment and Development, also called The Brundtland Commission, in 1987. Brundtland defined sustainable development as that which "meets the needs of the present generation without compromising the needs of future generations."

**Syndication**  An arrangement whereby a collection of banks, usually organized by one or a few lead institutions, divide responsibility for financing a major loan package. Syndication was often used in lending to Third World countries during the 1970s. Syndication agreements typically stipulate that agreement among the participating banks is required before any renegotiation of debt arrangements can be implemented.

**Tied Aid**  A condition attached to foreign economic assistance which requires that the aid extended to a recipient country be spent on goods and/or services produced by firms residing in the donor country.

**Trade Surplus/Deficit**  A situation in a nation's balance of payments when exports exceed imports (surplus) or when imports exceed exports (deficit).

**Transfer Pricing**  An accounting practice by which multinational corporations adjust prices on intrafirm trade in order to shift profits from subsidiaries located in high-tax countries to those residing in low-tax countries or to escape restrictions of the repatriation of profits imposed by host-country governments.

**World Bank**  This term actually refers to a group of related international financial institutions, including the International Bank for Reconstruction and Development (IBRD), the International Development Agency (IDA), and the International Finance Corporation (IFC). Funded largely by capital infusions from Northern governments, these agencies provide financing for Third World development projects or programs.

**World Trade Organization**  A global trade organization created to oversee the implementation of agreements emerging out of the Uruguay Round of international trade negotiations.

***Zaibatsu/keiretsu***  Two related forms of industrial organization in Japan in which family-centered holding companies act to organize and integrate many different firms. Often, large banks operate to supply capital and in other cases complex systems of manufacturers and suppliers are the main forms of organization. *Zaibatsu* refers to such enterprise systems prior to 1945; *keiretsu* refers to such systems after 1945.

# Acronyms

**AID** Agency for International Development

**APEC** Asian-Pacific Economic Cooperation

**ARPA** Advanced Research Projects Agency

**ASEAN** Association of Southeast Asian Nations

**BRITE** Basic Research for Industrial Technology in Europe

**CAP** Common Agricultural Policy

**CGIAR** Consultative Group on International Agricultural Research

**CIMMYT** Centro Internacional de Major-amiento de Maiz y Trige

**CIS** Commonwealth of Independent States

**CMEA** Council for Mutual Economic Assistance

**DAC** Development Assistance Council

**EAEC** East Asian Economic Caucus

**EC** European Community

**ECU** European Currency Unit

**EEC** European Economic Community

**EFTA** European Free Trade Area

**ELI** Export Led Industrialization

**EMS** European Monetary System

**EMU** Economic and Monetary Union

**ERM** Exchange Rate Mechanism

**ESPRIT** European Strategic Programme for Research and Development

**EU** European Union

**EUREKA** European Research Coordination Agency

**FDI** Foreign Direct Investment

**FTA** Free Trade Agreement

**G-5** Group of Five

**G-7** Group of Seven

**GATT** General Agreement on Tariffs and Trade

**GDP/GNP** Gross Domestic Product/ Gross National Product

**GEF** Global Environmental Fund

**IBM** International Business Machines

**IBRD** International Bank for Reconstruction and Development

**IMF** International Monetary Fund

**IRRI** International Rice Research Institute

**ISI** Import Substitution Industrialization

**JESSI** Joint European Semiconductor Silicon

**MITI** Ministry of International Trade and Industry

**MNC** Multinational Corporation

**MOF** Ministry of Finance

**NAFTA** North American Free Trade Agreement

**NIC** Newly Industrializing Country

**NIEO** New International Economic Order

**NTB** Non-Tariff Barriers

**ODA** Official Development Assistance

**OECD** Organization of Economic Co-operation and Development

**OMA** Orderly Marketing Agreement

**OPEC** Organization of Petroleum Exporting Countries

**PPP** Purchasing Power Parity

**R&D** Research and Development

**RACE** R&D in Advanced Communications-Technologies in Europe

**RTAA** Reciprocal Trade Agreements Act

**SDR** Special Drawing Rights

**SEA** Single European Act

**SEZs** Special Economic Zones

**TEU** Treaty on European Union

**TVEs** Township and Village Enterprises

**UNDP** United Nations Development Program

**VER** Voluntary Export Restraint

**WTO** World Trade Organization

# INDEX